ADVANTAGE EDITION

WORLD HISTORY

EIGHTH EDITION

ADVANTAGE EDITION

WORLD HISTORY

EIGHTH EDITION

Volume I: To 1800

William J. Duiker
The Pennsylvania State University

Jackson J. Spielvogel
The Pennsylvania State University

CENGAGE
Learning·

Australia • Brazil • Mexico • Singapore • United Kingdom • United States

CENGAGE
Learning·

Cengage Advantage Books:
World History, Vol. I: To 1800,
Eighth Edition
William Duiker and
Jackson Spielvogel

Product Manager: Cara St.
Hilaire

Content Developer: Cara Swan

Product Assistant: Andrew
Newton

Market Development Manager:
Kyle Zimmerman

IP Analyst: Alexandra Ricciardi

Manufacturing Planner: Sandee
Milewski

Art and Design Direction,
Production Management,
and Composition:
Lumina Datamatics, Inc.

Cover Image: Trade in the
Middle Ages: activities one day
walking in a city. Thumbnail
objection of Justinian Code
(Codex Justinianus), a collection
of laws and institutions, written
under the Roman Emperor
Justinian I of Byzantium (483-565),
1350. Bibliotheque Nationale
Torino. © Electa/Leemage/
Lebrecht

For product information and
technology assistance, contact us at **Cengage Learning
Customer & Sales Support, 1-800-354-9706.**

For permission to use material from this text or product,
submit all requests online at **www.cengage.com/permissions.**
Further permissions questions can be e-mailed to
permissionrequest@cengage.com.

Library of Congress Control Number: 2015936370

Student Edition:

ISBN: 978-1-305-09172-6

Cengage Learning
20 Channel Center Street
Boston, MA 02210
USA

Cengage Learning is a leading provider of customized learning
solutions with employees residing in nearly 40 different countries
and sales in more than 125 countries around the world. Find your
local representative at **www.cengage.com**.

Cengage Learning products are represented in Canada by
Nelson Education, Ltd.

To learn more about Cengage Learning Solutions, visit
www.cengage.com.

Purchase any of our products at your local college store or at our
preferred online store **www.cengagebrain.com.**

Printed in the United States of America
Print Number: 02   Print Year: 2015

Brief Contents

Preface **xiii**

A Note to Students About Language and the Dating of Time **xxv**

Themes for Understanding World History **xxvii**

About the Authors **xxix**

PART ONE The First Civilizations and the Rise of Empires (Prehistory to 500 C.E.) *1*

1 Early Humans and the First Civilizations *5*

2 Ancient India *47*

3 China in Antiquity *78*

4 The Civilization of the Greeks *114*

5 The Roman World Empire *153*

PART TWO New Patterns of Civilization (500–1500 C.E.) *187*

6 The Americas *191*

7 Ferment in the Middle East: The Rise of Islam *219*

8 Early Civilizations in Africa *251*

9 The Expansion of Civilization in South and Southeast Asia *279*

10 The Flowering of Traditional China *313*

11 The East Asian Rimlands: Early Japan, Korea, and Vietnam *350*

12 The Making of Europe *376*

13 The Byzantine Empire and Crisis and Recovery in the West *414*

PART THREE The Emergence of New World Patterns (1500–1800) *449*

14 New Encounters: The Creation of a World Market *453*

15 Europe Transformed: Reform and State Building *487*

16 The Muslim Empires *519*

17   The East Asian World   *553*

18   The West on the Eve of a New World Order   *585*

Chapter Notes   **N-1**

Index   **I-1**

Contents

Preface   xiii

A Note to Students About Language and the Dating of Time   xxv

Themes for Understanding World History   xxvii

About the Authors   xxix

PART 1

THE FIRST CIVILIZATIONS AND THE RISE OF EMPIRES (PREHISTORY TO 500 C.E.)   1

1

EARLY HUMANS AND THE FIRST CIVILIZATIONS   5

The First Humans   6

COMPARATIVE ESSAY: From Hunter-Gatherers and Herders to Farmers   11

The Emergence of Civilization   12

Civilization in Mesopotamia   14

Egyptian Civilization: "The Gift of the Nile"   20

OPPOSING VIEWPOINTS: The Great Flood: Two Versions   22

New Centers of Civilization   33

The Rise of New Empires   39

OPPOSING VIEWPOINTS: The Governing of Empires: Two Approaches   42

2

ANCIENT INDIA   47

The Emergence of Civilization in India: Harappan Society   48

COMPARATIVE ESSAY: Writing and Civilization   51

The Aryans in India   53

Escaping the Wheel of Life: The Religious World of Ancient India   62

OPPOSING VIEWPOINTS: The Search for Truth   64

The Exuberant World of Indian Culture   72

3

CHINA IN ANTIQUITY   78

The Dawn of Chinese Civilization   79

COMPARATIVE ESSAY: The Use of Metals   84

The Zhou Dynasty   85

OPPOSING VIEWPOINTS: A Debate over Good and Evil   92

The First Chinese Empire: The Qin Dynasty   95

The Glorious Han Dynasty (202 B.C.E.–221 C.E.)   99

Daily Life in Ancient China   105

Chinese Culture   108

4

THE CIVILIZATION OF THE GREEKS   114

Early Greece   115

The Greek City-States (c. 750–c. 500 B.C.E.)   119

The High Point of Greek Civilization: Classical Greece   125

COMPARATIVE ESSAY: The Axial
    Age *134*

OPPOSING VIEWPOINTS: Women in Athens
    and Sparta *138*

The Rise of Macedonia and the
    Conquests of Alexander *140*

FILM & HISTORY: Alexander *(2004)*   *142*

The World of the Hellenistic
    Kingdoms *144*

5

THE ROMAN WORLD
EMPIRE   **153**

Early Rome and the Republic *154*

The Roman Empire at Its
    Height *163*

OPPOSING VIEWPOINTS: Women in the
    Roman and Han Empires *172*

FILM & HISTORY: Gladiator *(2000)*   *174*

Crisis and the Late Empire *176*

Transformation of the Roman
    World: The Development of
    Christianity *178*

COMPARATIVE ESSAY: Rulers and
    Gods *180*

OPPOSING VIEWPOINTS: Roman
    Authorities and a Christian
    on Christianity *182*

A Comparison of the Roman and Han
    Empires *184*

PART 2

NEW PATTERNS OF CIVILIZATION
(500–1500 C.E.)   **187**

6

THE AMERICAS   **191**

The Peopling of the Americas *192*

Early Civilizations in Central
    America *193*

The First Civilizations in South
    America *207*

COMPARATIVE ESSAY: History and the
    Environment *210*

Stateless Societies in the
    Americas *214*

7

FERMENT IN THE MIDDLE EAST: THE
RISE OF ISLAM   **219**

The Rise of Islam *220*

FILM & HISTORY: The Message
    (Muhammad: The Messenger
    of God) *(1976)*   *222*

The Arab Empire and Its
    Successors *225*

Islamic Civilization *238*

COMPARATIVE ESSAY: Trade and
    Civilization *241*

8

EARLY CIVILIZATIONS IN
AFRICA   **251**

The Emergence of Civilization *252*

COMPARATIVE ESSAY: The Migration of
    Peoples *258*

The Coming of Islam *260*

States and Noncentralized Societies
    in Central and Southern
    Africa *269*

African Society *271*

African Culture *274*

9

THE EXPANSION OF CIVILIZATION
IN SOUTH AND SOUTHEAST
ASIA   **279**

The Silk Road *280*

India After the Mauryas *282*
The Arrival of Islam *287*
Society and Culture *290*

COMPARATIVE ESSAY: Caste, Class, and Family 294

The Golden Region: Early Southeast Asia *301*

10

THE FLOWERING OF TRADITIONAL CHINA 313

China After the Han *314*

China Reunified: The Sui, the Tang, and the Song *314*

OPPOSING VIEWPOINTS: Action or Inaction: An Ideological Dispute in Medieval China 322

COMPARATIVE ESSAY: The Spread of Technology 326

Explosion in Central Asia: The Mongol Empire *333*

FILM & HISTORY: The Adventures of Marco Polo *(1938) and* Marco Polo *(2007)* 338

The Ming Dynasty *340*
In Search of the Way *342*
The Apogee of Chinese Culture *345*

11

THE EAST ASIAN RIMLANDS: EARLY JAPAN, KOREA, AND VIETNAM 350

Japan: Land of the Rising Sun *351*

COMPARATIVE ESSAY: Feudal Orders Around the World 356

Korea: Bridge to the East *368*

Vietnam: The Smaller Dragon *370*

12

THE MAKING OF EUROPE 376

The Emergence of Europe in the Early Middle Ages *377*

Europe in the High Middle Ages *385*

FILM & HISTORY: The Lion in Winter *(1968)* 390

OPPOSING VIEWPOINTS: Two Views of Trade and Merchants 392

COMPARATIVE ESSAY: Cities in the Medieval World 395

Medieval Europe and the World *409*

13

THE BYZANTINE EMPIRE AND CRISIS AND RECOVERY IN THE WEST 414

From Eastern Roman to Byzantine Empire *415*

The Zenith of Byzantine Civilization (750–1025) *424*

The Decline and Fall of the Byzantine Empire (1025–1453) *426*

The Crises of the Fourteenth Century in the West *431*

COMPARATIVE ESSAY: The Role of Disease in History 432

Recovery: The Renaissance *438*

OPPOSING VIEWPOINTS: The Renaissance Prince: The Views of Machiavelli and Erasmus 444

PART 3
THE EMERGENCE OF NEW WORLD PATTERNS (1500–1800)   449

14
NEW ENCOUNTERS: THE CREATION OF A WORLD MARKET   453
An Age of Exploration and Expansion   454
The Portuguese Maritime Empire   458
The Conquest of the "New World"   462
FILM & HISTORY: The Mission (1986)   468
OPPOSING VIEWPOINTS: The March of Civilization   472
Africa in Transition   472
COMPARATIVE ESSAY: The Columbian Exchange   474
Southeast Asia in the Era of the Spice Trade   481

15
EUROPE TRANSFORMED: REFORM AND STATE BUILDING   487
The Reformation of the Sixteenth Century   488
OPPOSING VIEWPOINTS: A Reformation Debate: Conflict at Marburg   494
COMPARATIVE ESSAY: Marriage in the Early Modern World   498
Europe in Crisis, 1560–1650   501
Response to Crisis: The Practice of Absolutism   508
England and Limited Monarchy   513
The Flourishing of European Culture   514

16
THE MUSLIM EMPIRES   519
The Ottoman Empire   520
COMPARATIVE ESSAY: The Changing Face of War   522
The Safavids   533
The Grandeur of the Mughals   536
OPPOSING VIEWPOINTS: The Capture of Port Hoogly   543

17
THE EAST ASIAN WORLD   553
China at Its Apex   554
Changing China   561
COMPARATIVE ESSAY: Population Explosion   563
Tokugawa Japan   569
OPPOSING VIEWPOINTS: Some Confucian Commandments   576
Korea and Vietnam   581

18
THE WEST ON THE EVE OF A NEW WORLD ORDER   585
Toward a New Heaven and a New Earth: An Intellectual Revolution in the West   586
COMPARATIVE ESSAY: The Scientific Revolution   590
Economic Changes and the Social Order   597
Colonial Empires and Revolution in the Americas   600
Toward a New Political Order and Global Conflict   603

The French Revolution   607

FILM & HISTORY: Marie Antoinette
(2006)   610

OPPOSING VIEWPOINTS: The Natural Rights
of the French People: Two
Views   613

The Age of Napoleon   618

Chapter Notes   N-1

Index   I-1

Preface

For several million years after primates first appeared on the surface of the earth, human beings lived in small communities, seeking to survive by hunting, fishing, and foraging in a frequently hostile environment. Then suddenly, in the space of a few thousand years, there was an abrupt change of direction as humans in a few widely scattered areas of the globe began to master the art of cultivating food crops. As food production increased, the population in those areas rose correspondingly, and people began to congregate in larger communities. Governments arose to provide protection and other needed services to the local population. Cities appeared and became the focal point of cultural and religious development. Historians refer to this process as the beginnings of civilization.

For generations, historians in Europe and the United States pointed to the rise of such civilizations as marking the origins of the modern world. Courses on Western civilization conventionally began with a chapter or two on the emergence of advanced societies in Egypt and Mesopotamia and then proceeded to ancient Greece and the Roman Empire. From Greece and Rome, the road led directly to the rise of modern civilization in the West.

There is nothing inherently wrong with this approach. Important aspects of our world today can indeed be traced back to these early civilizations, and all human beings the world over owe a considerable debt to their achievements. But all too often this interpretation has been used to imply that the course of civilization has been linear, leading directly from the emergence of agricultural societies in ancient Mesopotamia to the rise of advanced industrial societies in Europe and North America. Until recently, most courses on world history taught in the United States routinely focused almost exclusively on the rise of the West, with only a passing glance at other parts of the world, such as Africa, India, and East Asia. The contributions made by those societies to the culture and technology of our own time were often passed over in silence.

Two major reasons have been advanced to justify this approach. Some people have argued that it is more important that young minds understand the roots of their own heritage than that of peoples elsewhere in the world. In many cases, however, the motivation for this Eurocentric approach has been the belief that since the time of Socrates and Aristotle, Western civilization has been the main driving force in the evolution of human society.

Such an interpretation, however, represents a serious distortion of the process. During most of the course of human history, the most advanced civilizations have been in East Asia or the Middle East, not in the West. A relatively brief period of European dominance culminated with the era of imperialism in the late nineteenth century, when the political, military, and economic power of the advanced nations of the West spanned the globe. During recent generations, however, that dominance has gradually eroded, partly as a result of changes taking place in Western societies and partly because new centers of development are emerging elsewhere on the globe—notably in Asia, especially with the growing economic strength of China and India.

World history, then, has been a complex process in which many branches of the human community have played an active part, and the dominance of any one area of the world has been a temporary rather than a permanent phenomenon. It will be our purpose in this book to present a balanced picture of this story, with all respect for the richness and diversity of the tapestry of the human experience. Due attention must be paid to the rise of the West, of course, since that has been the most dominant aspect of world history in recent centuries. But the contributions made by other peoples must be given adequate consideration as well, not only in the period prior to 1500, when the major centers of civilization were located in Asia, but also in our own day, where a multipolar picture of development is clearly beginning to emerge.

Anyone who wishes to teach or write about world history must decide whether to present the topic as an integrated whole or as a collection of different cultures. The world that we live in today, of course, is in many respects an interdependent one in terms of economics as well as culture and communications, a reality that is often expressed by the phrase "global village." The convergence of peoples across the surface of the earth into an integrated world system began in early times and intensified after the rise of capitalism in the early modern era. In recognition of this trend, historians trained in global history, as well as instructors in the growing number of world history courses, have now begun to speak and write of a "global approach" that gives less attention to the study of individual civilizations and focuses instead on the "big picture" or, as the world historian Fernand Braudel termed it, interpreting world history as a river with no banks.

On the whole, this development is to be welcomed as a means of bringing the common elements of the evolution of human society to our attention. But this approach also involves two problems. For the vast majority of their time on earth, human beings have lived in partial or virtually total isolation from each other. Differences in climate, location, and geographic features have created human societies very different from each other in culture and historical experience. Only in relatively recent times (the commonly accepted date has long been the beginning of the age of European exploration at the end of the fifteenth century, but some would now push it back to the era of the Mongol Empire or even earlier) have cultural interchanges begun to create a common "world system," in which events taking place in one part of the world are rapidly transmitted throughout the globe, often with momentous consequences. In recent generations, of course, the process of global interdependence has been proceeding even more rapidly. Nevertheless, even now the process is by no means complete, as ethnic and regional differences continue to exist and to shape the course of world history. The tenacity of these differences and sensitivities is reflected not only in the rise of internecine conflicts in such divergent areas as Africa, India, and eastern Europe but also in the emergence in recent years of such regional organizations as the African Union, the Association for the Southeast Asian Nations, and the European Union.

The second problem is a practical one. College students today often are not well informed about the distinctive character of civilizations such as China and India and, without sufficient exposure to the historical evolution of such societies, will assume all too readily that the peoples in these countries have had historical experiences similar to ours and will respond to various stimuli in a similar fashion to those living in western Europe or the United States. If it is a mistake to ignore those forces that link us together, it is equally a mistake to underestimate those factors that continue to divide us and to differentiate us into a world of diverse peoples.

Our response to this challenge has been to adopt a global approach to world history while at the same time attempting to do justice to the distinctive character and development of individual civilizations and regions of the world. The presentation of individual cultures is especially important in Parts I and II, which cover a time when it is generally agreed that the process of global integration was not yet far advanced. Later chapters adopt a more comparative and thematic approach, in deference to the greater number of connections that have been established among the world's peoples since the fifteenth and sixteenth centuries. Part V consists of a series of chapters that center on individual regions of the world while at the same time focusing on common problems related to the Cold War and the rise of global problems such as overproduction and environmental pollution.

We have sought balance in another way as well. Many textbooks tend to simplify the content of history courses by emphasizing an intellectual or political perspective or, most recently, a social perspective, often at the expense of sufficient details in a chronological framework. This approach is confusing to students whose high school social studies programs have often neglected a systematic study of world history. We have attempted to write a well-balanced work in which political, economic, social, religious, intellectual, cultural, and military history are integrated into a chronologically ordered synthesis.

FEATURES OF THE TEXT

To enliven the past and let readers see for themselves the materials that historians use to create their pictures of the past, we have included **primary sources** (boxed documents) in each chapter that are keyed to the seven major themes of world history and relate to the surrounding discussion in the text. The documents include examples of the religious, artistic, intellectual, social, economic, and political aspects of life in different societies and reveal in a vivid fashion what civilization meant to the individual men and women who shaped it by their actions. A question at the end of each box helps to guide students in analyzing the documents. The Opposing Viewpoints feature (see full description later in the Preface) provides additional primary source materials.

A chronology at the end of each chapter enables students to see the major developments of an era at a glance. **Map captions** are designed to enrich students' awareness of the importance of geography to history, **Chapter Outlines** at the beginning of each chapter give students a useful overview and guide them to the main subjects of each chapter. A **guide to pronunciation** is now provided in parentheses in the text, following the first mention of a complex name or term.

Comparative Essays, keyed to the seven major themes of world history, enable us to draw more concrete comparisons and contrasts across geographic, cultural, and chronological lines. **Comparative Illustrations,** also keyed to the seven major themes, continue to be a feature in some chapters. Both the Comparative Essays and the Comparative Illustrations conclude with focus questions to help students develop their analytical skills. We hope that the Comparative Essays and the Comparative Illustrations will assist instructors who wish to encourage their students to adopt a comparative approach to their understanding of the human experience.

The **Film & History** feature, now appearing in many chapters, presents a brief analysis of the plot as well as the historical significance, value, and accuracy of popular films. New features have been added on films such as *Gladiator, The Young Victoria,* and *The Iron Lady.*

The **Opposing Viewpoints** feature, which has proven popular with reviewers and their students since its introduction in the sixth edition, presents a comparison of two or three primary sources to facilitate student analysis of historical documents. This feature has been expanded and now appears in almost every chapter. Focus questions are included to help students evaluate the documents.

NEW TO THIS EDITION

After reexamining the entire book and analyzing the comments and reviews of many colleagues who have found the book to be a useful instrument for introducing their students to world history, we have also made a number of other changes for the eighth edition.

We have continued to strengthen the global framework of the book, but not at the expense of reducing the attention assigned to individual regions of the world. New material has been added to most chapters to help students be aware of similar developments globally, including new comparative sections.

The enthusiastic response to the primary sources (boxed documents) led us to evaluate the content of each document carefully and add new documents throughout the text, including new comparative documents in the **Opposing Viewpoints** feature.

New **historiographical subsections** (often marked by headings in question format), which examine how and why historians differ in their interpretation of specific topics, have also been added. To keep up with the ever-growing body of historical scholarship, new or revised material has been added throughout the book on many topics (see specific notes below).

CHAPTER-BY-CHAPTER CONTENT REVISIONS

Chapter 1 New and revised material on religion in Neolithic societies and the role of ritual in ancient Egypt; new Opposing Viewpoints features, "The Great Flood: Two Versions," and "The Governing of Empires: Two Approaches"; new historiographical subsection, "What Were the Causes of Civilization?"

Chapter 2 New document, "A Singular Debate"; new information on early forms of currency in India.

Chapter 3 New information on early writing and currency. Addition of material and document "A Prescription for the Emperor" on Han dynasty (moved from Chapter 5 and revised).

Chapter 4 New and revised material on the following: the role of the phalanx and colonies in the rise of democracy in Greece, helots and women in Sparta, the political system in Sparta, Sophocles, and sports and violence in ancient Greece; new document, "Sophocles: 'The Miracle of Man.'"

Chapter 5 The section on Han China has been moved back to Chapter 3; new material on the following: Roman children and early Christianity, especially Christian women; new subsection: "The Struggle of the Orders: Social Division in the Roman Republic"; new subsection: "The Nature of Roman Imperialism"; new subsection: "Prosperity in the Early Empire: Trade with China and India," focusing on the Silk Road and contact between Romans and Chinese; new section, "A Comparison of the Roman and Han Empires"; new Opposing Viewpoints feature, "Women in the Roman and Han Empires"; new Comparative Illustration, "Emperors, West and East."

Chapter 6 New document "Aztec Religion Through Spanish Eyes"; added material on early civilizations in South America.

Chapter 7 New document "The Spread of the Muslim Faith" on the meaning of *jihad* in the Qur'an; new material on Arab science and philosophy, the arrival of the Turks in the Middle East, and early Arab seafaring technology.

Chapter 8 New document "The Slave Trade in Ancient Africa"; enhanced treatment of West Africa.

Chapter 9 Two new documents, "Chinese Traders in the Philippines" and "The Spread of Buddhism in Southeast Asia"; new historiographical interpretation question, "The Indian Economy: Promise Unfulfilled?"; added information on the Kushan state.

Chapter 10 Two new documents, "Choosing the Best and Brightest" and "Proper Etiquette in Tang Dynasty China"; added material on Chinese cartography and trade relations.

Chapter 11 New document, "A Plea to the New Emperor"; updated information on Korea.

Chapter 12 New material on the *missi dominici*, the role of peasant women, commercial capitalism, and women in medieval cities; new document, "Pollution in a Medieval City"; new Opposing Viewpoints feature, "Two Views of Trade and Merchants"; new historiographical subsection, "What Was the Significance of Charlemagne?"

Chapter 13 New section, "Women in the Byzantine Empire"; new material on Italian Renaissance art; new subsection, "Machiavelli and Political Power in the Renaissance"; new Opposing Viewpoints feature, "The Renaissance Prince: The Views of Machiavelli and Erasmus."

Chapter 14 Revised Opposing Viewpoints feature, "The March of Civilization"; added material on cartography and navigation, and the "maroon" slave communities in the Americas.

Chapter 15 New material on Judith Leyster; new document, "Queen Elizabeth I: 'I Have the Heart of a King'"; new historiographical subsection, "Was There a Military Revolution?"

Chapter 16 New historiographical subsection, "The Ottoman Empire: A Civilization in Decline?"; new material on Indian textile industry.

Chapter 17 New Opposing Viewpoints feature, "Some Confucian Commandments"; new document, "A Plea for Women's Education"; revised material on Chinese and Japanese foreign trade; new material on galleon and impact of silver in China; references to Yi Dynasty changed to Choson Dynasty.

Chapter 18 New material on the following: a consumer revolution in the eighteenth century and the finances of the French court; new document, "The State of French Finances."

Because courses in world history at American and Canadian colleges and universities follow different chronological divisions, the text is available in both one-volume comprehensive and two-volume versions to fit the needs of instructors. Teaching and learning ancillaries include the following.

INSTRUCTOR RESOURCES

MindTap™

MindTap for *World History* is a personalized, online digital learning platform providing students with an immersive learning experience that builds critical thinking skills. Through a carefully designed chapter-based learning path, MindTap allows students to easily identify the chapter's learning objectives, complete reading activities organized into short, manageable blocks, and test their content knowledge with Aplia™ Critical Thinking Activities developed for the most important concepts in each chapter (see Aplia description below).

- *Setting the Scene:* Each chapter of the MindTap begins with a brief video that introduces the chapter's major themes in a compelling, visual way that encourages students to think critically about the subject matter.

- *Aplia:* The Aplia Critical Thinking assignments will include at least one map-based exercise, one primary source–based exercise, and an exercise summarizing the content and themes of the chapter.

- *Reflection Activity:* Every chapter ends with an assignable, gradable reflection activity, intended as a brief writing assignment to be shared with the class as an online discussion, through which students can apply a theme or idea they've just studied.

MindTap also provides a set of web applications known as MindApps to help you create the most engaging course for your students. The MindApps range from ReadSpeaker (which reads the text out loud to students) to Kaltura (allowing you to insert inline video and audio into your curriculum) to ConnectYard (allowing you to create digital "yards" through social media—all without "friending" your students). MindTap for *World History* goes well beyond an eBook, a homework solution/digital supplement, a resource center website, or a Learning Management System. It is truly a Personal Learning Experience that allows you to synchronize the text reading and engaging assignments. To learn more, ask your Cengage Learning sales representative to demo it for you, or go to www.Cengage.com /MindTap.

Aplia™

Aplia is an online interactive learning solution that improves comprehension and outcomes by increasing student effort and engagement. Founded by a professor to enhance his own courses, Aplia provides automatically graded assignments with detailed, immediate explanations on every question. The interactive assignments have been developed to address the major concepts covered in *World History* and are designed to promote critical thinking and engage students more fully in learning. Question types include questions built around animated maps, primary sources such as newspaper extracts, or imagined scenarios, like engaging in a conversation with a historical figure or finding a diary and being asked to fill in some blanks; more in-depth primary source question sets address a major topic with a number of related primary sources and questions that promote deeper analysis of historical evidence. Many of the questions incorporate images, video clips, or audio clips. Students get immediate feedback on their work (not only what they got right or wrong, but why), and they can choose to see another set of related questions if they want more practice. A searchable eBook is available inside the course as well so that students can easily reference it as they work. Map-reading and writing tutorials are also available to get students off to a good start.

Aplia's simple-to-use course management interface allows instructors to post announcements, upload course materials, host student discussions, e-mail students, and manage the gradebook. A knowledgeable and friendly support team offers assistance and personalized support in customizing assignments to the instructor's course schedule. To learn more and view a demo for this book, visit www.aplia .com.

Instructor Companion Website

This website is an all-in-one resource for class preparation, presentation, and testing for instructors. Accessible through Cengage.com/login with your faculty account, you will find an Instructor's Manual, PowerPoint presentations (descriptions below), and test bank files (please see Cognero description).

Instructor's Manual   For each chapter, this manual contains chapter outlines, lecture suggestions, primary source discussion questions, student research topics, and web and video resources.

PowerPoint® Lecture Tools   These presentations are ready-to-use, visual outlines of each chapter. They are easily customized for your lectures. There are presentations of only lectures or only images, as well as combined lecture and image presentations. Also available is a per-chapter JPEG library of images and maps.

Test Bank   Cengage Learning Testing, powered by Cognero®, for *World History* was prepared by Kathleen Addison of California State University, Northridge, and is accessible through Cengage.com/login with your faculty account. This test bank contains multiple-choice and essay questions for each chapter. Cognero® is a flexible, online system that allows you to author, edit, and manage test bank content for *World History*, eighth edition. Create multiple test versions instantly and deliver them through your LMS from your classroom, or wherever you may be, with no special installs or downloads required.

The following format types are available for download from the Instructor Companion Site: Blackboard, Angel, Moodle, Canvas, and Desire2Learn. You can import these files directly into your LMS to edit, manage questions, and create tests. The test bank is also available in PDF format from the Instructor Companion Website.

MindTap Reader for *World History*

MindTap Reader is an eBook specifically designed to address the ways students assimilate content and media assets. MindTap Reader combines thoughtful navigation ergonomics, advanced student annotation, note-taking, search tools, and embedded media assets such as video and MP3 chapter summaries, primary source documents with critical thinking questions, and interactive (zoomable) maps. Students can use the eBook as their primary text or as a multimedia companion to their printed book. The MindTap Reader eBook is available within the MindTap found at www.cengagebrain.com.

CourseReader

CourseReader is an online collection of primary and secondary sources that lets you create a customized electronic reader in minutes. With an easy-to-use interface and assessment tool, you can choose exactly what your students will be assigned—simply search or browse Cengage Learning's extensive document database to preview and select your customized collection of readings. In addition to print sources of all types (letters, diary entries, speeches, newspaper accounts, etc.), their collection includes a growing number of images and video and audio clips. Each primary source document includes a descriptive headnote that puts the reading into context and is further supported by both critical thinking and multiple-choice questions designed to reinforce key points. For more information, visit www.cengage.com/coursereader.

Reader Program

Cengage Learning publishes a number of readers, some containing exclusively primary sources, others containing a combination of primary and secondary sources, and some designed to guide students through the process of historical inquiry. Visit Cengage.com/history for a complete list of readers.

Cengagebrain.com

Save your students time and money. Direct them to www.cengagebrain.com for choice in formats and savings and a better chance to succeed in your class. Cengagebrain.com, Cengage Learning's online store, is a single destination for more than 10,000 new textbooks, eTextbooks, eChapters, study tools, and audio supplements. Students have the freedom to purchase a la carte exactly what they need when they need it. Students can save 50 percent on the electronic textbook and can pay as little as $1.99 for an individual eChapter.

Custom Options

Nobody knows your students like you, so why not give them a text that is tailored to their needs? Cengage Learning offers custom solutions for your course—whether it's making a small modification to *World History* to match your syllabus or combining multiple sources to create something truly unique. You can pick and choose chapters, include your own material, and add additional map exercises along with the Rand McNally Atlas to create a text that fits the way you teach. Ensure that your students get the most out of their textbook dollar by giving them exactly what they need. Contact your Cengage Learning representative to explore custom solutions for your course.

STUDENT RESOURCES

MindTap Reader

MindTap Reader is an eBook specifically designed to address the ways students assimilate content and media assets. MindTap Reader combines thoughtful navigation ergonomics, advanced student annotation, note-taking, search tools, and embedded media assets such as video and MP3 chapter summaries, primary source documents with critical thinking questions, and interactive (zoomable) maps. Students can use the eBook as their primary text or as a multimedia companion to their printed book. The MindTap Reader eBook is available within the MindTap found at www.cengagebrain.com.

Reader Program

Cengage Learning publishes a number of readers, some containing exclusively primary sources, others containing a combination of primary and secondary sources, and some designed to guide students through the process of historical inquiry. Visit Cengage.com/history for a complete list of readers.

Cengagebrain.com

Save time and money! Go to www.cengagebrain.com for choice in formats and savings and a better chance to succeed in your class. Cengagebrain.com, Cengage Learning's online store, is a single destination for more than 10,000 new textbooks, eTextbooks, eChapters, study tools, and audio supplements. Students have the freedom to purchase a la carte exactly what they need when they need it. Students can save 50 percent on the electronic textbook and can pay as little as $1.99 for an individual eChapter.

Writing for College History, 1e [ISBN: 9780618306039]

Prepared by Robert M. Frakes, Clarion University. This brief handbook for survey courses in American history, Western Civilization/European history, and world civilization guides students through the various types of writing assignments they encounter in a history class. Providing examples of student writing and candid assessments of student work, this text focuses on the rules and conventions of writing for the college history course.

The History Handbook, 2e [ISBN: 9780495906766]

Prepared by Carol Berkin of Baruch College, City University of New York, and Betty Anderson of Boston University. This book teaches students both basic and history-specific study skills such as how to read primary sources, research historical topics, and correctly cite sources. Substantially less expensive than comparable skill-building texts, *The History Handbook* also offers tips for Internet research and evaluating online sources.

Doing History: Research and Writing in the Digital Age, 2e [ISBN: 9781133587880]

Prepared by Michael J. Galgano, J. Chris Arndt, and Raymond M. Hyser of James Madison University. Whether you're starting down the path as a history major or simply looking for a straightforward and systematic guide to writing a successful paper, you'll find this text to be an indispensable handbook to historical research. This text's "soup to nuts" approach to researching and writing about history addresses every step of the process, from locating your sources and gathering information, to writing clearly and making proper use of various citation styles to avoid plagiarism. You'll also learn how to make the most of every tool available to you—especially the technology that helps you conduct the process efficiently and effectively.

The Modern Researcher, 6e [ISBN: 9780495318705]

Prepared by Jacques Barzun and Henry F. Graff of Columbia University. This classic introduction to the techniques of research and the art of expression is used widely in history courses, but is also appropriate for writing and research methods courses in other departments. Barzun and Graff thoroughly cover every aspect of research, from the selection of a topic through the gathering, analysis, writing, revision, and publication of findings, presenting the process not as a set of rules but through actual cases that put the subtleties of research in a useful context. Part One covers the principles and methods of research; Part Two covers writing, speaking, and getting one's work published.

ACKNOWLEDGMENTS

Both authors gratefully acknowledge that without the generosity of many others, this project could not have been completed.

William Duiker would like to thank Kumkum Chatterjee and On-cho Ng for their helpful comments about issues related to the history of India and premodern China. His longtime colleague Cyril Griffith, now deceased, was a cherished friend and a constant source of information about modern Africa. Art Goldschmidt has been of invaluable assistance in reading several chapters of the manuscript, as well as in unraveling many of the mysteries of Middle Eastern civilization. He has benefited from comments by Charles Ingrao on Spanish policies in Latin America, and from Tony Hopkins and Dan Baugh on British imperial policy. Dale Peterson has been an unending source of useful news items. Finally, he remains profoundly grateful to his wife, Yvonne V. Duiker, Ph.D. She has not only given her usual measure of love and support when this appeared to be an insuperable task, but she has also contributed her own time and expertise to enrich the sections on art and literature, thereby adding life and sparkle to this edition, as well as the earlier editions, of the book. To her, and to his daughters Laura and Claire, he will be forever thankful for bringing joy to his life.

Jackson Spielvogel would like to thank Art Goldschmidt, David Redles, and Christine Colin for their time and ideas. Daniel Haxall of Kutztown University provided valuable assistance with materials on postwar art, popular culture, Post-modern art and thought, and the digital age. He is especially grateful to Kathryn Spielvogel for her work as editorial associate. Above all, he thanks his family for their support. The gifts of love, laughter, and patience from his daughters, Jennifer and Kathryn; his sons, Eric and Christian; his daughters-in-law, Liz and Laurie; and his sons-in-law, Daniel and Eddie, were especially valuable. He also wishes to acknowledge his grandchildren, Devyn, Bryn, Drew, Elena, Sean, Emma, and Jackson, who bring great joy to his life. Diane, his wife and best friend, provided him with editorial assistance, wise counsel, and the loving support that made a project of this magnitude possible.

The authors are truly grateful to the people who have helped us to produce this book. We especially want to thank Clark Baxter, whose faith in our ability to do this project was inspiring. Margaret McAndrew Beasley thoughtfully, wisely, effi-ciently, and cheerfully guided the overall development of the eighth edition. We also thank Brooke Barbier for her suggestions and valuable insights. Abbie Baxter provided valuable assistance in suggesting illustrations and obtaining permissions for the illustrations. Anne Talvacchio was as cooperative and cheerful as she was competent in matters of production management.

A Note to Students About Language and the Dating of Time

One of the most difficult challenges in studying world history is coming to grips with the multitude of names, words, and phrases in unfamiliar languages. Unfortunately, this problem has no easy solution. We have tried to alleviate the difficulty, where possible, by providing an English-language translation of foreign words or phrases, and a pronunciation guide. The issue is especially complicated in the case of Chinese because two separate systems are commonly used to transliterate the spoken Chinese language into the Roman alphabet. The Wade-Giles system, invented in the nineteenth century, was the more frequently used until recent years, when the pinyin system was adopted by the People's Republic of China as its own official form of transliteration. We have opted to use the latter, as it appears to be gaining acceptance in the United States.

In our examination of world history, we also need to be aware of the dating of time. In recording the past, historians try to determine the exact time when events occurred. World War II in Europe, for example, began on September 1, 1939, when Adolf Hitler sent German troops into Poland, and ended on May 7, 1945, when Germany surrendered. By using dates, historians can place events in order and try to determine the development of patterns over periods of time.

If someone asked you when you were born, you would reply with a number, such as 1996. In the United States, we would all accept that number without question because it is part of the dating system followed in the Western world (Europe and the Western Hemisphere). In this system, events are dated by counting backward or forward from the birth of Jesus Christ (assumed to be the year 1). An event that took place 400 years before the birth of Christ would most commonly be dated 400 B.C. (before Christ). Dates after the birth of Christ are labeled as A.D. These letters stand for the Latin words *anno Domini*, which mean "in the year of the Lord" (the year since the birth of Christ). Thus, an event that took place 250 years after the birth of Christ is written A.D. 250. It can also be written as 250, just as you would not give your birth year as "A.D. 1996" but simply as "1996."

Many historians now prefer to use the abbreviations B.C.E. ("before the common era") and C.E. ("common era") instead of B.C. and A.D. This is especially true of world historians who prefer to use symbols that are not so Western or Christian oriented. The dates, of course, remain the same. Thus, 1950 B.C.E. and 1950 B.C. refer to the same year, as do A.D. 40 and 40 C.E. In keeping with the current usage by world historians, this book uses the terms B.C.E. and C.E.

Historians also make use of other terms to refer to time. A decade is 10 years, a century is 100 years, and a millennium is 1,000 years. The phrase "fourth century B.C.E." refers to the fourth period of 100 years counting backward from 1, the assumed date of the birth of Christ. Since the first century B.C.E. would be the years 100 B.C.E. to 1 B.C.E., the fourth century B.C.E. would be the years 400 B.C.E. to

301 B.C.E. We could say, then, that an event in 350 B.C.E. took place in the fourth century B.C.E.

The phrase "fourth century C.E." refers to the fourth period of 100 years after the birth of Christ. Since the first period of 100 years would be the years 1 to 100, the fourth period or fourth century would be the years 301 to 400. We could say, then, for example, that an event in 350 took place in the fourth century. Likewise, the first millennium B.C.E. refers to the years 1000 B.C.E. to 1 B.C.E., and the second millennium C.E. refers to the years 1001 to 2000.

The dating of events can also vary from people to people. Most people in the Western world use the Western calendar, also known as the Gregorian calendar after Pope Gregory XIII, who refined it in 1582. The Hebrew calendar uses a different system in which the year 1 is the equivalent of the Western year 3760 B.C.E., once calculated to be the date of the creation of the world, according to the Old Testament. Thus, the Western year 2013 corresponds to the year 5773 on the Jewish calendar. The Islamic calendar begins year 1 on the day Muhammad fled from Mecca, which is the year 622 on the Western calendar.

Themes for Understanding World History

As they pursue their craft, historians often organize their material on the basis of themes that enable them to ask and try to answer basic questions about the past. Such is our intention here. In preparing the eighth edition of this book, we have selected several major themes that we believe are especially important in understanding the course of world history. These themes transcend the boundaries of time and space and have relevance to all cultures since the beginning of the human experience.

In the chapters that follow, we will refer to these themes frequently as we advance from the prehistoric era to the present. Where appropriate, we shall make comparisons across cultural boundaries or across different time periods. To facilitate this process, we have included a Comparative Essay in each chapter that focuses on a particular theme within the specific time period discussed in that section of the book. For example, the Comparative Essays in Chapters 1 and 6 deal with the human impact on the natural environment during the premodern era, while those in Chapters 22 and 30 discuss the issue during the age of imperialism and in the contemporary world. Each Comparative Essay is identified with a particular theme, although it should be noted that many essays deal with several themes at the same time.

We have sought to illustrate these themes through the use of Comparative Illustrations in each chapter. These illustrations are comparative in nature and seek to encourage the reader to think about thematic issues in cross-cultural terms, while not losing sight of the unique characteristics of individual societies. Our seven themes, each divided into two subtopics, are listed below.

1. *Politics and Government* The study of politics seeks to answer certain basic questions that historians have about the structure of a society: How were people governed? What was the relationship between the ruler and the ruled? What people or groups of people (the political elites) held political power? What actions did people take to guarantee their security or change their form of government?

2. *Art and Ideas* We cannot understand a society without looking at its culture, or the common ideas, beliefs, and patterns of behavior that are passed on from one generation to the next. Culture includes both high culture and popular culture. High culture consists of the writings of a society's thinkers and the works of its artists. A society's popular culture is the world of ideas and experiences of ordinary people. Today, the media have embraced the term *popular culture* to describe the current trends and fashionable styles.

3. *Religion and Philosophy* Throughout history, people have sought to find a deeper meaning in human life. How have the world's great religions, such as Hinduism, Buddhism, Judaism, Christianity, and Islam, influenced people's lives? How have they spread to create new patterns of culture in other parts of the world?

4. *Family and Society* The most basic social unit in human society has always been the family. From a study of family and social patterns, we learn about the different social classes that make up a society and their relationships with one another. We also learn about the role of gender in individual societies. What different roles did men and women play in their societies? How and why were those roles different?

5. *Science and Technology* For thousands of years, people around the world have made scientific discoveries and technological innovations that have changed our world. From the creation of stone tools that made farming easier to advanced computers that guide our airplanes, science and technology have altered how humans have related to their world.

6. *Earth and the Environment* Throughout history, peoples and societies have been affected by the physical world in which they live. Climatic changes alone have been an important factor in human history. Through their economic activities, peoples and societies, in turn, have also made an impact on their world. Human activities have affected the physical environment and even endangered the very existence of entire societies and species.

7. *Interaction and Exchange* Many world historians believe that the exchange of ideas and innovations is the driving force behind the evolution of human societies. Knowledge of agriculture, writing and printing, metalworking, and navigational techniques, for example, spread gradually from one part of the world to other regions and eventually changed the face of the entire globe. The process of cultural and technological exchange took place in various ways, including trade, conquest, and the migration of peoples.

About the Authors

WILLIAM J. DUIKER is liberal arts professor emeritus of East Asian studies at The Pennsylvania State University. A former U.S. diplomat with service in Taiwan, South Vietnam, and Washington, D.C., he received his doctorate in Far Eastern history from Georgetown University in 1968, where his dissertation dealt with the Chinese educator and reformer Cai Yuanpei. At Penn State, he has written widely on the history of Vietnam and modern China, including the widely acclaimed *Communist Road to Power in Vietnam* (revised edition, Westview Press, 1996), which was selected for a Choice Outstanding Academic Book Award in 1982–1983 and 1996–1997. Other recent books are *China and Vietnam: The Roots of Conflict* (Berkeley, 1987), *U.S. Containment Policy and the Conflict in Indochina* (Stanford, 1995), *Sacred War: Nationalism and Revolution in a Divided Vietnam* (McGraw-Hill, 1995), and *Ho Chi Minh* (Hyperion, 2000), which was nominated for a Pulitzer Prize in 2001. Although his research specialization is in the field of nationalism and Asian revolutions, his intellectual interests are considerably more diverse. He has traveled widely and has taught courses on the history of communism and non-Western civilizations at Penn State, where he was awarded a Faculty Scholar Medal for Outstanding Achievement in the spring of 1996. In 2002 the College of Liberal Arts honored him with an Emeritus Distinction Award.

TO YVONNE,
FOR ADDING SPARKLE TO THIS BOOK AND TO MY LIFE
W.J.D.

JACKSON J. SPIELVOGEL is associate professor emeritus of history at The Pennsylvania State University. He received his Ph.D. from The Ohio State University, where he specialized in Reformation history under Harold J. Grimm. His articles and reviews have appeared in such journals as *Moreana, Journal of General Education, Catholic Historical Review, Archiv für Reformationsgeschichte*, and *American Historical Review*. He has also contributed chapters or articles to *The Social History of the Reformation, The Holy Roman Empire: A Dictionary Handbook, Simon Wiesenthal Center Annual of Holocaust Studies*, and *Utopian Studies*. His work has been supported by fellowships from the Fulbright Foundation and the Foundation for Reformation Research. At Penn State, he helped inaugurate the Western civilization course as well as a popular course on Nazi Germany. His book *Hitler and Nazi Germany* was published in 1987 (seventh edition, 2014). He is the author of

Western Civilization, published in 1991 (ninth edition, 2015). Professor Spielvogel has won five major university-wide teaching awards. During the year 1988–1989, he held the Penn State Teaching Fellowship, the university's most prestigious teaching award. In 1996, he won the Dean Arthur Ray Warnock Award for Outstanding Faculty Member and in 2000 received the Schreyer Honors College Excellence in Teaching Award.

TO DIANE,
WHOSE LOVE AND SUPPORT MADE IT ALL POSSIBLE
J.J.S.

WORLD HISTORY

EIGHTH EDITION

Part One

THE FIRST CIVILIZATIONS
AND THE RISE OF EMPIRES
(PREHISTORY TO 500 C.E.)

CHAPTER 1
Early Humans and the First Civilizations

CHAPTER 2
Ancient India

CHAPTER 3
China in Antiquity

CHAPTER 4
The Civilization of the Greeks

CHAPTER 5
The Roman World Empire

For hundreds of thousands of years, human beings lived in small groups or villages, seeking to survive by hunting, fishing, and foraging in an often hostile environment. Then, in the space of a few thousand years, an abrupt change occurred as people in a few areas of the globe began to master the art of cultivating food crops. As food production increased, the population in these areas grew, and people began to live in larger communities. Cities appeared and became centers of cultural and religious development. Historians refer to these changes as the beginnings of civilization.

How and why did the first civilizations arise? What role did cross-cultural contacts play in their development? What was the nature of the relationship between these permanent settlements and nonagricultural peoples living elsewhere in the world? Finally, what brought about the demise of these early civilizations, and what legacy did they leave for their successors in the region? The first civilizations that emerged in Mesopotamia, Egypt, India, and China in the fourth and third millennia B.C.E. all shared a number of basic characteristics. Perhaps most important was that each developed in a river valley that was able to provide the agricultural resources needed to maintain a large population.

The emergence of these sedentary societies had a major impact on the social organizations, religious beliefs, and ways of life of the peoples living in them. As population increased and cities sprang up, centralized authority became a necessity. And in the cities, new forms of livelihood arose to satisfy the growing demand for social services and consumer goods. Some people became artisans or merchants, while others became warriors, scholars, or priests. In some cases, the early cities reflected the hierarchical character of the society as a whole, with a central royal palace surrounded by an imposing wall to separate the rulers from the remainder of the urban population.

Although the emergence of the first civilizations led to the formation of cities governed by elites, the vast majority of the population consisted of peasants or slaves working on the lands of the wealthy. In general, rural peoples were less affected by the changes than their urban counterparts. Farmers continued to live in simple mud-and-thatch huts, and many continued to face legal restrictions on their freedom of action and movement. Slavery was common in virtually all ancient societies.

Within these civilizations, the nature of social organization and relationships also began to change. As the concept of private property spread, people were less likely to live in large kinship groups, and the nuclear family became increasingly prevalent. Gender roles came to be differentiated, with men working in the fields or at various specialized occupations and women remaining in the home. Wives were less likely to be viewed as partners than as possessions under the control of their husbands.

These new civilizations were also the sites of significant religious and cultural developments. All of them gave birth to new religions that sought to explain and even influence the forces of nature. Winning the approval of the gods was deemed crucial to a community's success, and a professional class of priests emerged to handle relations with the divine world.

Writing was an important development in the evolution of these new civilizations. Eventually, all of them used writing as both a means of communication and an avenue of creative expression.

From the beginnings of the first civilizations around 3000 B.C.E., the trend was toward the creation of larger territorial states with more sophisticated systems of control. This process reached a high point in the first millennium B.C.E. Between 1000 and 500 B.C.E., the Assyrians and Persians amassed empires that encompassed large areas of the Middle East. The conquests of Alexander the Great in the fourth century B.C.E. created an even larger, if short-lived, empire that soon divided into four kingdoms. Later, the western portion of these kingdoms, along with the Mediterranean world and much of western Europe, fell subject to the mighty empire of the Romans. At the same time, much of India became part of the Mauryan Empire. Finally, in the last few centuries B.C.E., the Qin and Han dynasties of China governed a unified Chinese empire.

At first, these new civilizations had relatively little contact with peoples in the surrounding regions. But regional trade had started to take hold in the Middle East, and probably in southern and eastern Asia as well, at a very early date. As the population increased, the volume of trade rose with it, and the new civilizations moved outward to acquire new lands and access needed resources. As they expanded, they began to encounter peoples along the periphery of their empires.

Little evidence has survived to know the nature of these first encounters, but it is likely that the results varied according to time and place. In some cases, the growing civilizations found it relatively easy to absorb isolated communities of agricultural or food-gathering peoples that they encountered. Such was the case in southern China and southern India. But in other instances, notably among the nomadic or seminomadic peoples in the central and northeastern parts of Asia, the problem was more complicated and often resulted in bitter and extended conflict.

Over a long period of time, contacts between these nomadic or seminomadic peoples and settled civilizations gradually developed. Often the relationship, at least at the outset, was mutually beneficial, as each needed goods produced by the other. Nomadic peoples in Central Asia also served as an important link for goods and ideas transported over long distances between sedentary civilizations as early as 3000 B.C.E. Overland trade throughout southwestern Asia was already well established by the third millennium B.C.E.

Eventually, the relationship between the settled peoples and the nomadic peoples became increasingly tense. Where conflict occurred, the governments of the sedentary civilizations used a variety of techniques to resolve the problem, including negotiations, conquest, or alliance with other pastoral peoples to isolate their primary tormentors.

In the end, these early civilizations collapsed not only as a result of nomadic invasions but also because of their own weaknesses, which made them increasingly vulnerable to attacks along the frontier. Some of their problems were political, and others were related to climatic change or environmental problems.

The fall of the ancient empires did not mark the end of civilization, of course, but rather served as a transition to a new stage of increasing complexity in the evolution of human society.

1

EARLY HUMANS AND THE FIRST CIVILIZATIONS

© Nik Wheeler/CORBIS

Excavation of Warka showing the ruins of Uruk

CHAPTER OUTLINE

• The First Humans • The Emergence of Civilization • Civilization in Mesopotamia • Egyptian Civilization: "The Gift of the Nile" • New Centers of Civilization • The Rise of New Empires

THE FIRST HUMANS

Historians rely mostly on documents to create their pictures of the past, but no written records exist for the prehistory of humankind. In their absence, the story of early humanity depends on archaeological and, more recently, biological information, which anthropologists and archaeologists use to formulate theories about our early past. Although modern science has given us more precise methods for examining prehistory, much of our understanding of early humans still relies on considerable conjecture.

The earliest humanlike creatures—known as **hominids**—lived in Africa some 3 to 4 million years ago. Called Australopithecines (aw-stray-loh-PITH-uh-synz), or "southern ape-men," by their discoverers, they flourished in eastern and southern Africa and were the first hominids to make simple stone tools. Australopithecines may also have been bipedal—that is, they may have walked upright on two legs, a trait that would have enabled them to move over long distances and make use of their arms and legs for different purposes.

In 1959, Louis and Mary Leakey discovered a new form of hominid in Africa that they labeled *Homo habilis* ("skillful human"). The Leakeys believed that *Homo habilis*, which had a brain almost 50 percent larger than that of the Australopithecines, was the earliest toolmaking hominid. Their larger brains and ability to walk upright allowed these hominids to become more sophisticated in searching for meat, seeds, and nuts for nourishment.

A new phase in early human development occurred around 1.5 million years ago with the emergence of *Homo erectus* ("upright human"). A more advanced human form, *Homo erectus* made use of larger and more varied tools and was the first hominid to leave Africa and move into Europe and Asia.

The Emergence of *Homo sapiens* Around 250,000 years ago, a crucial stage in human development began with the emergence of *Homo sapiens* (HOH-moh SAY-pee-unz) ("wise human being"). The first anatomically modern humans, known as *Homo sapiens sapiens* ("wise, wise human being"), appeared in Africa between 200,000 and 150,000 years ago. Recent evidence indicates that they began to spread outside Africa around 70,000 years ago. Map 1.1 shows probable dates for different movements, although many of these are still controversial.

These modern humans, who were our direct ancestors, soon encountered other hominids, such as the Neanderthals, whose remains were first found in the Neander valley in Germany. Neanderthal remains have since been found in both Europe and western Asia and have been dated to between 200,000 and 30,000 B.C.E. Neanderthals relied on a variety of stone tools and were the first early people to bury their dead. By 30,000 B.C.E., *Homo sapiens sapiens* had replaced the Neanderthals, who had largely become extinct.

The Spread of Humans: Out of Africa or Multiregional?   The movements of the first modern humans were rarely sudden or rapid. Groups of people advanced

MAP 1.1 The Spread of *Homo sapiens sapiens*

Homo sapiens sapiens spread from Africa beginning about 70,000 years ago. Living and traveling in small groups, these anatomically modern humans were hunter-gatherers.

beyond their old hunting grounds at a rate of only 2 to 3 miles per generation. This was enough, however, to populate the world in some tens of thousands of years. Some scholars, who advocate a multiregional theory, have suggested that advanced human creatures may have emerged independently in different parts of the world, rather than in Africa alone. But the latest genetic, archaeological, and climatic evidence strongly supports the out-of-Africa theory as the most likely explanation of human origin. In any case, by 10,000 B.C.E., members of the *Homo sapiens sapiens* species could be found throughout the world. By that time, it was the only human species left. All humans today, be they Europeans, Australian Aborigines, or Africans, belong to the same subspecies of human being.

The Hunter-Gatherers of the Paleolithic Age

One of the basic distinguishing features of the human species is the ability to make tools. The earliest tools were made of stone, and so this early period of human history (c. 2,500,000–10,000 B.C.E.) has been designated the **Paleolithic Age** (*paleolithic* is Greek for "old stone").

For hundreds of thousands of years, humans relied on gathering and hunting for their daily food. Paleolithic peoples had a close relationship with the world around them, and over a period of time, they came to know which plants to eat and which animals to hunt. They did not know how to grow crops or raise animals, however. They gathered wild nuts, berries, fruits, and a variety of wild grains and green plants. Around the world, they captured and consumed various animals, including buffalo, horses, bison, wild goats, reindeer, and fish.

The gathering of wild plants and the hunting of animals no doubt led to certain patterns of living. Archaeologists and anthropologists have speculated that Paleolithic people lived in small bands of twenty to thirty individuals. They were nomadic, moving from place to place to follow animal migrations and vegetation cycles. Hunting depended on careful observation of animal behavior patterns and required a group effort for success. Over the years, tools became more refined and more useful. The invention of the spear and later the bow and arrow made hunting considerably easier. Harpoons and fishhooks made of bone increased the catch of fish.

Both men and women were responsible for finding food—the chief work of Paleolithic people. Since women bore and raised the children, they generally stayed close to the camps, but they played an important role in acquiring food by gathering berries, nuts, and grains. Men hunted for wild animals, an activity that often took them far from camp. Because both men and women played important roles in providing for the band's survival, many scientists believe that a rough equality existed between men and women. Indeed, some speculate that both men and women made the decisions that governed the activities of the Paleolithic band.

Some groups of Paleolithic peoples found shelter in caves, but over time, they also created new types of shelter. Perhaps the most common was a simple structure of wood poles or sticks covered with animal hides. Where wood was scarce, Paleolithic hunter-gatherers might use the bones of mammoths for the framework and cover it with animal hides. The systematic use of fire, which archaeologists believe began around 500,000 years ago, made it possible for the caves and human-made structures to have a source of light and heat. Fire also enabled early humans to cook their food, making it taste better, last longer, and in the case of some plants, such as wild grains, easier to chew and digest.

The making of tools and the use of fire—two important technological innovations of Paleolithic peoples—remind us how crucial the ability to adapt was to human survival. Changing physical conditions during periodic ice ages posed a considerable threat to human existence. Paleolithic peoples used their technological innovations to change their physical environment. By working together, they found a way to survive. And by passing on their common practices, skills, and material products to their children, they ensured that later generations, too, could survive in a harsh environment.

But Paleolithic peoples did more than just survive. The cave paintings of large animals found in southwestern France and northern Spain bear witness to the cultural activity of Paleolithic peoples. A cave discovered in southern France in 1994—known as the Chauvet (shoh-VAY) cave after the leader of the expedition that found it—contains more than three hundred paintings of lions, oxen, owls, bears, and other animals. Most of these are animals that Paleolithic people did not hunt, which suggests to some scholars that the paintings were made for religious or even decorative purposes. The discoverers were overwhelmed by what they saw: "There was a moment of ecstasy.... They overflowed with joy and emotion in their turn.... These were moments of indescribable madness."[1]

The Neolithic Revolution, c. 10,000–4000 B.C.E.

The end of the last ice age around 10,000 B.C.E. was followed by what is called the **Neolithic Revolution**, a significant change in living patterns that occurred in the New Stone Age (*neolithic* is Greek for "new stone"). The name "New Stone Age" is misleading, however. Although Neolithic peoples made a new type of polished stone axes, this was not the most significant change they introduced.

An Agricultural Revolution   The biggest change was the shift from gathering plants and hunting animals for sustenance (food gathering) to producing food by systematic agriculture (food production). The planting of grains and vegetables provided a regular supply of food, while the domestication of animals, such as sheep, goats, cattle, and pigs, added a steady source of meat, milk, and fibers such as wool for clothing. Larger animals could also be used as beasts of burden. The growing of crops and the taming of food-producing animals created a new relationship between humans and nature. Historians like to speak of this as an agricultural revolution. Revolutionary change is dramatic and requires great effort, but the ability to acquire food on a regular basis gave humans greater control over their environment. It enabled them to give up their nomadic ways of life and begin to live in settled communities. The increase in food supplies also led to a noticeable expansion of the population.

The shift from hunting and gathering to food producing was not as sudden as was once believed, however. The **Mesolithic Age** ("Middle Stone Age," c. 10,000–7000 B.C.E.) saw a gradual transition from a food-gathering and hunting economy

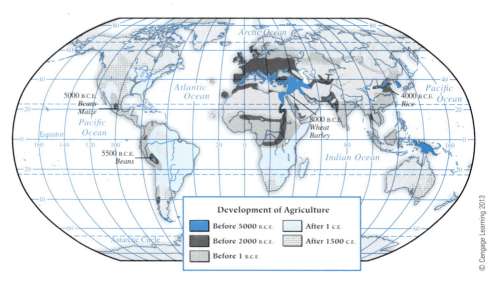

MAP 1.2 The Development of Agriculture

Agriculture first began between 8000 and 5000 B.C.E. in four different parts of the world. It allowed the establishment of permanent settlements where crops could be grown and domesticated animals that produced meat and milk could be easily tended.

to a food-producing one and witnessed a gradual domestication of animals as well. Likewise, the movement toward the use of plants and their seeds as an important source of nourishment was not sudden. Moreover, throughout the Neolithic period, hunting and gathering as well as nomadic herding remained ways of life for many people around the world.

Systematic agriculture developed independently in different areas of the world between 8000 and 5000 B.C.E. Inhabitants of the Middle East began cultivating wheat and barley and domesticating pigs, cattle, goats, and sheep by 8000 B.C.E. From the Middle East, farming spread into southeastern Europe and, by 4000 B.C.E., was well established in central Europe and the coastal regions of the Mediterranean. The cultivation of wheat and barley also spread from western Asia into the Nile Valley of Egypt by 6000 B.C.E. and soon moved up the Nile to other areas of Africa, especially Ethiopia. In the woodlands and tropical forests of West Africa, a separate agricultural system emerged, based on the cultivation of tubers or root crops such as yams. The cultivation of wheat and barley also moved eastward into the highlands of northwestern and central India between 7000 and 5000 B.C.E. By 5000 B.C.E., rice was being cultivated in southeastern Asia, and from there it spread into southern China. In northern China, the cultivation of millet and the domestication of pigs and dogs seem well established by 6000 B.C.E. In the Western Hemisphere, Mesoamericans (inhabitants of present-day Mexico and Central America) domesticated beans, squash, and maize (corn) as well as dogs and fowl between 7000 and 5000 B.C.E.

Neolithic Farming Villages   The growing of crops on a regular basis gave rise to more permanent settlements, which historians refer to as Neolithic farming villages or towns. Although Neolithic villages appeared in Europe, India, Egypt, China, and Mesoamerica, the oldest and most extensive ones were located in the Middle East. Jericho, in Canaan near the Dead Sea, was in existence by 8000 B.C.E. and covered several acres by 7000 B.C.E. It had a wall several feet thick that enclosed houses made of sun-dried mudbricks. Çatal Hüyük (chaht-ul hoo-YOOK), located in modern Turkey, was an even larger community. Its walls enclosed 32 acres, and its population probably reached six thousand inhabitants during its high point from 6700 to 5700 B.C.E. People lived in simple mudbrick houses that were built so close to one another that there were few streets. To get to their homes, people would walk along the rooftops and enter the house through a hole in the roof.

Archaeologists have discovered twelve cultivated products in Çatal Hüyük, including fruits, nuts, and three kinds of wheat. People grew their own food and stored it in storerooms in their homes. Domesticated animals, especially cattle, yielded meat, milk, and hides. Food surpluses also made it possible for people to engage in activities other than farming. Some people became artisans and made weapons and jewelry that were traded with neighboring peoples.

Religious shrines housing figures of gods and goddesses have been found at Çatal Hüyük, as have a number of female statuettes. Molded with noticeably large breasts and buttocks, these "earth mothers" perhaps symbolically represented the fertility of both "our mother" earth and human mothers. The shrines and the statues point to the important role of religious practices in the lives of these Neolithic peoples.

From Hunter–Gatherers and Herders to Farmers

EARTH & ENVIRONMENT

About ten thousand years ago, human beings began to practice the cultivation of crops and the domestication of animals. The exact time and place that crops were first cultivated successfully is uncertain. The first farmers undoubtedly used simple techniques and still relied primarily on other forms of food production, such as hunting, foraging, and pastoralism (herding). The real breakthrough came when farmers began to cultivate crops along the floodplains of river systems. The advantage was that crops grown in such areas were not as dependent on rainfall and therefore produced a more reliable harvest. An additional benefit was that the sediment carried by the river waters deposited nutrients in the soil, enabling the farmer to cultivate a single plot of land for many years without moving to a new location. Thus, the first truly sedentary societies were born.

The spread of river valley agriculture in various parts of Asia and Africa was the decisive factor in the rise of the first civilizations. The increase in food production in these regions led to a significant growth in population, while efforts to control the flow of water to maximize the irrigation of cultivated areas and to protect the local inhabitants from hostile forces outside the community provoked the first steps toward cooperative activities on a large scale. The need to oversee the entire process brought about the emergence of an elite that was eventually transformed into a government.

We shall investigate this process in the next several chapters as we explore the rise of civilizations in the Mediterranean, the Middle East, South Asia, China, and the Americas. We shall also raise a number of important questions: Why did human communities in some areas that had the capacity to support agriculture not take the leap to farming? Why did other groups that had managed to master the cultivation of crops not take the next step and create large and advanced societies? Finally, what happened to the existing communities of hunter-gatherers who were overrun or driven out as the agricultural revolution spread throughout the world?

Over the years, a number of possible explanations, some of them biological, others cultural or environmental, have been advanced to answer such questions. According to Jared Diamond, in *Guns, Germs, and Steel: The Fates of Human Societies*, the ultimate causes of such differences lie not within the character or cultural values of the resident population but in the nature of the local climate and topography. These influence the degree to which local crops and animals can be put to human use and then be transmitted to adjoining regions. In Mesopotamia, for example, the widespread availability of edible crops, such as wheat and barley, helped promote the transition to agriculture in the region. At the same time, the absence of land barriers between Mesopotamia and its neighbors to the east and west facilitated the rapid spread of agricultural techniques and crops to climatically similar regions in the Indus River valley and Egypt.

Q *What role did the development of agriculture play in the emergence of civilization?*

Consequences of the Neolithic Revolution   The Neolithic agricultural revolution had far-reaching consequences. Once people settled in villages or towns, they built houses for protection and other structures for the storage of goods. As organized communities stored food and accumulated material goods, they began to engage in trade. In the Middle East, for example, the new communities exchanged such objects as shells, flint, and semiprecious stones. People also began to specialize in certain crafts, and a division of labor developed. Pottery was made from clay and baked in fire to make it hard. The pots were used for cooking and to store grains. Woven baskets were also used for storage. Stone tools became refined as flint blades were used to make sickles and hoes for use in the fields. Obsidian—a volcanic glass that was easily flaked—was also used to create very sharp tools. In the course of the Neolithic Age, many of the food plants still in use today began to be cultivated. Moreover, vegetable fibers from such plants as flax and cotton were used to make thread that was woven into cloth.

The change to systematic agriculture in the Neolithic Age also had consequences for the relationship between men and women. Men assumed the primary responsibility for working in the fields and herding animals, jobs that kept them away from the home. Women remained behind, grinding grain into flour, caring for the children, weaving cloth, making cheese from milk, and performing other household tasks that required considerable labor. In time, as work outside the home was increasingly perceived as more important than work done in the home, men came to play the more dominant role in human society, which gave rise to the practice of **patriarchy** (PAY-tree-ark-ee), or a society dominated by men, a basic pattern that has persisted to our own times.

Other patterns set in the Neolithic Age also proved to be enduring elements of human history. Fixed dwellings, domesticated animals, regular farming, a division of labor, men holding power—all of these are part of the human story. For all of our scientific and technological progress, human survival still depends on the growing and storing of food, an accomplishment of people in the Neolithic Age. The Neolithic Revolution was truly a turning point in human history.

Between 4000 and 3000 B.C.E., significant technical developments began to transform the Neolithic towns. The invention of writing enabled records to be kept, and the use of metals marked a new level of human control over the environment and its resources. Already before 4000 B.C.E., artisans had discovered that metal-bearing rocks could be heated to liquefy the metal, which could then be cast in molds to produce tools and weapons that were more useful than stone instruments. Although copper was the first metal to be used for producing tools, after 4000 B.C.E., metalworkers in western Asia discovered that a combination of copper and tin produced bronze, a much harder and more durable metal than copper. Its widespread use has led historians to call the period from around 3000 to 1200 B.C.E. the Bronze Age; thereafter, bronze was increasingly replaced by iron.

At first, Neolithic settlements were hardly more than villages. But as their inhabitants mastered the art of farming, more complex human societies gradually emerged. As wealth increased, these societies sought to protect it from being plundered by outsiders and so began to develop armies and to build walled cities. By the beginning of the Bronze Age, the concentration of larger numbers of people in river valleys was leading to a whole new pattern for human life.

The Emergence of Civilization

As we have seen, early human beings formed small groups that developed a simple culture that enabled them to survive. As human societies grew and developed greater complexity, civilization came into being. A **civilization** is a complex culture in which large numbers of people share a variety of common elements. Historians have identified a number of basic characteristics of civilization, including the following:

1. *An urban focus.* Cities became the centers for political, economic, social, cultural, and religious development. The cities that emerged were much larger than the Neolithic towns that preceded them.
2. *New political and military structures.* An organized government bureaucracy arose to meet the administrative demands of the growing population, and armies were organized to gain land and power and for defense.
3. *A new social structure based on economic power.* While kings and an upper class of priests, political leaders, and warriors dominated, there also existed large groups of free common people (farmers, artisans, craftspeople) and, at the very bottom of the social hierarchy, a class of slaves.
4. *The development of more complexity in a material sense.* Surpluses of agricultural crops freed some people to work in occupations other than farming. Demand among ruling elites for luxury items encouraged the creation of new products. And as urban populations exported finished goods in exchange for raw materials from neighboring populations, organized trade grew substantially.
5. *A distinct religious structure.* The gods were deemed crucial to the community's success, and a professional priestly class, serving as stewards of the gods' property, regulated relations with the gods.
6. *The development of writing.* Kings, priests, merchants, and artisans used writing to keep records.
7. *New forms of significant artistic and intellectual activity.* For example, monumental architectural structures, usually religious, occupied a prominent place in urban environments.

Early Civilizations Around the World

The first civilizations that developed in Mesopotamia and Egypt will be examined in detail in this chapter. But civilizations also developed independently in other parts of the world. Between 3000 and 1500 B.C.E., the valleys of the Indus River in India supported a flourishing civilization that extended hundreds of miles from the Himalayas to the coast of the Arabian Sea. Two major cities—Harappa and Mohenjo-Daro—were at the heart of this advanced civilization, which flourished for hundreds of years. As in the city-states that arose in Mesopotamia and along the Nile, the Harappan economy was based primarily on farming, but Harappan civilization also carried on extensive trade with Mesopotamia. Textiles and food were imported from the Mesopotamian city-states in exchange for copper, lumber, precious stones, cotton, and various types of luxury goods.

Another river valley civilization emerged along the Yellow River in northern China about four thousand years ago. Under the Shang dynasty of kings, which ruled from 1570 to 1045 B.C.E., this civilization contained impressive cities with huge city walls, royal palaces, and large royal tombs. A system of irrigation enabled early Chinese civilization to maintain a prosperous farming society ruled by an aristocratic class whose major concern was war.

Scholars have long believed that civilization emerged only in four areas—the fertile river valleys of the Tigris and Euphrates, the Nile, the Indus, and the Yellow River—that is, in Southwest Asia, Egypt, India, and China. Recently, however, archaeologists have discovered other early civilizations. One of these flourished in Central Asia (in what are now the republics of Turkmenistan and Uzbekistan) around four thousand years ago. People in this civilization built mudbrick buildings, raised sheep and goats, had bronze tools, used a system of irrigation to grow wheat and barley, and developed a writing system.

Another early civilization was discovered in the Supe River valley of Peru. At the center of this civilization was the city of Caral, which flourished around 2600 B.C.E. It contained buildings for officials, apartment buildings, and grand residences, all built of stone. The inhabitants of Caral also developed a system of irrigation by diverting a river more than a mile upstream into their fields. This Peruvian culture reached its height during the first millennium B.C.E.

What Were the Causes of Civilization? Why civilizations developed remains difficult to explain. Since civilizations developed independently in different parts of the world, can general causes be identified that would tell us why all of these civilizations emerged? A number of possible explanations have been suggested. One theory maintains that challenges forced human beings to make efforts that resulted in the rise of civilization. Some scholars have argued that material forces, such as the accumulation of food surpluses, made possible the specialization of labor and development of large communities with bureaucratic organization. But some areas were not naturally conducive to agriculture. Abundant food could be produced only through a massive human effort to manage the water, an undertaking that required organization and bureaucratic control and led to civilized cities. Other historians have argued that nonmaterial forces, primarily religious, provided the sense of unity and purpose that made such organized activities possible. Finally, some scholars doubt that we will ever discover the actual causes of early civilization.

CIVILIZATION IN MESOPOTAMIA

The Greeks called the valley between the Tigris and Euphrates Rivers Mesopotamia (mess-uh-puh-TAY-mee-uh), the land "between the rivers." The region receives little rain, but the soil of the plain of southern Mesopotamia was enlarged and enriched over the years by layers of silt deposited by the two rivers. In late spring, the Tigris and Euphrates overflow their banks and deposit their fertile silt, but since this flooding depends on the melting of snows in the upland mountains where the rivers begin, it is irregular and sometimes catastrophic. In such circumstances, farming could be accomplished only with human intervention in the form of irrigation and drainage ditches. A complex system was required to control the flow of the rivers and produce the crops. Large-scale irrigation made possible the expansion of agriculture in this region, and the abundant food provided the material base for the emergence of civilization in Mesopotamia.

The City-States of Ancient Mesopotamia The creators of the first Mesopotamian civilization were the Sumerians (soo-MER-ee-unz *or* soo-MEER-ee-unz), a people whose origins remain unclear. By 3000 B.C.E., they had established a number of independent cities in southern Mesopotamia, including Eridu, Ur, Uruk, Umma, and Lagash. As the cities expanded, they came to exercise political and economic control over the surrounding countryside, forming city-states, which were the basic units of Sumerian civilization.

Sumerian Cities Sumerian cities were surrounded by walls. Uruk, for example, was encircled by a wall 6 miles long with defense towers located every 30 to 35 feet along it. City dwellings, built of sun-dried bricks, included both the small flats of peasants and the larger dwellings of the civic and priestly officials. Although Mesopotamia had little stone or wood for building purposes, it did have plenty of mud. Mudbricks, easily shaped by hand, were left to bake in the hot sun until they were hard enough to use for building. People in Mesopotamia were remarkably innovative with mudbricks, inventing the arch and the dome and constructing some of the largest brick buildings in the world.

© Cengage Learning 2013

MAP 1.3 The Ancient Near East

The Fertile Crescent encompassed land with access to water. Employing flood management and irrigation systems, the peoples of the region established civilizations based on agriculture. These civilizations developed writing, law codes, and economic specialization.

The most prominent building in a Sumerian city was the temple, which was dedicated to the chief god or goddess of the city and often built atop a massive stepped tower called a **ziggurat** (ZIG-uh-rat). The Sumerians believed that gods and goddesses owned the cities, and much wealth was used to build temples as well as elaborate houses for the priests and priestesses who served the deities. Priests and priestesses, who supervised the temples and their property, had great power. In fact, historians believe that in the early stages of certain city-states, priests and priestesses may have had an important role in governance. The Sumerians believed that the gods ruled the cities, making the state a **theocracy** (government by a divine authority). Ruling power, however, was primarily in the hands of worldly figures known as kings.

Kingship   Sumerians viewed kingship as divine in origin—kings, they believed, derived their power from the gods and were the agents of the gods. As one person said in a petition to his king, "You in your judgment, you are the son of Anu [god of the sky]; your commands, like the word of a god, cannot be reversed; your words, like rain pouring down from heaven, are without number."[2] Regardless of their origins, kings had power—they led armies and organized workers for the irrigation projects on which Mesopotamian farming depended. The army, the government bureaucracy, and the priests and priestesses all aided the kings in their rule. Befitting their power, Sumerian kings lived in large palaces with their wives and children.

Economy and Society   The economy of the Sumerian city-states was primarily agricultural, but commerce and industry became important as well. The people of Mesopotamia produced woolen textiles, pottery, and metalwork. The Sumerians imported copper, tin, and timber in exchange for dried fish, wool, barley, wheat, and metal goods. Traders traveled by land to the eastern Mediterranean in the west and by sea to India in the east. The introduction of the wheel, which had been invented around 3000 B.C.E. by nomadic people living in the region north of the Black Sea, led to carts with wheels that made the transport of goods easier.

Sumerian city-states probably contained four major social groups: elites, dependent commoners, free commoners, and slaves. Elites included royal and priestly officials and their families. Dependent commoners included the elites' clients, who worked for the palace and temple estates. Free commoners worked as farmers, merchants, fishers, scribes, and craftspeople. Probably 90 percent or more of the population were farmers. Slaves belonged to palace officials, who used them in building projects; to temple officials, who used mostly female slaves to weave cloth and grind grain; and to rich landowners, who used them for agricultural and domestic work.

Empires in Ancient Mesopotamia   As the number of Sumerian city-states grew and the states expanded, new conflicts arose as city-state fought city-state for control of land and water. The fortunes of various city-states rose and fell over the centuries. The constant wars, with their burning and sacking of cities, left many Sumerians in deep despair, as is evident in the words of this Sumerian poem from the city of Ur:

Ur is destroyed, bitter is its lament.
The country's blood now fills its holes like hot bronze in a mold.
Bodies dissolve like fat in the sun.
Our temple is destroyed, the gods have abandoned us, like migrating birds.
Smoke lies on our city like a shroud.[3]

The Akkadian Empire   Located in the flat land of Mesopotamia, the Sumerian city-states were also open to invasion. To the north of the Sumerian city-states were the Akkadians (uh-KAY-dee-unz). We call them a Semitic people because of the type of language they spoke. Around 2340 B.C.E., Sargon, leader of the Akkadians, overran the Sumerian city-states and established a dynastic empire. Sargon used the former rulers of the conquered city-states as his governors. His power was based on the military, namely, his standing army of 5,400 men. Sargon's empire, including all of Mesopotamia as well as lands westward to the Mediterranean, inspired generations of Near Eastern leaders to emulate his accomplishment. Even in the first millennium B.C.E., Sargon was still remembered in chronicles as a king of Akkad who "had no rival or equal, spread his splendor over all the lands, and crossed the sea in the east. In his eleventh year, he conquered the western land to its furthest point, and brought it under his sole authority."[4] Attacks from neighboring hill peoples eventually caused the Akkadian empire to fall, and its end by 2100 B.C.E. brought a return to independent city-states and the conflicts between them. It was not until 1792 B.C.E. that a new empire came to control much of Mesopotamia under Hammurabi (ham-uh-RAH-bee), who ruled over the Amorites or Old Babylonians, a large group of Semitic-speaking seminomads.

Hammurabi's Empire   Hammurabi (1792–1750 B.C.E.) employed a well-disciplined army of foot soldiers who carried axes, spears, and copper or bronze daggers. He learned to divide his opponents and subdue them one by one. Using such methods, he gained control of Sumer and Akkad, creating a new Mesopotamian kingdom. After his conquests, he called himself "the sun of Babylon, the king who has made the four quarters of the world subservient," and established a new capital at Babylon.

Hammurabi, the man of war, was also a man of peace. A collection of his letters, found by archaeologists, reveals that he took a strong interest in state affairs. He built temples, defensive walls, and irrigation canals; encouraged trade; and brought about an economic revival. Indeed, Hammurabi saw himself as a shepherd to his people: "I am indeed the shepherd who brings peace, whose scepter is just. My benevolent shade was spread over my city. I held the people of the lands of Sumer and Akkad safely on my lap."[5] After his death, however, a series of weak kings were unable to keep Hammurabi's empire united, and it finally fell to new invaders.

The Code of Hammurabi: Society in Mesopotamia   Hammurabi is best remembered for his law code, a collection of 282 laws. Although many scholars today view Hammurabi's collection less as a code of laws and more as an attempt by Hammurabi to portray himself as the source of justice to his people, the code still gives us a glimpse of the Mesopotamian society of his time.

The Code of Hammurabi reveals a society with a system of strict justice. Penalties for criminal offenses were severe and varied according to the social class of the victim. A crime against a member of the upper class (a noble) by a member of the lower class (a commoner) was punished more severely than the same offense against a member of the lower class. Moreover, the principle of "an eye for an eye, a tooth for a tooth" was fundamental to this system of justice. This meant that punishments should fit the crime: "If a freeman has destroyed the eye of a member of the aristocracy, they shall destroy his eye" (Code of Hammurabi, No. 196). Hammurabi's code also had an impact on legal ideas in Southwest Asia for hundreds of years, as the following verse from the Hebrew Bible (Leviticus 24:19–20) demonstrates: "If anyone injures his neighbor, whatever he has done must be done to him: fracture for fracture, eye for eye, tooth for tooth. As he has injured the other, so he is to be injured."

The largest category of laws in the Code of Hammurabi focused on marriage and the family. Parents arranged marriages for their children. After marriage, the parties involved signed a marriage contract; without it, no one was considered legally married. While the husband provided a bridal payment to the bride's parents, the woman's parents were responsible for a dowry to the new husband.

As in many patriarchal societies, women possessed far fewer privileges and rights in the married relationship than men. A woman's place was in the home, and failure to fulfill her expected duties was grounds for divorce. If she was not able to bear children, her husband could divorce her. Furthermore, a wife who was a "gadabout, ... neglecting her house [and] humiliating her husband, shall be prosecuted" (No. 143). We do know that in practice not all women remained at home. Some worked in the fields and others in business, where they were especially prominent in running taverns.

Women were guaranteed some rights, however. If a woman was divorced without good reason, she received the dowry back. A woman could seek a divorce and get her dowry back if her husband was unable to show that she had done anything wrong. In theory, a wife was guaranteed the use of her husband's legal property in the event of his death. A mother could also decide which of her sons would receive an inheritance.

Sexual relations were strictly regulated as well. Husbands, but not wives, were permitted sexual activity outside marriage. A wife and her lover caught committing adultery were pitched into the river, although if the husband pardoned his wife, the king could pardon the guilty man. Incest was strictly forbidden. If a father had incestuous relations with his daughter, he would be banished. Incest between a son and his mother resulted in both being burned.

Fathers ruled their children as well as their wives. Obedience was duly expected: "If a son has struck his father, they shall cut off his hand" (No. 195). If a son committed a serious enough offense, his father could disinherit him, although fathers were not permitted to disinherit their sons arbitrarily.

The Culture of Mesopotamia

A spiritual worldview was of fundamental importance to Mesopotamian culture. To the peoples of Mesopotamia, the gods were living realities who affected all aspects of life. It was crucial, therefore, that the correct hierarchies be observed. Leaders could prepare armies for war, but success really depended on a favorable relationship with the gods. This helps explain the importance of the priestly class and is the reason why even the kings took great care to dedicate offerings and monuments to the gods.

The Importance of Religion   The physical environment had an obvious impact on the Mesopotamian view of the universe. Ferocious floods, heavy downpours, scorching winds, and oppressive humidity were all part of the Mesopotamian climate. These conditions and the resulting famines easily convinced Mesopotamians that this world was controlled by supernatural forces and that the days of human beings "are numbered; whatever he may do, he is but wind," as *The Epic of Gilgamesh* put it. In the presence of nature, Mesopotamians could easily feel helpless, as this poem relates:

> *The rampant flood which no man can oppose,*
> *Which shakes the heavens and causes earth to tremble,*
> *In an appalling blanket folds mother and child,*
> *Beats down the canebrake's full luxuriant greenery,*
> *And drowns the harvest in its time of ripeness.*[6]

The Mesopotamians discerned cosmic rhythms in the universe and accepted its order but perceived that it was not completely safe because of the presence of willful, powerful cosmic powers that they identified with gods and goddesses.

With its numerous gods and goddesses animating all aspects of the universe, Mesopotamian religion was a form of **polytheism**. The four most important deities were An, god of the sky and hence the most important force in the universe; Enlil (EN-lil), god of wind; Enki (EN-kee), god of the earth, rivers, wells, and canals as well as inventions and crafts; and Ninhursaga (nin-HUR-sah-guh), a goddess associated with soil, mountains, and vegetation, who came to be worshiped as a mother goddess, a "mother of all children," who manifested her power by giving birth to kings and conferring the royal insignia on them.

Human relationships with the gods were based on subservience since, according to Sumerian myth, human beings were created to do the manual labor the gods were unwilling to do for themselves. Moreover, humans were insecure because they could never predict the gods' actions. But humans did attempt to relieve their anxiety by discovering the intentions of the gods through **divination**.

Divination took a variety of forms. A common form, at least for kings and priests who could afford it, involved killing animals, such as sheep or goats, and examining their livers or other organs. Supposedly, features seen in the organs of the sacrificed animals foretold events to come. Thus, one handbook states that if the animal organ has shape x, the outcome of the military campaign will be y. The Mesopotamian arts of divination arose out of the desire to discover the purposes of the gods. If people could decipher the signs that foretold events, the events would be predictable and humans could act wisely.

The Cultivation of Writing and Sciences   The realization of writing's great potential was another aspect of Mesopotamian culture. The oldest Mesopotamian texts date to around 3000 B.C.E. and were written by the Sumerians, who used a

cuneiform ("wedge-shaped") system of writing. Using a reed stylus, they made wedge-shaped impressions on clay tablets, which were then baked or dried in the sun. Once dried, these tablets were virtually indestructible, and the several hundred thousand that have been found so far have been a valuable source of information for modern scholars. Sumerian writing evolved from pictures of concrete objects to simplified and stylized signs, leading eventually to a phonetic system that made possible the written expression of abstract ideas.

Mesopotamian peoples used writing primarily for record keeping, but cuneiform texts were also used in schools set up to teach the cuneiform system of writing. The primary goal of scribal education was to produce professionally trained scribes for careers in the temples and palaces, the military, and government service. Pupils were male and primarily from wealthy families.

Writing was important because it enabled a society to keep records and maintain knowledge of previous practices and events. Writing also made it possible for people to communicate ideas in new ways, which is especially evident in the most famous piece of Mesopotamian literature, *The Epic of Gilgamesh*, an epic poem that records the exploits of a legendary king of Uruk. Gilgamesh (GILL-guh-mesh), wise, strong, and perfect in body, part man and part god, befriends a hairy beast named Enkidu. Together they set off in pursuit of heroic deeds. When Enkidu dies, Gilgamesh experiences the pain of mortality and begins a search for the secret of immortality. He finds Utnapishtim, who was granted immortality by the gods after he survived the Great Flood sent by the gods to destroy humankind. Utnapishtim tries to help Gilgamesh gain immortality, but his efforts fail, and Gilgamesh remains mortal. The desire for immortality, one of humankind's great searches, ends in complete frustration. "Everlasting life," as this Mesopotamian epic makes clear, is only for the gods.

Mesopotamians also made outstanding achievements in mathematics and astronomy. In math, the Sumerians devised a number system based on 60, using combinations of 6 and 10 for practical solutions. Geometry was used to measure fields and erect buildings. In astronomy, the Sumerians made use of units of 60 and charted the heavenly constellations. Their calendar was based on twelve lunar months and was brought into harmony with the solar year by adding an extra month from time to time.

EGYPTIAN CIVILIZATION: "THE GIFT OF THE NILE"

"The Egyptian Nile," wrote one Arab traveler, "surpasses all the rivers of the world in sweetness of taste, in length of course and usefulness. No other river in the world can show such a continuous series of towns and villages along its banks." The Nile River was crucial to the development of Egyptian civilization. Egypt, like Mesopotamia, was a river valley civilization.

The Impact of Geography   The Nile is a unique river, beginning in the heart of Africa and coursing northward for thousands of miles. It is the longest river in the world. The Nile was responsible for creating an area several miles wide on both banks of the river that was fertile and capable of producing abundant harvests. The "miracle" of the Nile was its annual flooding.

Early Writing

RMN-Grand Palais/Art Resource, NY

© Sandro Vannini/CORBIS

ART & IDEAS

Pictured at the top is the upper part of the cone of Uruinimgina, covered in cuneiform script from an early Sumerian dynasty. The first Egyptian writing was also pictographic, as shown in the hieroglyphs in the detail from the mural in the tomb of Ramesses I shown below. In Central America, the Mayan civilization had a well-developed writing system, also based on hieroglyphs.

Q *What common feature is evident in these early writing systems? How might you explain that?*

The Great Flood: Two Versions

Both the Mesopotamian poem, *The Epic of Gilgamesh*, and the Hebrew Bible (Old Testament) include accounts of a great flood. In the first selection, taken from the *The Epic of Gilgamesh*, Utnapishtim tells Gilgamesh the story of how he survived the flood unleashed by the gods to destroy humankind. Utnapishtim recounts how the god Ea advised him to build a boat and how he came to land the boat at the end of the flood. The second selection is the account of the great flood that appears in the book of Genesis in the Hebrew Bible. The biblical Noah appears to be a later version of the Mesopotamian Utnapishtim.

The Epic of Gilgamesh

In those days the world teemed, the people multiplied, the world bellowed like a wild bull, and the great god was aroused by the clamor. Enlil heard the clamor and he said to the gods in council, "The uproar of mankind is intolerable and sleep is no longer possible by reason of the babel." So the gods agreed to exterminate mankind. Enlil did this, but Ea [Sumerian Enki, god of the waters] because of his oath warned me in a dream ... "tear down your house and build a boat, abandon possessions and look for life, despise worldly goods and save your soul alive.

Tear down your house, I say, and build a boat.... Then take up into the boat the seed of all living creatures...." [Utnapishtim did as he was told, and then the destruction came.]

For six days and six nights the winds blew, torrent and tempest and flood overwhelmed the world, tempest and flood raged together like warring hosts. When the seventh day dawned the storm from the south subsided, the sea grew calm, the flood was stilled; I looked at the face of the world and there was silence, all mankind was turned to clay. The surface of the sea stretched as flat as a rooftop; I opened a hatch and the light fell on my face. Then I bowed low, I sat down and I wept, the tears streamed down my face, for on every side was the waste of water. I looked for land in vain, but fourteen leagues distant there appeared a mountain, and there the boat grounded; on the mountain of Nisir the boat held fast, she held fast and did not budge.

... When the seventh day dawned I loosed a dove and let her go. She flew away, but finding no resting-place she returned. Then I loosed a swallow, and she flew away but finding no resting-place she returned. I loosed a raven, she saw that the waters had retreated, she ate, she flew around, she cawed, and she did not come back. Then I threw everything

---

The river rose in the summer from rains in Central Africa, crested in Egypt in September and October, and left a deposit of silt that enriched the soil. The Egyptians called this fertile land the "Black Land" because it was dark in color from the silt and the crops that grew on it so densely. Beyond these narrow strips of fertile fields lay the deserts (the "Red Land"). About 100 miles before it empties into the Mediterranean, the river splits into two major branches, forming the delta, a triangular-shaped territory called Lower Egypt to distinguish it from Upper Egypt, the land upstream to the south. Egypt's important cities developed at the tip of the open to the four winds, I made a sacrifice and poured out a libation on the mountain top.

Genesis 6:11–15, 17–19; 7:24; 8:3, 13–21

Now the earth was corrupted in God's sight and was full of violence. God saw how corrupt the earth had become, for all the people on earth had corrupted their ways. So God said to Noah, "I am going to put an end to all people, for the earth is filled with violence because of them. I am surely going to destroy both them and the earth. So make yourself an ark of cypress wood: make rooms in it and coat it with pitch inside and out.... I am going to bring flood waters on the earth to destroy all life under the heavens, every creature that has the breath of life in it. Everything on earth will perish. But I will establish my covenant with you, and you will enter the ark—you and your sons and your wife and your sons' wives with you. You are to bring into the ark two of all living creatures, male and female, to keep them alive with you...."

The waters flooded the earth for a hundred and fifty days.... By the first day of the first month of Noah's six hundred and first year, the water had dried up from the earth. Noah then removed the covering from the ark and saw that the surface of the ground was dry....

Then God said to Noah, "Come out of the ark, you and your wife and your sons and their wives. Bring out every kind of living creature that is with you—the birds, the animals, and all the creatures that move along the ground—so they can multiply on the earth and be fruitful and increase in number upon it." So Noah came out, together with his sons and his wife and his sons' wives ... [and all the animals]. Then Noah built an altar to the Lord and, taking some of all the clean animals and clean birds, he sacrificed burnt offerings on it. The Lord smelled the pleasing aroma and said in his heart, "Never again will I curse the ground because of man, even though every inclination of his heart is evil from childhood. And never again will I destroy all living creatures, as I have done."

Q *What does the selection from* The Epic of Gilgamesh *tell you about the relationship between the Mesopotamians and their gods? How might you explain the similarities and differences between this account and the biblical flood story in* Genesis?

Sources: From *The Epic of Gilgamesh* translated by N. K. Sandars (Penguin Classics 1960, Third Edition 1972). *The Holy Bible, New International Version®*, NIV® Copyright © 1973, 1978, 1984, 2011 by Biblica, Inc.® Used by permission. All rights reserved worldwide.

delta. Even today, most of Egypt's people are crowded along the banks of the Nile River.

Unlike Mesopotamia's rivers, the flooding of the Nile was gradual and usually predictable, and the river itself was seen as life-enhancing, not life-threatening. Although a system of organized irrigation was still necessary, the small villages along the Nile could create such systems without the massive state intervention that was required in Mesopotamia. Egyptian civilization consequently tended to remain more rural, with many small population centers congregated along a narrow band on both sides of the Nile.

MAP 1.4 Ancient Egypt

Egyptian civilization centered on the life-giving water and flood silts of the Nile River, with most of the population living in Lower Egypt, where the river splits to form the Nile delta. Most of the pyramids, built during the Old Kingdom, are clustered south and west of Cairo.

The surpluses of food that Egyptian farmers grew in the fertile Nile Valley made Egypt prosperous. But the Nile also served as a unifying factor in Egyptian history. In ancient times, the Nile was the fastest way to travel through the land, making both transportation and communication easier. Winds from the north pushed sailboats south, and the current of the Nile carried them north.

Unlike Mesopotamia, which was subject to constant invasion, Egypt had natural barriers that fostered isolation, protected it from invasion, and gave it a sense of security. These barriers included deserts to the west and east; cataracts (rapids) on the southern part of the river, which made defense relatively easy; and the Mediterranean Sea to the north. These barriers, however, were effective only when combined with Egyptian fortifications at strategic locations. Nor did these barriers prevent the development of trade. Indeed, there is evidence of very early trade between Egypt and Mesopotamia.

The regularity of the Nile floods and the relative isolation of the Egyptians created a sense of security and a feeling of changelessness. To the ancient Egyptians, when the Nile flooded each year, "the fields laugh, and people's faces light up." Unlike people in Mesopotamia, Egyptians faced life with a spirit of confidence in the stability of things. Ancient Egyptian civilization was characterized by a remarkable degree of continuity for thousands of years.

The Old and Middle Kingdoms

Modern historians have divided Egyptian history into three major periods, known as the Old Kingdom, the Middle Kingdom, and the New Kingdom. These were periods of long-term stability characterized by strong monarchical authority, competent bureaucracy, freedom from invasion, much construction of temples and pyramids, and considerable intellectual and cultural activity. But between the periods of stability were intervals known as the Intermediate Periods, characterized by weak political structures and rivalry for leadership, invasions, a decline in building activity, and a restructuring of society.

The Old Kingdom

According to the Egyptians' own tradition, their land consisted initially of numerous populated areas ruled by tribal chieftains. Around 3100 B.C.E., the first Egyptian royal dynasty, under a king called Menes, united Upper and Lower Egypt into a single kingdom. Henceforth, the king would be called "king of Upper and Lower Egypt," and a royal crown, the Double Crown, was created, combining the White Crown of Upper Egypt and the Red Crown of Lower Egypt. Just as the Nile served to unite Upper and Lower Egypt physically, the king served to unite the two areas politically.

The Old Kingdom encompassed the fourth through eighth dynasties of Egyptian kings, lasting from around 2575 to 2125 B.C.E. It was an age of prosperity and splendor, made visible in the construction of the greatest and largest pyramids in Egypt's history. The capital of the Old Kingdom was located at Memphis, south of the delta.

Kingship was a divine institution in ancient Egypt and formed part of a universal cosmic scheme: "What is the king of Upper and Lower Egypt? He is a god by whose dealings one lives, the father and mother of all men, alone by himself, without an equal."[7] In obeying their king, subjects helped maintain the cosmic order. A breakdown in royal power could only mean that citizens were offending divinity and weakening the universal structure. Among the various titles of Egyptian kings, that of **pharaoh** (originally meaning "great house" or "palace") eventually came to be the most common.

Although they possessed absolute power, Egyptian kings were supposed to rule not arbitrarily but according to set principles. The chief principle was called *Ma'at* (MAH-ut), a spiritual precept that conveyed the ideas of truth and justice and especially right order and harmony. To ancient Egyptians, this fundamental order and harmony had existed throughout the universe since the beginning of time. Pharaohs were the divine instruments who maintained it and were themselves subject to it.

Although theoretically absolute in their power, in practice Egyptian kings did not rule alone. Initially, members of the king's family performed administrative tasks, but by the fourth dynasty, a bureaucracy with regular procedures had developed. Especially important was the office of vizier, "steward of the whole land." Directly responsible to the king, the vizier was in charge of the bureaucracy. For administrative purposes, Egypt was divided into provinces, or *nomes* as they were later called by the Greeks—twenty-two in Upper Egypt and twenty in Lower Egypt. A governor, called by the Greeks a *nomarch*, was head of each nome and was responsible to the king and vizier. Nomarchs, however, tended to build up large holdings of land and power within their nomes, creating a potential rivalry with the pharaohs.

The Middle Kingdom   Despite the theory of divine order, the Old Kingdom eventually collapsed, ushering in a period of disarray. Finally, a new royal dynasty managed to pacify all Egypt and inaugurated the Middle Kingdom, a period of stability lasting from around 2010 to 1630 B.C.E. Egyptians later portrayed the Middle Kingdom as a golden age, a clear indication of its stability. Several factors contributed to its vitality. The nome structure was reorganized. The boundaries of each nome were now settled precisely, and the obligations of the nomes to the state were clearly delineated. Nomarchs were confirmed as hereditary officeholders but with the understanding that their duties must be performed faithfully. These included the collection of taxes for the state and the recruitment of labor forces for royal projects, such as stone quarrying.

The Middle Kingdom was characterized by a new concern of the pharaohs for the people. In the Old Kingdom, the pharaoh had been viewed as an inaccessible god-king. Now he was portrayed as the shepherd of his people with the responsibility to build public works and provide for the public welfare. As one pharaoh expressed it, "He [a particular god] created me as one who should do that which he had done, and to carry out that which he commanded should be done. He appointed me herdsman of this land, for he knew who would keep it in order for him."[8]

Society and Economy in Ancient Egypt   Egyptian society had a simple structure in the Old and Middle Kingdoms; basically, it was organized along hierarchical lines with the god-king at the top. An upper class of nobles and priests aided the king and participated in the elaborate rituals of life that surrounded the pharaoh. This ruling class ran the government and managed its own landed estates, which provided much of its wealth.

Below the upper classes were merchants and artisans. Merchants engaged in an active trade up and down the Nile as well as in town and village markets. Some merchants also engaged in international trade; the king sent them to Crete and

Syria, where they obtained wood and other products. Expeditions traveled into Nubia for ivory and down the Red Sea to Punt for incense and spices. Eventually, trade links were established between ports in the Red Sea and countries as far away as the Indonesian archipelago. Egyptian artisans made an incredible variety of well-built and beautiful goods: stone dishes; painted boxes made of clay; wooden furniture; gold, silver, and copper tools and containers; paper and rope made of papyrus; and linen clothes.

By far the largest number of people in Egypt simply worked the land. In theory, the king owned all the land but granted portions of it to his subjects. Large sections were in the possession of nobles and the temple complexes. Most of the lower classes were serfs, or common people bound to the land, who cultivated the estates. They paid taxes in the form of crops to the king, nobles, and priests; lived in small villages or towns; and provided military service and forced labor for building projects.

The Culture of Egypt

Egypt produced a culture that dazzled and awed its later conquerors. The Egyptians' technical achievements, especially visible in the construction of the pyramids, demonstrated a measure of skill unequaled in the world at that time. To the Egyptians, all of these achievements were part of a cosmic order suffused with the presence of the divine.

Spiritual Life in Egyptian Society

The Egyptians had no word for religion because it was an inseparable element of the entire world order to which Egyptian society belonged. Egypt was part of the universal cosmic scheme, and the pharaoh was the divine being whose function was to maintain Egypt's stability within the cosmic order.

This perspective helps explain the importance of ritual in ancient Egypt. Through their rituals, Egyptians worked to maintain the cosmic order by appeasing the gods and goddesses who controlled the universe. Egyptian ritual ceremonies focused on an image of a deity, providing it with food and sustenance and thereby performing an act of ritual worship to appease the god. The pharaoh was at the heart of Egypt's ritual life. He supervised the sacred ceremonies that were performed in the temples, although it was the pharaoh's religious deputies—the priests—who executed the daily ceremonies.

The Egyptians had a remarkable number of gods associated with heavenly bodies and natural forces, hardly unusual in view of the importance to Egypt's well-being of the sun, the river, and the fertile land along its banks. The sun was the source of life and hence worthy of worship. A sun cult developed, and the sun god took on different forms and names, depending on his specific role. He was worshiped as Atum in human form and also as Re, who had a human body but the head of a falcon. The pharaoh took the title of "Son of Re" because he was regarded as the earthly embodiment of Re.

River and land deities included Osiris (oh-SY-russ) and Isis (Y-sis) with their child Horus, who was related to the Nile and to the sun as well. Osiris became especially important as a symbol of resurrection or rebirth. A famous Egyptian myth told of the struggle between Osiris, who brought civilization to Egypt, and his evil brother Seth, who killed him, cut his body into fourteen parts, and tossed them into the Nile River. Isis, the faithful wife of Osiris, found the pieces and, with help from other gods, restored Osiris to life. As a symbol of resurrection and as judge of the dead, Osiris took on an important role for the Egyptians. By identifying with Osiris, one could hope to gain new life just as Osiris had done. The dead, embalmed and mummified, were placed in tombs (in the case of kings, in pyramidal tombs), given the name of Osiris, and by a process of magical identification became Osiris. Like Osiris, they could then be reborn. The flood of the Nile and the new life it brought to Egypt were symbolized by Isis gathering all of the parts of Osiris together and were celebrated each spring in the Festival of the New Land.

Later Egyptian spiritual practice began to emphasize morality by stressing the role of Osiris as judge of the dead. The dead were asked to give an account of their earthly deeds so that Osiris could determine whether they deserved a reward. At first, the Osiris cult was reserved for the very wealthy, who could afford to take expensive measures to preserve the body after death. During the Middle Kingdom, however, the cult became "democratized" and was extended to all Egyptians who aspired to an afterlife.

The Pyramids   One of the great achievements of Egyptian civilization, the building of pyramids, occurred in the time of the Old Kingdom. Pyramids were built as part of a larger complex of buildings dedicated to the dead—in effect, a city of the dead. The area included a large pyramid for the king's burial, smaller pyramids for his family, and *mastabas*, rectangular structures with flat roofs, as tombs for the pharaoh's noble officials.

The tombs were well prepared for their residents, their rooms furnished and stocked with numerous supplies, including chairs, boats, chests, weapons, games, dishes, and a variety of foods. The Egyptians believed that human beings had two bodies, a physical one and a spiritual one they called the *ka*. If the physical body was properly preserved (by mummification) and the tomb was furnished with all the objects of regular life, the *ka* could return, surrounded by earthly comforts, and continue its life despite the death of the physical body.

To preserve the physical body after death, the Egyptians practiced mummification, a process of slowly drying a dead body to prevent it from decomposing. Special workshops, run by priests, performed this procedure, primarily for the wealthy families who could afford it. According to an ancient Greek historian who visited Egypt around 450 B.C.E., "The most refined method is as follows: first of all they draw out the brain through the nostrils with an iron hook.... Then they make an incision in the flank with a sharp Ethiopian stone through which they extract all the internal organs."[9] The liver, lungs, stomach, and intestines were placed in four special jars that were put in the tomb with the mummy. The priests then covered the corpse with a natural salt that absorbed the body's water. Later, they filled the body with spices and wrapped it with layers of linen soaked in resin. At the end of the process, which took about seventy days, a lifelike mask was placed over the head and shoulders of the mummy, which was then sealed in a case and placed in its tomb.

Pyramids were tombs for the mummified bodies of the pharaohs. The largest and most magnificent of all the pyramids was built under King Khufu. Constructed at Giza around 2540 B.C.E., this famous Great Pyramid covers 13 acres, measures

756 feet at each side of its base, and stands 481 feet high. Its four sides are almost precisely oriented to the four points of the compass. The interior included a grand gallery to the burial chamber, which was built of granite with a lidless sarcophagus for the pharaoh's body. The Great Pyramid still stands as a visible symbol of the power of Egyptian kings and the spiritual conviction that underlay Egyptian society. No pyramid built later ever matched its size or splendor. The pyramid was not only the king's tomb; it was also an important symbol of royal power. It could be seen from miles away, a visible reminder of the glory and might of the ruler who was a living god on earth.

Art and Writing   Commissioned by kings or nobles for use in temples and tombs, Egyptian art was largely functional. Wall paintings and statues of gods and kings in temples served a strictly spiritual purpose. They were an integral part of the performance of ritual, which was thought necessary to preserve the cosmic order and hence the well-being of Egypt. Likewise, the mural scenes and sculptured figures found in the tombs had a specific function: they were supposed to assist the journey of the deceased into the afterworld.

Egyptian art was also formulaic. Artists and sculptors observed a strict canon of proportions that determined both form and presentation. This canon gave Egyptian art a distinctive appearance for thousands of years. Especially characteristic was the convention of combining the profile, semiprofile, and frontal views of the human body in relief work and painting in order to represent each part of the body accurately. The result was an art that was highly stylized yet still allowed distinctive features to be displayed.

Writing emerged in Egypt during the first two dynasties. The Greeks later called Egyptian writing **hieroglyphics** (HY-uh-roh-glif-iks), meaning "priest-carvings" or "sacred writings." Hieroglyphs were signs that depicted objects and had a sacred value at the same time. Although hieroglyphs were later simplified into two scripts for writing purposes, they never developed into an alphabet. Egyptian hieroglyphs were initially carved in stone, but later the two simplified scripts were written on papyrus, a paper made from the reeds that grew along the Nile. Most of the ancient Egyptian literature that has come down to us was written on papyrus rolls and wooden tablets.

Disorder and a New Order: The New Kingdom   The Middle Kingdom came to an end around 1650 B.C.E. with the invasion of Egypt by a people from western Asia known to the Egyptians as the Hyksos. The Hyksos used horse-drawn war chariots and overwhelmed the Egyptian soldiers, who fought from donkey carts. For almost a hundred years, the Hyksos ruled much of Egypt, but the conquered took much from their conquerors. From the Hyksos, the Egyptians learned to use bronze in making new farming tools and weapons. They also mastered the military skills of the Hyksos, especially the use of horse-drawn war chariots.

The Egyptian Empire   Eventually, a new line of pharaohs—the eighteenth dynasty—made use of the new weapons to throw off Hyksos domination, reunite Egypt, establish the New Kingdom (c. 1539–1069 B.C.E.), and launch the Egyptians along a new militaristic and imperialistic path, characterized by the development of a more professional army. During the period of the New Kingdom, Egypt assembled an empire and became the most powerful state in the Middle East.

Massive wealth aided the power of the New Kingdom pharaohs. The Egyptian rulers showed their wealth by building new temples. Queen Hatshepsut (hat-SHEP-soot) (c. 1503–1480 B.C.E.), in particular, one of the first women to become pharaoh in her own right, built a great temple at Deir el Bahri (dayr ahl BAH-ree) near Thebes. As pharaoh, Hatshepsut sent out military expeditions, encouraged mining, fostered agriculture, and sent a trading expedition up the Nile. Hatshepsut's official statues sometimes show her clothed and bearded like a king. She was referred to as "His Majesty." Hatshepsut was succeeded by her nephew, Thutmosis (thoot-MOH-suss) III (c. 1480–1450 B.C.E.), who led seventeen military campaigns into Syria and Canaan and even reached the Euphrates River. Egyptian forces occupied Canaan and Syria and also moved westward into Libya.

Akhenaten and Religious Change   The eighteenth dynasty was not without its troubles, however. Amenhotep (ah-mun-HOH-tep) IV (c. 1353–1336 B.C.E.) introduced the worship of Aten, god of the sun disk, as the supreme god and, later in his reign, as the only god. In the pharaoh's eyes, he and Aten had become co-rulers of Egypt. Changing his own name to Akhenaten (ah-kuh-NAH-tun) ("servant of Aten"), the pharaoh closed the temples of other gods and especially endeavored to lessen the power of the priesthood dedicated to the god Amon-Re at Thebes. Akhenaten strove to reduce the priests' influence by replacing Thebes as the capital of Egypt with Akhetaten (ah-kuh-TAH-tun) ("horizon of Aten"), a new city located at modern Tell el-Amarna, 200 miles north of Thebes. The pharaoh decreed that Akhetaten, not Thebes, would be his final resting place.

Akhenaten's attempt at religious change failed. It was too much to ask Egyptians to give up their traditional ways and beliefs, especially since they saw the destruction of the old gods as subversive of the very cosmic order on which Egypt's survival and continuing prosperity depended. Moreover, the priests at Thebes were unalterably opposed to the changes, which had diminished their influence and power. At the same time, Akhenaten's preoccupation with religion caused him to ignore foreign affairs and led to the loss of both Syria and Canaan. Akhenaten's changes were soon undone after his death by those who influenced his successor, the boy-pharaoh Tutankhamun (too-tang-KAH-mun) (c. 1332–1322 B.C.E.). Tutankhamun returned the government to Thebes and restored the old gods. The Aten experiment had failed to take hold, and the eighteenth dynasty itself soon came to an end.

Decline of the Egyptian Empire   The nineteenth dynasty managed to restore Egyptian power one more time. Under Ramesses (RAM-uh-seez) II (c. 1279–1213 B.C.E.), the Egyptians went on the offensive, regained control of Canaan, and restored Egypt as an imperial power. During his long sixty-seven year reign, Ramesses II provided visible demonstrations of his power by constructing mammoth new temple buildings, many of which were characterized by colossal statues of himself.

Statues of Ramesses II at Abu Simbel. *After being driven out of Canaan and Syria by the Hittites, the Egyptian empire grew to power one final time under Ramesses II. He succeeded in reconquering Canaan but was unable to restore the boundaries of the previous empire. The massive Temple of Ramesses II, located at Abu Simbel, was carved out of a cliff of Nubian sandstone. The giant statues represent Ramesses II.*

Bildarchiv Steffens/The Bridgeman Art Library

After the death of Ramesses II, struggles for the throne weakened the government, and new invasions in the thirteenth century by the "Sea Peoples," as the Egyptians called them, destroyed Egyptian power in Canaan and drove the Egyptians back within their old frontiers. The days of Egyptian empire were ended, and the New Kingdom itself expired with the end of the twentieth dynasty in 1069 B.C.E. For the next thousand years, despite periodical revivals of strength, Egypt was dominated by Libyans, Nubians, Assyrians, Persians, and finally Macedonians, after the conquest of Alexander the Great. In the first century B.C.E., Egypt became a province in Rome's mighty empire.

Daily Life in Ancient Egypt: Family and Marriage

Ancient Egyptians had a very positive attitude toward daily life on earth and followed the advice of the wisdom literature, which suggested that people marry young and establish a home and family. Monogamy was the general rule, although a husband was allowed to keep additional wives if his first wife was childless. Pharaohs were entitled to harems; the queen, however, was acknowledged as the "great wife," with a status higher than that of the other wives. The husband was master in the house, but wives were very much respected and in charge of the household and the education of the children. From a book of wise sayings (which the Egyptians called "instructions") came this advice:

If you are a man of standing, you should found your household and love your wife at home as is fitting. Fill her belly; clothe her back. Ointment is the prescription for her body. Make her heart glad as long as you live. She is a profitable field for her lord. You should not contend with her at law, and keep her far from gaining control.... Let her heart be soothed through what may accrue to you; it means keeping her long in your house.[10]

Women's property and inheritance remained in their hands, even in marriage. Although most careers and public offices were closed to women, some women did operate businesses. Peasant women worked long hours in the fields and at numerous domestic tasks. Upper-class women could function as priestesses, and a few queens, such as Hatshepsut, even became pharaohs in their own right.

Parents arranged marriages. The primary concerns were family and property, and the chief purpose of marriage was to produce children, especially sons. From the New Kingdom came this piece of wisdom: "Take to yourself a wife while you are [still] a youth, that she may produce a son for you."[11] Daughters were not slighted, however. Numerous tomb paintings show the close and affectionate relationship parents had with both sons and daughters. Marriages could and did end in divorce, which was allowed, apparently with compensation for the wife. Adultery, however, was strictly prohibited, with stiff punishments—especially for women, who could have their noses cut off or be burned at the stake.

The Spread of Egyptian Influence: Nubia

The civilization of Egypt had an impact on other peoples in the lands of the eastern Mediterranean. Egyptian products have been found in Crete and Cretan products in Egypt. Egyptian influence is also evident in early Greek statues. The Egyptians also had an impact to the south in Nubia (the northern part of modern Sudan). In fact, some archaeologists have recently suggested that the African kingdom of Nubia may have arisen even before the kingdoms of Egypt.

It is clear that contacts between the upper and lower Nile had been established by the late third millennium B.C.E., when Egyptian merchants traveled to Nubia to obtain ivory, ebony, frankincense, and leopard skins. A few centuries later, Nubia had become an Egyptian tributary. At the end of the second millennium B.C.E., Nubia profited from the disintegration of the Egyptian New Kingdom to become the independent state of Kush. Egyptian influence continued, however, as Kushite culture borrowed extensively from Egypt, including religious beliefs, the practice of interring kings in pyramids, and hieroglyphs.

But in the first millennium B.C.E., Kush also had a direct impact on Egypt. During the second half of the eighth century B.C.E., Kushite monarchs took control of Egypt and formed the twenty-fifth dynasty of Egyptian rulers. It was not until 663 B.C.E. that the last Kushite ruler was expelled from Egypt. During this period, the Kushite rulers of Egypt even aided the Israelites in their struggle with the Assyrians.

Although its economy was probably founded primarily on agriculture and animal husbandry, Kush developed into a major trading state in Africa that endured for hundreds of years. Its commercial activities were stimulated by the discovery of iron ore in a floodplain near the river at Meroë. Strategically located at the point where a land route across the desert to the south intersected the Nile River, Meroë eventually became the capital of a new state. In addition to iron products, Kush and Meroë supplied goods from Central and East Africa, notably ivory, gold, ebony, and slaves, to the Romans, Arabia, and India. At first, goods were transported by donkey caravans to the point where the river north was navigable. By the last centuries of the first millennium B.C.E., however, the donkeys were being replaced by camels, newly introduced from the Arabian peninsula.

New Centers of Civilization

Mesopotamia and Egypt have dominated our story of civilization so far, but significant developments were also taking place on the fringes of these civilizations. Farming had spread into the Balkan peninsula of Europe by 6500 B.C.E., and by 4000 B.C.E., it was well established in southern France, central Europe, and the coastal regions of the Mediterranean. Although migrating farmers from the Anatolian peninsula may have brought some farming techniques into Europe, some historians believe that the Neolithic peoples of Europe domesticated animals and began to farm largely on their own.

One outstanding feature of late Neolithic Europe was the erection of **megaliths** (*megalith* is Greek for "large stone"). Radiocarbon dating, a technique that allows scientists to determine the age of objects, shows that the first megalithic structures were constructed around 4000 B.C.E., more than a thousand years before the great pyramids were built in Egypt. Between 3200 and 1500 B.C.E., standing stones, placed in circles or lined up in rows, were erected throughout the British Isles and northwestern France. Other megalithic constructions have been found as far north as Scandinavia and as far south as the islands of Corsica, Sardinia, and Malta. Archaeologists have demonstrated that the stone circles were used as observatories to detect not only such simple astronomical phenomena as the midwinter and midsummer sunrises but also such sophisticated phenomena as the major and minor standstills of the moon.

Nomadic Peoples: Impact of the Indo-Europeans   On the fringes of civilization lived nomadic peoples who depended on hunting and gathering, herding, and sometimes a bit of farming for their survival. Most important were the pastoral nomads who on occasion overran civilized communities and forged their own empires. Pastoral nomads domesticated animals for both food and clothing and moved along regular migratory routes to provide steady sources of nourishment for their animals.

The Indo-Europeans were among the most important nomadic peoples. These groups spoke languages derived from a single parent tongue. Indo-European languages include Greek, Latin, Persian, Sanskrit, and the Germanic and Slavic tongues. The original Indo-European-speaking peoples were probably based in the steppe region north of the Black Sea or in southwestern Asia, in modern Iran or Afghanistan, but around 2000 B.C.E., they began to move into Europe, India, and western Asia. The domestication of horses and the importation of the wheel and wagon from Mesopotamia facilitated the Indo-European migrations to other lands.

MAP 1.5   The Spread of the Indo-Europeans

From their probable homeland in the steppe region north of the Black Sea, Indo-European-speaking peoples moved eventually into Europe, India, and western Asia. The languages shown on the map are all Indo-European languages.

The Hittites   One group of Indo-Europeans who moved into Asia Minor and Anatolia (modern Turkey) around 1750 B.C.E. coalesced with the native peoples to form the Hittite kingdom, with its capital at Hattusha (Bogazköy in modern Turkey). Between 1600 and 1200 B.C.E., the Hittites formed their own empire in western Asia and even threatened the power of the Egyptians.

The Hittites were the first of the Indo-European peoples to make use of iron, enabling them to construct weapons that were stronger and cheaper to make because of the widespread availability of iron ore. During its height, the Hittite Empire also demonstrated an interesting ability to assimilate other cultures into its own. In language, literature, art, law, and religion, the Hittites borrowed much from Mesopotamia as well as from the native peoples they had subdued. Recent scholarship has stressed the important role of the Hittites in transmitting Mesopotamian culture, as they transformed it, to later civilizations in the Mediterranean area, especially to the Mycenaean Greeks.

Territorial States in Western Asia: The Phoenicians   During its heyday, the Hittite Empire was one of the great powers in western Asia. Constant squabbling over succession to the throne, however, tended to weaken royal authority at times. Especially devastating, however, were attacks by the Sea Peoples from the west and aggressive neighboring tribes. By 1190 B.C.E., Hittite power had come to an end. The destruction of the Hittite kingdom and the weakening of Egypt around 1200 B.C.E. left no dominant powers in western Asia, allowing a patchwork of petty kingdoms and city-states to emerge, especially in the area of Syria and Canaan. The Phoenicians (fuh-NEE-shunz) were one of these peoples.

A Semitic-speaking people, the Phoenicians lived in the area of Canaan along the Mediterranean coast on a narrow band of land 120 miles long. Their newfound political independence after the demise of Hittite and Egyptian power helped the Phoenicians expand the trade that was already the foundation of their prosperity. The chief cities of Phoenicia—Byblos, Tyre, and Sidon—were ports on the eastern Mediterranean, but they also served as distribution centers for the lands to the east in Mesopotamia. The Phoenicians themselves produced a number of goods for foreign markets, including purple dye, glass, wine, and lumber from the famous cedars of Lebanon. In addition, the Phoenicians improved their ships and became great international sea traders. They charted new routes, not only in the Mediterranean but also in the Atlantic Ocean, where they reached Britain and sailed south along the west coast of Africa. The Phoenicians established a number of colonies in the western Mediterranean, including settlements in southern Spain, Sicily, and Sardinia. Carthage, the Phoenicians' most famous colony, was located on the north coast of Africa.

Culturally, the Phoenicians are best known as transmitters. Instead of using pictographs or signs to represent whole words and syllables as the Mesopotamians and Egyptians did, the Phoenicians simplified their writing by using twenty-two different signs to represent the sounds of their speech. These twenty-two characters or letters could be used to spell out all the words in the Phoenician language. Although the Phoenicians were not the only people to invent an alphabet, theirs would have special significance because it was eventually passed on to the Greeks. From the Greek alphabet was derived the Roman alphabet that we still use today. The Phoenicians achieved much while independent, but they ultimately fell subject to the Assyrians and Persians.

The Hebrews: The "Children of Israel"   To the south of the Phoenicians lived another group of Semitic-speaking people known as the Hebrews. Although they were a minor factor in the politics of the region, their **monotheism**—belief in but one God—later influenced both Christianity and Islam and flourished as a world religion in its own right. The Hebrews had a tradition concerning their origins and history that was eventually written down as part of the Hebrew Bible, known to Christians as the Old Testament. Describing them as a nomadic people, the Hebrews' own tradition states that they were descendants of the patriarch Abraham, who had migrated from Mesopotamia to the land of Canaan, where the Hebrews became identified as the "Children of Israel." Moreover, according to tradition, a drought in Canaan caused many Hebrews to migrate to Egypt, where they lived peacefully until they were enslaved by pharaohs who used them as laborers on building projects. The Hebrews remained in bondage until Moses led his people out of Egypt in the well-known "exodus," which some historians believe occurred in the first half of the thirteenth century B.C.E. According to the biblical account, the Hebrews then wandered for many years in the desert until they entered Canaan. Organized into twelve tribes, the Hebrews became embroiled in conflict with the Philistines, who had settled along the coast of Canaan but were beginning to move inland.

Many scholars today doubt that the biblical account reflects the true history of the early Israelites. They argue that the early books of the Bible, written centuries after the events described, preserve only what the Israelites came to believe about themselves and that recent archaeological evidence often contradicts the details of the biblical account. Some of these scholars have even argued that the Israelites were not nomadic invaders but indigenous peoples in the Canaanite hill country. What is generally agreed, however, is that between 1200 and 1000 B.C.E., the Israelites emerged as a distinct group of people, possibly organized into tribes or a league of tribes.

Was There a United Kingdom of Israel?   According to the Hebrew Bible, the Israelites established a united kingdom of Israel beginning with Saul (c. 1020–1000 B.C.E.), who supposedly achieved some success in the ongoing struggle with the Philistines. But after his death, a brief period of anarchy ensued until one of Saul's lieutenants, David (c. 1000–970 B.C.E.), reunited the Israelites, defeated the Philistines, and established control over all of Canaan. Among David's conquests was the city of Jerusalem, which he supposedly made into the capital of a united kingdom.

According to the biblical account, David's son Solomon (c. 970–930 B.C.E.) did even more to strengthen royal power. He expanded the political and military establishments and extended the trading activities of the Israelites. Solomon is portrayed as a great builder who was responsible for the Temple in the city of Jerusalem. The Israelites viewed the Temple as the symbolic center of their religion and hence of the kingdom of Israel itself. Under Solomon, ancient Israel supposedly reached the height of its power.

The accuracy of this biblical account of the united kingdom of Israel under Saul, David, and Solomon has recently been challenged by a new generation of archaeologists and historians. Although they mostly accept Saul, David, and Solomon as historical figures, they view them more as chief warlords than as kings. If a kingdom of Israel did exist during these years, it was not as powerful or as well organized as the Hebrew Bible says. Furthermore, they argue, there is no definitive archaeological evidence that Solomon built the Temple in Jerusalem.

The Kingdoms of Israel and Judah   There may or may not have been a united kingdom of Israel, but after the death of Solomon, tensions between northern and southern tribes in Israel led to the establishment of two separate kingdoms—the kingdom of Israel, composed of the ten northern tribes, with its capital eventually at Samaria, and the southern kingdom of Judah, consisting of two tribes, with its capital at Jerusalem. In 722 or 721 B.C.E., the Assyrians (uh-SEER-ee-unz) destroyed Samaria, overran the kingdom of Israel, and deported many Hebrews to other parts of the Assyrian Empire. These dispersed Hebrews (the "ten lost tribes") merged with neighboring peoples and gradually lost their identity.

The southern kingdom of Judah was also forced to pay tribute to Assyria but managed to retain its independence as Assyrian power declined. A new enemy, however, appeared on the horizon. The Chaldeans (kal-DEE-unz) defeated Assyria,

MAP 1.6 The Israelites and Their Neighbors in the First Millennium B.C.E.

After the death of Solomon, tensions between the tribes in Israel led to the creation of two kingdoms—a northern kingdom of Israel and a southern kingdom of Judah. With power divided, the Israelites could not resist invasions that dispersed many of them from Canaan. Some, such as the "ten lost tribes," never returned. Others were sent to Babylon but were later allowed to return under the rule of the Persians.

conquered the kingdom of Judah, and completely destroyed Jerusalem in 586 B.C.E. Many upper-class people from Judah were deported to Babylonia; the memory of their exile is still evoked in the stirring words of Psalm 137:

> *By the rivers of Babylon, we sat and wept when we remembered Zion....*
> *How can we sing the songs of the Lord while in a foreign land?*
> *If I forget you, O Jerusalem, may my right hand forget its skill.*
> *May my tongue cling to the roof of my mouth if I do not remember you,*
> *If I do not consider Jerusalem my highest joy.*[12]

But the Babylonian captivity of the people of Judah did not last. A new set of conquerors, the Persians, destroyed the Chaldean kingdom and allowed the people of Judah to return to Jerusalem and rebuild their city and Temple. The revived kingdom of Judah remained under Persian control until the conquests of Alexander the Great in the fourth century B.C.E. The people of Judah survived, eventually becoming known as the Jews and giving their name to Judaism, the religion of Yahweh (YAH-way), the Israelite God.

The Spiritual Dimensions of Israel   The spiritual perspective of the Israelites evolved over time. Early Israelites probably worshiped many gods, including nature spirits dwelling in trees and rocks. For some Israelites, Yahweh was the chief god of Israel, but many, including kings of Israel and Judah, worshiped other gods as well. It was among the Babylonian exiles in the sixth century B.C.E. that Yahweh— the God of Israel—came to be seen as the only God. After these exiles returned to Judah, their point of view eventually became dominant, and pure monotheism came to be the major tenet of Judaism.

According to the Hebrew conception, there is but one God, called Yahweh, who created the world and everything in it. Yahweh ruled the world and was subject to nothing. This omnipotent creator was not removed from the life he had created, however, but was a just and good God who expected goodness from his people. If they did not obey his will, they would be punished. But he was primarily a God of mercy and love: "The Lord is gracious and compassionate, slow to anger and rich in love. The Lord is good to all; he has compassion on all he has made."[13] Each individual could have a personal relationship with this being.

Three aspects of the Hebrew religious tradition had special significance: the covenant, the law, and the prophets. The Israelites believed that during the exodus from Egypt, when Moses, according to biblical tradition, led his people out of bondage and into the Promised Land, God made a covenant or contract with the tribes of Israel, who believed that Yahweh had spoken to them through Moses. The Israelites promised to obey Yahweh and follow his law. In return, Yahweh promised to take special care of his chosen people, "a peculiar treasure unto me above all people."

This covenant between Yahweh and his chosen people could be fulfilled, however, only by obedience to the law of God. Most important were the ethical concerns that stood at the center of the law. Sometimes these took the form of specific standards of moral behavior: "You shall not murder. You shall not commit adultery. You shall not steal."[14] True freedom consisted of following God's moral standards voluntarily. If people chose to ignore the good, suffering and evil would follow.

The Israelites believed that certain religious teachers, called prophets, were sent by God to serve as his voice to his people. The golden age of prophecy began in the mid-eighth century B.C.E. and continued during the time when the people of Israel and Judah were threatened by Assyrian and Chaldean conquerors. The "men of God" went through the land warning the Israelites that they had failed to keep God's commandments and would be punished for breaking the covenant: "I will punish you for all your iniquities."

Out of the words of the prophets came new concepts that enriched the Jewish tradition. The prophets embraced a concern for all humanity. All nations would someday come to the God of Israel: "All the earth shall worship thee." This vision encompassed the elimination of war and the establishment of peace for all nations. In the words of the prophet Isaiah, "He will judge between the nations and will settle disputes for many people. They will beat their swords into plowshares and their spears into pruning hooks. Nation will not take up sword against nation, nor will they train for war anymore."[15]

Although the prophets developed a sense of universalism, the demands of the Jewish religion (the need to obey God) eventually encouraged a separation between the Jews and their non-Jewish neighbors. Unlike most other peoples of the Middle East, Jews could not simply be amalgamated into a community by accepting the gods of their conquerors and their neighbors. To remain faithful to the demands of their God, they might even have to refuse loyalty to political leaders.

THE RISE OF NEW EMPIRES

Small and independent states could exist only as long as no larger state dominated western Asia. New empires soon arose, however, and conquered vast stretches of the ancient world.

The Assyrian Empire   The first of these empires was formed in Assyria, located on the upper Tigris River, an area that brought it into both cultural and political contact with southern Mesopotamia. The Assyrians were a Semitic-speaking people who exploited the use of iron weapons, first developed by the Hittites, to establish an empire that by 700 B.C.E. included Mesopotamia, parts of the Iranian Plateau, sections of Asia Minor, Syria, Canaan, and Egypt down to Thebes. Ashurbanipal (ah-shur-BAH-nuh-pahl) (669–627 B.C.E.) was one of the strongest Assyrian rulers, but during his reign it was already becoming apparent that the Assyrian Empire was greatly overextended. Moreover, subject peoples, such as the Babylonians, greatly resented Assyrian rule and rebelled against it. Soon after Ashurbanipal's reign, the Assyrian Empire began to disintegrate. The capital city of Nineveh fell to a coalition of Chaldeans and Medes in 612 B.C.E., and in 605 B.C.E., the rest of the empire was finally divided between the two powers.

At its height, the Assyrian Empire was ruled by kings whose power was considered absolute. Under their leadership, the empire came to be well organized. Local officials were directly responsible to the king. The Assyrians also developed an efficient system of communication to administer their empire more effectively. A network of staging posts was established throughout the empire that used relays of horses (mules or donkeys in mountainous terrain) to carry messages. The system was so effective that a provincial governor anywhere in the empire (except Egypt) could send a question and receive an answer from the king in his palace within a week.

The Assyrians' ability to conquer and maintain an empire was due to a combination of factors. Over many years of practice, the Assyrians developed effective military leaders and fighters. They were able to enlist and deploy troops numbering in the hundreds of thousands, although most campaigns were not on such a large

MAP 1.7 The Assyrian and Persian Empires

Cyrus the Great united the Persians and led them in a successful conquest of much of the Near East, including most of the lands of the Assyrian Empire. By the time of Darius, the Persian Empire was the largest the world had yet seen.

scale. Size alone was not decisive, however. The Assyrian army was well organized and disciplined. It included a standing army of infantry as its core, accompanied by cavalry and horse-drawn war chariots that were used as mobile platforms for shooting arrows. In addition to fighting set battles on open ground, the Assyrian army was also capable of waging guerrilla warfare in the mountains and laying siege to cities.

Another factor in the effectiveness of the Assyrian military machine was its use of terror as an instrument of warfare. As a matter of regular policy, the Assyrians laid waste to the land in which they were fighting, smashing dams, looting and destroying towns, setting crops on fire, and cutting down trees, particularly fruit trees. They were especially known for committing atrocities on their captives. King Ashurnasirpal (ah-shur-NAH-zur-pahl) recorded this account of his treatment of prisoners:

> 3000 of their combat troops I felled with weapons…. Many of the captives taken from them I burned in a fire. Many I took alive; from some of these I cut off their hands to the wrist, from others I cut off their noses, ears and fingers; I put out the eyes of many of the soldiers…. I burned their young men and women to death.[16]

After conquering another city, the same king wrote, "I fixed up a pile of corpses in front of the city's gate. I flayed the nobles, as many as had rebelled, and spread their skins out on the piles…. I flayed many within my land and spread their skins out on the walls."[17] It should be noted that this policy of extreme cruelty to prisoners was not used against all enemies but was primarily reserved for those who were already part of the empire and then rebelled against Assyrian rule.

Assyrian Society   Assyrian deportation policies created a polyglot society in which ethnic differences were not very important. What gave identity to the Assyrians themselves was their language, although even that was akin to the language of their southern neighbors in Babylonia, who also spoke a Semitic tongue. Religion was also a cohesive force. Assyria was literally "the land of Ashur," a reference to its chief god. The king, as Ashur's representative on earth, provided a final unifying focus.

Agriculture formed the principal basis of Assyrian life. Assyria was a land of farming villages with relatively few significant cities, especially in comparison to southern Mesopotamia. Unlike the river valleys, where farming required the minute organization of large numbers of people to control irrigation, Assyrian farms received sufficient moisture from regular rainfall.

Trade was second to agriculture in economic importance. For internal trade, metals—including gold, silver, copper, and bronze—were used as a medium of exchange. Various agricultural products also served as a form of payment or exchange. Because of their geographic location, the Assyrians served as intermediaries and participated in an international trade, importing timber, wine, and precious metals and stones while exporting textiles produced in palaces, temples, and private workshops.

Assyrian Culture   The Assyrians assimilated much of Mesopotamian civilization and saw themselves as guardians of Sumerian and Babylonian culture. Assyrian kings also tried to maintain old traditions when they rebuilt damaged temples by constructing the new buildings on the original foundations rather than in new locations.

Among the best-known objects of Assyrian art are the relief sculptures found in the royal palaces in three of the Assyrian capital cities, Nimrud, Nineveh, and Khorsabad. These reliefs, which were begun in the ninth century B.C.E. and reached their high point in the reign of Ashurbanipal in the seventh, depicted two different kinds of subject matter: ritual or ceremonial scenes revolving around the king and scenes of hunting and war. The latter show realistic action scenes of the king and his warriors engaged in battle or hunting animals, especially lions. These images depict a strongly masculine world where discipline, brute force, and toughness are the enduring values—indeed, the very values of the Assyrian military monarchy.

The Persian Empire   After the collapse of the Assyrian Empire, the Chaldeans, under their king Nebuchadnezzar (neb-uh-kud-NEZZ-ur) II (605–562 B.C.E.), made Babylonia the leading state in western Asia. Nebuchadnezzar rebuilt Babylon as the center of his empire, giving it a reputation as one of the great cities of the ancient world. But the splendor of Chaldean Babylonia proved to be short-lived when Babylon fell to the Persians in 539 B.C.E.

The Persians were an Indo-European-speaking people who lived in southwestern Iran. Primarily nomadic, the Persians were organized into tribes until the

OPPOSING VIEWPOINTS

The Governing of Empires: Two Approaches

Both the Assyrians and the Persians created large empires that encompassed large areas of the ancient Near East. Although both Assyrian and Persian rulers used military force and violence to attain their empires, their approaches to conquest and ruling sometimes differed. Assyrian rulers were known for their terror tactics and atrocities, as described in the first two selections. Although the kings of Persia also used terror when needed, they also had a reputation for less cruelty and more tolerance. Especially noteworthy was Cyrus, as is evident in this selection from a decree (known as the Cyrus Cylinder) that he issued in 538 B.C.E. The propaganda value of his words is also apparent, however.

King Sennacherib (704–681 B.C.E.) Describes His Siege of Jerusalem (701 B.C.E.)

As to Hezekiah, the Jew, he did not submit to my yoke, I laid siege to 46 of his strong cities, walled forts and to the countless small villages in their vicinity, and conquered them by means of well-stamped earth-ramps, and battering-rams brought thus near to the walls combined with the attack by foot soldiers, using mines, breaches as well as sapper work. I drove out of them 200,150 people, young and old, male and female, horses, mules, donkeys, camels, big and small cattle beyond counting, and considered them booty. Himself I made a prisoner in Jerusalem, his royal residence, like a bird in a cage. I surrounded him with earthwork in order to molest those who were leaving his city's gate.

King Ashurbanipal (669–627 B.C.E.) Describes His Treatment of Conquered Babylon

I tore out the tongues of those whose slanderous mouths had uttered blasphemies against my god Ashur and had plotted against me, his god-fearing prince; I defeated them completely. The others, I smashed alive with the very same statues of protective deities with which they had smashed my own grandfather

Achaemenid (ah-KEE-muh-nud) dynasty managed to unify them. One of the dynasty's members, Cyrus (559–530 B.C.E.), created a powerful Persian state that rearranged the political map of western Asia.

Cyrus the Great   In 550 B.C.E., Cyrus extended Persian control over the Medes, making Media the first Persian **satrapy** (SAY-truh-pee), or province. Three years later, Cyrus defeated the prosperous Lydian kingdom in western Asia Minor, and Lydia became another Persian satrapy. Cyrus's forces then went on to conquer the Greek city-states that had been established on the Ionian coast. Cyrus then turned eastward, subduing the eastern part of the Iranian Plateau, Sogdia, and even western India. His eastern frontiers secured, Cyrus entered Mesopotamia in 539 and captured Babylon. His treatment of Babylonia showed remarkable restraint and wisdom. Babylonia was made into a Persian province under a Persian **satrap** (SAY-trap), or governor, but many government officials were kept in their positions.

Sennacherib—now finally as a belated burial sacrifice for his soul. I fed their corpses, cut into small pieces, to dogs, pigs, ... vultures, the birds of the sky and also to the fish of the ocean. After I ... thus made quiet again the hearts of the great gods, my lords, I removed the corpses of those whom the pestilence had felled, whose leftovers after the dogs and pigs had fed on them were obstructing the streets, filling the places of Babylon, and of those who had lost their lives through the terrible famine.

The Cyrus Cylinder

I am Cyrus, king of the world, great king, legitimate king, king of Babylon, king of Sumer and Akkad, king of the four corners of the earth....

When I entered Babylon as a friend and when I established the seat of the government in the palace of the ruler under jubilation and rejoicing, Marduk, the great lord [the chief Babylonian god], caused the magnanimous inhabitants of Babylon to love me, and I was daily endeavoring to worship him. My numerous troops walked around in Babylon in peace. I did not allow anybody to terrorize any place of the country of Sumer and Akkad. I strove for peace in Babylon and in all his other sacred cities. As to the inhabitants of Babylon ... I brought relief to their dilapidated housing, putting thus an end to their main complaints....

As to the region from as far as Ashur and Susa ... I returned to these sacred cities on the other side of the Tigris, the sanctuaries of which have been ruins for a long time, the images which used to live therein and established for them permanent sanctuaries. I also gathered all their former inhabitants and returned to them their dwellings.

Both Ashurbanipal and Cyrus entered Babylon as conquerors. How did their treatment of the conquered city differ? How do you explain the differences? Which method do you think was more effective? Why?

Sources: Pritchard, James B., ed., *Ancient Near Eastern Texts Relating to the Old Testament*, Third Edition with Supplement. © 1950, 1955, 1969, renewed 1978 by Princeton University Press. Reprinted by permission of Princeton University Press.

Cyrus took the title "King of All, Great King, Mighty King, King of Babylon, King of the Land of Sumer and Akkad, King of the Four Rims [of the earth], the Son of Cambyses the Great King, King of Anshan"[18] and insisted that he stood in the ancient, unbroken line of Babylonian kings. By appealing to the vanity of the Babylonians, he won their loyalty. Cyrus also issued an edict permitting the Jews, who had been brought to Babylon in the sixth century B.C.E., to return to Jerusalem with their sacred objects and to rebuild their Temple as well.

To his contemporaries, Cyrus deserved to be called Cyrus the Great. The Greek historian Herodotus recounted that the Persians viewed him as a "father," a ruler who was "gentle, and procured them all manner of goods."[19] Cyrus must have been an unusual ruler for his time, a man who demonstrated considerable wisdom and compassion in the conquest and organization of his empire. He won approval by using not only Persians but also native peoples as government officials in their own states. Unlike the Assyrian rulers of an earlier empire, he had a reputation for mercy. Medes, Babylonians, and Jews all accepted him as their legitimate ruler. Indeed, the Jews regarded him as the anointed one of God: "I am the Lord who says of Cyrus, 'He is my shepherd and will accomplish all that I please'; he will say of Jerusalem, 'Let it be rebuilt'; and of the Temple, 'Let its foundations be laid.' This is what the Lord says to his anointed, to Cyrus, whose right hand I take hold of to subdue nations before him."[20]

Expanding the Empire   Cyrus's successors extended the territory of the Persian Empire. His son Cambyses (kam-BY-seez) (530–522 B.C.E.) undertook a successful invasion of Egypt. Darius (duh-RY-uss) (521–486 B.C.E.) added a new Persian province in western India that extended to the Indus River and moved into Europe proper, conquering Thrace and making the Macedonian king a vassal. A revolt of the Ionian Greek cities in 499 B.C.E. resulted in temporary freedom for these communities in western Asia Minor. Aid from the Greek mainland, most notably from Athens, encouraged the Ionians to invade Lydia and burn Sardis, center of the Lydian satrapy. This event led to Darius's involvement with the mainland Greeks. After reestablishing control of the Ionian Greek cities, Darius undertook an invasion of the Greek mainland, which culminated in the Athenian victory in the Battle of Marathon, in 490 B.C.E.

Governing the Empire   By the reign of Darius, the Persians had assembled the largest empire the world had yet seen. It not only included all the old centers of power in Egypt and western Asia but also extended into Thrace and Asia Minor in the west and into India in the east. For administrative purposes, the empire had been divided into approximately twenty satrapies. Each province was ruled by a satrap, literally a "protector of the kingdom." Satraps collected tributes, were responsible for justice and security, raised military levies for the royal army, and normally commanded the military forces within their satrapies. In terms of real power, the satraps were miniature kings who created courts imitative of the Great King's.

An efficient system of communication was crucial to sustaining the Persian Empire. Well-maintained roads facilitated the rapid transit of military and government personnel. One in particular, the so-called Royal Road, stretched from Sardis, the center of Lydia in Asia Minor, to Susa, the chief capital of the Persian Empire. Like the Assyrians, the Persians established staging posts equipped with fresh horses for the king's messengers.

The Great King   In this vast administrative system, the Persian king occupied an exalted position. Although not considered a god in the manner of an Egyptian pharaoh, he was nevertheless the elect one or regent of the Persian god Ahuramazda (uh-HOOR-uh-MAHZ-duh). All subjects were the king's servants, and he was the source of all justice, possessing the power of life and death over everyone. Persian kings were largely secluded and not easily accessible. They resided in a series of splendid palaces. Darius in particular was a palace builder on a grand scale.

The policies of Darius also tended to widen the gap between the king and his subjects. As the Great King himself said of all his subjects, "What was said to them by me, night and day it was done."[21] Over a period of time, the Great Kings in their greed came to hoard immense quantities of gold and silver in treasuries located in the capital cities. Both their hoarding of wealth and their later over-taxation of their subjects were crucial factors in the ultimate weakening of the Persian Empire.

In its heyday, however, the empire stood supreme, and much of its power depended on the military. By the time of Darius, the Persian monarchs had created a standing army of professional soldiers. This army was truly international, composed of contingents from the various peoples who made up the empire. At its core was a cavalry force of ten thousand and an elite infantry force of ten thousand Medes and Persians known as the Immortals because they were never allowed to fall below ten thousand in number. When one was killed, he was immediately replaced.

Persian Religion   Of all the Persians' cultural contributions, the most original was their religion, **Zoroastrianism**. According to Persian tradition, Zoroaster (ZOR-oh-ass-tur) was born in 660 B.C.E. After a period of wandering and solitude, he experienced revelations that caused him to be revered as a prophet of the "true religion." His teachings were eventually written down in the third century B.C.E. in the *Zend Avesta*, the sacred book of Zoroastrianism.

Zoroaster's spiritual message was basically monotheistic. To Zoroaster, the religion he preached was the only perfect one, and Ahuramazda was the only god. Ahuramazda ("Wise Lord") was the supreme deity, "creator of all things." According to Zoroaster, Ahuramazda also possessed qualities that all humans should aspire to, such as good thought, right action, and piety. Although Ahuramazda was supreme, he was not unopposed; this gave a dualistic element to Zoroastrianism. At the beginning of the world, the good spirit of Ahuramazda was opposed by the evil spirit, later identified as Ahriman.

Humans also played a role in this cosmic struggle between good and evil. Ahuramazda, the creator, gave all humans free will and the power to choose between right and wrong. The good person chooses the right way of Ahuramazda. Zoroaster taught that there would be an end to the struggle between good and evil. Ahuramazda would eventually triumph, and at the last judgment at the end of the world, the final separation of good and evil would occur. Individuals, too, would be judged. Each soul faced a final evaluation of its actions. The soul of a person who had performed good deeds would achieve paradise; but if deeds had been evil, the person would be thrown into an abyss of torment. Some historians believe that Zoroastrianism, with its emphasis on good and evil, heaven and hell, and a last judgment, had an impact on Christianity, a religion that eventually surpassed it in significance.

CHRONOLOGIES

THE FIRST HUMANS

c. 3–4 million years ago	Australopithecines flourished
c. 1–4 million years ago	*Homo habilis* flourished
c. 100,000–1.5 million years ago	*Homo erectus* flourished
c. 200,000–30,000 B.C.E.	Neanderthals flourished
c. 200,000 B.C.E.	*Homo sapiens sapiens* emerged

THE BIRTH OF EARLY CIVILIZATIONS

c. 3100 B.C.E.	Egypt
c. 3000 B.C.E.	Mesopotamia
c. 3000 B.C.E.	India
c. 2600 B.C.E.	Peru
c. 2000 B.C.E.	China
c. 2000 B.C.E.	Central Asia

THE EGYPTIANS

c. 3100–2575 B.C.E.	Early Dynastic Period (Dynasties 1–3)
c. 2575–2125 B.C.E.	Old Kingdom (Dynasties 4–8)
c. 2125–2010 B.C.E.	First Intermediate Period (Dynasties 9–11)
c. 2010–1630 B.C.E.	Middle Kingdom (Dynasties 12–13)
c. 1630–1539 B.C.E.	Second Intermediate Period (Dynasties 14–17)
c. 1539–1069 B.C.E.	New Kingdom (Dynasties 18–20)
c. 1069–30 B.C.E.	Post-Empire (Dynasties 21–31)

EARLY EMPIRES

The Assyrians

700 B.C.E.	Height of power
669–627 B.C.E.	Ashurbanipal
612 B.C.E.	Fall of Nineveh
605 B.C.E.	Assyrian Empire destroyed

The Persians

600s B.C.E.	Unification under Achaemenid dynasty
550 B.C.E.	Persian control over Medes
559–530 B.C.E.	Conquests of Cyrus the Great
530–522 B.C.E.	Cambyses and conquest of Egypt
521–486 B.C.E.	Reign of Darius

 MindTap™

MindTap is a fully online, highly personalized learning experience built upon Cengage Learning content. MindTap combines student learning tools—readings, multimedia, activities, and assessments—into a singular Learning Path that guides students through their course.

2

ANCIENT INDIA

Krishna and Arjuna preparing for battle

CHAPTER OUTLINE

• The Emergence of Civilization in India: Harappan Society • The Aryans in India • Escaping the Wheel of Life: The Religious World of Ancient India • The Exuberant World of Indian Culture

The Emergence of Civilization in India: Harappan Society

Like the civilizations of Mesopotamia and Egypt, the earliest civilizations in India arose in river valleys and were shaped, in part, by their environment. Thus, from its beginnings, Indian civilization has been intimately associated with the geography of the subcontinent.

A Land of Diversity   India was and still is a land of diversity. This diversity is evident in its languages and cultures as well as in its physical characteristics. India possesses an incredible array of languages. It has a deserved reputation, along with the Middle East, as a cradle of religion. Two of the world's major religions, Hinduism and Buddhism, originated in India, and a number of others, including Sikhism and Islam (the latter of which entered the South Asian subcontinent in the ninth or tenth century C.E.), continue to flourish there.

In its size and geographical complexity, India seems more like a continent than a nation. That complexity begins with the physical environment. The Indian subcontinent, shaped like a spade hanging from the southern ridge of Asia, is composed of a number of core regions. In the far north are the Himalayan and Karakoram mountain ranges, home of the highest peaks in the world. Directly to the south of the Himalayas and the Karakoram range is the rich valley of the Ganges, India's "holy river" and one of the core regions of Indian culture. To the west is the Indus River valley. Today, the latter is a relatively arid plateau that forms the backbone of the modern state of Pakistan, but in ancient times it enjoyed a more balanced climate and served as the cradle of Indian civilization.

South of India's two major river valleys lies the Deccan, a region of hills and an upland plateau that extends from the Ganges Valley to the southern tip of the Indian subcontinent. The interior of the plateau is relatively hilly and dry, but the eastern and western coasts are occupied by lush plains, which have historically been among the most densely populated regions of India. Off the southeastern coast is the island known today as Sri Lanka. Although Sri Lanka is now a separate country quite distinct politically and culturally from India, the island's history is intimately linked with that of its larger neighbor.

In this vast region live a rich mixture of peoples: people speaking one of the languages in the Dravidian family, who may have descended from the Indus River culture that flourished at the dawn of Indian civilization more than four thousand years ago; Aryans, descended from the pastoral peoples who flooded southward from Central Asia in the second millennium B.C.E.; and hill peoples, who may be the descendants of the first migrants passing through the area and hence may have been the earliest inhabitants of all. Although today this beautiful mosaic of peoples and cultures has been broken up into a number of separate independent states, the region still possesses a coherent history that is recognizably Indian.

Harappan Civilization: A Fascinating Enigma   In the 1920s, archaeologists discovered the existence of agricultural settlements dating back more than six thousand years in the lower Indus River valley in modern Pakistan. Those small mudbrick villages eventually gave rise to the

MAP 2.1 Ancient Harappan Civilization

This map shows the location of the first civilization that arose in the Indus River valley, which today is located in Pakistan.

sophisticated human communities that historians call Harappan civilization. Although today the area is relatively arid, during the third and fourth millennia B.C.E., it evidently received much more abundant rainfall, and the valleys of the Indus River and its tributaries supported a thriving civilization that may have covered a total area of more than 600,000 square miles, from the Himalayas to the Indian Ocean. More than seventy sites have been unearthed since the area was discovered in the 1850s, but the main sites are at the two major cities, Harappa, in the Punjab, and Mohenjo-Daro, nearly 400 miles to the south near the mouth of the Indus River.

Political and Social Structures In several respects, Harappan civilization closely resembled the cultures of Mesopotamia and the Nile Valley. Like them, it probably began in tiny farming villages scattered throughout the river valley, some dating back to as early as 6500 or 7000 B.C.E. These villages thrived and grew until by the middle of the third millennium B.C.E. they could support a privileged ruling elite living in walled cities of considerable magnitude and affluence. The center of power was the city of Harappa, which was surrounded by a brick wall over 40 feet thick at its base and more than 3.5 miles in circumference. The city was laid out on an essentially rectangular grid, with some streets as wide as 30 feet. Most buildings were constructed of kiln-dried mudbricks and were square in shape, reflecting the grid pattern. At its height, the city may have had as many as 80,000 inhabitants, making it as large as some of the most populous Sumerian urban centers.

Both Harappa and Mohenjo-Daro were divided into large walled neighborhoods, with narrow lanes separating the rows of houses. Houses varied in size, with some as high as three stories, but all followed the same general plan based on a square courtyard surrounded by rooms. Bathrooms featured an advanced drainage system, which carried wastewater out to drains located under the streets and thence to sewage pits beyond the city walls. But the cities also had the equivalent of the modern slum. At Harappa, tiny dwellings for workers have been found near metal furnaces and the open areas used for pounding grain.

Unfortunately, Harappan writing has not yet been deciphered, so historians know relatively little about the organization of the Harappan state. Recent archaeological evidence suggests, however, that unlike its contemporaries in Egypt and Sumer, Harappa was not a centralized monarchy with a theocratic base but a collection of more than 1,500 towns and cities loosely connected by ties of trade and alliance and ruled by a coalition of landlords and rich merchants. There were no royal precincts or imposing burial monuments, and there are few surviving stone or terra-cotta images that might represent kings, priests, or military commanders. It is possible that religion had advanced beyond the stage of spirit worship to belief in a single god or goddess of fertility. Presumably, priests at court prayed to this deity to maintain the fertility of the soil and guarantee the annual harvest.

As in Mesopotamia and Egypt, the Harappan economy was based primarily on agriculture. Wheat, barley, rice, and peas were apparently the primary crops. The presence of cotton seeds at various sites suggests that the Harappan peoples may have been the first to master the cultivation of this useful crop and possibly introduced it, along with rice, to other societies in the region. But Harappa also developed an extensive trading network that extended to Sumer and other civilizations to the west. Textiles and foodstuffs were apparently imported from Sumer in exchange for metals such as copper, lumber, precious stones, and various types of luxury goods. Much of this trade was conducted by ship via the Persian Gulf, although some undoubtedly went by land.

Harappan Culture   Archaeological remains indicate that the Indus Valley peoples possessed a culture as sophisticated in some ways as that of the Sumerians to the west. Although Harappan architecture was purely functional and shows little artistic sensitivity, the aesthetic quality of some of the pottery and sculpture is superb. Harappan painted pottery, wheel-turned and kiln-fired, rivals equivalent work produced elsewhere. Sculpture, however, was the Harappans' highest artistic achievement. Some artifacts possess a wonderful vitality of expression. Fired clay seals show a deft touch in carving animals such as elephants, tigers, rhinoceroses, and antelope, and figures made of copper or terra-cotta show a lively sensitivity and a sense of grace and movement that is almost modern.

Writing was another achievement of Harappan society and dates back at least to the beginning of the third millennium B.C.E. Unfortunately, the only surviving examples of Harappan writing are the pictographic symbols inscribed on clay seals. The script contained more than four hundred characters, but most are too stylized to be identified by their shape, and as noted earlier, scholars have been

COMPARATIVE ESSAY

Writing and Civilization

ART & IDEAS

In the year 3250 B.C.E., King Scorpion of Egypt issued an edict announcing a major victory for his army over rival forces in the region. Inscribed in limestone on a cliff face in the Nile River valley, that edict is perhaps the oldest surviving historical document in the world today.

According to prehistorians, human beings invented the first spoken language about 50,000 years ago. As human beings spread from Africa to other continents, that initial language gradually fragmented and evolved into innumerable separate tongues. By the time the agricultural revolution began about 10,000 B.C.E., there were perhaps nearly twenty distinct language families in existence around the world.

During the later stages of the agricultural revolution, the first writing systems also began to emerge in various places around the world. The first successful efforts were apparently achieved in Mesopotamia and Egypt, but knowledge of writing soon spread to peoples along the shores of the Mediterranean and in the Indus River valley in South Asia. Wholly independent systems were also invented in China and Mesoamerica. Writing was used for a variety of purposes. King Scorpion's edict suggests that one reason was to enable a ruler to communicate with his subjects on matters of official concern. In other cases, the purpose was to enable human beings to communicate with supernatural forces. In China and Egypt, for example, priests used writing to communicate with the gods. In Mesopotamia and in the Indus River valley, merchants used writing to record commercial and other legal transactions. Finally, writing was also used to present ideas in new ways, giving rise to such early Mesopotamian literature as *The Epic of Gilgamesh*.

How did these early written languages evolve into the complex systems in use today? In almost all cases, the first systems consisted of pictographs, pictorial images of various concrete objects such as trees, water, cattle, body parts, and the heavenly bodies. Eventually, the pictographs became more stylized to facilitate transcription—much as we often use a cursive script instead of block printing today. Finally, and most important for their future development, these pictorial images began to take on specific phonetic meanings so that they could represent sounds in the written language. Most sophisticated written systems eventually evolved to a phonetic script, based on an alphabet of symbols to represent all sounds in the spoken language, but others went only part of the way by adding phonetic signs to the individual character to suggest pronunciation while keeping the essence of the original pictograph to indicate meaning. Most of the latter systems, such as hieroglyphics in Egypt and cuneiform in Mesopotamia, eventually became extinct, but the ancient Chinese writing system survives today, in greatly altered form.

Q *What are the various purposes for which writing systems were developed in the ancient world? What appears to have been the initial purpose for the development of the Harappan script?*

unable to decipher them. There are no apparent links with Mesopotamian scripts, although, as in Mesopotamia, the primary purpose of writing may have been to record commercial transactions. Until the script is deciphered, much about the Harappan civilization must remain, as one historian termed it, a fascinating enigma.

The Collapse of Harappan Civilization   One of the great mysteries of Harappan civilization is how it came to an end. Archaeologists working at Mohenjo-Daro have discovered signs of first a gradual decay and then a sudden destruction of the city and its inhabitants around 1500 B.C.E. Many of the surviving skeletons have been found in postures of running or hiding, reminiscent of the ruins of the Roman city of Pompeii, destroyed by the eruption of Mount Vesuvius in 79 C.E.

These tantalizing signs of flight before a sudden catastrophe once led scholars to surmise that the city of Mohenjo-Daro (the name was applied by archaeologists and means "city of the dead") and perhaps the remnants of Harappan civilization were destroyed by the Aryans, pastoral peoples from the north who arrived in the subcontinent around the middle of the second millennium B.C.E. Although the Aryans were considered to be less sophisticated culturally than the Harappans, like many nomadic peoples they excelled at the art of war. As in Mesopotamia and the Nile Valley, contacts between pastoral and agricultural peoples proved unstable and often ended in armed conflict. Today, however, historians are doubtful that the Aryan peoples were directly responsible for the final destruction of Mohenjo-Daro. More likely, Harappan civilization had already fallen on hard times, perhaps as a result of climatic change in the Indus Valley. Archaeologists have found clear signs of social decay, including evidence of trash in the streets, neglect of public services, and overcrowding in urban neighborhoods. Mohenjo-Daro itself may have been destroyed by an epidemic or by natural phenomena such as floods, an earthquake, or a shift in the course of the Indus River. If that was the case, any migrating peoples arrived in the area after the greatness of Harappan civilization had already passed.

Who Were the Aryans?   Historians know relatively little about the origins and culture of the Aryans. The traditional view is that they were Indo-European-speaking peoples who inhabited vast areas in the steppes north and east of the Black and Caspian Seas. The Indo-Europeans were pastoral peoples who migrated from season to season in search of fodder for their herds. Historians have credited them with a number of technological achievements, including the invention of horse-drawn chariots and the stirrup, both of which were eventually introduced throughout much of the Eurasian supercontinent.

Whereas many other Indo-European-speaking peoples moved westward and eventually settled throughout Europe, the Aryans moved south across the Hindu Kush into the plains of northern India. Between 1500 and 1000 B.C.E., they gradually advanced eastward from the Indus Valley, across the fertile plain of the Ganges, and later southward into the Deccan Plateau. Eventually, they extended their political mastery over the entire subcontinent and its Dravidian-speaking inhabitants, although the indigenous culture survived to remain a prominent element in the evolution of traditional Indian civilization.

In recent years, a new theory has been proposed by some Indian historians, who contend that the Aryan peoples did not migrate into the Indian subcontinent from Central Asia, but were in fact descendants of the indigenous population that had originally created the Indus River civilization. Most scholars, however,

MAP 2.2 Writing Systems in the Ancient World

One of the chief characteristics of the first civilizations was the development of a system of written communication.

continue to support the migration hypothesis, although the evidence is not conclusive. They point out that the spoken language of the Aryan people, known as Sanskrit, is widely recognized as a branch of the Indo-European family of languages. Moreover, the earliest account produced by the Aryan people themselves, known as the Rig Veda (RIK VAY-duh), describes a culture based primarily on pastoralism, a pursuit not particularly suited to the Indus River valley. A definitive solution to the debate will have to await further evidence.

THE ARYANS IN INDIA

After they settled in India, the Aryans gradually adapted to the geographic realities of their new homeland and abandoned the pastoral life for agricultural pursuits. They were assisted by the introduction of iron, which probably came from the Middle East, where it had been introduced by the Hittites about 1500 B.C.E. The invention of the iron plow, along with the development of irrigation, allowed the Aryans and their indigenous subjects to clear the dense jungle growth along the Ganges River and transform the Ganges Valley into one of the richest agricultural regions in South Asia. The Aryans also developed their first writing system, based on the Aramaic script of the Middle East, and were thus able to transcribe the legends that previously had been passed down from generation to generation by memory. Most of what is known about the early Aryans is based on oral traditions passed on in the Rig Veda, an ancient work that was written down after the Aryans arrived in India (it is one of several Vedas, or collections of sacred instructions and rituals).

From Chieftains to Kings   As in other Indo-European societies, each of the various Aryan tribes was led by a chieftain, called a **raja** (RAH-juh), who was assisted by a council of elders composed of other leading members of the community; like them, he was normally a member of the warrior class, called the *kshatriya* (kshuh-TREE-yuh). The chief derived his power from his ability to protect his people from rival groups, a skill that was crucial in the warring kingdoms and shifting alliances that were typical of early Aryan society. Though the rajas claimed to be representatives of the gods, they were not viewed as gods themselves.

As Aryan society grew in size and complexity, the chieftains began to be transformed into kings, usually called **maharajas** (mah-huh-RAH-juhs) ("great rajas"). Nevertheless, the tradition that the ruler did not possess absolute authority remained strong. Like all human beings, the ruler was required to follow the *dharma* (DAR-muh), a set of laws that set behavioral standards for all individuals and classes in Indian society.

The Impact of the Greeks   While competing groups squabbled for precedence in India, powerful new empires were rising to the west. First came the Persian Empire of Cyrus and Darius. Then came the Greeks. After two centuries of sporadic rivalry and warfare, the Greeks achieved a brief period of regional dominance in the late fourth century B.C.E. with the rise of Macedonia under Alexander the Great. Alexander had heard of the riches of India, and in 330 B.C.E., after conquering Persia, he launched an invasion of the east. In 326, his armies arrived in the plains of northwestern India and the Indus River valley. They departed almost as suddenly as they had come, leaving in their wake Greek administrators and a veneer of cultural influence that would affect the area for generations to come.

The Mauryan Empire   The Alexandrian conquest was a brief interlude in the history of the Indian subcontinent, but it played a formative role, for on the heels of Alexander's departure came the rise of the first dynasty to control much of the region. The founder of the new state, who took the royal title Chandragupta Maurya (chun-druh-GOOP-tuh MOWR-yuh) (324–301 B.C.E.), drove out the Greek administrators that Alexander had left behind and solidified his control over the northern Indian plain. He established the capital of his new Mauryan Empire at Pataliputra (pah-tah-lee-POO-truh) (modern Patna) in the Ganges Valley. Little is known of his origins, although some sources say he had originally fought on the side of the invading Greek forces but then angered Alexander with his outspoken advice.

Little, too, is known of Chandragupta Maurya's empire. Most accounts of his reign rely on the scattered remnants of a lost work written by Megasthenes (muh-GAS-thuh-neez), a Greek ambassador to the Mauryan court, in about 302 B.C.E. Chandragupta Maurya was apparently advised by a brilliant court official named Kautilya (kow-TIL-yuh), whose name has been attached to a treatise on politics called the *Arthasastra*. The work actually dates from a later time, but it may well reflect Kautilya's ideas.

Although the author of the *Arthasastra* follows Aryan tradition in stating that the happiness of the king lies in the happiness of his subjects, the treatise also asserts that when the sacred law of the *dharma* and practical politics collide, the latter must take precedence: "Whenever there is disagreement between history and sacred law or between evidence and sacred law, then the matter should be settled in accordance with sacred law. But whenever sacred law is in conflict with rational law, then reason shall be held authoritative."[1] The *Arthasastra* also emphasizes ends rather than means, achieved results rather than the methods employed. For this reason, it has often been compared to Machiavelli's famous political treatise of the Italian Renaissance, *The Prince*, written more than a thousand years later.

As described in the *Arthasastra*, Chandragupta Maurya's government was highly centralized and even despotic: "It is power and power alone which, only when exercised by the king with impartiality, and in proportion to guilt, over his son or his enemy, maintains both this world and the next."[2] The king possessed a large army and a secret police responsible to his orders (according to the Greek ambassador Megasthenes, Chandragupta Maurya was chronically fearful of assassination, a not unrealistic concern for someone who had allegedly come to power by violence). Reportedly, all food was tasted in his presence, and he made a practice of never sleeping twice in the same bed in his sumptuous palace. To guard against corruption, a board of censors was empowered to investigate cases of possible malfeasance and incompetence within the bureaucracy.

The ruler's authority beyond the confines of the capital may often have been limited, however. The empire was divided into provinces that were ruled by governors. At first, most of these governors were appointed by and reported to the ruler, but later the position became hereditary. The provinces themselves were divided into districts, each under a chief magistrate appointed by the governor. At the base of the government pyramid was the village, where the vast majority of the Indian people lived. The village was governed by a council of elders; membership in the council was normally hereditary and was shared by the wealthiest families in the village.

Caste and Class: Social Structures in Ancient India

When the Aryans arrived in India, they already possessed a social system based on a ruling warrior class and other groupings characteristic of a pastoral society. In the subcontinent, they encountered peoples living by farming or, in some cases, by other pursuits such as fishing, hunting, or food gathering. Although the immediate consequences of this mixture of cultures are still unclear, the ultimate result was the emergence of a set of social institutions that continues to have relevance down to the present day.

The Class System   At the crux of the social system was the concept of a hierarchical division of society that placed each individual within a ritual framework that defined the person's occupation and status within the broader community. In part, this division may have been an outgrowth of attitudes held by the Aryan peoples with regard to the indigenous population. The Aryans, who followed primarily pastoral pursuits, tended to look askance at their new neighbors, who lived by tilling the soil. Further, the Aryans, a mostly light-skinned people, were contemptuous of the indigenous peoples, who were darker. Light skin came to imply high status, whereas dark skin suggested the opposite.

The concept of color, however, was only the physical manifestation of a division that took place in Indian society on the basis of economic functions. Indian classes (called **varna**, literally, "color," and commonly but mistakenly translated as "castes" in English) did not simply reflect an informal division of labor. Instead, at least in theory, they were a set of rigid social classifications that determined not only one's occupation but also one's status in society and one's hope for ultimate salvation. There were five major *varna* in Indian society in ancient times. At the top were two classes, collectively viewed as the aristocracy, which represented the ruling elites in Aryan society prior to their arrival in India: the priests and the warriors.

The priestly class, known as the **brahmins**, was usually considered to be at the top of the social scale. Descended from seers who had advised the ruler on religious matters in Aryan tribal society—*brahmin* meant "one possessed of **Brahman**" (BRAH-mun), a term for the supreme god—they were eventually transformed into an official class after their religious role declined in importance. Megasthenes described this class as follows:

> From the time of their conception in the womb they are under the care and guardianship of learned men who go to the mother and ... give her prudent hints and counsels, and the women who listen to them most willingly are thought to be the most fortunate in their offspring. After their birth the children are in the care of one person after another, and as they advance in years their masters are men of superior accomplishments. The philosophers reside in a grove in front of the city within a moderate-sized enclosure. They live in a simple style and lie on pallets of straw and [deer] skins. They abstain from animal food and sexual pleasures, and occupy their time in listening to serious discourse and in imparting knowledge to willing ears.[3]

The second class was the *kshatriya*, the warriors. Although often listed below the *brahmins* in social status, many *kshatriyas* were probably descended from the ruling warrior class in Aryan society prior to the conquest of India and thus may have originally ranked socially above the *brahmins*, although they were ranked lower in religious terms. Like the *brahmins*, the *kshatriyas* were originally identified with a single occupation—fighting—but as the character of Aryan society changed, they often switched to other forms of employment. At the same time, new families from other classes were sometimes tacitly accepted into the ranks of the warriors.

The third-ranked class in Indian society was the **vaisya** (VISH-yuh) (literally, "commoner"). The *vaisyas* were usually viewed in economic terms as the merchant class. Some historians have speculated that the *vaisyas* were originally guardians of the tribal herds but that after settling in India, many moved into commercial pursuits. Megasthenes noted that members of this class "alone are permitted to hunt and keep cattle and to sell beasts of burden or to let them out on hire. In return for clearing the land of wild beasts and birds which infest sown fields, they receive an allowance of corn from the king. They lead a wandering life and dwell in tents."[4] Although this class was ranked below the first two in social status, it shared with them the privilege of being considered "**twice-born**," a term referring to a ceremony at puberty whereby young males were initiated into adulthood and introduced into Indian society. After the ceremony, male members of the top three classes were allowed to wear the "sacred thread" for the remainder of their lives.

Below the three "twice-born" classes were the **sudras** (SOO-druhs *or* SHOO-druhs), who represented the great bulk of the Indian population. The *sudras* were not considered fully Aryan, and the term probably originally referred to the indigenous population. Most *sudras* were peasants or artisans or worked at other forms of manual labor. They had only limited rights in society. In recent years, DNA samples have revealed that most upper-class South Indians share more genetic characteristics with Europeans than their lower-class counterparts do, a finding that supports the hypothesis that the Aryans established their political and social dominance over the indigenous population.

At the lowest level of Indian society, and in fact not even considered a legitimate part of the class system, were the untouchables (also known as outcastes or **pariahs**). The untouchables probably originated as a slave class consisting of prisoners of war, criminals, ethnic minorities, and other groups considered outside Indian society. Even after slavery was outlawed, the untouchables were given menial and degrading tasks that other Indians would not accept, such as collecting trash, handling dead bodies, or serving as butchers or tanners. One historian estimates that they may have accounted for a little more than 5 percent of the total population of India in antiquity.

The lives of the untouchables were extremely demeaning. They were regarded as being not fully human, and their very presence was considered polluting to members of the other *varna*. No Indian would touch or eat food handled or prepared by an untouchable. Untouchables lived in ghettos and, according to a foreign observer, were required to tap two sticks together to announce their approach when they traveled outside their quarters so that others could avoid them.

Technically, these class divisions were absolute. Individuals supposedly were born, lived, and died in the same class. In practice, upward or downward mobility probably took place, and there was undoubtedly some flexibility in economic functions. But throughout most of Indian history, class taboos remained strict. Members generally were not permitted to marry outside their class (although in practice, men were occasionally allowed to marry below their class but not above it). At first, attitudes toward the handling of food were relatively loose, but eventually that taboo grew stronger, and social mores dictated that sharing meals and marrying outside one's class were unacceptable.

The *Jati* The people of ancient India did not belong to a particular class as individuals but as part of a larger kin group commonly referred to as the ***jati*** (JAH-tee) (in Portuguese, *casta*, which evolved into the English term *caste*), a system of extended families that originated in ancient India and still exists in somewhat changed form today. Although the origins of the *jati* system are unknown (there are no indications of strict class distinctions in Harappan society), the *jati* eventually became identified with a specific kinship group living in a specific area and carrying out a specific function in society. Each *jati* was identified with a particular *varna*, and each had its own separate economic function.

Jatis were thus the basic social organization into which traditional Indian society was divided. Each *jati* was composed of hundreds or thousands of individual nuclear families and was governed by its own council of elders. Membership in this ruling council was usually hereditary and was based on the wealth or social status of particular families within the community.

In theory, each *jati* was assigned a particular form of economic activity. Obviously, though, not all families in a given *jati* could take part in the same vocation, and as time went on, members of a single *jati* commonly engaged in several different lines of work. Sometimes an entire *jati* would have to move its location in order to continue a particular form of activity. In other cases, a *jati* would adopt an entirely new occupation in order to remain in a certain area. Such changes in habitat or occupation introduced the possibility of movement up or down the social scale. In this way, an entire *jati* could sometimes engage in upward mobility, even though that normally was not possible for individuals, who were tied to their class identity for life.

The class system in ancient India may sound highly constricting, but there were persuasive social and economic reasons why it survived for so many centuries. In the first place, it provided an identity for individuals in a highly hierarchical society. Although an individual might rank lower on the social scale than members of other classes, it was always possible to find others ranked even lower. Class was also a means for new groups, such as mountain tribal people, to achieve a recognizable place in the broader community. Perhaps equally important, the *jati* was a primitive form of welfare system. Each *jati* was obliged to provide for any of its members who were poor or destitute. It also provided an element of stability in a society that all too often was in a state of political turmoil.

Daily Life in Ancient India

Beyond these rigid social stratifications was the Indian family. Not only was life centered around the family, but the family, not the individual, was the most basic unit in society.

The Family The ideal social unit was an extended family, with three generations living under the same roof. It was essentially patriarchal, except along the Malabar coast, near the southwestern tip of the subcontinent, where a matriarchal form of social organization prevailed down to modern times. In the rest of India, the oldest male traditionally possessed legal authority over the entire family unit.

The family was linked together in a religious sense to its ancestral members by a series of commemorative rites. Family ceremonies were conducted to honor the departed and to link the living and the dead. The male family head was responsible for leading the ritual. At his death, his eldest son had the duty of conducting the funeral rites.

The importance of the father and the son in family ritual underlined the importance of males in Indian society. Male superiority was expressed in a variety of ways. Women could not serve as priests (although some were accepted as seers), nor were they normally permitted to study the Vedas. In general, males had a monopoly on education, since the primary goal of learning to read was to conduct family rituals. In high-class families, young men, after having been initiated into the sacred thread, began Vedic studies with a **guru** (teacher). Some then went on to higher studies in one of the major cities. The goal of such an education might be either professional or religious. Such young men were not supposed to marry until after twelve years of study.

Marriage   In general, only males could inherit property, except in a few cases when there were no sons. According to law, a woman was always considered a minor. Divorce was prohibited, although it sometimes took place. According to the *Arthasastra*, a wife who had been deserted by her husband could seek a divorce. Polygamy was fairly rare and apparently occurred mainly among the higher classes, but husbands were permitted to take a second wife if the first was barren. Producing children was an important aspect of marriage, both because children provided security for their parents in old age and because they were a physical proof of male potency. Child marriage was common for young girls, whether because of the desire for children or because daughters represented an economic liability to their parents. But perhaps the most graphic symbol of women's subjection to men was the ritual of *sati* (suh-TEE) (often written *suttee*), which encouraged the wife to throw herself on her dead husband's funeral pyre. The Greek visitor Megasthenes reported "that he had heard from some persons of wives burning themselves along with their deceased husbands and doing so gladly; and that those women who refused to burn themselves were held in disgrace."[5] All in all, it was undoubtedly a difficult existence. According to the *Law of Manu*, an early treatise on social organization and behavior in ancient India, probably written in the first or second century B.C.E., a woman was subordinated to men throughout her life—first to her father, then to her husband, and finally to her sons:

> She should do nothing independently
>   even in her own house.
> In childhood subject to her father,
>   in youth to her husband,
> and when her husband is dead to her sons,
>   she should never enjoy independence....
> Though he be uncouth and prone to pleasure,
>   though he have no good points at all,
> the virtuous wife should ever
>   worship her lord as a god.[6]

The Role of Women   At the root of female subordination to the male was the practical fact that as in most agricultural societies, men did most of the work in the fields. Females were viewed as having little utility outside the home and indeed were considered an economic burden, since parents were obliged to provide a dowry to acquire a husband for a daughter. Female children also appeared to offer little advantage in maintaining the family unit, since they joined the families of their husbands after the wedding ceremony.

Despite all of these indications of female subjection to the male, there are numerous signs that in some ways women often played an influential role in Indian society, and the code of behavior set out in the *Law of Manu* stressed that they should be treated with respect. Indians appeared to be fascinated by female sexuality, and tradition held that women often used their sexual powers to achieve domination over men. The author of the Mahabharata, a vast epic of early Indian society, complained that "the fire has never too many logs, the ocean never too many rivers, death never too many living souls, and fair-eyed woman never too many men." Despite the legal and social constraints, women often played an

Female Earth Spirit.
This earth spirit, carved on a gatepost of the Buddhist stupa at Sanchi 2,200 years ago, illustrates how earlier representations of the fertility goddess were incorporated into Buddhist art. Women were revered as powerful fertility symbols and considered dangerous when menstruating or immediately after giving birth. Voluptuous and idealized, the earth spirit was believed to be able to cause a tree to blossom by wrapping her leg around its trunk or even merely touching a branch with her arm.

Atlantide Phototravel/Corbis

important role within the family unit, and many were admired and honored for their talents. It is probably significant that paintings and sculpture from ancient and medieval India frequently show women in a role equal to that of men, and the tradition of the henpecked husband is as prevalent in India as in many Western societies today.

The Economy   The arrival of the Aryans did not drastically change the economic character of Indian society. Not only did most Aryans eventually take up farming, but it is likely that agriculture expanded rapidly under Aryan rule with the invention of the iron plow and the spread of northern Indian culture into the Deccan Plateau. One consequence of this process was to shift the focus of Indian culture from the Indus Valley farther eastward to the Ganges River valley, which even today is one of the most densely populated regions on earth. The flatter areas in the Deccan Plateau and in the coastal plains were also turned into cropland.

Indian Farmers   For most Indian farmers, life was harsh. Among the most fortunate were those who owned their own land, although they were required to pay taxes to the state. Many others were sharecroppers or landless laborers. They were subject to the vicissitudes of the market and often paid exorbitant rents to their landlord. Concentration of land in large holdings was limited by the tradition of dividing property among all the sons, but large estates worked by hired laborers or rented out to sharecroppers were not uncommon, particularly in areas where local rajas derived much of their wealth from their property.

Another problem for Indian farmers was the unpredictability of the climate. India is in the monsoon zone. The monsoon is a seasonal wind pattern in southern Asia that blows from the southwest during the summer months and from the northeast during the winter. The southwest monsoon, originating in the Indian Ocean, is commonly marked by heavy rains. When the rains were late, thousands starved, particularly in the drier areas, which were especially dependent on rainfall. Strong governments attempted to deal with such problems by building state-operated granaries and maintaining the irrigation works, but strong governments were rare, and famine was probably all too common. The staple crops in the north were wheat, barley, and millet, with wet rice common in the fertile river valleys. In the south, grain and vegetables were supplemented by various tropical products, cotton, and spices such as pepper, ginger, cinnamon, and saffron.

Trade and Manufacturing   By no means were all Indians farmers. As time passed, India became one of the most advanced trading and manufacturing civilizations in the ancient world. After the rise of the Mauryas, India's role in regional trade began to expand, and the subcontinent became a major transit point in a vast commercial network that extended from the rim of the Pacific Ocean to the Middle East and the Mediterranean Sea. This regional trade went both by sea and by camel caravan. Maritime trade across the Indian Ocean may have begun as early as the fifth century B.C.E. It extended eastward as far as Southeast Asia and China and southward as far as the straits between Africa and the island of Madagascar. Westward to Egypt went spices, teakwood, perfumes, jewels, textiles, precious stones and ivory, and wild animals. In return, India received gold, tin, lead, and wine. The subcontinent had become a major crossroads of trade in the ancient world.

India's expanding role as a manufacturing and commercial hub was undoubtedly a spur to the growth of the state. Under Chandragupta Maurya, the central government became actively involved in commercial and manufacturing activities. It owned mines and land and undoubtedly earned massive profits from its role in regional commerce. Separate government departments were established for trade, agriculture, mining, and the manufacture of weapons, and the movement of private goods was vigorously taxed. Nevertheless, a significant private sector also flourished; it was dominated by great caste guilds, which monopolized key sectors of the economy. A money economy probably came into operation during the second century B.C.E., when copper and gold coins were introduced from the Middle East. This in turn led to the development of banking. But village trade continued to be conducted by means of cowry shells (highly polished shells used as a medium of exchange throughout much of Africa and Asia) or barter throughout the ancient period.

ESCAPING THE WHEEL OF LIFE: THE RELIGIOUS WORLD OF ANCIENT INDIA

Like Indian politics and society, Indian religion is a blend of Aryan and Dravidian culture. The intermingling of those two civilizations gave rise to an extraordinarily complex set of religious beliefs and practices, filled with diversity and contrast. Out of this cultural mix came two of the world's great religions, Buddhism and Hinduism, and several smaller ones, including Jainism and Sikhism. Early Aryan religious beliefs, however, are known to historians as **Brahmanism**. In time, Brahmanical beliefs and practices would give rise to Hinduism. Here we will focus on the earliest religious traditions and on the origins of Buddhism.

Brahmanism

Evidence about the earliest religious beliefs of the Aryan peoples comes primarily from sacred texts such as the Vedas, four collections of hymns and religious ceremonies transmitted by memory through the centuries by Aryan priests. Many of these religious ideas were probably common to all of the Indo-European peoples before their separation into different groups at least four thousand years ago. Early Aryan beliefs were based on the common concept of a pantheon of gods and goddesses representing great forces of nature similar to the immortals of Greek mythology. The Aryan ancestor of the Greek father-god Zeus, for example, may have been the deity known in early Aryan tradition as Dyaus.

The parent god Dyaus was a somewhat distant figure, however, who was eventually overshadowed by other, more functional gods possessing more familiar human traits. For a while, the primary Aryan god was the great warrior god Indra. Indra summoned the Aryan tribal peoples to war and was represented in nature by thunder. Later, Indra declined in importance and was replaced by Varuna, lord of justice. Other gods and goddesses represented various forces of nature or the needs of human beings, such as fire, fertility, and wealth.

The concept of sacrifice was a key element in Aryan religious belief in Vedic times. As in many other ancient cultures, the practice may have begun as human sacrifice, but later animals were used as substitutes. The priestly class, the *brahmins*, played a key role in these ceremonies.

Another element of Indian religious belief in ancient times was the ideal of *asceticism*. Although there is no reference to such practices in the Vedas, by the sixth century B.C.E., self-discipline or subjecting oneself to painful stimuli had begun to replace sacrifice as a means of placating or communicating with the gods. Apparently, the original motive for asceticism was to achieve magical powers, but later, in the Upanishads—a set of commentaries on the Vedas compiled in the sixth century B.C.E.—it was seen as a means of spiritual meditation that would enable the practitioner to reach beyond material reality to a world of truth and bliss beyond earthly joy and sorrow. It is possible that another motive was to permit those with strong religious convictions to communicate directly with meta-physical reality without having to rely on the priestly class at court.

Asceticism, of course, has been practiced in other religions, including Christianity and Islam, but it seems particularly identified with Hinduism, the religion that emerged from the early Indian religious tradition. Eventually, asceticism evolved into the modern practice of body training that we know as *yoga* ("union"), which is accepted today as a meaningful element of Hindu religious practice.

Reincarnation   Another new concept that probably began to appear around the time the Upanishads were written was **reincarnation**. This is the idea that the individual soul is reborn in a different form after death and progresses through several existences on the wheel of life until it reaches its final destination in a union with the Great World Soul, *Brahman*. Because life is harsh, this final release is the objective of all living souls. From this concept comes the term *Brahmanism*, referring to the early Aryan religious tradition.

A key element in this process is the idea of ***karma***—that one's rebirth in a next life is determined by one's actions (*karma*) in this life. Hinduism, as it emerged from Brahmanism, placed all living species on a vast scale of existence, including the four classes and the untouchables in human society. The current status of an individual soul, then, is not simply a cosmic accident but the inevitable result of actions that that soul has committed in its past existence.

At the top of the scale are the *brahmins*, who by definition are closest to ultimate release from the law of reincarnation. The *brahmins* are followed in descending order by the other classes in human society and the world of the beasts. Within the animal kingdom, an especially high position is reserved for the cow, which even today is revered by Hindus as a sacred beast. Some scholars have speculated that the unique role played by the cow in Hinduism derives from the value of cattle in Aryan pastoral society. But others have pointed out that cattle were a source of both money and food and suggest that the cow's sacred position may have descended from the concept of the sacred bull in Harappan culture.

The concept of *karma* is governed by the *dharma*, or the law. A law regulating human behavior, the *dharma* imposes different requirements on different individuals depending on their status in society. Those high on the social scale, such as *brahmins* and *kshatriyas*, are held to a stricter form of behavior than *sudras* are. The *brahmin*, for example, is expected to abstain from eating meat, because that would entail the killing of another living being, thus interrupting its *karma*.

How the concept of reincarnation originated is not known, although it was apparently not unusual for early peoples to believe that the individual soul would be reborn in a different form in a later life. In any case, in India the concept may have had practical causes as well as consequences. In the first place, it tended to provide religious sanction for the rigid class divisions that had begun to emerge in Indian society after the arrival of the Aryans, and it provided moral and political justification for the privileges of those on the higher end of the scale.

At the same time, the concept of reincarnation provided certain compensations for those lower on the ladder of life. For example, it gave hope to the poor that if they behaved properly in this life, they might improve their condition in the next. It also provided a means for unassimilated groups such as ethnic minorities to find a

OPPOSING VIEWPOINTS

The Search for Truth

RELIGION & PHILOSOPHY

At the time the Rig Veda was originally composed in the second millennium B.C.E., *brahmins* at court believed that the best way to communicate with the gods was through sacrifice, a procedure that was carried out through the intermediation of the fire god Agni. The first selection is an incantation uttered by priests at the sacrificial ceremony.

By the middle of the first millennium B.C.E., however, the tradition of offering sacrifices had come under attack by opponents, who argued that the best way to seek truth and tranquility was by renouncing material existence and adopting the life of a wandering mendicant. In the second selection, from the Mundaka Upanishad, an advocate of this position forcefully presents his views. The similarity with the fervent believers of early Christianity, who renounced the corrupting forces of everyday life by seeking refuge in isolated monasteries in the desert, is striking.

The Rig Veda

I extol Agni, the household priest, the divine minister of the sacrifice, the chief priest, the bestower of blessings.

May that Agni, who is to be extolled by ancient and modern seers, conduct the gods here.

Through Agni may one gain day by day wealth and welfare which is glorious and replete with heroic sons.

O Agni, the sacrifice and ritual which you encompass on every side, that indeed goes to the gods.

May Agni, the chief priest, who possesses the insight of a sage, who is truthful, widely renowned, and divine, come here with the gods.

O Agni, O Angiras ["messenger"], whatever prosperity you bring to the pious is indeed in accordance with your true function.

O Agni, illuminator of darkness, day by day we approach you with holy thought bringing homage to you.

Presiding at ritual functions, the brightly shining custodian of the cosmic order [*rta*], thriving in your own realm.

O Agni, be easy of access to us as a father to his son. Join us for our well-being.

The Mundaka Upanishad

Unsteady, indeed, are those boats in the form of sacrifices, eighteen in number, in

place in Indian society while at the same time permitting them to maintain their distinctive way of life.

The ultimate goal of achieving "good" *karma*, as we have seen, was to escape the cycle of existence. To the sophisticated, the nature of that release was a spiritual union of the individual soul with the Great World Soul, *Brahman*, described in the Upanishads as a form of dreamless sleep, free from earthly desires.

Popular Religion   Little is known about the religious beliefs of the vast majority of the Indian people during this formative stage in South Asian society. In all likelihood, popular religion during the first millennium B.C.E. was a distant reflection of its counterpart in India today, which is peopled with a which is prescribed only the inferior work. The fools who delight in this sacrificial ritual as the highest spiritual good go again and again through the cycle of old age and death.

Abiding in the midst of ignorance, wise only according to their own estimate, thinking themselves to be learned, but really obtuse, these fools go round in a circle like blind men led by one who is himself blind.

Abiding manifoldly in ignorance they, all the same, like immature children think to themselves: "We have accomplished our aim." Since the performers of sacrificial ritual do not realize the truth because of passion, therefore, they, the wretched ones, sink down from heaven when the merit that qualified them for the higher world becomes exhausted.

Regarding sacrifice and merit as most important, the deluded ones do not know of any other higher spiritual good. Having enjoyed themselves only for a time on top of the heaven won by good deeds [sacrifice, etc.] they reenter this world or a still lower one.

Those who practice penance [tapas] and faith in the forest, the tranquil ones, the knowers of truth, living the life of wandering mendicancy—they depart, freed from passion, through the door of the sun, to where dwells verily ... the imperishable Soul [atman].

Having scrutinized the worlds won by sacrificial rites, a *brahmin* should arrive at nothing but disgust. The world that was not made is not won by what is done [i.e., by sacrifice]. For the sake of that knowledge he should go with sacrificial fuel in hand as a student, in all humility to a preceptor [*guru*] who is well versed in the [Vedic] scriptures and also firm in the realization of Brahman.

Unto him who has approached him in proper form, whose mind is tranquil, who has attained peace, does the knowing teacher teach, in its very truth, that knowledge about Brahman by means of which one knows ... the only Reality.

Q *In which passages in these two documents do you find a reference to the idea of karma? Which document makes use of the concept, and how? What role does asceticism play in these documents?*

Source: From *Sources of Indian Tradition*, Vol. 1, 2e, by Ainslee Embree. Copyright © 1988 by Columbia University Press.

multitude of very human gods and goddesses. It has been estimated that the Hindu pantheon contains more than 33,000 deities. Only a small number are primary ones, however, notably the so-called trinity of gods: Brahman the Creator, Vishnu the Preserver, and Shiva (SHIV-uh) (originally the Vedic god Rudra) the Destroyer. Although Brahman (sometimes in his concrete form called Brahma) is considered to be the highest god, Vishnu and Shiva take precedence in the devotional exercises of many Hindus, who can be roughly divided into Vishnuites and Shaivites. In addition to the trinity of gods, all of whom have wives with readily identifiable roles and personalities, there are countless minor deities, each again with his or her own specific function. A notable example is Ganesha, described in Indian literature as a son of Shiva who was accidentally beheaded by his father in a fit of anger. When

Shiva repented of his action, he provided his son with the head of an elephant. Even today the widely revered Ganesha is often viewed as the god of good fortune.

The rich variety and the earthy character of many of these deities are somewhat misleading, however, for Hindus regard the multitude of gods simply as different manifestations of one ultimate reality. The various deities also provide a way for ordinary Indians to personify their religious feelings. Even though some individuals among the early Aryans attempted to communicate with the gods through animal sacrifice or asceticism, most Indians undoubtedly sought to satisfy their own individual religious needs through devotion, which they expressed through ritual ceremonies and offerings at a temple. Such offerings were not only a way of seeking salvation but also a means of satisfying all the aspirations of daily life.

Over the centuries, Indian religious belief changed radically from its origins in Aryan pastoral society. An early belief in deities representing forces of nature gradually gave way to a more elitist system, with a priestly class at court performing sacrifices in order to obtain heavenly favors. During the first millennium B.C.E., religious belief began to evolve into a more personal experience, with an emphasis on ethics as a means of obtaining a union between the individual soul (**Atman**) and the ultimate reality (*Brahman*).[7]

Such a concept, however, was probably too ethereal for the average Indian, who looked for a more concrete form of heavenly salvation, a place of beauty and bliss after a life of disease and privation. In later centuries, the Brahmanical beliefs and practices of early Aryan society would gradually be replaced by a more popular faith that would henceforth become known as Hinduism.

Buddhism: The Middle Path

In the sixth century B.C.E., a new doctrine appeared in northern India that would eventually begin to rival the popularity of Brahmanical beliefs throughout the subcontinent. This new doctrine was called **Buddhism**.

The Life of Siddhartha Gautama

The historical founder of Buddhism, Siddhartha Gautama (si-DAR-tuh GAW-tuh-muh) (c. 560–480 B.C.E.), was a native of a small kingdom in the foothills of the Himalaya Mountains in what is today southern Nepal. He was born in the mid-sixth century B.C.E., the son of a ruling *kshatriya* family. According to tradition, the young Siddhartha was raised in affluent surroundings and trained, like many other members of his class, in the martial arts. On reaching maturity, he married and began to raise a family. At the age of twenty-nine, however, he suddenly discovered the pain of illness, the sorrow of death, and the degradation caused by old age in the lives of ordinary people and exclaimed, "Would that sickness, age, and death might be forever bound!" From that time on, he decided to dedicate his life to determining the cause and seeking the cure for human suffering.

To find the answers to these questions, Siddhartha abandoned his home and family and traveled widely. At first he tried to follow the model of the ascetics, but he eventually decided that self-mortification did not lead to a greater understanding of life and abandoned the practice. Then one day after a lengthy period of meditation under a tree, he achieved enlightenment as to the meaning of life and spent the remainder of his life preaching it. His conclusions, as embodied in his teachings, became the philosophy (or as some would have it, the religion) of Buddhism. According to legend, the Devil (the Indian term is *Mara*) attempted desperately to tempt him with political power and the company of beautiful girls. But Siddhartha Gautama resisted:

> *Pleasure is brief as a flash of lightning*
> *Or like an autumn shower, only for a moment....*
> *Why should I then covet the pleasures you speak of?*
> *I see your bodies are full of all impurity:*
> *Birth and death, sickness and age are yours.*
> *I seek the highest prize, hard to attain by men—*
> *The true and constant wisdom of the wise.*[8]

Buddhism and Brahmanism   How much the modern doctrine of Buddhism resembles the original teachings of Siddhartha Gautama is open to debate, for much time has elapsed since his death and original texts relating his ideas are lacking. Nor is it certain that Siddhartha even intended to found a new religion or doctrine. In some respects, his ideas could be viewed as a reformist form of Brahmanism, designed to transfer responsibility from the priests to the individual, much as the sixteenth-century German monk Martin Luther saw his ideas as a reformation of Christianity. Siddhartha accepted much of the belief system of Brahmanism, if not all of its practices. For example, he accepted the concept of reincarnation and the role of *karma* as a means of influencing the movement of individual souls up and down the scale of life. He praised nonviolence and borrowed the idea of living a life of simplicity and chastity from the ascetics. Moreover, his vision of metaphysical reality—commonly known as **Nirvana**—is closer to the Aryan concept of *Brahman* than it is to the Christian concept of heavenly salvation. Nirvana, which involves an extinction of selfhood and a final reunion with the Great World Soul, is sometimes likened to a dreamless sleep or to a kind of "blowing out" (as of a candle). Buddhists occasionally remark that someone who asks for a description does not understand the concept.

At the same time, the new doctrine differed from existing practices in a number of key ways. In the first place, Siddhartha denied the existence of an individual soul. To him, the concept of *Atman*—the individual soul—meant that the soul was subject to rebirth and thus did not achieve a complete liberation from the cares of this world. In fact, Siddhartha denied the ultimate reality of the material world in its entirety and taught that it was an illusion that had to be transcended. Siddhartha's idea of achieving Nirvana was based on his conviction that the pain, poverty, and sorrow that afflict human beings are caused essentially by their attachment to the things of this world. Once worldly cares are abandoned, pain and sorrow can be overcome. With this knowledge comes ***bodhi***, or wisdom (source of the term *Buddhism* and the familiar name for Gautama the Wise: Gautama Buddha).

Achieving this understanding is a key step on the road to Nirvana, which, as in Brahmanism, is a form of release from the wheel of life. According to tradition, Siddhartha transmitted this message in a sermon to his disciples in a deer park at Sarnath, not far from the modern city of Varanasi (Benares). Like so many messages, it is deceptively simple and is enclosed in four noble truths: life is suffering,

suffering is caused by desire, the way to end suffering is to end desire, and the way to end desire is to avoid the extremes of a life of vulgar materialism and a life of self-torture and to follow the **Middle Path**. Also known as the Eightfold Way, the Middle Path calls for right knowledge, right purpose, right speech, right conduct, right occupation, right effort, right awareness, and right meditation.

Another characteristic of Buddhism was its relative egalitarianism. Although Siddhartha accepted the idea of reincarnation (and hence the idea that human beings differ as a result of *karma* accumulated in a previous existence), he rejected the division of humanity into rigidly defined classes based on previous reincarnations and taught that all human beings could aspire to Nirvana as a result of their behavior in this life—a message that likely helped Buddhism win support among people at the lower end of the social scale.

In addition, Buddhism was much simpler than existing beliefs. Siddhartha rejected the panoply of gods that had become identified with Brahmanism and forbade his followers to worship his person or his image after his death. In fact, many Buddhists view Buddhism as a philosophy rather than a religion.

After Siddhartha Gautama's death in 480 B.C.E., dedicated disciples carried his message the length and breadth of India. Buddhist monasteries were established throughout the subcontinent, and temples and **stupas** (STOO-puhs) (stone towers housing relics of the Buddha) sprang up throughout the countryside.

Women were permitted to join the monastic order but only in an inferior position. As Siddhartha had explained, women are "soon angered," "full of passion," and "stupid": "That is the reason ... why women have no place in public assemblies ... and do not earn their living by any profession." Still, the position of women tended to be better in Buddhist societies than it was elsewhere in ancient India.

Jainism   During the next centuries, Buddhism began to compete actively with the existing Aryan beliefs, as well as with another new faith known as Jainism. **Jainism** (JY-ni-zuhm) was founded by Mahavira (mah-hah-VEE-ruh), a contemporary of Siddhartha Gautama. Resembling Buddhism in its rejection of the reality of the material world, Jainism was more extreme in practice. Where Siddhartha Gautama called for the "middle way" between passion and luxury on one extreme and pain and self-torture on the other, Mahavira preached a doctrine of extreme simplicity to his followers, who kept no possessions and relied on begging for a living. Some even rejected clothing and wandered through the world naked. Perhaps because of its insistence on a life of poverty, Jainism failed to attract enough adherents to become a major doctrine and never received official support. According to tradition, however, Chandragupta Maurya accepted Mahavira's doctrine after abdicating the throne and fasted to death in a Jain monastery.

Ashoka, a Buddhist Monarch   Buddhism received an important boost when Ashoka (uh-SHOH-kuh), the grandson of Chandragupta Maurya, converted to Buddhism in the third century B.C.E. Ashoka (r. 269–232 B.C.E.) is widely considered the greatest ruler in the history of India. By his own admission, as noted in rock edicts placed around his kingdom, Ashoka began his reign conquering, pillaging, and killing, but after his conversion to Buddhism, he began to regret his blood-thirsty past and attempted to rule benevolently.

Ashoka directed that banyan trees and shelters be placed along the road to provide shade and rest for weary travelers. He sent Buddhist missionaries throughout India and ordered the erection of stone pillars with official edicts and Buddhist inscriptions to instruct people in the proper way. In time, much of the population living under Mauryan rule may have converted to Buddhism.

MAP 2.3 The Empire of Ashoka

Ashoka, the greatest Indian monarch, ruled over much of the subcontinent in the third century B.C.E. This map shows the extent of his empire and the locations of the pillar edicts that were erected along major trade routes.

A Singular Debate

RELIGION & PHILOSOPHY

One of the key points of contention between advocates of Brahmanism and Buddhism was the belief on the part of the former that members of the highest social class—the Brahmins—were purer than those lower on the social scale, based on their past actions (*karma*). Siddhartha Gautama, however, had argued that all humans were inherently equal at birth and could obtain Nirvana—the state of release from earthly cares—as a consequence of their behavior in this life.

In this passage from the *Tripitaka* (Three Baskets), a collection of Buddhist writings collated by Theravada Buddhists on the island of Sri Lanka, Siddhartha Gautama confronts a devotee of Brahmanism and demonstrates the superiority of Buddhist teachings. Whether the debate actually took place is unlikely, and the date of the passage is uncertain, but it effectively singles out one of the key points of difference between the two teachings.

The Tripitaka

Once when the Lord was staying at Savatthi there were five hundred brahmans from various countries in the city ... and they thought: "This ascetic Gautama preaches that all four classes are pure. Who can refute him?"

At that time there was a young brahman named Assalayana in the city, ... a youth of sixteen, thoroughly versed in the Vedas ... and in all brahmanic learning. "He can do it!", thought the brahmans, and so they asked him to try; ... he agreed, and so, surrounded by a crowd of brahmans, he went to the Lord, and, after greeting him, sat down and said:

"Brahmans maintain that only they are the highest class, and the others are below them. They are white, the others black; only they are pure, and not the others. Only they are the true sons of Brahma, born from his mouth, born of Brahma, creations of Brahma, heirs of Brahma. Now what does the worthy Gautama say to that?"

"Do the brahmans really maintain this Assalayana, when they're born of women

According to tradition, his son converted the island of Sri Lanka to Buddhism, and the peoples there accepted a tributary relationship with the Mauryan Empire.

After Ashoka: The Rule of the Fishes After Ashoka's death in 232 B.C.E., the Mauryan Empire began to decline. In 183 B.C.E., the last Mauryan ruler was overthrown by one of his military commanders, and India began to fragment into separate states. A number of new kingdoms, some of them perhaps influenced by the memory of the Alexandrian conquests, arose along the fringes of the subcontinent in Bactria, known today as Afghanistan. In the first century C.E., Indo-European-speaking peoples fleeing from the nomadic Xiongnu (SHYAHNG-noo) just like anyone else, of brahman women who have their periods and conceive, give birth and nurse their children, just like any other women?"

"For all you say, this is what they think...."

...

"Again if a man is a murderer, a thief, or an adulterer, or commits other grave sins, when his body breaks up on death does he pass on to purgatory if he's a kshatriya, vaishya, or shudra, but not if he's a brahman?"

"No, Gautama. In such a case, the same fate is in store for all men, whatever their class."

...

"And is a brahman capable of developing a mind of love without hate or ill will, but not a man of the other classes?"

"No, Gautama. All four classes are capable of doing so."

"Can only a brahman go down to a river and wash away dust and dirt, and not men of the other classes?"

"No, Gautama. All four classes can."

...

"Suppose there are two young brahman brothers, one a scholar and the other uneducated. Which of them would be served first at memorial feasts, festivals, and sacrifices, or when entertained as guests?"

"The scholar, of course; for what great benefit would accrue from entertaining the uneducated one?"

"But suppose the scholar is ill-behaved and wicked, while the uneducated one is well-behaved and virtuous?"

"Then the uneducated one would be served first, for what great benefit would accrue from entertaining an ill-behaved and wicked man?"

"First, Assalayana, you based your claim on birth, then you gave up birth for learning, and finally you have come round to my way of thinking, that all four classes are equally pure!"

At this Assalayana sat silent ... his shoulders hunched, his eyes cast down, thoughtful in mind, and with no answer at hand.

Q *What arguments does the Brahmanic scholar present to Siddhartha Gautama? How does the latter respond?*

Source: Ainslee T. Embree (ed.), *Sources of Indian Tradition*, volume I (New York: Columbia University Press, 1988), pp. 140–141.

warriors in Central Asia seized power in the area and proclaimed the new Kushan (koo-SHAHN) kingdom. For the next two centuries, the Kushans extended their political sway over northern India as far as the central Ganges Valley, while other kingdoms scuffled for predominance elsewhere on the subcontinent. India would not see unity again for another five hundred years.

Several reasons for India's failure to maintain a unified empire have been proposed. Some historians suggest that a decline in regional trade during the first millennium C.E. may have contributed to the growth of small land-based kingdoms, which drew their primary income from agriculture. The tenacity of the Aryan tradition, with its emphasis on tribal rivalries, may also have contributed. Although the Mauryan rulers tried to impose a more centralized organization, clan loyalties once again came to the fore after the collapse of the Mauryan dynasty. Furthermore, the behavior of the ruling class was characterized by what Indians call the "rule of the fishes," which glorified warfare as the natural activity of the king and the aristocracy. The *Arthasastra*, which set forth a model of a centralized Indian state, assumed that war was the "sport of kings." Still, this was not an uneventful period in the history of India, as Indo-Aryan ideas continued to spread southward and both Brahmanism and Buddhism evolved in new directions.

THE EXUBERANT WORLD OF INDIAN CULTURE

Few cultures in the world are as rich and varied as that of India. Most societies excel in some forms of artistic and literary achievement and not in others, but India has produced great works in almost all fields of cultural endeavor—art and sculpture, science, architecture, literature, and music.

Literature   The earliest known Indian literature consists of the four Vedas, which were passed down orally from generation to generation until they were finally written down after the Aryans arrived in India. The Rig Veda dates from the second millennium B.C.E. and consists of more than a thousand hymns that were used at religious ceremonies. The other three Vedas were written considerably later and contain instructions for performing ritual sacrifices and other ceremonies. The Brahmanas and the Upanishads served as commentaries on the Vedas.

The language of the Vedas was **Sanskrit** (SAN-skrit), one of the Indo-European family of languages. After the arrival of the Aryans in India, Sanskrit gradually declined as a spoken language and was replaced in northern India by a simpler tongue known as **Prakrit** (PRAH-krit). Nevertheless, Sanskrit continued to be used as the language of the bureaucracy and of literary expression for many centuries after that and, like Latin in medieval Europe, served as a common language of communication between various regions of India. In the south, a variety of Dravidian languages continued to be spoken.

As early as the fifth century B.C.E., Indian grammarians had codified Sanskrit to preserve the authenticity of the Vedas for the spiritual edification of future generations. A famous grammar written by the scholar Panini in the fourth century B.C.E. set forth four thousand grammatical rules prescribing the correct usage of the spoken and written language. This achievement is particularly impressive in that Europe did not have a science of linguistics until the nineteenth century, when it was developed partly as a result of the discovery of the works of Panini and later Indian linguists.

After the development of a writing system in the first millennium B.C.E., India's holy literature was probably inscribed on palm leaves stitched together into a book somewhat similar to the first books produced on papyrus or parchment in the Mediterranean region. Also written for the first time were India's great historical epics, the Mahabharata and the Ramayana (rah-mah-YAH-nah). Both of these epics may have originally been recited at religious ceremonies, but they are essentially histories that recount the martial exploits of great Aryan rulers and warriors.

The Mahabharata, consisting of more than 90,000 stanzas, was probably written about 100 B.C.E. and describes in great detail a war between cousins for control of the kingdom nine hundred years earlier. Interwoven in the narrative are many fantastic legends of the gods. Above all, the Mahabharata is a tale of moral confrontations and an elucidation of the ethical precepts of the *dharma*. The most famous section of the book is the so-called Bhagavad Gita, a sermon by the legendary Indian figure Krishna on the eve of a major battle. In this sermon, Krishna sets forth one of the key ethical maxims of Indian society: in taking action, one must be indifferent to success or failure and consider only the moral rightness of the act itself.

The Ramayana, written at about the same time, is much shorter than the Mahabharata. It is an account of a semilegendary ruler named Rama (RAH-mah) who, as a result of a palace intrigue, is banished from the kingdom and forced to live as a hermit in the forest. Later he fights the demon-king of Sri Lanka, who has kidnapped his beloved wife, Sita (SEE-tuh). Like the Mahabharata, the Ramayana is strongly imbued with religious and moral significance. Rama is portrayed as the ideal Aryan hero, a perfect ruler and an ideal son, while Sita projects the supreme duty of female chastity and wifely loyalty to her husband. The Ramayana is a story of the triumph of good over evil, duty over self-indulgence, and generosity over selfishness. It combines filial and erotic love, conflicts of human passion, character analysis, and poetic descriptions of nature.

The Ramayana also has all the ingredients of an enthralling adventure: giants, wondrous flying chariots, invincible arrows and swords, and magic potions and mantras. One of the real heroes of the story is the monkey-king Hanuman, who flies from India to Sri Lanka to set the great battle in motion. It is no wonder that for millennia the Ramayana has remained a favorite among Indians of all age groups, often performed at festivals today and inspiring a hugely popular TV version produced in recent years.

Architecture and Sculpture

After literature, the greatest achievements of early Indian civilization were in architecture and sculpture. Some of the earliest examples of Indian architecture stem from the time of Emperor Ashoka, when Buddhism became the religion of the state. Until the time of the Mauryas, Aryan buildings had been constructed of wood. With the rise of the empire, stone began to be used as artisans arrived in India seeking employment after the destruction of the Persian Empire by Alexander. Many of these stone carvers accepted the patronage of Emperor Ashoka, who used them to spread Buddhist ideas throughout the subcontinent.

There were three main types of religious structures: the pillar, the stupa, and the rock chamber. As noted earlier, during Ashoka's reign, many stone columns were erected alongside roads to commemorate the events in the Buddha's life and mark pilgrim routes to holy places. Weighing up to 50 tons each and rising as high as 32 feet, these polished sandstone pillars were topped with a carved capital, usually depicting lions uttering the Buddha's message. Ten remain standing today.

COMPARATIVE ILLUSTRATION

The Buddha and Jesus

© William J. Duiker

**RELIGION &
PHILOSOPHY**

As Buddhism evolved, transforming Siddhartha Gautama, known as the Buddha, from mortal to god, Buddhist art changed as well. Statuary and relief panels began to illustrate the story of his life.

On the left, in a frieze from the second century C.E., the infant Siddhartha is seen emerging from the hip of his mother, Queen Maya. Although dressed in draperies that reflect Greek influences from Alexander the Great's brief incursion into northwestern

Erich Lessing/Art Resource, NY

India, her sensuous stance and the touching of the tree evoke the female earth spirit of traditional Indian art.

On the right is a Byzantine painting depicting the infant Jesus with his mother, the Virgin Mary, dating from the sixth century C.E. Notice that a halo surrounds the head of both the Buddha and Jesus. The halo—a circle of light—is an ancient symbol of divinity. In Hindu, Greek, and Roman art, the heads of gods were depicted emitting sun-like divine radiances. Early kings adopted crowns made of gold and precious gems to symbolize their own divine authority.

Q *What similarities and differences do you see in these depictions of the mothers of key religious figures?*

A stupa was originally meant to house a relic of the Buddha, such as a lock of his hair or a branch of the famous Bodhi tree (the tree beneath which Siddhartha Gautama had first achieved enlightenment), and was constructed in the form of a burial mound (the pyramids in Egypt also derived from burial mounds). Eventually, the stupa became a place for devotion and the most familiar form of Buddhist architecture. Stupas rose to considerable heights and were surmounted with a spire, possibly representing the stages of existence en route to Nirvana. According to legend, Ashoka ordered the construction of 84,000 stupas throughout India to promote the Buddha's message. A few survive today, including the famous stupa at Sanchi, begun under Ashoka and completed two centuries later.

The final form of early Indian architecture is the rock chamber carved out of a cliff on the side of a mountain. Ashoka began the construction of these chambers to provide rooms to house monks or wandering ascetics and to serve as halls for religious ceremonies. The chambers were rectangular, with pillars, an altar, and a vault, reminiscent of Roman basilicas in the West. The three most famous chambers of this period are at Bhaja, Karli, and Ajanta (uh-JUHN-tuh); the last one contains twenty-nine rooms.

All three forms of architecture were embellished with detailed reliefs and free-standing statues of deities, other human figures, and animals that are permeated with a sense of nature and the vitality of life. Many reflect an amalgamation of popular and sacred themes, of Buddhist, Vedic, and pre-Aryan religious motifs, such as male and female earth spirits. Until the second century C.E., Siddhartha Gautama was represented only through symbols, such as the wheel of life, the Bodhi tree, and the footprint, perhaps because artists deemed it improper to portray him in human form, since he had escaped his corporeal confines into enlightenment. After the spread of Mahayana Buddhism in the second century, when the Buddha was no longer portrayed as a teacher but rather as a god, his image began to appear in stone as an object for divine worship.

By this time, India had established its own unique religious art. The art is permeated by sensuousness and exuberance and is often overtly sexual. These scenes are meant to express otherworldly delights, not the pleasures of this world. The sensuous paradise that adorned the religious art of ancient India represented salvation and fulfillment for the ordinary Indian.

Science

Our knowledge of Indian science is limited by the paucity of written sources, but it is evident that ancient Indians had amassed an impressive amount of scientific knowledge in a number of areas. Especially notable was their work in mathematics, where they devised the numerical system that we know as Arabic numbers and use today, and in astronomy, where they charted the movements of the heavenly bodies and recognized the spherical nature of the earth at an early date. Their ideas of physics were similar to those of the Greeks; matter was divided into the five elements of earth, air, fire, water, and ether. Many of their technological achievements are impressive, notably the quality of their textiles and the massive stone pillars erected during the reign of Ashoka. As noted, the pillars weighed up to 50 tons each and were transported many miles to their final destination.

CHRONOLOGY

ANCIENT INDIA

c. 2600–1900 B.C.E.	Harappan civilization
c. 1500 B.C.E.	Arrival of the Aryans
c. 560–480 B.C.E.	Life of Gautama Buddha
326 B.C.E.	Invasion of India by Alexander the Great
324 B.C.E.	Mauryan dynasty founded
324–301 B.C.E.	Reign of Chandragupta Maurya
269–232 B.C.E.	Reign of Ashoka
183 B.C.E.	Collapse of Mauryan dynasty
c. first century C.E.	Rise of Kushan kingdom

MindTap is a fully online, highly personalized learning experience built upon Cengage Learning content. MindTap combines student learning tools—readings, multimedia, activities, and assessments—into a singular Learning Path that guides students through their course.

3

CHINA IN ANTIQUITY

政始自始皇乙卯即王位庚辰併天下稱皇帝
年居王位二十五年即帝位十二年壽五十

Image Asset Management Ltd./Alamy

The First Emperor of Qin

CHAPTER OUTLINE

• The Dawn of Chinese Civilization • The Zhou Dynasty • The First Chinese Empire: The Qin Dynasty • The Glorious Han Dynasty (202 B.C.E.–221 C.E.) • Daily Life in Ancient China • Chinese Culture

THE DAWN OF CHINESE CIVILIZATION

According to a familiar legend, Chinese society was founded by a series of rulers who brought the first rudiments of civilization to the region nearly five thousand years ago. The first was Fu Xi (foo SHEE), the ox-tamer, who "knotted cords for hunting and fishing," domesticated animals, and introduced the beginnings of family life. The second was Shen Nong (shun NOONG), the divine farmer, who "bent wood for plows and hewed wood for plowshares." He taught the people the techniques of agriculture. Last came Huang Di (hwahng DEE), the Yellow Emperor, who "strung a piece of wood for the bow, and whittled little sticks of wood for the arrows." Legend credits Huang Di with creating the Chinese system of writing, as well as with inventing the bow and arrow.[1] Modern historians, of course, do not accept the literal accuracy of such legends but view them instead as part of the process whereby early peoples attempt to make sense of the world and their role in it. Nevertheless, such re-creations of a mythical past often contain an element of truth. Although there is no clear evidence that the "three sovereigns" actually existed, their achievements do symbolize some of the defining characteristics of Chinese civilization: the interaction between nomadic and agricultural peoples, the importance of the family as the basic unit of Chinese life, and the development of a unique system of writing.

The Land and People of China   Although human communities have existed in China for several hundred thousand years, the first *Homo sapiens* arrived in the area sometime after 40,000 B.C.E. as part of the great migration out of Africa. At least as early as the eighth millennium B.C.E., the early peoples living along the riverbanks of northern and central China began to master the cultivation of crops. A number of these early agricultural settlements were in the neighborhood of the Yellow River, where they gave birth to two Neolithic societies known to archaeologists as the **Yangshao** (yahng-SHOW ["ow" as in "how"]) and the **Longshan** (loong-SHAHN) cultures (sometimes identified in terms of their pottery as the painted and black pottery cultures, respectively). Similar communities began to appear in the Yangzi Valley in central China and along the coast to the south. The southern settlements were based on the cultivation of rice, which had been introduced in China as early as the sixth millennium B.C.E., rather than dry crops such as millet, barley, and wheat (the last was an import from the Middle East in the second millennium B.C.E.), but they were as old as those in the north. Thus, agriculture, and perhaps other elements of early civilization, may have developed spontaneously in several areas of China rather than radiating outward from one central region.

At first, these simple Neolithic communities were hardly more than villages, but as the inhabitants mastered the rudiments of agriculture, they gradually gave rise to more sophisticated and complex societies. In a pattern that we have already seen elsewhere, civilization gradually spread from these nuclear settlements in the valleys of the Yellow and Yangzi Rivers to other lowland areas of eastern and central China. The two great river valleys, then, can be considered the core regions in the development of Chinese civilization.

Although these densely cultivated valleys eventually became two of the great food-producing areas of the ancient world, China is more than a land of fertile fields. In fact, only 12 percent of the total land area is arable, compared with 23 percent in the United States. Much of the remainder consists of mountains and deserts that ring the country on its northern and western frontiers.

This often arid and forbidding landscape is a dominant feature of Chinese life and has played a significant role in Chinese history. The geographic barriers served to isolate the Chinese people from advanced agrarian societies in other parts of Asia. The frontier regions in the Gobi (GOH-bee) Desert, Central Asia, and the Tibetan plateau were sparsely inhabited by peoples of Mongolian, Indo-European, or Turkish extraction. Most were pastoral societies, and like the contacts between other ancient river valley civilizations and their neighbors, relations between the Chinese and the steppe peoples were intermittent and frequently unstable. Sometimes the two sides engaged in productive trade relations, swapping grain and

© Cengage Learning 2013

MAP 3.1 Neolithic China

Like the ancient civilizations that arose in North Africa and western Asia, early Chinese society emerged along the banks of two major river systems, the Yellow and the Yangtze. China was separated from the other civilizations by snow-capped mountains and forbidding deserts, however, and thus was compelled to develop essentially on its own, without contacts from other societies going through a similar process.

manufactured goods for hides and other animal products. On other occasions, however, mutual suspicion and contrasting interests led to conflict. Although less numerous than the Chinese, many of the peoples along the frontiers possessed impressive skills in war and were sometimes aggressive in seeking wealth or territory in the settled regions south of the Gobi Desert. Over the next two thousand years, the northern frontier became one of the great fault lines of conflict in Asia as Chinese armies attempted to protect precious farmlands from marauding peoples from beyond the frontier. In turn, nomadic peoples often took offense at Chinese efforts to encroach on their grazing lands. When China was unified and blessed with capable rulers, it could usually keep the nomadic intruders at bay and even bring them under a loose form of Chinese administration. But in times of internal weakness, China was vulnerable to attack from the north, and on several occasions, nomadic peoples succeeded in overthrowing native Chinese rulers and setting up their own dynastic regimes.

From other directions, China normally had little to fear. To the east lay the China Sea, a lair for pirates and the source of powerful typhoons that occasionally ravaged the Chinese coast but otherwise rarely a source of concern. South of the Yangzi River was a hilly region inhabited by a mixture of peoples of varied linguistic and ethnic stock who lived by farming, fishing, or food gathering. They were gradually absorbed in the inexorable expansion of Chinese civilization.

The Shang Dynasty

Historians of China have traditionally dated the beginning of Chinese civilization to the founding of the Xia (shee-AH) dynasty more than four thousand years ago. Although the precise date for the rise of the Xia is in dispute, recent archaeological evidence confirms its existence. Legend maintains that the founder was a ruler named Yu, who is also credited with introducing irrigation and draining the floodwaters that periodically threatened to inundate the North China plain. The Xia dynasty was replaced by a second dynasty, the Shang (SHAHNG), around the sixteenth century B.C.E. The late Shang capital at Anyang (ahn-YAHNG), just north of the Yellow River in north-central China, has been excavated by archaeologists. Among the finds were thousands of so-called oracle bones, ox and chicken bones or turtle shells that were used by Shang rulers for divination and to communicate with the gods. The inscriptions on these oracle bones—a form of pictographic writing similar to those we have encountered in Egypt and Mesopotamia—are the earliest known form of Chinese writing and provide much of our information about the beginnings of civilization in China. They describe a culture gradually emerging from the Neolithic to the early Bronze Age.

Political Organization

China under the Shang dynasty was a predominantly agricultural society ruled by an aristocratic class whose major occupation was war and control over key resources such as metals and salt. One ancient chronicler complained that "the big affairs of state consist of sacrifice and soldiery."[2] Combat was carried on by means of two-horse chariots. The appearance of chariots in China in the mid-second millennium B.C.E. coincides roughly with similar developments elsewhere, leading some historians to suggest that the Shang ruling class may

COMPARATIVE ILLUSTRATION

The Afterlife and Prized Possessions

RELIGION & PHILOSOPHY

Like the pharaohs in Egypt, Chinese rulers filled their tombs with prized possessions from daily life. It was believed that if a tomb was furnished and stocked with supplies, including chairs, boats, chests, weapons, games, and dishes, the spiritual body could continue its life despite the death of the physical body. In the photo above, we see the remains of a chariot and horses in a burial pit in China's Hebei province that dates from the early Zhou dynasty. The tradition of

Lowell Georgia/Corbis

providing items of daily use for the departed continues today in Chinese communities throughout Asia. The papier-mâché vehicle in the photo below, will be burned so that it will ascend in smoke to the world of the spirits.

Q *How did ancient Chinese tombs compare with the tombs of Egyptian pharaohs? What do the differences tell you about these two societies? What do the items shown here have in common?*

© William J. Duiker

originally have invaded China from elsewhere in Asia. But items found in Shang burial mounds are similar to Longshan pottery, implying that the Shang ruling elites were linear descendants of the indigenous Neolithic peoples in the area. If that was the case, the Shang may have acquired their knowledge of horse-drawn chariots through contact with the peoples of neighboring regions.

Some recent support for that assumption has come from evidence unearthed in the sandy wastes of Xinjiang (SHIN-jyahng), China's far-northwestern province. There archaeologists have discovered corpses dating back as early as the second millennium B.C.E. with physical characteristics resembling those of Europeans. They are also clothed in textiles similar to those worn at the time in central Asia and eastern Europe, suggesting that they may have been members of a migration by Indo-European peoples from areas much farther to the west. If that is the case, they were probably familiar with advances in chariot making that occurred a few hundred years earlier in southern Russia and Kazakhstan (ka-zak-STAN *or* kuh-zahk-STAHN). By about 2000 B.C.E., spoked wheels were being deposited at grave sites in Ukraine and also in the Gobi Desert, just north of the great bend of the Yellow River. It is thus likely that the new technology became available to the founders of the Shang dynasty and may have aided their rise to power in northern China.

The Shang king ruled with the assistance of a central bureaucracy in the capital city. His realm was divided into a number of territories governed by aristocratic chieftains, but the king appointed these chieftains and could apparently depose them at will. He was also responsible for the defense of the realm and controlled large armies that often fought on the fringes of the kingdom. The transcendent importance of the ruler was graphically displayed in the ritual sacrifices undertaken at his death, when hundreds of his retainers were buried with him in the royal tomb.

As the inscriptions on the oracle bones make clear, the Shang ruling elite believed in the existence of supernatural forces and thought that they could communicate with those forces to obtain divine intervention on matters of this world. In fact, the main purpose of the oracle bones seems to have been to communicate with the gods. Supreme among the heavenly forces was the sky god, known as Di. Evidence from the oracle bones also suggests that the king was already being viewed as an intermediary between heaven and earth. An early Shang character for king (王) consists of three horizontal lines connected by a single vertical line; the middle horizontal line represents the king's place between human society and the divine forces in nature.

The early Chinese also had a clear sense of life in the hereafter. Though some of the human sacrifices discovered in the royal tombs were presumably intended to propitiate the gods, others were meant to accompany the king or members of his family on the journey to the next world. From this conviction would come the concept of **veneration of ancestors** (mistakenly known in the West as "ancestor worship") and the practice, which continues to the present day in many Chinese communities, of burning replicas of physical objects to accompany the departed on their journey to the next world.

Social Structures In the Neolithic period, the farming village was apparently the basic social unit of China, at least in the core region of the Yellow River valley. Villages were organized by clans rather than by nuclear family units, and all residents probably took the common clan name of the entire village. In some cases, a village may have included more than one clan. At Banpo, an archaeological site near the modern city of Xian (shih-AHN) that dates back at least seven thousand years, the houses in the village are separated by a ditch, which some scholars think may have served as a divider between two clans. The individual dwellings at Banpo housed nuclear families, but a larger building in the village was apparently used as a clan meeting hall. The clan-based origins of Chinese society may help

COMPARATIVE ESSAY

The Use of Metals

SCIENCE & TECHNOLOGY

Around 6000 B.C.E., people in western Asia discovered how to use metals. They soon realized the advantage of using metal instead of stone to make both tools and weapons. Metal could be shaped more precisely, allowing artisans to make more refined tools and weapons with sharper edges and more regular shapes. Copper, silver, and gold, which were commonly found in their elemental form, were the first metals to be used. These were relatively soft and could be easily pounded into different shapes. But an important step was taken when people discovered that a rock that contained metal could be heated to liquefy the metal (a process called smelting). The liquid metal could then be poured into molds of clay or stone to make precisely shaped tools and weapons.

Copper was the first metal to be used in making tools. The first known copper smelting furnace, dated to 3800 B.C.E., was found in the Sinai. Within the next century, artisans in western Asia discovered that tin could be added to copper to make bronze. Bronze has a lower melting point that makes it easier to cast, but it is also a harder metal than copper and corrodes less. Eventually the technique spread eastward, and by 1400 B.C.E., the Chinese were making bronze decorative objects as well as battle-axes and helmets. The widespread use of bronze has led historians to speak of the period from around 3000 to 1200 B.C.E. as the Bronze Age, although this is somewhat misleading in that many peoples continued to use stone tools and weapons even after bronze became available.

But there were limitations to the use of bronze. Tin was not as available as copper, so bronze tools and weapons were expensive. After 1200 B.C.E., bronze was increasingly replaced by iron, which was probably first used around 1500 B.C.E. in western Asia, where the Hittites made weapons from it. Between 1500 and 600 B.C.E., iron-making spread across Europe, North Africa, and Asia. Bronze continued to be used, but mostly for jewelry and other domestic purposes. Iron was used to make tools and weapons with sharp edges. Because iron weapons were cheaper than bronze ones, more warriors could be armed, and wars could be fought on a larger scale.

Iron was handled differently from bronze: it was heated until it could be beaten into a desired shape. Each hammering made the metal stronger. This wrought iron, as it was called, was typical of iron manufacturing in the West until the late Middle Ages. In China, however, the use of heat-resistant clay in the walls of blast furnaces raised temperatures to 1,537 degrees Celsius, enabling artisans already in the fourth century B.C.E. to liquefy iron so that it too could be cast in molds. Europeans would not develop such blast furnaces until the fifteenth century C.E.

Q *What were the advantages of making objects out of bronze versus iron in the ancient world? Which metal ultimately triumphed in China?*

explain the continued importance of the joint family in traditional China, as well as the relatively small number of family names in Chinese society. Even today there are only about four hundred commonly used family names in a society of more than one billion people, and a colloquial expression for the common people in China today is "the old hundred names."

By Shang times, the classes were becoming increasingly differentiated. It is likely that some poorer peasants did not own their farms but were obliged to work the land of the chieftain and other elite families in the village. The aristocrats not only made war and served as officials (indeed, the first Chinese character for *official* originally meant "warrior"), but they were also the primary landowners. In addition to the aristocratic elite and the peasants, there were a small number of merchants and artisans, as well as slaves, probably consisting primarily of criminals or prisoners taken in battle.

The Shang are perhaps best known for their mastery of the art of casting bronze. Utensils, weapons, and ritual objects made of bronze have been found in royal tombs in urban centers throughout the area known to be under Shang influence. It is also clear that the Shang had achieved a fairly sophisticated writing system that would eventually spread throughout East Asia and evolve into the written language that is still used in China today.

The Shang Dynasty: China's "Mother Culture"?   Until recently, the prevailing wisdom among historians—both Chinese and non-Chinese—was that the Yellow River valley was the ancient heartland of Chinese civilization and that technological and cultural achievements gradually radiated from there to other areas in East Asia. Here, it was thought, occurred the first technological breakthroughs, including the development of a writing system, advanced farming techniques, and the ability to make bronze ritual vessels. Supporting this idea was the fact that the first significant archaeological finds in China, including the last Shang capital at Anyang, were made in that region.

Today, this **diffusion hypothesis**, as it is sometimes called, is no longer so widely accepted. The remains of early agricultural communities have now been unearthed in the Yangzi River valley and along the southern coast, and a rich trove of bronze vessels has been discovered in grave sites in central Sichuan (suh-CHWAHN) province. Such finds suggest that although the Yellow River civilization may have taken the lead in some areas, such as complex political organization and the development of writing, similar advances were already occurring in other parts of China, suggesting that communication between regions was already well under way.

THE ZHOU DYNASTY

In the eleventh century B.C.E., the Shang dynasty was overthrown by an aggressive young state located to the west of Anyang, the Shang capital, and near the great bend of the Yellow River as it begins to flow directly eastward to the sea. The new dynasty, which called itself the Zhou, survived for about eight hundred years, making it the longest-lived dynasty in the history of China. According to tradition, the last of the Shang rulers was a tyrant who oppressed the people (Chinese sources assert that he was a degenerate who built "ponds of wine" and ordered the composing of lustful music that "ruined the morale of the nation"),[3] leading the ruler of the principality of Zhou to revolt and establish a new dynasty.

The Zhou located their capital in their home territory, near the present-day city of Xian. Later they established a second capital city at modern Luoyang

(LWOH-yahng), farther to the east, to administer new territories captured from the Shang. This established a pattern of eastern and western capitals that would endure off and on in China for nearly two thousand years.

Political Structures   The Zhou dynasty (1045–221 B.C.E.) adopted the political system of its predecessors, with some changes. The Shang practice of dividing the kingdom into a number of territories governed by officials appointed by the king was continued under the Zhou. At the apex of the government hierarchy was the Zhou king, who was served by a bureaucracy of growing size and complexity. It now included several ministries responsible for rites, education, law, and public works. Beyond the capital, the Zhou kingdom was divided into a number of principalities, governed by members of the hereditary aristocracy, who were appointed by the king and were at least theoretically subordinated to his authority.

The Mandate of Heaven   But the Zhou kings also introduced some innovations. According to the *Rites of Zhou*, one of the oldest surviving documents on statecraft, the Zhou dynasty ruled China because it possessed the **mandate of Heaven**. According to this concept, Heaven (now viewed as an impersonal law of nature rather than as an anthropomorphic deity) maintained order in the universe through the Zhou king, who thus ruled as a representative of Heaven but not as a divine being. The king, who was selected to rule because of his talent and virtue, was then responsible for governing the people with compassion and efficiency. It was his duty to appease the gods in order to protect the people from natural calamities or bad harvests. But if the king failed to rule effectively, he could, theoretically at least, be overthrown and replaced by a new ruler. As noted earlier, this idea was used to justify the Zhou conquest of the Shang. Eventually, the concept of the heavenly mandate would become a cardinal principle of Chinese statecraft.[4] Each founder of a new dynasty would routinely assert that he had earned the mandate of Heaven, and who could disprove it except by overthrowing the king? As a pragmatic Chinese proverb put it, "He who wins is the king; he who loses is the rebel."

In asserting that the ruler had a direct connection with the divine forces presiding over the universe, Chinese tradition reflected a belief that was prevalent in all ancient civilizations. But whereas in some societies, notably in Mesopotamia and Greece, the gods were seen as capricious and not subject to human understanding, in China, Heaven was viewed as an essentially benevolent force devoted to universal harmony and order that could be influenced by positive human action. Was this attitude a consequence of the fact that China, though subject to some of the same climatic vicissitudes that plagued other parts of the world, experienced a somewhat more predictable and beneficial environment than regions like the Middle East?

Later Chinese would regard the period of the early Zhou dynasty, as portrayed in the *Rites of Zhou* (which, of course, is no more an unbiased source than any modern government document), as a golden age when there was harmony in the world and all was right under Heaven. Whether the system functioned in such an ideal manner, of course, is open to question. In any case, the golden age did not last, whether because it never existed in practice or because of the increasing complexity of Chinese civilization. Perhaps, too, its disappearance was a consequence of the intellectual and moral weakness of the rulers of the Zhou royal house.

By the sixth century B.C.E., the Zhou dynasty began to decline. As the power of the central government disintegrated, bitter internal rivalries arose among the various principalities, where the governing officials had succeeded in making their positions hereditary at the expense of the king. As the power of these officials grew, they began to regulate the local economy and seek reliable sources of revenue for their expanding armies, such as a uniform tax system and government monopolies on key commodities such as salt and iron. A century later, the Zhou rulers had lost all pretense of authority, and China was divided into a cauldron of squabbling states, an era known to Chinese historians as the "Period of the Warring States."

Economy and Society   During the Zhou dynasty, the essential characteristics of Chinese economic and social institutions began to take shape. The Zhou continued the pattern of land ownership that had existed under the Shang: the peasants worked on lands owned by their lord but also had land that they cultivated for their own use. The practice was called the **well-field system** because the Chinese character for "well" (井) calls to mind the division of land into nine separate segments. Each peasant family tilled an outer plot for its own use and joined with other families to work the inner one for the hereditary lord. How widely this system was used is unclear, but it represented an ideal described by Confucian scholars of a later day. As the following passage from *The Book of Songs* indicates, the life of the average farmer was a difficult one. The "big rat" is probably the government or a lord who has imposed high taxes on the peasants.

> Big rat, big rat,
> Do not eat my millet!
> Three years I have served you,
> But you will not care for me.
> I am going to leave you
> And go to that happy land;
> Happy land, happy land,
> Where I will find my place.[5]

Trade and manufacturing were carried out by merchants and artisans, who lived in walled towns under the direct control of the local lord. Merchants did not operate independently but were considered the property of the local lord and on occasion could even be bought and sold like chattels. A class of slaves performed a variety of menial tasks and perhaps worked on local irrigation projects. Most of them were probably prisoners of war captured during conflicts with the neighboring principalities. Scholars do not know how extensive slavery was in ancient times, but slaves probably did not constitute a large portion of the total population.

The period of the later Zhou, from the sixth to the third century B.C.E., was an era of significant economic growth and technological innovation, especially in agriculture. During that time, large-scale water control projects were undertaken to regulate the flow of rivers and distribute water evenly to the fields, as well as to construct canals to facilitate the transport of goods from one region to another. Perhaps the most impressive technological achievement of the period was the construction of a massive water control project on the Min River, a tributary of the Yangzi. This system of canals and spillways, put into operation by the state of Qin a few years prior to the end of the Zhou dynasty, diverted excess water from the river into the local irrigation network and watered an area populated by as many as 5 million people. The system is still in use today, more than two thousand years later.

Food production was also stimulated by a number of advances in farm technology. By the mid-sixth century B.C.E., the introduction of iron had led to the development of iron plowshares, which permitted deep plowing for the first time. Other innovations dating from the later Zhou were the use of natural fertilizer, the collar harness, and the technique of leaving land fallow to preserve or replenish nutrients in the soil. By the late Zhou dynasty, the cultivation of wet rice had become one of the prime sources of food in China. Although rice was difficult and time-consuming to produce, it replaced other grain crops in areas with a warm climate because of its good taste, relative ease of preparation, and high nutritional value.

The advances in agriculture, which enabled the population of China to rise as high as 20 million people during the late Zhou era, were also undoubtedly a major factor in the growth of commerce and manufacturing. During the late Zhou, economic wealth began to replace noble birth as the prime source of power and influence. Tools made of iron became more common, and trade developed in a variety of useful commodities, including cloth, salt, and manufactured goods.

One of the most important items of trade in ancient China was silk. There is evidence of silkworms being raised as early as the Neolithic period. Remains of silk material have been found on Shang bronzes, and a large number of fragments have been recovered in tombs dating from the mid-Zhou era. Silk cloth was used not only for clothing and quilts but also to wrap the bodies of the dead prior to burial. Fragments have been found throughout Central Asia and as far away as Greece, suggesting that the famous Silk Road stretching from Central China westward to the Middle East and the Mediterranean Sea was in operation as early as the fifth century B.C.E.

Initially, however, jade was probably a more important item of trade carried along the Silk Road. Blocks of the precious stone were mined in the mountains of northern Tibet as early as the sixth millennium B.C.E. and began to appear in China during the Shang dynasty. Praised by Confucius as a symbol of purity and virtue, jade assumed an almost sacred quality among Chinese during the Zhou dynasty.

With the development of trade and manufacturing, China began to move toward a money economy. The first form of money, as in much of the rest of the world, may have been cowries or other seashells (the Chinese character for goods or property contains the ideographic symbol for "shell" 貝), but by the Zhou dynasty, pieces of iron shaped like a knife or round coins with a hole in the middle so they could be carried in strings of a thousand were being used. Most ordinary Chinese, however, simply used a system of barter. Taxes, rents, and even the salaries of government officials were normally paid in grain.

The Hundred Schools of Ancient Philosophy   In China, as in other great river valley societies, the birth of civilization was accompanied by the emergence of an organized effort to comprehend the nature of the cosmos and the role of human beings within it. Speculation over such questions began in the very early stages of civilization and culminated at the end of the Zhou era in the "hundred schools" of ancient philosophy, a wide-ranging debate over the nature of human beings, society, and the universe.

Early Beliefs   The first hint of religious belief in ancient China comes from relics found in royal tombs of Neolithic times. By then, the Chinese had already developed a religious sense beyond the primitive belief in the existence of spirits in nature. The Shang had begun to believe in the existence of one transcendent god, known as Shang Di, who presided over all the forces of nature. As time went on, the Chinese concept of religion evolved from a vaguely anthropomorphic god to a somewhat more impersonal symbol of universal order known as Heaven (*Tian*). There was also much speculation among Chinese intellectuals about the nature of the cosmic order. One of the earliest ideas was that the universe was divided into two primary forces of good and evil, light and dark, male and female, called the *yang* and the *yin*, represented symbolically by the sun (*yang*) and the moon (*yin*). According to this theory, somewhat reminiscent of the religion of Zoroastrianism in Persia, life was a dynamic process of interaction between the forces of *yang* and *yin*. Early Chinese could only attempt to understand the process and perhaps to have some minimal effect on its operation. They could not hope to reverse it. It is sometimes asserted that this belief has contributed to the heavy element of fatalism in Chinese popular wisdom. The Chinese have traditionally believed that bad times will be followed by good times and vice versa.

The belief that there was some mysterious "law of nature" that could be interpreted by human beings led to various attempts to predict the future, such as the Shang oracle bones and other methods of divination. Philosophers invented ways to interpret the will of nature, while shamans, playing a role similar to the *brahmins* in India, were employed at court to assist the emperor in his policy deliberations until at least the fifth century C.E. One of the most famous manuals used for this purpose was the *Yi Jing*, known in English as the *Book of Changes*.

Confucianism   Efforts to divine the mysterious purposes of Heaven notwithstanding, Chinese thinking about metaphysical reality also contained a strain of pragmatism, readily apparent in the ideas of the great philosopher Confucius. Confucius (*Kung fuci*, or "Master Kung") was born in the state of Lu, in the modern province of Shandong (SHAHN-doong), in 551 B.C.E. After reaching maturity, he apparently hoped to find employment as a political adviser in one of the principalities into which China was divided at that time, but he had little success in finding a patron. Nevertheless, his ideas, as contained in the *Analects* and other works attributed to him, made an indelible mark on Chinese history and culture.

In conversations with his disciples contained in the *Analects*, Confucius often adopted a detached and almost skeptical view of Heaven. "If you are unable to serve men," he commented on one occasion, "how can you serve the spirits? If you don't understand life, how can you understand death?" In many instances, he appeared to advise his followers to revere the deities and the ancestral spirits but to keep them at a distance. Confucius believed it was useless to speculate too much about metaphysical questions. It was better by far to assume that there was a rational order to the universe and then concentrate on ordering the affairs of this world.[6]

Confucius's interest in philosophy, then, was essentially political and ethical. The universe was constructed in such a way that if human beings could act harmoniously in accordance with its purposes, their own affairs would prosper. Much of his concern was with human behavior. The key to proper behavior was to behave in accordance with the **Dao** (DOW) (Way). Confucius assumed that all human beings had their own *Dao*, depending on their individual role in life, and it was their duty to follow it. Even the ruler had his own *Dao*, and he ignored it at his peril, for to do so could mean the loss of the mandate of Heaven. The idea of the *Dao* is reminiscent of the concept of *dharma* in ancient India and played a similar role in governing the affairs of society.

Two elements in the Confucian interpretation of the *Dao* are particularly worthy of mention. The first is the concept of duty. It was the responsibility of all individuals to subordinate their own interests and aspirations to the broader need of the family and the community. Confucius assumed that if each individual worked hard to fulfill his or her assigned destiny, the affairs of society as a whole would prosper as well. In this respect, it was important for the ruler to set a good example. If he followed his "kingly way," the beneficial effects would radiate throughout society.

The second key element is the idea of humanity, sometimes translated as "human-heartedness." This concept involves a sense of compassion and empathy for others. It is similar in some ways to Christian concepts, but with a subtle twist. Where Christian teachings call on human beings to "behave toward others as you would have them behave toward you," the Confucian maxim is put in a different way: "Do not do unto others what you would not wish done to yourself." To many Chinese, this attitude symbolizes an element of tolerance in the Chinese character that has not always been practiced in other societies.[7]

Confucius may have considered himself a failure because he never attained the position he wanted, but many of his contemporaries found his ideas appealing, and in the generations after his death, his message spread widely throughout China. Confucius was an outspoken critic of his times and lamented the disappearance of what he regarded as the golden age of the early Zhou. One classical source quoted him as follows:

> The practice of the Great Way, the illustrious men of the Three Dynasties—these I shall never know in person. And yet they inspire my ambition. When the Great Way was practiced, the world was shared by all alike. The worthy and the able were promoted to office and practiced good faith and lived in affection. There they did not regard as parents only their own parents, or as sons only their own sons. The aged found a fitting close to their lives, the robust their proper employment; the young were provided with an upbringing and the widow and widower, the orphaned and the sick, with proper care. Men had their talks and women their hearths. They hated to see goods lying about in waste, yet they did not hoard them for themselves; they disliked the thought that their energies were not fully used, yet they used them not for private ends. Therefore all evil plotting was prevented and thieves and rebels did not arise, so that people could leave their outer gates unbolted. This was the age of Grand Unity.[8]

Yet Confucius was not just another disgruntled Chinese conservative mourning the passing of the good old days; rather, he was a revolutionary thinker, many of whose key ideas looked forward rather than backward. Perhaps his most striking political idea was that the government should be open to all men of superior quality, not limited to those of noble birth. As one of his disciples reports in the *Analects*, "The Master said, by their nature, men are quite similar; in practice, they become far apart."[9] Confucius undoubtedly had himself in mind as one of those "superior" men, but the rapacity of the hereditary lords must have added strength to his convictions.

The concept of rule by merit was, of course, not an unfamiliar idea in the China of his day; the *Rites of Zhou* had clearly stated that the king deserved to rule because of his talent and virtue, not as the result of noble birth. In practice, however, aristocratic privilege must often have opened the doors to political influence, and many of Confucius's contemporaries must have regarded his appeal for government by talent as both exciting and dangerous. Confucius did not explicitly question the right of the hereditary aristocracy to play a leading role in the political process, nor did his ideas have much effect in his lifetime. Still, they introduced a new concept that was later implemented in the form of a bureaucracy selected through a civil service examination.

Confucius's ideas, passed on to later generations through the *Analects* as well as through writings attributed to him, had a strong impact on Chinese political thinkers of the late Zhou period, a time when the existing system was in disarray and open to serious question. But as with most great thinkers, Confucius's ideas were sufficiently ambiguous to be interpreted in contradictory ways. Some, like the philosopher Mencius (MEN-shuss) (370–290 B.C.E.), stressed the humanistic side of Confucian ideas, arguing that human beings were by nature good and hence could be taught their civic responsibilities by example. He also stressed that the ruler had a duty to govern with compassion:

> Here is the way to win the empire: win the people and you win the empire. Here is the way to win the people: win their hearts and you win the people. Here is the way to win their hearts: give them and share with them what they like, and do not do to them what they do not like. The people turn to a humane ruler as water flows downward or beasts take to wilderness.[10]

Here is a prescription for political behavior that could win wide support in our own day. Other thinkers, however, rejected Mencius's rosy view of human nature and argued for a different approach.

Legalism   A school of thought that became quite popular during the "hundred schools" era in ancient China was the philosophy of **Legalism**. Taking issue with the view of Mencius and other disciples of Confucius that human nature was essentially good, the Legalists argued that human beings were by nature evil and would follow the correct path only if coerced by harsh laws and stiff punishments. These thinkers were referred to as the School of Law because they rejected the Confucian view that government by "superior men" could solve society's problems and argued instead for a system of impersonal laws.

OPPOSING VIEWPOINTS

A Debate over Good and Evil

RELIGION &
PHILOSOPHY

During the latter part of the Zhou dynasty, one of the major preoccupations of Chinese philosophers was to determine the essential qualities of human nature. In the *Analects*, Confucius was cited as asserting that humans' moral instincts were essentially neutral at birth; their minds must be cultivated to bring out the potential goodness therein. In later years, the master's disciples elaborated on this issue. The great humanitarian philosopher Mencius maintained that human nature was essentially good. But his rival Xunzi (SHYOON-zuh) took the opposite tack, arguing that evil is inherent in human nature and could be eradicated only by rigorous training at the hands of an instructor. Later, Xunzi's views would be adopted by the Legalist philosophers of the Qin dynasty, although his belief in the efficacy of education earned him a place in the community of Confucian scholars.

The Book of Mencius

Mencius said, ... "The goodness of human nature is like the downward course of water. There is no human being lacking in the tendency to do good, just as there is no water lacking in the tendency to flow downward. Now by striking water and splashing it, you may cause it to go over your head, and by damming and channeling it, you can force it to flow uphill. But is this the nature of water? It is the force that makes this happen. While people can be made to do what is not good, what happens to their nature is like this....

"All human beings have a mind that cannot bear to see the sufferings of others....

"Here is why.... Now, if anyone were suddenly to see a child about to fall into a well, his mind would always be filled with alarm, distress, pity, and compassion. That he would react accordingly is not because he would use the opportunity to ingratiate himself with the child's parents, nor because he would seek commendation from neighbors and friends, nor because he would hate the adverse reputation. From this it may be seen that one who lacks a mind that feels pity and compassion would not be human; one who lacks a mind that feels shame and aversion would not be human; one who lacks a mind that feels modesty and compliance would not be human; and one who lacks a mind that knows right and wrong would not be human.

The Legalists also disagreed with the Confucian belief that the universe has a moral core. They therefore argued that only firm action by the state could bring about social order. Fear of harsh punishment, more than the promise of material reward, could best motivate the common people to serve the interests of the ruler. Because human nature was essentially corrupt, officials could not be trusted to carry out their duties in a fair and even-handed manner, and only a strong ruler could create an orderly society. All human actions should be subordinated to the effort to create a strong and prosperous state subject to his will.

Daoism   One of the most popular alternatives to **Confucianism** was the philosophy of **Daoism** (DOW-iz-uhm) (frequently spelled Taoism). According to Chinese

"The mind's feeling of pity and compassion is the beginning of humaneness; the mind's feeling of shame and aversion is the beginning of rightness; the mind's feeling of modesty and compliance is the beginning of propriety; and the mind's sense of right and wrong is the beginning of wisdom."

The Book of Xunzi

Human nature is evil; its goodness derives from conscious activity. Now it is human nature to be born with a fondness for profit. Indulging this leads to contention and strife, and the sense of modesty and yielding with which one was born disappears. One is born with feelings of envy and hate, and, by indulging these, one is led into banditry and theft, so that the sense of loyalty and good faith with which he was born disappears. One is born with the desires of the ears and eyes and with a fondness for beautiful sights and sounds, and by indulging these, one is led to licentiousness and chaos, so that the sense of ritual, rightness, refinement, and principle with which one was born is lost. Hence, following human nature and indulging human emotions will inevitably lead to contention and strife, causing one to rebel against one's proper duty, reduce principle to chaos, and revert to violence. Therefore one must be transformed by the example of a teacher and guided by the way of ritual and right before one will attain modesty and yielding, accord with refinement and ritual and return to order. From this perspective it is apparent that human nature is evil and that its goodness is the result of conscious activity.

Mencius said, "Now human nature is good, and [when it is not] this is always a result of having lost or destroyed one's nature." I say that he was mistaken to take such a view. Now, it is human nature that, as soon as a person is born, he departs from his original substance and from his rational disposition so that he must inevitably lose and destroy them. Seen in this way, it is apparent that human nature is evil.

Q *What arguments do these two Confucian thinkers advance to support their point of view about the essential elements of human nature? In your view, which argument is more persuasive?*

Source: Excerpt from William Theodore de Bary and Irene Bloom, *Sources of Chinese Tradition*, Vol. I, 2nd ed. (New York, 1999). Copyright © 1999 by Columbia University Press.

tradition, the Daoist school was founded by a contemporary of Confucius popularly known as Lao Zi (LOW ["ow" as in "how"] dzuh), or the Old Master. Many modern scholars, however, are skeptical that Lao Zi actually existed.

Obtaining a clear understanding of the original concepts of Daoism is difficult because its primary document, a short treatise known as the *Dao De Jing* (DOW deh JING) (sometimes translated as *The Way of the Tao*), is an enigmatic book whose interpretation has baffled scholars for centuries. The opening line, for example, explains less what the *Dao* is than what it is not: "The Tao [Way] that can be told of is not the eternal Tao. The name that can be named is not the eternal name."[11]

Nevertheless, the basic concepts of Daoism are not especially difficult to understand. Like Confucianism, Daoism does not anguish over the underlying meaning of the cosmos. Rather, it attempts to set forth proper forms of behavior for human beings here on earth. In most other respects, however, Daoism presents a view of life and its ultimate meaning that is almost diametrically opposed to that of Confucianism. Whereas Confucian doctrine asserts that it is the duty of human beings to work hard to improve life here on earth, Daoists contend that the true way to interpret the will of Heaven is not action but inaction (*wu wei*). The best way to act in harmony with the universal order is to act spontaneously and let nature take its course.

Such a message could be very appealing to people who were uncomfortable with the somewhat rigid flavor of the Confucian work ethic and preferred a more individualistic approach. This image would eventually find graphic expression in Chinese landscape painting, which in its classic form would depict naturalistic scenes of mountains, water, and clouds and underscore the fragility and smallness of individual human beings.

Daoism achieved considerable popularity in the waning years of the Zhou dynasty. It was especially popular among intellectuals, who may have found it appealing as an escapist antidote in a world characterized by growing disorder.

Popular Beliefs   Daoism also played a second role as a framework for popular spiritualistic and animistic beliefs among the common people. Popular Daoism was less a philosophy than a religion; it comprised a variety of rituals and behaviors that were regarded as a means of achieving heavenly salvation or even a state of immortality on earth. Daoist sorcerers practiced various types of exercises for training the mind and body in the hope of achieving power, sexual prowess, and long life. It was primarily this form of Daoism that survived into a later age.

The philosophical forms of Confucianism and Daoism did not provide much meaning to the mass of the population, for whom philosophical debate over the ultimate meaning of life was less important than the daily struggle for survival. Even among the elites, interest in the occult and in astrology was high, and many royal courts included a hereditary astrologer to help predict the intentions of the heavenly forces. Throughout the ancient period, magico-religious ideas coexisted with interest in natural science and humanistic philosophy.

For most Chinese, Heaven was not a vague, impersonal law of nature, as it was for many Confucian and Daoist intellectuals. Instead, it was a terrain peopled with innumerable gods and spirits of nature, both good and evil, who existed in trees, mountains, and streams as well as in heavenly bodies. As human beings mastered the techniques of farming, they called on divine intervention to guarantee a good harvest. Other gods were responsible for the safety of fishers, transportation workers, or prospective mothers.

Another aspect of popular religion was the belief that the spirits of deceased human beings lived in the atmosphere for a time before ascending to heaven or descending to hell. During that period, surviving family members had to care for the spirits through proper ritual, or they would become evil spirits and haunt the survivors.

Thus, in ancient China, human beings were offered a variety of interpretations of the nature of the universe. Confucianism satisfied the need for a rational doctrine of nation building and social organization at a time when the existing political and social structure was beginning to disintegrate. Philosophical Daoism provided a more sensitive approach to the vicissitudes of fate and nature and a framework for a set of diverse animistic beliefs at the popular level. But neither could satisfy the deeper emotional needs that sometimes inspire the human spirit. Neither could effectively provide solace in a time of sorrow or the hope of a better life in the hereafter. Something else would be needed to fill the gap.

THE FIRST CHINESE EMPIRE: THE QIN DYNASTY

During the last two centuries of the Zhou dynasty (the fourth and third centuries B.C.E.), the authority of the king became increasingly nominal, and several of the small principalities into which the Zhou kingdom had been divided began to evolve into powerful states that presented a potential challenge to the Zhou ruler himself. Chief among these were Qu (CHOO) in the central Yangzi Valley, Wu (WOO) in the Yangzi delta, and Yue (yoo-EH) along the southeastern coast. At first, their mutual rivalries were held in check, but by the late fifth century B.C.E., competition intensified into civil war, giving birth to the so-called Period of the Warring States. Powerful principalities vied with each other for preeminence and largely ignored the now purely titular authority of the Zhou court. New forms of warfare also emerged with the invention of iron weapons and the introduction of the foot soldier. Cavalry, too, made its first appearance, armed with the powerful crossbow. Cities were now threatened by larger and more competent armies. When they sought to protect themselves by erecting high walls, their opponents countered by developing new techniques in siege warfare.

Eventually, the relatively young state of Qin (CHIN), located in the original homeland of the Zhou, emerged as a key player in these conflicts. By the mid-fourth century B.C.E., it had become a major force in the contest for hegemony in late-Zhou China by adopting a number of reforms in agriculture, government administration, military organization, and fiscal policy. As a result of policies put into effect by the adviser Shang Yang (SHAHNG yahng) in the mid-fourth century B.C.E., Qin society was ruled with ruthless efficiency. In the words of Sima Qian (SUH-mah chee-AHN), a famous historian of the Han dynasty:

> He commanded that the people be divided into tens and fives and that they supervise each other and be mutually liable. Anyone who failed to report criminal activity would be chopped in two at the waist, while those who reported it would receive the same reward as that for obtaining the head of an enemy.[12]

Benefiting from a strong defensive position in the mountains to the west of the great bend of the Yellow River, as well as from their control of the rich Sichuan plains, the Qin gradually subdued their main rivals through conquest or diplomatic maneuvering. In 221 B.C.E., the Qin ruler declared the establishment of a new dynasty, the first truly unified government in Chinese history.

MAP 3.2 China During the Period of the Warring States

From the fifth to the third centuries B.C.E., China was locked in a time of civil strife known as the Period of the Warring States. This map shows the Zhou dynasty capital at Luoyang, along with the major states that were squabbling for precedence in the region.

The Qin Dynasty (221–206 B.C.E.)   One of the primary reasons for the triumph of the Qin was probably the character of the Qin ruler, known to history as Qin Shi Huangdi, or the First Emperor of Qin. A man of forceful personality and immense ambition, Qin Shi Huangdi had ascended to the throne of Qin in 246 B.C.E. at the age of thirteen. Described by the Han dynasty historian Sima Qian as having "the chest of a bird of prey, the voice of a jackal, and the heart of a tiger," the new king found the Legalist views of his adviser Li Su (lee SUH) all too appealing. In 221 B.C.E., Qin Shi Huangdi defeated the last of his rivals and founded a new dynasty with himself as emperor.

Political Structures   The Qin dynasty transformed Chinese politics. Philosophical doctrines that had proliferated during the late Zhou period were prohibited, and Legalism was adopted as the official ideology. Those who opposed the policies of the new regime were punished and sometimes executed, while books presenting ideas contrary to the official orthodoxy were publicly put to the torch, perhaps the first example of book burning in history.

Legalistic theory gave birth to a number of fundamental administrative and political developments, some of which would survive the Qin and serve as a model for future dynasties. In the first place, unlike the Zhou, the Qin was a highly centralized state. The central bureaucracy was divided into three primary ministries: a civil authority, a military authority, and a censorate, whose inspectors surveyed the efficiency of officials throughout the system. This would later become standard administrative procedure for future Chinese dynasties.

Below the central government were two levels of administration: provinces and counties. Unlike the Zhou system, officials at these levels did not inherit their positions but were appointed by the court and were subject to dismissal at the emperor's whim. A penal code provided for harsh punishments for all wrongdoers. Officials were watched by the censors, who reported directly to the throne. Those guilty of malfeasance in office were executed.

Society and the Economy   Qin Shi Huangdi, who had a passion for centralization, unified the system of weights and measures, standardized the monetary system and the written forms of Chinese characters, and ordered the construction of a system of roads extending throughout the empire. He also attempted to eliminate the remaining powers of the landed aristocrats and divided their estates among the peasants, who were now taxed directly by the state. He thus eliminated potential rivals and secured tax revenues for the central government. Members of the aristocratic clans were required to live in the capital city at Xianyang (shi-AHN-yahng), just north of modern Xian, so that the court could monitor their activities. Such a system may not have been advantageous to the peasants in all respects, however, since the central government could now collect taxes more effectively and mobilize the peasants for military service and for various public works projects.

The Qin dynasty was equally unsympathetic to the merchants, whom it viewed as parasites. Private commercial activities were severely restricted and heavily taxed, and many vital forms of commerce and manufacturing, including mining, wine making, and the distribution of salt, were placed under a government monopoly.

Qin Shi Huangdi was equally aggressive in foreign affairs. His armies continued the gradual advance to the south that had taken place during the final years of the Zhou dynasty, extending the border of China to the edge of the Red River in modern Vietnam. To supply the Qin armies operating in the area, a canal was dug that provided direct inland navigation from the Yangzi River in central China to what is now the modern city of Guangzhou (gwahng-JOE) (Canton) in the south.

Beyond the Frontier: The Nomadic Peoples and the Great Wall   The main area of concern for the Qin emperor, however, was in the north, where a nomadic people, known to the Chinese as the Xiongnu (SHYAHNG-noo) and possibly related to the Huns or to Indo-European-speaking people in the area, had become increasingly active in the area of the Gobi Desert. The area north of the Yellow River had been sparsely inhabited since prehistoric times. During the Qin period, the climate of northern China was somewhat milder and moister than it is today, and parts of the region were heavily forested. The local population probably lived by hunting and fishing, practicing limited forms of agriculture, or herding animals such as cattle or sheep.

As the climate gradually became drier, people were forced to rely increasingly on animal husbandry as a means of livelihood. Their response was to master the art of riding on horseback and to adopt the nomadic life. Organized loosely into communities consisting of a number of kinship groups, they ranged far and wide in search of pasture for their herds of cattle, goats, or sheep. As they moved seasonally from one pasture to another, they often traveled several hundred miles carrying their goods and their circular felt tents, called *yurts*.

But the new way of life presented its own challenges. Increased food production led to a growing population, which in times of drought outstripped the available resources. Rival groups then competed for the best pastures. After they mastered the art of fighting on horseback in the middle of the first millennium B.C.E., territorial warfare became commonplace throughout the entire frontier region, from the Pacific Ocean to Central Asia.

By the end of the Zhou dynasty in the third century B.C.E., the nomadic Xiongnu had unified many of the groups operating in the region and began to pose a serious threat to the security of China's northern frontier. A number of Chinese principalities in the area began to build walls and fortifications to keep them out, but warriors on horseback possessed significant advantages over the infantry of the Chinese.

Qin Shi Huangdi's answer to the problem was to introduce mounted archers into his military units stationed in the north to counter nomad attacks while strengthening the walls to keep the marauders out. In Sima Qian's words:

> First Emperor of the [Qin] ... seized control of all the lands south of the Yellow River and established border defenses along the river, constructing forty-four walled district cities overlooking the river and manning them with convict laborers transported to the border for garrison duty. Thus, he utilized the natural mountain barriers to establish the border defenses, scooping out the valleys and constructing ramparts and building installations at other points where they were needed. The whole line of defenses stretched over ten thousand *li* [a *li* is one-third of a mile]....[13]

Today, of course, we know Qin Shi Huangdi's project as the Great Wall, which extends nearly 4,000 miles from the sandy wastes of Central Asia to the sea. It is constructed of massive granite blocks, and its top is wide enough to serve as a roadway for horse-drawn chariots. Although the wall that appears in most photographs today was built 1,500 years after the Qin, during the Ming dynasty, some of the walls built by the Qin remain standing. Their construction was a massive project that required the efforts of thousands of laborers, many of whom met their deaths there and, according to legend, are buried within the wall.

The Fall of the Qin   The Legalist system put in place by the First Emperor of Qin was designed to achieve maximum efficiency as well as total security for the state. It did neither. Qin Shi Huangdi was apparently aware of the dangers of factions within the imperial family and established a class of **eunuchs** (castrated males) who served as personal attendants for himself and female members of the royal family. The original idea may have been to restrict the influence of male courtiers, and the eunuch system later became a standard feature of the Chinese imperial system. But as confidential advisers to the royal family, eunuchs were in a position of influence. The rivalry between the "inner" imperial court and the "outer" court of bureaucratic officials led to tensions that persisted until the end of the imperial system.

By ruthlessly gathering control over the empire into his own hands, Qin Shi Huangdi had hoped to establish a rule that, in the words of Sima Qian, "would be enjoyed by his sons for ten thousand generations." In fact, his centralizing zeal alienated many key groups. Landed aristocrats and Confucian intellectuals, as well as the common people, groaned under the censorship of thought and speech, harsh taxes, and forced labor projects. "He killed men," recounted the historian, "as though he thought he could never finish, he punished men as though he were afraid he would never get around to them all, and the whole world revolted against him."[14] Shortly after the emperor died in 210 B.C.E., the dynasty descended into factional rivalry, and four years later it was overthrown.

THE GLORIOUS HAN DYNASTY (202 B.C.E.–221 C.E.)

The fall of the Qin dynasty in 206 B.C.E. was followed by a brief period of civil strife as aspiring successors competed for hegemony. Out of this strife emerged one of the greatest and most durable dynasties in Chinese history—the Han (HAHN). The Han dynasty would later become so closely identified with the advance of Chinese civilization that even today the Chinese sometimes refer to themselves as "people of Han" and to their language as the "language of Han."

The founder of the Han dynasty was Liu Bang (lyoo BAHNG), a commoner of peasant origin who would be known historically by his imperial title of Han Gaozu (HAHN gow-DZOO), or Exalted Emperor of Han. Under his strong rule and that of his successors, the new dynasty quickly moved to consolidate its control over the empire and promote the welfare of its subjects. Efficient and benevolent, at least by the standards of the time, Gaozu maintained the centralized political institutions of the Qin but abandoned its harsh Legalistic approach to law enforcement. Han rulers discovered in Confucian principles a useful foundation for the creation of a new state philosophy. Under the Han, Confucianism, supplemented by elements from the surviving classics of the "hundred schools" period, began to take on the character of an official ideology.

Confucianism and the State   The integration of Confucian doctrine with Legalist institutions, creating a system generally known as **State Confucianism**, took a while to accomplish. At first, the founding emperor Han Gaozu departed from the Qin policy of centralized rule by rewarding some of his key allies with vast fiefdoms, restricting his own territory to lands around the new capital of Chang'an (CHENG-AHN). But chronic unrest throughout the countryside eventually forced a change in policy. By the mid-second century B.C.E., the influence of unruly aristocratic forces had been curbed, and once again power was concentrated at the imperial court.

Once this was accomplished, the Han rulers sought to restore key components of the Qin system of centralized government. For example, they borrowed the

A Prescription for the Emperor

**POLITICS &
GOVERNMENT**

Jia Yi (JYAH YEE) (201–168?
B.C.E.) was a counselor to
Emperor Wendi (wen-DEE)
(r. 181–157 B.C.E.), one of the
early rulers of the Han dynasty. His words
of advice to his sovereign, excerpted in this
selection, bear witness to the strong tradition of popular sovereignty in Confucian
thought that had earlier been expressed by
the well-known fourth-century B.C.E. philosopher Mencius. Following Mencius's
example, Jia Yi declared that the desires
of the people should be paramount in
forming the basis of government. In his
opinion, a ruler who did not defer to the
wishes of his subjects did not merit the
mandate of Heaven. Jia's views on the role
of the supernatural in human affairs are
particularly striking, as he declared that it
was not the will of Heaven, but good or
bad deeds undertaken here on earth,
that brought fortune or misfortune to the
people of China.

"People Are in Every Way the Root"

It is said that in government, the people
are in every way the root (base). For the
state, the ruler, and the officials, the people constitute the root. Thus the security
of the state or its endangerment depends
on them [the people]; the prestige of the
ruler or his disgrace depends on them; and
the honor of the officials or their debase-
ment is contingent on them. This is what
is meant by saying the people are in every
way the root. Then again, it is said that in
government, the people constitute in every
way the mandate. For the state, the ruler,
and the officials all depend on the people
for their mandate. The life or death of the
state depends on the people, the vision or
blindness of the ruler depends on them,
and whether officials are respected or

not depends on them. This is why the people are in every way the mandate....

Still further it is said that the people
are the power on which the state, the
ruler, and the officials all depend for
their power. If victory is won, it is because
the people want to be victorious; if an
attack succeeds, it is because the people
want it so; if defense succeeds, it is
because the people want to survive.... If
the people are fearful of the enemy, they
will surely retreat and defeat will surely
come. Disaster and fortune, as we see,
are determined not in Heaven but by the
officers and the people....

Good deeds will in the end bring good
fortune, and bad deeds will inevitably
bring misfortune. Those who are blessed
by Heaven need not thank Heaven, and
those who suffer from natural disasters
need not blame Heaven, for it is all one's
own doing.... Heaven will present good fortune to the virtuous and disaster to those
who deprive the people. Even the lowest of
people should not *be slighted, and the most
foolish among them should not be taken
advantage of.* Thus, throughout history,
those who oppose the people sooner or
later are defeated by the people.... How
can anyone think of behaving with arrogance and self-deception? The enlightened
ruler and the noble person will vie to practice
good when they perceive it, and they will
treat evil like an enemy if they hear of it.

Q *Are Jia Yi's views implicit in the teachings
of Confucius, as expressed in the Analects
and other sources discussed in this chapter?
How do his views compare with the advice
offered to rulers in other ancient societies?*

Source: From *Sources of Chinese Tradition*, 2nd ed.,
Vol. 1, by Wm. T. DeBary and Irene Bloom. Copyright © 1999 Columbia University Press. Reprinted
with permission of the publisher.

tripartite division of the central government into civilian and military authorities and a censorate. The government was headed by a "grand council" including representatives from all three segments of government. The Han also retained the system of local government, dividing the empire into provinces and districts.

Finally, the Han sought to apply the Qin system of selecting government officials on the basis of merit rather than birth. Shortly after founding the new dynasty, Han Gaozu decreed that local officials would be asked to recommend promising candidates for public service. Thirty years later, in 165 B.C.E., the first known **civil service examination** was administered to candidates for positions in the bureaucracy. Shortly after that, an academy was established to train candidates. The first candidates were almost all from aristocratic or other wealthy families, and the Han bureaucracy itself was still dominated by the traditional hereditary elite. Still, the principle of selecting officials on the basis of talent had been established and would eventually become standard practice. By the end of the first century B.C.E., as many as 30,000 students were enrolled at the academy.

Driven by government policies that used tax incentives to promote large families, the population of the empire increased rapidly—by some estimates rising from about 20 million to more than 60 million at the height of the dynasty—creating a growing need for a large and efficient bureaucracy to maintain the state in proper working order. Unfortunately, the Han were unable to resolve all of the problems left over from the past. Factionalism at court remained a serious problem and undermined the efficiency of the central government. Equally important, despite their efforts, the Han rulers were never able to restrain the great aristocratic families, who continued to play a dominant role in political and economic affairs. The failure to curb the power of the wealthy clans eventually became a major factor in the collapse of the dynasty.

The Economy

Han rulers unwittingly contributed to their own problems by adopting fiscal policies that led eventually to greater concentration of land in the hands of the wealthy. They were aware that a free peasantry paying taxes directly to the state would both limit the wealth and power of the great noble families and increase the state's revenues. The Han had difficulty, however, in preventing the recurrence of the economic inequities that had characterized the last years of the Zhou. Land taxes were not especially high but had to be paid in cash rather than in grain to make collection easier. In years of bad harvests, poor farmers were unable to pay their taxes and were forced to sell their land and become tenant farmers, paying rents of up to half the annual harvest. Although food production increased steadily due to the application of natural fertilizer and the use of iron tools that brought new lands under the plow, the trebling of the population under the early Han eventually reduced the average size of a family's farm plot to about one acre per person, barely enough for survival.

Farm families also faced a number of other exactions, including compulsory military service for adult males and forced labor of up to one month annually. As rural protests escalated during the first decades of Han rule, the imperial government finally ended military conscription and began to rely on professional armies, recruited primarily among non-Chinese minorities living along the periphery of the empire. That strategy, however, would eventually lead to its own problems.

Manufacturing and Trade   Although such economic problems contributed to the eventual downfall of the dynasty, in general the period of the early Han was one of unparalleled productivity and prosperity, marked by a major expansion of trade, both domestic and foreign. This was not necessarily due to official encouragement. In fact, the Han were as suspicious of private merchants as their predecessors had been and levied stiff taxes on trade in an effort to limit commercial activities. Merchants were also subject to severe social constraints. They were disqualified from seeking office, restricted in their place of residence, and generally viewed as parasites providing little true value to Chinese society.

The state itself directed much trade and manufacturing; it manufactured weapons, for example, and operated shipyards, granaries, and mines. The system of roads was expanded and modernized, and new bridges, rest houses, and post stations for changing horses were added. Unlike the Romans, however, the Han rulers relied on waterways for the bulk of their transportation needs. To supplement the numerous major rivers crisscrossing the densely populated heartland of China, new canals were dug to facilitate the moving of goods from one end of the vast empire to the other.

The Han dynasty also began to move cautiously into foreign trade, mostly with neighboring areas in Central and Southeast Asia, although trade relations were established with countries as far away as India and the Mediterranean, where active contacts were maintained with the Roman Empire. Some of this long-distance trade was carried by sea through southern ports like Guangzhou (gwahng-JOE), but more was transported by overland caravans on the Silk Road and other routes that led westward into Central Asia.

New technology contributed to the economic prosperity of the Han era. Significant progress was achieved in such areas as textile manufacturing, water mills, and iron casting; skill at ironworking led to the production of steel a few centuries later. Paper was invented under the Han, and the development of the rudder and fore-and-aft rigging permitted ships to sail into the wind for the first time. Thus equipped, Chinese merchant ships carrying heavy cargoes could sail throughout the islands of Southeast Asia and into the Indian Ocean.

Imperial Expansion and the Origins of the Silk Road   The Han emperors continued the process of territorial expansion and consolidation that had begun under the Zhou and the Qin. Han rulers, notably Han Wudi (HAHN woo-DEE), or "Martial Emperor of Han," who ruled from 141 to 87 B.C.E., successfully completed the assimilation into the empire of the regions south of the Yangzi River, including the Red River delta in what is today northern Vietnam. Han armies also marched westward as far as the Caspian Sea, pacifying nomadic tribal peoples and extending China's boundary far into Central Asia.

The latter project apparently was originally planned as a means to fend off pressure from the nomadic Xiongnu peoples, who periodically threatened Chinese lands from their base area north of the Great Wall. In 138 B.C.E., Han Wudi dispatched the courtier Zhang Qian (JANG chee-AHN) on a mission westward into Central Asia to seek alliances with peoples living in the area against the common Xiongnu menace. Zhang Qian returned home with ample information about political and economic conditions in Central Asia. The new knowledge permitted the Han court to establish the first Chinese military presence in the area of the Taklimakan (tah-kluh-muh-KAHN) Desert and the Tian Shan (TEE-en SHAHN) (Heavenly Mountains). Eventually, this area would become known to the Chinese people as Xinjiang, or "new region."

Chinese commercial exchanges with peoples in Central Asia now began to expand dramatically. Eastward into China came grapes, precious metals, glass objects, and horses from Persia and Central Asia. Horses were of particular significance because Chinese military strategists had learned of the importance of cavalry in their battles against the Xiongnu and sought the sturdy Ferghana horses of Bactria to increase their own military effectiveness. In return, China exported goods, especially silk, to countries to the west.

Silk, a filament recovered from the cocoons of silkworms, had been produced in China since the fourth millennium B.C.E. Eventually, knowledge of the wonder product reached the outside world, and Chinese silk exports began to rise dramatically. By the second century B.C.E., the first items made from silk reached the Mediterranean Sea, stimulating the first significant contacts between China and Rome, its great counterpart in the west. The bulk of the trade went overland through Central Asia (thus earning this route its modern name, the Silk Road), although significant exchanges also took place via the maritime route. Silk became

MAP 3.3   The Han Empire

This map shows the territory under the control of the Han Empire at its greatest extent during the first century B.C.E. Note the Great Wall's placement relative to nomadic peoples.

a craze among Roman elites, leading to a vast outflow of silver from Rome to China and provoking the Roman emperor Tiberius to grumble that "the ladies and their baubles are transferring our money to foreigners."

The silk trade also stimulated a degree of mutual curiosity between China and other civilizations farther to the west. Roman authors such as Pliny the Elder and the geographer Strabo (who speculated that silk was produced from the leaves of a "silk tree") wrote of a strange land called "Seres" far to the east, while Chinese sources mentioned the empire of "Great Qin" at the far end of the Silk Road to the west. Of more immediate consequence was the increased communication that took place with societies in the South Asian subcontinent. The Han dynasty's adoption of Confucianism did not have much direct impact on the religious beliefs of the Chinese people, who continued to worship the pantheon of local deities and spirits of nature connected with popular Daoism. But in the first century C.E., a new salvationist faith appeared on the horizon as merchants from Central Asia brought Buddhist teachings to China for the first time. At first, its influence was limited, as no Buddhist text was translated into Chinese until the fifth century C.E. But the terrain was ripe for the introduction of a new religion into China, and the first Chinese monks departed for India shortly after the end of the Han dynasty.

The Decline and Fall of the Han   In 9 C.E., the reformist official Wang Mang (wahng MAHNG), who was troubled by the plight of the peasants, seized power from the Han court and declared the foundation of the Xin (SHEEN) (New) dynasty. The empire had been crumbling for decades. As frivolous or depraved rulers amused themselves with the pleasures of court life, the power and influence of the central government began to wane, and the great noble families filled the vacuum, amassing vast landed estates and transforming free farmers into tenants. Wang Mang tried to confiscate the great estates, restore the ancient well-field system, and abolish slavery. In so doing, however, he alienated powerful interests, who conspired to overthrow him. In 23 C.E., beset by administrative chaos and a collapse of the frontier defenses, Wang Mang was killed in a coup d'état.

For a time, strong leadership revived some of the glory of the early Han. (Chinese historians refer to the period after the Wang Mang revolt as the Later Han dynasty.) The court did attempt to reduce land taxes and carry out land resettlement programs. The growing popularity of nutritious crops like rice, wheat, and soybeans, along with the introduction of new crops such as alfalfa and grapes, helped boost food production. But the great landed families' firm grip on land and power continued. Weak rulers were isolated within their imperial chambers and dominated by eunuchs and other powerful court insiders. Official corruption and the concentration of land in the hands of the wealthy led to widespread peasant unrest.

The Han also continued to have problems with the Xiongnu beyond the Great Wall to the north. Professional armies recruited from among non-Chinese peoples along the periphery of the empire proved to be unreliable in both performance and loyalty. After attempts to pacify the Xiongnu leaders through negotiations failed to resolve the situation, Han rulers turned once again to military force. The threat from the north did not abate until the end of the first century C.E., when the alliance among the various nomadic groups fractured into disunity. The respite proved to be short-lived, however, as raids on Chinese territory continued intermittently up to the end of the dynasty, sometimes reaching almost to the gates of the capital city.

Buffeted by insurmountable problems within and without, in the late second century C.E., the dynasty entered a period of inexorable decline. The population, which had been estimated at about 60 million in China's first census in the year 2 C.E., had shrunk to less than one-third that number two hundred years later. In the early third century C.E., the dynasty was finally brought to an end when power was seized by Cao Cao (TSOW tsow), a general known to later generations as one of the main characters in the famous Chinese epic *The Romance of the Three Kingdoms*. But Cao Cao was unable to consolidate his power, and China entered a period of almost constant anarchy and internal divisions, compounded by invasions of northern nomadic peoples. The next great dynasty did not arise until the beginning of the seventh century, four hundred years later.

DAILY LIFE IN ANCIENT CHINA

Few social institutions have been as closely identified with China as the family. As in most agricultural civilizations, the family served as the basic economic and social unit in society. In traditional China, however, it took on an almost sacred quality as a microcosm of the entire social order.

The Role of the Family

In Neolithic times, the farm village, organized around the clan, was the basic social unit in China, at least in the core region of the Yellow River valley. Even then, however, the smaller family unit was becoming more important, at least among the nobility, who attached considerable significance to the veneration of their ancestors.

During the Zhou dynasty, the family took on increasing importance, in part because of the need for cooperation in agriculture. Rice had become the primary crop along the Yangzi River and in the provinces to the south because of its taste, its productivity, and its high nutrient value. But the cultivation of rice is highly labor-intensive. The seedlings must be planted in several inches of water in a nursery bed and then transferred individually to the paddy beds, which must be irrigated constantly. During the harvest, the stalks must be cut and the kernels carefully separated from the stalks and husks. As a result, children—and the labor they supplied—were considered essential to the survival of the family, not only during their youthful years but also later, when sons were expected to provide for their parents. Loyalty to family members came to be considered even more important than loyalty to the broader community or the state. Confucius commented that it is the mark of a civilized society that a son should protect his father even if the latter has committed a crime against the community.

At the crux of the concept of family was the idea of **filial piety**, which called on all members of the family to subordinate their personal needs and desires to the patriarchal head of the family. More broadly, it created a hierarchical system in which every family member had a place. All Chinese learned the **five relationships** that were the key to a proper social order. The son was subordinate to the father, the wife to her husband, the younger brother to the older brother, and all were subject to their king. The final relationship was the proper one between friend and friend. Only if all members of the family and the community as a whole behaved in a properly filial manner would society function effectively.

A stable family system based on obedient and hardworking members can serve as a bulwark for an efficient government, but putting loyalty to the family and the clan over loyalty to the state can also present a threat to a centralizing monarch. For that reason, the Qin dynasty attempted to destroy the clan system in China and assert the primacy of the state. Legalists even imposed heavy taxes on any family with more than two adult sons in order to break down the family concept. The Qin reportedly also originated the practice of organizing several family units into larger groups of five and ten families that would exercise mutual control and surveillance. Later dynasties continued the practice under the name of the **Bao-jia** (BOW-jah ["ow" as in "how"]) **system.**

But the efforts of the Qin to eradicate or at least reduce the importance of the family system ran against tradition and the dynamics of the Chinese economy, and under the Han dynasty, which followed the Qin, the family revived and increased in importance. With official encouragement, the family system began to take on the character that it would possess until our own day. The family was not only the basic economic unit; it was also the basic social unit for education, religious observances, and training in ethical principles.

Lifestyles

We know much more about the lifestyle of the elites than that of the common people in ancient China. The first houses for the former were probably constructed of wooden planks, but later Chinese mastered the art of building in tile and brick. By the first millennium B.C.E., most public buildings and the houses of the wealthy were probably constructed in this manner. The latter often had several wings surrounding a central courtyard to provide space for several generations under one roof, a style that continued down to modern times. By the second century B.C.E., most Chinese, however, probably lived in simple houses of mud, wooden planks, or brick with thatch or occasionally tile roofs. But in some areas, especially the loess (LESS) (a type of soil common in North China) regions of northern China, cave dwelling remained common down to modern times. The most famous cave dweller of modern times was Mao Zedong, who lived in a cave in Yan'an (yuh-NAHN) during his long struggle against Chiang Kai-shek.

Chinese houses usually had little furniture; most people squatted or sat with their legs spread out on the packed-mud floor. Chairs were apparently not introduced until the sixth or seventh century C.E. Clothing was simple, consisting of cotton trousers and shirts in the summer and wool or burlap in the winter.

The staple foods were millet in the north and rice in the south. Other common foods were wheat, barley, soybeans, mustard greens, and bamboo shoots. In early times, such foods were often consumed in a porridge, but by the Zhou dynasty, stir-frying in a wok was becoming common. When possible, the Chinese family would vary its diet of grain foods with vegetables, fruit (including pears, peaches, apricots, and plums), and fish or meat; but for most, such additions to the daily plate of rice, millet, or soybeans were a rare luxury.

Alcohol in the form of ale was drunk at least by the higher classes and by the early Zhou era had already begun to inspire official concern. According to the *Book of History*, "King Wen admonished ... the young nobles ... that they should not ordinarily use spirits; and throughout all the states he required that they should be drunk only on occasion of sacrifices, and that then virtue should preside so that there might be no drunkenness."[15] For the poorer classes, alcohol in any form was probably a rare luxury. Chinese legend hints that tea—a plant originally found in upland regions in southern China and Southeast Asia—was introduced by the mythical emperor Shen Nong. In fact, however, tea drinking did not become widespread in China until around 500 c.e. By then tea was lauded for its medicinal qualities and its capacity to soothe the spirit.

Cities

With the rise to power of the Qin, cities began to take on the central importance they would hold through later Chinese history. Urban centers were divided into neighborhoods—perhaps a forerunner of the grid pattern assumed by imperial cities under later dynasties—as a means of facilitating control over the population. As mentioned earlier, landed aristocrats, many of them former opponents of the Qin, were forcibly resettled in the new capital of Xianyang—a pattern that we shall see repeated, notably in France and Japan, in later centuries. Their villas and gardens aped the splendor of the imperial palace, which formed the centerpiece of the urban landscape.

Under the Qin and the Han, as never before, cities became the cultural hub of Chinese society, although their residents made up only a tiny proportion of the total population. In the crowded streets, haughty nobles sought to avoid rubbing shoulders with commoners, while merchants, workers, wandering gangs, and prostitutes relentlessly imitated the mannerisms of the elite. As a poem of the time satirically noted:

In the city, if they love to have their hair dressed up high,
Then everywhere else they dress their hair an inch higher.
In the city, if they love to enlarge their eyebrows,
Then everywhere else they will make their eyebrows cover half their
*   foreheads.*
In the city, if they love large sleeves,
Then everywhere else they will use up whole bolts of silk.[16]

The Humble Estate: Women in Ancient China

Male dominance was a key element in the social system of ancient China. As in many traditional societies, the male was considered of transcendent importance because of his role as food procurer or, in the case of farming communities, food producer. In ancient China, men worked in the fields and women raised children and served in the home. This differential in gender roles goes back to prehistoric times and is embedded in Chinese creation myths. According to legend, Fu Xi's wife Nu Wa (noo WAH) assisted her husband in organizing society by establishing the institution of marriage and the family. Yet Nu Wa was not just a household drudge. After Fu Xi's death, she became China's first female sovereign.

During ancient times, women apparently did not normally occupy formal positions of authority, but they often became a force in politics, especially at court, where wives of the ruler or other female members of the royal family were often influential in palace intrigues. Such activities were frowned on, however, as the following passage from *The Book of Songs* attests:

A clever man builds a city,
A clever woman lays one low;
With all her qualifications, that clever woman
Is but an ill-omened bird.
A woman with a long tongue
Is a flight of steps leading to calamity;
For disorder does not come from heaven,
But is brought about by women.
Among those who cannot be trained or taught
Are women and eunuchs.[17]

The nature of gender relationships was also graphically demonstrated in the Chinese written language. The character for man (男) combines the symbols for strength and rice field, while the character for woman (女) represents a person in a posture of deference and respect. The character for peace (安) is a woman under a roof. A wife is symbolized by a woman with a broom. Male chauvinism has deep linguistic roots in China.

Confucian thought, while not denigrating the importance of women as mothers and homemakers, accepted the dual roles of men and women in Chinese society. Men governed society. They carried on family ritual through the veneration of ancestors. They were the warriors, scholars, and ministers. Their dominant role was firmly enshrined in the legal system. Men were permitted to have more than one wife and to divorce a spouse who did not produce a male child. Women were denied the right to own property, and there was no dowry system in ancient China that would have provided the wife with a degree of financial security from her husband and his family. However, there were exceptions, including Ban Zhao (bahn ZHOW), who, although a woman, was one of the most prominent historians of the Han dynasty. But even she conceded that a woman's role in China was to be "humble, yielding, respectful and reverential" in her dealings with others. As the third-century C.E. poet Fu Xuan (foo SHWAHN), a woman, lamented:

How sad it is to be a woman
Nothing on earth is held so cheap.
No one is glad when a girl is born.
By her the family sets no store.
No one cries when she leaves her home
Sudden as clouds when the rain stops.[18]

CHINESE CULTURE

Modern knowledge about artistic achievements in ancient civilizations is limited because often little has survived the ravages of time. Fortunately, many ancient civilizations, such as Egypt and Mesopotamia, were located in relatively arid areas where many artifacts were preserved, even over thousands of years. In more humid regions, such as China and South Asia, the cultural residue left by the civilizations of antiquity has been adversely affected by climate.

As a result, relatively little remains of the cultural achievements of the prehistoric Chinese aside from Neolithic pottery and the relics found at the site of the Shang dynasty capital at Anyang. In recent years, a rich trove from the time of the Qin Empire has been unearthed near the tomb of Qin Shi Huangdi near Xian and at Han tombs nearby. But little remains of the literature of ancient China and almost none of the painting, architecture, and music.

Metalwork and Sculpture

Discoveries at archaeological sites indicate that ancient China was a society rich in cultural achievement. The pottery found at Neolithic sites such as Longshan and Yangshao exhibits a freshness and vitality of form and design, and the ornaments, such as rings and beads, show a strong aesthetic sense.

Bronze Casting

The pace of Chinese cultural development began to quicken during the Shang dynasty, which ruled in northern China from the sixteenth to the eleventh century B.C.E. At that time, objects cast in bronze began to appear. Various bronze vessels were produced for use in preparing and serving food and drink in the ancestral rites. Later vessels were used for decoration or for dining at court.

The method of casting used was one reason for the extraordinary quality of Shang bronze work. Bronze workers in most ancient civilizations used the lost-wax method, in which a model was first made in wax. After a clay mold had been formed around it, the model was heated so that the wax would melt away, and the empty space was filled with molten metal. In China, clay molds composed of several sections were tightly fitted together prior to the introduction of the liquid bronze. This technique, which had evolved from ceramic techniques used during the Neolithic period, enabled the artisans to apply the design directly to the mold and thus contributed to the clarity of line and rich surface decoration of the Shang bronzes.

Bronze casting became a large-scale business, and more than ten thousand vessels of an incredible variety of form and design survive today. Factories were located not only in the Yellow River valley but also in Sichuan province, in southern China. The art of bronze working continued into the Zhou dynasty, but the quality and originality declined. The Shang bronzes remain the pinnacle of creative art in ancient China.

One reason for the decline of bronze casting in China was the rise in popularity of iron. Ironmaking developed in China around the ninth or eighth century B.C.E., much later than in the Middle East, where it had been mastered almost a thousand years earlier. Once familiar with the process, however, the Chinese quickly moved to the forefront. Ironworkers in Europe and the Middle East, lacking the technology to achieve the high temperatures necessary to melt iron ore for casting, were forced to work with wrought iron, a cumbersome and expensive process. By the fourth century B.C.E., the Chinese had invented the technique of the blast furnace, powered by a worker operating a bellows. They were therefore able to manufacture cast iron ritual vessels and agricultural tools centuries before an equivalent technology appeared in the West.

Another reason for the deterioration of the bronze-casting tradition was the development of cheaper materials such as lacquerware and ceramics. Lacquer, made from resins obtained from the juices of sumac trees native to the region, had been produced since Neolithic times, and by the second century B.C.E. it had become a popular method of applying a hard coating to objects made of wood or fabric. Pottery, too, had existed since early times, but technological advances led to the production of a high-quality form of pottery covered with a brown or gray-green glaze, the latter known popularly as celadon. By the end of the first millennium B.C.E., both lacquerware and pottery had replaced bronze in popularity, much as plastic goods have replaced more expensive materials in our own time. This trend continued into the Han dynasty, as bronze was increasingly replaced by iron as the medium of choice. Less expensive to produce, iron was better able to satisfy the growing popular demand during a time of increasing economic affluence. Also during the Han, painting—often in the form of wall frescoes—became increasingly popular in the homes and tombs of the wealthy, although little has survived the ravages of time.

The First Emperor's Tomb   In 1974, in a remarkable discovery, farmers digging a well about 35 miles east of Xian unearthed a number of terra-cotta figures in an underground pit about one mile east of the burial mound of the First Emperor of Qin. Chinese archaeologists sent to work at the site discovered a vast terra-cotta army that they believed was a recreation of Qin Shi Huangdi's imperial guard, which was to accompany the emperor on his journey to the next world.

One of the astounding features of the terra-cotta army is its size. The army is enclosed in four pits that were originally encased in a wooden framework, which has disintegrated. More than a thousand figures have been unearthed in the first pit, along with horses, wooden chariots, and seven thousand bronze weapons. Archaeologists estimate that there are more than six thousand figures in that pit alone.

Equally impressive is the quality of the work. Slightly larger than life size, the figures were molded of finely textured clay and then fired and painted. The detail on the uniforms is realistic and sophisticated, but the most striking feature is the individuality of the facial features of the soldiers. Apparently, ten different head shapes were used and were then modeled further by hand to reflect the variety of ethnic groups and personality types in the army.

The discovery of the terra-cotta army also shows that the Chinese had come a long way from the human sacrifices that had taken place at the death of Shang sovereigns more than a thousand years earlier. But the project must have been ruinously expensive and is additional evidence of the burden the Qin ruler imposed on his subjects. One historian has estimated that one-third of the national income in Qin times may have been spent on preparations for the ruler's afterlife. The emperor's mausoleum has not yet been unearthed, but it is enclosed in a mound nearly 250 feet high surrounded by a rectangular wall extending for nearly 4 miles. According to the Han historian Sima Qian, the ceiling was a replica of the heavens, while the floor contained a relief model of the entire Qin kingdom, with rivers flowing in mercury. According to tradition, traps were set within the mausoleum to prevent intruders, and the workers applying the final touches were buried alive in the tomb with its secrets.

Language and Literature

Precisely when writing developed in China cannot be determined, but certainly by Shang times, as the oracle bones demonstrate, the Chinese had developed a simple but functional script. Like many other languages of antiquity, it was primarily ideographic and pictographic in form. Symbols, usually called characters, were created to represent an idea or to form a picture of the object to be represented. For example, the Chinese characters for mountain (山), the sun (日), and the moon (月) were meant to represent the objects themselves. Other characters, such as "big" (大) (a man with his arms outstretched), represent an idea. The character for "east" (東) symbolizes the sun coming up behind the trees.

Each character, of course, would be given a sound by the speaker when pronounced. In other cultures, this process led to the abandonment of the system of ideographs and the adoption of a written language based on phonetic symbols. The Chinese language, however, has never entirely abandoned its original ideographic format, although the phonetic element has developed into a significant part of the individual character. In that sense, the Chinese written language is virtually unique in the world today.

One reason the language retained its ideographic quality may have been the aesthetics of the written characters. By the time of the Qin dynasty, if not earlier, the written language came to be seen as an art form as well as a means of communication, and calligraphy became one of the most prized forms of painting in China.

	sun	hill	water	man	woman
Mesopotamian Cuneiform					
Egyptian Hieroglyphics					
Oracle Bone Script					
Modern Chinese	日	山	水	男	女

Ripley Center, Smithsonian Institution, Washington, DC/Photo © William J. Duiker

Pictographs in Ancient Cultures. *Virtually all written language evolved from pictographs—representations of physical objects that were eventually stylized and tied to sounds in the spoken language. This chart shows pictographs that originated independently in three ancient cultures and the stylized modern characters into which the Chinese oracle pictographs evolved.*

Even more important, if the written language had developed in the direction of a phonetic alphabet, it could no longer have served as the written system for all the peoples of the expanding Chinese civilization. Although the vast majority spoke a tongue derived from a parent Sinitic language (a system distinguished by variations in pitch, a characteristic that gives Chinese its lilting quality even today), the languages spoken in various regions of the country differed from each other in pronunciation and to a lesser degree in vocabulary and syntax; for the most part, they were (and are today) mutually unintelligible.

The Chinese answer to this problem was to give all the spoken languages the same writing system. Although any character might be pronounced differently in different regions of China, that character would be written the same way (after the standardization undertaken under the Qin). Written characters could therefore be read by educated Chinese from one end of the country to the other. This became the language of the bureaucracy and the vehicle for the transmission of Chinese culture from the Great Wall to the southern border and beyond. The written language was not identical to the spoken form, however; it eventually evolved its own vocabulary and grammatical structure, and as a result, users of written Chinese required special training.

The earliest extant form of Chinese literature dates from the Zhou dynasty. It was written on silk or strips of bamboo and consisted primarily of historical records such as the *Rites of Zhou*, philosophical treatises such as the *Analects* and *The Way of the Tao*, and poetry, as recorded in *The Book of Songs* and the *Song of the South*. In later years, when Confucian principles had been elevated to a state ideology, the key works identified with the Confucian school were integrated into a set of so-called Confucian Classics. These works became required reading for generations of Chinese schoolchildren and introduced them to the forms of behavior that would be required of them as adults.

By the Han dynasty, there was considerable experimentation with new forms of expression in literature. Poetry and philosophical essays continued to be popular, but historical writing became the primary form of literary creativity. Historians such as Sima Qian and Ban Gu (the dynasty's official historian and the older brother of the female historian Ban Zhao) wrote works that became models for later dynastic histories. These historical works combined political and social history with biographies of key figures. Like so much literary work in China, their primary purpose was moral and political—to explain the underlying reasons for the rise and fall of individual human beings and dynasties.

Music

From early times in China, music was viewed not just as an aesthetic pleasure but also as a means of achieving political order and refining the human character. In fact, music may have originated as an accompaniment to sacred rituals at the royal court. According to the *Historical Records*, written during the Han dynasty, "When our sage-kings of the past instituted rites and music, their objective was far from making people indulge in the ... amusements of singing and dancing.... Music is produced to purify the heart, and rites introduced to rectify the behavior."[19] Eventually, however, music began to be appreciated for its own sake as well as to accompany singing and dancing.

A wide variety of musical instruments were used, including flutes, various stringed instruments, bells and chimes, drums, and gourds. Bells cast in bronze were first used as musical instruments in the Shang period; they were hung in rows and struck with a wooden mallet. The finest were produced during the mid-Zhou era and are considered among the best examples of early bronze work in China. Some weighed more than two tons and, in combination, covered a range of several octaves. Bronze bells have not been found in any other contemporary civilization and are considered one of the great cultural achievements of ancient China. The largest known bell dating from the Roman Empire, for example, is less than 3 inches high.

By the late Zhou era, bells had begun to give way as the instrument of choice to strings and wind instruments, and the purpose of music shifted from ceremony to entertainment. This led conservative critics to rail against the onset of an age of debauchery.

Ancient historians stressed the relationship between music and court life, but it is highly probable that music, singing, and dancing were equally popular among the common people. The *Book of History*, purporting to describe conditions in the late third millennium B.C.E., suggests that ballads emanating from the popular culture were welcomed at court. Nevertheless, court music and popular music differed in several respects. Among other things, popular music was more likely to be motivated by the desire for pleasure than for the purpose of law and order and moral uplift. Those differences continued to be reflected in the evolution of music in China down to modern times.

CHRONOLOGY

ANCIENT CHINA

?–c. 1570 B.C.E.	Xia dynasty
c. 1570–c. 1045 B.C.E.	Shang dynasty
c. 1045–221 B.C.E.	Zhou dynasty
551–479 B.C.E.	Life of Confucius
403–221 B.C.E.	Period of the Warring States
370–290 B.C.E.	Life of Mencius
221–206 B.C.E.	Qin dynasty
259–210 B.C.E.	Life of the First Emperor of Qin
202 B.C.E–221 C.E.	Han Dynasty

MindTap is a fully online, highly personalized learning experience built upon Cengage Learning content. MindTap combines student learning tools—readings, multimedia, activities, and assessments—into a singular Learning Path that guides students through their course.

4

THE CIVILIZATION OF THE GREEKS

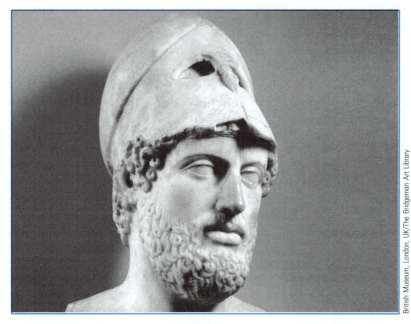

A bust of Pericles

British Museum, London, UK/The Bridgeman Art Library

CHAPTER OUTLINE

• Early Greece • The Greek City-States (c. 750–c. 500 B.C.E.) • The High Point of Greek Civilization: Classical Greece • The Rise of Macedonia and the Conquests of Alexander • The World of the Hellenistic Kingdoms

EARLY GREECE

Geography played an important role in Greek history. Compared to Mesopotamia and Egypt, Greece occupied a small area, a mountainous peninsula that encompassed only 45,000 square miles of territory, about the size of the state of Louisiana. The mountains and the sea were especially significant. Much of Greece consists of small plains and river valleys surrounded by mountain ranges 8,000 to 10,000 feet high. The mountains isolated Greeks from one another, causing Greek communities to follow their own separate paths and develop their own ways of life. Over a period of time, these communities became so fiercely attached to their independence that they were willing to fight one another to gain advantage. No doubt the small size of these independent Greek communities fostered participation in political affairs and unique cultural expressions, but the rivalry among them also led to the bitter warfare that ultimately devastated Greek society.

The sea also influenced Greek society. Greece had a long seacoast, dotted by bays and inlets that provided numerous harbors. The Greeks also inhabited a number of islands to the west, south, and east of the Greek mainland. It is no accident that the Greeks became seafarers who sailed out into the Aegean and Mediterranean Seas to make contact with the outside world and later to establish colonies that would spread Greek civilization throughout the Mediterranean region.

Topography helped determine the major territories into which Greece was ultimately divided. South of the Gulf of Corinth was the Peloponnesus (pell-uh-puh-NEE-suss), virtually an island attached by a tiny isthmus to the mainland. Consisting mostly of hills, mountains, and small valleys, the Peloponnesus was the location of Sparta, as well as the site of Olympia, where athletic games were held. Northeast of the Peloponnesus was the Attic peninsula (or Attica), the home of Athens, hemmed in by mountains to the north and west and surrounded by the sea to the south and east. Northwest of Attica was Boeotia (bee-OH-shuh) in central Greece, with its chief city of Thebes (THEEBZ). To the north of Boeotia was Thessaly, which contained the largest plains and became a great producer of grain and horses. To the north of Thessaly lay Macedonia, which was not of much importance in Greek history until 338 B.C.E., when a Macedonian king Philip II conquered the Greeks.

Minoan Crete   The earliest civilization in the Aegean region emerged on the large island of Crete, southeast of the Greek mainland. A Bronze Age civilization that used metals, especially bronze, in making weapons had been established there by 2800 B.C.E. This civilization was discovered at the turn of the twentieth century by the English archaeologist Arthur Evans, who named it "Minoan" (mih-NOH-uhn) after Minos (MY-nuss), a legendary king of Crete. In language and religion, the Minoans were not Greek, although they did have some influence on the peoples of the Greek mainland.

Evans's excavations on Crete unearthed an enormous palace complex at Knossus (NOSS-suss), near modern Iràklion (Heracleion), that was most likely the center of a far-ranging "sea empire," probably largely commercial. We know from the archaeological remains that the people of Minoan Crete were accustomed to sea travel and had made contact with the more advanced civilization of Egypt. Egyptian

MAP 4.1 Ancient Greece (c. 750–338 B.C.E.)

Between 750 and 500 B.C.E., Greek civilization witnessed the emergence of the city-state as the central institution in Greek life and the Greeks' colonization of the Mediterranean and Black Seas. Classical Greece lasted from about 500 to 338 B.C.E. and encompassed the high points of Greek civilization in arts, science, philosophy, and politics, as well as the Persian Wars and the Peloponnesian War.

products have been found in Crete and Cretan products in Egypt. Minoan Cretans also had contacts with and exerted influence on the Greek-speaking inhabitants of the Greek mainland.

The Minoan civilization reached its height between 2000 and 1450 B.C.E. The palace at Knossus, the royal seat of the kings, was an elaborate structure that included numerous private living rooms for the royal family and workshops for making decorated vases, ivory figurines, and jewelry. Even bathrooms with elaborate drains, like those found at Mohenjo-Daro in India, were part of the complex. The rooms were decorated with brightly colored frescoes showing sporting events and nature scenes. Storerooms in the palace held enormous jars of oil, wine, and grain, paid as taxes in kind to the king.

The centers of Minoan civilization on Crete eventually suffered a collapse. Many historians believe that a tsunami triggered by a powerful volcanic eruption on the island of Thera was responsible for destroying towns and ships on the north coast of Crete, while volcanic ash devastated the land. Although people began to rebuild, there is evidence that mainland Greeks, known as the Mycenaeans, invaded and pillaged many centers, including Knossus, which was destroyed around 1450 B.C.E.

The First Greek State: Mycenae The term *Mycenaean* (my-suh-NEE-un) is derived from Mycenae (my-SEE-nee), a remarkable fortified site excavated by the amateur German archaeologist Heinrich Schliemann (HYN-rikh SHLEE-mahn) starting in 1870. Mycenae was one center in a Mycenaean Greek civilization that flourished between 1600 and 1100 B.C.E. The Mycenaean Greeks were part of the Indo-European family of peoples who spread from their original location into southern and western Europe, India, and Persia. One group entered the territory of Greece from the north around 1900 B.C.E. and eventually managed to gain control of the Greek mainland and develop a civilization.

Mycenaean civilization, which reached its high point between 1400 and 1200 B.C.E., consisted of a number of powerful monarchies centered in fortified palace complexes. Like Mycenae itself, the palaces were built on hills and surrounded by gigantic stone walls. These various centers of power probably formed a loose confederacy of independent states, with Mycenae the strongest.

The Mycenaeans were above all a warrior people who prided themselves on their heroic deeds in battle. Archaeological evidence indicates that the Mycenaean monarchies also developed an extensive commercial network. Mycenaean pottery has been found throughout the Mediterranean basin, in Syria and Egypt to the east and Sicily and southern Italy to the west. But some scholars also believe that the Mycenaeans, led by Mycenae itself, spread outward militarily, conquering Crete and making it part of the Mycenaean world. The most famous of all their supposed military adventures has come down to us in the epic poetry of Homer. Did the Mycenaean Greeks, led by Agamemnon, king of Mycenae, sack the city of Troy on the northwestern coast of Asia Minor around 1250 B.C.E.? Scholars have debated this question ever since Schliemann began his excavations in 1870. Some believe that Homer's account does have a basis in fact, although there is little archaeological evidence to support it.

By the late thirteenth century, Mycenaean Greece was showing signs of serious trouble. Mycenae itself was burned around 1190 B.C.E., and other Mycenaean centers show a similar pattern of destruction as new waves of Greek-speaking invaders moved into Greece from the north. By 1100 B.C.E., the Mycenaean culture was coming to an end, and the Greek world was entering a new period of considerable insecurity.

The Greeks in a Dark Age (c. 1100–c. 750 B.C.E.) After the collapse of Mycenaean civilization, Greece entered a difficult era of declining population and falling food production. Because of the difficult conditions and our lack of knowledge about the period, historians refer to it as the Dark Age. Not until 850 B.C.E. did farming—and Greece itself—revive.

During the Dark Age, large numbers of Greeks left the mainland and migrated across the Aegean Sea to various islands and especially to the southwestern shore of Asia Minor, a strip of territory that came to be called Ionia (y-OH-nee-uh). Two other major groups of Greeks settled in established parts of Greece. The Aeolian (ee-OH-lee-un) Greeks of northern and central Greece colonized the large island of Lesbos and the adjacent territory of the mainland. The Dorians (DOR-ee-unz) established themselves in southwestern Greece, especially in the Peloponnesus, as well as on some of the south Aegean islands, including Crete.

As trade and economic activity began to recover, iron replaced bronze in the construction of weapons, making them affordable for more people. At some point in the eighth century B.C.E., the Greeks adopted the Phoenician alphabet to give themselves a new system of writing. And near the very end of the Dark Age appeared the work of Homer, who has come to be viewed as one of the greatest poets of all time.

Homer and Homeric Greece   The *Iliad* and the *Odyssey*, the first great epic poems of early Greece, were based on stories that had been passed down from generation to generation. It is generally assumed that Homer made use of these oral traditions to compose the *Iliad*, his epic poem of the Trojan War. The war was sparked by Paris, a prince of Troy, who kidnapped Helen, wife of the king of the Greek state of Sparta, outraging all the Greeks. Under the leadership of the Spartan king's brother, Agamemnon of Mycenae, the Greeks attacked Troy. After ten years of combat, the Greeks finally sacked the city. The *Iliad* is not so much the story of the war itself, however, as it is the tale of the Greek hero Achilles (uh-KIL-eez) and how the "wrath of Achilles" led to disaster. The *Odyssey*, Homer's other masterpiece, is an epic romance that recounts the journeys of one of the Greek heroes, Odysseus, from the fall of Troy until his eventual return to his wife, Penelope, twenty years later.

Although the *Iliad* and the *Odyssey* supposedly deal with the heroes of the Mycenaean age of the thirteenth century B.C.E., many scholars believe that they really describe the social conditions of the Dark Age. According to the Homeric view, Greece was a society based on agriculture in which a landed warrior-aristocracy controlled much wealth and exercised considerable power. Homer's world reflects the values of aristocratic heroes.

Homer's Enduring Importance   This, of course, explains the importance of Homer to later generations of Greeks. Homer did not so much record history as make it. The Greeks regarded the *Iliad* and the *Odyssey* as authentic history. They gave the Greeks an idealized past, somewhat like the concept of the golden age in ancient China, with a legendary age of heroes, and the poems came to be used as standard texts for the education of generations of Greek males. As one Athenian stated, "my father was anxious to see me develop into a good man ... and as a means to this end he compelled me to memorize all of Homer."[1] The values Homer inculcated were essentially the aristocratic values of courage and honor. It was important to strive for the excellence befitting a hero, which the Greeks called *arete*. In the warrior-aristocratic world of Homer, *arete* is won in a struggle or contest. Through his willingness to fight, the hero protects his family and friends, preserves his own honor and his family's, and earns his reputation.

In the Homeric world, aristocratic women, too, were expected to pursue excellence. Penelope, for example, the wife of Odysseus (oh-DISS-ee-uss), the hero of the *Odyssey*, remains faithful to her husband and displays great courage and intelligence in preserving their household during her husband's long absence. Upon his return, Odysseus praises her for her excellence: "Madame, there is not a man in the wide world who could find fault with you. For your fame has reached heaven itself, like that of some perfect king, ruling a populous and mighty state with the fear of god in his heart, and upholding the right."[2]

To later generations of Greeks, these heroic values formed the core of aristocratic virtue, a fact that explains the tremendous popularity of Homer as an educational tool. Homer gave to the Greeks a single universally accepted model of heroism, honor, and nobility. But in time, as a new world of city-states emerged in Greece, new values of cooperation and community also transformed what the Greeks learned from Homer.

THE GREEK CITY-STATES (C. 750–C. 500 B.C.E.)

During the Dark Age, Greek villages gradually expanded and evolved into independent city-states. In the eighth century B.C.E., Greek civilization burst forth with new energies, beginning the period that historians have called the Archaic Age of Greece. Two major developments stand out in this era: the evolution of the city-state, or what the Greeks called a **polis** (plural, *poleis*), as the central institution in Greek life and the Greeks' colonization of the Mediterranean and Black Seas.

The *Polis*

In the most basic sense, a *polis* (POH-liss) could be defined as a small but autonomous political unit in which all major political, social, and religious activities were carried out at one central location. The *polis* encompassed a town or city or even village and its surrounding countryside. But each had a central place where the citizens of the *polis* could assemble for political, social, and religious activities. In some *poleis*, this central meeting point was a hill, like the Acropolis in Athens, which could serve as a place of refuge during an attack and later at some sites came to be the religious center on which temples and public monuments were erected. Below the acropolis would be an *agora*, an open space that served both as a market and as a place where citizens could assemble.

Poleis varied greatly in size, from a few square miles to a few hundred square miles. They also varied in population. Athens had a population of about 250,000 by the fifth century B.C.E. But most *poleis* were much smaller, consisting of only a few hundred to several thousand people.

Although our word *politics* is derived from the Greek term *polis*, the *polis* itself was much more than a political institution. It was a community of citizens in which all political, economic, social, cultural, and religious activities were focused. As a community, the *polis* consisted of citizens with political rights (adult males), citizens with no political rights (women and children), and noncitizens (slaves and resident aliens). All citizens of a *polis* possessed rights, but these rights were coupled with responsibilities. The Greek philosopher Aristotle argued that the citizen did not just belong to himself: "We must rather regard every citizen as belonging to the state." However, the loyalty that citizens had to their city-states also had a negative side. City-states distrusted one another, and the division of Greece into fiercely patriotic independent units helped bring about its ruin.

A New Military System: The Greek Way of War   As the *polis* developed, so did a new military system. In earlier times, wars in Greece had been fought by aristocratic cavalry soldiers—nobles on horseback. These aristocrats, who were large landowners, also dominated the political life of their *poleis*. But by the end of the eighth century B.C.E., a new military order came into being that was based on **hoplites** (HAHP-lyts), heavily armed infantrymen who wore bronze or leather helmets, breastplates, and greaves (shin guards). Each carried a round shield, a short sword, and a thrusting spear about 9 feet long. Hoplites advanced into battle as a unit, shoulder to shoulder, forming a **phalanx** (a rectangular formation) in tight order, usually eight ranks deep. As long as the hoplites kept their order, were not outflanked, and did not break, they either secured victory or, at the very least, suffered no harm. The phalanx was easily routed, however, if it broke its order. Thus, the safety of the phalanx depended above all on the solidarity and discipline of its members. As one seventh-century B.C.E. poet noted, a good hoplite was "a short man firmly placed upon his legs, with a courageous heart, not to be uprooted from the spot where he plants his legs."[3]

The hoplite force had political as well as military repercussions. The aristocratic cavalry was now outdated. Since each hoplite provided his own armor, men of property, both aristocrats and small farmers, made up the new phalanx. Those who could become hoplites and fight for the state could also challenge aristocratic control. Thus, the development of the hoplite and phalanx became an important factor in the rise of democracy in Greece.

In the world of the Greek city-states, war became an integral part of the Greek way of life. The Greek philosopher Plato described war as "always existing by nature between every Greek city-state."[4] The Greeks created a tradition of warfare that became a prominent element of Western civilization. For example, the Greeks devised excellent weapons and body armor, making effective use of technological improvements. Greek armies included a wide number of citizen-soldiers, who gladly accepted the need for training and discipline, giving them an edge over their opponents' often far-larger armies of mercenaries. Moreover, the Greeks displayed a willingness to engage the enemy head-on, thus deciding a battle quickly and with as few casualties as possible. Finally, the Greeks demonstrated the effectiveness of heavy infantry in determining the outcome of a battle. All these features of Greek warfare remained part of Western warfare for centuries.

Colonization and the Growth of Trade   Between 750 and 550 B.C.E., large numbers of Greeks left their homeland to settle in distant lands. The growing gulf between rich and poor, overpopulation, and the development of trade were all factors that spurred the establishment of colonies.

Each colony was founded as a *polis* and was usually independent of the mother *polis* (the *metropolis*) that had established it.

In the western Mediterranean, new Greek settlements were established along the coastline of southern Italy, southern France, eastern Spain, and northern Africa west of Egypt. To the north, the Greeks set up colonies in Thrace, where they sought good agricultural lands to grow grains. Greeks also settled along the shores of the Black Sea and secured the approaches to it with cities on the Hellespont and Bosporus, most notably Byzantium, site of the later Constantinople (Istanbul). In establishing these settlements, the Greeks spread their culture throughout the Mediterranean basin. Moreover, colonization helped the Greeks foster a greater sense of Greek identity. Before the eighth century, Greek communities were mostly isolated from one another, and many neighboring states were on unfriendly terms. Once Greeks from different communities went abroad and found peoples with unfamiliar languages and customs, they became more aware of their own linguistic and cultural similarities.

Colonization also led to increased trade and industry. The Greeks on the mainland sent their pottery, wine, and olive oil to the colonized areas; in return, they received grains and metals from the west and fish, timber, wheat, metals, and slaves from the Black Sea region. In many *poleis*, the expansion of trade and industry created a new group of rich men who perceived that the decisions of the *polis* could affect their businesses. They now desired new political privileges but found them impossible to gain because of the power of the ruling aristocrats. This desire for change soon led to political crisis in many Greek states.

Tyranny in the Greek *Polis* The aspirations of the new industrial and commercial groups laid the groundwork for the rise of **tyrants** in the seventh and sixth centuries B.C.E. They were not necessarily oppressive or wicked, as the modern English word *tyrant* connotes. Greek tyrants were rulers who came to power in an unconstitutional way; a tyrant was not subject to the law. Many tyrants were actually aristocrats who opposed the control of the ruling aristocratic faction in their cities. The support for the tyrants, however, came from the new rich who made their money in trade and industry, as well as from poor peasants who were becoming increasingly indebted to landholding aristocrats. Both groups were opposed to the domination of political power by aristocratic **oligarchies** (*oligarchy* means "rule by the few").

Once in power, the tyrants built new marketplaces, temples, and walls that not only glorified the city but also enhanced their own popularity. Tyrants also favored the interests of merchants and traders. Despite these achievements, however, **tyranny** was largely extinguished by the end of the sixth century B.C.E. Greeks believed in the rule of law, and tyranny made a mockery of that ideal.

Although tyranny did not last, it played a significant role in the evolution of Greek history by ending the rule of narrow aristocratic oligarchies. Once the tyrants were eliminated, the door was opened to the participation of new and more people in governing the affairs of the community. Although this trend culminated in the development of democracy in some communities, in other states expanded oligarchies of one kind or another managed to remain in power. Greek states exhibited considerable variety in their governmental structures; this can perhaps best be seen by examining the two most famous and most powerful Greek city-states, Sparta and Athens.

Sparta

Located in the southeastern Peloponnesus, Sparta, like other Greek states, faced the need for more land. Instead of sending its people out to found new colonies, the Spartans conquered the neighboring Laconians and later, beginning around 730 B.C.E., undertook the conquest of neighboring Messenia despite its larger size and population. Messenia possessed a large, fertile plain ideal for growing grain. After its conquest in the seventh century B.C.E., the Messenians, like the Laconians earlier, were reduced to serfdom—they were known as **helots** (HEL-uts), a name derived from a Greek word for "capture"—and forced to work for the Spartans. But the helots drastically outnumbered the Spartan citizens (some estimates are ten to one) and constantly threatened to revolt. To ensure control over them, the Spartans made a conscious decision to create a military state.

The New Sparta   Between 800 and 600 B.C.E., the Spartans instituted a series of reforms that are associated with the name of the lawgiver Lycurgus (ly-KUR-guss). Although historians are not sure that Lycurgus ever existed, there is no doubt about the result of the reforms that were made: the lives of Spartans were now rigidly organized and tightly controlled (to this day, the word *spartan* means "highly self-disciplined"). Boys were taken from their mothers at the age of seven and put under control of the state. They lived in military-style barracks, where they were subjected to harsh discipline to make them tough and given an education that stressed military training and obedience to authority. At twenty, Spartan males were enrolled in the army for regular military service. Although allowed to marry, they continued to live in the barracks and ate all their meals in public dining halls with their fellow soldiers. Meals were simple; the famous Spartan black broth consisted of a piece of pork boiled in blood, salt, and vinegar, causing a visitor who ate in a public mess to remark that he now understood why Spartans were not afraid to die. At thirty, Spartan males were recognized as mature and allowed to vote in the assembly and live at home, but they remained in military service until the age of sixty.

While their husbands remained in military barracks until age thirty, Spartan women lived at home. Because of this separation, Spartan women had greater freedom of movement. Permitted to own and inherit land, Spartan women had greater power in the household than was common for women elsewhere in Greece and could even supervise large estates. They were encouraged to exercise and remain fit to bear and raise healthy children. Like the men, Spartan women engaged in athletic exercises in the nude. Many Spartan women upheld the strict Spartan values, expecting their husbands and sons to be brave in war. The story is told that as a Spartan mother was burying her son, an old woman came up to her and said, "You poor woman, what a misfortune." "No," replied the mother, "because I bore him so that he might die for Sparta, and that is what has happened, as I wished."[5]

The Spartan State   The so-called Lycurgan reforms also reorganized the Spartan government, creating an oligarchy. Two kings from different families were primarily responsible for military affairs and served as the leaders of the Spartan army on its campaigns. A group of five men, known as the *ephors* (EFF-urz), were elected each year and were responsible for the education of youth and the conduct of all citizens. A council of elders, composed of the two kings and twenty-eight male citizens over the age of sixty, decided on the issues that would be presented to an assembly. This assembly of all male citizens did not debate but only voted on the proposals put before it by the council of elders. The assembly also elected the council of elders and the ephors.

To make their new military state secure, the Spartans deliberately turned their backs on the outside world. Foreigners, who might bring in new ideas, were discouraged from visiting Sparta. Nor were Spartans, except for military reasons, allowed to travel abroad, where they might pick up new ideas dangerous to the stability of the state. Likewise, Spartan citizens were discouraged from studying philosophy, literature, or the arts—subjects that might encourage new thoughts. The art of war was the Spartan ideal, and all other arts were frowned on.

In the sixth century, Sparta used its military might and the fear it inspired to gain greater control of the Peloponnesus by organizing an alliance of almost all the Peloponnesian states. Sparta's strength enabled it to dominate this Peloponnesian League and determine its policies. By 500 B.C.E., the Spartans had organized a powerful military state that maintained order and stability in the Peloponnesus. Raised from early childhood to believe that total loyalty to the Spartan state was the basic reason for existence, the Spartans viewed their strength as justification for their militaristic ideals and regimented society.

Athens

By 700 B.C.E., Athens had established a unified *polis* on the peninsula of Attica. Although early Athens had been ruled by a monarchy, by the seventh century B.C.E. it had fallen under the control of its aristocrats. They possessed the best land and controlled political and religious life by means of a council of nobles, assisted by a board of nine officials called archons. Although there was an assembly of full citizens, it possessed few powers.

Near the end of the seventh century B.C.E., Athens faced political turmoil because of serious economic problems. Increasing numbers of Athenian farmers found themselves sold into slavery when they were unable to repay loans they had obtained from their aristocratic neighbors, pledging themselves as collateral. Repeatedly, there were cries to cancel the debts and give land to the poor.

The Reforms of Solon

The ruling Athenian aristocrats responded to this crisis by choosing Solon (SOH-lun), a reform-minded aristocrat, as sole archon in 594 B.C.E. and giving him full power to make changes. Solon canceled all land debts, outlawed new loans based on humans as collateral, and freed people who had fallen into slavery for debts. He refused, however, to carry out land redistribution and hence failed to deal with the basic cause of the economic crisis.

Like his economic reforms, Solon's political measures were also a compromise. Though by no means eliminating the power of the aristocracy, they opened the door to the participation of new people, especially the nonaristocratic wealthy, in the government. But Solon's reforms, though popular, did not solve Athens's problems. Aristocratic factions continued to vie for power, and the poorer peasants resented Solon's failure to institute land redistribution. Internal strife finally led to the very institution Solon had hoped to avoid—tyranny. Pisistratus (puh-SIS-truh-tuss), an aristocrat, seized power in 560 B.C.E. Pursuing a foreign policy that aided Athenian trade, Pisistratus remained popular with the mercantile and industrial classes. But the Athenians rebelled against his son and ended the tyranny in 510 B.C.E. Although the aristocrats attempted to reestablish an aristocratic oligarchy, Cleisthenes (KLYSS-thuh-neez), another aristocratic reformer, opposed this plan and, with the backing of the Athenian people, gained the upper hand in 508 B.C.E.

The Reforms of Cleisthenes   Cleisthenes created the Council of Five Hundred, chosen by lot by the ten tribes in which all citizens had been enrolled. The council was responsible for the administration of both foreign and financial affairs and prepared the business that would be handled by the assembly. This assembly of all male citizens had final authority in the passing of laws after free and open debate; thus, Cleisthenes's reforms had reinforced the central role of the assembly of citizens in the Athenian political system.

The reforms of Cleisthenes created the foundations for Athenian democracy. More changes would come in the fifth century, when the Athenians themselves would begin to use the word *democracy* to describe their system (from the Greek words *demos*, "people," and *kratia*, "power"). By 500 B.C.E., Athens was more united than it had been and was on the verge of playing a more important role in Greek affairs.

Foreign Influence on Early Greek Culture   As the Greeks moved out into the eastern Mediterranean, they came into increased contact with the older civilizations of the Near East and Egypt, which had a strong impact on early Greek culture. The Greeks adopted new gods and goddesses as well as new myths—such as the story of the flood—from Mesopotamian traditions. Greek pottery in the eighth and seventh centuries began to use new motifs—such as floral designs—borrowed from the Near East. Greek sculpture, particularly that of the Ionian Greek settlements in southwestern Asia Minor, demonstrates the impact of the considerably older Egyptian civilization. There we first see the life-size stone statues of young male nudes known as *kouros* (KOO-rohss) figures. The *kouros* bears a strong resemblance to Egyptian statues of the New Kingdom. The figures are not realistic but stiff, the face bearing the hint of a smile; one leg is advanced ahead of the other, and the arms are held rigidly at the sides of the body.

Greek literature was also the beneficiary of a Greek alphabet that owed much to the Phoenicians. The Greeks adopted some of the twenty-two Phoenician consonants as Greek consonants and used other symbols to represent vowel sounds, which the Phoenicians did not have. In the process, the Greeks created a truly phonetic alphabet, probably between 800 and 750 B.C.E., thus making the Greek language easier to read and write than Egyptian hieroglyphics and Mesopotamian cuneiform. Greek could be used to record laws and commercial transactions and to write the poetry, philosophical treatises, and other literary works that distinguish Greek culture.

THE HIGH POINT OF GREEK CIVILIZATION: CLASSICAL GREECE

Classical Greece is the name given to the period of Greek history from around 500 B.C.E. to the conquest of Greece by the Macedonian king Philip II in 338 B.C.E. Many of the cultural contributions of the Greeks occurred during this period. The age began with a mighty confrontation between the Greek states and the mammoth Persian Empire.

The Challenge of Persia   As the Greeks spread throughout the Mediterranean, they came into contact with the Persian Empire to the east. In his play *The Persians*, the Greek playwright Aeschylus reflected what some Greeks perceived to be the essential difference between themselves and the Persians. The Persian queen, curious to find out more about the Athenians, asks, "Who commands them? Who is shepherd of their host?" The chorus responds: "They are slaves to none, nor are they subject."[6] Thus, at least, some Greeks saw the struggle with the Persians as a contest between freedom and slavery. To the Greeks, a person was a citizen of the state, not a subject.

The Ionian Greek cities in western Asia Minor had already fallen subject to the Persian Empire by the mid-sixth century B.C.E. An unsuccessful revolt by the Ionian cities in 499 B.C.E.—assisted by the Athenian navy—led the Persian ruler Darius (duh-RY-uss) to seek revenge by attacking the mainland Greeks. In 490 B.C.E., the Persians landed an army on the plain of Marathon, only 26 miles from Athens. The Athenians and their allies were clearly outnumbered, but led by Miltiades (mil-TY-uh-deez), one of the Athenian leaders who insisted on attacking, the Greek hoplites charged across the plain of Marathon and crushed the Persian forces.

Xerxes (ZURK-seez), the new Persian monarch after the death of Darius in 486 B.C.E., vowed revenge and planned to invade. In preparation for the attack, some of the Greek states formed a defensive league under Spartan leadership. The Athenians, in the meantime, had acquired a new leader, Themistocles (thuh-MISS-tuh-kleez), who persuaded his fellow citizens to pursue a new military policy, namely, the development of a navy. By the time of the Persian invasion in 480 B.C.E., the Athenians had produced a fleet of about two hundred vessels, primarily triremes (TRY-reemz) (ships with three banks of oars).

Xerxes led a massive invasion force into Greece: close to 150,000 troops, almost seven hundred naval ships, and hundreds of supply ships to keep the large army fed. The Greeks tried to delay the Persians at the pass of Thermopylae (thur-MAHP-uh-lee), along the main road into central Greece. A Greek force numbering close to nine thousand, under the leadership of the Spartan king, Leonidas, and his contingent of three hundred Spartans, held off the Persian army for two days. The Spartan troops were especially brave. When told that Persian arrows would darken the sky in battle, one Spartan warrior supposedly responded, "That is good news. We will fight in the shade!" Unfortunately for the Greeks, a traitor told the Persians how to use a mountain path to outflank the Greek force. The Spartans fought to the last man.

The Athenians, now threatened by the onslaught of the Persian forces, abandoned their city. While the Persians sacked and burned Athens, the Greek fleet remained offshore near the island of Salamis (SAH-luh-miss) and challenged the

Persian navy to fight. Although the Greeks were outnumbered, they managed to outmaneuver the Persian fleet and utterly defeated it. A few months later, early in 479 B.C.E., the Greeks formed the largest Greek army seen up to that time and decisively defeated the Persian army at Plataea (pluh-TEE-uh), northwest of Attica. The Greeks had won the war and were now free to pursue their own destiny.

The Growth of an Athenian Empire in the Age of Pericles   After the defeat of the Persians, Athens took over the leadership of the Greek world by forming a defensive alliance against the Persians called the Delian League in the winter of 478–477 B.C.E. Its main headquarters was on the island of Delos, but its chief officials, including the treasurers and commanders of the fleet, were Athenian. Under the leadership of the Athenians, the Delian League pursued the attack against the Persian Empire. Virtually all of the Greek states in the Aegean were liberated from Persian control. Arguing that the Persian threat was now over, some members of the Delian League wished to withdraw. But the Athenians forced them to remain in the league and to pay tribute. In 454 B.C.E., the Athenians moved the treasury of the league from Delos to Athens. By controlling the Delian League, Athens had created an empire.

At home, Athenians favored the new imperial policy, especially after 461 B.C.E., when politics came to be dominated by a political faction led by a young aristocrat named Pericles (PER-i-kleez). Under Pericles, who remained a leading figure in Athenian politics for more than three decades, Athens embarked on a policy of expanding democracy at home and its new empire abroad. This period of Athenian and Greek history, which historians have subsequently labeled the Age of Pericles, witnessed the height of Athenian power and the culmination of its brilliance as a civilization.

During the Age of Pericles, the Athenians became deeply attached to their democratic system. The sovereignty of the people was embodied in the assembly, which consisted of all male citizens over eighteen years of age. In the 440s, that was probably a group of about 43,000. Not all attended, however, and the number present at the meetings, which were held every ten days on a hillside east of the Acropolis, seldom reached 6,000. The assembly passed all laws and made final decisions on war and foreign policy.

Routine administration of public affairs was handled by a large body of city magistrates, usually chosen by lot without regard to class and usually serving only one-year terms. This meant that many male citizens held public office at some time in their lives. A board of ten officials known as generals (*strategoi* [strah-tay-GOH-ee]) was elected by public vote to guide affairs of state, although their power depended on the respect they had earned. Generals were usually wealthy aristocrats, even though the people were free to select otherwise. The generals could be reelected, enabling individual leaders to play an important political role. Pericles's frequent reelection (fifteen times) as one of the ten generals made him one of the leading politicians between 461 and 429 B.C.E.

Pericles expanded the Athenians' involvement in democracy, which is what by now the Athenians had come to call their form of government. Power was in the hands of the people; male citizens voted in the assemblies and served as jurors in the courts. Lower-class citizens were now eligible for public offices formerly closed to them. Pericles also introduced state pay for officeholders, including the widely held jury duty. This meant that even poor citizens could afford to participate in public affairs and hold public office. Nevertheless, although the Athenians developed a system of government that was unique in its time in which citizens had equal rights and the people were the government, aristocrats continued to hold the most important offices, and many people, including women, slaves, and foreigners residing in Athens, were not given the same political rights.

Under Pericles, Athens became the leading center of Greek culture. The Persians had destroyed much of the city during the Persian Wars, but Pericles used the treasury money of the Delian League to set in motion a massive rebuilding program. New temples and statues soon made the greatness of Athens more visible. Art, architecture, and philosophy flourished, and Pericles broadly boasted that Athens had become the "school of Greece." But the achievements of Athens alarmed the other Greek states, especially Sparta, and soon all of Greece was confronting a new war.

The Great Peloponnesian War and the Decline of the Greek States

During the forty years after the defeat of the Persians, the Greek world came to be divided into two major camps: Sparta and its supporters and the Athenian maritime empire. Sparta and its allies feared the growing Athenian Empire. Then, too, Athens and Sparta had created two very different kinds of societies, and neither state was able to tolerate the other's system. A series of disputes finally led to the outbreak of war in 431 B.C.E.

At the beginning of the war, both sides believed they had winning strategies. The Athenians planned to remain behind the protective walls of Athens while the overseas empire and the navy would keep them supplied. Pericles knew that the Spartans and their allies could beat the Athenians in open battles, which was the chief aim of the Spartan strategy. The Spartans and their allies invaded Attica and ravaged the fields and orchards, hoping that the Athenians would send out their army to fight beyond the walls. But Pericles was convinced that Athens was secure behind its walls and stayed put.

In the second year of the war, however, plague devastated the crowded city of Athens and wiped out possibly one-third of the population. Pericles himself died the following year (429 B.C.E.), a severe loss to Athens. Despite the losses from the plague, the Athenians fought on in a struggle that dragged on for another twenty-seven years. A final crushing blow came in 405 B.C.E., when the Athenian fleet was destroyed at Aegospotami (ee-guh-SPOT-uh-my) on the Hellespont. Athens was besieged and surrendered in 404. Its walls were torn down, the navy was disbanded, and the Athenian Empire was no more. The great war was finally over.

The Great Peloponnesian War weakened the major Greek states and destroyed any possibility of cooperation among the states. The next seventy years of Greek history are a sorry tale of efforts by Sparta, Athens, and Thebes, a new Greek power, to dominate Greek affairs. Focused on their petty wars, the Greek states remained oblivious to the growing power of Macedonia to their north.

The Culture of Classical Greece   Classical Greece was a period of remarkable intellectual and cultural growth throughout the Greek world, and Periclean Athens was the most important center of Classical Greek culture.

The Writing of History

History as we know it, as the systematic analysis of past events, was introduced to the Western world by the Greeks. Herodotus (huh-ROD-uh-tuss) (c. 484–c. 425 B.C.E.) wrote *History of the Persian Wars*, which is commonly regarded as the first real history in Western civilization. The central theme of Herodotus's work was the conflict between the Greeks and the Persians, which he viewed as a struggle between freedom and despotism. Herodotus traveled extensively and questioned many people to obtain his information. He was a master storyteller and sometimes included considerable fanciful material, but he was also capable of exhibiting a critical attitude toward the materials he used.

Thucydides (thoo-SID-uh-deez) (c. 460–c. 400 B.C.E.) was a better historian by far; indeed, he is considered the greatest historian of the ancient world. Thucydides was an Athenian and a participant in the Peloponnesian War. He had been elected a general, but a defeat in battle led the fickle Athenian assembly to send him into exile, which gave him the opportunity to write his *History of the Peloponnesian War*.

Unlike Herodotus, Thucydides was not concerned with underlying divine forces or gods as explanatory causal factors in history. He saw war and politics in purely rational terms, as the activities of human beings. He examined the causes of the Peloponnesian War in a clear, methodical, objective fashion, placing much emphasis on accuracy and the precision of his facts. As he stated:

> With regard to my factual reporting of the events of the war I have made it a principle not to write down the first story that came my way, and not even to be guided by my own general impressions; either I was present myself at the events which I have described or else I heard of them from eyewitnesses whose reports I have checked with as much thoroughness as possible.[7]

Thucydides also provided remarkable insight into the human condition. He believed that political situations recur in similar fashion and that the study of history is therefore of great value in understanding the present.

Greek Drama

Drama as we know it in Western culture was originated by the Greeks. Plays were presented in outdoor theaters as part of religious festivals. The plays followed a fairly stable form. Three male actors who wore masks acted all the parts. A chorus, also male, spoke lines that explained what was going on. Action was very limited because the emphasis was on the story and its meaning.

The first Greek dramas were tragedies, plays based on the suffering of a hero and usually ending in disaster. Aeschylus (ESS-kuh-luss) (525–456 B.C.E.) is the first tragedian whose plays are known to us. As was customary in Greek tragedy, his plots are simple, and the entire drama focuses on a single tragic event and its meaning. Greek tragedies were sometimes presented in a trilogy (a set of three plays) built around a common theme. The only complete trilogy we possess, called the *Oresteia* (uh-res-TY-uh), was written by Aeschylus. The theme of this trilogy is derived from Homer. Agamemnon, the king of Mycenae, returns a hero from the defeat of Troy. His wife, Clytemnestra, avenges the sacrificial death of her daughter Iphigenia by murdering Agamemnon, who had been responsible for Iphigenia's death. In the second play of the trilogy, Agamemnon's son Orestes avenges his father by killing his mother. Orestes is then pursued by the avenging Furies, who torment him for killing his mother. Evil acts breed evil acts, and suffering is one's lot, suggests Aeschylus. But Orestes is put on trial and acquitted by Athena, the patron goddess of Athens. Personal vendetta has been eliminated, and law has prevailed.

The most successful writer of Greek tragedies was the Athenian playwright Sophocles (SAHF-uh-kleez) (c. 496–406 B.C.E.), whose most famous work was *Oedipus the King*. In this play, the oracle of Apollo foretells that a man (Oedipus) will kill his own father and marry his mother. Despite all attempts at prevention, the tragic events occur. Although it appears that Oedipus suffered the fate determined by the gods, Oedipus also accepts that he himself as a free man must bear responsibility for his actions: "It was Apollo, friends, Apollo, that brought this bitter bitterness, my sorrows to completion. But the hand that struck me was none but my own."[8]

In *Antigone* (an-TIG-oh-nee), the daughter of Oedipus is caught in the dilemma of following her religious obligations to bury the body of her brother Polynices (pol-ee-NICE-eez), who has died in an attempt to seize the throne of Thebes. Antigone's uncle, Cleon, the king of Thebes, however, has forbidden his burial as a traitor to the state. Should Antigone adhere to her principles and fulfill her obligation to the gods by burying her brother or face death by defying the authority of the state? In this confrontation between Cleon and Antigone, Sophocles bears witness to the complexity of human existence.

Another outstanding Athenian tragedian, Euripides (yoo-RIP-uh-deez) (c. 485–406 B.C.E.), moved beyond his predecessors by creating more realistic characters. His plots also became more complex, with a greater interest in real-life situations. Euripides was controversial because he questioned traditional moral and religious values. For example, he was critical of the traditional view that war was glorious. Instead, he portrayed war as brutal and barbaric.

Greek tragedies dealt with universal themes still relevant to our day. They probed such problems as the nature of good and evil, the rights of the individual, the nature of divine forces, and the nature of human beings. Over and over, the tragic lesson was repeated: humans were free and yet could operate only within limitations imposed by the gods. Striving to do the best may not always gain a person success in human terms but is nevertheless worthy of the endeavor. Greek pride in human accomplishment and independence was real. As the chorus chants in Sophocles's *Antigone*: "Is there anything more wonderful on earth, our marvelous planet, than the miracle of man?"[9]

Greek comedy developed later than tragedy. The plays of Aristophanes (ar-is-STAH-fuh-neez) (c. 450–c. 385 B.C.E.), who used both grotesque masks and obscene jokes to entertain the Athenian audience, are examples of Old Comedy. But comedy in Athens was also more clearly political than tragedy. It was used to attack or savagely satirize both politicians and intellectuals. Of special importance to Aristophanes was his opposition to the Peloponnesian War.

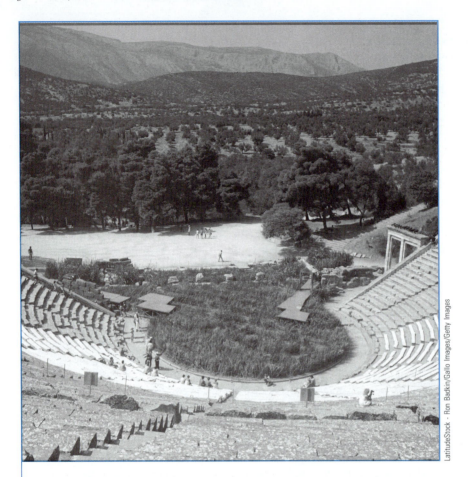

The Amphitheater at Epidaurus. *The photo shows the ancient Greek amphitheater at Epidaurus in the eastern Peloponnesus. It held eighteen thousand onlookers for the theatrical presentations and athletic games that were part of the religious festivals dedicated to Asclepius, the god of healing.*

The Arts: The Classical Ideal   The artistic standards established by the Greeks of the Classical period have largely dominated the arts of the Western world. Greek art was concerned with expressing eternally true ideals. Its subject matter was basically the human being, expressed harmoniously as an object of great beauty. The Classical style, based on the ideals of reason, moderation, symmetry, balance, and harmony in all things, was meant to civilize the emotions.

In architecture, the most important form was the temple dedicated to a god or goddess. At the center of Greek temples were walled rooms that housed the statues of deities and treasuries in which gifts to the gods and goddesses were safeguarded. These central rooms were surrounded by a screen of columns that made Greek temples open structures rather than closed ones. The columns were originally made of wood but were changed to marble in the fifth century B.C.E.

Sophocles: "The Miracle of Man"

RELIGION & PHILOSOPHY

In *Antigone*, Sophocles presents a thoughtful analysis of the painful dilemmas in human existence. In one outstanding passage, the chorus expresses an exalted message on human resourcefulness and the achievements of human beings.

Sophocles, *Antigone*

*Is there anything more wonderful on
      earth,
Our marvelous planet,
Than the miracle of man!
With what arrogant ease
He rides the dangerous seas,
From the waves' towering summit
To the yawning trough beneath.
The earth mother herself, before time
      began,
The oldest of the ageless gods,
Learned to endure his driving plough,
Turning the earth and breaking the
      clods
Till by the sweat of his brow
She yielded up her fruitfulness....*

*He has mastered the mysteries of
      language:
And thought, which moves faster
      than the wind,
He has tamed, and made rational.
Political wisdom too, all the
      knowledge
Of people and States, all the practical
Arts of government he has studied
      and refined,
Built cities to shelter his head
Against rain and anger and cold*

*And ordered all things in his mind.
There is no problem he cannot
      resolve
By the exercise of his brains or his
      breath,
And the only disease he cannot salve
Or cure, is death.*

*In action he is subtle beyond
      imagination,
Limitless is his skill, and these gifts
Are both enemies and friends,
As he applies them, with equal
      determination,
To good or evil ends.
All men honor, and the State
      uplifts
That man to the heights of glory,
      whose powers
Uphold the constitution, and the
      gods, and their laws.
His city prospers. But if he shifts
His ground, and takes the wrong
      path,
Despising morality, and blown up
      with pride,
Indulges himself and his power, at
      my hearth
May he never warm himself, or sit at
      my side.*

Q *What is Sophocles's view of humans
and their accomplishments? What are the
limitations to these human
accomplishments?*

Source: From Sophocles, *Antigone*, trans. Don Taylor (London: Methuen, 2006), pp. 17–18.

Some of the finest examples of Greek Classical architecture were built in fifth-century Athens. The most famous building, regarded as the finest example of the Classical Greek temple, was the Parthenon, built between 447 and 432 B.C.E. Consecrated to Athena, the patron goddess of Athens, the Parthenon was also dedicated to the glory of the city-state and its inhabitants. The Parthenon typifies the

principles of Classical architecture: calmness, clarity, and the avoidance of superflu-
ous detail.

Greek sculpture developed a Classical style that differed significantly from the
artificial stiffness of the figures of earlier times, which had been influenced by Egyptian sculpture. Statues of the male nude, the favorite subject of Greek sculptors,
now exhibited more relaxed attitudes; their faces were self-assured, their bodies
flexible and smooth-muscled. Although the figures possessed natural features that
made them lifelike, Greek sculptors sought to achieve not realism but a standard
of ideal beauty. Polyclitus (pahl-ee-KLY-tuss), a fifth-century sculptor, wrote a treatise (now lost) on a canon of proportions that he illustrated in a work known as the
Doryphoros (doh-RIF-uh-rohss). His theory maintained that the use of ideal proportions, based on mathematical ratios found in nature, could produce an ideal human
form, beautiful in its perfected and refined features. This search for ideal beauty
was the dominant feature of the Classical standard in sculpture.

The Greek Love of Wisdom   *Philosophy* is a Greek word that originally meant
"love of wisdom." Early Greek philosophers were concerned with the development
of critical or rational thought about the nature of the universe and the place of
divine forces and souls in it.

Much of early Greek philosophy focused on the attempt to explain the universe
on the basis of unifying principles. Many Greeks, however, were simply not interested in such speculations. The **Sophists** were a group of philosophical teachers in
the fifth century B.C.E. who rejected such speculation as foolish. Like their near contemporary Confucius in China, they argued that understanding the universe was
beyond the reach of the human mind. It was more important for individuals to
improve themselves, so the only worthwhile object of study was human behavior.
The Sophists were wandering scholars who sold their services as professional teachers to the young men of Greece, especially those of Athens. The Sophists stressed
the importance of **rhetoric** (the art of persuasive oratory) in winning debates and
swaying an audience, a skill that was especially valuable in democratic Athens.
Unlike Confucius, however, the Sophists tended to be skeptics who questioned the
traditional values of their societies. To the Sophists, there was no absolute right or
wrong. True wisdom consisted of being able to perceive and pursue one's own
good. Many people, however, viewed the Sophists as harmful to society and considered their ideas especially dangerous to the values of young people.

In Classical Greece, Athens became the foremost intellectual and artistic center.
Its reputation is perhaps strongest of all in philosophy. Socrates, Plato, and Aristotle raised basic questions that have been debated for two thousand years, for the
most part the very same philosophical questions we wrestle with today.

Socrates (SAHK-ruh-teez) (469–399 B.C.E.) left no writings, but we know about
him from his pupils. Socrates was a stonemason whose true love was philosophy.
He taught a number of pupils, but not for pay, because he believed that the goal
of education was to improve the individual. His approach, still known as the
Socratic method, employs a question-and-answer technique to lead pupils to see
things for themselves using their own reason. Socrates believed that all knowledge
is within each person; only critical examination was needed to call it forth. This
was the real task of philosophy, since "the unexamined life is not worth living."

Socrates questioned authority and criticized some traditional Athenian values, and this soon led him into trouble. Athens had had a tradition of free thought and inquiry, but its defeat in the Peloponnesian War had created an environment intolerant of open debate and soul-searching. Socrates was accused of corrupting the youth of Athens by his teaching. An Athenian jury convicted him and sentenced him to death.

One of Socrates's disciples was Plato (PLAY-toh) (c. 429–347 B.C.E.), considered by many the greatest philosopher of Western civilization. Unlike his master Socrates, who wrote nothing, Plato wrote a great deal. He was fascinated with the question of reality: How do we know what is real? According to Plato, a higher world of eternal, unchanging Ideas or Forms has always existed. To know these Forms is to know truth. These ideal Forms constitute reality and can be apprehended only by a trained mind—which, of course, is the goal of philosophy. The objects that we perceive with our senses are simply reflections of the ideal Forms. They are shadows; reality is in the Forms themselves.

Plato's ideas of government were set out in his dialogue titled *The Republic*. Based on his experience in Athens, Plato had come to distrust the workings of democracy. It was obvious to him that individuals could not attain an ethical life unless they lived in a just and rational state. In *The Republic*, he constructed such an ideal state, in which the population was divided into three basic groups. At the top was an upper class, a ruling elite, the philosopher-kings: "Unless ... political power and philosophy meet together ..., there can be no rest from troubles ... for states, nor yet, as I believe, for all mankind."[10] The second group consisted of the courageous; they would be the warriors who protected the society. All the rest made up the masses, essentially people driven not by wisdom or courage but by desire. They would be the producers—the artisans, tradespeople, and farmers. Contrary to common Greek custom, Plato also believed that men and women should have the same education and equal access to all positions.

Plato established a school at Athens known as the Academy. One of his pupils, who studied there for twenty years, was Aristotle (AR-iss-tot-ul) (384–322 B.C.E.), who later became a tutor to Alexander the Great. Aristotle did not accept Plato's theory of ideal Forms. Instead, he believed that by examining individual objects, we can perceive their form and arrive at universal principles, but these principles do not exist as a separate higher world of reality beyond material things; rather they are a part of things themselves. Aristotle's interests, then, lay in analyzing and classifying things based on thorough research and investigation. His interests were wide-ranging, and he wrote treatises on an enormous number of subjects: ethics, logic, politics, poetry, astronomy, geology, biology, and physics.

Like Plato, Aristotle wished for an effective form of government that would rationally direct human affairs. Unlike Plato, he did not seek an ideal state based on the embodiment of an ideal Form of justice but tried to find the best form of government by a rational examination of existing governments. For his *Politics*, Aristotle examined the constitutions of 158 states and arrived at general categories for organizing governments. He identified three good forms of government: monarchy, aristocracy, and constitutional government. But based on his examination, he warned that monarchy can easily turn into tyranny, aristocracy into oligarchy, and

COMPARATIVE ESSAY

The Axial Age

ART & IDEAS

By the fourth century B.C.E., important regional civilizations existed in China, India, Southwest Asia, and the Mediterranean. During their formative periods between 700 and 300 B.C.E., all were characterized by the emergence of religious and philosophical thinkers who established ideas—or "axes"—that remained the basis for religions and philosophical thought in those societies for hundreds of years. Hence, some historians have referred to the period when these ideas developed as "the Axial Age."

During the fifth and fourth centuries in Greece, the philosophers Socrates, Plato, and Aristotle not only proposed philosophical and political ideas crucial to the Greek world and later to Roman and Western civilization but also conceived of a rational method of inquiry that became important to modern science. By the seventh century B.C.E., concepts of monotheism had developed in Persia through the teachings of Zoroaster and in Canaan through the Hebrew prophets. In Judaism, the Hebrews developed a world religion that influenced the later religions of Christianity and Islam.

During the sixth century, two major schools of thought—Confucianism and Daoism—emerged in China. Both sought to spell out the principles that would create a stable order in society. And although their views of reality were diametrically opposed, both came to have an impact on Chinese civilization that lasted into the twentieth century.

Two of the world's greatest religions, Hinduism and Buddhism, began in India during the Axial Age. Hinduism was an outgrowth of the religious beliefs of the Aryan peoples who settled in India. These ideas were expressed in the sacred texts known as the Vedas and in the Upanishads, which were commentaries on the Vedas compiled in the sixth century B.C.E. With its belief in reincarnation, Hinduism provided justification for India's rigid class system. Buddhism was the product of one man, Siddhartha Gautama, known as the Buddha, who lived in the sixth century B.C.E. The Buddha's simple message of achieving wisdom created a new spiritual philosophy that would rival Hinduism. Although a product of India, Buddhism also spread to other parts of the world.

Although these philosophies and religions developed in different areas of the world, they had some features in common. Like the Chinese philosophers Confucius and Lao Tzu, the Greek philosophers Plato and Aristotle had different ideas about the nature of reality. Thinkers

constitutional government into radical democracy or anarchy. He favored constitutional government as the best form for most people.

Aristotle's philosophical and political ideas played an enormous role in the development of Western thought during the Middle Ages. So did his ideas on women. Aristotle maintained that women were biologically inferior to men: "A woman is, as it were, an infertile male. She is female in fact on account of a kind of inadequacy." Therefore, according to Aristotle, women must be subordinated to men, not only in the community but also in marriage: "The association between husband and wife is clearly an aristocracy. The man rules by virtue of merit, and in the sphere that is his by right; but he hands over to his wife such matters as are suitable for her."[11]

in India and China also developed rational methods of inquiry similar to those of Plato and Aristotle. And regardless of their origins, when we speak of Judaism, Hinduism, Buddhism, Confucianism, Daoism, or Greek philosophical thought, we realize that the ideas of the Axial Age not only spread around the world at different times but are also still an integral part of our world today.

Q *What do historians mean when they speak of the Axial Age? What do you think could explain the emergence of similar ideas in different parts of the world during this period?*

Erich Lessing/Art Resource, NY

Philosophers in the Axial Age. *This mosaic from Pompeii re-creates a gathering of Greek philosophers at the school of Plato.*

Greek Religion   As was the case throughout the ancient world, religion played an important role in Greek society and was intricately connected to every aspect of daily life; it was both social and practical. Public festivals, which originated from religious practices, served specific functions: boys were prepared to be warriors, girls to be mothers. Because religion was related to every aspect of life, citizens had to have a proper attitude toward the gods. Religion was a civic cult necessary for the well-being of the state. Temples dedicated to a god or goddess were the major buildings in Greek cities.

The poetry of Homer gave an account of the gods that provided Greek religion with a definite structure. Over a period of time, all Greeks came to accept a basic polytheistic religion with twelve chief gods who supposedly lived on Mount Olympus, the highest mountain in Greece. Among the twelve were Zeus (**ZOOSS**), the chief deity and father of the gods; Athena, goddess of wisdom and crafts; Apollo, god of the sun and poetry; Aphrodite, goddess of love; and Poseidon, brother of Zeus and god of the seas and earthquakes. Although the twelve Olympian gods were common to all Greeks, each *polis* usually singled out one of the twelve as a guardian deity for the community. Athena was the patron goddess of Athens, for example.

Because the Greeks wanted the gods to look favorably on their activities, ritual assumed enormous proportions in Greek religion. Prayers were often combined with gifts to the gods based on the principle "I give so that you, the gods, will give in return." Ritual meant sacrifices, whether of animals or agricultural products. Animal sacrifices were burned on an altar in front of a temple or on a small altar in front of a home.

As another practical side of Greek religion, Greeks wanted to know the will of the gods. To do so, they made use of the *oracle*, a sacred shrine dedicated to a god or goddess who revealed the future. The most famous was the oracle of Apollo at Delphi, located on the side of Mount Parnassus, overlooking the Gulf of Corinth. At Delphi, a priestess listened to questions while in a state of ecstasy that was believed to be induced by Apollo. Her responses were interpreted by the priests and given in verse form to the person asking questions. Representatives of states and individuals traveled to Delphi to consult the oracle of Apollo. States might inquire whether they should undertake a military expedition; individuals might raise such questions as "Heracleidas asks whether he will have offspring from the wife he has now." Responses were often enigmatic and at times even politically motivated. Croesus (KREE-suss), the king of Lydia in Asia Minor who was known for his incredible wealth, sent messengers to the oracle at Delphi, asking whether he should go to war with the Persians. The oracle replied that if Croesus attacked the Persians, he would destroy a mighty empire. Overjoyed to hear these words, Croesus made war on the Persians but was crushed. A mighty empire was indeed destroyed—his own.

Festivals also developed as a way to honor the gods and goddesses. Some of these (the Panhellenic celebrations) came to have international significance and were held at special locations, such as those dedicated to the worship of Zeus at Olympia or to Apollo at Delphi. The great festivals incorporated numerous events in honor of the gods, including athletic competitions to which all Greeks were invited.

According to tradition, such athletic games were first held at the Olympic festival in 776 B.C.E. and then held every four years thereafter to honor Zeus. Initially, the Olympic contests consisted of foot races and wrestling, but later boxing, javelin throwing, and various other contests were added. Competitions were always between individuals, not groups. The Greeks looked upon winning athletes as great heroes and often rewarded them with parades, as well as money and free rents for life.

Olympic games were not without danger to the participants. Athletes competed in the nude, and rules were rather relaxed. Wrestlers, for example, were allowed to gouge eyes and even pick up their competitors and bring them down head first onto a hard surface. Boxers wrapped their hands and forearms with heavy leather thongs, making their blows damaging. Some athletes were killed during the games.

Given the hatred that often existed between city-states in ancient Greece, their deaths were not always accidental.

The Greek Olympic games came to an end in 393 C.E., when a Christian Roman emperor banned them as pagan exercises. Fifteen hundred years later, the games were revived through the efforts of a French baron, Pierre de Coubertin (PYAYR duh koo-ber-TANH). In 1896, the first modern Olympic games were held in Athens, Greece.

Life in Classical Athens

The *polis* was above all a male community: only adult male citizens took part in public life. In Athens, this meant the exclusion of women, slaves, and foreign residents, or roughly 85 percent of the total population in Attica. There were probably 150,000 citizens in Athens, of whom about 43,000 were adult males who exercised political power. Resident foreigners, who numbered about 35,000, received the protection of the laws but were also subject to some of the responsibilities of citizens, namely, military service and the funding of festivals. The remaining social group, the slaves, numbered around 100,000. Most slaves in Athens worked in the home as cooks and maids or toiled in the fields. Some were owned by the state and worked on public construction projects.

Economy and Lifestyle

The Athenian economy was based largely on agriculture and trade. Athenians grew grains, vegetables, and fruit for local consumption. Grapes and olives were cultivated for wine and olive oil, which were used locally and also exported. The Athenians raised sheep and goats for wool and dairy products. Because of the size of the population in Attica and the lack of abundant fertile land, Athens had to import 50 to 80 percent of its grain, a staple in the Athenian diet. Trade was thus very important to the Athenian economy. Perhaps that is one reason why the Greeks were among the first to mint silver coins.

The Athenian lifestyle was basically simple. Athenian houses were furnished with necessities bought from artisans, such as beds, couches, tables, chests, pottery, stools, baskets, and cooking utensils. Wives and slaves made clothes and blankets at home. The Athenian diet was rather plain and relied on such basic foods as barley, wheat, millet, lentils, grapes, figs, olives, almonds, bread made at home, vegetables, eggs, fish, cheese, and chicken. Olive oil was widely used, not only for eating but also for burning in lamps and rubbing on the body after washing and exercise. Although country houses kept animals, they were used for reasons other than their flesh: oxen for plowing, sheep for wool, and goats for milk and cheese.

Family and Relationships

The family was a central institution in ancient Athens. It was composed of husband, wife, and children (a nuclear family), although other dependent relatives and slaves were regarded as part of the family economic unit. The family's primary social function was to produce new citizens. Strict laws enacted in the fifth century stipulated that a citizen must be the offspring of a legally acknowledged marriage between two Athenian citizens whose parents were also citizens.

OPPOSING VIEWPOINTS

Women in Athens and Sparta

EARTH &
ENVIRONMENT

In Classical Athens, a woman's place was in the home. She had two major responsibilities as a wife—bearing and raising children and managing the household. In the first selection, from a dialogue on estate management, Xenophon (ZEN-uh-fuhn) relates the instructions of an Athenian to his new wife. Although women in Sparta had the same responsibilities as women in Athens, they assumed somewhat different roles as a result of the Spartan lifestyle. The second, third, and fourth selections demonstrate these differences as seen in the accounts of three ancient Greek writers.

Xenophon, *Oeconomicus*

[Ischomachus addresses his new wife:] For it seems to me, dear, that the gods with great discernment have coupled together male and female, as they are called, chiefly in order that they may form a perfect partnership in mutual service. For, in the first place that the various species of living creatures may not fail, they are joined in wedlock for the production of children. Secondly, offspring to support them in old age is provided by this union, to human beings, at any rate. Thirdly, human beings live not in the open air, like beasts, but obviously need shelter. Nevertheless, those who mean to win stores to fill the covered place, have need of someone to work at the open-air occupations; since plowing, sowing, planting and grazing are all such open-air employments; and these supply the needful food. For he made the man's body and mind

more capable of enduring cold and heat, and journeys and campaigns; and therefore imposed on him the outdoor tasks. To the woman, since he had made her body less capable of such endurance, I take it that God has assigned the indoor tasks. And knowing that he had created in the woman and had imposed on her the nourishment of the infants, he meted out to her a larger portion of affection for newborn babes than to the man....

Your duty will be to remain indoors and send out those servants whose work is outside, and superintend those who are to work indoors, and to receive the incomings, and distribute so much of them as must be spent, and watch over so much as is to be kept in store, and take care that the sum laid by for a year be not spent in a month. And when wool is brought to you, you must see that cloaks are made for those that want them. You must see too that the dry corn is in good condition for making food. One of the duties that fall to you, however, will perhaps seem rather thankless: you will have to see that any servant who is ill is cared for.

Xenophon, *Constitution of the Spartans*

First, to begin at the beginning, I will start with the begetting of children. Elsewhere those girls who are going to have children and are considered to have been well brought up are nourished with the plainest diet which is practicable and the smallest amount of luxury good possible; wine

Adult female citizens could participate in most religious cults and festivals but were otherwise excluded from public life. They could not own property beyond personal items and always had a male guardian. An Athenian woman was expected to be a good wife. Her foremost obligation was to bear children, especially male is certainly not allowed them at all, or only if well diluted. Just as the majority of craftsmen are sedentary, the other Greeks expect their girls to sit quietly and work wool. But how can one expect girls brought up like this to give birth to healthy babies? Lycurgus considered slave girls quite adequate to produce clothing, and thought that for free women the most important job was to bear children. In the first place, therefore, he prescribed physical training for the female sex no less than for the male; and next, just as for men, he arranged competitions of racing and strength for women also, thinking that if both parents were strong their children would be more robust.

Aristotle, *Politics*

Now, this license of the [Spartan] women, from the earliest times, was to be expected. For the men were absent from home for long periods of time on military expeditions, fighting the war against the Argives and again against the Arkadians and Messenians.... And nearly two-fifths of the whole country is in the hands of women, both because there have been numerous heiresses, and because large dowries are customary. And yet it would have been better to have regulated them, and given none at all or small or even moderate ones. But at present it is possible for a man to give an inheritance to whomever he chooses.

Plutarch, *Lycurgus*

Since Lycurgus regarded education as the most important and finest duty of the

legislator, he began at the earliest stage by looking at matters relating to marriages and births. For he exercised the girls' bodies with races and wrestling and discus and javelin throwing, so that the embryos formed in them would have a strong start in strong bodies and develop better, and they would undergo their pregnancies with vigor and would cope well and easily with childbirth. He got rid of daintiness and sheltered upbringing and effeminacy of all kinds, by accustoming the girls no less than the young men to walking naked in processions and dancing and singing at certain festivals, when young men were present and watching. The nudity of the girls had nothing disgraceful in it for modesty was present and immorality absent, but rather it made them accustomed to simplicity and enthusiastic as to physical fitness, and gave the female sex a taste of noble spirit, in as much as they too had a share in valor and ambition.

Q *In what ways were the lifestyles of Athenian and Spartan women the same? In what ways were they different? How did the Athenian and Spartan views of the world shape their conceptions of gender and gender roles, and why were those conceptions different?*

Sources: From *Ancient Greece: Social and Historical Documents from Archaic Times to the Death of Socrates*, edited by Matthew Dillon and Lynda Garland. London: Routledge, 1994, pp. 393–95. Copyright © 1994 Matthew and Lynda Garland. From *Aristotle, A Treatise on Government*, trans. William Ellis (J. M. Dent & Sons Ltd.: London, 1912), p. 1270a. From *Ideal Commonwealths: Plutarch's Lycurgus*, ed. Henry Morley, 5th ed. (George Rutledge and Sons, Limited, London, 1890).

children who would preserve the family line. A wife was also to take care of her family and her house, either doing the household work herself or supervising the slaves who did the actual work.

Women were kept under strict control. Because they were married at fourteen or fifteen, they were taught about their responsibilities at an early age. Although many managed to learn to read and play musical instruments, they were not given any formal education. And women were expected to remain at home out of sight unless attending funerals or festivals. If they left the house, they were to be accompanied. A woman working alone in public was either poverty-stricken or not a citizen.

Male homosexuality was also a prominent feature of Athenian life. The Greek homosexual ideal was a relationship between a mature man and a young male. It is most likely that this was an aristocratic ideal and not one practiced by the common people. While the relationship was frequently physical, the Greeks also viewed it as educational. The older male (the "lover") won the love of his "beloved" through his value as a teacher and the devotion he demonstrated in training his charge. In a sense, this love relationship was seen as a way of initiating young males into the male world of political and military dominance. The Greeks did not feel that the coexistence of homosexual and heterosexual predilections created any special problems for individuals or their society.

THE RISE OF MACEDONIA AND THE CONQUESTS OF ALEXANDER

While the Greek city-states were continuing to fight each other, to their north a new and ultimately powerful kingdom was emerging in its own right. Its people, the Macedonians, were mostly rural folk, organized in tribes, not city-states, and were viewed as barbarians by their southern neighbors, the Greeks. Not until the end of the fifth century B.C.E. did Macedonia emerge as an important kingdom. But when Philip II (359–336 B.C.E.) came to the throne, he built an efficient army and turned Macedonia into the strongest power of the Greek world—one that was soon drawn into the conflicts among the Greeks.

The Athenians at last took notice of the new contender. Fear of Philip led them to ally with a number of other Greek states and confront the Macedonians at the Battle of Chaeronea (ker-uh-NEE-uh), near Thebes, in 338 B.C.E. The Macedonian army crushed the Greeks, and Philip was now free to consolidate his control over the Greek peninsula. The Greek states were joined together in an alliance that we call the Corinthian League because they met at Corinth. All members took an oath of loyalty: "I swear by Zeus, Earth, Sun, Poseidon, Athena, Ares, and all the gods and goddesses. I will abide by the peace, and I will not break the agreements with Philip the Macedonian, nor will I take up arms with hostile intent against any one of those who abide by the oaths either by land or by sea."[12] Philip insisted that the Greek states end their bitter rivalries and cooperate with him in a war against Persia. Before Philip could undertake his invasion of Asia, however, he was assassinated, leaving the task to his son Alexander.

Alexander the Great   Alexander was only twenty when he became king of Macedonia. He had in many ways been prepared to rule by his father, who had taken Alexander along on military campaigns and had given him control of the cavalry at the important battle of Chaeronea. After his father's assassination, Alexander moved quickly to assert his authority, securing the Macedonian frontiers and smothering a rebellion in Greece. He then turned to his father's dream, the invasion of the Persian Empire.

Alexander's Conquests   There is no doubt that Alexander was taking a chance in attacking the Persian Empire, which was still a strong state. In the spring of 334 B.C.E., Alexander entered Asia Minor with an army of 37,000 men. About half were Macedonians, the rest Greeks and other allies. The cavalry, which would play an important role as a strike force, numbered about 5,000.

Alexander's first confrontation with the Persians, at a battle at the Granicus River in 334 B.C.E., almost cost him his life but resulted in a major victory. By the following spring, the entire western half of Asia Minor was in Alexander's hands. Meanwhile, the Persian king, Darius III, mobilized his forces to stop Alexander's army. Although the Persian troops outnumbered Alexander's, the Battle of Issus (ISS-uss) was fought on a narrow field that canceled the advantage of superior numbers and resulted in another Macedonian success. After his victory at Issus in 333 B.C.E., Alexander turned south, and by the winter of 332, Syria, Palestine, and Egypt were under his domination. He took the traditional title of pharaoh of Egypt and founded the first of a series of cities named after him (Alexandria) as the Greek administrative capital of Egypt. It became (and remains today) one of the most important cities in Egypt and in the Mediterranean world.

In 331 B.C.E., Alexander renewed his offensive, moved into the territory of the ancient Mesopotamian kingdoms, and fought a decisive battle with the Persians at Gaugamela (gaw-guh-MEE-luh), northwest of Babylon. After his victory, Alexander entered Babylon and then proceeded to the Persian capitals at Susa and Persepolis,

MAP 4.2 The Conquests of Alexander the Great

In just twelve years, Alexander the Great conquered vast territories. Dominating lands from west of the Nile to east of the Indus, he brought the Persian Empire, Egypt, and much of the Middle East under his control.

FILM & HISTORY

Alexander (2004)

Alexander is a product of director Oliver Stone's lifelong fascination with Alexander, the king of Macedonia who conquered the Persian Empire in the fourth century B.C.E. and launched the Hellenistic era. Stone's epic film cost $150 million, which resulted in an elaborate and in places visually beautiful film. Narrated by the aging Ptolemy (Anthony Hopkins), Alexander's Macedonian general who took control of Egypt after his death, the film tells the story of Alexander (Colin Farrell) through an intermix of battle scenes, scenes showing the progress of Alexander and his army through the Middle East and India, and flashbacks to his early years. Stone portrays Alexander's relationship with his mother, Olympias (Angelina Jolie), as instrumental in his early development while also focusing on his rocky relationship with his father, King Philip II (Val Kilmer). The movie elaborates on the major battle at Gaugamela in 331 B.C.E., where the Persian leader Darius is forced to flee, and then follows Alexander as he conquers the rest of the Persian Empire and continues east into India. After his troops begin to mutiny, Alexander returns to Babylon, where he dies on June 10, 323 B.C.E.

The enormous amount of money spent on the film enabled Stone to achieve a stunning visual spectacle, but as history, the film leaves much to be desired. The character of Alexander is never developed in depth. He is shown at times as a weak character who is plagued by doubts over his decisions and often seems obsessed with his desire for glory. Alexander is also portrayed as an idealistic leader who believed that the people he conquered wanted change, that he was "freeing the people of the world," and that Asia and Europe would grow together into a single entity. But was Alexander an idealistic dreamer, as Stone apparently believes, or was he a military leader who, following the dictum that "fortune favors the bold," ran roughshod over the wishes of his soldiers in order to follow his dream and was responsible for mass slaughter in the process? The latter is a perspective that Stone glosses over, but Ptolemy probably expresses the more realistic notion that "none of us believed in his dream." The movie also does not elaborate on Alexander's wish to be a god. Certainly, Alexander aspired to divine honors; at one point he sent instructions to the

where he acquired the Persian treasuries and took possession of vast quantities of gold and silver. By 330, Alexander was again on the march, pursuing Darius. After Darius was killed by one of his own men, Alexander took the title and office of Great King of the Persians.

But Alexander was not content to rest with the spoils of the Persian Empire. Over the next three years, he moved east and northeast, as far as modern Pakistan. By the summer of 327 B.C.E., he had entered India, which at that time was divided into a number of warring states. In 326 B.C.E., Alexander and his armies arrived in the plains of northwestern India. At the Battle of the Hydaspes River, Alexander won a brutally fought battle. When Alexander made clear his determination to march east to conquer more of India, his soldiers, weary of campaigning year after

Greek cities to "vote him a god." Stone's portrayal of Alexander is perhaps most realistic in presenting his drinking binges and his bisexuality, which was common in the Greco-Roman world. The movie shows not only his marriage to Roxane (Rosario Dawson), daughter of a Bactrian noble, but also his love for his lifelong companion, Hephaestion (Jared Leto), and his sexual relationship with the Persian male slave Bagoas (Francisco Bosch).

The film contains a number of inaccurate historical details. Alexander's first encounters with the Persian royal princesses and Bagoas did not occur when he entered Babylon for the first time. Alexander did not kill Cleitas in India, and he was not wounded in India at the Battle of the Hydaspes River but at the siege of Malli. Specialists in Persian history have also argued that the Persian military forces were much more disciplined than they are depicted in the film.

Alexander (Colin Farrell) reviews his troops before the Battle of Gaugamela.

The Kobal Collection at Art Resource, NY

year, mutinied and refused to go on. Reluctantly, Alexander turned back, leading his men across the arid lands of southern Persia. Conditions in the desert were appalling; the blazing sun and lack of water led to thousands of deaths before Alexander and his remaining troops reached Babylon. Alexander planned still more campaigns, but in June 323 B.C.E., weakened from wounds, fever, and probably excessive alcohol consumption, he died at the age of thirty-two.

The Legacy: Was Alexander Great?   Alexander is one of the most puzzling significant figures in history. Historians relying on the same sources draw vastly different pictures of him. For some, his military ability, extensive conquests, and creation of a new empire alone justify calling him Alexander the Great. Other historians also praise Alexander's love of Greek culture and his intellectual brilliance, especially in matters of warfare. In the lands that he conquered, Alexander attempted to fuse the Macedonians, Greeks, and Persians into a new ruling class. Did he do this because he was an idealistic visionary who believed in a concept of universal humanity, as some suggest? Or was he merely trying to bolster his power and create an autocratic monarchy?

Those historians who see Alexander as aspiring to autocratic monarchy present a very different portrait of him as a ruthless Machiavellian. One has titled his biography *Alexander the Great Failure*. These critics ask whether a man who slaughtered indigenous peoples, who risked the lives of his soldiers for his own selfish reasons, whose fierce temper led him to kill his friends, and whose neglect of administrative duties weakened his kingdom can really be called great.

But how did Alexander view himself? We know that he sought to imitate Achilles, the warrior-hero of Homer's *Iliad*. Alexander kept a copy of the *Iliad*—and a dagger—under his pillow. He also claimed to be descended from Heracles, the Greek hero who came to be worshiped as a god.

Regardless of his ideals, motives, or views about himself, one fact stands out: Alexander ushered in a completely new age, the Hellenistic era. The word *Hellenistic* is derived from a Greek word meaning "to imitate Greeks." It is an appropriate way, then, to describe an age that saw the extension of the Greek language and ideas to the non-Greek world of the Middle East. Alexander's destruction of the Persian monarchy created opportunities for Greek engineers, intellectuals, merchants, soldiers, and administrators. Those who followed Alexander and his successors participated in a new political unity based on the principle of monarchy. His successors used force to establish military monarchies that dominated the Hellenistic world after his death. Autocratic power became a regular feature of those Hellenistic monarchies and was part of Alexander's political legacy to the Hellenistic world. His vision of empire no doubt inspired the Romans, who were, of course, Alexander's real heirs.

But Alexander also left a cultural legacy. As a result of his conquests, Greek language, art, architecture, and literature spread throughout the Middle East. The urban centers of the Hellenistic Age, many founded by Alexander and his successors, became springboards for the diffusion of Greek culture. While the Greeks spread their culture in the east, they were also inevitably influenced by eastern ways. Thus, Alexander's legacy included one of the basic characteristics of the Hellenistic world: the clash and fusion of different cultures.

THE WORLD OF THE HELLENISTIC KINGDOMS

The united empire that Alexander created by his conquests disintegrated after his death. All too soon, Macedonian military leaders were engaged in a struggle for power, and by 301 B.C.E., all hope of unity was dead.

Hellenistic Monarchies   Eventually, four Hellenistic kingdoms emerged as the successors to Alexander. In Macedonia, the struggle for power led to the extermination of Alexander the Great's dynasty. Not until 276 B.C.E. did Antigonus Gonatus (an-TIG-oh-nuss guh-NAH-tuss), the grandson of one of Alexander's generals, succeed in establishing the Antigonid (an-TIG-uh-nid) dynasty as rulers of Macedonia and Greece. Another Hellenistic

MAP 4.3 The World of the Hellenistic Kingdoms

Alexander died unexpectedly at the age of thirty-two and did not designate a successor. After his death, his generals struggled for power, eventually establishing four monarchies that spread Hellenistic culture and fostered trade and economic development.

kingdom emerged in Egypt, where a Macedonian general named Ptolemy (TAHL-uh-mee) established himself as king in 305 B.C.E., initiating the Ptolemaic (tahl-uh-MAY-ik) dynasty of pharaohs. A third Hellenistic kingdom came into being in 230 B.C.E. when Attalus I declared himself king of Pergamum (PURR-guh-mum) in Asia Minor and established the Attalid (AT-uh-lid) dynasty.

The Seleucid Kingdom and India   By far the largest of the Hellenistic kingdoms was founded by the general Seleucus (suh-LOO-kuss), who established the Seleucid dynasty of Syria, which controlled much of the old Persian Empire from Turkey in the west to India in the east. The Seleucids, however, found it increasingly difficult to maintain control of the eastern territories. In fact, the Indian ruler Chandragupta Maurya (chun-druh-GOOP-tuh MOWR-yuh) created a new Indian state, the Mauryan Empire, in 324 B.C.E. and drove out the Seleucid forces. His grandson Ashoka (uh-SHOH-kuh) extended the empire to include most of India. A pious Buddhist, Ashoka sought to convert the remaining Greek communities in northwestern India to his religion.

The Seleucid rulers maintained relations with the Mauryan Empire. Trade was fostered, especially in such luxuries as spices and jewels. Seleucus also sent Greek and Macedonian ambassadors to the Mauryan court. Best known of these was Megasthenes (muh-GAS-thuh-neez), whose report on the people of India remained one of the West's best sources of information until the Middle Ages.

Political Institutions   The Hellenistic monarchies created a semblance of stability for several centuries, even though Hellenistic kings refused to accept the status quo and periodically engaged in wars to alter it. At the same time, an underlying strain always existed between the new Greco-Macedonian ruling class and the native populations. Together these factors created a certain degree of tension that was never truly ended until the Roman state to the west stepped in and imposed a new order.

Although Alexander the Great had apparently planned to fuse Greeks and easterners—he used Persians as administrators, encouraged his soldiers to marry easterners, and did so himself—Hellenistic monarchs who succeeded him relied primarily on Greeks and Macedonians to form the new ruling class. Even those easterners who did advance to important administrative posts had learned Greek (all government business was transacted in Greek) and had become Hellenized in a cultural sense. The Greek ruling class was determined to maintain its privileged position.

Hellenistic Cities   Cities played an especially important role in the Hellenistic kingdoms. Throughout his conquests, Alexander had founded new cities and military settlements, and Hellenistic kings did likewise. The new population centers varied considerably in size and importance. Military settlements were meant to maintain order and might consist of only a few hundred men strongly dependent on the king. But there were also new independent cities with thousands of inhabitants. Alexandria in Egypt was the largest city in the Mediterranean region by the first century B.C.E. Seleucus was especially active in founding new cities, according to one ancient writer:

> The other kings have exulted in destroying existing cities; he, on the other hand, arranged to build cities which did not yet exist. He established so many ... that they were enough to carry the names of towns in Macedonia as well as the names of those in his family.... One can go to Phoenicia to see his cities; one can go to Syria and see even more.[13]

Hellenistic rulers encouraged a massive spread of Greek colonists to the Middle East because of their intrinsic value to the new monarchies. Greeks (and Macedonians) provided not only recruits for the army but also a pool of civilian administrators and workers who contributed to economic development. Even architects, engineers, dramatists, and actors were in demand in the new Greek cities. Many Greeks and Macedonians were quick to see the advantages of moving to the new urban centers and gladly sought their fortunes in the Middle East. The Greek cities of the Hellenistic era were the chief agents in the spread of Greek culture in the Middle East—as far, in fact, as modern Afghanistan and India.

The Greeks' belief in their own cultural superiority provided an easy rationalization for their political dominance of the eastern cities. But Greek control of the new cities was also necessary because the kings frequently used the cities as instruments of government, enabling them to rule considerable territory without an extensive bureaucracy. At the same time, for security reasons, the Greeks needed the support of the kings. After all, the Hellenistic cities were islands of Greek culture in a sea of non-Greeks.

The Importance of Trade   Agriculture was still of primary importance to both the native populations and the new Greek cities of the Hellenistic world. The Greek cities continued their old agrarian patterns. A well-defined citizen body owned land and worked it with the assistance of slaves. But these farms were isolated units in a vast area of land ultimately owned by the king or assigned to large estate owners and worked by native peasants dwelling in villages.

Commerce expanded considerably in the Hellenistic era. Indeed, trading contacts linked much of the Hellenistic world. The decline in the number of political barriers encouraged more commercial traffic. Although Hellenistic monarchs still fought wars, the conquests of Alexander and the policies of his successors made possible greater trade between east and west. Two major trade routes connected the east with the Mediterranean. The major route proceeded by sea from India to the Persian Gulf and then up the Tigris River to Seleucia on the Tigris. Overland routes from Seleucia then led to Antioch and Ephesus. A southern route also began by sea from India but went around Arabia and up the Red Sea to Petra and later Berenice. Caravan routes then led overland to Coptos on the Nile, thence to Alexandria and the Mediterranean.

An incredible variety of products were traded: gold and silver from Spain; salt from Asia Minor; timber from Macedonia; ebony, gems, ivory, and spices from India; frankincense (used on altars) from Arabia; slaves from Thrace, Syria, and Asia Minor; fine wines from Syria and western Asia Minor; olive oil from Athens; and numerous exquisite foodstuffs, such as the famous prunes of Damascus. The greatest trade, however, was in the basic staple of life—grain.

Social Life: New Opportunities for Women   The development of the kingdom as the focus of political life in the Hellenistic era resulted in fewer restrictions on the role of women. In many cities, for example, women of all classes had a new freedom of movement. However, the most notable gains, especially for upper-class women, came in the economic realm. Documents show increasing numbers of women involved in managing slaves, selling property, and making loans. Even then, legal contracts made by women had to include their official male guardians. Only in Sparta were women free to control their own economic affairs. Many Spartan women were noticeably wealthy; females owned 40 percent of Spartan land.

Spartan women, however, were an exception, especially on the Greek mainland. Women in Athens, for example, still remained highly restricted and supervised. Although a few philosophers welcomed female participation in men's affairs, many philosophers rejected equality between men and women and asserted that the traditional roles of wives and mothers were most satisfying for women. And although they were now less restricted, peasant women experienced no real benefit from this freedom because they were still subject to a lifetime of hard work. The large group of women who were condemned to the practice of prostitution faced an even harsher reality.

But the opinions of philosophers did not prevent upper-class women from making gains in areas other than the economic sphere. New possibilities for females arose when women in some areas of the Hellenistic world were allowed to pursue education in the traditional fields of literature, music, and even athletics. Education, then, provided new opportunities for women: female poets appeared in the third century B.C.E., and there are instances of women involved in both scholarly and artistic activities.

The creation of the Hellenistic monarchies, which represented a considerable departure from the world of the city-state, also gave new scope to the role played by the monarchs' wives, the Hellenistic queens. In Macedonia, a pattern of alliances between mothers and sons provided openings for women to take an active role in politics, especially in political intrigue. In Egypt, opportunities for royal women were even greater because the Ptolemaic rulers reverted to an Egyptian custom of kings marrying their own sisters. Of the first eight Ptolemaic rulers, four wed their sisters. Ptolemy II and his sister-wife Arsinoë (ahr-SIN-oh-ee) II were both worshiped as gods in their lifetimes. Arsinoë played an energetic role in government and was involved in the expansion of the Egyptian navy. She was also the first Egyptian queen whose portrait appeared on coins with that of her husband.

Culture in the Hellenistic World

Although the Hellenistic kingdoms encompassed vast territories and many diverse peoples, the diffusion of Greek culture throughout the Hellenistic world provided a sense of unity. The Hellenistic era was a period of considerable accomplishment in many areas—literature, art, science, and philosophy. Although these achievements occurred throughout the Hellenistic world, certain centers, especially the great cities of Alexandria and Pergamum, stood out. In both cities, cultural developments were encouraged by the rulers themselves. Rich Hellenistic monarchs had considerable resources with which to patronize culture.

New Directions in Literature and Art   The Hellenistic Age produced an enormous quantity of literature, most of which has not survived. Hellenistic monarchs, who held literary talent in high esteem, subsidized writers on a grand scale. The Ptolemaic rulers of Egypt were particularly lavish. The combination of their largesse and a famous library with more than 500,000 scrolls drew a host of scholars and authors to Alexandria, including a circle of poets. Theocritus (thee-AHK-ruh-tuss) (c. 315–250 B.C.E.), originally a native of the island of Sicily, wrote "little poems" known as *idylls* dealing with erotic subjects, lovers' complaints, and pastoral themes expressing love of nature and appreciation of nature's beauties.

In the Hellenistic era, Athens remained the theatrical center of the Greek world. Tragedy had fallen by the wayside, but a new style of comedy came to the fore. New Comedy completely rejected political themes and sought only to entertain and amuse. The Athenian playwright Menander (muh-NAN-dur) (c. 342–291 B.C.E.) was perhaps the best representative of New Comedy. Plots were simple: typically, a hero falls in love with a not-really-so-bad prostitute, who turns out eventually to be the long-lost daughter of a rich neighbor. The hero marries her, and they live happily ever after.

In addition to being patrons of literary talent, the Hellenistic monarchs were eager to spend their money to beautify and adorn the cities within their states. The founding of new cities and the rebuilding of old ones provided numerous opportunities for Greek architects and sculptors. The buildings of the Greek home-land—gymnasia, baths, theaters, and, of course, temples—lined the streets of these cities.

Both Hellenistic monarchs and rich citizens patronized sculptors. Thousands of statues, many paid for by the people honored, were erected in towns and cities all over the Hellenistic world. Sculptors traveled throughout this world, attracted by the material rewards offered by wealthy patrons. As a result, Hellenistic sculpture was characterized by a considerable degree of uniformity. Hellenistic artistic styles even affected artists in India. While maintaining the technical skill of the Classical period, Hellenistic sculptors moved away from the idealism of fifth-century classicism to a more emotional and realistic art, seen in numerous statues of old women, drunkards, and little children at play.

A Golden Age of Science   The Hellenistic era witnessed a more conscious separation of science from philosophy. In Classical Greece, what we would call the physical and life sciences had been divisions of philosophical inquiry. Nevertheless, by the time of Aristotle, the Greeks had already established an important principle of scientific investigation: empirical research, or systematic observation as the basis for generalization. In the Hellenistic Age, the sciences tended to be studied in their own right.

One of the traditional areas of Greek science was astronomy, and two Alexandrian scholars continued this exploration. Aristarchus (ar-iss-TAR-kus) of Samos (c. 310–230 B.C.E.) developed a *heliocentric* view of the universe, contending that the sun and the fixed stars remain stationary while the earth rotates around the sun in a circular orbit. He also argued that the earth rotates around its own axis. This view was not widely accepted, and most scholars clung to the earlier *geocentric* view of the Greeks, which held that the earth was at the center of the universe. Another astronomer, Eratosthenes (er-uh-TAHSS-thuh-neez) (c. 275–194 B.C.E.), determined that the earth was round and calculated its circumference at 24,675 miles—within 200 miles of the actual figure.

A third Alexandrian scholar was Euclid (YOO-klid), who lived around 300 B.C.E. He established a school in Alexandria but is primarily known for his work titled *Elements*. This was a systematic organization of the fundamental elements of geometry as they had already been worked out; it became the standard textbook of plane geometry and was used up to modern times.

By far the most famous scientist of the period was Archimedes (ahr-kuh-MEE-deez) (287–212 B.C.E.) of Syracuse. Archimedes was especially important for his work on the geometry of spheres and cylinders and for establishing the value of the mathematical constant pi. Archimedes was also a practical inventor. He may have devised the so-called Archimedean screw, used to pump water out of mines and to lift irrigation water. During the Roman siege of Syracuse, he constructed a number of devices to thwart the attackers. According to Plutarch's account, the Romans became so frightened "that if they did but see a little rope or a piece of wood from the wall, instantly crying out, that there it was again, Archimedes was about to let fly some engine at them, they turned their backs and fled."[14] Archimedes's accomplishments inspired a wealth of semilegendary stories. Supposedly, he discovered specific gravity by observing the water he displaced in his bath and became so excited by his realization that he jumped out of the water and ran home naked, shouting, "Eureka!" ("I have found it!"). He is said to have emphasized the importance of levers by proclaiming to the king of Syracuse, "Give me a lever and a place to stand, and I will move the earth." The king was so impressed that he encouraged Archimedes to lower his sights and build defensive weapons instead.

Philosophy: New Schools of Thought   While Alexandria and Pergamum became the renowned cultural centers of the Hellenistic world, Athens remained the prime center for philosophy. After Alexander the Great, the home of Socrates, Plato, and Aristotle continued to attract the most illustrious philosophers from the Greek world, who chose to establish their schools there. New schools of philosophical thought reinforced Athens's reputation as a philosophical center.

Epicurus (ep-i-KYOOR-uss) (341–270 B.C.E.), the founder of **Epicureanism** (ep-i-kyoo-REE-uh-ni-zum), established a school in Athens near the end of the fourth century B.C.E. Epicurus believed that human beings were free to follow self-interest as a basic motivating force. Happiness was the goal of life, and the means to achieve it was the pursuit of pleasure, the only true good. But the pursuit of pleasure was not meant in a physical, hedonistic sense (as our word *epicurean* has come to mean). Pleasure was not satisfying one's desire in an active, gluttonous fashion but rather freedom from emotional turmoil, freedom from worry—the freedom that came from a mind at rest. To achieve this kind of pleasure, one had to free oneself from public affairs and politics. But this was not a renunciation of all social life, for to Epicurus, a life could be complete only when it was based on friendship. His own life in Athens was an embodiment of his teachings. Epicurus and his friends created their own private community where they could pursue their ideal of true happiness.

Another school of thought was **Stoicism** (STOH-i-siz-um), which became the most popular philosophy of the Hellenistic world and later flourished in the Roman Empire as well. It was the product of a teacher named Zeno (ZEE-noh) (335–263 B.C.E.), who came to Athens and began to teach in a public colonnade known as the Painted Portico (the *Stoa Poikile*—hence the name *Stoicism*). Like Epicureanism, Stoicism was concerned with how individuals find happiness. But Stoics took a radically different approach to the problem. To them, happiness, the supreme good, could be found only by living in harmony with the divine will, by which people gained inner peace. Life's problems could not disturb these people, and they could bear whatever life offered (hence our word *stoic*). Unlike Epicureans, Stoics did not believe in the need to separate oneself from the world and politics. Public service was regarded as noble, and the real Stoic was a good citizen and could even be a good government official.

Both Epicureanism and Stoicism focused primarily on human happiness, and their popularity would suggest a fundamental change in the Greek lifestyle. In the Classical Greek world, the happiness of individuals and the meaning of life were closely associated with the life of the *polis*. One found fulfillment in the community. In the Hellenistic kingdoms, the sense that one could find satisfaction and fulfillment through life in the *polis* had weakened. People sought new philosophies that offered personal happiness, and in the cosmopolitan world of the Hellenistic states, with their mixture of peoples, a new openness to thoughts of universality could also emerge. For some people, Stoicism embodied this larger sense of community. The appeal of new philosophies in the Hellenistic era can also be explained by the apparent decline in certain aspects of traditional religion.

Religion in the Hellenistic World   When the Greeks spread throughout the Hellenistic kingdoms, they took their gods with them. But over a period of time, there was a noticeable decline in the vitality of the traditional Greek religion, which left Greeks receptive to the numerous religious cults of the eastern world. The eastern religions that appealed most to Greeks, however, were the **mystery religions**. What was the source of their attraction?

Mystery cults, with their secret initiations and promises of individual salvation, were not new to the Greek world. But the Greeks of the Hellenistic era were also strongly influenced by eastern mystery cults, such as those of Egypt, which offered a distinct advantage over the Greek mystery religions. The latter had usually been connected to specific locations (such as Eleusis), which meant that a would-be initiate had to undertake a pilgrimage in order to participate in the rites. In contrast, the eastern mystery religions were readily available since temples to their gods and goddesses were located throughout the Greek cities of the east. All of the mystery religions were based on the same fundamental premises. Individuals could pursue a path to salvation and achieve eternal life by being initiated into a union with a savior god or goddess who had died and risen again.

The Egyptian cult of Isis (Y-sis) was one of the most popular mystery religions. Isis was the goddess of women, marriage, and children; as one of her hymns states, "I am she whom women call goddess. I ordained that women should be loved by men: I brought wife and husband together, and invented the marriage contract. I ordained that women should bear children."[15] Isis was also portrayed as the giver of civilization, who had brought laws and letters to all humankind. The cult of Isis offered a precious commodity to its initiates—the promise of eternal life. In many ways, the cult of Isis and the other mystery religions of the Hellenistic era helped pave the way for Christianity.

CHRONOLOGIES

THE PERSIAN WARS

499–494 B.C.E.	Rebellion of Greek cities in Asia Minor
490 B.C.E.	Battle of Marathon
480–479 B.C.E.	Xerxes invades Greece
480 B.C.E.	Battles of Thermopylae and Salamis
479 B.C.E.	Battle of Plataea

THE RISE OF MACEDONIA AND THE CONQUESTS OF ALEXANDER

359–336 B.C.E.	Reign of Philip II
338 B.C.E.	Battle of Chaeronea; Philip II conquers Greece
336–323 B.C.E.	Reign of Alexander the Great
334 B.C.E.	Alexander invades Asia; Battle of Granicus River
333 B.C.E.	Battle of Issus
331 B.C.E.	Battle of Gaugamela
330 B.C.E.	Fall of Persepolis, the Persian capital
327 B.C.E.	Alexander enters India
326 B.C.E.	Battle of Hydaspes River
323 B.C.E.	Death of Alexander

MindTap is a fully online, highly personalized learning experience built upon Cengage Learning content. MindTap combines student learning tools—readings, multimedia, activities, and assessments—into a singular Learning Path that guides students through their course.

5

THE ROMAN WORLD EMPIRE

Musei Capitolini, Rome, Italy/Giraudon/The Bridgeman Art Library

*Horatius defending the bridge, as envisioned by Tommaso Laureti,
a sixteenth-century Italian painter.*

CHAPTER OUTLINE

• Early Rome and the Republic • The Roman Empire at Its Height • Crisis
and the Late Empire • Transformation of the Roman World: The Development
of Christianity • A Comparison of the Roman and Han Empires

EARLY ROME AND THE REPUBLIC

Italy is a peninsula extending about 750 miles from north to south. It is not very wide, however, averaging about 120 miles across. The Apennines form a ridge down the middle of Italy that divides west from east. Nevertheless, Italy has some fairly large fertile plains that are ideal for farming. Most important are the Po River valley in the north; the plain of Latium (LAY-shee-um), on which Rome was located; and Campania to the south of Latium. To the east of the Italian peninsula is the Adriatic Sea and to the west the Tyrrhenian Sea, bounded by the large islands

© Cengage Learning 2013

MAP 5.1 Ancient Italy

Ancient Italy was home to several groups. Both the Etruscans in the north and the Greeks in the south had a major influence on the development of Rome.

Cincinnatus Saves Rome: A Roman Morality Tale

POLITICS & GOVERNMENT

There is perhaps no better account of how the virtues of duty and simplicity enabled good Roman citizens to prevail during the travails of the fifth century B.C.E. than Livy's account of Cincinnatus (sin-suh-NAT-uss). He was chosen dictator, supposedly in 457 B.C.E., to defend Rome against the attacks of the Aequi (EYE-kwee or EE-kwy). The position of dictator was a temporary expedient used only in emergencies; the consuls would resign, and a leader with unlimited power would be appointed for a specified period (usually six months). In this account, Cincinnatus did his duty, defeated the Aequi, and returned to his simple farm in just fifteen days.

Livy, *The Early History of Rome*

The city was thrown into a state of turmoil, and the general alarm was as great as if Rome herself were surrounded. Nautius was sent for, but it was quickly decided that he was not the man to inspire full confidence; the situation evidently called for a dictator, and, with no dissentient voice, Lucius Quinctius Cincinnatus was named for the post.

Now I would solicit the particular attention of those numerous people who imagine that money is everything in this world, and that rank and ability are inseparable from wealth: let them observe that Cincinnatus, the one man in whom Rome reposed all her hope of survival, was at that moment working a little three-acre farm ... west of the Tiber, just opposite the spot where the shipyards are today. A mission from the city found him at work on his land—digging a ditch, maybe, or plowing. Greetings were exchanged, and he was asked—with a prayer for divine blessing on himself and his country—to put on his toga and hear the Senate's instructions. This naturally surprised him, and, asking if all were well, he told his wife Racilia to run to their cottage and fetch his toga. The toga was brought, and wiping the grimy sweat from his hands and face he put it on; at once the envoys from the city saluted him, with congratulations, as Dictator, invited him to enter Rome, and informed him of the terrible danger of Municius's army. A state vessel was waiting for him on the river, and on the city bank he was welcomed by his three sons who had come to meet him, then by other kinsmen and friends, and finally by nearly the whole body of senators. Closely attended by all these people and preceded by his lictors he was then escorted to his residence through streets lined with great crowds of common folk who, be it said, were by no means so pleased to see the new Dictator, as they thought his power excessive and dreaded the way in which he was likely to use it....

[Cincinnatus proceeds to raise an army, march out, and defeat the Aequi.]

In Rome the Senate was convened by Quintus Fabius the City Prefect, and a decree was passed inviting Cincinnatus to enter in triumph with his troops. The chariot he rode in was preceded by the enemy commanders and the military standards, and followed by his army loaded with its spoils.... Cincinnatus finally resigned after holding office for fifteen days, having originally accepted it for a period of six months.

Q *What values did Livy emphasize in his account of Cincinnatus? How important were those values to Rome's success? Why did Livy say he wrote his history?*

Source: From *The Early History of Rome* by Livy, translated by Aubrey de Selincourt (Penguin Classics, 1960).

of Corsica and Sardinia. Sicily lies just west of the "toe" of the boot-shaped Italian peninsula.

Geography had an impact on Roman history. Although the Apennines bisected Italy, they were less rugged than the mountain ranges of Greece and did not divide the peninsula into small isolated communities. Italy also possessed considerably more productive agricultural land than Greece, enabling it to support a large population. Rome's location was favorable from a geographic perspective. Located 18 miles inland on the Tiber River, Rome had access to the sea and yet was far enough inland to be safe from pirates. Built on seven hills, it was easily defended. Because the Tiber could be readily forded, Rome became a natural crossing point for north-south traffic in western Italy. All in all, Rome had a good central location in Italy from which to expand.

Moreover, the Italian peninsula juts into the Mediterranean, making Italy an important crossroads between the western and eastern ends of the sea. Once Rome had unified Italy, involvement in Mediterranean affairs was natural. And after the Romans had conquered their Mediterranean empire, governing it was made easier by Italy's central location.

Early Rome

According to Roman legend, Rome was founded by twin brothers, Romulus and Remus, in 753 B.C.E., and archaeologists have found that by around that time, a village of huts had been built on the tops of Rome's hills. The early Romans, basically a pastoral people, spoke Latin, which, like Greek, belongs to the Indo-European family of languages. The Roman historical tradition also maintained that early Rome (753–509 B.C.E.) had been under the control of seven kings and that two of the last three had been Etruscans (i-TRUSS-kunz), people who lived north of Rome in Etruria. Historians believe that the king list may have some historical accuracy. What is certain is that Rome did fall under the influence of the Etruscans for about a hundred years during the period of the kings and that by the beginning of the sixth century, under Etruscan influence, Rome began to emerge as a city. The Etruscans were responsible for an outstanding building program. They constructed the first roadbed of the chief street through Rome, the Sacred Way, before 575 B.C.E. and oversaw the development of temples, markets, shops, streets, and houses. By 509 B.C.E., supposedly when the monarchy was overthrown and a republican form of government was established, a new Rome had emerged, essentially a result of the fusion of Etruscan and native Roman elements.

The Roman Republic

The transition from monarchy to a republican government was not easy. Rome felt threatened by enemies from every direction and, in the process of meeting these threats, embarked on a military course that led to the conquest of the entire Italian peninsula.

The Roman Conquest of Italy

At the beginning of the Republic, Rome was surrounded by enemies, including the Latin communities on the plain of Latium. If we are to believe Livy (LIV-ee), one of the chief ancient sources for the history of the early Roman Republic, Rome was engaged in almost continuous warfare with these enemies for the next hundred years. In his account, Livy provided a detailed narrative of Roman efforts. Many of his stories were legendary in character; writing in the first century B.C.E., he used his stories to teach Romans the moral values and virtues that had made Rome great. These included tenacity, duty, courage, and especially discipline.

By 338 B.C.E., Rome had crushed the Latin states in Latium. During the next fifty years, the Romans waged a successful struggle with hill peoples from central Italy and then came into direct contact with the Greek communities. The Greeks had arrived on the Italian peninsula in large numbers during the age of Greek colonization (750–550 B.C.E.). Initially, the Greeks settled in southern Italy and then crept around the coast and up the peninsula. They also occupied the eastern two-thirds of Sicily.

The Greeks had much influence on Rome. They cultivated olives and grapes, passed on their alphabet, and provided artistic and cultural models through their sculpture, architecture, and literature. By 267 B.C.E., the Romans had completed the conquest of southern Italy by defeating the Greek cities. After crushing the remaining Etruscan states to the north in 264 B.C.E., Rome had conquered most of Italy.

To rule Italy, the Romans devised the Roman Confederation in 338 B.C.E. Under this system, Rome allowed some peoples—especially the Latins—to have full Roman citizenship. Most of the remaining communities were made allies. They were free to run their own local affairs but were required to provide soldiers for Rome. Moreover, the Romans made it clear that loyal allies could improve their status and even have hope of becoming Roman citizens. The Romans had found a way to give conquered peoples a stake in Rome's success.

In the course of their expansion throughout Italy, the Romans had pursued consistent policies that help explain their success. The Romans were superb diplomats who excelled in making the correct diplomatic decisions. While firm and even cruel when necessary—rebellions were crushed without mercy—they were also shrewd in extending their citizenship and allowing autonomy in domestic affairs. In addition, the Romans were not only good soldiers but also persistent ones. The loss of an army or a fleet did not cause them to quit but spurred them on to raise new armies and build new fleets. Finally, the Romans had a practical sense of strategy. As they conquered, the Romans established colonies—fortified towns—at strategic locations throughout Italy. By building roads to these settlements and connecting them, the Romans created an impressive communications and military network that enabled them to rule effectively and efficiently. By insisting on military service from the allies in the Roman Confederation, Rome essentially mobilized the entire military manpower of all Italy for its wars.

The Roman State   After the overthrow of the monarchy, Roman nobles, eager to maintain their position of power, established a republican form of government. The chief executive officers of the Roman Republic were the **consuls** (KAHN-sulls) and **praetors** (PREE-turs). Two consuls, chosen annually, administered the government and led the Roman army into battle. The office of praetor was created in 366 B.C.E. The praetor was in charge of civil law (law as it applied to Roman citizens), but he could also lead armies and govern Rome when the consuls were away from the city. As the Romans' territory expanded, they added another praetor to judge cases in which one or both people were noncitizens. The Roman state also had a number of administrative officials who handled specialized duties, such as the administration of financial affairs and supervision of the public games of Rome.

The Roman **senate** came to hold an especially important position in the Roman Republic. The senate or council of elders was a select group of about three hundred men who served for life. The senate could only advise the magistrates, but this advice was not taken lightly and by the third century B.C.E. had virtually the force of law.

The Roman Republic had a number of popular assemblies. By far the most important was the **centuriate assembly**. Organized by classes based on wealth, it was structured in such a way that the wealthiest citizens always had a majority. This assembly elected the chief magistrates and passed laws. Another assembly, the **council of the plebs**, came into being in 471 B.C.E.

The Roman Republic, then, witnessed the interplay of three major elements. Two consuls and later other elected officials served as magistrates and ran the state. An assembly of adult males (the centuriate assembly), controlled by the wealthiest citizens, elected these officials, while the senate, a small group of large landowners, advised them. Thus, the Roman state was an aristocratic republic controlled by a relatively small group of privileged people.

The Struggle of the Orders: Social Divisions in the Roman Republic

The most noticeable element in the social organization of early Rome was the division between two groups—the patricians and the plebeians. The **patricians** were descendants of the original senators appointed during the period of the kings and were great landowners, who constituted an aristocratic governing class. Only they could be consuls, magistrates, and senators. Through their patronage of large numbers of dependent clients, they controlled the centuriate assembly and many other facets of Roman life. The **plebeians** constituted the considerably larger group of nonpatrician large landowners, less wealthy landholders, artisans, merchants, and small farmers. Although they, too, were citizens, they did not have the same rights as the patricians. Both patricians and plebeians could vote, but only the patricians could be elected to governmental offices. Both had the right to make legal contracts and marriages, but intermarriage between patricians and plebeians was forbidden. At the beginning of the fifth century B.C.E., the plebeians began to seek both political and social equality with the patricians.

The struggle between the patricians and plebeians dragged on for hundreds of years, but the plebeians ultimately were successful. The council of the plebs, a popular assembly for plebeians only, was created in 471 B.C.E., and new officials, known as **tribunes of the plebs**, were given the power to protect plebeians against arrest by patrician magistrates. A new law allowed marriages between patricians and plebeians, and in the fourth century B.C.E., plebeians were permitted to become consuls. Finally, in 287 B.C.E., the council of the plebs received the right to pass laws for all Romans.

The struggle between the patricians and plebeians, then, had a significant impact on the development of the Roman state. Plebeians could now hold the highest offices of state, they could intermarry with the patricians, and they could pass laws binding on the entire Roman community. Theoretically, by 287 B.C.E., all Roman citizens were equal under the law, and all could strive for political office. But in reality, as a result of the right of intermarriage, a select number of patrician and plebeian families formed a new senatorial aristocracy that came to dominate the political offices. The Roman Republic had not become a democracy.

The Roman Conquest of the Mediterranean (264–133 B.C.E.)   After their conquest of the Italian peninsula, the Romans found themselves face to face with a formidable Mediterranean power—Carthage (KAHR-thij). Founded around 800 B.C.E. on the coast of North Africa by Phoenicians, Carthage had flourished and assembled an enormous empire in the western Mediterranean. By the third century B.C.E., the Carthaginian Empire included the coast of northern Africa, southern Spain, Sardinia, Corsica, and western Sicily. The presence of Carthaginians in Sicily, so close to the Italian coast, made the Romans apprehensive. In 264 B.C.E., the two powers began a lengthy struggle for control of the western Mediterranean.

The Punic Wars   In the First Punic (PYOO-nik) War (the Latin word for Phoenician was *Punicus*), the Romans resolved to conquer Sicily. The Romans—a land power—realized that they could not win the war without a navy and promptly developed a substantial naval fleet. After a long struggle, a Roman fleet defeated the Carthaginian navy off Sicily, and the war quickly came to an end. In

MAP 5.2   Roman Conquests in the Mediterranean, 264–133 B.C.E.

Beginning with the Punic Wars, Rome expanded its holdings, first in the western Mediterranean at the expense of Carthage and later in Greece and western Asia Minor.

241 B.C.E., Carthage gave up all rights to Sicily and had to pay an indemnity. Sicily became the first Roman province.

Carthage vowed revenge and extended its domains in Spain to compensate for the territory lost to Rome. When the Romans encouraged one of Carthage's Spanish allies to revolt against Carthage, Hannibal (HAN-uh-bul), the greatest of the Carthaginian generals, struck back, beginning the Second Punic War (218–201 B.C.E.).

This time, the Carthaginian strategy aimed at bringing the war home to the Romans and defeating them in their own backyard. Hannibal crossed the Alps with an army of 30,000 to 40,000 men and inflicted a series of defeats on the Romans. At Cannae (KAH-nee) in 216 B.C.E., the Romans lost an army of almost 40,000 men. The Romans seemed on the brink of disaster but refused to give up, raised yet another army, and began to reconquer some of the Italian cities that had gone over to Hannibal's side. More important, the Romans pursued a strategy aimed at undermining the Carthaginian Empire in Spain. By 206 B.C.E., the Romans had pushed the Carthaginians out of Spain.

The Romans then took the war directly to Carthage, forcing the Carthaginians to recall Hannibal from Italy. At the Battle of Zama (ZAH-muh) in 202 B.C.E., the Romans crushed Hannibal's forces, and the war was over. By the peace treaty signed in 201 B.C.E., Carthage lost Spain, which became another Roman province. Rome had become the dominant power in the western Mediterranean.

Fifty years later, the Romans fought their third and final struggle with Carthage. A technical breach in the peace treaty gave the Romans the opportunity to carry out a policy advocated by a number of Romans, especially the conservative politician Cato, who ended every speech he made to the senate with the words, "And I think Carthage must be destroyed." In 146 B.C.E., Carthage was destroyed. For ten days, Roman soldiers burned and pulled down all of the city's buildings. The inhabitants—50,000 men, women, and children—were sold into slavery. The territory of Carthage became a Roman province called Africa.

The Eastern Mediterranean   During its struggle with Carthage, Rome also had problems with the Hellenistic states in the eastern Mediterranean, and after the defeat of Carthage, Rome turned its attention there. In 148 B.C.E., Macedonia was made a Roman province, and two years later, Greece was placed under the control of the Roman governor of Macedonia. In 133 B.C.E., the king of Pergamum deeded his kingdom to Rome, giving Rome its first province in Asia. Rome was now master of the Mediterranean Sea.

The Nature of Roman Imperialism   Rome's empire was built in three stages: the conquest of Italy, the conflict with Carthage and expansion into the western Mediterranean, and the involvement with and domination of the Hellenistic kingdoms in the eastern Mediterranean. The Romans did not possess a master plan for the creation of an empire. Much of their expansion was opportunistic; once involved in a situation that threatened their security, the Romans did not hesitate to act. And the more they expanded, the more threats to their security appeared on the horizon, involving them in yet more conflicts. Indeed, the Romans liked to portray themselves as declaring war only for defensive reasons or to protect allies.

That is only part of the story, however. It is likely, as some historians have suggested, that at some point a group of Roman aristocratic leaders emerged who favored expansion both for the glory it offered and for the economic benefits it provided. Certainly, by the second century B.C.E., aristocratic senators perceived new opportunities for lucrative foreign commands, enormous spoils of war, and an abundant supply of slave labor for their growing landed estates. By that same time, as the destruction of Carthage indicates, Roman imperialism had become more arrogant and brutal as well. Rome's foreign success also had enormous repercussions for the internal development of the Roman Republic.

The Roman Army   By the fourth century B.C.E., the Roman army consisted of four legions, each made up of four thousand to five thousand men; each legion had about three hundred cavalry and the rest infantry. In the early Republic, the army was recruited from citizens between the ages of eighteen and forty-six who had the resources to equip themselves for battle. Since most of them were farmers, they enrolled only for a year, campaigned during the summer months, and returned home in time for the fall harvest. Later, during the Punic Wars of the third century B.C.E., the period of service had to be extended, although this was resisted by farmers whose livelihoods could be severely harmed by a long absence. Nevertheless, after the disastrous Battle of Cannae in 216 B.C.E., the Romans were forced to recruit larger armies, and the number of legions rose to twenty-five. Major changes in recruitment would not come until the first century B.C.E. with the military reforms of Marius.

The Decline and Fall of the Roman Republic (133–31 B.C.E.)   By the middle of the second century B.C.E., Roman domination of the Mediterranean Sea was complete. Yet the process of creating an empire had weakened the internal stability of Rome, leading to a series of crises that plagued the Republic for the next hundred years.

Growing Inequality and Unrest   By the second century B.C.E., the senate had become the effective governing body of the Roman state. It comprised three hundred men, drawn primarily from the landed aristocracy; they remained senators for life and held the chief magistracies of the Republic. The senate directed the wars of the third and second centuries and took control of both foreign and domestic policy, including financial affairs.

Of course, these aristocrats formed only a tiny minority of the Roman people. The backbone of the Roman state and army had traditionally been the small farmers. But over time, many small farmers had found themselves unable to compete with large, wealthy landowners and had lost their lands. By taking over state-owned land and by buying out small peasant owners, these landed aristocrats had amassed large estates, called *latifundia* (lat-i-FOON-dee-uh), that used slave labor. Thus, the rise of the *latifundia* contributed to a decline in the number of small farmers. Since the latter group traditionally provided the foundation of the Roman army, the number of men available for military service declined. Moreover, many of these small farmers drifted to the cities, especially Rome, forming a large class of landless poor.

Some aristocrats tried to remedy this growing economic and social crisis. Two brothers, Tiberius and Gaius Gracchus (ty-BEER-ee-uss and GY-uss GRAK-us), came to believe that the underlying cause of Rome's problems was the decline of the small farmer. To help the landless poor, they bypassed the senate by having the council of the plebs pass land reform bills that called for the government to reclaim public land held by large landowners and to distribute it to landless Romans. Many senators, themselves large landowners whose estates included broad tracts of public land, were furious. A group of senators took the law into their own hands and murdered Tiberius in 133 B.C.E. Twelve years later, Gaius suffered the same fate. The attempts of the Gracchus brothers to bring reforms had opened the door to further violence. Changes in the Roman army soon brought even worse problems.

A New Role for the Roman Army   In the closing years of the second century B.C.E., a Roman general named Marius (MAR-ee-uss) began to recruit his armies in a new way. The Roman army had traditionally been a conscript army of small farmers who were landholders. Marius, who held the consulship from 104 to 100 B.C.E., recruited volunteers from both the urban and rural poor who possessed no property. These volunteers swore an oath of loyalty to the general, not the senate, and thus constituted a professional-type army that might no longer be subject to the state. Moreover, to recruit these men, the generals would promise them land, forcing the generals to play politics in order to get laws passed that would provide the land promised to their veterans. Marius had created a new system of military recruitment that placed much power in the hands of the individual generals.

Lucius Cornelius Sulla was the next general to take advantage of the new military system. The senate had given him command of a war in Asia Minor, but when the council of the plebs tried to transfer command of this war to Marius, a civil war broke out. Sulla won and seized Rome itself in 82 B.C.E., conducting a reign of terror to wipe out all opposition. Then Sulla restored power to the hands of the senate and eliminated most of the powers of the popular assemblies. Sulla hoped that he had created a firm foundation for the traditional Republic governed by a powerful senate, but his real legacy was quite different from what he had intended. His example of using an army to seize power would prove most attractive to ambitious men.

The Collapse of the Republic   For the next fifty years, Roman history was characterized by two important features: the jostling for dominance of a number of powerful individuals and the civil wars generated by their conflicts. Three individuals came to hold enormous military and political power—Crassus (KRASS-uss), Pompey (PAHM-pee), and Julius Caesar. Crassus was known as the richest man in Rome and led a successful military command against a major slave rebellion. Pompey had returned from a successful military command in Spain in 71 B.C.E. and had been hailed as a military hero. Julius Caesar also had a military command in Spain. In 60 B.C.E., Caesar joined with Crassus and Pompey to form a coalition that historians call the First Triumvirate (*triumvirate* means "three-man rule").

The combined wealth and influence of these three men was enormous, enabling them to dominate the political scene and achieve their basic aims: Pompey received a command in Spain, Crassus a command in Syria, and Caesar a special military command in Gaul (modern France). When Crassus was killed in battle in 53 B.C.E., his death left two powerful men with armies in direct competition. Caesar had conquered all of Gaul and gained fame, wealth, and military experience as well as an army of seasoned veterans who were loyal to him. When leading senators endorsed Pompey as the less harmful to their cause and voted for Caesar to lay down his command and return as a private citizen to Rome, Caesar refused. He chose to keep his army and moved into Italy illegally by crossing the Rubicon, the river that formed the southern boundary of his province. Caesar marched on Rome and defeated the forces of Pompey and his allies, leaving Caesar in complete control of the Roman government.

Caesar was officially made **dictator** in 47 B.C.E. and three years later was named dictator for life. Realizing the need for reforms, he gave land to the poor and increased the senate to nine hundred members. By filling it with many of his supporters and increasing the membership, he effectively weakened the power of the senate. He also reformed the calendar by introducing the Egyptian solar year of 365 days (with later changes in 1582, it became the basis of our own calendar). Caesar planned much more in the way of building projects and military adventures in the east, but in 44 B.C.E., a group of leading senators assassinated him.

Within a few years after Caesar's death, two men had divided the Roman world between them—Octavian (ahk-TAY-vee-un), Caesar's grandnephew and adopted son, took the western portion and Antony, Caesar's ally and assistant, the eastern half. But the empire of the Romans, large as it was, was still too small for two masters, and Octavian and Antony eventually came into conflict. Antony allied himself closely with the Egyptian queen, Cleopatra VII. At the Battle of Actium in Greece in 31 B.C.E., Octavian's forces smashed the army and navy of Antony and Cleopatra, who both fled to Egypt, where they committed suicide a year later. Octavian, at the age of thirty-two, stood supreme over the Roman world. The civil wars had ended. And so had the Republic.

THE ROMAN EMPIRE AT ITS HEIGHT

With the victories of Octavian, peace finally settled on the Roman world. Although civil conflict still erupted occasionally, the new imperial state constructed by Octavian experienced remarkable stability for the next two hundred years. The Romans imposed their peace on the largest empire established in antiquity.

The Age of Augustus (31 B.C.E.–14 C.E.)   In 27 B.C.E., Octavian proclaimed the "restoration of the Republic." He understood that only traditional republican forms would satisfy the senatorial aristocracy. At the same time, Octavian was aware that the Republic could not be fully restored. Although he gave some power to the senate, in fact, Octavian became the first Roman emperor. The senate awarded him the title of Augustus, "the revered one"—a fitting title, in view of his power, that had previously been reserved for gods. Augustus proved highly popular, but the chief source of his power was his continuing control of the army. The senate also gave Augustus the title of *imperator* (im-puh-RAH-tur), or commander in chief. *Imperator* is Latin for our word *emperor*.

Augustus maintained a standing army of twenty-eight legions, or about 150,000 men (a legion was a military unit of about 5,000 troops). Only Roman citizens could be legionaries, while subject peoples could serve as auxiliary forces, which numbered around 130,000 under Augustus. Augustus was also responsible for setting up a **praetorian guard** of roughly 9,000 men who had the important task of guarding the emperor. Eventually, the praetorian guard would play a weighty role in making and deposing emperors.

While claiming to have restored the Republic, Augustus inaugurated a new system for governing the provinces. Under the Republic, the senate had appointed the governors of the provinces. Now certain provinces were given to the emperor, who assigned deputies known as legates to govern them. The senate continued to name the governors of the remaining provinces, but the authority of Augustus enabled him to overrule the senatorial governors and establish a uniform imperial policy.

Augustus also stabilized the frontiers of the Roman Empire. He conquered the central and maritime Alps and then expanded Roman control of the Balkan peninsula up to the Danube River. His attempt to conquer Germany failed when three Roman legions, led by a general named Varus, were massacred in 9 C.E. by a coalition of German tribes. His defeats in Germany taught Augustus that Rome's power was not unlimited and also devastated him; for months, he would beat his head on a door, shouting, "Varus, give me back my legions!"

Augustus died in 14 C.E. after dominating the Roman world for forty-five years. He had created a new order while placating the old by restoring traditional values, a fitting combination for a leader whose favorite maxim was "make haste slowly." By the time of his death, his new order was so well established that few agitated for an alternative. Indeed, as the Roman historian Tacitus (TASS-i-tuss) pointed out, "Practically no one had ever seen truly Republican government.... Political equality was a thing of the past; all eyes watched for imperial commands."[1] The Republic was now only a memory—and given its last century of warfare, an unpleasant one at that. The new order was here to stay.

The Early Empire (14–180)

There was no serious opposition to Augustus's choice of his stepson Tiberius (ty-BEER-ee-uss) as his successor. By his actions, Augustus established the Julio-Claudian dynasty; the next four successors of Augustus were related either to his own family or that of his wife, Livia.

Several major tendencies emerged during the reigns of the Julio-Claudians (14–68 C.E.). In general, more and more of the responsibilities that Augustus had given to the senate tended to be taken over by the emperors, who also instituted an imperial bureaucracy, staffed by talented freedmen, to run the government on a daily basis. As the Julio-Claudian successors of Augustus acted more openly as real rulers rather than "first citizens of the state," the opportunity for arbitrary and corrupt acts also increased. Nero (NEE-roh) (54–68), for example, freely eliminated people he wanted out of the way, including his own mother, whose murder he arranged. Without troops, the senators proved unable to oppose these excesses, but the Roman legions finally revolted. Abandoned by his guards, Nero chose to commit suicide by stabbing himself in the throat after uttering his final words, "What an artist the world is losing in me!"

The Five Good Emperors (96–180)   Many historians regard the **Pax Romana** (PAKS *or* PAHKS ro-MAH-nuh) (the "Roman peace") and the prosperity it engendered as the chief benefits of Roman rule during the first and second centuries C.E. These benefits were especially noticeable during the reigns of the five so-called **good emperors**. These rulers treated the ruling classes with respect, maintained peace in the empire, and supported generally beneficial domestic policies. Though absolute monarchs, they were known for their tolerance and diplomacy. By adopting capable men as their sons and successors, the first four of these emperors reduced the chances of succession problems.

Under the five good emperors, the powers of the emperor continued to expand at the expense of the senate. Increasingly, imperial officials appointed and directed by the emperor took over the running of the government. The good emperors also extended the scope of imperial administration to areas previously untouched by the imperial government. Trajan (TRAY-jun) (98–117) implemented an alimentary program that provided state funds to assist poor parents in raising and educating their children.

The good emperors were widely praised for their extensive building programs. Trajan and Hadrian (HAY-dree-un) (117–138) were especially active in constructing public works—aqueducts, bridges, roads, and harbor facilities—throughout the provinces and in Rome. Trajan built a new forum in Rome to provide a setting for his celebrated victory column. Hadrian's Pantheon, a temple of "all the gods," is one of the grandest ancient buildings surviving in Rome.

Frontiers and the Provinces   Although Trajan extended Roman rule into Dacia (modern Romania), Mesopotamia, and the Sinai peninsula, his successors recognized that the empire was overextended and returned to Augustus's policy of defensive imperialism. Hadrian withdrew Roman forces from much of Mesopotamia. Although he retained Dacia and Arabia, he went on the defensive in his frontier policy by reinforcing the fortifications along a line connecting the Rhine and Danube Rivers and building a defensive wall 80 miles long across northern Britain to keep the Scots out of Roman Britain. By the end of the second century, the Roman forces were established in permanent bases behind the frontiers. But when one frontier was attacked, troops had to be drawn from other frontiers, leaving them vulnerable to attack.

At its height in the second century C.E., the Roman Empire was one of the greatest states the world had seen. It covered about 3.5 million square miles and had a population, like that of Han China, estimated at more than 50 million. While the emperors and the imperial administration provided a degree of unity, considerable leeway was given to local customs, and the privileges of Roman citizenship were extended to many people throughout the empire. In 212, the emperor Caracalla (kar-uh-KAL-uh) completed the process by giving Roman citizenship to every free inhabitant of the empire. Latin was the language of the western part of the empire, while Greek was used in the east. Roman culture spread to all parts of

MAP 5.3 The Roman Empire from Augustus Through Trajan (14–117)

Augustus and later emperors continued the expansion of the Roman Empire, adding more resources but also increasing the tasks of administration and keeping the peace. Compare this map with Map 5.2.

the empire and freely mixed with Greek culture, creating what has been called Greco-Roman civilization.

The administration and cultural life of the Roman Empire depended greatly on cities and towns. A provincial governor's staff was not large, so it was left to local city officials to act as Roman agents in carrying out many government functions, especially those related to taxes. Most towns and cities were not large by modern standards. The largest was Rome, but there were also some large cities in the east: Alexandria in Egypt numbered more than 300,000 inhabitants. In the west, cities were usually small, with only a few thousand inhabitants. Cities were important in the spread of Roman culture, law, and the Latin language, and they resembled one another with their temples, markets, amphitheaters, and other public buildings.

The process of Romanization in the provinces was reflected in significant changes in the governing classes of the empire. In the course of the first century, there was a noticeable decline in the number of senators from Italian families. By the end of the second century, Italian senators made up less than 50 percent of the total. Increasingly, the Roman senate was being recruited from wealthy provincial families. The provinces also provided many of the legionaries for the Roman army and, beginning with Trajan, supplied many of the emperors.

Prosperity in the Early Empire: Trade with China and India   The Early Empire was a period of considerable prosperity. Internal peace resulted in unprecedented levels of trade. Merchants from all over the empire came to the chief Italian ports of Puteoli on the Bay of Naples and Ostia at the mouth of the Tiber River. Long-distance trade beyond the Roman frontiers also developed during the Early Empire. Economic expansion in both the Roman and Chinese Empires helped foster the growth of this trade. Although both empires built roads chiefly for military pur-poses, the roads also came to facilitate trade. Moreover, by creating large empires, the Romans and Chinese not only established internal stability but also pacified bordering territories, thus reducing the threat that bandits posed to traders. As a result, merchants developed a network of trade routes that brought these two great empires into commercial contact.

Most important was the overland Silk Road, a regular caravan route between West and East. Silk, a filament recovered from the cocoons of silkworms, had been produced in China since the fourth millennium B.C.E. Eventually, knowledge of this special product reached the outside world, and Chinese silk exports began to rise. By the second century B.C.E., the first clothing made from silk reached the Mediter-ranean Sea, stimulating the contacts between China and the Roman Empire. The bulk of the trade went overland through Central Asia (thus earning this route its modern name, the Silk Road). By the first century C.E., large quantities of silk were being delivered to markets in Rome through the Silk Road trade. Silk became a craze among Roman elites, leading to a vast outflow of silver from Rome to China and causing the Roman scholar Pliny the Elder to remark that the Roman treasury was being depleted because wealthy Roman women were purchasing so much silk clothing.

The silk trade also stimulated a degree of mutual curiosity between the two great empires but not much mutual knowledge. The Roman geographer Strabo wrote of a strange land called "Seres" far to the east, while Chinese sources men-tioned the empire of "Great Qin" at the far end of the Silk Road to the west. So far as is known, no personal or diplomatic contacts between the two civilizations ever took place. But two great empires at either extreme of the Eurasian supercontinent had for the first time been linked in a commercial relationship.

After the takeover of Egypt in the first century C.E., Roman merchants also began an active trade with India, from where they received precious pearls as well as pepper and other spices used in the banquets of the wealthy. The Romans even established a trading post in southern India where their merchants built warehouses and docks.

Prosperity in the Early Empire: Industry and Farming   Increased trade helped stimulate manufacturing. The cities of the east still produced the items made in Hel-lenistic times. The first two centuries of the empire also witnessed the high point of industrial development in Italy. Some industries became concentrated in certain areas, such as bronze work in Capua and pottery in Arretium in Etruria. Other industries, such as brick making, were pursued in rural areas as by-products of large landed estates.

Despite the profits from trade and commerce, agriculture remained the chief pursuit of most people and the underlying basis of Roman prosperity. Although the large *latifundia* still dominated agriculture, especially in southern and central Italy, small peasant farms continued to flourish, particularly in Etruria and the Po Valley. Although large estates depended on slaves for the raising of sheep and cattle, the lands of some *latifundia* were also worked by free tenant farmers who paid rent in labor, produce, or sometimes cash.

Despite the prosperity of the Roman world, an enormous gulf existed between rich and poor. The development of towns and cities, so important to the creation of any civilization, is based largely on the agricultural surpluses of the countryside. In ancient times, the margin of surplus produced by each farmer was relatively small. Therefore, the upper classes and urban populations had to be supported by the labor of a large number of agricultural producers, who never found it easy to produce much more than they needed for themselves. In lean years, when there were no surpluses, the townspeople often took what they wanted, leaving little for the peasants.

Culture and Society in the Roman World

One of the notable characteristics of Roman culture and society is the impact of the Greeks. Greek ambassadors, merchants, and artists traveled to Rome and spread Greek thought and practices. After their conquest of the Hellenistic kingdoms, Roman generals shipped Greek manuscripts and artworks back to Rome. Multitudes of educated Greek slaves labored in Roman households. Rich Romans hired Greek tutors and sent their sons to Athens to study. As the Roman poet Horace (HOR-uss) said, "Captive Greece took captive her rude conqueror." Greek thought captivated Roman minds, and the Romans became willing transmitters of Greek culture.

Roman Literature   The high point of Latin literature was reached in the Age of Augustus, often called the golden age of Latin literature. The most distinguished poet of the Augustan Age was Virgil (VUR-jul) (70–19 B.C.E.). The son of a small landholder in northern Italy, he welcomed the rule of Augustus and wrote his greatest work in the emperor's honor. Virgil's masterpiece was the *Aeneid*, an epic poem clearly intended to rival the work of Homer. The connection between Troy and Rome is made in the poem when Aeneas, a hero of Troy, survives the destruction of that city and eventually settles in Latium—establishing a link between Roman civilization and Greek history. Aeneas is portrayed as the ideal Roman—his virtues are duty, piety, and faithfulness. Virgil's overall purpose was to show that Aeneas had fulfilled his mission to establish the Romans in Italy and thereby start Rome on its divine mission to rule the world.

> Let others fashion from bronze more lifelike,
>   breathing images—
> For so they shall—and evoke living faces from marble;
> Others excel as orators, others track with their
>   instruments
> The planets circling in heaven and predict when
>   stars will appear.
> But, Romans, never forget that government is your
>   medium!

Be this your art:—to practice men in the habit of peace,
Generosity to the conquered, and firmness against
    aggressors.[2]

As Virgil expressed it, ruling was Rome's gift.

Roman Art   The Romans were also dependent on the Greeks for artistic inspiration. The Romans developed a taste for Greek statues, which they placed not only in public buildings but also in their private houses. The Romans' own portrait sculpture was characterized by an intense realism that included even unpleasant physical details. Wall paintings and frescoes in the homes of the rich realistically depicted landscapes, portraits, and scenes from mythological stories.

The Romans excelled in architecture, a highly practical art. Although they continued to adapt Greek styles and made use of colonnades and rectangular structures, the Romans were also innovative. They made considerable use of curvilinear forms: the arch, vault, and dome. The Romans were also the first people in antiquity to use concrete on a massive scale. By combining concrete and curvilinear forms, they were able to construct huge buildings—public baths, such as those of Caracalla, and amphitheaters capable of seating 50,000 spectators. These large buildings were made possible by Roman engineering skills. These same skills were put to use in constructing roads, aqueducts, and bridges: a network of 50,000 miles of roads linked all parts of the empire, and in Rome, almost a dozen aqueducts kept the population of one million supplied with water.

Roman Law   One of Rome's chief gifts to the Mediterranean world of its day and to later generations was its system of law. Rome's first code of laws was the Twelve Tables of 450 B.C.E., but that was designed for a simple farming society and proved inadequate for later needs. So, from the Twelve Tables, the Romans developed a system of civil law that applied to all Roman citizens. As Rome expanded, problems arose between citizens and noncitizens and also among noncitizen residents of the empire. Although some of the rules of civil law could be used in these cases, special rules were often needed. These rules gave rise to a body of law known as the *law of nations*, defined as the part of the law that applied to both Romans and foreigners. Under the influence of Stoicism, the Romans came to identify their law of nations with **natural law**, a set of universal laws based on reason. This enabled them to establish standards of justice that applied to all people.

These standards of justice included principles that we would immediately recognize. A person was regarded as innocent until proved otherwise. People accused of wrongdoing were allowed to defend themselves before a judge. A judge, in turn, was expected to weigh evidence carefully before arriving at a decision. These principles lived on long after the fall of the Roman Empire.

The Roman Family   At the heart of the Roman social structure stood the family, headed by the ***paterfamilias*** (pay-tur-fuh-MEE-lee-uss)—the dominant male. The household also included the wife, sons with their wives and children, unmarried daughters, and slaves. Like the Greeks, Roman males believed that females needed male guardians. The *paterfamilias* exercised that authority; on his death, sons or nearest male relatives assumed the role of guardians.

Fathers arranged the marriages of daughters. In the Republic, women married "with legal control" passing from father to husband. By the mid-first century B.C.E., the dominant practice had changed to "without legal control," which meant that married daughters officially remained within the father's legal power. Since the fathers of most married women died sooner or later, not being in the "legal control" of a husband made possible independent property rights that forceful women could translate into considerable power within the household and outside it.

Like the Greeks, the Romans did not always raise all the children born into their families. Not only were deformed children abandoned to die of exposure, but infant mortality rates were high—as many as half of all infants did not survive into childhood. Nevertheless, upper-class families did take good care of their surviving children. The father was largely responsible for providing for the education of his children. Roman boys learned reading and writing, moral principles and family values, law, and physical training to prepare them to be soldiers. Girls learned at home what they needed to know to be good wives and mothers.

The end of childhood for Roman males came at the age of sixteen, when a young man exchanged his purple-edged toga for a plain white toga—the toga of manhood—and soon after began his career. For Roman girls, childhood ended at age fourteen, the common age of marriage. Although some Roman doctors warned that early pregnancies could be dangerous for young girls, early marriages persisted because women died at a relatively young age. A good example is Tullia, Cicero's beloved daughter. She was married at sixteen, widowed at twenty-two, remarried one year later, divorced at twenty-eight, remarried at twenty-nine, and divorced at thirty-three. She died at thirty-four, which was not unusually young for women in Roman society.

By the second century C.E., significant changes were occurring in the Roman family. The *paterfamilias* no longer had absolute authority over his children; he could no longer sell his children into slavery or have them put to death. Moreover, the husband's absolute authority over his wife had also disappeared, and by the late second century, women were no longer required to have guardians.

Upper-class Roman women in the Early Empire had considerable freedom and independence. They had acquired the right to own, inherit, and dispose of property. Upper-class women could attend races, the theater, and events in the amphitheater, although in the latter two places they were forced to sit in separate female sections. Women still could not participate in politics, but the Early Empire saw a number of important women who influenced politics through their husbands or sons, including Livia, the wife of Augustus, and Plotina, the wife of Trajan.

Slaves and Their Masters   Although slavery was a common institution throughout the ancient world, no people possessed more slaves or relied so much on slave labor as the Romans eventually did. Slaves were used in many ways in Roman society. The rich owned the most and the best. In the late Roman Republic, it became a badge of prestige to be attended by many slaves. Greek slaves were in much demand as tutors, musicians, doctors, and artists. Roman businessmen would employ them as shop assistants or craftspeople. Slaves were also used as farm laborers; in fact, huge gangs of slaves worked the large landed estates under pitiful conditions. Many slaves of all nationalities were used as menial household workers, such as cooks, waiters, cleaners, and gardeners. Contractors used slave labor to build roads, aqueducts, and other public structures.

The treatment of Roman slaves varied. There are numerous instances of humane treatment by masters and even reports of slaves who protected their owners from danger out of gratitude and esteem. But slaves were also subject to severe punishments, torture, abuse, and hard labor that drove some to run away, despite stringent laws against aiding a runaway slave. Some slaves revolted against their owners and even murdered them, causing some Romans to live in unspoken fear of their slaves.

Near the end of the second century B.C.E., large-scale slave revolts occurred in Sicily, where enormous gangs of slaves were subjected to horrible working conditions on large landed estates. The most famous uprising on the Italian peninsula occurred in 73 B.C.E. Led by a gladiator named Spartacus (SPAR-tuh-kuss), the revolt broke out in southern Italy and involved 70,000 slaves. Spartacus managed to defeat several Roman armies before being trapped and killed in southern Italy in 71 B.C.E. Six thousand of his followers were crucified, the traditional form of execution for slaves.

Imperial Rome   At the center of the colossal Roman Empire was the ancient city of Rome. A true capital city, Rome had the largest population of any city in the empire, close to one million by the time of Augustus. Only Chang'an (CHENG-AHN), the imperial capital of the Han Empire in China, had a comparable population during this time.

An enormous gulf existed between rich and poor in the city of Rome. While the rich had comfortable villas, the poor lived in apartment blocks called *insulae*, which might be six stories high. Constructed of concrete, they were often poorly built and prone to collapse. The use of wooden beams in the floors and movable stoves, torches, candles, and lamps for heat and light created a constant danger of fire. Once started, fires were extremely difficult to put out. The famous conflagration of 64, which Nero was unjustly accused of starting, devastated a good part of the city. Besides the hazards of collapse and fire, living conditions were miserable. High rents forced entire families into one room. In the absence of plumbing and central heating, conditions were so uncomfortable that poorer Romans spent most of their time outdoors in the streets.

Though the center of a great empire, Rome was also a great parasite. Beginning with Augustus, the emperors accepted responsibility for providing food for the urban populace, with about 200,000 people receiving free grain. But even the free grain did not relieve the grim condition of the poor. Early in the second century C.E., a Roman doctor claimed that rickets was common among the city's children.

In addition to food, entertainment was also provided on a grand scale for the inhabitants of Rome. The poet Juvenal (JOO-vuh-nul) said of the Roman masses, "But nowadays, with no vote to sell, their motto is 'Couldn't care less.' Time was when their plebiscite elected generals, heads of state, commanders of legions: but now they've pulled in their horns, there's only two things that concern them: Bread

Women in the Roman and Han Empires

FAMILY &
SOCIETY

These two excerpts are taken from the works of writers in two of the ancient world's great empires: one is a male philosopher living in the Roman Empire and the other is a female writer in Han China. Although they reflect different cultures, they have similar ideas about the role and education of women. Gaius Musonius Rufus was a philosopher who taught Stoicism in Rome in the first century C.E. His students wrote down some of his philosophical opinions. The excerpt here is taken from his thoughts on whether women should study philosophy. Ban Zhao was a well-educated woman from a prominent aristocratic family. She wrote *Admonitions for Women* as a guide for upper-class women in the proper performance of their wifely duties.

Gaius Musonius Rufus, "That Women Too Should Study Philosophy"

When he was asked whether women ought to study philosophy, he began to answer.... Women have received from the gods the same ability to reason that men have.... Likewise women have the same senses as men, sight, hearing, smell, and the rest.... Since that is so, why is it appropriate for men to seek out and examine how they might live well, that is, to practice philosophy, but not women? ...

Let us consider in detail the qualities that a woman who seeks to be good must possess, for it will be apparent that she could acquire each of these qualities from the practice of philosophy.

In the first place a woman must run her household and pick out what is beneficial for her home and take charge of the household slaves.... Next a woman must be chaste, and capable of keeping herself free from illegal love affairs, ... and not enjoy quarrels, not be extravagant or occupied with her appearance.... There are still other requirements: she must control anger, and not be overcome by grief, and be stronger than every kind of emotion....

[When asked if sons and daughters should be given the same education, he replied,] There are not different sets of virtues for men and women. First, men and women both need to be sensible.... Second, both need to live just lives.... Third, a wife ought to be chaste, and so should a husband....

Well, then, suppose someone says, "Do you think that men ought to learn spinning like women and that women ought to practice gymnastics like men?" No, that is not what I suggest. I say that because in the case of the human race, the males are naturally stronger, and the women weaker, appropriate work ought to be assigned to each, and the heavier task be given to the stronger, and the lighter to the weaker. For this reason, spinning is more appropriate work for women than for men, and household management. Gymnastics are more appropriate for men than for women, and outdoor work likewise.... Some tasks are more appropriate for one nature, others for the other. For that reason some jobs are called men's work, and others women's....

and Circuses."[3] The emperor and other state officials provided public spectacles as part of the great festivals—most of them religious in origin—celebrated by the state. The festivals included three major types of entertainment. At the Circus Maximus, horse and chariot races attracted hundreds of thousands, while dramatic and other

Without philosophy no man and no woman either can be well educated. I do not mean to say that women need to have clarity with or facility in argument, because they will use philosophy as women use it.... My point is that women ought to be good and noble in their characters, and that philosophy is no other than the training for that nobility.

Ban Zhao, *Admonitions for Women*

Let a woman modestly yield to others; let her respect others, let her put others first, herself last. Should she do something good, let her not mention it; should she do something bad, let her not deny it. Let her bear contempt; let her even endure when others speak or do evil to her....

Let a woman retire late to bed, but rise early to her duties; let her not dread tasks by day or night. Let her not refuse to perform domestic duties whether easy or difficult. That which must be done, let her finish completely, tidily and systematically....

Let a woman be composed in demeanor and upright in bearing in the service of her husband. Let her live in purity and quietness and keep watch over herself. Let her not love gossip and silly laughter. Let her cleanse, purify and arrange in order the wine and the food for the offerings to the ancestors....

Now examine the gentlemen of the present age. They only know that wives must be controlled and that the husband's authority must be maintained. They therefore teach their boys to read books and study histories.... Yet only to teach men and not to teach women—is this not ignoring the reciprocal relation between them?

Book learning begins at the age of eight, and at the age of fifteen one goes off to school. Why, however, should this principle not apply to girls as well as boys....

In womanly behavior there are four things ... womanly virtue, womanly speech, womanly appearance, and womanly work.

To guard carefully her chastity, to control circumspectly her behavior, in every motion to exhibit modesty, ... : this may be called womanly virtue.

To choose her words with care, to avoid vulgar language, to speak at appropriate times, and not to be offensive to others may be called womanly speech.

To wash and scrub dirt and grime, to keep clothes and ornaments fresh and clean, to wash the head and bathe the body regularly, ... may be called womanly appearance.

With wholehearted devotion to sew and weave, not to love gossip and silly laughter, to prepare the wine and food for serving guests may be called womanly work.

Q *What are the views of Gaius Musonius Rufus and Ban Zhao on the responsibilities of a woman? In what ways do they agree? In what ways do they disagree? How do you explain the differences? From your point of view, what are the strengths and weaknesses in each argument?*

Sources: Lefkowitz, Mary R. and Maureen B. Fant, eds. *Women's Life in Greece and Rome: A Source Book in Translation*, 2nd ed. pp. 50–54 © 1992 M. B. Fant and M. R. Lefkowitz. Reprinted with permission of Johns Hopkins University Press and Bloomsbury Academic. From *Sources of Chinese Tradition*, 2nd ed., Vol. 1, by Wm. T. DeBary and Irene Bloom. Copyright © 1999 Columbia University Press. Reprinted with permission of the publisher.

performances were held in theaters. But the most famous of all the public spectacles were the gladiatorial shows.

The Gladiatorial Shows   The gladiatorial shows were an integral part of Roman society. They took place in amphitheaters. Perhaps the most famous was the

FILM & HISTORY

Gladiator (2000)

The film *Gladiator*, directed by Ridley Scott, is a fictional story set in the Roman Empire near the end of the second century C.E. In the movie, Emperor Marcus Aurelius (Richard Harris) informs his son Commodus (Joaquin Phoenix) that he

DreamWorks/Courtesy Everett Collection

Maximus (Russell Crowe) triumphs in the Roman Colosseum.

amphitheater known as the Colosseum, constructed in Rome to seat 50,000 spectators. In most cities and towns, amphitheaters were the biggest buildings, rivaled only by the circuses (arenas) for races and the public baths.

Gladiatorial games were held from dawn to dusk. Contests to the death between trained fighters formed the central focus of these games, but the games included other forms of entertainment as well. Criminals of all ages and both genders were sent into the arena without weapons to face certain death from intends to turn over imperial power to his successful and respected general, Maximus (Russell Crowe), in the hope that this decent and honest man can restore the Roman senate and revive the Republic. Commodus reacts by killing his father, assuming the position of emperor, and ordering the deaths of Maximus, his wife, and son. Maximus escapes but returns too late to Spain to save his wife and child. He is captured and then sold into slavery to Proximo (Oliver Reed), who trains him to be a gladiator. Maximus is eventually sent to Rome, where he becomes a superhero in the gladiatorial games in the Roman Colosseum, all the while awaiting an opportunity to avenge the death of his wife and son by killing Commodus. Maximus becomes involved in a plot with Lucilla (Connie Nielsen), the emperor's sister, and Gracchus (Derek Jacobi), a Roman senator, to rejoin his army, march on Rome, and overthrow the emperor. When Commodus discovers the plot, he challenges the captured Maximus to a duel in the Colosseum but stabs him first to ensure his own success. Despite his injury, Maximus kills the emperor in combat.

Gladiator is a relatively exciting story, but how much of it is based on historical facts? With the exception of Marcus Aurelius, Commodus, and Lucilla, all of the characters are fictional. Marcus Aurelius was a kind emperor with a love of philosophy and died in 180, probably from plague, and certainly not by his son's hands, as depicted in the film. Commodus ruled from 180 to 192, although he was only eighteen when he became emperor, not in his late twenties as in the movie; and he had blond hair, not dark hair. Commodus was an unstable and cruel young man who was strongly attracted to gladiatorial contests. He was obsessed with performing in the arena, especially with slaughtering animals. He was not killed in the Colosseum, however, but strangled by his wrestling partner on the last day of 192.

Contrary to the movie, Marcus Aurelius had no intention of restoring the Republic; by 180, most Romans had become well accustomed to the empire. In fact, Marcus Aurelius had already made his son Commodus a joint ruler in 177. Nor had Marcus Aurelius banned gladiatorial games, as the movie claims. And although Commodus's sister Lucilla did enter into a plot with some senators to assassinate her brother, the plot of 182 failed, and the conspirators, including Lucilla, were executed.

Although *Gladiator* shows little concern for historical facts, the movie did demonstrate that many people are still interested in ancient history. It became one of the highest earning films of 2000 and won numerous awards including Academy Awards for Best Picture and Best Actor for Russell Crowe. Moreover, the film helped renew interest in Roman history—sales of biographies of historical Roman figures and of Marcus Aurelius's *Meditations* increased noticeably in the years after the movie was released.

wild animals who would tear them to pieces. Numerous types of animal contests were also held: wild beasts against each other, such as bears against buffaloes; staged hunts with men shooting safely from behind iron bars; and gladiators in the arena with bulls, tigers, and lions. It is recorded that five thousand beasts were killed in one day of games when Emperor Titus inaugurated the Colosseum in 80 C.E.

These bloodthirsty spectacles were extremely popular with the Roman people. But the gladiatorial games served a purpose beyond mere entertainment. Like the other forms of public entertainment, the games fulfilled both a political and a social function. Certainly, the games served to divert the idle masses from political unrest. It was said of the emperor Trajan that he understood that although the distribution of grain and money satisfied the individual, spectacles were necessary for the "contentment of the masses."

Disaster in Southern Italy   Gladiatorial spectacles were contrived by humans, but the Roman Empire also experienced some spectacular natural disasters. One of the greatest was the eruption of Mount Vesuvius (vuh-SOO-vee-uss) on August 24, 79 C.E. Although known to be a volcano, Vesuvius was thought to be extinct, its hillsides green with flourishing vineyards. Its eruption threw up thousands of tons of lava and ash. Toxic fumes killed many people, and the nearby city of Pompeii (pahm-PAY) was quickly buried under volcanic ash. To the west, Herculaneum (hur-kyuh-LAY-nee-um) and other communities around the Bay of Naples were submerged beneath a mud flow. Not for another 1,700 years were systematic excavations begun on the buried towns. Through examination of their preserved remains, archaeologists have been able to reconstruct the everyday life and art of these Roman towns. Their discovery in the eighteenth century was an important force in stimulating both scholarly and public interest in Classical antiquity and helped give rise to the Neoclassical style of that century.

CRISIS AND THE LATE EMPIRE

During the reign of Marcus Aurelius, the last of the five good emperors, a number of natural catastrophes struck Rome. To many Romans, these natural disasters seemed to portend an ominous future for Rome. New problems arose soon after the death of Marcus Aurelius in 180.

Crises in the Third Century   In the course of the third century, the Roman Empire came near to collapse. Military monarchy under the Severan rulers (193–235), which restored order after a series of civil wars, was followed by military anarchy. For the next fifty years (235–284), the empire was mired in the chaos of continual civil war. Contenders for the imperial throne found that bribing soldiers was an effective way to become emperor. In these five decades, there were twenty-seven emperors, only four of whom did not meet a violent end. At the same time, the empire was beset by a series of invasions, no doubt exacerbated by the civil wars. In the east, the Sassanid (suh-SAN-id) Persians made inroads into Roman territory. Germanic tribes also poured into the empire. Not until the end of the third century were most of the boundaries restored.

Invasions, civil wars, and plague came close to causing an economic collapse of the Roman Empire in the third century. There was a noticeable decline in trade and small industry, and the labor shortage caused by the plague affected both military recruiting and the economy. Farm production deteriorated significantly as fields were ravaged by invaders or, even more often, by the defending Roman armies. The monetary system began to collapse as a result of debased coinage and inflation. Armies were needed more than ever, but financial strains made it difficult to pay and enlist more soldiers. By the mid-third century, the state had to hire Germans to fight under Roman commanders.

The Late Roman Empire At the end of the third and beginning of the fourth centuries, the Roman Empire gained a new lease on life through the efforts of two strong emperors, Diocletian (dy-uh-KLEE-shun) and Constantine (KAHN-stun-teen). Under their rule, the empire was transformed into a new state, the so-called Late Empire, distinguished by a new governmental structure, a rigid economic and social system, and a new state religion—Christianity.

The Reforms of Diocletian and Constantine Both Diocletian (284–305) and Constantine (306–337) extended imperial control by strengthening and expanding the administrative bureaucracies of the Roman Empire. A hierarchy of officials exercised control at the various levels of government. The army was enlarged, and mobile units were set up that could be quickly moved to support frontier troops when the borders were threatened.

Constantine's biggest project was the construction of a new capital city in the east, on the site of the Greek city of Byzantium on the shores of the Bosporus. Eventually renamed Constantinople (modern Istanbul), the city was developed for defensive reasons and had an excellent strategic location. Calling it his "New Rome," Constantine endowed the city with a forum, large palaces, and a vast amphitheater.

The political and military reforms of Diocletian and Constantine also greatly increased two institutions—the army and the civil service—that drained most of the public funds. Though more revenues were needed to pay for the army and the bureaucracy, the population was not growing, so the tax base could not be expanded. To ensure the tax base and keep the empire going despite the shortage of labor, the emperors issued edicts that forced people to remain in their designated vocations. Basic jobs, such as baker or shipper, became hereditary. The fortunes of free tenant farmers also declined. Soon they found themselves bound to the land by large landowners who took advantage of depressed agricultural conditions to enlarge their landed estates.

In general, the economic and social policies of Diocletian and Constantine were based on an unprecedented degree of control and coercion. Though temporarily successful, such authoritarian polices in the long run stifled the very vitality the Late Empire needed to revive its sagging fortunes.

The End of the Western Empire Constantine had reunited the Roman Empire and restored a semblance of order. After his death, however, the empire continued to divide into western and eastern parts, which had become two virtually independent states by 395. In the course of the fifth century, while the empire in the east remained intact under the Roman emperor in Constantinople, the administrative structure of the empire in the west collapsed and was replaced by an assortment of Germanic kingdoms. The process was a gradual one, beginning with the movement of Germans into the empire.

Although the Romans had established a series of political frontiers along the Rhine and Danube Rivers, Romans and Germans often came into contact across these boundaries. Until the fourth century, the empire had proved capable of absorbing these people without harm to its political structure. In the late fourth century, however, the Germanic tribes came under new pressure when the Huns, a fierce tribe of nomads from the steppes of Asia who may have been related to the Xiongnu (SHYAHNG-noo), the invaders of the Han Empire in China, moved into the Black Sea region, possibly attracted by the riches of the empire to its south. One of the groups displaced by the Huns was the Visigoths (VIZ-uh-gahthz), who moved south and west, crossed the Danube into Roman territory, and settled down as Roman allies. But the Visigoths soon revolted, and the Roman attempt to stop them at Adrianople in 378 led to a crushing defeat for Rome.

Increasing numbers of Germans now crossed the frontiers. In 410, the Visigoths sacked Rome. Vandals poured into southern Spain and Africa, Visigoths into Spain and Gaul. The Vandals crossed into Italy from North Africa and ravaged Rome again in 455. By the middle of the fifth century, the western provinces of the Roman Empire had been taken over by Germanic peoples who set up their own independent kingdoms. At the same time, a semblance of imperial authority remained in Rome, although the real power behind the throne tended to rest in the hands of important military officials known as masters of the soldiers. These military commanders controlled the government and dominated the imperial court. In 476, Odoacer (oh-doh-AY-sur), a new master of the soldiers, himself of German origin, deposed the Roman emperor, the boy Romulus Augustulus (RAHM-yuh-lus ow-GOOS-chuh-luss). To many historians, the deposition of Romulus signaled the end of the Roman Empire in the west. Of course, this is only a symbolic date, as much of direct imperial rule had already been lost in the course of the fifth century.

What Caused the Fall of the Western Roman Empire?   The end of the Roman Empire in the west has given rise to numerous theories that attempt to provide a single, all-encompassing reason for the "decline and fall of the Roman Empire." These include the following: Christianity's emphasis on a spiritual kingdom undermined Roman military virtues and patriotism; traditional Roman values declined as non-Italians gained prominence in the empire; lead poisoning caused by water pipes and cups made of lead resulted in a mental decline; plague decimated the population; Rome failed to advance technologically because of slavery; and Rome was unable to achieve a workable political system. There may be an element of truth in each of these theories, but all of them have also been challenged. History is an intricate web of relationships, causes, and effects. No single explanation will ever suffice to explain historical events. One thing is clear, however. Weakened by a shortage of manpower, the Roman army in the west was simply not able to fend off the hordes of people invading Italy and Gaul. In contrast, the Eastern Roman Empire, which would survive for another thousand years, remained largely free from invasion.

TRANSFORMATION OF THE ROMAN WORLD: THE DEVELOPMENT OF CHRISTIANITY

The rise of Christianity marked a fundamental break with the dominant values of the Greco-Roman world. To understand the rise of Christianity, we must first examine both the religious environment of the Roman world and the Jewish background from which Christianity emerged.

The Religious World of the Roman Empire   The Roman state religion focused on the worship of a pantheon of Greco-Roman gods and goddesses, including Juno, the patron goddess of women; Minerva, the goddess of craftspeople; Mars, the god of war; and Jupiter Optimus Maximus (JOO-puh-tur AHP-tuh-muss MAK-suh-muss) ("best and greatest"), who became the patron deity of Rome and assumed a central place in the religious life of the city. The Romans believed that the observance of proper ritual by state priests brought them into a right relationship with the gods, thereby guaranteeing security, peace, and prosperity, and that their success in creating an empire confirmed that they enjoyed the favor of the gods. As the first-century B.C.E. politician Cicero claimed, "We have overcome all the nations of the world because we have realized that the world is directed and governed by the gods."[4]

The polytheistic Romans were extremely tolerant of other religions. They allowed the worship of native gods and goddesses throughout their provinces and even adopted some of the local deities. In addition, beginning with Augustus, emperors were often officially made gods by the Roman senate, thus bolstering support for the emperors.

The desire for a more emotional spiritual experience led many people to the mystery religions of the Hellenistic east, which flooded into the western Roman world during the Early Empire. The mystery religions offered their followers entry into a higher world of reality and the promise of a future life superior to the present one.

The Jewish Background   In addition to the mystery religions, the Romans' expansion into the eastern Mediterranean also brought them into contact with the Jews. Roman involvement with the Jews began in 63 B.C.E., and by 6 C.E., Judaea (which embraced the old Jewish kingdom of Judah) had been made a province and placed under the direction of a Roman procurator. But unrest continued, augmented by divisions among the Jews themselves. One group, the Essenes, awaited a Messiah who would save Israel from oppression, usher in the kingdom of God, and establish paradise on earth. Another group, the Zealots, were militant extremists who advocated the violent overthrow of Roman rule. A Jewish revolt in 66 C.E. was crushed by the Romans four years later. The Jewish Temple in Jerusalem was destroyed, and Roman power once more stood supreme in Judaea.

The Rise of Christianity   Jesus of Nazareth (c. 6 B.C.E.–c. 29 C.E.) was a Palestinian Jew who grew up in Galilee, an important center of the militant Zealots. Jesus's message was simple. He reassured his fellow Jews that he did not plan to undermine their traditional religion. What was important was not strict adherence to the letter of the law but the transformation of the inner person: "So in everything, do to others what you would have them do to you, for this sums up the Law and the Prophets."[5] God's command was simply to love God and one another: "Love the Lord your God with all your heart and with all your soul and with all your mind and with all your strength. The second is this: Love your neighbor as yourself."[6] In his teachings, Jesus presented the ethical concepts—humility, charity, and brotherly love—that would form the basis of the value system of medieval Western civilization.

Rulers and Gods

RELIGION & PHILOSOPHY

All of the world's earliest civilizations believed that there was a close relationship between rulers and gods. In Egypt, pharaohs were considered gods whose role was to maintain the order and harmony of the universe in their own kingdom. In the words of an Egyptian hymn, "What is the king of Upper and Lower Egypt? He is a god by whose dealings one lives, the father and mother of all men, alone by himself, without an equal." In Mesopotamia, India, and China, rulers were thought to rule with divine assistance. Kings were often seen as rulers who derived their power from the gods and acted as the agents or representatives of the gods. In ancient India, rulers claimed to be representatives of the gods because they were descended from Manu, the first man who had been made a king by Brahman, the chief god. Many Romans believed that their success in creating an empire was a visible sign of divine favor.

Their supposed connection to the gods also caused rulers to seek divine aid in the affairs of the world. This led to the art of divination, an organized method to discover the intentions of the gods. In Mesopotamian and Roman society, one form of divination involved the examination of the livers of sacrificed animals; features seen in the livers were interpreted to foretell events to come. The Chinese used oracle bones to receive advice from supernatural forces that were beyond the power of human beings. Questions for the gods were scratched on turtle shells or animal bones, which were then exposed to fire. Shamans examined the resulting cracks on the surface of the shells or bones and interpreted their meaning as messages from supernatural forces. The Greeks divined the will of the gods by use of the oracle, a sacred shrine dedicated to a god or goddess who revealed the future in response to a question.

Underlying all of these divinatory practices was a belief in a supernatural universe, that is, a world in which divine forces were in charge and on which humans were dependent for their own well-being. It was not until the Scientific Revolution of the modern world that many people began to believe in a natural world that was not governed by spiritual forces.

Q *What role did spiritual forces play in early civilizations?*

To the Roman authorities of Palestine, however, Jesus was a potential revolutionary who might transform Jewish expectations of a messianic kingdom into a revolt against Rome. Therefore, Jesus found himself denounced on many sides, and the procurator Pontius Pilate ordered his crucifixion. But that did not solve the problem. A few loyal followers of Jesus spread the story that Jesus had overcome death, had been resurrected, and had then ascended into heaven. The belief in Jesus's resurrection became an important tenet of Christian doctrine. Jesus was now hailed as "the anointed one" (*Christus* in Greek), the Messiah who would return and usher in the kingdom of God on earth.

Christianity began, then, as a religious movement within Judaism and was viewed that way by Roman authorities for many decades. One of the prominent figures in early Christianity, however, Paul of Tarsus (c. 5–c. 67), believed that the message of Jesus should be preached not only to Jews but to Gentiles (non-Jews) as well. Paul taught that Jesus was the savior, the son of God, who had come to earth to save all humans, who were all sinners as a result of Adam's sin of disobedience against God. By his death, Jesus had atoned for the sins of all humans and made possible their reconciliation with God and hence their salvation. By accepting Jesus as their savior, they too could be saved.

The Spread of Christianity   Christianity spread slowly at first. Although the teachings of early Christianity were mostly disseminated by preaching, written materials also appeared. Among them were a series of epistles (letters) written by Paul outlining Christian beliefs for different Christian communities. Some of Jesus's disciples may also have preserved some of the sayings of the master in writing and would have passed on personal memories that became the basis of the written *gospels*—the "good news" concerning Jesus—of Matthew, Mark, Luke, and John, which by the end of the first century C.E. had become the authoritative record of Jesus's life and teachings and formed the core of the New Testament. Recently, some scholars have argued that other gospels, such as that of Thomas, were rejected because they deviated from the beliefs about Jesus held by the emerging church leaders.

Although Jerusalem was the first center of Christianity, its destruction by the Romans in 70 C.E. dispersed the Christians and left individual Christian churches with considerable independence. By 100, Christian churches had been established in most of the major cities of the east and in some places in the western part of the empire. Many early Christians came from the ranks of Hellenized Jews and the Greek-speaking populations of the east. But in the second and third centuries, an increasing number of followers came from Latin-speaking peoples.

Initially, the Romans did not pay much attention to the Christians, whom they regarded as simply another Jewish sect. As time passed, however, the Roman attitude toward Christianity began to change. The Romans tolerated other religions as long as they did not threaten public order or public morals. Many Romans came to view Christians as harmful to the Roman state because they refused to worship the state gods and emperors. Nevertheless, Roman persecution of Christians in the first and second centuries was only sporadic and local, never systematic. In the second century, Christians were largely ignored as harmless. By the end of the reigns of the five good emperors, Christians still represented a small minority within the empire, but one of considerable strength.

The Triumph of Christianity   Christianity grew slowly in the first century, took root in the second, and by the third had spread widely. Why was the new faith able to attract so many followers? First, the Christian message had much to offer the Roman world. The promise of salvation, made possible by Jesus's death and resurrection, made a resounding impact on a world full of suffering and injustice. Christianity seemed to imbue life with a meaning and purpose beyond the simple material things of everyday reality. Second, Christianity seemed familiar. It was regarded as simply another mystery religion, offering immortality as the result of

Roman Authorities and a Christian on Christianity

RELIGION &
PHILOSOPHY

At first, Roman authorities were uncertain how to deal with the Christians. In the second century, Christians were often viewed as harmless and yet were subject to persecution if they persisted in their beliefs. Pliny was governor of the province of Bithynia in northwestern Asia Minor **(present-day Turkey)**. He wrote to the emperor for advice about how to handle people accused of being Christians. Trajan's response reflects the general approach toward Christians by the emperors of the second century. The final selection is taken from *Against Celsus*, written about 246 by Origen of Alexandria. In it, Origen defended the value of Christianity against Celsus, a philosopher who had launched an attack on Christians and their teachings.

An Exchange Between Pliny and Trajan

Pliny to Trajan

It is my custom. Sir, to refer to you in all cases where I do not feel sure, for who can better direct my doubts or inform my ignorance? I have never been present at any legal examination of the Christians, and I do not know, therefore, what are the usual penalties passed upon them or the limits of those penalties, or how searching an inquiry should be made.... In the meantime, this is the plan which

I have adopted in the case of those Christians who have been brought before me. I ask them if they are Christians. If they say they are, then I repeat the question a second and a third time, warning them of the penalties it entails, and if they still persist, I order them to be taken away to prison. For I do not doubt that, whatever the character of the crime may be which they confess, their pertinacity and inflexible obstinacy certainly ought to be punished.

As is usually the way, the very fact of my taking up this question led subsequently to a great increase of accusations, and a variety of cases were brought before me.... So I postponed my examination, and immediately consulted you.

The matter seems to me worthy of your consideration, especially as there are so many people involved in the danger. Many persons of all ages, and of both sexes alike, are being brought into peril of their lives by their accusers, and the process will go on. For the contagion of this superstition has spread, not only through the free cities, but into the villages and the rural districts.

Trajan to Pliny

You have adopted the proper course, my dear Pliny, in examining into the cases of those who have been denounced to you as Christians, for no hard and fast rule can be laid down to meet a question of such wide extent. The Christians are not to be

the sacrificial death of a savior-god. At the same time, it offered more than the other mystery religions did. Jesus had been a human figure, not a mythological one, and people could relate to him. Finally, Christianity fulfilled the human need to belong. Christians formed communities bound to one another in which people could express their love by helping each other and offering assistance to the poor, sick, widowed, and orphaned. Christianity satisfied the need to belong in a way that the huge, impersonal, and remote Roman Empire never could.

hunted out. If they are brought before you and the offense is proved, they are to be punished, but with this reservation—that if anyone denies that he is a Christian and makes it clear that he is not, by offering prayers to our deities, then he is to be pardoned because of his recantation, however suspicious his past conduct may have been. But pamphlets published anonymously must not carry any weight whatever, no matter what the charge may be, for they are not only a precedent of the very worst type but they are not in consonance with the spirit of our age.

Origen, *Against Celsus*

[Celsus] says that Christians perform their rites and teach their doctrines in secret, and they do this with good reason to escape the death penalty that hangs over them. He compares the danger to the risks encountered for the sake of philosophy as by Socrates.... I reply to this that in Socrates's cases the Athenians at once regretted what they had done, and cherished no grievance against him.... But in the case of the Christians the Roman Senate, the contemporary emperors, the army, ... and the relatives of believers fought against the gospel and would have hindered it; and it would have been defeated by the combined force of so many unless it had overcome and risen above the opposition by divine power, so that it has conquered the whole world that was conspiring against it....

He [also] ridicules our teachers of the gospel who try to elevate the soul in every way to the Creator of the universe.... He compares them [Christians] to ... the most obtuse yokels, as if they called children quite in infancy and women to evil practices, telling them to leave their father and teachers and to follow them. But let Celsus ... tell us how we make women and children leave noble and sound teaching, and call them to wicked practices. But he will not be able to prove anything of any kind against us. On the contrary, we deliver women from licentiousness and from perversion caused by their associates, ... while we make boys self-controlled when they come to the age of puberty and burn with desires for sexual pleasure, showing them not only the disgrace of their sins, but also what a state these pleasures produce in the souls of bad men, and what penalties they will suffer and how they will be punished.

Q *What were Pliny's personal opinions of Christians? Why was he willing to execute them? What was Trajan's response, and what were its consequences for the Christians? What major points did Origen make about the benefits of the Christian religion? Why did the Roman authorities consider these ideas dangerous to the Roman state?*

Source: From *Readings in Ancient History*, Hutton Webster (D.C. Health and Co.: Boston 1919), p. 250. From Origen, *Contra Celsum*. Trans. Henry Chadwick. Copyright © 1953 Cambridge University Press.

Christianity proved attractive to all classes. The promise of eternal life was for all—rich, poor, aristocrats, slaves, men, and women. Christianity emphasized a sense of spiritual equality for all people. Many women, in fact, found that Christianity offered them new roles and new forms of companionship with other women. Christian women fostered the new religion in their homes and preached their convictions to other people in their towns and villages. Many also died for their faith. Perpetua was an aristocratic woman who converted to Christianity. Her pagan family begged her to renounce her new faith, but she refused. Arrested by the Roman authorities, she chose instead to die for her faith and was one of a group of Christians who were slaughtered by wild beasts in the arena at Carthage on March 7, 203.

Moreover, the sporadic persecution of Christians by the Romans in the first and second centuries not only did little to stop the growth of Christianity, but in fact served to strengthen it as an institution in the second and third centuries by causing it to become more organized. Crucial to this change was the emerging role of the bishops, who began to assume more control over church communities. The Christian church was creating a well-defined hierarchical structure in which the bishops and clergy were salaried officers separate from the laity or regular church members.

As the Christian church became more organized, some emperors in the third century responded with more systematic persecutions, but their schemes failed. The last great persecution was at the beginning of the fourth century, but by that time, Christianity had become too strong to be eradicated by force. After Constantine became the first Christian emperor, Christianity flourished. Although Constantine was not baptized until the end of his life, in 313 he issued the Edict of Milan officially tolerating Christianity. Under Theodosius (thee-uh-DOH-shuss) the Great (378–395), it was made the official religion of the Roman Empire. In less than four centuries, Christianity had triumphed.

A COMPARISON OF THE ROMAN AND HAN EMPIRES

At the beginning of the first millennium C.E., two great empires—the Roman Empire in the West and the Han Empire in the East—dominated large areas of the world. Although there was little contact between them, the two empires exhibited some remarkable similarities. Both lasted for centuries, and both were extremely successful in establishing centralized control. Both built elaborate systems of roads in order to rule efficiently and relied on provincial officials, and especially on towns and cities, for local administration. Architectural features found in the capital cities of Rome and Chang'an were also transferred on a smaller scale to provincial towns and cities. In both empires, settled conditions led to a high level of agricultural production that sustained large populations, estimated at between 50 and 60 million in each empire. Although both empires expanded into areas with different languages, ethnic groups, and ways of life, they managed to extend their legal and political institutions, their technical skills, and their languages throughout their empires. In this way, they integrated local communities into a common political and cultural framework.

The Roman and Han Empires also had similar social and economic structures. The family stood at the heart of the social structure, and the male head of the family was all-powerful. The family also inculcated the values that helped make the empires strong—duty, courage, obedience, and discipline. The wealth of both societies also depended on agriculture. Although a free peasantry provided a backbone of strength and stability in each empire, wealthy landowners were able to gradually convert the free peasants into tenant farmers and thereby ultimately to undermine the power of the imperial governments.

Of course, there were also significant differences. The empires came into existence in different ways. Han China inherited an ideal of imperial culture on which to build. The Romans, on the other hand, began with a small city-state ruled

COMPARATIVE ILLUSTRATION

Emperors, West and East

Werner Forman Archive/The Bridgeman Art Library

Art Archive, The/SuperStock

POLITICS & GOVERNMENT

Two great empires with strong central governments dominated much of the ancient world—the Roman Empire in the West and the Han Empire in the East. Shown here are two emperors from these empires. The Roman emperor Hadrian, who ruled from 117 to 138, was the third of the five good emperors. He had been adopted by the emperor Trajan to serve as his successor. Hadrian was a strong and intelligent ruler who took his responsibilities seriously. Between 121 and 132, he visited all of the provinces in the empire. Liu Bang **(lyoo BAHNG)** came from the peasant class, but through his military prowess, he defeated all rivals in the civil wars that followed the death of the First Emperor of Qin. Liu Bang, who is known historically by his title of Han Gaozu **(HAHN gow-DZOO)**, was the first emperor of the Han dynasty, which ruled China for four hundred years. He won the support of his subjects by reducing their tax burden. He was also responsible for bringing China back under central control but was killed in a frontier battle in 195 B.C.E.

Q *What similarities do you see in the lives of these two rulers?*

collectively by its prominent citizens. As the Romans expanded throughout Italy and the Mediterranean, they eventually created a single imperial state.

There were also economic and social differences. Merchants were more highly regarded and allowed more freedom in Rome than they were in China. One key reason for this difference is that whereas many inhabitants of the Roman Empire depended to a considerable degree on commerce to obtain such staples as wheat, olives, wine, cloth, and timber, the vast majority of Chinese were subsistence farmers whose needs—when they were supplied—could normally be met by the local environment. As a result, there was undoubtedly less social mobility in China than in Rome, and many Chinese peasants spent their entire lives without venturing far beyond the village gate.

Another difference is that over the four hundred years of the empires' existence, Chinese imperial authority was far more stable. With a more cohesive territory and a strong dynastic tradition, Chinese rulers could easily pass on their authority to other family members. In contrast in the Roman Empire, political instability was a chronic problem, at least in some periods. Although Roman emperors were accorded divine status by the Roman senate after death, accession to the Roman imperial throne depended less on solid dynastic principles and more on pure military force.

Despite the differences, one major inescapable similarity remains: both empires eventually faced overwhelming problems. Both suffered from overexpansion, and both fortified their long borders with walls, forts, and military garrisons to guard against invasions of nomadic people. Both empires were periodically beset by invasions of nomadic peoples: the Han dynasty was weakened by the incursions of the Xiongnu, and the Western Roman Empire eventually collapsed in the face of incursions by the Germanic peoples.

Nevertheless, one inescapable difference between these two contemporary empires also remains. Although the Han dynasty collapsed, the Chinese imperial tradition, along with the class structure and set of values that sustained that tradition, survived, and the Chinese Empire, under new dynasties, continued well into the twentieth century as a single political entity. In stark contrast, the Roman Empire in the west collapsed and lived on only as an idea.

CHRONOLOGY

THE ROMAN CONQUEST OF ITALY AND THE MEDITERRANEAN

340 B.C.E.	Conquest of Latins completed
338 B.C.E.	Creation of the Roman Confederation
264–241 B.C.E.	First Punic War
218–201 B.C.E.	Second Punic War
216 B.C.E.	Battle of Cannae
206 B.C.E.	Roman seizure of Spain
202 B.C.E.	Battle of Zama
149–146 B.C.E.	Third Punic War
148 B.C.E	Macedonia made a Roman province
146 B.C.E.	Destruction of Carthage
133 B.C.E.	Kingdom of Pergamum to Rome

MindTap is a fully online, highly personalized learning experience built upon Cengage Learning content. MindTap combines student learning tools—readings, multimedia, activities, and assessments—into a singular Learning Path that guides students through their course.

Part Two

▼

NEW PATTERNS OF CIVILIZATION (500–1500 C.E.)

CHAPTER 6
The Americas

CHAPTER 7
Ferment in the Middle East: The Rise of Islam

CHAPTER 8
Early Civilizations in Africa

CHAPTER 9
The Expansion of Civilization in South and Southeast Asia

CHAPTER 10
The Flowering of Traditional China

CHAPTER 11
The East Asian Rimlands: Early Japan, Korea, and Vietnam

CHAPTER 12
The Making of Europe

CHAPTER 13
The Byzantine Empire and Crisis and Recovery in the West

By the beginning of the first millennium C.E., many of the great states of the ancient world were in decline; some were even at the point of collapse. On the ruins of these ancient empires, new patterns of civilization began to take shape between 400 and 1500 C.E. In some cases, these new societies were built on the political and cultural foundations laid down by their predecessors. The Tang Dynasty in China and the Guptas in India both looked back to the ancient period to provide an ideological model for their own time. The Byzantine Empire carried on parts of the Classical Greek tradition while also adopting the powerful creed of Christianity from the Roman Empire. In other cases, new states incorporated some elements of the former classical civilizations while heading in markedly different directions, as was the case with the Arabic states in the Middle East and the new European civilization of the Middle Ages. In Europe, however, the Renaissance, which began in the fifteenth century, sought to bring about a revival of parts of the old Greco-Roman culture.

During this period, a number of significant forces were at work in human society. The accoutrements of a more technologically advanced society gradually spread from the heartland regions of the Middle East, the Mediterranean basin, the South Asian subcontinent, and China into new areas of the world—sub-Saharan Africa, central and western Europe, Southeast Asia, and even the islands of Japan, off the eastern edge of the Eurasian landmass. Across the oceans, unique but advanced civilizations continued to take shape in isolation in the Americas. In the meantime, the vast migrations of peoples continued, leading not only to bitter conflicts but also to increased interchanges of technology and ideas. The result was the transformation of separate and distinct cultures and civilizations into an increasingly complex and vast world system embracing not only technology and trade but also ideas and religious beliefs.

As had been the case during antiquity, the Middle East was at the heart of this activity. The Arab empire, which took shape after the death of the Prophet Muhammad in the early seventh century, brought a measure of renewed stability to the region and provided the key link in the revived trade routes that threaded their way throughout Africa and much of the Eurasian supercontinent. The new religion of Islam became the cement that held the disparate peoples of the region together. Muslim traders—both Arab and Berber—opened contacts with West African societies south of the Sahara, while their ships followed the monsoon winds eastward as far as the Spice Islands in Southeast Asia. Traders from Central Asia, some of them Muslim, carried goods back and forth along the Silk Road between the Middle East and China. For the next several hundred years, the great cities of the Middle East— Mecca, Damascus, and Baghdad—became among the wealthiest in the known world.

Islam's contributions to the human experience during this period were cultural and technological as well as economic. Muslim philosophers preserved the works of the ancient Greeks for posterity, Muslim scientists and mathematicians made new discoveries about the nature of the universe and the human body, and Muslim cartographers and historians mapped the known world and speculated about the fundamental forces in human society.

But the Middle East was not the only or necessarily even the primary contributor to world trade and civilization during this period. While the Arab empire became the linchpin of trade between the Mediterranean and eastern and southern Asia, another center of primary importance in world trade was emerging in East Asia, focused on China. China had been a major participant in regional trade during the Han dynasty, when its silks were already being transported to Rome via Central Asia, but its role had declined after the fall of the Han. Now, with the rise of the great Tang and Song Dynasties, China reemerged as a major commercial power in East Asia, trading by sea with Southeast Asia and Japan and by land with the nomadic peoples of Central Asia.

Like the Middle East, China was also a prime source of new technology. From China came paper, printing, the compass, and gunpowder. The double-hulled Chinese junks that entered the Indian Ocean during the Ming Dynasty were slow and cumbersome but extremely seaworthy and capable of carrying substantial quantities of goods over long distances. Many inventions arrived in Europe by way of India or the Middle East, and their Chinese origins were therefore unknown in the West.

Increasing trade on a regional or global basis also led to the exchange of ideas. Buddhism was brought to China by merchants, and Islam first arrived in sub-Saharan Africa and the Indonesian archipelago in the same manner. Merchants were not the only means by which religious and cultural ideas spread, however. Sometimes migration, conquest, or relatively peaceful processes played a part. The case of the Bantu-speaking peoples in Central Africa is apparently an example of peaceful expansion; and while Islam sometimes followed the path of Arab warriors, they seldom imposed their religion by force on the local population. In some instances, as with the Mongols, the conquerors made no effort to convert others to their own religions. By contrast, Christian monks, motivated by missionary fervor, converted many of the peoples of central and eastern Europe. Roman Catholic monks brought Latin Christianity to the Germanic and western Slavic peoples, and monks from the Byzantine Empire largely converted the southern and eastern Slavic populations to Eastern Orthodox Christianity.

Another characteristic of the period between 500 and 1500 C.E. was the almost constant migration of nomadic and seminomadic peoples. Dynamic forces in the Gobi Desert, Central Asia, the Arabian peninsula, and Central Africa provoked vast numbers of peoples to abandon their homelands and seek their livelihood elsewhere. Sometimes the migration was peaceful. More often, however, migration produced political instability and sometimes invasion and subjugation. As had been the case during antiquity, the most active source of migrants was Central Asia. The region later gave birth to the fearsome Mongols, whose armies advanced to the gates of central Europe and conquered China in the thirteenth century. Wherever they went, they left a trail of enormous destruction and loss of life. Inadvertently, the Mongols were also the source of a new wave of epidemics that swept through much of Europe and the Middle East in the fourteenth century. The spread of the plague—known at the time as the Black Death—took much of the population of Europe to an early grave.

But there was another side to the era of nomadic expansion. Even the invasions of the Mongols—the "scourge of God," as Europeans of the thirteenth and fourteenth centuries called them—had constructive as well as destructive consequences. After their initial conquests, for a brief period of three generations, the Mongols provided an avenue for trade throughout the most extensive empire (known as the *Pax Mongolica*) the world had yet seen.

6

THE AMERICAS

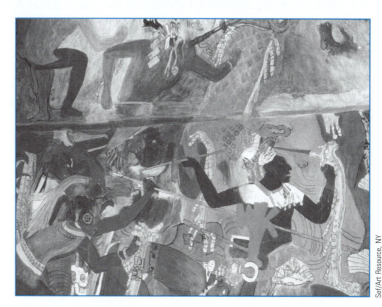

Warriors raiding a village to capture prisoners for the ritual of sacrifice

Sef/Art Resource, NY

CHAPTER OUTLINE

- The Peopling of the Americas • Early Civilizations in Central America
- The First Civilizations in South America • Stateless Societies
in the Americas

THE PEOPLING OF THE AMERICAS

The Maya (MY-uh) were only the latest in a series of sophisticated societies that had sprung up at various locations in North and South America since human beings first crossed the Bering Strait several millennia earlier. Most of these early peoples, today often referred to as **Amerindians,** lived by hunting and fishing or by food gathering. But eventually organized societies, based on the cultivation of agriculture, began to take root in Central and South America. One key area of development was on the plateau of central Mexico. Another was in the lowland regions along the Gulf of Mexico and extending into modern Guatemala. A third was in the central Andes Mountains, adjacent to the Pacific coast of South America. Others were just beginning to emerge in the vast Amazon River basin and in the river valleys and Great Plains of North America.

For two thousand years, these societies developed in isolation from their counterparts elsewhere in the world. This lack of contact with other human populations deprived them of access to technological and cultural developments taking place in Africa, Asia, and Europe. They did not know of the wheel, for example, and their written languages were rudimentary compared to those in complex civilizations elsewhere around the globe. They did not benefit from the presence of the horse (which had died out in the Americas thousands of years previously) and of other draft animals such as the ox and the water buffalo. Still, in many respects, their cultural achievements were the equal of those realized elsewhere. When the first European explorers arrived in the region at the turn of the sixteenth century, they described much that they observed in glowing terms.

The First Americans   When the first human beings arrived in the Western Hemisphere has long been a matter of conjecture. In the centuries following the voyages of Christopher Columbus (1492–1504), speculation centered on the possibility that the first settlers to reach the American continents had crossed the Atlantic Ocean. Were they the lost tribes of Israel? Were they Phoenician seafarers from Carthage? Were they refugees from the legendary lost continent of Atlantis? In all cases, the assumption was that they were relatively recent arrivals.

By the mid-nineteenth century, under the influence of the Darwinian concept of evolution, a new theory developed. It proposed that the peopling of America had taken place much earlier as a result of the migration of small groups across the Bering Strait, at a time when the area was a land bridge uniting the continents of Asia and North America. Recent evidence, including numerous physical similarities between most early Americans and contemporary peoples living in northeastern Asia, has confirmed this hypothesis. The debate on when the migrations began continues, however. The archaeologist Louis Leakey, one of the pioneers in the search for the origins of humankind in Africa, suggested that the first hominids may have arrived in America as long as 100,000 years ago. Most scholars today, however, estimate that the first Americans were *Homo sapiens sapiens* who crossed from Asia by foot between 10,000 and 15,000 years ago in pursuit of herds of bison and caribou that moved into the area in search of grazing land at the end of the last ice age. Some suggest that early migrants from Asia may have followed a maritime route down the western coast of the Americas, supporting themselves by fishing and feeding on other organisms floating in the sea.

In recent years, a number of fascinating new possibilities have opened up. A number of sites discovered at such disparate locations as Cactus Hill in Virginia, Buttermilk Creek in Texas, and Paisley Cave in Oregon show signs of human habitation as long as 15,000 years ago. Other recent discoveries raise the possibility that some early settlers may have originally come from Africa or from the South Pacific rather than from Asia. The question has not yet been answered definitively.

Nevertheless, it is now generally accepted that human beings were living in the Americas at least 15,000 years ago. They gradually spread throughout the North American continent and had penetrated almost to the southern tip of South America by about 11,000 B.C.E. These first Americans were hunters and food gatherers who lived in small nomadic communities close to the sources of their food supply. Although it is not known when agriculture was first practiced, beans and squash seeds have been found at sites that date back at least 10,000 years, implying that farming arose in America almost as early as in the Middle East. The cultivation of maize (corn), and perhaps other crops as well, appears to have been under way as early as 5000 B.C.E. in the Tehuacán (teh-hwah-KAHN) Valley in central Mexico. Archaeologists have traced the ancestry of corn back at least 9,000 years to a wild Mexican grass called teosinte (tay-oh-SIN-tee). Through a lengthy process of experimentation, local farmers transformed it into a highly productive food crop that enabled the rise of the first civilizations in the Americas. A similar process may have occurred in the lowland regions near the modern city of Veracruz and in the Yucatán (yoo-kuh-TAHN) peninsula farther to the east. There, in the region that archaeologists call Mesoamerica, one of the first civilizations in the Americas began to appear.

EARLY CIVILIZATIONS IN CENTRAL AMERICA

The first signs of civilization in Mesoamerica appeared at the end of the second millennium B.C.E., with the emergence of what is called Olmec (AHL-mek *or* OHL-mek) culture in the hot and swampy lowlands along the coast of the Gulf of Mexico south of Veracruz.

The Olmecs: In the Land of Rubber   Olmec civilization was characterized by intensive agriculture along the muddy riverbanks in the area and by the carving of stone ornaments, tools, and monuments at sites such as San Lorenzo and La Venta. The site at La Venta contains a ceremonial precinct with a 30-foot-high earthen pyramid, the largest of its date in all Mesoamerica. The Olmec peoples organized a widespread trading network, carried on religious rituals, and devised an as yet undeciphered system of hieroglyphics that is similar in some respects to later Mayan writing and may be the ancestor of the first true writing systems in the Americas.

Olmec society apparently consisted of several classes, including a class of skilled artisans who produced a series of massive stone heads, some of which are more than 10 feet high. The Olmec peoples supported themselves primarily by cultivating crops, such as corn and beans, but also engaged in fishing and hunting. The Olmecs

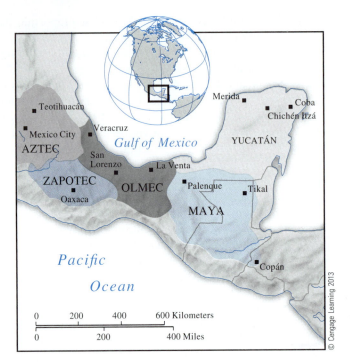

MAP 6.1 Early Mesoamerica

Mesoamerica was home to some of the first civilizations in the Western Hemisphere. This map shows the major urban settlements in the region.

apparently played a ceremonial game on a stone ball court, a ritual that would later be widely practiced throughout the region. The ball was made from the sap of a local rubber tree, thus providing the name *Olmec*: "people of the land of rubber."

Trade between the Olmecs and their neighbors was apparently quite extensive, and rubber was one of the products most desired by peoples in nearby regions. It was used not only for the manufacture of balls, but also for rubber bands and footwear, as the Olmec learned how to mix the raw latex (the sap of the rubber tree) with other ingredients to make it more supple.

Eventually, Olmec civilization began to decline, and it apparently collapsed around the fourth century B.C.E. During its heyday, however, it extended from Mexico City to El Salvador and perhaps to the shores of the Pacific Ocean.

The Zapotecs   Parallel developments were occurring at Monte Albán (MON-tee ahl-BAHN), on a hillside overlooking the modern city of Oaxaca (wah-HAH-kuh), in central Mexico. Around the middle of the first millennium B.C.E., the Zapotec (zah-puh-TEK) peoples created an extensive civilization that flourished for several hundred years in the highlands. Like the Olmec sites, Monte Albán contains a number of temples and pyramids, but they are located in much more awesome surroundings on a massive stone terrace atop a 1,200-foot-high mountain overlooking the Oaxaca valley. The majority of the population, estimated at about 20,000, dwelled on terraces cut into the sides of the mountain known to local residents as Danibaan, or "sacred mountain."

The government at Monte Albán was apparently theocratic, with an elite class of nobles and priests ruling over a population composed primarily of farmers and artisans. Like the Olmecs, the Zapotecs devised a written language that has not been deciphered. Zapotec society survived for several centuries following the collapse of the Olmecs, but Monte Albán was abandoned for unknown reasons in the late eighth century C.E.

Teotihuacán: America's First Metropolis   The first major metropolis in Mesoamerica was the city of Teotihuacán (tay-oh-tee-hwah-KAHN), capital of an early state about 30 miles northeast of Mexico City that arose around the third century B.C.E. and flourished for nearly a millennium until it collapsed under mysterious circumstances about 800 C.E. Along the main thoroughfare were temples and palaces, all dominated by the massive Pyramid of the Sun, under which archaeologists have discovered the remains of sacrificial victims, probably put to death during the dedication of the structure. In the vicinity are the remains of a large market where goods from distant regions as well as agricultural produce grown by farmers in the vicinity were exchanged. The products traded included cacao, rubber, feathers, and various types of vegetables and meat. Pulque (POOL-kay), a liquor extracted from the agave (uh-GAH-vee) plant, was used in religious ceremonies. An obsidian mine nearby may explain the location of the city; obsidian is a volcanic glass that was prized in Mesoamerica for use in tools, mirrors, and the blades of sacrificial knives.

Most of the city consisted of one-story stucco apartment compounds; some were as large as 35,000 square feet, sufficient to house more than a hundred people. Each apartment was divided into several rooms, and the compounds were covered by flat roofs made of wooden beams, poles, and stucco. The compounds were separated by wide streets laid out on a rectangular grid and were entered through narrow alleys.

Living in the fertile Valley of Mexico, an upland plateau surrounded by magnificent snowcapped mountains, the inhabitants of Teotihuacán probably obtained the bulk of their wealth from agriculture. At that time, the valley floor was filled with swampy lakes containing the water runoff from the surrounding mountains. The combination of fertile soil and adequate water made the valley one of the richest farming areas in Mesoamerica.

Sometime during the eighth century C.E., perhaps because of drought or the overcultivation of the land, the wealth and power of the city began to decline, and eventually its ruling class departed, with the priests carrying stone images of local deities on their backs. The next two centuries were a time of troubles throughout the region as principalities fought over limited farmland. The problem was later compounded when peoples from surrounding areas, attracted by the rich farmlands, migrated into the Valley of Mexico and began to compete for territory with small city-states already established there. As the local population expanded, farmers began to engage in more intensive agriculture. They drained the lakes to build *chinampas* (chee-NAM-pahs), swampy islands crisscrossed by canals that provided water for their crops and easy transportation to local markets for their excess produce.

COMPARATIVE ILLUSTRATION

The Pyramid

**RELIGION &
PHILOSOPHY**

The building of monumental structures known as pyramids was characteristic of a number of civilizations that arose in antiquity. The pyramid symbolized the link between the world of human beings and the realm of deities and was often used to house the tomb of a deceased ruler. Shown here are two prominent examples. The upper photo shows the pyramids of Giza, Egypt, built in the third millennium B.C.E. and located near the modern city of Cairo. The second photo shows the Pyramid of the Sun at Teotihuacán, erected in central Mexico in the fifth century C.E. Similar structures of various sizes were built throughout the Western Hemisphere. The concept of the pyramid was also widely applied in parts of Asia. Scholars still debate the technical aspects of constructing such pyramids.

Q *How do the pyramids erected in the Western Hemisphere compare with similar structures in other parts of the world? What were their symbolic meanings to the builders?*

PATSTOCK/age fotostock/SuperStock

SuperStock

The Olmecs: Mother Culture or First Among Equals?

What were the relations among these early societies in Mesoamerica? Trade contacts were quite active, as the Olmecs exported rubber to their neighbors in exchange for salt and obsidian. During its heyday, Olmec influence extended throughout the region, leading some historians to surmise that it was a "mother culture," much as the Shang Dynasty was once thought to be in ancient China.

A seventh-century B.C.E. pyramid recently unearthed in the southern Mexican state of Chiapas (chee-AH-pahs) contained tomb objects that bore some resemblance to counterparts in the Olmec site of La Venta, but also displayed characteristics unique to the Zoque (ZOH-kay) culture that was prevalent in that region at the time. Some scholars point to such indigenous elements to suggest that perhaps the Olmec were merely first among equals. This issue has not yet been resolved.

The Maya

Far to the east of the Valley of Mexico, another major civilization had arisen in what is now the state of Guatemala and the Yucatán peninsula. This was the civilization of the Maya ("those who grow maize" in the Mayan language), which was older and just as sophisticated as the society at Teotihuacán.

Origins It is not known when human beings first inhabited the Yucatán peninsula, but peoples contemporaneous with the Olmecs were already cultivating such crops as corn, yams, and manioc in the area during the first millennium B.C.E. As the population increased, an early civilization began to emerge along the Pacific coast directly to the south of the peninsula and in the highlands of modern Guatemala. Contacts were already established with the Olmecs to the west.

Since the area was a source for cacao trees and obsidian, the inhabitants soon developed relations with other early civilizations in the region. Cacao trees (whose name derives from the Mayan word *kakaw*) were the source of chocolate, which was drunk as a beverage by the upper classes, while cocoa beans, the fruit of the cacao tree, were used as currency in markets throughout the region. A fermented beer was produced from the pulp of the fruit. The chocolate consumed in ancient Mesoamerican cultures was roasted and had a bitter taste. The flavor survives today in a classic sauce—mole (moh-LAY)—that includes unsweetened chocolate and chili peppers among its ingredients and is served with poultry and other meats. Chocolate did not develop its familiar sweet taste until the seventeenth century when cocoa beans were brought to Europe and sugar and milk were added.

As the population in the area increased, the inhabitants began to migrate into the central Yucatán peninsula and farther to the north. The overcrowding forced farmers in the lowland areas to shift from slash-and-burn cultivation to swamp agriculture of the type practiced in the lake region of the Valley of Mexico. By the middle of the first millennium C.E., the entire area was honeycombed with a patchwork of small city-states competing for land and resources. The largest urban centers such as Tikal (tee-KAHL) may have had 100,000 inhabitants at their height and displayed a level of technological and cultural achievement that was unsurpassed in the region. By the end of the third century C.E., Mayan civilization had begun to enter its classical phase.

Political Structures   The power of Mayan rulers was impressive. One of the monarchs at Copán (koh-PAHN)—known to scholars as "18 Rabbit" from the hieroglyphs composing his name—ordered the construction of a grand palace requiring more than 30,000 person-days of labor. Around the ruler was a class of aristocrats whose wealth was probably based on the ownership of land farmed by their poorer relatives. Eventually, many of the nobles became priests or scribes at the royal court or adopted honored professions as sculptors or painters. As the society's wealth grew, so did the role of artisans and traders, who began to form a small middle class.

The majority of the population on the peninsula, however (estimated at roughly 3 million at the height of Mayan prosperity), were farmers. They lived on their *chinampa* plots or on terraced hills in the highlands. Houses were built of adobe and thatch and probably resembled the houses of the majority of the population in the area today. There was a fairly clear-cut division of labor along gender lines. The men were responsible for fighting and hunting, the women for home-making and the preparation of cornmeal, the staple food of much of the population.

Some noblewomen, however, seem to have played important roles in both political and religious life. In the seventh century C.E., for example, Pacal (pa-KAL) became king of Palenque (pah-LEN-kay), one of the most powerful of the Mayan city-states, through the royal line of his mother and grandmother, thereby breaking the patrilineal descent twice. His mother ruled Palenque for three years and was the power behind the throne for her son's first twenty-five years of rule. Pacal legitimized his kingship by transforming his mother into a divine representation of the "first mother" goddess.

Mayan Religion   Like some of the early religious beliefs in Asia and the Mediterranean, Mayan religion was polytheistic. Although the names were different, Mayan gods shared many of the characteristics of deities of nearby cultures. The supreme god was named Itzamna (eet-SAHM-nuh) ("Lizard House"). Viewed as the creator of all things, he was credited with bringing the knowledge of maize, cacao, medicine, and writing to the Mayan people.

Deities were ranked in order of importance and had human characteristics, as in ancient Greece and India. Some, like the jaguar god of night, were evil rather than good. Many of the nature deities may have been viewed as manifestations of one supreme godhead. As at Teotihuacán, human sacrifice (normally by decapitation) was practiced to propitiate the heavenly forces.

Mayan cities were built around a ceremonial core dominated by a central pyramid surmounted by a shrine to the gods. Nearby were other temples, palaces, and a sacred ball court. Like many of their modern counterparts, Mayan cities suffered from urban sprawl, with separate suburbs for the poor and the middle class, and even strip malls stretched along transportation routes, where merchants hawked their wares to pedestrians passing by.

The ball court was a rectangular space surrounded by vertical walls with metal rings through which the contestants attempted to drive a hard rubber ball. Although the rules of the game are only imperfectly understood, it apparently had religious significance, and the vanquished players were sacrificed in ceremonies held after the close of the game. Most of the players were men, although there may have been some women's teams. Similar courts have been found at sites throughout Central and South America, with the earliest, located near Veracruz, dating back to around 1500 B.C.E.

Mayan Hieroglyphs and Calendars The Mayan writing system, developed during the mid-first millennium B.C.E., was based on hieroglyphs that remained undeciphered until scholars recognized that symbols appearing in many passages represented dates in the Mayan calendar. This elaborate calendar, which measures time back to a particular date in August 3114 B.C.E., required a sophisticated understanding of astronomical events and mathematics to compile. Starting with these known symbols as a foundation, modern scholars have gradually deciphered the script. Like the scripts of the Sumerians and ancient Egyptians, the Mayan hieroglyphs were both ideographic and phonetic and were becoming more phonetic as time passed.

The responsibility for compiling official records in the Mayan city-states was given to a class of scribes, who wrote on deerskin or strips of tree bark. Unfortunately, virtually all such records have fallen victim to the ravages of a humid climate or were deliberately destroyed by Spanish missionaries after their arrival in the sixteenth century. As one Spanish bishop remarked at the time, "We found a large number of books in these characters and, as they contained nothing in which there were not to be seen superstition and lies of the devil, we burned them all, which they regretted to an amazing degree, and which caused them much affliction."[1]

As a result, almost the only surviving written records dating from the classical Mayan era are those that were carved in stone. One of the most important repositories of Mayan hieroglyphs is at Palenque, an archaeological site deep in the jungles in the neck of the Mexican peninsula, considerably to the west of the Yucatán. In a chamber located under the Temple of Inscriptions, archaeologists discovered a royal tomb and a massive limestone slab covered with hieroglyphs. By deciphering the message on the slab, archaeologists for the first time identified a historical figure in Mayan history. He was the ruler named Pacal, known from his glyph as "The Shield"; Pacal ordered the construction of the Temple of Inscriptions in the mid-seventh century, and it was his body that was buried in the tomb at the foot of the staircase leading down into the crypt.

As befits their intense interest in the passage of time, the Maya also had a sophisticated knowledge of astronomy and kept voluminous records of the movements of the heavenly bodies (according to some knowledgeable observers, Mayan pyramids, known as *huacas*, were situated to observe the stars). There were practical reasons for their concern. The arrival of the planet Venus in the evening sky, for example, was a traditional time to prepare for war. The Maya also devised the so-called Long Count, a system of calculating time based on a lunar calendar that called for the end of the current cycle of 5,200 years in the year 2012 of the Western solar-based Gregorian calendar.

Scholars once believed that the Maya were a peaceful people who rarely engaged in violence. Now, however, it is thought that rivalry among Mayan city-states was endemic and often involved bloody clashes. Scenes from paintings and rock carvings depict a society preoccupied with war and the seizure of captives for sacrifice. During the seventh century C.E., two powerful city-states, Tikal and Calakmul (kah-lahk-MOOL), competed for dominance throughout the region, setting up

MAP 6.2 The Maya Heartland

During the classical era, Mayan civilization was centered on modern-day Guatemala and the lower Yucatán peninsula. After the ninth century, new centers of power like Chichén Itzá and Uxmal began to emerge farther north.

puppet regimes and waging bloody wars that wavered back and forth for years but ultimately resulted in the total destruction of Calakmul at the end of the century.

The Mystery of Mayan Decline   Sometime in the eighth or ninth century, the classical Mayan civilization in the central Yucatán peninsula began to decline. At Copán, for example, it ended abruptly in 822 C.E., when work on various stone sculptures ordered by the ruler suddenly ceased. The end of Palenque soon followed, and the city of Tikal was abandoned by 870 C.E. Whether the decline was caused by overuse of the land, incessant warfare, internal revolt, or a natural disaster such as a volcanic eruption is a question that has puzzled archaeologists for decades. Recent evidence supports the theory that overcultivation of the land due to a growing population gradually reduced crop yields. A long drought, which lasted throughout most of the ninth and tenth centuries C.E., may have played a major role, although the city-state of Tikal, blessed with fertile soil and the presence of nearby Lake Petén, does not appear to have suffered from a lack of water. In general, though, as arable land and water became increasingly scarce, conflict among the various mini-states in the region may have intensified, accelerating the process leading to a final collapse.

Whatever the case, cities such as Tikal and Palenque were abandoned to the jungles. In their place, newer urban centers in the northern part of the peninsula, such as Uxmal (oosh-MAHL) and Chichén Itzá (chee-CHEN eet-SAH), continued to prosper, although the level of cultural achievement in this postclassical era did not match that of previous years. According to local history, this latter area was taken over by peoples known as the Toltecs (TOHL-teks), led by a man known as Kukulcan (koo-kul-KAHN), who migrated to the peninsula from Teotihuacán in central Mexico sometime in the tenth century. Some scholars believe this flight was associated with the legend of the departure from that city of Quetzalcoatl (KWET-sul-koh-AHT-ul), a deity in the form of a feathered serpent who promised that he would someday return to reclaim his homeland.

The Toltecs apparently controlled the upper peninsula from their capital at Chichén Itzá for several centuries, but this area was less fertile and more susceptible to drought than the earlier regions of Mayan settlement, and eventually they too declined. By the early sixteenth century, the area was divided into a number of small principalities, and the cities, including Uxmal and Chichén Itzá, had been abandoned.

The Aztecs

Among the groups moving into the Valley of Mexico after the fall of Teotihuacán were the Mexica (meh-SHEE-kuh). No one knows their origins, although folk legend held that their original homeland was an island in a lake called Aztlán. From that legendary homeland comes the name *Aztec*, by which they are known to the modern world. Sometime during the early twelfth century, the Aztecs left their original habitat and, carrying an image of their patron deity, Huitzilopochtli (WEET-see-loh-POHSHT-lee), began a lengthy migration that climaxed with their arrival in the Valley of Mexico sometime late in the century.

Less sophisticated than many of their neighbors, the Aztecs were at first forced to seek alliances with stronger city-states. They were excellent warriors, however, and (like Sparta in ancient Greece and the state of Qin in Zhou dynasty China) theirs had become the dominant city-state in the lake region by the early fifteenth century. Establishing their capital at Tenochtitlán (teh-nahch-teet-LAHN), on an island in the middle of Lake Texcoco (tess-KOH-koh), they set out to bring the entire region under their domination.

For the remainder of the fifteenth century, the Aztecs consolidated their control over much of what is modern Mexico, from the Atlantic to the Pacific Ocean and as far south as the Guatemalan border. The new kingdom was not a centralized state but a collection of semiautonomous territories. To provide a unifying focus for the kingdom, the Aztecs promoted their patron god, Huitzilopochtli, as the guiding deity of the entire population, which now numbered several million.

Politics Like all great empires in ancient times, the Aztec state was authoritarian. Power was vested in the monarch, whose authority had both a divine and a secular character. The Aztec ruler claimed descent from the gods and served as an intermediary between the material and the metaphysical worlds. Unlike many of his counterparts in other ancient civilizations, however, the monarch did not obtain his position by a rigid law of succession. On the death of the ruler, his successor was

MAP 6.3 The Valley of Mexico Under Aztec Rule

The Aztecs were one of the most advanced peoples in pre-Columbian Central America. Their capital at Tenochtitlán—Tlaltelolco (tuh-lahl-teh-LOH-koh)—was located at the site of modern-day Mexico City. Of the five lakes shown here, only Lake Texcoco remains today.

selected from within the royal family by a small group of senior officials, who were also members of the family and were therefore eligible for the position. Once placed on the throne, the Aztec ruler was advised by a small council of lords, headed by a prime minister who served as the chief executive of the government, and a bureaucracy. Beyond the capital, the power of the central government was limited. Rulers of territories subject to the Aztecs were allowed considerable autonomy in return for paying tribute, in the form of goods or captives, to the central government. The most important government officials in the provinces were the tax collectors, who collected the tribute. They used the threat of military action against those who failed to carry out their tribute obligations and therefore, understandably, were not popular with the taxpayers. According to Bernal Díaz, a Spaniard who recorded his impressions of Aztec society during a visit in the early sixteenth century:

All these towns complained about Montezuma [Moctezuma, the Aztec ruler] and his tax collectors, speaking in private so that the Mexican ambassadors should not hear them, however. They said these officials robbed them of all they possessed, and that if their wives and daughters were pretty they would violate them in front of their fathers and husbands and carry them away. They also said that the Mexicans [that is, the representatives from the capital] made the men work like slaves, compelling them to carry pine trunks and stone and firewood and maize overland and in canoes, and to perform other tasks, such as planting maize fields, and that they took away the people's lands as well for the service of their idols.[2]

Social Structures   Positions in the government bureaucracy were the exclusive privilege of the hereditary nobility, all of whom traced their lineage to the founding family of the Aztec clan. Male children in noble families were sent to temple schools, where they were exposed to a harsh regimen of manual labor, military training, and memorization of information about Aztec society and religion. On reaching adulthood, they would select a career in the military service, the government bureaucracy, or the priesthood. As a reward for their services, senior officials received large estates from the government, and they alone had the right to hire communal labor.

The remainder of the population consisted of commoners, indentured workers, and slaves. Most indentured workers were landless laborers who contracted to work on the nobles' estates, while slaves served in the households of the wealthy. Slavery was not an inherited status, and the children of slaves were considered free citizens. Commoners might sell themselves into slavery when in debt and then later purchase their freedom.

The vast majority of the population consisted of commoners. All commoners were members of large kinship groups called **calpullis** (kal-PUL-eez). Each *calpulli*, often consisting of as many as a thousand members, was headed by an elected chief, who ran its day-to-day affairs and served as an intermediary with the central government. Each *calpulli* was responsible for providing taxes (usually in the form of goods) and conscript labor to the state.

Each *calpulli* maintained its own temples and schools and administered the land held by the community. Farmland within the *calpulli* was held in common and could not be sold, although it could be passed down within the family. In the cities, each *calpulli* occupied a separate neighborhood, where its members often performed a particular function, such as metalworking, stonecutting, weaving, carpentry, or commerce. Apparently, a large proportion of the population engaged in some form of trade, at least in the densely populated Valley of Mexico, where an estimated half of the people lived in an urban environment. Many farmers, who cultivated their crops in *chinampas* as their predecessors had for centuries, brought their goods to the markets via the canals and sold them directly to retailers.

The *calpulli* compounds themselves were divided into smaller family units. Individual families lived in small flat-roofed dwellings containing one or two rooms. Each house was separate from its neighbors and had direct access to the surrounding streets and canals. The houses of farmers living on the *chinampas* were set on raised dirt platforms built above the surrounding fields to prevent flooding.

Gender roles within the family were rigidly stratified. Male children were trained for war and were expected to serve in the army on reaching adulthood.

Women were expected to work in the home, weave textiles, and raise children, although, like their brothers, they were permitted to enter the priesthood. According to Bernal Díaz, a female deity presided over the rites of marriage. As in most traditional societies, chastity and obedience were desirable female characteristics. Although women in Aztec society enjoyed more legal rights than women in some other traditional civilizations, they were still not equal to men. Women were permitted to own and inherit property and to enter into contracts. Marriage was usually monogamous, although noble families sometimes practiced **polygyny** (having more than one wife at a time). Wedding partners were normally selected from within the lineage group but not the immediate family. As in most societies at the time, parents usually selected their child's spouse, often for purposes of political or social advancement.

Classes in Aztec society were rigidly stratified. Commoners were not permitted to enter the nobility, although some occasionally rose to senior positions in the army or the priesthood as the result of exemplary service. As in medieval Europe, such occupations often provided a route of upward mobility for ambitious commoners. A woman of noble standing would sometimes marry a commoner because the children of such a union would inherit her higher status, and she could expect to be treated better by her husband's family, who would be proud of the marriage relationship.

Land of the Feathered Serpent: Aztec Religion and Culture   The Aztecs, like their contemporaries throughout Mesoamerica, lived in an environment populated by a multitude of gods. Scholars have identified more than a hundred deities in the Aztec pantheon; some of them were nature spirits, like the rain god, Tlaloc (tuh-lah-LOHK), and some were patron deities, like the symbol of the Aztecs themselves, Huitzilopochtli. A supreme deity, called Ometeotl (oh-met-tee-AH-tul), represented the all-powerful and omnipresent forces of the heavens, but he was rather remote, and other gods, notably the feathered serpent Quetzalcoatl, had a more direct impact on the lives of the people. Representing the forces of creation, virtue, and learning and culture, Quetzalcoatl bears a distinct similarity to Shiva in Hindu belief. According to Aztec tradition, this godlike being had left his homeland in the Valley of Mexico in the tenth century, promising to return in triumph.

Aztec cosmology was based on a belief in the existence of two worlds, the material and the divine. The earth was the material world and took the form of a flat disk surrounded by water on all sides. The divine world, which consisted of both heaven and hell, was the abode of the gods. Human beings could aspire to a form of heavenly salvation but first had to pass through a transitional stage, somewhat like Christian purgatory, before reaching their final destination, where the soul was finally freed from the body. To prepare for the final day of judgment, as well as to help them engage in proper behavior through life, all citizens underwent religious training at temple schools during adolescence and took part in various rituals throughout their lives. The most devout were encouraged to study for the priesthood. Once accepted, they served at temples ranging from local branches at the *calpulli* level to the highest shrines in the ceremonial precinct at Tenochtitlán. In some respects, however, Aztec society may have been undergoing a process of secularization. By late Aztec times, athletic contests at the ball court had apparently lost some of their religious significance. Gambling was increasingly common, and wagering on the results of the matches was widespread. One province reportedly sent 16,000 rubber balls to the capital city of Tenochtitlán as its annual tribute to the royal court.

Aztec religion contained a distinct element of fatalism that was inherent in the creation myth, which described an unceasing struggle between the forces of good and evil throughout the universe. This struggle led to the creation and destruction of four worlds, or suns. The world was now living in the time of the fifth sun. But that world, too, was destined to end with the destruction of this earth and all that is within it:

> *Even jade is shattered,*
> *Even gold is crushed,*
> *Even quetzal plumes are torn....*
> *One does not live forever on this earth:*
> *We endure only for an instant!*[3]

In an effort to postpone the day of reckoning, the Aztecs practiced human sacrifice. The Aztecs believed that by appeasing the sun god, Huitzilopochtli, with sacrifices, they could delay the final destruction of their world. Victims were prepared for the ceremony through elaborate rituals and then brought to the holy shrine, where their hearts were ripped out of their chests and presented to the gods as a holy offering. It was an honor to be chosen for sacrifice, and captives were often used as sacrificial victims, since they represented valor, the trait the Aztecs prized most.

Art and Culture   Like the art of the Olmecs, most Aztec architecture, art, and sculpture had religious significance. At the center of the capital city of Tenochtitlán was the sacred precinct, dominated by the massive pyramid dedicated to Huitzilopochtli and the rain god, Tlaloc. According to Bernal Díaz, at its base the pyramid was equal to the plots of six large European town houses and tapered from there to the top, which was surmounted by a platform containing shrines to the gods and an altar for performing human sacrifices. The entire pyramid was covered with brightly colored paintings and sculptures.

Although little Aztec painting survives, it was evidently of high quality. Díaz compared the best work with that of Michelangelo. Artisans worked with stone and with soft metals such as gold and silver, which they cast using the lost-wax technique. They did not have the knowledge for making implements in bronze or iron, however. Stoneworking consisted primarily of representations of the gods and bas-reliefs depicting religious ceremonies. Among the most famous is the massive disk called the Stone of the Fifth Sun, carved for use at the central pyramid at Tenochtitlán.

The Aztecs had devised a form of writing based on hieroglyphs that represented an object or a concept. The symbols had no phonetic significance and did not constitute a writing system as such but could give the sense of a message and were probably used by civilian or religious officials as notes or memorandums for their orations. Although many of the notes simply recorded dates in the complex calendar that had evolved since Olmec times, others provide insight into the daily lives of the Aztec peoples. A trained class of scribes carefully painted the notes on paper made from the inner bark of fig trees. Unfortunately, many of these notes were destroyed by the Spaniards as part of their effort to eradicate all aspects of Aztec religion and culture.

Aztec Religion Through Spanish Eyes

ART & IDEAS

When the first European explorers arrived in Mexico in the early sixteenth century, they reported their impressions of Aztec society in diaries and letters to their compatriots back home. The following passage from Father Diego Duran's *The Aztecs: The History of the Indies of New Spain* describes the ritual of human sacrifice as a central part of Aztec religion. The Aztecs believed that only the gift of human hearts would appease their god Huitzilopochtli and prevent him from bringing disaster to their civilization. Although some modern-day scholars doubt the accuracy of such reports, it is now widely accepted that human sacrifice was a common practice in many Amerindian societies, as it had once been in other parts of the world as well.

Diego Duran, *The Aztecs: The History of the Indies of New Spain*

When the day of the feast arrived, Moteczoma and Tlacaelel blackened their bodies with soot and applied it in such a way that it caught the light.... They placed crowns of fine feathers, adorned with gold and precious stones, upon their heads, and on each arm they wore a sheath of gold reaching from the elbow to the shoulder. On their feet were richly worked jaguar skin sandals, inlaid with gold and gems. They also were robed in splendid royal mantles.... Jeweled plugs were attached to holes in their noses, and both these lords carried flint knives in their hands.

The king and Tlacaelel now appeared before the assembly and went to stand upon the stone which was the likeness and image of the sun, one having ascended by one staircase and the other by another. The five priests of sacrifice followed them. They were to hold down the feet, hands and heads of the victims, and they were painted all over with red ocher, even their loincloths and tunics. Upon their heads they wore paper crowns surmounted by little shields which hung to the middle of their foreheads, also painted in ocher. On the top of their heads they wore long stiff feathers which had been tied to their hair and which stood straight up. On their feet were very common, worthless sandals....

The five priests entered and claimed the prisoner who stood first in the line at the skull rack. Each prisoner they took to the place where the king stood and, when they had forced him to stand upon the stone which was the figure and likeness of the sun, they threw him upon his back. One took him by the right arm, another by the left, one by his left foot, another by his right, while the fifth priest tied his neck with a cord and held him down so that he could not move.

The king lifted the knife on high and made a gash in his breast. Having opened it he extracted the heart and raised it high with his hand as an offering to the sun. When the heart had cooled he tossed it into the circular depression, taking some of the blood in his hand and sprinkling it in the direction of the sun. In this way the sacrificers killed four, one by one; then Tlacaelel came and killed another four in his turn. And so, four by four, the prisoners were slain, till every last man that had been brought from the Mixteca had perished.

Q *What other societies encountered in this book engaged in human sacrifices as an aspect of their religious practices?*

Source: From Diego Duran, *The Aztecs: The History of the Indies of New Spain*, Doris Heyden and Fernando Horcasitas, trans. (New York: Orion Press, 1964), pp. 120–121.

The First Civilizations in South America

South America is a vast continent, characterized by extremes in climate and geography. The north is dominated by the mighty Amazon River, which flows through dense tropical rain forests carrying a larger flow of water than any other river system in the world. Farther to the south, the forests are replaced by prairies and steppes stretching westward to the Andes Mountains, which extend the entire length of the continent, from the Isthmus of Panama to the Strait of Magellan. Along the Pacific coast, on the western slopes of the mountains, are some of the driest desert regions in the world.

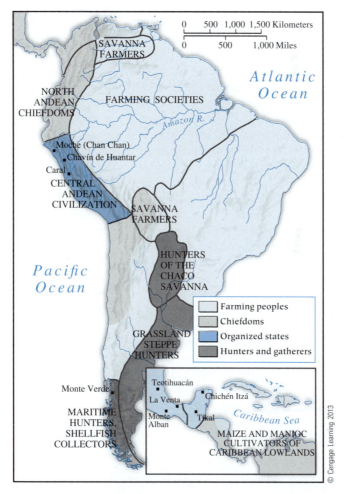

MAP 6.4   Early Peoples and Cultures of Central and South America

This map shows regions of early human settlements in Central and South America. Urban conglomerations appear in Mesoamerica (see inset) and along the western coast of South America.

South America has been inhabited by human beings for more than 12,000 years. Wall paintings discovered at the so-called Cavern of the Painted Rock in the Amazon region suggest that Stone Age peoples were living in the area at least 11,000 years ago, and a site at Monte Verde, along the central coast of Chile, has been dated to 10,500 B.C.E. Early peoples lived by hunting, fishing, and food gathering, but there are indications that irrigated farming was being practiced on the western slopes of the Andes Mountains more than 5,000 years ago.

Caral

By the third millennium B.C.E., complex societies had begun to emerge in the coastal regions of modern-day Peru and Ecuador. Some settlements were located along the coast, but the remnants of farming communities watered by canals have also been found in the valleys of rivers flowing down from the Andes Mountains. Fish, reeds, and various other maritime products were traded to inland peoples for agricultural produce, wool, and salt.

The most vivid example of this process can be seen along the Pacific coast of modern-day Peru. By 3500 B.C.E.—more than a thousand years earlier than the earliest known cities in Mesoamerica—the first urban settlements appeared in the region. At Caral, a highly publicized site located 14 miles inland from the coast, the remnants of a 4,500-year-old city sit on the crest of a 60-foot-high plateau just above the fertile valley of the Supe River. Several pyramids similar to those built in Mesoamerica were erected at the site, along with plazas, sunken altars, residential areas, and structures that were evidently used for astronomical observation. Nearly twenty similar settlements are scattered over an area of 66 hectares on both sides of the Supe River as it makes it way westward to the sea.

The inhabitants of these ancient settlements raised squash, beans, and tomatoes in the river valley below, and provided such agricultural produce, as well as cotton and salt, to fishing communities along the nearby coast, where the cotton material was used to make fishnets. In return, they received maritime products and reeds for baskets. They were sophisticated farmers, as evidenced by the remnants of ancient irrigation canals found in the vicinity. Some maritime trade was apparently conducted along the Pacific coast, as evidenced by the presence of *Spondylus* shells from Ecuador (used for religious ceremonies) and various plants not found in the vicinity.

The exact nature of these early communities is not yet clear. Indeed, it is not known whether these early settlements were actual villages or merely ceremonial centers, although there is convincing evidence of the existence of distinct social classes, a ruling elite, specialized labor, and organized religious beliefs, as well as cultural activities such as music and crafts. There are even indications of the appearance of a primitive writing system.

Although the reasons for eventual decline are not yet clear, this culture apparently reached its height during the first millennium B.C.E. with the emergence of the Chavín style, named for a site near the modern city of Chavín de Huantar (chah-VEEN day HWAHN-tar). The ceremonial precinct at the site contained an impressive stone temple complete with interior galleries, a stone-block ceiling, and a system of underground canals that probably channeled water into the temple complex for ceremonial purposes. The structure was surrounded by stone figures depicting various deities and two pyramids. Evidence of metallurgy has also been found, with objects made of copper and gold. Another impressive technological achievement was the building in 300 B.C.E. of the first solar observatory in the Americas in the form of thirteen stone towers on a hillside north of Lima, Peru.

Moche

Chavín society had broken down by 200 B.C.E., but early in the first millennium C.E., another advanced civilization appeared in northern Peru, in the valley of the Moche River, which flows from the foothills of the Andes into the Pacific Ocean. It occupied an area of more than 2,500 square miles, and its capital city, large enough to contain more than 10,000 people, was dominated by two massive adobe pyramids nearly 100 feet high. The larger one, known today as the Pyramid of the Sun, covered a total of 15 acres. The other, built on the side of a mountain and known as the Pyramid of the Moon, was adorned with painted murals depicting battles, ritual sacrifices, and various local deities.

Artifacts found at Moche (moh-CHAY), especially the metalwork and stone and ceramic figures, exhibit a high quality of artisanship. They were imitated at river valley sites throughout the surrounding area, which suggests that the influence of the Moche rulers may have extended as far as 400 miles along the coast. The artifacts also indicate that the people at Moche, like those in Central America, were preoccupied with warfare. Paintings and pottery as well as other artifacts in stone, metal, and ceramics frequently portray warriors, prisoners, and sacrificial victims. The Moche were also fascinated by the heavens, and much of their art consisted of celestial symbols and astronomical constellations.

Environmental Problems   The Moche River valley is extremely arid, normally receiving less than an inch of rain annually. The peoples in the area compensated by building a sophisticated irrigation system to carry water from the river to the parched fields. At its zenith, Moche culture was spectacular. By the eighth century C.E., however, the civilization was in a state of collapse, the irrigation canals had been abandoned, and the remaining population had left the area and moved farther inland or suffered from severe malnutrition.

What had happened to bring Moche culture to this untimely end? Archaeologists speculate that environmental disruptions, perhaps brought on by changes in the temperature of the Pacific Ocean known as **El Niño**, led to alternating periods of drought and flooding of coastal regions, which caused the irrigated fields to silt up. The warm water created by El Niño conditions also killed local marine life, severely damaging the local fishing industry.

Wari and Chimor   A few hundred miles to the south of Moche, a people known as the Wari (WAH-ree) culture began to expand from their former home in the Andes foothills and established communities along the coast in the vicinity of modern Lima, Peru. As the state of Moche declined, the Wari gradually spread northward in the eighth century and began to occupy many of the urban sites in the Moche valley. According to some scholars, they may even have made use of the Moche's sacred buildings and appropriated their religious symbolism. In the process, the Wari created the most extensive land empire yet seen in South America. In the end, however, they too succumbed to the challenge posed by unstable environmental conditions.

COMPARATIVE ESSAY

History and the Environment

EARTH &
ENVIRONMENT

In *The Decline and Fall of the Roman Empire*, published in 1788, the British historian Edward Gibbon raised a question that has fascinated historians ever since: What brought about the collapse of that once powerful civilization that dominated the Mediterranean region for more than five centuries? Traditional explanations have centered on political or cultural factors, such as imperial overreach, moral decay, military weakness, or the impact of invasions. Recently, however, some historians have suggested that environmental problems, such as poisoning due to the use of lead water pipes and cups, the spread of malaria, or a lengthy drought in wheat-growing regions in North Africa, might have at least contributed to Rome's collapse.

The current interest in the impact of the environment on the Roman Empire reflects a growing awareness among historians that environmental conditions may have been a key factor in the fate of several of the great societies in the ancient world. Climatic changes or natural disasters almost certainly led to the decline and collapse of Harappan civilization in the Indus River valley. In the Americas, massive flooding brought about by the El Niño effect (environmental conditions triggered by changes in water temperature in the Pacific Ocean) appears to be one possible cause for the collapse of the Moche civilization in what is today Peru, while drought and overcultivation of the land are often cited as reasons for the decline of the Maya in Mesoamerica.

Climatic changes continued to affect the fate of nations and peoples in later eras as well. Drought conditions and overuse of the land may have led to the gradual decline of Mesopotamia as a focal point of advanced civilization in the Middle East, while soil erosion and colder conditions doomed an early attempt by the Vikings to establish a foothold in Greenland and North America. Sometimes the problems were self-inflicted, as on Easter Island, a remote outpost in the Pacific Ocean, where Polynesian settlers migrating from the west about 900 C.E. may have denuded the landscape that by the fifteenth century, what had been a reasonably stable and peaceful society had descended into civil war and cannibalism.

Climatic changes, of course, have not always been detrimental to the health and prosperity of human beings. A warming trend that took place at the end of the last ice age eventually made much of the world more habitable for farming peoples about ten thousand years ago. The effects of El Niño may be beneficial to people living in some areas and disastrous in others. But human misuse of land and water resources is always dangerous to settled societies, especially those living in fragile environments.

Q *Many ancient civilizations throughout the world were weakened or destroyed by changes taking place in the environment. What are some examples in the pre-Columbian Americas?*

Around 1100, a new power, the kingdom of Chimor (chee-MAWR), with its capital at Chan Chan (CHAHN CHAHN), at the mouth of the Moche River, emerged in the area. Built almost entirely of adobe, Chan Chan housed an estimated 30,000 residents in an area of more than 12 square miles that included a number of palace compounds surrounded by walls nearly 30 feet high. One compound contained an intricate labyrinth that wound its way progressively inward until it ended in a central chamber, probably occupied by the ruler. Like the Moche before them, the people of Chimor—the Chimú (chee-MOO)—relied on irrigation to funnel the water from the river into their fields. An elaborate system of canals brought the water through hundreds of miles of hilly terrain to the fields near the coast. Nevertheless, by the fifteenth century, Chimor, too, had disappeared, a victim of floods and a series of earthquakes that destroyed the intricate irrigation system that had been the basis of its survival.

These early civilizations in the Andes were by no means isolated from other societies in the region. As early as 2000 B.C.E., local peoples had been venturing into the Pacific Ocean on wind-powered rafts constructed of balsa wood. By the late first millennium C.E., seafarers from the coast of Ecuador had established a vast trading network that extended southward to central Peru and as far north as western Mexico, more than 2,000 miles away. Items transported included jewelry, beads, and metal goods. In all likelihood, technological exchanges were an important by-product of the relationship.

Transportation by land, however, was more difficult. Although roads were constructed to facilitate communication between communities, the forbidding terrain in the mountains was a serious obstacle, and the only draft animal on the entire continent was the llama, which is considerably less hardy than the cattle, horses, and water buffalo used in much of Asia. Such problems undoubtedly hampered the development of regular contacts with distant societies in the Americas, as well as the exchange of goods and ideas that had lubricated the rise of civilizations from China to the Mediterranean Sea.

The Inka

The Chimor kingdom was eventually succeeded in the late fifteenth century by an invading force from the mountains far to the south. In the late fourteenth century, the Inka were a small community in the area of Cuzco (KOOS-koh), a city located at an altitude of 10,000 feet in the mountains of southern Peru. In the 1440s, however, under the leadership of their powerful ruler Pachakuti (pah-chah-KOO-tee) (sometimes called Pachacutec, or "he who transforms the world"), the Inka launched a campaign of conquest that eventually brought the entire region under their authority. Under Pachakuti and his immediate successors, Topa Inka (TOH-puh INK-uh) and Huayna Inka (WY-nuh INK-uh) (the word *Inka* means "ruler"), the boundaries of the empire were extended as far as Ecuador, central Chile, and the edge of the Amazon basin.

The Four Quarters: Inka Politics and Society

Pachakuti created a highly centralized state. With a stunning concern for mathematical precision, he divided his empire, called Tahuantinsuyu (tuh-HWAHN-tin-SOO-yoo), or "the world of the four quarters," into provinces and districts. Each province contained about ten thousand residents (at least in theory) and was ruled by a governor related to the royal family. Excess inhabitants were transferred to other locations. The capital of Cuzco was divided into four quarters, or residential areas, and the social status and economic functions of the residents of each quarter were rigidly defined.

The state was built on forced labor. Often entire communities of workers were moved from one part of the country to another to open virgin lands or engage in massive construction projects. Under Pachakuti, Cuzco was transformed from a

MAP 6.5 The Inka Empire About 1500 C.E.

The Inka were the last civilization to flourish in South America before the arrival of the Spanish. The impressive system of roads constructed to facilitate communication shows the extent of Inka control throughout the Andes Mountains.

city of mud and thatch into an imposing metropolis of stone. The walls, built of close-fitting stones without the use of mortar, were a wonder to early European visitors. The most impressive structure in the city was a temple dedicated to the sun. According to a Spanish observer, "All four walls of the temple were covered from top to bottom with plates and slabs of gold."[4] Equally impressive are the ruins of the abandoned city of Machu Picchu (MAH-choo PEE-choo), built on a lofty hilltop far above the Urubamba River.

Another major construction project was a system of 24,800 miles of highways and roads that extended from the border of modern Colombia to a point south of modern Santiago, Chile. Two major roadways extended in a north-south direction, one through the Andes Mountains and the other along the coast, with connecting routes between them. Rest houses and storage depots were placed along the roads. Suspension bridges made of braided fiber and fastened to stone abutments on

Virgins with Red Cheeks

FAMILY & SOCIETY

A letter from a Peruvian chief to King Philip III of Spain written four hundred years ago gives us a firsthand account of the nature of traditional Inkan society. The purpose of author Huaman Poma was both to justify the history and culture of the Inka peoples and to record their sufferings under Spanish domination. In his letter, Poma describes Inkan daily life from birth to death in minute detail. He explains the different tasks assigned to men and women, beginning with their early education. Whereas boys were taught to watch the flocks and trap animals, girls were taught to dye, spin, and weave cloth and perform other domestic chores. Most interesting, perhaps, was the emphasis that the Inka placed on virginity, as is evident in the document presented here. The Inka's tradition of temple virgins is reminiscent of similar practices in ancient Rome, where young girls from noble families were chosen as priestesses to tend the sacred fire in the Temple of Vesta for thirty years. If an Inkan temple virgin lost her virginity, she was condemned to be buried alive in an underground chamber.

Huaman Poma, Letter to a King

During the time of the Incas certain women, who were called *accla* or "the chosen," were destined for lifelong virginity. Mostly they were confined in houses and they belonged to one of two main categories, namely sacred virgins and common virgins.

The so-called "virgins with red cheeks" entered upon their duties at the age of twenty and were dedicated to the service of the Sun, the Moon, and the Day-Star. In their whole life they were never allowed to speak to a man.

The virgins of the Inca's own shrine of Huanacauri were known for their beauty as well as their chastity. The other principal shrines had similar girls in attendance. At the less important shrines there were the older virgins who occupied themselves with spinning and weaving the silklike clothes worn by their idols. There was a still lower class of virgins, over forty years of age and no longer very beautiful, who performed unimportant religious duties and worked in the fields or as ordinary seamstresses.

Daughters of noble families who had grown into old maids were adept at making girdles, headbands, string bags, and similar articles in the intervals of their pious observances.

Girls who had musical talent were selected to sing or play the flute and drum at Court, weddings and other ceremonies, and all the innumerable festivals of the Inca year.

There was yet another class of *accla* or "chosen," only some of whom kept their virginity and others not. These were the Inca's beautiful attendants and concubines, who were drawn from noble families and lived in his palaces. They made clothing for him out of material finer than taffeta or silk. They also prepared a maize spirit of extraordinary richness, which was matured for an entire month, and they cooked delicious dishes for the Inca. They also lay with him, but never with any other man.

Q *According to this selection, one of the chief duties of a woman in Inkan society was to spin and weave. In what other traditional societies was textile making a woman's work? Why do you think this was the case?*

Source: From *Letter to a King* by Guaman Poma de Ayala. Translated and edited by Christopher Dilke. Published by E. P. Dutton, New York, 1978.

opposite banks were built over ravines and waterways. Use of the highways was restricted to official and military purposes. Trained runners carried messages rapidly from one way station to another, enabling information to travel up to 140 miles in a single day.

In rural areas, the population lived mainly by farming. In the mountains, the most common form was terraced agriculture, watered by irrigation systems that carried precise amounts of water into the fields, which were planted with maize, potatoes, and other crops. The plots were tilled by collective labor regulated by the state. Like other aspects of Inkan society, marriage was strictly regulated, and men and women were required to select a marriage partner from within the immediate tribal group. For women, there was one escape from a life of domestic servitude: fortunate maidens were selected to serve as "chosen virgins" in temples throughout the country. Noblewomen were eligible to compete for service in the Temple of the Sun at Cuzco, while commoners might hope to serve in temples in the provincial capitals. Punishment for breaking the vow of chastity was harsh, and few evidently took the risk.

Inka Culture   Like many other civilizations in pre-Columbian Latin America, the Inka state was built on war. Soldiers for the 200,000-man Inka army, the largest and best armed in the region, were raised by universal male conscription. Military units were moved rapidly along the highway system and were bivouacked in the rest houses located along the roadside. Because the Inka had no wheeled vehicles, supplies were carried on the backs of llamas. Once an area was placed under Inka authority, the local inhabitants were instructed in the Quechua (KEH-chuh-wuh) language, which became the lingua franca of the state, and were introduced to the state religion. The Inka had no writing system but kept records using a system of knotted strings called **quipu** (KEE-poo), maintained by professionally trained officials, that were able to record all data of a numerical nature. What could not be recorded in such a manner was committed to memory and then recited when needed. The practice was apparently not invented by the Inka. Fragments of *quipu* have been found at Caral and dated at approximately five thousand years ago. Nor apparently was the experiment limited to the Americas. A passage in the Chinese classic *The Way of the Tao* declares, "Let the people revert to communication by knotted cords."

As in the case of the Aztecs and the Maya, the lack of a fully developed writing system did not prevent the Inka from realizing a high level of cultural achievement. Most of what survives was recorded by the Spanish and consists of entertainment for the elites. The Inka had a highly developed tradition of court theater, including both tragic and comic works. There was also some poetry, composed in blank verse and often accompanied by music played on reed instruments.

STATELESS SOCIETIES IN THE AMERICAS

Beyond Central America and the high ridges of the Andes Mountains, on the Great Plains of North America, along the Amazon River in South America, and on the islands of the Caribbean Sea, other communities of Amerindians were also beginning to master the art of agriculture and to build organized societies.

Although human beings had occupied much of the continent of North America during the early phase of human settlement, the switch to farming as a means of survival did not occur until the third millennium B.C.E. at the earliest, and much later in most areas of the continent. Until that time, most Amerindian communities lived by hunting, fishing, or foraging. As the supply of large animals began to diminish, they turned to smaller game and to fishing and foraging for wild plants, fruits, and nuts.

The Eastern Woodlands

It was probably during the third millennium B.C.E. that peoples in the Eastern Woodlands (the land in eastern North America from the Great Lakes to the Gulf of Mexico) began to cultivate indigenous plants for food in a systematic way. As wild game and food became scarce, some communities began to place more emphasis on cultivating crops. This shift first occurred in the Mississippi River valley from Ohio, Indiana, and Illinois down to the Gulf of Mexico. Among the most commonly cultivated crops were maize, squash, beans, and various grasses.

As the population in the area increased, people began to congregate in villages, and sedentary communities began to develop in the alluvial lowlands, where the soil could be cultivated for many years at a time because of the nutrients deposited by the river water.

Village councils were established to adjudicate disputes, and in a few cases, several villages banded together under the authority of a local chieftain. Urban centers began to appear, some of them inhabited by ten thousand people or more. At the same time, regional trade increased. The people of the **Hopewell culture** in Ohio ranged from the shores of Lake Superior to the Appalachian Mountains and the Gulf of Mexico in search of metals, shells, obsidian, and manufactured items to support their economic needs and religious beliefs.

Cahokia

At the site of Cahokia, near the modern city of East Saint Louis, Illinois, archaeologists found a burial mound more than 98 feet high with a base larger than that of the Great Pyramid in Egypt. A hundred smaller mounds were also found in the vicinity. The town itself, which covered almost 300 acres and was surrounded by a wooden stockade, was apparently the administrative capital of much of the surrounding territory until its decline in the 1200s. With a population of more than 20,000, it was reportedly the largest city in North America until Philadelphia surpassed that number in the early nineteenth century. Cahokia carried on extensive trade with other communities throughout the region, and there are some signs of regular contacts with the civilizations in Mesoamerica, such as the presence of ball courts in the Central American style. But wars were not uncommon, leading the Iroquois, who inhabited much of the modern states of Pennsylvania and New York as well as parts of southern Canada, to create a tribal alliance called the League of Iroquois.

The Ancient Pueblo Peoples

West of the Mississippi River basin, most Amerindian peoples lived by hunting or food gathering. During the first millennium C.E., knowledge of agriculture gradually spread up the rivers to the Great Plains, and farming was practiced as far west as southwestern Colorado, where an agricultural community was established in an area extending from northern New Mexico and Arizona to southwestern Colorado and parts of southern Utah. Although they apparently never discovered the wheel or used beasts of burden, these Ancient Pueblo peoples (formerly known by the Navajo name "Anasazi," or "alien ancient ones") created a system of roads that facilitated an extensive exchange of technology, products, and ideas throughout the region. By the ninth century, they had mastered the art of irrigation, which allowed them to expand their productive efforts to squash and beans, and had established an important urban center at Chaco Canyon, in southern New Mexico, where they built a walled city with dozens of three-story adobe communal houses, today called **pueblos** with timbered roofs. Community religious functions were carried out in two large circular chambers called *kivas* (KEE-vuhs). Clothing was made from hides or cotton cloth. At its height, **Pueblo Bonito** contained several hundred compounds housing several thousand residents.

In the mid-twelfth century, the Ancient Pueblo peoples moved north to Mesa Verde, in southwestern Colorado. At first, they settled on top of the mesa, but eventually they expanded onto the cliffs of surrounding canyons.

Sometime during the late thirteenth century, however, Mesa Verde was also abandoned, and the inhabitants migrated southward. Their descendants, the Zuni and the Hopi, now occupy pueblos in central Arizona and New Mexico (thus leading them to adopt their new name). For years, archaeologists surmised that a severe drought was the cause of the migration, but new evidence has raised doubts that decreasing rainfall, by itself, was a sufficient explanation. An increase in internecine warfare, perhaps brought about by climatic changes, may also have played a role in the decision to relocate. Some archaeologists point to evidence that cannibalism was practiced at Pueblo Bonito and suggest that migrants from the south may have arrived in the area, provoking bitter rivalries within Ancient Pueblo society. In any event, with increasing aridity and the importation of the horse by the Spanish in the sixteenth century, hunting revived, and mounted nomads like the Apache and the Navajo came to dominate much of the Southwest. Prior to their relocation, however, the Pueblo Bonito peoples maintained commercial contacts with their counterparts in Mexico and even as far south as the Pacific Coast of South America.

South America: The Arawak   East of the Andes Mountains in South America, other Amerindian societies were beginning to make the transition to agriculture. Perhaps the most prominent were the Arawak (AR-uh-wahk), a people living along the Orinoco River in modern Venezuela. Having begun to cultivate manioc (a tuber also known as *cassava* or *yuca*, the source of tapioca) along the banks of the river, they gradually migrated down to the coast and then proceeded to move eastward along the northern coast of the continent. Some occupied the islands of the Caribbean Sea. In their new island habitat, they lived by a mixture of fishing, hunting, and cultivating maize, beans, manioc, and squash, as well as other crops such as peanuts, peppers, and pineapples. As the population increased, a pattern of political organization above the village level appeared, along with recognizable social classes headed by a chieftain (*cacique*) whose authority included control over the economy. The Arawak practiced human sacrifice, and some urban centers contained ball courts, suggesting the possibility of contacts with Mesoamerica.

Eventually, new peoples from South America began to migrate into the islands of the Caribbean Sea. Known as Caribs, they tended to be more warlike than their predecessors and often drove the previous arrivals to seek refuge on islands farther

Jason Langley/AGE Fotostock

Cliff Palace at Mesa Verde. *Mesa Verde is one of the best-developed sites of the Ancient Pueblo peoples in southwestern North America. At one time they were farmers who tilled the soil atop the mesas, but eventually they were forced to build their settlements in more protected locations. At Cliff Palace, shown here, adobe houses were hidden on the perpendicular face of the mesa. Access was achieved only by a perilous descent via indented finger- and toeholds on the rock face.*

to the north. A Carib community survives today on the island of Dominica, in the Lesser Antilles.

In most such societies, where clear-cut class stratifications had not as yet taken place, men and women were considered of equal status. Men were responsible for hunting, warfare, and dealing with outsiders, while women were accountable for the crops, the distribution of food, maintaining the household, and bearing and raising the children. Their roles were complementary and were often viewed as a divine division of labor. In such cases, women in the stateless societies of North America held positions of greater respect than their counterparts in the river valley civilizations of the ancient world.

Amazonia   Substantial human activity was also apparently taking place in the Amazon River valley. Scholars have been skeptical that advanced societies could take shape in the region because the soil was believed to lack adequate nutrients to support a large population. Recent archaeological evidence, however, suggests that in some areas where decaying organic matter produces a rich soil suitable for farming—such as the region near the modern river port of Santarem—large agricultural societies may once have existed. More information about this previously unknown culture must await further archaeological evidence.

CHRONOLOGIES

EARLY MESOAMERICA

At least 15,000 years ago	Arrival of human beings in America
c. 8000 B.C.E.	Agriculture first practiced
1200 B.C.E.	Rise of Olmec culture
Fourth century B.C.E.	End of Olmec era
First millennium C.E.	Origins of Mayan civilization
c. 300 B.C.E.–800 C.E.	Teotihuacán civilization
300–900 C.E.	Classical era of Mayan culture
870 C.E.	Tikal abandoned
Late 1100s	Migration of Mexica to Valley of Mexico
1300s–1400s	Kingdom of the Aztecs

EARLY SOUTH AMERICA

10,500 B.C.E.	Monte Verde
c. 3500 B.C.E.	First organized societies in the Andes
c. 3200 B.C.E.	Agriculture first widely practiced
c. 2500 B.C.E.	Founding of Caral
First millennium B.C.E.	Chavín style
c. 150–800 C.E.	Moche civilization
c. 500–1000 C.E.	Wari culture
c. 1100–1450	Civilization of Chimor
1400s	Inka takeover in central Andes

MindTap is a fully online, highly personalized learning experience built upon Cengage Learning content. MindTap combines student learning tools—readings, multimedia, activities, and assessments—into a singular Learning Path that guides students through their course.

7

FERMENT IN THE MIDDLE EAST: THE RISE OF ISLAM

Muhammad rises to heaven

CHAPTER OUTLINE

• The Rise of Islam • The Arab Empire and Its Successors • Islamic
Civilization

THE RISE OF ISLAM

The Arabs were a Semitic-speaking people of southwestern Asia with a long history. They were mentioned in Greek sources of the fifth century B.C.E. and even earlier in the Old Testament. The Greek historian Herodotus had applied the name *Arab* to the entire peninsula, calling it Arabia. In 106 B.C.E., the Romans extended their authority to the Arabian peninsula, transforming it into a province of their growing empire.

During Roman times, the region was inhabited primarily by the **Bedouin** (BED-oo-un *or* BED-wuhn) Arabs, nomadic peoples who came originally from the northern part of the peninsula. Bedouin society was organized on a tribal basis. The ruling member of the tribe was called the **sheikh** (SHAYK *or* SHEEK) and was selected from one of the leading families by a council of elders called the **majlis** (MAHJ-liss). The *sheikh* ruled the tribe with the consent of the council. Each tribe was autonomous but felt a general sense of allegiance to the larger unity of all the clans in the region. In early times, the Bedouins had supported themselves primarily by sheepherding or by raiding passing caravans, but after the domestication of the camel during the second millennium B.C.E., the Bedouins began to participate in the caravan trade themselves and became major carriers of goods between the Persian Gulf and the Mediterranean Sea.

The Arabs of pre-Islamic times were polytheistic, with a supreme god known as Allah presiding over a community of spirits. It was a communal faith, involving all members of the tribe, and had no priesthood. Spirits were believed to inhabit natural objects, such as trees, rivers, and mountains, while the supreme deity was symbolized by a sacred stone. Each tribe possessed its own stone, but by the time of Muhammad, a massive black meteorite, housed in a central shrine called the Ka'aba (KAH-buh) in the commercial city of Mecca, had come to possess especially sacred qualities.

In the fifth and sixth centuries C.E., the economic importance of the Arabian peninsula began to increase. As a result of the political disorder in Mesopotamia— a consequence of the constant wars between the Eastern Roman (Byzantine) and Sassanian Persian Empires—and in Egypt, the trade routes that ran directly across the peninsula or down the Red Sea became increasingly perilous, and a third route, which passed from the Mediterranean through Mecca to Yemen and then by ship across the Indian Ocean, became more popular. The communities in that part of the peninsula benefited from the change and took a larger share of the caravan trade between the Mediterranean and the countries on the other side of the Indian Ocean. As a consequence, relations between the Bedouins of the desert and the increasingly wealthy merchant class of the towns began to become strained.

The Role of Muhammad   Into this world came Muhammad (also known as Mohammed), a man whose spiritual visions unified the Arab world with a speed no one would have suspected possible. Unfortunately, there is almost no verifiable evidence relating to Muhammad's life. As a result, historians must rely on a limited number of sources, including the Qur'an and testimonials about his life by his followers (the *Hadith*). These sources were extensively revised after his death, however, and may have been shaped so as to favor the interests of his successors. Consequently, to many historians of the Middle East, the first years of Islam remain a matter of debate and conjecture.

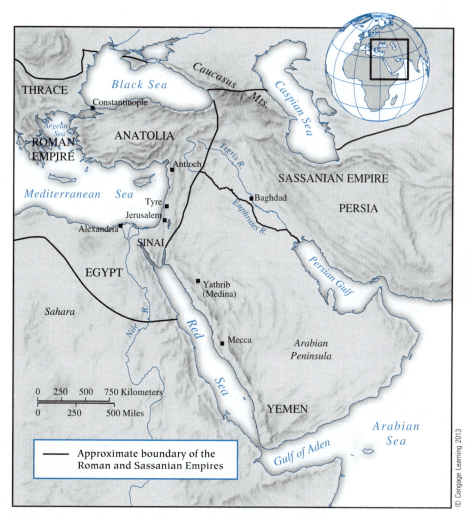

MAP 7.1 The Middle East in the Time of Muhammad

When Islam began to spread throughout the Middle East in the early seventh century, the dominant states in the region were the Roman Empire in the eastern Mediterranean and the Sassanian Empire in Persia.

Born in Mecca to a merchant family and orphaned at the age of six, Muhammad (570–632) grew up to become a caravan manager and eventually married a rich widow, Khadija (kah-DEE-juh), who was also his employer. A member of the local Hashemite (HASH-uh-myt) clan of the Quraishi (koo-RY-shee) tribe, he lived in Mecca as a merchant for several years but, according to tradition, was apparently troubled by the growing gap between the Bedouin values of honesty and generosity and the acquisitive behavior of the affluent commercial elites in the city. Deeply concerned, he began to visit the nearby hills to meditate in isolation. It was there that he encountered the angel Gabriel, who commanded him to preach the revelations that he would be given.

FILM & HISTORY

The Message (Muhammad: The Messenger of God) (1976)

Over the years, countless commercial films depicting the early years of Christianity have been produced in Hollywood. In contrast, cinematic portrayals of the birth of other world religions such as Buddhism, Hinduism, and Islam have been rare. In the case of Islam, the reluctance has been based in part on Muslims' traditional prohibition against depicting the face and figure of the Prophet Muhammad. Reactions to depictions of the Prophet in European media in recent years have demonstrated that this issue remains highly sensitive in Muslim communities worldwide.

In the 1970s, a Syrian-American filmmaker, Moustapha Akkad, himself a Muslim, was dismayed at the widespread ignorance of the tenets of Islam in Western countries. He therefore sought to produce a full-length feature film on the life of Muhammad for presentation in Europe and the United States. Failing to obtain financial help from U.S. sources, he sought aid abroad and finally won the support of the Libyan leader Muammar Qaddafi, and

the film was released in both English and Arabic versions in 1976.

The film seeks to present an accurate and sympathetic account of the life of the Prophet from his spiritual awakening in 610 to his return to Mecca in 630. To assuage Muslim concerns, neither the figure nor the voice of Muhammad appears in the film. None of his wives, daughters, or sons-in-law appear onscreen. The narrative is carried on through the comments and actions of his friends and disciples, notably the Prophet's uncle Hamza, ably played by the American veteran actor Anthony Quinn.

The film, shot on location in Libya and Morocco, is a sometimes moving account of the emergence of Islam in early-seventh-century Arabia. Although it does not dwell on the more esoteric aspects of Muslim beliefs, it stresses many of the humanistic elements of Islam, including respect for women and opposition to slavery, as well as the equality of all human beings in the eyes of God. Muhammad and his followers are shown as

It is said that Muhammad was acquainted with Jewish and Christian beliefs and came to believe that while Allah had already revealed himself in part through Moses and Jesus—and thus through the Hebraic and Christian traditions—the final revelations were now being given to him. Out of his revelations, which were eventually dictated to scribes, came the Qur'an (meaning "recitation"; also spelled Koran), the holy scriptures of Islam (meaning "submission," implying submission to the will of Allah). The Qur'an contained the guidelines by which followers of Allah, known as Muslims (practitioners of Islam), were to live. Like the Christians and the Jews, Muslims (also known as Moslems) were a "people of the Book," believers in a faith based on scripture.

Muslims believe that after returning home, Muhammad set out to comply with Gabriel's command by preaching to the residents of Mecca about his revelations. At first, many were convinced that he was a madman or a charlatan. Others likely concerned that his vigorous attacks on traditional beliefs and the corrupt society around him might severely shake the social and political order. After three years of proselytizing, he had only thirty followers.

messengers of peace who are aroused to violence only in order to protect themselves from the acts of their enemies.

Though slow-moving in spots and somewhat lengthy in the manner of the genre, *The Message* (also known as *Muhammad: Messenger of God*) is beautifully filmed and contains a number of stirring battle scenes. Viewers come away with a fairly accurate and sympathetic portrait of the life of the Prophet and his message to the faithful.

John Bryson/Time Life Pictures/Getty Images

Hamza, Muhammad's uncle (left, played by Anthony Quinn), is shown defending Muhammad's followers in the early years of Islam.

Discouraged, perhaps, by the systematic persecution of his followers, which was allegedly undertaken with a brutality reminiscent of the cruelties suffered by early Christians, as well as the failure of the Meccans to accept his message, in 622 Muhammad and some of his closest supporters (mostly from his own Hashemite clan) left the city and retreated north to the rival city of Yathrib, later renamed Medina (muh-DEE-nuh), or "city of the Prophet." That flight, known in history as the **Hegira** (huh-JY-ruh *or* HEH-juh-ruh) (*Hijrah*), marks the first date on the official calendar of Islam. At Medina, Muhammad failed in his original purpose—to convert the Jewish community in Medina to his beliefs. But he was successful in winning support from many residents of the city as well as from Bedouins in the surrounding countryside. From this mixture, he formed the first Muslim community—the *umma* (UM-mah). Returning to his birthplace at the head of a considerable military force, Muhammad conquered Mecca and converted the townspeople to the new faith. In 630, he made a symbolic visit to the Ka'aba, where he declared it a sacred shrine of Islam and ordered the destruction of the idols of the traditional faith.

"Draw Their Veils over Their Bosoms"

RELIGION & PHILOSOPHY

Before the Islamic era, many upper-class women greeted men on the street, entertained their husband's friends at home, went on pilgrimages to Mecca, and even accompanied their husbands to battle. Such women were neither veiled nor secluded. Muhammad, however, specified that his own wives, who (according to the Qur'an) were "not like any other women," should be modestly attired and should be addressed by men from behind a curtain. Over the centuries, Muslim theologians, fearful that female sexuality could threaten the established order, interpreted Muhammad's references to "modest attire" and curtains to mean that all Muslim women should remain in segregated seclusion and conceal their bodies. In fact, one strict scholar in fourteenth-century Cairo went so far as to prescribe that, ideally, a woman should leave her home only three times in her life: on entering her husband's home after marriage, after the death of her parents, and after her own death.

In traditional Islamic societies, veiling and seclusion were more prevalent among urban women than among their rural counterparts. The latter, who worked in the fields and rarely saw people outside their extended family, were less restricted. In this excerpt from the Qur'an, women are instructed to "guard their modesty" and "draw veils over their bosoms." Nowhere in the Qur'an, however, does it stipulate that women should be sequestered or covered from head to toe.

Qur'an, Sura 24: "The Light"

And say to the believing women
That they should lower
Their gaze and guard
Their modesty: that they
Should not display their
Beauty and ornaments except
What [must ordinarily] appear
Thereof: that they should
Draw their veils over
Their bosoms and not display
Their beauty except
To their husbands, their fathers,
Their husbands' fathers, their sons,
Their husbands' sons,
Their brothers or their brothers'
*   sons,*
Or their sisters' sons,
Or their women, or the slaves
Whom their right hands
Possess, or male servants
Free of physical needs,
Or small children who
Have no sense of the shame
Of sex; and that they
Should not strike their feet
In order to draw attention
To their hidden ornaments.

Q *How does the role of women in Islam compare with what we have seen in other traditional societies, such as India, China, and the Americas?*

Source: The Holy Quran, 24:32.

The Teachings of Muhammad   Like Christianity and Judaism, Islam is monotheistic. Allah is the all-powerful being who created the universe and everything in it. Islam is also concerned with salvation and offers the hope of an afterlife. Those who hope to achieve it must subject themselves to the will of Allah. Unlike Christianity, Islam makes no claim to the divinity of its founder. Muhammad, like Abraham, Moses, and other figures of the Old

Testament, was a prophet, but he was also a man like other men. Because, according to the Qur'an, earlier prophets had corrupted his revelations, Allah sent his complete revelation through Muhammad.

At the heart of Islam is the Qur'an, with its basic message that there is no God but Allah and Muhammad is his Prophet. Consisting of 114 *suras* (SUR-uhz) (chapters) drawn together by a committee established after Muhammad's death, the Qur'an is not only the sacred book of Islam but also an ethical guidebook and a code of law and political theory combined.

As it evolved, Islam developed a number of fundamental tenets. Of primary importance is the need to obey the will of Allah. This means following a basic ethical code that consists of what are popularly termed the **Five Pillars of Islam**: belief in Allah and Muhammad as his Prophet; standard prayer five times a day and public prayer on Friday at midday to worship Allah; observance of the holy month of **Ramadan** (RAH-muh-dan), including fasting from dawn to sunset; making a pilgrimage—known as the *hajj* (HAJ)—to Mecca at least once in one's lifetime, if possible; and giving alms, called *zakat* (zuh-KAHT), to the poor and unfortunate. The faithful who observe the law are guaranteed a place in an eternal paradise (a vision of a luxurious and cool garden shared by some versions of Eastern Christianity) with the sensuous delights so obviously lacking in the Arabian desert.

Islam is not just a set of religious beliefs but a way of life as well. After the death of Muhammad, a panel of Muslim scholars, known as the **ulama** (OO-luh-mah *or* oo-LAH-muh), drew up a law code, called the **Shari'a** (shah-REE-uh), to provide believers with a set of prescriptions to regulate their daily lives. Much of the *Shari'a* was drawn from existing legal regulations or from the **Hadith** (hah-DEETH), a collection of the sayings of the Prophet that was used to supplement the revelations contained in the holy scriptures.

Believers are subject to strict behavioral requirements. In addition to the Five Pillars, Muslims are forbidden to gamble, eat pork, drink alcoholic beverages, or engage in dishonest behavior. Sexual mores are also strict. Contacts between unmarried men and women are discouraged, and ideally, marriages are arranged by the parents. In accordance with Bedouin custom, polygyny is permitted, but Muhammad attempted to limit the practice by restricting males to no more than four wives.

The degree to which the traditional account of the exposition and inner meaning of the Qur'an can stand up to historical analysis is a matter of debate. As explained earlier, the circumstances surrounding the life of Muhammad and his role in founding the religion of Islam remain highly speculative, and many Muslims may be concerned that the consequences of rigorous examination might undercut key tenets of the Muslim faith. One problem is that the earliest known versions of the Qur'an available today do not contain the diacritical marks that modern Arabic uses to clarify meaning, so much of the sacred text is ambiguous and open to varying interpretations.

THE ARAB EMPIRE AND ITS SUCCESSORS

The death of Muhammad presented his followers with a dilemma. Although Muhammad had not claimed divine qualities, Muslims saw no separation between political and religious authority. Submission to the will of Allah meant submission to his Prophet, Muhammad. According to the Qur'an, "Whoso obeyeth the messenger obeyeth Allah."[1] Muhammad's charismatic authority and political skills had been at the heart of his success. But Muslims have never agreed on whether he named a successor, and although he had several daughters, he left no sons. In the male-oriented society of his day, who would lead the community of the faithful?

Shortly after Muhammad's death, a number of his closest followers selected Abu Bakr (ah-boo BAHK-ur), a wealthy merchant from Medina who was Muhammad's father-in-law and one of his first supporters, as **caliph** (KAY-liff) (*khalifa*, literally "successor"). The caliph was the temporal leader of the Islamic community and was also considered, in general terms, to be a religious leader, or **imam** (ih-MAHM). Under Abu Bakr's prudent leadership, the movement succeeded in suppressing factional tendencies among some of the Bedouin tribes in the peninsula and began to direct its attention to wider fields. Muhammad had used the Arabic tribal custom of the *razzia* (RAZZ-ee-uh), or raid, in the struggle against his enemies. Now his successors turned to the same custom to expand the authority of the movement.

When historians of the Middle East today discuss the expansion of Islam after the death of Muhammad, the Arabic term ***jihad*** (jee-HAHD) is often used to describe the process. The word appears in the Qur'an on several occasions, and it appears to have had multiple meanings, much as the word *crusade* does in English. Sometimes *jihad* is used in the sense of "striving in the way of the Lord," as a means of exhorting believers to struggle against the evil within themselves. In other cases, however, it has been translated as "holy war," justifying hostile action against the enemies of Islam. In that sense, the word can be used to describe the expansion of the world of Islam into the realm of the unbelievers. Many Islamic terrorist movements of the present day clearly view *jihad* in the latter sense, an interpretation that many other Muslims vigorously reject. Because the word is so heavily laden with emotional connotations, it clearly should be used sparingly and with care.

Creation of an Empire

Once the Arabs had become unified under Muhammad's successor, they began directing against neighboring peoples the energy they had formerly directed against each other. The Byzantine and Sassanian Empires were the first to feel the strength of the newly united Arabs, now aroused to a peak of zeal by their common faith. In 636, the Muslims defeated the Byzantine army on the Yarmuk (yahr-MOOK) River, north of the Dead Sea. Four years later, they took possession of the Byzantine province of Syria. In 640, they conquered Cairo. To the east, the Arabs defeated a Persian force in 637 and then went on to conquer the entire empire of the Sassanids by 650. In the meantime, the rest of Egypt and other areas of North Africa were also brought under Arab authority.

What accounts for this rapid expansion of the Arabs after the rise of Islam in the early seventh century? Historians have proposed various explanations, ranging from a prolonged drought on the Arabian Peninsula to the desire of Islam's leaders to channel the energies of their new converts. Others have suggested that the Byzantine Empire had been weakened by a plague epidemic that had not affected the desert regions farther to the east. Still another hypothesis is that the expansion was deliberately planned by the ruling elites in Mecca to extend their trade routes and bring surplus-producing regions under their control. Whatever the case, Islam's

The Spread of the Muslim Faith

RELIGION &
PHILOSOPHY

Like Christianity, Islam is not an exclusive religion, intended solely for members of a particular social or ethnic group, but is universalist in form, with all humans eligible to join the ranks of the believers. As a result, the sacred books of both religions—the Bible and the Qur'an—contain passages that encourage the spread of faith by whatever means are necessary and appropriate. In this selection from the Qur'an, Muslims are called upon to take part in the proselytizing effort, sometimes known in Arabic as *jihad*. While the vast majority of Muslims today believe that conversion to Islam should only take place by peaceful means, militants cite this passage from Chapter 47 as justification for their decision to make war on "unbelievers."

The Qur'an: Chapter 47, "Muhammad, Revealed at Medina"

Allah will bring to nothing the deeds of those who disbelieve and debar others from His path. As for the faithful who do good works and believe in what is revealed to Muhammad—which is the truth from their Lord—He will forgive them their sins and ennoble their state.

This, because the unbelievers follow falsehood, while the faithful follow the truth from their Lord. Thus Allah coins their sayings for mankind.

When you meet the unbelievers in the battlefield strike off their heads and, when you have laid them low, bind your captives firmly. Then grant them their freedom or take ransom from them, until War shall lay down her armour.

Thus shall you so. Had Allah willed, He could Himself have punished them; but He has ordained it thus that He might test you, the one by the other.

As for those who are slain in the cause of Allah, He will not allow their works to perish. He will vouchsafe them guidance and ennoble their state; He will admit them to the Paradise He has made known to them.

Believers, if you help Allah, Allah will help you and make you strong. But the unbelievers shall be consigned to perdition. He will bring their deeds to nothing. Because they opposed His revelations, He will frustrate their works.

Have they never journeyed through the land and seen what was the end of those who have gone before them? Allah destroyed them utterly. A similar fate awaits the unbelievers because Allah is the protector of the faithful; because the unbelievers have no protector.

Allah will admit those who embrace the true faith and do good works to gardens watered by running streams. The unbelievers take their fill of pleasure and eat as the beasts eat: but Hell shall be their home....

This is the Paradise which the righteous have been promised. There shall flow in it rivers of unpolluted water, and rivers of milk forever fresh; rivers of delectable wine and rivers of clearest honey. They shall eat therein of every fruit and receive forgiveness from their Lord. Is this like the lot of those who shall abide in Hell forever and drink scalding water which will tear their bowels? ...

Know that there is no god but Allah. Implore Him to forgive your sins and to forgive the true believers, men and women. Allah knows your busy haunts and resting places.

Q *According to this passage, what is the fate of those who adhere to the teachings of the Prophet Muhammad? How should unbelievers be treated?*

Source: From *The Koran*, trans. N. J. Dawood (Penguin Classics, 1956, 5th rev. ed. 1990). Copyright © N. J. Dawood.

ability to unify the Bedouin peoples certainly played a role. Although the Arab triumph was made substantially easier by the ongoing conflict between the Byzantine and Persian Empires, which had weakened both powers, the strength and mobility of the Bedouin armies with their much vaunted cavalry should not be overlooked. Led by a series of brilliant generals, the Arabs assembled a large, highly motivated army whose valor was enhanced by the belief that Muslim warriors who died in battle were guaranteed a place in paradise.

Once the army had prevailed, Arab civilian administration of the conquered areas was applied. Although early sources often portrayed the conquest in violent terms, many historians today portray the process as generally, but not universally, tolerant. Sometimes, due to a shortage of trained Arab administrators, government was left to local officials. Conversion to Islam was usually voluntary in accordance with the maxim in the Qur'an that "there shall be no compulsion in religion."[2] Those who chose not to convert, however, were required to submit to Muslim rule and to pay a head tax in return for exemption from military service, which was required of all Muslim males. Under such conditions, the local populations often regarded Arab rule as preferable to Byzantine rule or that of the Sassanid dynasty in Persia. Furthermore, the simple and direct character of the new religion and its egalitarian qualities (all people were viewed as equal in the eyes of Allah) were very likely attractive to peoples throughout the region.

The Rise of the Umayyads   The main challenge to the growing empire came from within. Some of Muhammad's followers had not agreed with the selection of Abu Bakr as the first caliph and promoted the candidacy of Ali, Muhammad's cousin and son-in-law, as an alternative. Ali's claim was ignored by other leaders, however, and after Abu Bakr's death, the office passed to Umar (oo-MAR), another of Muhammad's followers. In 656, Umar's successor, Uthman (ooth-MAHN), was assassinated, and Ali, who happened to be in Medina at the time, was finally selected for the position. But according to tradition, Ali's rivals were convinced that he had been implicated in the death of his predecessor, and a factional struggle broke out within the Muslim leadership. In 661, Ali himself was assassinated, and Mu'awiya (moo-AH-wee-yah), the governor of Syria and one of Ali's chief rivals, replaced him in office. Mu'awiya thereupon made the caliphate (KAY-luh-fayt) hereditary in his own family, called the Umayyads (oo-MY-ads), who were a branch of the Quraishi clan. The new caliphate, with its capital at Damascus, remained in power for nearly a century.

The factional struggle within Islam did not bring an end to Arab expansion. At the beginning of the eighth century, new attacks were launched at both the western and the eastern ends of the Mediterranean world. Arab armies advanced across North Africa, and conquered the Berbers, a primarily pastoral people living along the Mediterranean coast and in the mountains in the interior. Muslim fleets attacked several islands in the eastern Mediterranean. Then, around 710, Arab forces, supplemented by Berber allies under their commander, Tariq (tuh-REEK), crossed the Strait of Gibraltar and occupied southern Spain (thus the modern name of the Rock of Gibraltar—*Jebel Tariq*, or "Tariq's Mountain"). The Visigothic kingdom, already weakened by internecine warfare, quickly collapsed, and by 725, most of the Iberian Peninsula had become a Muslim state with its center

MAP 7.2 The Expansion of Islam

This map traces the expansion of the Islamic faith from its origins in the Arabian peninsula. Muhammad's followers carried the religion as far west as Spain and southern France and eastward to India and Southeast Asia.

in Andalusia (an-duh-LOO-zhuh). Seven years later, an Arab force, making a foray into southern France, was defeated by the army of Charles Martel between Tours (TOOR) and Poitiers (pwah-TYAY). For the first time, Arab horsemen had met their match, in a disciplined Frankish infantry. Some historians think that internal exhaustion would have forced the invaders to retreat even without their defeat at the hands of the Franks, the Germanic people who had established a kingdom in what is now France. In any event, the Battle of Tours (or Poitiers) would be the high-water mark of Arab expansion in Europe.

As Islamic power spread westward into the Mediterranean basin, the primary adversary for Arab forces was the Byzantine Empire. Because the Byzantines possessed a powerful fleet, many of the battles would inevitably take place at sea. Initially, the Arab ships would be at a substantial disadvantage, since the peoples of the peninsula—lacking protected harbors and sources of wood and iron for ships—had little experience at sea. They were quick to learn, however, and were soon competing on an equal basis with their opponents. Before the end of the seventh century, Arab fleets were able to seize a number of islands in the Mediterranean. In 717, a Muslim force launched an attack on Constantinople with the hope of destroying the Byzantine Empire. But the Byzantines' use of Greek fire, a petroleum-based compound containing quicklime and sulfur, destroyed the Muslim fleet, thereby saving the empire and indirectly Christian Europe, since the fall of Constantinople would have opened the door to an Arab invasion of eastern Europe.

The Byzantine Empire and Islam now established an uneasy frontier in southern Asia Minor.

Arab power also extended to the east, consolidating Islamic rule in Mesopotamia and Persia and northward into Central Asia. But factional disputes continued to plague the empire. Many Muslims of non-Arab extraction resented the favoritism toward Arabs shown by local administrators. In some cases, resentment led to revolt, as in Iraq, where Ali's second son, Hussein, disputed the legitimacy of the Umayyads and incited his supporters—to be known in the future as **Shi'ites** (SHEE-yts) (from the Arabic phrase *shi'at Ali*, "partisans of Ali")—to rise up against Umayyad rule in 680. Hussein's forces were defeated, and with the death of Hussein in the battle, a schism between Shi'ite and **Sunni** (SOON-nee) (usually translated "orthodox") Muslims had been created that continues to this day.

Umayyad rule created resentment, not only in Mesopotamia but also in North Africa, where Berber resistance continued, especially in the mountainous areas south of the coastal plains. According to critics, the Umayyads may have contributed to their own demise by their decadent behavior. One caliph allegedly swam in a pool of wine and then imbibed enough of the contents to lower the level significantly. Finally, in 750, a revolt led by Abu al-Abbas (ah-boo al-ah-BUSS), a descendant of Muhammad's uncle, led to the overthrow of the Umayyads and the establishment of the Abbasid (uh-BAH-sid *or* AB-uh-sid) dynasty (750–1258) in what is now Iraq.

The Abbasids   The Abbasid caliphs brought political, economic, and cultural change to the world of Islam. While seeking to implant their own version of religious orthodoxy, they tried to break down the distinctions between Arab and non-Arab Muslims. All Muslims were now allowed to hold both civil and military offices. This change helped open Islamic culture to the influences of the occupied civilizations. Some Arabs began to intermarry with the peoples they had conquered. In many parts of the Islamic world, notably North Africa and the eastern Mediterranean, most Muslim converts began to consider themselves Arabs. In 762, the Abbasids built a new capital city at Baghdad, on the Tigris River far to the east of the Umayyad capital at Damascus. The new capital was strategically positioned to take advantage of river traffic to the Persian Gulf and also lay astride the caravan route from the Mediterranean to Central Asia. The move eastward allowed Persian influence to come to the fore, encouraging a new cultural orientation. Under the Abbasids, judges, merchants, and government officials, rather than warriors, were regarded as the ideal citizens.

Abbasid Rule The new Abbasid caliphate experienced a period of splendid rule well into the ninth century. Best known of the caliphs of the time was Harun al-Rashid (hah-ROON al-rah-SHEED) (r. 786–809), or Harun "the Upright," whose reign is often described as the golden age of the Abbasid caliphate. His son al-Ma'mun (al-muh-MOON) (r. 813–833) was a patron of learning who founded an astronomical observatory and established a foundation for translating Classical Greek works. This was also a period of growing economic prosperity. The Arabs had conquered many of the richest provinces of the Roman Empire and now controlled the routes to the east. Baghdad became the center of an enormous commercial market that extended into Europe, Central Asia, and Africa, greatly adding to the

© Cengage Learning 2013

MAP 7.3   The Abbasid Caliphate at the Height of Its Power

The Abbasids arose in the eighth century as the defenders of the Muslim faith and established their capital at Baghdad. With its prowess as a trading state, the caliphate was the most powerful and extensive state in the region for several centuries. The "Zaidi imams" indicated on the map were a group of dissident Shi'ites who established an independent kingdom on the southern tip of the Arabian peninsula.

wealth of the Islamic world and promoting an exchange of culture, ideas, and technology from one end of the known world to the other. Paper was introduced from China and eventually passed on to North Africa and Europe. Crops from India and Southeast Asia, including rice, sugar, sorghum, and cotton, moved toward the west, while glass, wine, and indigo dye were introduced into China.

Under the Abbasids, the caliphs became more regal. More kings than spiritual leaders, described by such august phrases as the "caliph of God," they ruled by autocratic means similar to those used by the kings and emperors in neighboring civilizations. A thirteenth-century Chinese author, who compiled a world geography based on accounts by Chinese travelers, left the following description of one of the later caliphs:

> The king wears a turban of silk brocade and foreign cotton stuff [buckram]. On each new moon and full moon he puts on an eight-sided flat-topped headdress of pure gold, set with the most precious jewels in the world. His robe is of silk brocade and is bound around him with a jade girdle. On his feet he wears golden shoes.... The king's throne is set with pearls and precious stones, and the steps of the throne are covered with pure gold.[3]

As the caliph took on more of the trappings of a hereditary autocrat, the bureaucracy assisting him in administering the expanding empire grew more complex as well. The caliph was advised by a council—called a *diwan* (di-WAHN)—headed by a prime minister, known as a **vizier** (veh-ZEER) (*wazir*). The caliph did not attend meetings of the *diwan* in the normal manner but sat behind a screen and then communicated his divine will to the vizier. Some historians have ascribed the change in the caliphate to Persian influence, which permeated the empire after the capital was moved to Baghdad. Persian influence was indeed strong (the mother of the caliph al-Ma'mun, for example, was a Persian), but more likely, the increase in pomp and circumstance was a natural consequence of the growing power and prosperity of the empire.

Instability and Division   Nevertheless, an element of instability lurked beneath the surface. The lack of spiritual authority may have weakened the caliphate and given impetus to potential rivals, and disputes over the succession were common. At Harun's death, the rivalry between his two sons, Amin and al-Ma'mun, led to civil war and the destruction of Baghdad. As described by the tenth-century Muslim historian al-Mas'udi (al-muh-SOO-dee), "Mansions were destroyed, most remarkable monuments obliterated; prices soared.... Brother turned his sword against brother, son against father, as some fought for Amin, others for Ma'mun. Houses and palaces fueled the flames; property was put to the sack."[4]

Wealth contributed to financial corruption. By awarding important positions to court favorites, the Abbasid caliphs began to undermine the foundations of their own power and eventually became mere figureheads. Under Harun al-Rashid, members of his Hashemite clan received large pensions from the state treasury, and his wife Zubaida (zoo-BY-duh) reportedly spent huge sums while shopping on a pilgrimage to Mecca. One powerful family, the Barmakids, amassed vast wealth and power until Harun al-Rashid eliminated the entire clan in a fit of jealousy.

The life of luxury enjoyed by the caliph and other political and economic elites in Baghdad seemingly undermined the stern fiber of Arab society as well as the strict moral code of Islam. Strictures against sexual promiscuity were widely ignored, and caliphs were rumored to maintain thousands of concubines in their harems. Divorce was common, homosexuality was widely practiced, and alcohol was consumed in public despite Islamic law's prohibition against imbibing spirits.

The process of disintegration was accelerated by changes that were taking place within the armed forces and the bureaucracy of the empire. Given the shortage of qualified Arabs for key positions in the army and the administration, the caliphate began to recruit officials from among the non-Arab peoples in the empire, such as Persians and Turks from Central Asia. These people gradually became a dominant force in the army and administration.

Environmental problems added to the regime's difficulties. The Tigris and Euphrates river system, lifeblood of Mesopotamia for three millennia, was beginning to silt up. Bureaucratic inertia now made things worse, as many of the country's canals became virtually unusable, leading to widespread food shortages.

The fragmentation of the Islamic empire accelerated in the tenth century. Morocco became independent, and in 973, a new Shi'ite dynasty under the Fatimids (FAT-uh-mids) was established in Egypt with its capital at Cairo. With increasing disarray in the empire, the Islamic world was held together only by the common commitment to the Arabic language and the Qur'an.

The Seljuk Turks   In the eleventh century, the Abbasid caliphate faced yet another serious threat in the form of the Seljuk (SEL-jook) Turks. When the nomadic Xiongnu Empire fell apart early in the first millennium c.e., Turkish-speaking people in the area gradually migrated westward into Xinjiang and Central Asia. Some of them converted to Islam in the process. Eventually, one group, known as the Seljuk Turks, began to serve as military mercenaries for the Abbasid caliphate, where they were known for their ability as mounted archers. Moving gradually into Persia and Armenia as the Abbasids weakened, the Seljuk Turks grew in number until by the eleventh century, they were able to occupy the eastern provinces of the Abbasid Empire. In 1055, a Turkish leader captured Baghdad and assumed command of the empire with the title of **sultan** (SUL-tun) ("holder of power"). While the Abbasid caliph remained the chief representative of Sunni religious authority, the real military and political power of the state was in the hands of the Seljuk Turks. The latter did not establish their headquarters in Baghdad, which now entered a period of decline. As the historian Khatib Baghdadi (kah-TEEB bag-DAD-ee) described:

> There is no city in the world equal to Baghdad in the abundance of its riches, the importance of its business, the number of its scholars and important people, the distinctions of its leaders and its common people, the extent of its palaces, inhabitants, streets, avenues, alleys, mosques, baths, docks and caravansaries, the purity of its air, the sweetness of its water, the freshness of its dew and its shade, the temperateness of its summer and winter, the healthfulness of its spring and fall, and its great swarming crowds. The buildings and the inhabitants were most numerous during the time of Harun al-Rashid, when the city and its surrounding areas were full of cooled rooms, thriving places, fertile pastures, rich watering-places for ships. Then the riots began, an uninterrupted series of misfortunes befell the inhabitants, its flourishing conditions came to ruin to such extent that, before our time and the century preceding ours, it found itself, because of the perturbation and the decadence it was experiencing, in complete opposition to all capitals and in contradiction to all inhabited countries.[5]

Baghdad would revive, but it would no longer be the "Gift of God" of Harun al-Rashid.

By the last decades of the eleventh century, the Seljuks were exerting military pressure on Egypt and the Byzantine Empire. In 1071, when the Byzantines foolishly challenged the Turks, their army was routed at Manzikert (MANZ-ih-kurt), near Lake Van in eastern Turkey, and the victors took over much of the Anatolian peninsula. In dire straits, the Byzantine Empire turned to the west for help, setting in motion the papal pleas that led to the **crusades**.

In Europe, and undoubtedly within the Muslim world itself, the arrival of the Turks was initially regarded as a disaster. The Turks were viewed as barbarians who destroyed civilizations and oppressed populations. In fact, in many respects, Turkish rule in the Middle East was probably beneficial. After converting to Islam, the Turkish rulers temporarily brought an end to the fraternal squabbles between Sunni and Shi'ite Muslims while supporting the Sunnis. They put their energies into revitalizing Islamic law and institutions and provided much-needed political stability to the empire, which helped restore its former prosperity. Under Seljuk rule, Muslims began to organize themselves into autonomous brotherhoods, whose relatively tolerant practices characterized Islamic religious attitudes until the end of the nineteenth century, when increased competition with Europe led to confrontation with the West.

Seljuk political domination over the old Abbasid Empire, however, provoked resentment on the part of many Persian Shi'ites, who viewed the Turks as usurping

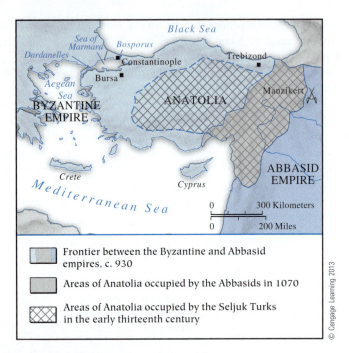

© Cengage Learning 2013

MAP 7.4 The Turkish Occupation of Anatolia

This map shows the expansion of Turkic-speaking peoples into the Anatolian peninsula. The Seljuk Turks seized much of the peninsula after the Battle of Manzikert in 1071. In the late thirteenth century, Seljuk power collapsed and was replaced by another Turkic-speaking people, the Ottoman Turks, who began to consolidate their power in the northwestern part of Anatolia. The Ottomans established their capital at Bursa in 1335 and eventually at Constantinople in 1453.

foreigners who had betrayed the true faith of Islam. Among the regime's most feared enemies was Hasan al-Sabahh (hah-SAHN al-SAH-bah), a Cairo-trained Persian who formed a rebel group, popularly known as "assassins" (guardians), who for several decades terrorized government officials and other leading political and religious figures from their base in the mountains south of the Caspian Sea. Like their modern-day equivalents, the members of the terrorist organization known as al-Qaeda, Sabahh's followers were highly motivated and were adept at infiltrating the enemy's camp to carry out their clandestine activities. The organization was finally eliminated by the invading Mongols in the thirteenth century.

The Crusades   Just before the end of the eleventh century, the Byzantine emperor Alexius I desperately called for assistance from other Christian states in Europe to protect his empire against the invading Seljuk Turks. As part of his appeal, he said that the Muslims were desecrating Christian shrines in the Holy Land and molesting Christian pilgrims en route to the shrines. In actuality, the Muslims had never threatened the shrines or cut off Christian access to them. But tension between Christendom and Islam was on the rise, and the Byzantine emperor's appeal received a ready response in Europe. Beginning in 1096 and continuing into the thirteenth century, a series of Christian raids on Islamic territories known as the crusades brought the Holy Land and adjacent areas on the Mediterranean coast from Antioch to the Sinai Peninsula under Christian rule.

At first, Muslim rulers in the area were taken aback by the invading crusaders, whose armored cavalry presented a new challenge to local warriors, and their response was ineffectual. The Seljuk Turks by that time were preoccupied with events taking place farther to the east and took no action themselves. But in 1169, Sunni Muslims under the leadership of Saladin (SAL-uh-din or Salah al-Din), vizier to the last Fatimid caliph, brought an end to the Fatimid dynasty. Proclaiming himself sultan, Saladin succeeded in establishing his control over both Egypt and Syria, thereby confronting the Christian states in the area with united Muslim power on two fronts. In 1187, Saladin's army invaded the kingdom of Jerusalem and destroyed the Christian forces concentrated there. Further operations reduced Christian occupation in the area to a handful of fortresses along the northern coast. Unlike the Christians of the First Crusade, who had slaughtered much of the population of Jerusalem when they captured the city, Saladin did not permit a massacre of the civilian population and even tolerated the continuation of Christian religious services in conquered territories. For a time, Christian occupation forces even carried on a lively trade relationship with Muslim communities in the region.

The Christians returned for another try a few years after the fall of Jerusalem, but the campaign succeeded only in securing some of the coastal cities. Although the Christians would retain a toehold on the coast for much of the thirteenth century (Acre, their last stronghold, fell to the Muslims in 1291), they were no longer a significant force in Middle Eastern affairs. In retrospect, the crusades had only minimal importance in the history of the Middle East, although they may have served to unite the forces of Islam against the foreign invaders, thus creating a residue of distrust toward Christians that continues to resonate through the Islamic world today. Far more important in their impact were the Mongols, a pastoral people who swept out of the Gobi Desert in the early thirteenth century to seize control over much of the known world. Beginning with the advances of Genghis Khan (JING-uss *or* GENG-uss KAHN) in northern China, Mongol armies later spread across Cetral Asia, and in 1258, under the leadership of Hulegu (HOO-lay-goo), brother of the more famous Khubilai Khan (KOO-bluh KAHN), they seized Persia and Mesopotamia, bringing an end to the caliphate at Baghdad.

The Mongols

Unlike the Seljuk Turks, the Mongols were not Muslims, and they found it difficult to adapt to the settled conditions that they found in the major cities in the Middle East. Their treatment of the local population in conquered territories was brutal (according to one historian, after conquering a city, they wiped out not only entire families but also their household pets) and destructive to the economy. Cities were razed to the ground, and dams and other irrigation works were destroyed, reducing prosperous agricultural societies to the point of mass starvation. The Mongols advanced as far as the Red Sea, but their attempt to seize Egypt failed, in part because of the effective resistance posed by the Mamluks (MAM-looks) (or Mamelukes, a Turkish military class originally composed of slaves), who had recently overthrown the administration set up by Saladin and seized power for themselves.

Eventually, the Mongol rulers in the Middle East began to assimilate the culture of the peoples they had conquered. Mongol elites converted to Islam, Persian influence became predominant at court, and the cities began to be rebuilt. By the fourteenth century, the Mongol empire had begun to split into separate kingdoms and then to disintegrate. In the meantime, however, the old Islamic empire originally established by the Arabs in the seventh and eighth centuries had long since come to an end. The new center of Islamic civilization was in Cairo, now about to promote a renaissance in Muslim culture under the sponsorship of the Mamluks.

To the north, another new force appeared on the horizon with the rise of the Ottoman Turks on the Anatolian peninsula. In 1453, Sultan Mehmet II seized Constantinople and brought an end to the Byzantine Empire. Then the Ottomans began to turn their attention to the rest of the Middle East.

Andalusia:
A Muslim
Outpost in
Europe

After the decline of Baghdad, perhaps the brightest star in the Muslim firmament was in Spain, where a member of the Umayyad dynasty had managed to establish himself after his family's rule in the Middle East had been overthrown in 750 C.E. Abd al-Rathman (AHB-d al-rahkh-MAHN) had escaped the carnage in Damascus and made his way to Spain, where Muslim power had recently replaced that of the Visigoths. By 756, he had legitimized his authority in southern Spain—known to the Arabs as *al-Andaluz* and to Europeans as Andalusia—and taken the title of **emir** (EH-meer) (commander), with his capital at Córdoba (KOR-duh-buh). There he and his successors sought to build a vibrant new center for Islamic culture in the region. With the primacy of Baghdad now at an end, Andalusian rulers established a new caliphate in 929.

Now that the seizure of Crete, Sardinia, Sicily, and the Balearic Islands had turned the Mediterranean Sea into a Muslim lake, Andalusia became part of a vast trade network that stretched all the way from the Strait of Gibraltar to the Red Sea and beyond. Valuable new agricultural products were introduced to the Iberian Peninsula, including cotton, sugar, olives, citrus, and the date palm.

Andalusia also flourished as an artistic and intellectual center. The court gave active support to writers and artists, creating a brilliant culture focused on the emergence of three world-class cities—Córdoba, Seville, and Toledo. Intellectual leaders arrived in the area from all parts of the Islamic world, bringing their knowledge of medicine, astronomy, mathematics, and philosophy. With the establishment of a paper factory near Valencia, the means of disseminating such information dramatically improved, and the libraries of Andalusia became the wonder of their time. Other wonders of the East that now began to become known in western Europe were glass mirrors and the private bath.

One major reason for the rise of Andalusia as a hub of artistic and intellectual activity was the atmosphere of tolerance in social relations fostered by the state. Although Islam was firmly established as the official faith and non-Muslims were required to pay a special tax and prohibited from proselytizing for their faith, the policy of *convivéncia* (con-vee-VEN-cee-uh) (commingling) provided an

A Pilgrimage to Mecca

RELIGION & PHILOSOPHY

The pilgrimage to Mecca, one of the Five Pillars of Islam, is the duty of every Muslim. Ibn Jubayr, a twelfth-century Spanish Muslim who was an ardent proponent of the view that Andalusian Islam had now become the leading force in global Islam with the decline of the Abbasids, left a description of his trip in his journal. The work is famous for its vivid and abundant detail. In this almost lyrical passage, Ibn Jubayr tells of reaching his final destination, the Ka'aba at Mecca, containing the Black Stone. The Qarmata were an extremist religious sect in ninth- and tenth-century Mesopotamia.

Ibn Jubayr, *The Travels of Ibn Jubayr*

The blessed Black Stone is encased in the corner [of the Ka'aba] facing east. The depth to which it penetrates it is not known, but it is said to extend two cubits into the wall. Its breadth is two-thirds of a span, its length one span and a finger joint. It has four pieces, joined together, and it is said that it was the Qarmata— may God curse them—who broke it. Its edges have been braced with a sheet of silver whose white shines brightly against the black sheen and polished brilliance of the Stone, presenting the observer a striking spectacle which will hold his gaze. The Stone, when kissed, has a softness and moistness which so enchants the mouth that he who puts his lips to it would wish them never to be removed. This is one of the special favors of Divine Providence, and it is enough that the Prophet— may God bless and preserve him—declare it to be a covenant of God on each. May God profit us by the kissing and touching of it. By His favor may all who yearn fervently for it be brought to it. In the sound piece of the stone, to the right of him who presents himself to kiss it, is a small white spot that shines and appears like a mole on the blessed surface. Concerning this white mole, there is a tradition that he who looks upon it clears his vision, and when kissing it one should direct one's lips as closely as one can to the place of the mole.

Q *What are the other Pillars of Islam? How does each task contribute to making a good Muslim?*

Source: Excerpt from *The Travels of Ibn Jubayr*, J. R. C. Broadhurst trans. (London: Jonathan Cape Ltd., 1952).

---

environment in which many Christians and Jews were able to maintain their religious beliefs and even obtain favors from the court.

A Time of Troubles Unfortunately, the primacy of Andalusia as a cultural center was short-lived. By the end of the tenth century, factionalism was beginning to undermine the foundations of the emirate. In 1009, the royal palace at Córdoba was totally destroyed in a civil war. Twenty years later, the caliphate itself disappeared as the emirate dissolved into a patchwork of city-states.

In the meantime, the Christian kingdoms that had managed to establish themselves in the north of the Iberian Peninsula were consolidating their position and beginning to expand southward. In 1085, Alfonso VI, the Christian king of Castile, seized Toledo, one of Andalusia's main intellectual centers. The new rulers continued to foster the artistic and intellectual activities of their predecessors, lead-ing eventually to the spread of such ideas northward to the great cities and univer-sities of central and western Europe. To recoup their losses, the Muslim rulers in Seville called on fellow Muslims, the Almoravids (al-MOR-uh-vids)—a Berber dynasty in Morocco—for help in halting the Christian advance. Berber mercenaries defeated Castilian forces at Badajoz (bah-duh-HOHZ) in 1086 but then remained in the area to establish their own rule over remaining Muslim-held areas in southern Spain.

A warrior culture with little tolerance for heterodox ideas, the Almoravids quickly brought an end to the era of religious tolerance and intellectual achieve-ment. But the presence of Andalusia's new warlike rulers was unable to stem the tide of Christian advance. In 1215, Pope Innocent III called for a new crusade to destroy Muslim rule in southern Spain. Over the next two hundred years, Christian armies advanced relentlessly southward, seizing the cities of Seville and Córdoba. But a single redoubt of Abd al-Rathman's glorious achievement remained: the remote mountain city of Granada (greh-NAH-duh), with its imposing hilltop for-tress, the Alhambra (al-HAM-bruh).

Moorish Spain: An Era of "Cultural Tolerance"?   In standard interpretations of European history, Western historians have usually described the *Reconquista* (ray-con-KEES-tuh) (reconquest) of southern Spain by the Christian kingdoms in the north as a positive development that freed the Spanish people from centuries of oppressive Muslim rule. In recent years, however, it has become fashionable to point to the Moorish era in Spain (the term *Moors* is often used to refer to the Muslims in Spain) as a period of "cultural tolerance," a time of diversity that was followed by the bloody era of the Spanish Inquisition, when the Catholic Church persecuted Muslims, Jews, and Christian heretics for their refusal to accept the true faith. This interpretation has been especially popular since the terrorist attacks in September 2001, as revisionist scholars seek to present a favorable image of Islam to counter the popular perception that all Muslims are sympathetic to terror-ism against the West.

Some historians, however, argue that this portrayal of the Moorish era as a period of "cultural tolerance" overstates the case. They point out that even under the relatively benign rule of Abd al-Rathman true religious tolerance was never achieved and that, in any case, any such era came to end with the arrival of the Almoravids and the Almohads (AL-moh-hads), a Berber dynasty that supplanted the Almoravids in Andalusia in the twelfth century. For historian J. S. Elliot, the era was, at best, one of "cultural interaction," which was eventually followed by a hardening of attitudes on both sides of the cultural spectrum. If there was an era of religious diversity in Spain under Muslim rule, it was all too brief.

Islamic Civilization

As Thomas Lippman, author of *Understanding Islam*, has remarked, the Muslim religion is based on behavior as well as belief. Although this generalization applies in broad terms to most major religions, it seems to be particularly true of Islam. To be a Muslim is not simply to worship Allah but also to live according to his law as revealed in the Qur'an, which is viewed as fundamental and immutable doctrine, not to be revised by human beings.

Thus, in Islamic society, there is no rigid demarcation between church and state, between the sacred and the secular. As Allah has decreed, so must human beings behave. Therefore, Islamic doctrine must be consulted to determine questions of politics, economic behavior, civil and criminal law, and social ethics.

Of course, to live entirely by God's law is difficult, if not impossible. Moreover, many issues of social organization and human behavior were not addressed in the Qur'an or in the *Hadith* or *Shari'a*. There was therefore some room for differing interpretations of holy scripture in accordance with individual preference and local practice. Still, the Islamic world is and has probably always been more homogeneous in terms of its political institutions, religious beliefs, and social practices than most of its contemporary civilizations.

Political Structures

For early converts, establishing political institutions and practices that conformed to Islamic doctrine was a daunting task. In the first place, the will of Allah, as revealed to his Prophet, was not precise about the relationship between religious and political authority, simply decreeing that human beings should "conduct their affairs by mutual consent." On a more practical plane, establishing political institutions for a large and multicultural empire presented a challenge for the Arabs, whose own political structures were relatively rudimentary and relevant only to small pastoral communities.

During the life of Muhammad, the problem could be avoided, since he was generally accepted as both the religious and the political leader of the Islamic community—the *umma*. His death, however, raised the question of how a successor should be chosen and what authority that person should have. As we have seen, Muhammad's immediate successors were called caliphs. Their authority was purely temporal, although they were also considered in general terms to be religious leaders, with the title of *imam*. At first, each caliph was selected informally by leading members of the *umma*. Soon succession became hereditary in the Umayyad clan, but their authority was still qualified, at least in theory, by the idea that they should consult with other leaders.

The Wealth of Araby: Trade and Cities in the Middle East

As we have noted, the Abbasid era was probably one of the most prosperous periods in the history of the Middle East. Trade flourished, not only in the Islamic world but also with China (now in a period of efflorescence during the Tang and Song Dynasties; with the Byzantine Empire, and with the trading societies in Southeast Asia. Trade goods were carried both by ship and by the "fleets of the desert," the camel caravans that traversed the arid land from Morocco in the far west to the countries beyond the Caspian Sea. From West Africa came gold and slaves; from China, silk and porcelain; from East Africa, gold, ivory, and rhinoceros horn; and from the lands of South Asia, sandalwood, cotton, wheat, sugar, and spices. Within the empire, Egypt contributed grain; Iraq, linens, dates, and precious stones; Spain, leather goods, olives, and wine; and western India, pepper and various textile goods. The exchange of goods was facilitated by the development of banking and the use of currency and letters of credit.

One of the key reasons for the Arab empire's emergence as a major participant in the regional trade network was its success in mastering the latest in naval technology. Arab ships—with hulls of teakwood and lateen sails appropriate for the sailing conditions in the Indian Ocean and beyond—were guided to their destinations by the astrolabe (an invention of the Greeks) and the compass (invented in China). Soon Muslim fleets were a familiar feature in the sea lanes from the western Mediterranean to the coast of southern China. In the process, Muslim merchants gradually replaced their Jewish or Persian counterparts in port cities throughout the region.

Under these conditions, urban areas flourished. While the Abbasids were in power, Baghdad was probably the greatest city in the empire, but after the rise of the Fatimids in Egypt, the focus of trade shifted to Cairo, described by the traveler Leo Africanus as "one of the greatest and most famous cities in all the whole world, filled with stately and admirable palaces and colleges, and most sumptuous temples."[6] Other great commercial cities included Basra at the head of the Persian Gulf, Aden at the southern tip of the Arabian peninsula, Damascus in modern Syria, and Marrakech in Morocco. In the cities, the inhabitants were generally segregated by religion, with Muslims, Jews, and Christians living in separate neighborhoods. But all were equally subject to the most common threats to urban life—fire, flood, and disease.

The most impressive urban buildings were usually the palace for the caliph or the local governor and the great mosque. Houses were often constructed of stone or

The Dhow: Workhorse of the Indian Ocean. *The dhow, a generic term for various types of sailing ships found in the Arabian Sea or along the east coast of Africa, has been the classic vessel for transporting goods in the Indian Ocean for over two millennia. Their lateen sails and narrow hulls composed of teak planking make them ideal for catching the monsoon winds that blow seasonally across the ocean between the Asian landmass and the coast of East Africa. The medieval painting on the left by an unknown artist is somewhat stylized, but the resemblance to modern-day vessels is clear, although many of the latter (like the cargo vessel plying the waters off the city of Dubai shown on the right) are motorized and thus no longer subject to the whims of the yearly monsoon winds. Wind-powered vessels of this type, however, remain common throughout the region.*

Trip/Art Directors & TRIP/Alamy

© William J. Duiker

COMPARATIVE ESSAY

Trade and Civilization

INTERACTION & EXCHANGE

In 2002, archaeologists unearthed the site of an ancient Egyptian port city on the shores of the Red Sea. Established sometime during the first millennium B.C.E., the city of Berenike linked the Nile River valley with ports as far away as the island of Java in Southeast Asia. The discovery of Berenike is only the latest piece of evidence confirming the importance of interregional trade in the ancient world. The exchange of goods between far-flung societies became a powerful engine behind the rise of advanced civilizations throughout the ancient world. Raw materials such as copper, tin, and obsidian; items of daily necessity such as salt, fish, and other foodstuffs; and luxury goods including gold, silk, and precious stones passed from one end of the Eurasian supercontinent to the other, across the desert from the Mediterranean Sea to sub-Saharan Africa. A similar network extended throughout much of the Americas. Less well known but also important was the maritime trade that stretched from the Mediterranean across the Indian Ocean to port cities on the distant coasts of Southeast and East Asia.

During the first millennium C.E., the level of interdependence among human societies intensified as three major trade routes—across the Indian Ocean, along the Silk Road, and by caravan across the Sahara—created the framework of a single system of trade. The new global network was not only commercial but informational as well, transmitting technology and ideas, such as the emerging religions of Buddhism, Christianity, and Islam, to new destinations.

There was a close relationship between missionary activities and trade. Buddhist merchants first brought the teachings of Siddhartha Gautama to China, and Muslim traders carried Muhammad's words to Southeast Asia and sub-Saharan Africa. Indian traders carried Hindu beliefs and political institutions to Southeast Asia.

What caused the rapid expansion of trade during this period? One key factor was the introduction of technology to facilitate transportation. The development of the compass, improved techniques in mapmaking and shipbuilding, and greater knowledge of wind patterns all contributed to the expansion of maritime trade. Caravan trade, once carried by wheeled chariots or on the backs of oxen, now used the camel as the preferred beast of burden through the deserts of Africa, Central Asia, and the Middle East.

Another reason for the expansion of commerce during this period was the appearance of several multinational empires that created zones of stability and affluence in key areas of the Eurasian landmass. Most important were the emergence of the Abbasid Empire in the Middle East and the prosperity of China during the Tang and Song Dynasties. The Mongol invasions in the thirteenth century temporarily disrupted the process but then established a new era of stability that fostered long-distance trade throughout the world.

The importance of interregional trade as a crucial factor in promoting the growth of human civilizations can be highlighted by comparing the social, cultural, and technological achievements of active trading states with those communities that have traditionally been cut off from contacts with the outside world. We shall encounter many of these communities in later chapters. Even in the Western Hemisphere, where regional trade linked societies from the great plains of North America to the Andes Mountains in present-day Peru, geographic barriers limited the exchange of inventions and ideas, placing these societies at a distinct disadvantage when the first contacts with peoples across the oceans occurred at the beginning of the modern era.

Q *What were the chief factors that led to the expansion of interregional trade during the first millennium C.E.? What role did Islamic peoples play in this process?*

brick on a timber frame. The larger houses were often built around an interior courtyard where the residents could retreat from the dust, noise, and heat of the city streets. Sometimes domestic animals such as goats or sheep would be stabled there. The houses of the wealthy were often multistoried, with balconies and windows covered with latticework to provide privacy. The poor in both urban and rural areas lived in simpler houses composed of clay or unfired bricks. The Bedouins lived in tents that could be dismantled and moved according to their needs.

The Arab empire was clearly more urbanized than most other areas of the known world at the time. Yet the bulk of the population continued to live in the countryside, supported by farming or herding animals. Farm productivity increased steadily throughout much of the empire, aided by reservoirs, new crops, and advanced water management techniques such as underground irrigation canals that had first been invented in the region thousands of years previously. During the early stages, most of the farmland was owned by independent peasants, but eventually some concentration of land in the hands of wealthy owners began to take place. Some lands were owned by the state or the court and were cultivated by slave labor, but plantation agriculture was not as common as it would be later in many areas of the world. In the valleys of rivers such as the Tigris, the Euphrates, and the Nile, the majority of the farmers were probably independent peasants. A Chinese account described life along the Nile:

> The peasants work their fields without fear of inundation or droughts; a sufficiency of water for irrigation is supplied by a river whose source is not known. During the seasons when no cultivation is in progress, the level of the river remains even with the banks; with the beginning of cultivation it rises day by day. Then it is that an official is appointed to watch the river and to await the highest water level, when he summons the people, who then plough and sow their fields. When they have had enough water, the river returns to its former level.[7]

Eating habits varied in accordance with economic standing and religious preference. Muslims did not eat pork, but those who could afford it often served other meats, including mutton, goat, poultry, or fish. Fruit, spices, and various sweets were delicacies. The poor were generally forced to survive on boiled millet or peas with an occasional lump of meat or fat. Bread—white or whole meal—could be found on tables throughout the region except in the deserts, where boiled grain was the staple food. Pasta was probably first introduced to the Italians by Arab traders operating in Sicily.

Islamic Society   In some ways, Arab society was probably one of the most egalitarian of its time. Both the principles of Islam, which held that all were equal in the eyes of Allah, and the importance of trade to the prosperity of the state certainly contributed to this egalitarianism. Although there was a fairly well defined upper class, consisting of the ruling families, senior officials, tribal elites, and the wealthiest merchants, there was no hereditary nobility as in many contemporary societies, and merchants enjoyed a degree of respect that they did not receive in Europe, China, or India.

Not all benefited from the high degree of social mobility in the Islamic world, however. Slavery was widespread. Since a Muslim could not be enslaved, the supply came from sub-Saharan Africa or from non-Islamic populations elsewhere in Asia. Most slaves were employed in the army (which was sometimes a road to power, as in the case of the Mamluks) or as domestic servants, who were occasionally permitted to purchase their freedom. The slaves who worked the large estates experienced the worst living conditions and rose in revolt on several occasions.

The Islamic principle of human equality also fell short, as in most other societies of its day, in the treatment of women. Although the Qur'an instructed men to treat women with respect, and women did have the right to own and inherit property, the male was dominant in Muslim society. Polygyny was permitted, and the right of divorce was in practice restricted to the husband, although some schools of legal thought permitted women to stipulate that their husband could have only one wife or to seek a separation in certain specific circumstances. Adultery and homosexuality were stringently forbidden (although such prohibitions were frequently ignored in practice), and Islamic custom required that women be cloistered in their homes and prohibited from social contacts with males outside their own family.

A prominent example of this custom is the harem, introduced at the Abbasid court during the reign of Harun al-Rashid. Members of the royal harem were drawn from non-Muslim female populations throughout the empire. The custom of requiring women to cover virtually all parts of their body when appearing in public was common in urban areas and continues to be practiced in many Islamic societies today. It should be noted, however, that these customs owed more to traditional Arab practice than to Qur'anic law.

The Culture of Islam

The Arabs were heirs to many elements of the remaining Greco-Roman culture of the Roman Empire, and they assimilated Byzantine and Persian culture just as readily. In the eighth and ninth centuries, numerous Greek, Syrian, and Persian scientific and philosophical works were translated into Arabic and eventually found their way to Europe. As the chief language in the southern Mediterranean and the Middle East, Arabic became an international language. Later, Persian and Turkish also came to be important in administration and culture.

The spread of Islam led to the emergence of a new culture throughout the Arab empire. This was true in all fields of endeavor, from literature to art and architecture. But pre-Islamic traditions were not extinguished and frequently combined with Muslim motifs, resulting in creative works of great imagination and originality.

Philosophy and Science During the centuries following the rise of the Arab empire, it was the Islamic world that was most responsible for preserving and spreading the scientific and philosophical achievements of ancient civilizations. At a time when ancient Greek philosophy was largely unknown in Europe, key works by Aristotle, Plato, and other Greek philosophers were translated into Arabic and stored in a "house of wisdom" in Baghdad, where they were read and studied by Muslim scholars. Eventually, many of these works were translated into Latin and were brought to Europe, where they exercised a profound influence on the later course of Christianity and Western philosophy.

The process began in the sixth century C.E., when the Byzantine ruler Justinian shut down the Platonic Academy in Athens, declaring that it promoted heretical ideas. Many of the scholars at the Academy fled to Baghdad, where their ideas and the Classical texts they brought with them soon aroused local interest and were translated into Persian or Arabic. Later such works were supplemented by acquisitions in Constantinople and possibly also from the famous library at Alexandria.

The academies where such translations were carried out—often by families specializing in the task—were not true universities like those that would later appear in Europe but were private operations under the sponsorship of a great patron, many of them highly cultivated Persians living in Baghdad or other major cities. Dissemination of the translated works was stimulated by the arrival of paper in the Middle East, brought by Buddhist pilgrims from China passing along the Silk Road. Knowledge of the new technique of block printing—also a recent invention in China—arrived in the Middle East at this time as well. Paper was much cheaper to manufacture than papyrus, and by the end of the eighth century, the first paper factories were up and running in Baghdad. Libraries and booksellers soon appeared, leading one recent scholar to suggest that Abbasid society was the first "book culture."

What motives inspired this ambitious literary preservation project? At the outset, it may have simply been an effort to provide philosophical confirmation for existing religious beliefs as derived from the Qur'an. Perhaps, also, the purpose was to train administrators for newly conquered lands in Europe by acquainting them with conditions in those areas. Eventually, however, more adventurous minds began to use the Classical texts not only to seek greater knowledge of the divine will but also to seek a better understanding of the laws of nature.

Such was the case with the physician and intellectual Ibn Sina (IB-un SEE-nuh) (980–1037), known in the West as Avicenna (av-i-SENN-uh), who in his own philosophical writings cited Aristotle to the effect that the world operated not only at the will of Allah but also by its own natural laws, laws that could be ascertained by human reason. Avicenna, a native of Balkh, was once imprisoned as punishment for publishing heterodox ideas, but the popularity of his writings caused them to spread nonetheless throughout the Islamic world and beyond.

Although Islamic scholars are justly praised for preserving much of Classical knowledge for the West, they also made considerable advances of their own. Nowhere is this more evident than in mathematics and the natural sciences. Islamic scholars adopted and passed on the numerical system of India, including the use of zero, and a ninth-century Persian mathematician founded the mathematical discipline of algebra (al-jabr, "the reduction"). Simplified "Arabic" numerals had begun to replace cumbersome Roman numerals in Italy by the thirteenth century.

In astronomy, Muslims set up an observatory at Baghdad to study the position of the stars. They were aware that the earth was round and in the ninth century produced a world map based on the tradition of the Greco-Roman astronomer Ptolemy.

Aided by the astrolabe, an instrument designed to enable sailors to track their position by means of the stars, Muslim fleets and caravans opened up new trading routes connecting the Islamic world with other civilizations, and Muslim travelers such as al-Mas'udi and Ibn Battuta provide modern readers with their most accurate descriptions of political and social conditions throughout the Middle East.

Muslim scholars also made many new discoveries in optics and chemistry and, with the assistance of texts on anatomy by the ancient Greek physician Galen (c. 180–200 C.E.), developed medicine as a distinctive field of scientific inquiry. Avicenna compiled a medical encyclopedia that, among other things, emphasized the contagious nature of certain diseases and showed how they could be spread by contaminated water supplies. After its translation into Latin, Avicenna's work became a basic medical textbook for medieval European university students.

Ultimately, though, the spurt of interest in Classical philosophy and science throughout much of the Muslim world proved somewhat abortive. The suggestion that reason could build a bridge to faith aroused the ire of traditional Muslim scholars, and although Classical works by such ancient writers as Euclid, Ptolemy, and Archimedes continued to be translated, the influence of Greek philosophy began to wane in Baghdad by the end of the eleventh century and did not recover. At the same time, the new technique of printing did not spread, perhaps because it allegedly lacked the aesthetic qualities of cursive script or was viewed as inappropriate for the dissemination of the words of Allah.

A similar pattern occurred in Spain, where philosophers such as Averroës (uh-VERR-oh-eez), whose Arabic name was Ibn Rushd (IB-un RUSH-ed *or* IB-un RUSHT), and Maimonides (my-MAH-nuh-deez) (Musa Ibn Maymun, a Jew who often wrote in Arabic) undertook their own translations and wrote in support of Avicenna's defense of the role of human reason. Both were born in Córdoba in the early twelfth century but were persecuted for their ideas by the Almohads, who had replaced the Almoravids in Andalusia, and both men ended their days in exile in North Africa.

By then, however, Christian rulers such as Alfonso X in Castile and Frederick II in Sicily were beginning to sponsor their own translations of Classical Greek works from Arabic into Latin, whence they made their way to the many new universities sprouting up all over western Europe. The end result of this period of cultural interaction would be an intellectual revolution that would transform the world of medieval Europe to its very core.

Islamic Literature   The literature of the Middle East is diverse, reflecting the many distinct cultures of the region. The Arabic and Persian works in particular represent a significant contribution to world literature. Arabic poetry prior to Muhammad extolled the Bedouin experience of tribal life, courage in battle, hunting, sports, and respect for the animals of the desert, especially the camel. Pre-Muslim Persia also boasted a long literary tradition, most of it oral and later written down using the Arabic alphabet. Lacking the desert tradition of the Arabs, Persian writers focused on legends of past kings, Zoroastrian religious themes, romances, fables, and folktales. The transcendent literary monument of early Persian literature is *The Book of Lords*, an early-sixth-century compilation of poetry about Persian myths and legendary heroes.

Islam brought major changes to the culture of the Middle East, not least to literature. Muslims regarded the Qur'an as their greatest literary work, but pre-Islamic traditions continued to influence writers throughout the region. Poetry is the Persian art par excellence. *The Book of Kings*, a ten-volume epic poem by the Persian poet Ferdowzi (fur-DOW-see) (940–1020), is one of the greatest achievements of Persian literature. It traces the history of the country from legendary times to the arrival of Islam. Iranian schoolchildren still learn its verses, which serve to reaffirm pride in their ancient heritage. But love poetry remained popular. One notable example was Rabe'a of Qozdar (rah-BAY-uh of kuz-DAHR), Persia's first known woman poet, whose writings in the second half of the tenth century expressed her anguish at the suffering love brings.

In the West, the most famous works of Middle Eastern literature are undoubtedly the *Rubaiyat* of Omar Khayyam (OH-mar ky-YAHM) and *Tales from 1001 Nights* (also called *The Arabian Nights*). Although these two works are not especially popular with Middle Eastern readers, they appealed to the taste of nineteenth-century Europeans, who developed a taste for stories set in exotic foreign places—a classic example of the tendency of Western observers to regard the customs and cultures of non-Western societies as strange or exotic.

Omar Khayyam's poetry, which he often composed orally over wine at a neighborhood tavern, is simple and down to earth. Key themes are the impermanence of life, the impossibility of knowing God, and disbelief in an afterlife. Among his most popular verses is the famous couplet: "Here with a loaf of bread beneath the bough, / A flask of wine, a book of verse, and thou." Ironically, recent translations of his work appeal to modern attitudes of skepticism and minimalist simplicity that may make him even more popular in the West:

> *In youth I studied for a little while;*
> *Later I boasted of my mastery.*
> *Yet this was all the lesson that I learned:*
> *We come from dust, and with the wind are gone....*
> *Drink wine by moonlight, darling, for the moon*
> *Will shine long after this, and find us not.*[8]

Like Omar Khayyam's verse, *The Arabian Nights* was loosely translated into European languages and adapted to Western tastes. A composite of folktales, fables, and romances of Indian and indigenous origin, the stories interweave the natural with the supernatural. The earliest stories were told orally and were later transcribed, with many later additions, in Arabic and Persian versions. The famous story of Aladdin and the Magic Lamp, for example, was an eighteenth-century addition. Nevertheless, *The Arabian Nights* has entertained readers for centuries, allowing them to enter a land of wish fulfillment through extraordinary plots, sensuality, comic and tragic situations, and a cast of unforgettable characters.

Sadi (sah-DEE) (1210–1292), considered the Persian Shakespeare, remains to this day the favorite author in Iran. His *Rose Garden* is a collection of entertaining stories written in prose sprinkled with verse. He is also renowned for his sonnetlike love poems, which set a model for generations to come. Sadi was a master of the pithy maxim:

> *A cat is a lion in catching mice*
> *But a mouse in combat with a tiger.*

> *He has found eternal happiness who lived a good life,*
> *Because, after his end, good repute will keep his name alive.*

> *When thou fightest with anyone, consider*
> *Whether thou wilt have to flee from him or he from thee.*[9]

Such maxims are typical of the Middle East, where the proverb, a one-line witty observation on the vagaries of life, has long been popular. Proverbs are not only a distinctive feature of Middle Eastern verse, especially Persian, but are also a part of daily life—a scholar recently recovered more than four thousand in one Lebanese village, including the following: "He who has money can eat sherbet in Hell." From Persia comes the cynical aphorism: "Trust in God, but tie up your camel."

Some Arabic and Persian literature reflected the deep spiritual and ethical concerns of the Qur'an. The thirteenth-century poet Rumi (ROO-mee), for example, embraced **Sufism** (SOO-fiz-uhm), a form of religious belief that called for a mystical relationship between Allah and human beings (the term *Sufism* stems from the Arabic word for "wool," referring to the rough wool garments that its adherents wore). Converted to Sufism by a wandering dervish (dervishes, from the word for "poor" in Persian, sought to achieve a mystical union with Allah through dancing and chanting in an ecstatic trance), Rumi abandoned orthodox Islam to embrace God directly through ecstatic love. Realizing that love transcends intellect, he sought to reach God through a trance attained by the whirling dance of the dervish, set to mesmerizing music. As he twirled, the poet extemporized some of the most passionate lyrical verse ever conceived. His faith and art remain an important force in Islamic society today.

The Islamic world also made a major contribution to historical writing, another discipline that was stimulated by the introduction of paper manufacturing. The first great Islamic historian was al-Mas'udi. Born in Baghdad in 896, he wrote about both the Muslim and the non-Muslim world, traveling widely in the process. His *Meadows of Gold* is the source of much of our knowledge about the golden age of the Abbasid caliphate. Translations of his work reveal a wide-ranging mind and a keen intellect, combined with a human touch that practitioners of the art in our century might find reason to emulate. Equaling al-Mas'udi in talent and reputation was the fourteenth-century historian Ibn Khaldun (IB-un kal-DOON). Combining scholarship with government service, Ibn Khaldun was one of the first historians to attempt a philosophy of history.

Islamic Art and Architecture   The art of Islam is a blend of Arab, Turkish, and Persian traditions. Although local influences can be discerned throughout the region, the Arabs, with their new religion and their writing system, served as a unifying force. Fascinated by the mathematics and astronomy they inherited from the Romans or the Babylonians, they developed a sense of rhythm and abstraction that found expression in their use of repetitive geometric ornamentation. The Turks made their own contribution with the use of abstraction in figurative and nonfigurative designs, while the Persians added their lyrical poetic mysticism.

The ultimate expression of Islamic art is to be found in magnificent architectural monuments beginning in the late seventh century. The first great example is the Dome of the Rock, built in 691 to proclaim the spiritual and political legitimacy of the new religion to the ancient world. Set in the sacred heart of Jerusalem on Muhammad's holy rock and touching both the Western Wall of the Jews and the city's oldest Christian church, the Dome of the Rock remains one of the most revered Islamic monuments. Constructed on Byzantine lines with an octagonal shape and marble columns and ornamentation, the interior reflects Persian motifs with mosaics of precious stones. Although rebuilt several times and incorporating influences from both East and West, this first monument to Islam represents the birth of a new art.

At first, desert Arabs, whether nomads or conquering armies, prayed in an open court, shaded along the *qibla* (KIB-luh) (the wall facing the holy city of Mecca) by a thatched roof supported by rows of palm trunks. There was also a ditch where the faithful could wash off the dust of the desert prior to prayer. As Islam became better established, enormous mosques, such as the one earlier discussed at Samarra, were constructed, but they were still modeled on the open court, which would be surrounded on all four sides with pillars supporting a wooden roof over the prayer area facing the *qibla* wall. Set in that wall was a niche, or **mihrab** (MEER-uhb), containing a decorated panel pointing to Mecca and representing Allah.

No discussion of mosques would be complete without mentioning the famous ninth-century mosque at Córdoba in southern Spain, which is still in remarkable condition. Its 514 columns supporting double horseshoe arches transform this architectural wonder into a unique forest of trees pointing upward, contributing to a light and airy effect. The unparalleled sumptuousness and elegance make the Córdoba mosque one of the wonders of world art, let alone Islamic art.

Since the Muslim religion combines spiritual and political power in one, palaces also reflected the glory of Islam. Beginning in the eighth century with the spectacular castles of Syria, the rulers constructed large brick domiciles reminiscent of Roman design, with protective walls, gates, and baths. With a central courtyard surrounded by two-story arcades and massive gate-towers, they resembled fortresses as much as palaces. The most impressive remaining Islamic palace is the fourteenth-century Alhambra in Spain. The extensive succession of courtyards, rooms, gardens, and fountains created a fairytale castle perched high above the city of Granada. Every inch of surface is decorated in intricate floral and semiabstract patterns; much of the decoration is done in carved plasterwork so fine that it resembles lace.

Since antiquity, one of the primary occupations of women has been the spinning and weaving of cloth to make clothing and other useful items for their families. In the Middle East, this skill reached an apogee in the art of the knotted woolen rug. Originating in the pre-Muslim era, rugs were initially used to insulate stone palaces against the cold as well as to warm shepherds' tents. Eventually, they were applied to religious purposes, since every practicing Muslim is required to pray five times a day on clean ground. Small rugs served as prayer mats for individual use, while larger and more elaborate ones were given by rulers as rewards for political favors. Bedouins in the Arabian desert covered their sandy floors with rugs to create a cozy environment in their tents.

In villages throughout the Middle East, the art of rug weaving has been passed down from mother to daughter over the centuries. Girls as young as four years old took part in the process by helping to spin and prepare the wool shorn from the family sheep. By the age of six, girls would begin their first rug, and before adolescence, their slender fingers would be producing fine carpets. Skilled artisanship represented an extra enticement to prospective bridegrooms, and rugs often became an important part of a woman's dowry to her future husband. After the wedding, the wife would continue to make rugs for home use, as well as for sale to augment the family income. Eventually, rugs began to be manufactured in workshops by professional artisans, who reproduced the designs from detailed painted diagrams.

Representation of the Prophet Muhammad, in painting or in any other art form, has traditionally been strongly discouraged. Although no passage of the Qur'an forbids representational painting, the *Hadith* warned against any attempt to imitate God through artistic creation or idolatry, and this has been interpreted as an outright ban on any such depictions. Accordingly, with the exception of Persian miniatures, where an earlier style involving human representation survived for a while, most decorations on all forms of Islamic art consisted of Arabic script and natural plant and figurative motifs. Repeated continuously in naturalistic or semi-abstract geometrical patterns called arabesques, these decorations completely covered the surface and left no area undecorated. This dense decor was also evident in brick, mosaic, and stucco ornamentation and culminated in the magnificent tile work of later centuries.

CHRONOLOGY

ISLAM: THE FIRST MILLENNIUM

570–632	Life of Muhammad
622	Flight to Medina
630	Conquest of Mecca
640	Fall of Cairo
650	Defeat of Persians
656	Election of Ali to caliphate
c. 710	Muslim entry into Spain
750–1258	Abbasid caliphate
762	Construction of city of Baghdad
786–809	Reign of Harun al-Rashid
929–1031	Umayyad caliphate in Spain
973	Founding of Fatimid dynasty in Egypt
1055	Capture of Baghdad by Seljuk Turks
1071	Seizure of Anatolia by Seljuk Turks
1096	First Crusade

1169	Saladin destroys Fatimid kingdom
1258	Mongols seize Baghdad
1453	Ottoman Turks capture Constantinople

MindTap is a fully online, highly personalized learning experience built upon Cengage Learning content. MindTap combines student learning tools—readings, multimedia, activities, and assessments—into a singular Learning Path that guides students through their course.

8

EARLY CIVILIZATIONS IN AFRICA

The Temple at Great Zimbabwe

CHAPTER OUTLINE

- The Emergence of Civilization • The Coming of Islam • States and Noncentralized Societies in Central and Southern Africa • African Society
- African Culture

THE EMERGENCE OF CIVILIZATION

After Asia, Africa is the largest of the continents. It stretches nearly 5,000 miles from the Cape of Good Hope in the south to the Mediterranean in the north and extends a similar distance from Cape Verde on the west coast to the Horn of Africa on the Indian Ocean.

The Land   Africa is as physically diverse as it is vast. The northern coast, washed by the Mediterranean Sea, is mountainous for much of its length. South of the mountains lies the greatest

MAP 8.1   Ancient Africa

Modern human beings, the primate species known as *Homo sapiens*, first evolved on the continent of Africa. Some key sites of early human settlement are shown on this map.

desert on earth, the Sahara, which stretches from the Atlantic to the Indian Ocean. To the east is the Nile River, heart of the ancient Egyptian civilization. Beyond that lies the Red Sea, separating Africa from Asia.

The Sahara acts as a great divide separating the northern coast from the rest of the continent. Africa south of the Sahara contains a number of major regions. In the west is the so-called hump of Africa, which juts like a massive shoulder into the Atlantic Ocean. Here the Sahara gradually gives way to grasslands in the interior and then to tropical rain forests along the coast. This region, dominated by the Niger River, is rich in natural resources and was the home of many ancient civilizations.

Far to the east, bordering the Indian Ocean, is a very different terrain of snow-capped mountains, upland plateaus, and lakes. Much of this region is grassland populated by wild beasts, which has caused many Westerners to view it as "safari country." Here, in the East African Rift Valley in the lake district of modern Kenya, early hominids began their long trek toward civilization several million years ago.

Directly to the west lies the Congo basin, with its rain forests watered by the mighty Congo River. The forests of equatorial Africa then fade gradually into the hills, plateaus, and deserts of the south. This rich land contains some of the most valuable mineral resources known today.

The First Farmers

It is not certain when agriculture was first practiced on the continent of Africa. Until recently, historians assumed that crops were first cultivated in the lower Nile Valley (the northern part near the Mediterranean) about seven or eight thousand years ago, when wheat and barley were introduced, possibly from the Middle East. Eventually, this area gave rise to the civilization of ancient Egypt.

Recent evidence, however, suggests that this hypothesis may need some revision. South of Egypt, near the junction of the White Nile and the Blue Nile, is an area historically known as Nubia. By the ninth millennium B.C.E., peoples living in this area began to domesticate animals, first wild cattle and then sheep and goats, which had apparently originated in the Middle East. In areas where the climate permitted, they supplemented their diet by gathering wild grains and soon learned how to cultivate grains such as sorghum and millet, while also growing gourds and melons.

Eventually, the practice of agriculture began to spread westward across the Sahara. At that time, the world's climate was much cooler and wetter than it is today, but a warm, humid climate prevailed in parts of the Sahara, creating lakes and ponds, as well as vast grasslands (known as savannas) replete with game. Hence, indigenous peoples living in the area were able to provide for themselves by hunting, food gathering, and fishing. By the seventh and sixth millennia B.C.E., however, conditions were becoming increasingly arid, forcing them to find new means of support. Rock paintings found in what are today some of the most uninhabitable parts of the region show that by the fourth millennium B.C.E. fishing and pastoralism in the heart of the Sahara were being supplemented by the limited cultivation of grain crops, including a drought-resistant form of dry rice.

Thus, the peoples of northern Africa, from Nubia westward into the heart of the Sahara, were among the earliest in the world to adopt settled agriculture as a means of subsistence. Shards of pottery found at archaeological sites in the area suggest that they were also among the first to manufacture clay pots, which allowed them to consume their cereals in the form of porridge rather than as bread baked from flour. By 5000 B.C.E., they were cultivating cotton plants for the purpose of manufacturing textiles.

After 3000 B.C.E., the desiccation (drying up) of the Sahara intensified, and the lakes began to dry up, forcing many local inhabitants to migrate eastward toward the Nile River and southward into the grasslands. As a result, farming began to spread into the savannas on the southern fringes of the desert and eventually into the tropical forest areas to the south, where crops were no longer limited to drought-resistant cereals but could include tropical fruits and tubers. In the meantime, the foundation was being laid for the emergence of an advanced civilization in Egypt along the banks of the Nile River.

Axum and Meroë   To the south of Egypt in Nubia, the kingdom of Kush had emerged as a major trading state by the end of the second millennium B.C.E. Kush adopted many of its political institutions and much of its culture from the kingdom of the pharaohs farther to the north and—at a time of Egyptian weakness in the eighth century B.C.E.—even managed to seize the city of Memphis and much of the Nile River Delta. Eventually, however, the Kushite rulers were driven out of lower Egypt and forced to retreat back to their original habitat in Nubia, where a new capital was established at Meroë (MER-oh-ee *or* MER-uh-wee), near the Fourth Cataract in the great bend of the Nile River.

The new capital was located near extensive iron deposits and, once smelting techniques had been developed, iron evidently provided the basis for much of the area's growing prosperity. Meroë eventually became a cultural center and a major trading hub for iron goods and other manufactures for the entire region. The prosperity of the area is attested to by the remnants of a number of pyramids, similar in design but smaller in size than their Egyptian counterparts, which were constructed to serve as tombs for the deceased rulers of the ruling dynasty. Recently, other pyramids, some as short as 3 feet high, have been located along the banks of the river, suggesting that local elites mimicked the ruling family in what one archaeologist called "the democratization of pyramids."

By the third century C.E., however, a competitor to Meroë's regional economic prominence began to arise a few hundred miles to the southeast, in the mountainous highlands of what today is known as Ethiopia. The founders of Axum (AHK-soom) claimed descent from migrants who arrived in Africa from the kingdom of Saba (SAH-buh) (also known as Sheba), across the Red Sea on the southern tip of the Arabian peninsula. During antiquity, Saba was a major trading state, serving as a transit point for goods carried from South Asia into the lands surrounding the Mediterranean. Biblical sources credited the "queen of Sheba" with vast wealth and resources. In fact, much of that wealth had originated much farther to the east and passed through Saba en route to the countries adjacent to the Mediterranean. Whether migrants from Saba were responsible for founding Axum is sheer conjecture, but a similarity in architectural styles suggests that there probably was some form of relationship between the two states.

After Saba declined, perhaps because of the desiccation of the Arabian Desert, Axum survived for centuries. Like Saba, Axum owed much of its prosperity to its location on the commercial trade route between India and the Mediterranean, and ships from Egypt stopped regularly at the port of Adulis (a-DOO-luss) on the Red Sea. Axum exported ivory, frankincense, myrrh, and slaves, while its primary imports were textiles, metal goods, wine, and olive oil. For a time, Axum competed for control of the ivory trade with the neighboring state of Meroë, and hunters from Axum armed with imported iron weapons scoured the entire region for elephants. Probably as a result of this competition, in the fourth century C.E., the Axumite ruler, claiming he had been provoked, launched an invasion of Meroë and conquered it, creating an empire that, in the view of some contemporaries, rivaled those of Rome and Persia.

One of the most distinctive features of Axumite civilization was its religion. Originally, the rulers of Axum (who claimed descent from King Solomon through the visit of the queen of Sheba to Israel in biblical times) followed the religion of Saba. But in the fourth century C.E., Axumite rulers adopted Christianity, possibly as the result of contacts with Egypt. This commitment to the Egyptian form of Christianity—often called **Coptic** (KAHP-tik) from the local language of the day—was retained even after the collapse of Axum and the expansion of Islam through

MAP 8.2 Ancient Ethiopia and Nubia

The first civilizations to appear on the African continent emerged in the Nile River valley. Early in the first century C.E., the state of Axum emerged in what is today the state of Ethiopia.

the area in later centuries. Later, Axum (renamed Ethiopia) would be identified by some Europeans as the "hermit kingdom" and the home of Prester John, a legendary Christian king of East Africa.

The Sahara and Its Environs Meroë and Axum were part of the ancient trading network that extended from the Mediterranean Sea to the Indian Ocean and were affected in various ways by the cross-cultural contacts that took place throughout that region. Elsewhere in Africa, somewhat different patterns prevailed; they varied from area to area, depending on the geography and climate.

Historians do not know when goods first began to be exchanged across the Sahara in a north-south direction, but during the first millennium B.C.E., the commercial center of Carthage on the Mediterranean had become a focal point of the trans-Saharan trade. The **Berbers**, a pastoral people of North Africa, served as intermediaries, carrying food products and manufactured goods from Carthage across the desert and exchanging them for salt, gold and copper, skins, various agricultural products, and perhaps slaves. Carthaginian fleets had for centuries also been actively searching for markets along the east African coast.

This trade initiated a process of cultural exchange that would exert a significant impact on the peoples of tropical Africa. Among other things, it may have spread the knowledge of ironworking south of the desert. Although historians once believed that ironworking knowledge reached sub-Saharan Africa from Meroë in the first centuries C.E., recent finds suggest that the peoples along the Niger River were smelting iron five or six hundred years earlier. Some scholars believe that the technique developed independently there, but others surmise that it was introduced by the Berbers, who had learned it from the Carthaginians.

Whatever the case, the **Nok** (NAHK) **culture** in northern Nigeria eventually became one of the most active ironworking societies in Africa. Excavations have unearthed numerous terra-cotta and metal figures, as well as stone and iron farm implements, dating back as far as 500 B.C.E. The remains of smelting furnaces confirm that the iron was produced locally.

Early in the first millennium C.E., the introduction of the camel from across the Red Sea in the Middle East provided a major stimulus to the trans-Saharan trade. With its ability to store considerable amounts of food and water, the camel was far better equipped to handle the arduous conditions of the desert than the donkey and the wheeled cart, which had been used previously. The camel caravans of the Berbers, arduously threading their way from the shores of the Mediterranean through the heart of the Sahara, became so essential to the local trade network that they became known as the "fleets of the desert."

The Garamantes Not all the peoples involved in trade across the Sahara were nomadic. Recent exploratory work in the Libyan Desert has revealed the existence of an ancient kingdom that for over a thousand years transported goods between societies along the Mediterranean Sea and sub-Saharan West Africa. The Garamantes (gar-uh-MAN-teez), as they were known to the Romans, carried salt, glass, metal, olive oil, and wine southward in return for gold, slaves, and various tropical products. To provide food for their communities in the heart of the desert, they constructed a complex irrigation system consisting of several thousand miles of underground channels. The technique is reminiscent of similar systems in Persia and Central Asia. Scholars believe that the kingdom declined as a result of the fall of the Roman Empire, which led to a drop in the exchange of goods throughout the area, and the desiccation of the desert. As the historian Felipe Fernández-Armesto has noted in his provocative study *Civilizations*, advanced societies do not easily thrive in desert conditions.[1]

East Africa   South of Axum, along the shores of the Indian Ocean and in the inland plateau that stretches from the mountains of Ethiopia through the lake district of Central Africa, lived a mixture of peoples. Some originally depended on hunting and food gathering, whereas others followed pastoral pursuits.

Beginning in the third millennium B.C.E., farming peoples speaking dialects of the Bantu **(BAN-too)** family of languages began to migrate from their original homeland in what today is Nigeria. Eventually, they reached East Africa, where they may have been responsible for introducing the widespread cultivation of crops and knowledge of ironworking, although there are signs of some limited iron smelting in the area before their arrival.

The Bantu settled in rural communities based on subsistence farming. The primary crops were millet and sorghum, along with yams, melons, and beans. In addition to stone implements, they often used iron tools, usually manufactured in a local smelter, to till the land. Some people kept domestic animals such as cattle, sheep, goats, or chickens or supplemented their diets by hunting and food gathering. Because the population was minimal and an ample supply of cultivable land was available, most settlements were relatively small, although there was apparently a readily visible set of class distinctions within the local population.

As early as the era of the New Kingdom in the second millennium B.C.E., Egyptian ships had plied the waters off the East African coast in search of gold, ivory, palm oil, and perhaps slaves. By the first century C.E., the region was an established part of a trading network that included the Mediterranean and the Red Sea. In that century, a Greek seafarer from Alexandria wrote an account of his travels down the coast from Cape Guardafui (GWAR-duh-fwee *or* GWAR-duh-foo-ee) at the tip of the Horn of Africa to the Strait of Madagascar (ma-duh-GAS-kur), thousands of miles to the south. Called the *Periplus* (PER-ih-pluss), this work provides descriptions of the peoples and settlements along the African coast and the trade goods they supplied.

According to the *Periplus*, the port of Rhapta (RAHP-tuh) (probably modern Dar es Salaam) was a commercial metropolis, exporting ivory, rhinoceros horn, and tortoise shell and importing glass, wine, grain, and metal goods such as weapons and tools. The identity of the peoples taking part in this trade is not clear, but it seems likely that the area was inhabited primarily by a mixture of local peoples supplemented by a small number of immigrants from the Arabian peninsula. Out of this mixture would eventually emerge a cosmopolitan **Swahili** (swah-HEE-lee) culture that continues to exist in coastal areas today. Beyond Rhapta was "unexplored ocean." Some contemporary observers believed that the Indian and Atlantic Oceans were connected. Others were convinced that the Indian Ocean was an enclosed sea

COMPARATIVE ESSAY

The Migration of Peoples

INTERACTION
& EXCHANGE

About 50,000 years ago, a small band of humans crossed the Sinai Peninsula from Africa and began to spread out across the Eurasian supercontinent. Thus began a migration of peoples that continued with accelerating speed throughout the ancient era and beyond. By 40,000 B.C.E., their descendants had spread across Eurasia as far as China and eastern Siberia and had even settled the distant continent of Australia.

Who were these peoples, and what provoked their decision to change their habitat? Undoubtedly, the first migrants were foragers or hunters in search of wild game, but with the advent of agriculture and the domestication of animals about 12,000 years ago, other peoples began to migrate vast distances in search of fertile farming and pasturelands.

The ever-changing climate was undoubtedly a major factor driving the process. Beginning in the fourth millennium B.C.E., the drying up of rich pasturelands in the Sahara forced the local inhabitants to migrate eastward toward the Nile River valley and the grasslands of East Africa. At about the same time, Indo-European-speaking farming peoples left the region of the Black Sea and moved gradually into central Europe in search of new farmlands. They were eventually followed by nomadic groups from Central Asia who began to occupy lands along the frontiers of the Roman Empire, while other bands of nomads threatened the plains of northern China from the Gobi Desert. In the meantime, Bantu-speaking farmers had migrated from the Niger River southward into the rain forests of Central Africa and beyond. Similar movements took place in Southeast Asia and the Americas.

This steady flow of migrating peoples often had a destabilizing effect on sedentary societies in their path. Nomadic incursions represented a constant menace to the security of China, Egypt, and the Roman Empire and ultimately brought them to an end. But these vast movements of peoples often had beneficial effects as well, spreading new technologies and means of livelihood. Although some migrants, like the Huns, came for plunder and left havoc in their wake, other groups, like the Celtic peoples and the Bantus, prospered in their new environments.

The most famous of all nomadic invasions is a case in point. In the thirteenth century C.E., the Mongols left their homeland in the Gobi Desert, advancing westward into the Russian steppes and southward into China and Central Asia, leaving death and devastation in their wake. At the height of their empire, the Mongols controlled virtually all of Eurasia except its western and southern

and that the continent of Africa could not be circumnavigated. Adverse winds and currents from the straits dividing Madagascar from Africa down to the southern tip of the continent made sailing conditions difficult.

Trade across the Indian Ocean and down the coast of East Africa, facilitated by the monsoon winds, would gradually become one of the most lucrative sources of commercial profit in the ancient and medieval worlds. Although the origins of the trade remain shrouded in mystery, traders eventually came by sea from as far away

Erich Lessing/Art Resource, NY

Rock Paintings of the Sahara. *Even before the Egyptians built their pyramids at Giza, other peoples far to the west in the vast wastes of the Sahara were creating their own art forms. These rock paintings, some of which date back to the fourth millennium B.C.E. and are reminiscent of similar examples from Europe, Asia, and Australia, provide a valuable record of a society that supported itself by a combination of farming, hunting, and herding animals. After the introduction of the horse from Arabia around 1200 B.C.E., subsequent rock paintings depicted chariots and horseback riding. Eventually, camels began to appear in the paintings, a consequence of the increasing desiccation of the Sahara.*

fringes, thereby creating a zone of stability in which a global trade and informational network could thrive that stretched from China to the shores of the Mediterranean.

Q *What have been some of the key reasons for the migration of large numbers of people throughout human history? Is the process still under way in our own day?*

as the mainland of Southeast Asia. Early in the first millennium C.E., Malay (mah-LAY) peoples bringing cinnamon to the Middle East began to cross the Indian Ocean directly and landed on the southeastern coast of Africa. Eventually, a Malay settlement was established on the island of Madagascar, where the population is still of mixed Malay-African origin. Historians suspect that Malay immigrants were responsible for introducing such Southeast Asian foods as the banana and the yam to Africa, although recent archaeological evidence suggests that such plants may have arrived in Africa as early as the third millennium B.C.E. The banana, with its high yield and ability to grow in uncultivated rain forest, became the preferred crop of many Bantu peoples.

THE COMING OF ISLAM

The rise of Islam during the first half of the seventh century C.E. had ramifications far beyond the Arabian peninsula. Arab armies swept across North Africa, incorporating it into the Arab empire and isolating the Christian state of Axum to the south. Although East Africa and West Africa south of the Sahara were not occupied by the Arab forces, Islam eventually penetrated these areas as well.

African Religious Beliefs Before Islam
When Islam arrived, most African societies already had well-developed systems of religious belief. Like other aspects of African life, early African religious beliefs varied from place to place, but certain characteristics appear to have been shared by most African societies. One of these common features was **pantheism**, belief in a single creator god from whom all things came. Sometimes the creator god was accompanied by a whole pantheon of lesser deities. The Ashanti (uh-SHAN-tee *or* uh-SHAHN-tee) people of Ghana (GAH-nuh) in West Africa believed in a supreme being called Nyame (NY-AH-may), whose sons were lesser gods. Each son served a different purpose: one was the rainmaker, another was the source of compassion, and a third was responsible for the sunshine. This heavenly hierarchy paralleled earthly arrangements: worship of Nyame was the exclusive preserve of the king through his priests; lesser officials and the common people worshiped Nyame's sons, who might intercede with their father on behalf of ordinary Africans.

Belief in an afterlife was closely connected to the importance of ancestors and the **lineage group**, or clan, in African society. Each lineage (LIH-nee-ij) group could trace itself back to a founding ancestor or group of ancestors. These ancestral souls would not be extinguished as long as the lineage group continued to perform rituals in their name. The rituals could also benefit the lineage group on earth, for the ancestral souls, being closer to the gods, had the power to influence the lives of their descendants, for good or evil.

Such beliefs were challenged but not always replaced by the arrival of Islam. In some ways, the tenets of Islam were in conflict with traditional African beliefs and customs. Although the concept of a single transcendent deity presented no problems in many African societies, Islam's rejection of spirit worship and a priestly class ran counter to the beliefs of many Africans and was often ignored in practice. Similarly, as various Muslim travelers observed, Islam's insistence on the separation of the sexes contrasted with the relatively informal relationships that prevailed in many African societies and was probably slow to take root. In the long run, imported ideas were synthesized with indigenous beliefs to create a unique brand of Africanized Islam.

The Arabs in North Africa
In 641, Arab forces advanced into Egypt, seized the delta of the Nile River, and brought two centuries of Byzantine rule to an end. To guard against attacks from the Byzantine fleet, the Arabs eventually built a new capital at Cairo, inland

from the previous Byzantine capital of Alexandria, and began to consolidate their control over the entire region.

On their arrival in Egypt, the Arab conquerors were probably welcomed by many, if not the majority, of the local inhabitants. Although Egypt had been a thriving commercial center under the Byzantines, the average Egyptian had not shared in this prosperity. Tax rates were generally high, and Christians were subjected to periodic persecution by the Byzantines, who viewed the local Coptic faith and other sects in the area as heresies. Although the new rulers continued to obtain much of their revenue from taxing the local farming population, tax rates were generally lower than they had been under the corrupt Byzantine government, and conversion to Islam brought exemption from taxation. During the next generations, many Egyptians converted to the Muslim faith, but Islam did not move into the upper Nile Valley until several hundred years later. As Islam spread southward, it was adopted by many lowland peoples, but it had less success in the mountains of Ethiopia, where Coptic Christianity continued to win adherents.

In the meantime, Arab rule was gradually being extended westward along the Mediterranean coast. When the Romans conquered Carthage in 146 B.C.E., they had called their new province Africa, thus introducing a name that would eventually be applied to the entire continent. After the fall of the Roman Empire, much of the area had reverted to the control of local Berber chieftains, but the Byzantines captured Carthage in the mid-sixth century C.E. In 690, the city was seized by the Arabs, who then began to extend their control over the entire area, which they called *al-Maghrib* (al-MAH-greb) ("the west").

At first, the local Berber peoples resisted their new conquerors. The Berbers were tough fighters, and for several generations, Arab rule was limited to the towns and lowland coastal areas. But Arab persistence eventually paid off, and by the early eighth century, the entire North African coast as far west as the Strait of Gibraltar was under Arab rule. The Arabs were now poised to cross the strait and expand into southern Europe and to push south beyond the fringes of the Sahara.

The Kingdom of Ethiopia: A Christian Island in a Muslim Sea   By the end of the sixth century C.E., the kingdom of Axum, long a dominant force in the trade network through the Red Sea, was in a state of decline. Overexploitation of farmland had played a role in the process, as had a shift in trade routes away from the Red Sea to the Arabian peninsula and Persian Gulf. By the beginning of the ninth century, the capital had been moved farther into the mountainous interior, and Axum was gradually transformed from a maritime power into an isolated agricultural society.

The rise of Islam on the Arabian peninsula hastened this process, as the Arab world increasingly began to serve as the focus of the regional trade passing through the area. By the eighth century, a number of Muslim trading states had been established on the African coast of the Red Sea, a development that contributed to the transformation of Axum into a landlocked society with primarily agricultural interests. At first, relations between Christian Axum and its Muslim neighbors were relatively peaceful, as the larger and more powerful Axumite kingdom attempted with some success to compel the coastal Islamic states to accept a tributary relationship. Axum's role in the local commercial network temporarily revived, and the area

COMPARATIVE ILLUSTRATION

Rock Architecture

ART & IDEAS

As we have seen, one of the earliest forms of religious architecture in India was the rock temple. One of the most famous examples is the eighth-century temple at Ellora, in central India. Named after Shiva's holy mountain in the Himalayas, the temple is approximately the size of the Parthenon in Athens but was literally carved out of a hillside, with its exquisite sculptures open to the sky (below photo).

William J. Duiker

became a prime source for ivory, gold, resins such as frankincense and myrrh, and slaves. Slaves came primarily from the south, where Axum had been attempting to subjugate restive tribal peoples living in the Amharic (am-HAR-ik) plateau beyond its southern border.

Beginning in the twelfth century, however, relations between Axum and its neighbors deteriorated as the Muslim states along the coast began to move inland to gain control over the growing trade in slaves and ivory. Axum responded with force and at first had some success in reasserting its hegemony over the area. But in the early fourteenth century, the Muslim state of Adal (a-DAHL), located at the juncture of the Indian Ocean and the Red Sea, launched a new attack on the Christian kingdom.

Axum also underwent significant internal change during this period. The Zagwe (ZAH-gweh) dynasty, which seized control of the country in the mid-twelfth century, centralized the government and extended the Christian faith throughout the kingdom, now known as Ethiopia. Military commanders or civilian officials who had personal

Werner Forman/Art Resource, NY

This form of architecture also found expression in parts of Africa. In 1200 C.E., Christian monks in Ethiopia began to construct a remarkable series of eleven churches carved out of solid volcanic rock (above photo). After a 40-foot trench was formed by removing the bedrock, the central block of stone was hewed into the shape of a Greek cross; then it was hollowed out and decorated. These churches, which are still in use today, testify to the fervor of Ethiopian Christianity, which plays a major role in preserving the country's cultural and national identity.

Q *Why do you think some early cultures made frequent use of the concept of rock architecture, while others did not? Why do you think the process was discontinued?*

or kinship ties with the royal court established vast landed estates to maintain security and facilitate the collection of taxes from the local population. In the meantime, Christian missionaries established monasteries and churches to propagate the faith in outlying areas. Close relations were reestablished with leaders of the Coptic church in Egypt and with Christian officials in the Holy Land. This process was continued by the Solomonids (sah-luh-MAHN-idz), who succeeded the Zagwe dynasty in 1270. But by the early fifteenth century, the state had become deeply involved in an expanding conflict with Muslim Adal to the east, a conflict that lasted for over a century and gradually took on the characteristics of a holy war.

East Africa: The Land of the Zanj The rise of Islam also had a lasting impact on the coast of East Africa, which the Greeks had called Azania and the Arabs called Zanj (ZANJ) referring to the "burnt skin" of the indigenous population. According to Swahili oral traditions, during the seventh and eighth centuries peoples from the Arabian peninsula and the Persian Gulf began to settle at ports along the coast and on the small islands offshore. Then, in the middle of the tenth century, a Persian from the city of Shiraz sailed to the area with his six sons. As his small fleet stopped along the coast, each son disembarked on one of the coastal islands and founded a small community; these settlements eventually grew into important commercial centers including Mombasa (mahm-BAH-suh), Pemba (PEM-buh), Zanzibar (ZAN-zi-bar) (literally, "the coast of the Zanj"), and Kilwa (KIL-wuh). Although this oral tradition may underestimate the indigenous population's growing involvement in local commerce, it also reflects the degree to which African merchants—who often served as middlemen between the peoples of the interior and the traders arriving from ports all around the Indian Ocean—saw themselves as part of an international commercial network.

In any case, by the ninth and tenth centuries, a string of trading ports had appeared stretching from Mogadishu (moh-guh-DEE-shoo) (today the capital of Somalia) in the north to Kilwa (south of present-day Dar es Salaam) in the south. Kilwa became especially important because it was near the southern limit for a ship hoping to complete the round-trip journey in a single season. Goods such as ivory, gold, and rhinoceros horn were exported across the Indian Ocean to countries as far away as China, while imports included iron goods, glassware, Indian textiles, and Chinese porcelain. Merchants in these cities often amassed considerable profit, as evidenced by their lavish stone palaces, some of which still stand in the modern cities of Mombasa and Zanzibar. Though now in ruins, Kilwa was one of the most magnificent cities of its day. The fourteenth-century Arab traveler Ibn Battuta (IB-un ba-TOO-tuh) described it as "amongst the most beautiful of cities and most elegantly built. All of it is of wood, and the ceilings of its houses are of *al-dis* [reeds]."[2] One particularly impressive structure was the Husini Kubwa (hoo-SEE-nee KOOB-wuh), a massive palace with vaulted roofs capped with domes and elaborate stone carvings, surrounding an inner courtyard. Ordinary townspeople and the residents in smaller towns did not live in such luxurious conditions, of course, but even so, affluent urban residents lived in spacious stone buildings, with indoor plumbing and consumer goods imported from as far away as China and southern Europe.

Most of the coastal states were self-governing, although sometimes several towns were grouped together under a single dominant authority. Government revenue came primarily from taxes imposed on commerce. Some trade went on between these coastal city-states and the peoples of the interior, who provided gold and iron, ivory, and various agricultural goods and animal products in return for textiles, manufactured articles, and weapons. Relations apparently varied, and the coastal merchants sometimes resorted to force to obtain goods from the inland peoples. A Portuguese visitor recounted that "the men [of Mombasa] are oft-times at war and but seldom at peace with those of the mainland, and they carry on trade with them, bringing thence great store of honey, wax, and ivory."[3]

By the twelfth and thirteenth centuries, a cosmopolitan culture, eventually known as Swahili, from the Arabic *sahel* (sah-HEL), meaning "coast," began to emerge throughout the seaboard area. Intermarriage between the small number of immigrants and the local population eventually led to the emergence of a ruling class of mixed heritage, some of whom had Arab or Persian ancestors. By this time, too, many members of the ruling class had converted to Islam. Middle Eastern urban architectural styles and other aspects of Arab culture were implanted within a society still predominantly African. Arabic words and phrases were combined with Bantu grammatical structures to form a distinct language, also known as Swahili; it is the national language of Kenya and Tanzania today.

The States of
West Africa
During the eighth century, merchants from the Maghrib began to carry Muslim beliefs to the savanna areas south of the Sahara. At first, conversion took place on an individual basis and primarily among local merchants, rather than through official encouragement. The first rulers to convert to Islam were the royal family of Gao (GAH-oh) at the end of the tenth century. Five hundred years later, most of the population in the grasslands south of the Sahara had accepted Islam.

The expansion of Islam into West Africa had a major impact on the political system. By introducing Arabic as the first written language in the region and Muslim law codes and administrative practices from the Middle East, Islam provided local rulers with the tools to increase their authority and the efficiency of their governments. Moreover, as Islam gradually spread throughout the region, a common religion united previously diverse peoples into a more coherent community.

When Islam arrived in the grasslands south of the Sahara, the region was beginning to undergo significant political and social change. As a partial consequence of the initiation of a new wet phase throughout the region in the early fourth century, a number of major trading states were in the making, and they eventually transformed the Sahara into one of the leading avenues of world trade, crisscrossed by caravan routes leading to destinations as far away as the Atlantic Ocean, the Mediterranean, and the Red Sea.

Ghana   The first of these great commercial states was Ghana, which emerged in the fifth century C.E. in the upper Niger Valley, a grassland region between the Sahara and the tropical forests along the West African coast. (The modern state of Ghana, which takes its name from this early trading society, is located in the forest region to the south.) The majority of the people in the area were farmers living in villages under the authority of a local chieftain. Gradually, these local communities were united to form the kingdom of Ghana.

Although the people of the region had traditionally lived from agriculture, a primary reason for Ghana's growing importance was gold. The heartland of the state was located near one of the richest gold-producing areas in all of Africa. Ghanaian merchants transported the gold to Morocco, whence it was distributed throughout the known world. The exchange of goods became quite ritualized. As the ancient Greek historian Herodotus relates:

> The Carthaginians also tell us that they trade with a race of men who live in a part of Libya beyond the Pillars of Heracles [the Strait of Gibraltar]. On reaching this country, they unload their goods, arrange them tidily along the beach, and then, returning to their boats, raise a smoke. Seeing the smoke, the natives come down to the beach, place on the ground a certain quantity of gold in exchange for the goods, and go off again to a distance. The Carthaginians then come ashore and take a look at the gold; and if they think it represents a fair price for their wares, they collect it and go away; if, on the

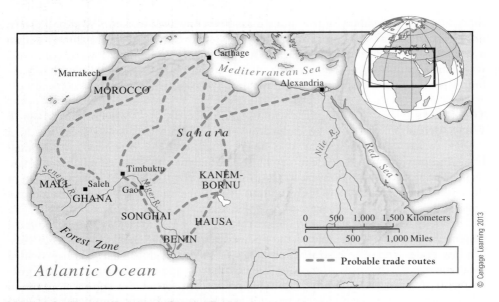

MAP 8.3 Trans-Saharan Trade Routes

Trade across the Sahara began during the first millennium B.C.E. With the arrival of the camel from the Middle East, trade expanded dramatically.

other hand, it seems too little, they go back aboard and wait, and the natives come and add to the gold until they are satisfied. There is perfect honesty on both sides; the Carthaginians never touch the gold until it equals in value what they have offered for sale, and the natives never touch the goods until the gold has been taken away.[4]

Later, Ghana became known to Arabic-speaking peoples in North Africa as "the land of gold." Actually, the name was misleading, for the gold did not come from Ghana but from a neighboring people, who sold it to merchants from Ghana.

Eventually, other exports from Ghana found their way to the bazaars of the Mediterranean coast and beyond—ivory, ostrich feathers, hides, leather goods, and ultimately slaves. The origins of the slave trade in the area probably go back to the first millennium B.C.E., when Berber tribesmen seized African villagers in the regions south of the Sahara and sold them to buyers in Europe and the Middle East. In return, Ghana imported metal goods (especially weapons), textiles, horses, and salt.

Much of the trade across the desert was still conducted by the nomadic Berbers, but Ghanaian merchants played an active role as intermediaries, trading tropical products such as bananas, kola nuts, and palm oil from the forest states of Guinea along the Atlantic coast to the south. By the eighth and ninth centuries, much of this trade was conducted by Muslim merchants, who purchased the goods from local traders (using iron and copper coins or cowrie shells from Southeast Asia as the primary means of exchange) and then sold them to Berbers, who carried them across the desert. The merchants who carried on this trade often became quite wealthy and lived in splendor in cities like Saleh (SAH-luh), the capital of Ghana. So did the king, of course, who taxed the merchants as well as the farmers and the producers.

Like other West African monarchs, the king of Ghana ruled by divine right and was assisted by a hereditary aristocracy composed of the leading members of the prominent clans, who also served as district chiefs responsible for maintaining law and order and collecting taxes. The king was responsible for maintaining the security of his kingdom, serving as an intermediary with local deities, and functioning as the chief law officer to adjudicate disputes. The kings of Ghana did not convert to Islam themselves, although they welcomed Muslim merchants and apparently did not discourage their subjects from adopting the new faith.

Mali   The empire of Ghana flourished for several hundred years, but by the twelfth century, weakened by ruinous wars with Berber marauders, it had begun to decline. The downfall of Ghana was a partial consequence of the emergence of the powerful Almoravid (al-MOR-uh-vid) dynasty in Morocco. The Almoravids were not only active in protecting the Moorish kingdoms in Andalusia, but also began to expand their activities southward in the desert from their new capital of Marrakech (mar-uh-KESH), a trading center founded in the eleventh century at a caravan stop near the Atlas Mountains. Attacks by mounted Berber forces on the weakening state of Ghana began shortly after, and it collapsed by the end of the following century.

In the ashes of the kingdom of Ghana rose a number of new trading societies, including large territorial empires like Mali (MAHL-ee) and Songhai (song-GY) in the west, Kanem-Bornu (KAH-nuhm-BOR-noo) in the east, and small commercial city-states like the Hausa states, located in what is today northern Nigeria.

The greatest of the empires that emerged after the destruction of Ghana was Mali. Extending from the Atlantic coast inland as far as the trading cities of Timbuktu (tim-buk-TOO) and Gao on the Niger River, Mali built its wealth and power on the gold trade. But the heartland of Mali was situated south of the Sahara in the savanna region, where there was sufficient moisture for farmers to grow such crops as sorghum, millet, and rice. The farmers lived in villages ruled by a local chieftain, called a ***mansa*** (MAHN-suh), who served as both religious and administrative leader and was responsible for forwarding tax revenues from the village to higher levels of government.

The primary wealth of the country was accumulated in the cities. Here lived the merchants, who were primarily of local origin, although many were now practicing Muslims. Commercial activities were taxed but were apparently so lucrative that both the merchants and the kings prospered. One of the most powerful kings of Mali was Mansa Musa (MAHN-suh MOO-suh) (r. 1312–1337), whose primary contribution to his people was probably not economic prosperity but the Muslim faith. Mansa Musa strongly encouraged the building of mosques and the study of the Qur'an in his kingdom and imported scholars and books to introduce his subjects to the message of Allah.

The city of Timbuktu ("well of Bouctu," a Taureg woman who lived in the area) is the most storied of the cities that emerged under the kingdom of Mali. It was founded by Berber tribal groups in 1100 C.E. as a seasonal camp for caravan

MAP 8.4 The Emergence of States in Africa

By the end of the first millennium C.E., organized states had begun to appear in various parts of Africa. The extensive empires of Ghana, Mali, and Songhai emerged at different times and did not exist simultaneously.

traders on the Niger River. Under Mansa Musa and his successors, the city gradually emerged as a major intellectual and cultural center in West Africa and the site of a renowned mosque, as well as schools of Islamic law, literature, and the sciences. Still, it was trade that drove the commerce of the city. As one Muslim historian later commented, "For Timbuktu, the great wealth was from salt.... Timbuktu would never have grown as important as it did if it hadn't been the main entrepôt for the merchants of Djenné, which sent here a large number of businessmen and men of letters."[5]

STATES AND NONCENTRALIZED SOCIETIES IN CENTRAL AND SOUTHERN AFRICA

In the southern half of the African continent, from the great basin of the Congo River to the Cape of Good Hope, states formed somewhat more slowly than in the north. Until the eleventh century C.E., most of the peoples in this region lived in what are sometimes called **noncentralized societies**, characterized by autonomous villages organized by clans and ruled by a local chieftain or clan head. Beginning in the eleventh century, in some parts of southern Africa, these independent villages gradually began to consolidate. Out of these groupings came the first states.

The Congo River Valley   One area where this process occurred was the Congo River valley, where the combination of fertile land and nearby deposits of copper and iron enabled the inhabitants to enjoy an agricultural surplus and engage in regional commerce. Two new states in particular underwent this transition. Sometime during the fourteenth century, the kingdom of Luba (LOOB-uh) was founded in the center of the continent, in a rich agricultural and fishing area near the shores of Lake Kisale. Luba had a relatively centralized government, in which the king appointed provincial governors, who were responsible for collecting tribute from the village chiefs. At about the same time, the kingdom of Kongo was formed just south of the mouth of the Congo River on the Atlantic coast.

These new states were primarily agricultural, although both had a thriving manufacturing sector and took an active part in the growing exchange of goods throughout the region. As time passed, both began to expand southward to absorb the mixed farming and pastoral peoples in the area of modern Angola. In the drier grassland area to the south, other small communities continued to support themselves by herding, hunting, or food gathering. A Portuguese sailor who encountered them in the late sixteenth century reported:

> These people are herdsmen and cultivators.... Their main crop is millet, which they grind between two stones or in wooden mortars to make flour.... Their wealth consists mainly in their huge number of dehorned cows.... They live together in small villages, in houses made of reed mats, which do not keep out the rain.[6]

Zimbabwe   Farther to the east, the situation was somewhat different. In the grassland regions immediately to the south of the Zambezi (zam-BEE-zee) River, a mixed economy involving farming, cattle herding, and commercial pursuits had begun to develop during the early centuries of the first millennium C.E. Characteristically, villages in this area were constructed inside walled enclosures to protect the animals at night. The most famous of these communities was Zimbabwe (zim-BAHB-way), located on the plateau of the same name between the Zambezi and Limpopo Rivers. From the twelfth century to the middle of the fifteenth, Zimbabwe was the most powerful and most prosperous state in the region and played a major role in the gold trade with the Swahili trading communities on the eastern coast.

The ruins of Zimbabwe's capital, known as Great Zimbabwe (*Zimbabwe* means "stone house" in the Bantu language), provide a vivid illustration of the kingdom's power and influence. Strategically situated between substantial gold reserves to the west and a small river leading to the coast, Great Zimbabwe was well placed to benefit from the expansion of trade between the coast and the interior. The town sits on a hill overlooking the river and is surrounded by stone walls, which enclosed an area large enough to hold over ten thousand residents. Like the Inka in South America, the local people stacked stone blocks without mortar to build their walls. The houses of the wealthy were built of cement on stone foundations, while those of the common people were of dried mud with thatched roofs. In the valley below is the royal palace, surrounded by a stone wall 30 feet high. Artifacts found at the site include household implements and ornaments made of gold and copper, as well as jewelry and porcelain imported from China.

Most of the royal wealth probably came from two sources: the ownership of cattle and the king's ability to levy heavy taxes on the gold that passed through the kingdom en route to the coast. By the middle of the fifteenth century, however, the city was apparently abandoned, possibly because of environmental damage caused by overgrazing. With the decline of Zimbabwe, the focus of economic power began to shift northward to the valley of the Zambezi River.

Southern Africa   South of the East African plateau and the Congo basin is a vast land of hills, grasslands, and arid desert stretching almost to the Cape of Good Hope at the tip of the continent. As Bantu-speaking farmers spread southward during the final centuries of the first millennium B.C.E., they began to encounter Neolithic peoples in the area who still lived primarily by hunting and foraging.

Available evidence suggests that early relations between these two peoples were relatively harmonious. Intermarriage between members of the two groups was apparently not unusual, and many of the hunter-gatherers were gradually absorbed into what became a dominantly Bantu-speaking pastoral and agricultural society that spread throughout much of southern Africa during the first millennium C.E.

The Khoi and the San   Two such peoples were the Khoi (KOI) and the San (SAHN). The two were related because of their language, known as Khoisan (KOI-sahn), distinguished by the use of "clicking" sounds. The Khoi were herders, while the San were hunter-gatherers who lived in small family communities of twenty to twenty-five members throughout southern Africa from Namibia in the west to the Drakensberg Mountains near the southeastern coast. Archaeologists have studied rock paintings found in caves throughout the area in their efforts to learn more about the early life of the San. These multicolored paintings, which predate the coming of the Europeans, were drawn with a brush made of small feathers fastened to a reed. They depict various aspects of the San's lifestyle, including their hunting techniques and religious rituals.

Africa: A Continent Without History?   Until the second half of the twentieth century, the prevailing view among Western historians was that Africa was a continent without history, a land of scattered villages isolated from the main currents of world affairs. But in the decades after the end of World War II, a new generation of historians trained in African studies, spurred on in part by the appearance in 1959 of Basil Davidson's path-breaking work, *Lost Cities of Africa*, began to contest that view.

Their studies have demonstrated that throughout history not only were many African societies actively in contact with peoples beyond their shores, but also that they created a number of advanced civilizations of their own.

Although the paucity of written sources continues to be a challenge for historians, other sources have been used with increasing success to throw light on the African historical experience. African peoples were at the forefront of the agricultural revolution in the ninth and eighth millennia B.C.E., and although some parts of the continent remained isolated from the main currents of world history, a number of other African societies began as early as the first millennium C.E. to play an active role in the expanding global trade network, which stretched from the Mediterranean Sea deep into the Sahara. Another major commercial trade route ran from the Arabian peninsula down the coast of East Africa along the shores of the Indian Ocean. Thus, it is becoming increasingly clear that from the dawn of history the peoples of Africa have made a significant contribution to the human experience.

AFRICAN SOCIETY

As noted earlier, generalizing about social organization, cultural development, and daily life in traditional Africa is difficult because of the extreme diversity of the continent and its inhabitants. One-quarter of all the languages in the world are spoken in Africa, and five of the major language families are located there. Ethnic divisions are equally pronounced. Because many of these languages did not have a system of writing until fairly recently, historians must rely on accounts by occasional visitors, such as al-Mas'udi and Ibn Battuta. Such travelers, however, tended to come into contact mostly with the wealthy and the powerful, leaving us to speculate about what life was like for ordinary Africans during this early period.

Urban Life   African towns often began as fortified walled villages and gradually evolved into larger communities serving several purposes. Here, of course, were the center of government and the teeming markets filled with goods from distant regions. Here also were artisans skilled in metalworking or woodworking, pottery making, and other crafts. Unlike the rural areas, where a village was usually composed of a single lineage group or clan, the towns drew their residents from several clans, although individual clans usually lived in their own compounds and were governed by their own clan heads.

In the states of West Africa, the focal point of the major towns was the royal precinct. The relationship between the ruler and the merchant class differed from the situation in most Asian societies, where the royal family and the aristocracy were largely isolated from the remainder of the population. In Africa, the chasm between the king and the common people was not so great. Often the ruler would hold an audience to allow people to voice their complaints or to welcome visitors from foreign countries. In the city-states of the East African coast, the rulers were often wealthy merchants who, as in the case of the town of Kilwa, "did not possess more country than the city itself."[7]

This is not to say that the king was not elevated above all others in status. In wealthier states, the walls of the audience chamber would be covered with sheets of beaten silver and gold, and the king would be surrounded by hundreds of armed soldiers and some of his trusted advisers. Nevertheless, the symbiotic relationship between the ruler and merchant class served to reduce the gap between the king and his subjects. The relationship was mutually beneficial, since the merchants received honors and favors from the palace while the king's coffers were filled with taxes paid by the merchants. Certainly, it was to the king's benefit to maintain law and order in his domain so that the merchants could ply their trade. As Ibn Battuta observed, among the good qualities of the peoples of West Africa was the prevalence of peace in the region. "The traveler is not afraid in it," he remarked, "nor is he who lives there in fear of the thief or of the robber by violence."[8]

Village Life   The vast majority of Africans lived in small rural villages. Their identities were established by their membership in a nuclear family and a lineage group. At the basic level was the nuclear family of parents and preadult children; sometimes it included an elderly grandparent and other family dependents as well. They lived in small, round huts constructed of packed mud and topped with a conical thatch roof. In most African societies, these nuclear family units were combined into larger kinship communities known as households or lineage groups.

The lineage group was similar in many respects to the clan in China or the *jati* in India in that it was normally based on kinship ties, although sometimes outsiders such as friends or other dependents may have been admitted to membership. Throughout the precolonial era, lineages served, in the words of one historian, as the "basic building blocks" of African society. The authority of the leading members of the lineage group was substantial. As in China, the elders had considerable power over the economic functions of the other people in the group, which provided mutual support for all members.

A village would usually be composed of a single lineage group, although some communities may have consisted of several unrelated families. At the head of the village was the familiar "big man," who was often assisted by a council of representatives of the various households in the community. Often the "big man" was believed to possess supernatural powers, and as the village grew in size and power, he might eventually be transformed into a local chieftain or monarch.

The Role of Women   Although generalizations are risky, we can say that women were usually subordinate to men in Africa, as in most early societies. In some cases, they were valued for the work they could do or for their role in increasing the size of the lineage group. Polygyny was not uncommon, particularly in Muslim societies. Women often worked in the fields while the men of the village tended the cattle or went on hunting expeditions. In some communities, the women specialized in commercial activities. In one area in southern Africa, young girls were sent into the mines to extract gold because of their smaller physiques.

But there were some key differences between the role of women in Africa and elsewhere. In many African societies, lineage was **matrilinear** rather than **patrilinear**. As Ibn Battuta observed during his travels in West Africa, "A man does not pass on inheritance except to the sons of his sister to the exclusion of his own sons."[9] He said he had never encountered this custom before except among the unbelievers of the Malabar coast in India. Women were often permitted to inherit property, and the husband was often expected to move into his wife's house.

The Slave Trade in Ancient Africa

FAMILY & SOCIETY

The practice of slavery was common throughout the African continent from ancient times, but information on the nature of the slave trade is relatively difficult to find. The following document is a contract for the purchase of a Nubian slave girl in sixth-century C.E. Egypt. Behind the legal terminology contained in the contract, probably a consequence of the adoption of Roman law in pre-Muslim Egypt, lies the poignant reality of a young Nubian girl, and perhaps her future children as well, sold into a lifetime of slavery. Tragically, the traffic in slaves continues in the region today as Muslim traders launch periodic raids on Christian villages in the southern Sudan.

Sale of a Nubian Slave Girl

Greeting. We acknowledge that we the aforementioned Pathermuthis and Anatolios, through this our written contract of sale, of our own free will and with voluntary intent and irrevocable and sincere resolution, with steadfast conscience, with correct intention, without any fraud or intimidation or violence or deceit or constraint of any bad faith or deception, that we have sold to you, the aforementioned most well-born Isidora, ... the girl who belongs to us and who has come to us ... from the other slave-traders of the Aithiopians, the black slave, Atalous by name, now renamed by you Eutukhia, about twelve years old more or less, an Aloan by race, which afore-mentioned black slave not being previously mortgaged

for any principal sum whatsoever or for any business or agreement or afflicted by any old injury or leprosy or beating or concealed ailment, ... for the mutually agreed, approved, resolved between us, full and just price [of] ... four gold solidi, of full weight, on the Alexandrian standard, which afore-mentioned price at once we, the vendors, Pathermuthis and Anatolios, have been paid by you ... for you to possess and to control and to own with every right of ownership, to acquire, to possess, to use her and, with God willing, her children, to manage and to administer concerning her, to sell, to put up as security, to give away, to exchange as dowry and to give ... and to give to your children and descendants, to leave behind and to transmit to your testamentary heirs, successors, and legal heirs, and in general to do and perform with her all such acts as the laws enjoin upon absolute owners to do with their own property unhindered and unimpeded, from now for ever, this perpetual warranty and clearance of title and defense of the present sale in regard to every warranty falling on us, the vendors.

Q *Based on what you have learned in this and previous chapters, to what sorts of duties would a young slave like Isidora be assigned? Did she have the option at some future date to obtain her freedom?*

Source: Reprinted from Richard Holton Pierce, "A Sale of an Alodian Slave Girl: a Reexamination of Papyrus Strassburg Inv. 1404," *Symbolae Osloenses* 70 (1995): 159–164, by permission of the publisher (Taylor & Francis Ltd, http://www.tandf.co.uk/journals).

Relations between the sexes were also sometimes more relaxed than in China or India, with none of the taboos characteristic of those societies. Again, in the words of Ibn Battuta, himself a Muslim:

With regard to their women, they are not modest in the presence of men, they do not veil themselves in spite of their perseverance in the prayers.... The women there have friends and companions amongst men outside the prohibited degrees of marriage [that is, other than brothers, fathers, or other closely related males]. Likewise for the men, there are companions from amongst women outside the prohibited degrees. One of them would enter his house to find his wife with her companion and would not disapprove of that conduct.[10]

When Ibn Battuta asked an African acquaintance about these customs, the latter responded, "Women's companionship with men in our country is honorable and takes place in a good way: there is no suspicion about it. They are not like the women in your country." Ibn Battuta noted his astonishment at such a "thoughtless" answer and did not accept further invitations to visit his friend's house.[11]

Such informal attitudes toward the relationship between the sexes were not found everywhere in Africa and were probably curtailed as many Africans converted to Islam. But it is a testimony to the tenacity of traditional customs that the relatively puritanical views about the role of women in society brought by Muslims from the Middle East made little impression even among Muslim families in West Africa.

Slavery

African slavery is often associated with the period after 1500. Indeed, the slave trade did reach enormous proportions in the seventeenth and eighteenth centuries, when European slave ships transported millions of unfortunate victims abroad to Europe or the Americas.

Slavery did not originate with the coming of the Europeans, however. It had been practiced in Africa since ancient times and probably originated when prisoners of war were forced into perpetual servitude. Slavery was common in ancient Egypt and became especially prevalent during the New Kingdom, when slaving expeditions brought back thousands of captives from the upper Nile to be used in labor gangs, for tribute, and even as human sacrifices.

Slavery persisted during the early period of state building, well past the tenth century C.E. Berber tribes may have regularly raided agricultural communities south of the Sahara for captives who were transported northward and eventually sold throughout the Mediterranean. Some were enrolled as soldiers, while others, often women, were put to work as domestic servants in the homes of the well-to-do. The use of captives for forced labor or exchange was apparently also common in African societies farther to the south and along the eastern coast.

Life was difficult for the average slave. The least fortunate were probably those who worked on plantations owned by the royal family or other wealthy land-owners. Those pressed into service as soldiers were sometimes more fortunate, since in Muslim societies in the Middle East, they might at some point win their freedom. Many slaves were employed in the royal household or as domestic servants in private homes. In general, these slaves probably had the most tolerable existence. Although they ordinarily were not permitted to purchase their freedom, their living conditions were often decent and sometimes practically indistinguishable from those of the free individuals in the household. In some societies in North Africa, slaves reportedly made up as much as 75 percent of the entire population. Elsewhere, the percentage was much lower, in some cases less than 10 percent.

AFRICAN CULTURE

In early Africa, as in much of the rest of the world at the time, creative expression, whether in the form of painting, literature, or music, was above all a means of serving religion and the social order. Though to the uninitiated a wooden mask or the bronze and iron statuary of southern Nigeria is simply a work of art, to the artist it was often a means of expressing religious convictions and communal concerns. Indeed, some African historians reject the use of the term *art* to describe such artifacts because they were produced for spiritual or moral rather than aesthetic purposes.

Painting and Sculpture   The oldest extant art forms in Africa are rock paintings. The most famous examples are in the Tassili Mountains in the central Sahara, where the earliest paintings may date back as far as 5000 B.C.E., though the majority are a millennium or so younger. Some of the later paintings depict the two-horse chariots used to transport goods prior to the introduction of the camel. Rock paintings are also found elsewhere in the continent, including the Nile Valley and eastern and southern Africa. Those of the San peoples of southern Africa are especially interesting for their illustrations of ritual ceremonies in which village shamans induce rain, propitiate the spirits, or cure illnesses.

More familiar, perhaps, are African wood carvings and sculpture. The remarkable statues, masks, and headdresses were carved from living trees, after the artist had made a sacrifice to the tree's spirit. These masks and headdresses were worn by costumed singers and dancers in performances to the various spirits, revealing the identification and intimacy of the African with the natural world. In Mali, for example, the 3-foot-tall Ci Wara (chee WAH-rah) headdresses, one female, the other male, expressed meaning in performances that celebrated the mythical hero who had introduced agriculture.

In the thirteenth and fourteenth centuries C.E., metal workers at Ife (EE-fay) in what is now southern Nigeria produced handsome bronze and iron statues using the lost-wax method, in which melted wax in a mold is replaced by molten metal. The Ife sculptures may in turn have influenced artists in Benin (bay-NEEN), in West Africa, who produced equally impressive works in bronze during the same period. The Benin sculptures include bronze heads, relief plaques depicting life at court, ornaments, and figures of various animals.

Westerners once regarded African wood carvings and metal sculpture as a form of "primitive art," but the label is not appropriate. The metal sculpture of Benin, for example, is highly sophisticated, and some of the best works are considered masterpieces. Such works were often created by artists in the employ of the royal court.

Music   Like sculpture and wood carving, African music and dance often served a religious function. With their characteristic heavy rhythmic beat, dances were a means of communicating with the spirits, and the frenzied movements that are often identified with African dance were intended to represent the spirits acting through humans.

African music during the traditional period varied from one society to another. A wide variety of instruments were used, including drums and other percussion instruments, xylophones, bells, horns and flutes, and stringed instruments like the fiddle, harp, and zither. Still, the music throughout the continent had sufficient common characteristics to justify a few generalizations. In the first place, a strong rhythmic pattern was an important feature of most African music, although the desired effect was achieved through a wide variety of means, including gourds, pots, bells, sticks beaten together, and hand clapping as well as drums.

Another important feature of African music was the integration of voice and instrument into a total musical experience. Musical instruments and the human voice were often woven together to tell a story, and instruments, such as the famous "talking drum," were often used to represent the voice. Choral music and individual voices were frequently used in a pattern of repetition and variation, sometimes known as "call and response." Through this technique, the audience participated in the music by uttering a single phrase over and over as a choral response to the changing call sung by the soloist. This tradition was carried by slaves to the Americas and survives to this day in the gospel music sung in many African American congregations. Sometimes instrumental music achieved a similar result.

Much music was produced in the context of social rituals, such as weddings and funerals, religious ceremonies, and official inaugurations. It could also serve an educational purpose by passing on to the young people information about the history and social traditions of the community. In the absence of written languages in sub-Saharan Africa (except for the Arabic script, used in Muslim societies in East and West Africa), music served as the primary means of transmitting folk legends and religious traditions from generation to generation. Oral tradition, which was usually undertaken by a priestly class or a specialized class of storytellers, served a similar function.

Architecture

No aspect of African artistic creativity is more varied than architecture. From the pyramids along the Nile to the ruins of Great Zimbabwe south of the Zambezi River, from the Moorish palaces at Zanzibar to the turreted mud mosques of West Africa, African architecture shows a striking diversity of approach and technique that is unmatched in other areas of creative endeavor.

The earliest surviving architectural form found in Africa is the pyramid. The kingdom of Meroë apparently adopted the pyramidal form from Egypt during the last centuries of the first millennium B.C.E. Although used for the same purpose as their earlier counterparts at Giza, the pyramids at Meroë were distinctive in style; they were much smaller and were topped with a flat platform rather than rising to a point. Remains of temples with massive carved pillars at Meroë also reflect Egyptian influence.

Farther to the south, the kingdom of Axum was developing its own architectural traditions. Most distinctive were the carved stone pillars, known as stelae (STEE-lee; singular STEE-luh) that were used to mark the tombs of dead kings. Some stood as high as 100 feet. The advent of Christianity eventually had an impact on Axumite architecture. During the Zagwe dynasty, churches carved out of solid rock were constructed throughout the country. The earliest may have been built in the eighth century C.E. Stylistically, they combined indigenous techniques inherited from the pre-Christian period with elements borrowed from Christian churches in the Holy Land.

In West Africa, buildings constructed in stone were apparently a rarity until the emergence of states during the first millennium C.E. At that time, the royal palace and other buildings of civic importance were often built of stone or cement, while the houses of the majority of the population continued to be constructed of dried mud. On his visit to the state of Guinea on the West African coast, the sixteenth-century traveler Leo Africanus noted that the houses of the ruler and other elites were built of chalk with roofs of straw. Even then, however, well into the state-building period, mosques were often built of mud.

Along the east coast, the architecture of the elite tended to reflect Middle Eastern styles. In the coastal towns and islands from Mogadishu to Kilwa, the houses of the wealthy were built of stone and reflected Arabic influence. As elsewhere, the common people lived in huts of mud, thatch, or palm leaves. Mosques were normally built of stone.

The most famous stone buildings in sub-Saharan Africa are those at Great Zimbabwe. Constructed without mortar, the outer wall and public buildings at Great Zimbabwe are an impressive monument to the architectural creativity of the peoples of the region.

Literature

Literature in the sense of written works did not exist in sub-Saharan Africa during the early traditional period, except in regions where Islam had brought the Arabic script from the Middle East. But African societies compensated for the absence of a written language with a rich tradition of oral lore. The **bard**, a professional storyteller, was an ancient African institution by which history was transmitted orally from generation to generation. In many West African societies, bards were highly esteemed and served as counselors to kings as well as protectors of local tradition. Bards were revered for their oratory and singing skills, phenomenal memory, and astute interpretation of history. As one African scholar wrote, the death of a bard was equivalent to the burning of a library.

Bards served several necessary functions in society. They were chroniclers of history, preservers of social customs and proper conduct, and entertainers who possessed a monopoly over the playing of several musical instruments, which accompanied their narratives. Because of their unique position above normal society, bards often played the role of mediator between hostile families or clans in a community. They were also credited with possessing occult powers and could read divinations and give blessings and curses. Traditionally, bards also served as advisers to the king, sometimes inciting him to action (such as going to battle) through the passion of their poetry. When captured by the enemy, bards were often treated with respect and released or compelled to serve the victor with their art.

One of the most famous West African poems is *The Epic of Son-Jara*. Passed down orally by bards for more than seven hundred years, it relates the heroic exploits of Son-Jara (sun-GAR-uh) (also known as Sunjata or Sundiata), the founder of Mali's empire and its ruler from 1230 to 1255. Although Mansa Musa is famous throughout the world because of his flamboyant pilgrimage to Mecca in the fourteenth century, Son-Jara is more celebrated in West Africa because of the dynamic and unbroken oral traditions of the West African peoples.

Like the bards, women were appreciated for their storytelling talents, as well as for their role as purveyors of the moral values and religious beliefs of African societies. In societies that lacked a written tradition, women represented the glue that held the community together. Through the recitation of fables, proverbs, poems, and songs, mothers conditioned the communal bonding and moral fiber of succeeding generations in a way that was rarely encountered in the patriarchal societies of

Europe, Asia, and the Middle East. Such activities were not only vital aspects of education in traditional Africa but also offered a welcome respite from the drudgery of everyday life and a spark to develop the imagination and artistic awareness of the young. Renowned for its many proverbs, Africa also offers the following: "A good story is like a garden carried in the pocket."

CHRONOLOGY

EARLY AFRICA

c. 9000–5000 B.C.E.	Origins of agriculture in Africa
c. 5000 B.C.E.	Desiccation of the Sahara begins
c. 1070 B.C.E.–350 B.C.E.	Kingdom of Kush in Nubia
c. Sixth century B.C.E.	Iron Age begins
c. First millennium B.C.E.	Beginning of trans-Saharan trade
c. 300 B.C.E.	Rise of Meroë
First century C.E.	Rise of Axum
Second century C.E.	Arrival of Malays on Madagascar
Early centuries C.E.	Arrival of Bantu in East Africa
Fourth century C.E.	Conquest of Meroë by Axum
Fifth century C.E.	Origins of Ghana
641 C.E.	Arab takeover of lower Nile Valley
c. First millennium C.E.	Development of Swahili culture
Seventh century C.E.	Spread of Islam across North Africa
Ninth century C.E.	Spread of Islam in Horn of Africa
Twelfth century C.E.	Decline of Ghana
c. 1100–c. 1450	Kingdom of Zimbabwe
c. 1150	Establishment of Zagwe dynasty in Ethiopia
c. 1250	Rise of Mali

MindTap is a fully online, highly personalized learning experience built upon Cengage Learning content. MindTap combines student learning tools—readings, multimedia, activities, and assessments—into a singular Learning Path that guides students through their course.

9

THE EXPANSION OF CIVILIZATION IN SOUTH AND SOUTHEAST ASIA

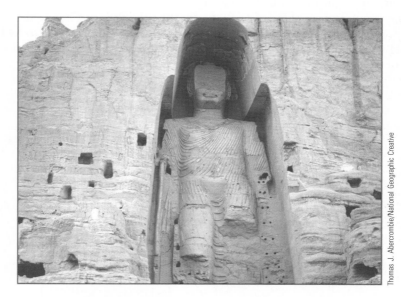

One of the two massive carved statues of the Buddha formerly at Bamiyan

Thomas J. Abercrombie/National Geographic Creative

CHAPTER OUTLINE

• The Silk Road • India After the Mauryas • The Arrival of Islam • Society and Culture • The Golden Region: Early Southeast Asia

THE SILK ROAD

The Kushan kingdom, with its power base beyond the Khyber Pass in modern Afghanistan, became the dominant political force in northern India in the centuries immediately after the fall of the Mauryas. Prior to being evicted from their original habitat by the Xiongnu, they had engaged in the silk trade with China from their base near Khotan (koh-TAHN), located on the southern route through the Taklimakan (tah-kluh-muh-KAHN) Desert. Now, with their position astride the main trade routes across the northern half of the Indian subcontinent, the Kushans thrived on the commerce that passed through the area. The bulk of that trade was between the Roman Empire and China and was transported along the route now known as the Silk Road, one segment of which passed through the mountains northwest of India. From there, goods were shipped to Rome through the Persian Gulf or the Red Sea. The importance of the trade with the Mediterranean region is attested to by the fact that gold and silver coins minted by the Kushan state were often imprinted with the figures of Iranian and Greek deities.

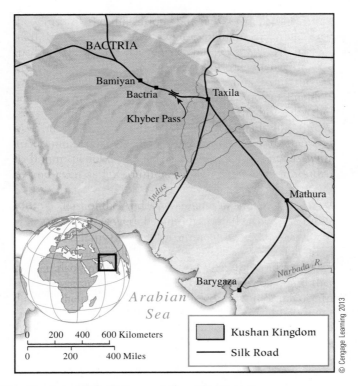

MAP 9.1   The Kushan Kingdom and the Silk Road

After the collapse of the Mauryan Empire, a new state formed by recent migrants from the north arose north of the Indus River valley. For the next four centuries, the Kushan kingdom played a major role in regional trade via the Silk Road until it declined in the third century C.E.

Trade between India and Europe had begun even before the rise of the Roman Empire, but it expanded rapidly in the first century C.E., when sailors mastered the pattern of the monsoon winds in the Indian Ocean (from the southwest in the summer and the northeast in the winter). Commerce between the Mediterranean and the Indian Ocean, as described in the *Periplus*, a first-century C.E. account by a Greek merchant, was extensive and often profitable, and it resulted in the establishment of several small trading settlements along the Indian coast. Rome imported ivory, indigo, textiles, precious stones, and pepper from India and silk from China. The Romans sometimes paid cash for these goods but also exported silver, wine, perfume, slaves, and glass and cloth from Egypt. Overall, Rome appears to have imported much more than it sold to the Far East.

The Silk Road was a conduit not only of material goods but also of technology and of ideas. The first Indian monks to visit China may have traveled over the road during the second century C.E. By the time of Fa Xian, a Buddhist monk who traveled from his native China to India in the early fifth century C.E. and whose observations are a valuable resource of the daily lives of the Indian people, Buddhist monks from China were beginning to arrive in increasing numbers to visit holy sites in India. The visits not only enriched the study of Buddhism in the two countries but also led to a fruitful exchange of ideas and technological advances in astronomy, mathematics, and linguistics. According to one scholar, the importation of Buddhist writings from India encouraged the development of printing in China, while the Chinese obtained lessons in health care from monks returned from the Asian subcontinent.

Indeed, the emergence of the Kushan kingdom as a major commercial power was due not only to its role as an intermediary in the Rome-China trade but also to the rising popularity of Buddhism. During the second century C.E., Kanishka (kuh-NISH-kuh), the greatest of the Kushan monarchs, began to patronize Buddhism. Under Kanishka and his successors, an intimate and mutually beneficial relationship was established between Buddhist monasteries and the local merchant community in thriving urban centers like Taxila (tak-SUH-luh) and Varanasi (vah-RAH-nah-see). Merchants were eager to build stupas and donate money to monasteries in return for social prestige and the implied promise of a better life in this world or the hereafter.

For their part, the wealthy monasteries ceased to be simple communities where monks could find a refuge from the material cares of the world; instead they became major consumers of luxury goods provided by their affluent patrons. Monasteries and their inhabitants became increasingly involved in the economic life of society, and Buddhist architecture began to be richly decorated with precious stones and glass purchased from local merchants or imported from abroad. The process was very similar to the changes that would later occur in the Christian church in medieval Europe.

It was from the Kushan kingdom that Buddhism began its long journey across the wastes of Central Asia to China and other societies in eastern Asia. As trade between the two regions increased, merchants and missionaries flowed from Bactria over the trade routes snaking through the mountains toward the northeast. At various stopping points on the trail, pilgrims erected statues and decorated mountain caves with magnificent frescoes depicting the life of the Buddha and his message to his followers. One of the most prominent of these centers was at Bamiyan, not far from modern-day Kabul, where believers carved two mammoth statues of the Buddha out of a sheer sandstone cliff. According to the Chinese pilgrim Fa Xian, when he visited the area in 400 C.E., more than a thousand monks were attending a religious ceremony at the site.

INDIA AFTER THE MAURYAS

The Kushan kingdom came to an end under uncertain conditions sometime in the third century C.E. In 320, a new state was established in the central Ganges Valley by a local raja named Chandragupta (chun-druh-GOOP-tuh) (no relation to Chandragupta Maurya, the founder of the Mauryan dynasty). Chandragupta located his capital at Pataliputra (pah-tah-lee-POO-truh), the site of the now decaying palace of the Mauryas. Under his successor, Samudragupta (suh-moo-druh-GOOP-tuh), the territory under Gupta (GOOP-tuh) rule was extended into surrounding areas, and eventually the new kingdom became the dominant political force throughout northern India. It also established a loose suzerainty over the Dravidian state of Pallava to the south, thus becoming the greatest state in the subcontinent since the decline of the Mauryan Empire. Under a succession of powerful, efficient, and highly cultured monarchs, notably Samudragupta (r. 335–375 C.E.) and Chandragupta II (r. 375–415 C.E.), India enjoyed a new "classical age" of civilization.

The Gupta Dynasty: A New Golden Age? Historians of India have traditionally viewed the Gupta era as a time of prosperity and thriving commerce with China, Southeast Asia, and the Mediterranean. Great cities, notable for their temples and Buddhist monasteries as well as for their economic prosperity, rose along the main trade routes throughout the subcontinent. The religious trade also prospered as pilgrims from across India and as far away as China came to visit the major religious centers.

As in the Mauryan Empire, much of the trade in the Gupta Empire was managed or regulated by the government. The Guptas owned mines and vast crown lands and earned massive profits from their commercial dealings. But there was also a large private sector, dominated by *jati* (caste) guilds that monopolized key sectors of the economy. A money economy had probably been in operation since the second century B.C.E., when copper and gold coins had been introduced from the Middle East. This in turn led to the development of banking. Nevertheless, there are indications that the circulation of coins was limited and that cowrie shells continued to be used for local trade. The Chinese missionary Xuan Zang (SHOO-wen ZAHNG), who visited India in the first half of the seventh century, remarked that most commercial transactions were conducted by barter.[1]

But the good fortunes of the Guptas proved to be relatively short-lived. Beginning in the late fifth century C.E., incursions by nomadic warriors from the northwest gradually reduced the power of the empire. Soon northern India was once more divided into myriad small kingdoms engaged in seemingly constant conflict. In the south, however, emerging states like Chola and Pallava prospered from their advantageous position athwart the regional trade network stretching from the Red Sea eastward into Southeast Asia.

MAP 9.2 The Gupta Empire

This map shows the extent of the Gupta Empire, the only major state to arise in the Indian subcontinent during the first millennium C.E. The arrow indicates the military campaign into southern India led by King Samudragupta.

The Transformation of Buddhism

The Chinese pilgrims who traveled to India during the Gupta era encountered a Buddhism that had changed in a number of ways in the centuries since the time of Siddhartha Gautama. They also found a doctrine that was beginning to decline in popularity in the face of the rise of Hinduism, as the Brahmanical religious beliefs of the Aryan people would eventually be called.

The transformation in Buddhism had come about in part because the earliest written sources were transcribed two centuries after Siddhartha's death and in part because his message was reinterpreted as it became part of the everyday life of the people. Abstract concepts of a Nirvana that cannot be described began to be replaced, at least in the popular mind, with more concrete visions of heavenly salvation, and Siddhartha was increasingly regarded as a divinity rather than as a sage.

As a sign of that transformation, the face of the Buddha began to be displayed in sacred sculptures, along with clear suggestions that, like Jesus, he was of divine birth. The Buddha's teachings that all four classes were equal gave way to the familiar Brahmanical conviction that some people, by reason of previous reincarnations, were closer to Nirvana than others.

Theravada   These developments led to a split in the movement. Purists emphasized what they insisted were the original teachings of the Buddha, describing themselves as the school of **Theravada** (thay-ruh-VAH-duh), or "the teachings of the elders." Followers of Theravada, many of them located in southern India and on the island of Sri Lanka, considered Buddhism a way of life, not a salvationist creed. Theravada stressed the importance of strict adherence to personal behavior and the quest for understanding as a means of release from the wheel of life.

Mahayana   In the meantime, another interpretation of Buddhist doctrine was emerging in the northwest. Here Buddhist believers, perhaps hoping to compete with other salvationist faiths circulating in the region, began to promote the view that Nirvana could be achieved through devotion and not just through painstaking attention to one's behavior. According to advocates of this school, eventually to be known as **Mahayana** (mah-huh-YAH-nuh) ("greater vehicle"), Theravada teachings were too demanding or too strict for ordinary people to follow and therefore favored the wealthy, who were more apt to have the time and resources to spend weeks or months away from their everyday occupations. Mahayana Buddhists referred to their rivals as **Hinayana** (hee-nuh-YAH-nuh), or "lesser vehicle," because in Theravada fewer would reach enlightenment. Mahayana thus attempted to provide hope for the masses in their efforts to reach Nirvana, but to the followers of Theravada, it did so at the expense of an insistence on proper behavior.

To advocates of the Mahayana school, salvation could also come from the intercession of a **bodhisattva** (boh-duh-SUT-vuh) ("he who possesses the essence of Buddhahood"). According to Mahayana beliefs, some individuals who had achieved *bodhi* and were thus eligible to enter the state of Nirvana after death chose instead, because of their great compassion, to remain on earth in spirit form to help all human beings achieve release from the life cycle. Followers of Theravada, who believed the concept of bodhisattva applied only to Siddhartha Gautama himself, denounced such ideas as "the teaching of demons." But to their proponents, such ideas extended the hope of salvation to the masses. Mahayana Buddhists revered the saintly individuals who, according to tradition, had become bodhisattvas at death and erected temples in their honor where the local population could pray and render offerings. The most famous bodhisattva was Avalokitesvara (uh-VAH-loh-kee-TESH-vuh-rah), a mythic figure whose name in Sanskrit means "Lord of Compassion." Perhaps because of the identification of Avalokitesvara with the concept of mercy, in China he was gradually transformed into a female figure known as Guan Yin (gwahn YIN).

A final distinguishing characteristic of Mahayana Buddhism was its reinterpretation of Buddhism as a religion rather than as a philosophy. Although Mahayana had philosophical aspects, its adherents increasingly regarded the Buddha as a divine figure, and an elaborate Buddhist cosmology developed. Nirvana was not a form of extinction but a true heaven with many rest stations along the way for the faithful.

Under Kushan rule, Mahayana achieved considerable popularity in northern India and for a while even made inroads in such Theravada strongholds as the island of Sri Lanka (sree LAHN-kuh). But in the end, neither Mahayana nor Theravada was able to retain its popularity in Indian society. By the seventh century C.E., Theravada had declined rapidly on the subcontinent, although it retained its foothold in Sri Lanka and across the Bay of Bengal in Southeast Asia, where it remained an influential force to modern times. Mahayana prospered in the northwest for centuries, but eventually it was supplanted by a revived Hinduism and later by a new arrival, Islam. But Mahayana too would find better fortunes abroad, as it was carried over the Silk Road or by sea to China and then to Korea and Japan. In all three countries, Buddhism has coexisted with Confucian doctrine and indigenous beliefs to the present.

The Decline of Buddhism in India   Why was Buddhism unable to retain its popularity in its native India, although it became a major force elsewhere in Asia? Some have speculated that in denying the existence of the soul, Buddhism ran counter to traditional Indian belief. Perhaps, too, one of Buddhism's strengths was also a weakness. In rejecting the class divisions that defined the Indian way of life, Buddhism appealed to those very groups who lacked an accepted place in Indian society, such as the untouchables. But at the same time, it represented a threat to those with a higher status. Moreover, by emphasizing the responsibility of each person to seek an individual path to Nirvana, Buddhism undermined the strong social bonds of the Indian class system.

Perhaps a final factor in the decline of Buddhism was the transformation of Brahmanism into a revised faith known as **Hinduism**. In its early development, Brahmanism had been highly elitist. Not only was observance of court ritual a monopoly of the *brahmin* class, but the major route to individual salvation, asceticism, was hardly realistic for the average Indian. In the centuries after the fall of the Mauryas, however, a growing emphasis on devotion—***bhakti*** (BAHK-tee)—as a religious observance brought the possibility of improving one's *karma* by means of ritual acts within the reach of Indians of all classes. Perhaps Hindu devotionalism rose precisely to combat the inroads of Buddhism and reduce the latter's appeal among the Indian population. The Chinese Buddhist missionary Fa Xian reported that mutual hostility between the Buddhists and the *brahmins* in the Gupta era was quite strong:

> Leaving the southern gate of the capital city, on the east side of the road is a place where Buddha once dwelt. Whilst here he bit [a piece from] the willow stick and fixed it in the earth; immediately it grew up seven feet high, neither more nor less. The unbelievers and Brahmans, filled with jealousy, cut it down and scattered the leaves far and wide, but yet it always sprang up again in the same place as before.[2]

For a while, Buddhism was probably able to stave off the Hindu challenge by its own salvationist creed of Mahayana, which also emphasized the role of devotion, but the days of Buddhism as a dominant faith in the subcontinent were numbered. By the eighth century C.E., Hindu missionaries spread throughout southern

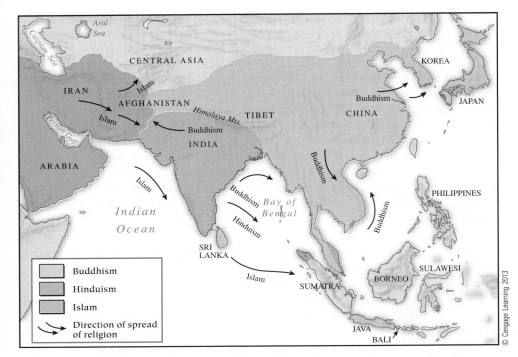

MAP 9.3   The Spread of Religions in Southern and Eastern Asia, 600–1900 C.E.

Between 600 and 1900, three of the world's great religions—Buddhism, Hinduism, and Islam—continued to spread from their original sources to various parts of southern and eastern Asia.

India, where their presence was spearheaded by new temples dedicated to Shiva at Kanchipuram (Kanchi), the site of a famous Buddhist monastery, and at Mamallapuram (muh-MAH-luh-poor-um).

When Did the Indians Become Hindus?

When did Brahmanism—the faith originally brought to India by the Aryan peoples in the second millennium B.C.E.—evolve into Hinduism, the religion practiced by the majority of the Indian people today? That question has aroused considerable interest among historians of India in recent years. Of course, the question does not have a single precise answer because the issue is partly a matter of definition and the transition was undoubtedly a gradual process.

Some observers point to the advent of Muslim rule in the northern parts of the subcontinent in the late first millennium C.E., when the indigenous people, labeled "Hindus" by the new arrivals, began to develop a greater sense of their distinct ethnic and cultural identity. Others point to the colonial era, when British colonial policies reinforced an Indian sense of being "the Other" and provoked them to come to the defense of their cultural and historical heritage.

Still other historians put the transition in the early centuries of the first millennium C.E., when the Brahmanical emphasis on court sacrifice and asceticism was gradually replaced by a more populist tradition focused on personal worship, known as **puja** (POO-juh), and the achievement of individual goals. In that interpretation, the change from Brahmanism to a faith more accessible to the mass of the population may initially have been stimulated by the egalitarian tendencies of early Buddhism. In any event, by the end of the first millennium c.e., the religious faith originally known as Brahmanism had fought off the challenges of alternative belief systems while transforming itself into the religion of the majority of the Indian people.

THE ARRIVAL OF ISLAM

While India was still undergoing a transition after the collapse of the Gupta Empire, a new and dynamic force in the form of Islam was arising in the Arabian peninsula to the west. As we have seen, during the seventh and eighth centuries, Arab armies carried the new faith westward to the Iberian Peninsula and eastward across the arid wastelands of Persia and into the rugged mountains of the Hindu Kush. Islam first reached India through the Arabs in the eighth century, but a second onslaught in the tenth and eleventh centuries by Turkic-speaking converts had a more lasting effect.

Although Arab merchants had been active along the Indian coasts for centuries, Arab armies did not reach India until the early eighth century. When Indian pirates attacked Arab shipping near the delta of the Indus River, the Muslim ruler in Mesopotamia demanded an apology from the ruler of Sind (SINNED), a Hindu state in the Indus Valley. When the latter refused, Muslim forces conquered lower Sind in 711 and then moved northward into the Punjab (pun-JAHB), bringing Arab rule into the frontier regions of the subcontinent for the first time.

The Empire of Mahmud of Ghazni   For the next three centuries, Islam made no further advances into India. But a second phase began at the end of the tenth century with the rise of the state of Ghazni (GAHZ-nee), located in the area of the old Kushan kingdom in present-day Afghanistan. The new kingdom was founded in 962 when Turkic-speaking slaves seized power from the Samanids, a Persian dynasty. When the founder of the new state died in 997, his son, Mahmud (MAHKH-mood) of Ghazni (r. 997–1030), succeeded him. Brilliant and ambitious, Mahmud used his patrimony as a base of operations for sporadic forays against neighboring Hindu kingdoms to the southeast. Before his death in 1030, he was able to extend his rule throughout the upper Indus Valley and as far south as the Indian Ocean. In wealth and cultural brilliance, his court at Ghazni rivaled that of the Abbasid Dynasty in Baghdad. But he was not universally admired. Describing Mahmud's conquests in northwestern India, the contemporary historian al-Biruni (al-buh-ROO-nee) wrote:

> Mahmud utterly ruined the prosperity of the country, and performed wonderful exploits by which the Hindus became like atoms scattered in all directions, and like a tale of old in the mouth of the people. Their scattered remains cherish, of course, the most inveterate aversion towards all Muslims. This is the reason, too, why Hindu sciences have retired far away from those parts of the country conquered by us, and have fled to places which our hand cannot yet reach, to Kashmir, Benares, and other places.[3]

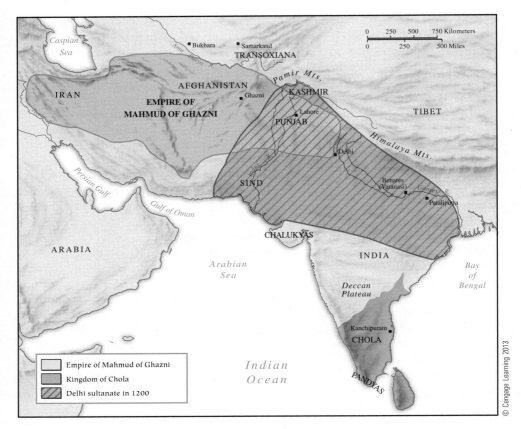

MAP 9.4   India, 1000–1200

Beginning in the tenth century, Turkic-speaking peoples invaded northwestern India and introduced Islam to the peoples in the area. Most famous was the empire of Mahmud of Ghazni.

Resistance against the advances of Mahmud and his successors into northern India was led by the Rajputs (RAHJ-pootz), aristocratic Hindu clans who were probably descended from tribal groups that had penetrated into northwestern India from Central Asia in earlier centuries. The Rajputs possessed a strong military tradition and fought bravely, but their military tactics, based on infantry supported by elephants, were no match for the fearsome cavalry of the invaders, whose ability to strike with lightning speed contrasted sharply with the slow-footed forces of their adversaries. Moreover, the incessant squabbling among the Rajput leaders put them at a disadvantage against the single-minded intensity and religious fervor of Mahmud's armies. Although the power of Ghazni declined after his death, a successor state in the area resumed the advance in the late twelfth century, and soon after 1200, Muslim power, in the form of a new Delhi (DEL-ee) sultanate, had been extended over the entire plain of northern India.

The Delhi
Sultanate

South of the Ganges River valley, Muslim influence spread more slowly and in fact had little immediate impact. Muslim armies launched occasional forays into the Deccan Plateau, but at first they had little success, even though the area was divided among a number of warring kingdoms, including the Cholas along the eastern coast and the Pandyas (PUHN-dee-ahz) far to the south.

One reason the Delhi sultanate failed to take advantage of the disarray of its rivals was the threat posed by the Mongols on the northwestern frontier. Mongol armies unleashed by the great tribal warrior Genghis Khan occupied Baghdad and destroyed the Abbasid caliphate in the 1250s, while other forces occupied the Punjab around Lahore (luh-HOR), from which they threatened Delhi on several occasions. For the next half-century, the attention of the sultanate was focused on the Mongols. That threat finally declined in the early fourteenth century with the gradual breakup of the Mongol Empire, and a new Islamic state emerged in the form of the Tughluq (tug-LUK) dynasty (1320–1413), which extended its power into the Deccan Plateau. In praise of his sovereign, the Tughluq monarch Ala-ud-din (uh-LAH-ud-DEEN), the poet Amir Khusrau (ah-MEER KOOS-roh) exclaimed:

> *Happy be Hindustan, with its splendor of religion,*
> *Where Islamic law enjoys perfect honor and dignity;*
> *In learning Delhi now rivals Bukhara;*
> *Islam has been made manifest by the rulers.*
> *From Ghazni to the very shore of the ocean*
> *You see Islam in its glory.*[4]

Such happiness was not destined to endure, however. During the latter half of the fourteenth century, the Tughluq dynasty gradually fell into decline. In 1398, a new military force crossed the Indus River from the northwest, raided the capital of Delhi, and then withdrew. According to some contemporary historians, as many as 100,000 Hindu prisoners were massacred before the gates of the city. Such was India's first encounter with Tamerlane (TAM-ur-layn).

Tamerlane

Tamerlane (b. 1330s), also known as Timur-i-lang (Timur the Lame), was the ruler of a Mongol khanate based in Samarkand (SAM-ur-kand) to the north of the Pamir (pah-MEER) Mountains. His kingdom had been founded on the ruins of the Mongol Empire, which had begun to disintegrate as a result of succession struggles in the thirteenth century. Tamerlane, the son of a local aristocrat and of mixed Turko-Mongolian heritage, seized power in Samarkand in 1369 and immediately launched a program of conquest. During the 1380s, he brought the entire region east of the Caspian Sea under his authority and then conquered Baghdad and occupied Mesopotamia. After his brief foray into northern India, he turned to the west and raided the Anatolian peninsula. Defeating the army of the Ottoman Turks, he advanced almost as far as the Bosporus before withdrawing. "The last of the great nomadic conquerors," as one modern historian described him, died in 1405 in a final military campaign.

The passing of Tamerlane removed a major menace from the diverse states of the Indian subcontinent. But the respite from external challenge was not long.

By the end of the fifteenth century, two new challenges had appeared from beyond the horizon: the Mughals, a newly emerging nomadic power beyond the Khyber Pass in the north, and the Portuguese traders, who arrived by sea from the eastern coast of Africa in search of gold and spices. Both, in different ways, would exert a major impact on the later course of Indian civilization.

SOCIETY AND CULTURE

The establishment of Muslim rule over the northern parts of the subcontinent had a significant impact on the society and culture of the Indian people.

Religion   Like their counterparts in other areas that came under Islamic rule, some Muslim rulers in India were relatively tolerant of other faiths and used peaceful means, if any, to encourage nonbelievers to convert to Islam. Even the more enlightened, however, could be fierce when their religious zeal was aroused. One ruler, on being informed that a Hindu fair had been held near Delhi, ordered the promoters of the event put to death. Hindu

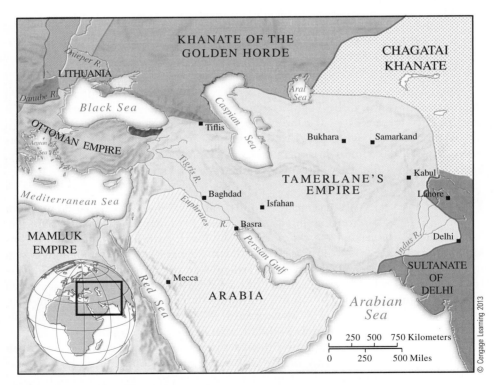

MAP 9.5   The Empire of Tamerlane

In the fourteenth century, Tamerlane, a feared conqueror of Mongolian extraction, established a brief empire in Central Asia with his capital at Samarkand.

temples were razed, and mosques were erected in their place. Eventually, however, most Muslim rulers realized that not all Hindus could be converted and recognized the necessity of accepting what to them was an alien and repugnant religion. While Hindu religious practices were generally tolerated, non-Muslims were compelled to pay a tax to the state. Some Hindus likely converted to Islam to avoid paying the tax, but they were then expected to make the traditional charitable contribution required of Muslims in all Islamic societies.

Over time, millions of Hindus did turn to the Muslim faith. Some were individuals or groups in the employ of the Muslim ruling class, such as government officials, artisans, or merchants catering to the needs of the court. But many others were probably peasants from the *sudra* class or even untouchables who found in the egalitarian message of Islam a way of removing the stigma of low-class status in the Hindu social hierarchy.

Seldom have two major religions been so strikingly different. Where Hinduism tolerated a belief in the existence of several deities (although admittedly they were all considered by some to be manifestations of one supreme god), Islam was uncompromisingly monotheistic. Where Hinduism was hierarchical, Islam was egalitarian. Where Hinduism featured a priestly class to serve as an intermediary with the ultimate force of the universe, Islam permitted no one to come between believers and their god. Such differences contributed to the mutual hostility that developed between the adherents of the two faiths in the Indian subcontinent, but more mundane issues, such as the Muslim habit of eating beef and the idolatry and sexual frankness of Hindu art, were probably a greater source of antagonism at the popular level.

In other cases, the two peoples borrowed from each other. Some Muslim rulers found the Indian idea of divine kingship appealing. In their turn, Hindu rajas

© William J. Duiker

Samarkand, Gem of the Empire. *The city of Samarkand has a long history. Originating during the first millennium* B.C.E. *as a caravan stop on the Silk Road, it was later occupied by Alexander the Great, the Abbasids, and the Mongols before becoming the capital of Tamerlane's expanding empire. Tamerlane expended great sums in creating a city worthy of his imperial ambitions. Shown here is the great square, known as the Registan. Site of a mosque, a library, and a Muslim university, all built in the exuberant Persian style, Samarkand was the jumping-off point for trade with China far to the east.*

The Islamic Conquest of India

INTERACTION & EXCHANGE

One consequence of the Muslim conquest of northern India was the imposition of many Islamic customs on Hindu society. In this excerpt, the fourteenth-century Muslim historian Zia-ud-din Barani **(ZEE-ah-ud-DIN buh-RAH-nee)** describes the attempt of one Muslim ruler, Ala-ud-din, to prevent the use of alcohol and gambling, two practices expressly forbidden in Muslim society. Ala-ud-din had seized power in Delhi from a rival in 1294.

A Muslim Ruler Suppresses Hindu Practices

He forbade wine, beer, and intoxicating drugs to be used or sold; dicing, too, was prohibited. Vintners and beer sellers were turned out of the city, and the heavy taxes which had been levied from them were abolished. All the china and glass vessels of the Sultan's banqueting room were broken and thrown outside the gate of Badaun, where they formed a mound. Jars and casks of wine were emptied out there till they made mire as if it were the season of the rains. The Sultan himself entirely gave up wine parties. Self-respecting people at once followed his example; but the ne'er-do-wells went on making wine and spirits and hid the leather bottles in loads of hay or firewood and by various such tricks smuggled it into the city. Inspectors and gate-keepers and spies diligently sought to seize the contraband and the smugglers; and when seized the wine was given to the elephants, and the importers and sellers and drinkers [were] flogged and given short terms of imprisonment. So many were they, however, that holes had to be dug for their incarceration outside the great thoroughfare of the Badaun gate, and many of the wine bibbers died from the rigor of their confinement and others were taken out half-dead and were long in recovering their health. The terror of these holes deterred many from drinking. Those who could not give it up had to journey ten or twelve leagues [30 to 36 miles] to get a drink, for at half that distance, four or five leagues from Delhi, wine could not be publicly sold or drunk. The prevention of drinking proving very difficult, the Sultan enacted that people might distill and drink privately in their own homes, if drinking parties were not held and the liquor not sold. After the prohibition of drinking, conspiracies diminished.

Q *How does the approach of the ruler described here, a Muslim establishing regulations for moral behavior in a predominantly Hindu society, compare with the approaches adopted by Muslim rulers in African societies?*

Source: Excerpt from *A History of India: From the Earliest Times to the Present Day* by Michael Edwardes (London: Thames & Hudson, 1961), p. 108.

learned by bitter experience the superiority of cavalry mounted on horses instead of elephants, the primary assault weapon in early India. Some upper-class Hindu males were attracted to the Muslim tradition of **purdah** (PUR-duh *or* POOR-duh) and began to keep their women in seclusion (termed locally "behind the curtain") from everyday society. Hindu sources claimed that one reason for adopting the custom was to protect Hindu women from the roving eyes of foreigners. But it is likely that many Indian families adopted the practice for reasons of prestige or because they were convinced that *purdah* was a practical means of protecting female virtue. Adult Indian women had already begun to cover their heads with a scarf during the Gupta era.

All in all, Muslim rule probably did not have a significant impact on the lives of most Indian women. *Purdah* was more commonly practiced among high castes than among the lower castes. Though it was probably of little consolation, relations between the genders were relatively egalitarian in poor and low-class families, as men and women worked together on press gangs or in the fields. Muslim customs apparently had little effect on the Hindu tradition of *sati* (widow burning). In fact, in many respects, Muslim women had more rights than their Hindu counterparts. They had more property rights than Hindu women and were legally permitted to divorce under certain conditions and to remarry after the death of their husband. The primary role for Indian women in general, however, was to produce children. Sons were preferred over daughters, not only because they alone could conduct ancestral rites but also because a daughter was a financial liability. A father had to provide a costly dowry for his daughter when she married, yet after the wedding, she would transfer her labor and assets to her husband's family. Still, women shared with men a position in the Indian religious pantheon. The cult of the mother-goddess, which had originated in the Harappan era, revived during the Gupta era stronger than ever. The Hindu female deity known as Devi (DAY-vee) was celebrated by both men and women as the source of cosmic power, bestower of wishes, and symbol of fertility.

Overall, the Muslims continued to view themselves as foreign conquerors and generally maintained a strict separation between the Muslim ruling class and the mass of the Hindu population. Although a few Hindus rose to important positions in the local bureaucracy, most high posts in the central government and the provinces were reserved for Muslims. Only with the founding of the Mughal Dynasty was a serious effort undertaken to reconcile the differences.

One result of this effort was the religion of the Sikhs (SEEKS *or* see-ikhz) ("disciples"). Founded by the guru Nanak (NAH-nuhk) in the early sixteenth century in the Punjab, Sikhism attempted to integrate the best of the two faiths in a single religion. Sikhism originated in the devotionalist movement in Hinduism, which taught that God was the single true reality. All else is illusion. But Nanak rejected the Hindu tradition of asceticism and mortification of the flesh and, like Muhammad, taught his disciples to participate in the world. Sikhism achieved considerable popularity in northwestern India, where Islam and Hinduism confronted each other directly, and eventually evolved into a militant faith that fiercely protected its adherents against its two larger rivals. In the end, Sikhism did not reconcile Hinduism and Islam but provided an alternative to them.

Class and Caste   One complication for both Muslims and Hindus as they tried to come to terms with the existence of a mixed society was the problem of class and caste. Could non-Hindus form castes, and if so, how were these castes related to the Hindu castes? Where did the Turkic-speaking elites who made up the ruling class in many of the Islamic states fit into the equation?

The problem was resolved in a pragmatic manner that probably followed an earlier tradition of assimilating non-Hindu tribal groups into the system.

COMPARATIVE ESSAY

Caste, Class, and Family

FAMILY & SOCIETY

Why have men and women played such different roles throughout human history? Why have some societies historically adopted the nuclear family, while others preferred the joint family or the clan? Such questions are controversial and often subject to vigorous debate, yet they are crucial to our understanding of the human experience.

As we know, the first human beings practiced hunting and foraging, living in small bands composed of one or more lineage groups and moving from place to place in search of sustenance. Individual members of the community were assigned different economic and social roles—usually with men as the hunters and women as the food gatherers—but such roles were not rigidly defined. The concept of private property did not exist, and all members shared the goods possessed by the community according to need.

The agricultural revolution brought about dramatic changes in human social organizations. Although women, as food gatherers, may have been the first farmers, men—now increasingly deprived of their traditional role as hunters—began to replace them in the fields. As communities gradually adopted a sedentary lifestyle, women were increasingly assigned to domestic tasks in the home while raising the children. As farming communities grew in size and prosperity, vocational specialization and the concept of private property appeared, leading to the family as a legal entity and the emergence of a class system composed of elites, commoners, and slaves. Women were deemed inferior to men and placed in a subordinate status.

This trend toward job specialization and a rigid class system was less developed in pastoral societies, some of which still practiced a nomadic style of life and shared communal goods on a roughly equal basis within the community. Even within sedentary societies, there was considerable variety in the nature of social organizations. In some areas, the nuclear family consisted of parents and their dependent children. Other societies, however, adopted (either in theory or in practice) the idea of the joint family (ideally consisting of three generations of a family living under one roof) and sometimes, even going a step further, linked several families under the larger grouping of the caste or the clan. Prominent examples of the latter tendency include India and China, although the degree to which reality conformed to such concepts is a matter of debate.

Such large social organizations, where they occurred, often established a rigid hierarchy of status within the community, including the subordination of women. At the same time, they sometimes played a useful role in society, providing a safety net or a ladder of upward mobility for disadvantaged members of the group, as well as a source of stability in societies where legitimate and effective authority at the central level was lacking.

Q *What were some of the unique aspects of community and family life in traditional India? What do you think accounts for these unique characteristics?*

Members of the Turkic ruling groups formed social groups that were roughly equivalent to the Hindu *brahmin* or *kshatriya* class. During the Delhi sultanate in the north, members of the local Rajput nobility who converted to Islam were occasionally permitted to join such class groupings. Ordinary Indians who converted to Islam also formed Muslim castes, although at a lower level on the social scale. Many who did so were probably artisans who converted en masse to obtain the privileges that conversion could bring.

In most of India, then, Muslim rule did not substantially disrupt the class and caste system, although it may have become more fluid than was formerly the case. One perceptive European visitor in the early sixteenth century reported that in Malabar (MAL-uh-bar), along the southwestern coast, there were separate castes for fishing, pottery making, weaving, carpentry and metalworking, salt mining, sorcery, and labor on the plantations. There were separate castes for doing the laundry, one for the elite and the other for the common people.

Economy and Daily Life   India's landed and commercial elites lived in the cities, often in conditions of considerable opulence. The rulers possessed the most wealth. One maharaja of a relatively small state in southern India, for example, had more than 100,000 soldiers in his pay along with 900 elephants and 20,000 horses. Another maintained a thousand high-caste women to serve as sweepers of his palace. Each carried a broom and a brass basin containing a mixture of cow dung and water and followed him from one house to another, plastering the path where he was to tread. Most urban dwellers, of course, did not live in such style. Xuan Zang, the Chinese Buddhist missionary, left us a description of ordinary homes in seventh-century urban areas:

> Their houses are surrounded by low walls.... The earth being soft and muddy, the walls of the towns are mostly built of brick or tiles. The towers on the walls are constructed of wood or bamboo; the houses have balconies and belvederes, which are made of wood, with a coating of lime or mortar, and covered with tiles. The different buildings have the same form as those in China; rushes, or dry branches, or tiles, or boards are used for covering them. The walls are covered with lime and mud, mixed with cow's dung for purity. At different seasons they scatter flowers about. Such are some of their different customs.[5]

Agriculture   The majority of India's population (estimated at slightly more than 100 million by the year 1000), however, lived on the land. Most were peasants who tilled small plots with a wooden plow pulled by oxen and paid a percentage of the harvest to their landlord. The landlord in turn forwarded part of the payment to the local ruler. In effect, the landlord functioned as a tax collector for the king, who retained ultimate ownership of all farmland in his domain. At best, most peasants lived at the subsistence level. At worst, they were forced into debt and fell victim to moneylenders who charged exorbitant rates of interest.

In the north and in the upland regions of the Deccan Plateau, the primary grain crops were wheat and barley. In the Ganges Valley and the southern coastal plains, the main crop was rice. Vegetables were grown everywhere, and southern India produced many spices and fruits, as well as sugarcane and cotton, both of which were gradually transported westward by the Arabs. Although sugarcane was first cultivated in Southeast Asia, the cotton plant apparently originated in the Indus River valley and spread from there. Although some cotton was cultivated in Spain and North Africa by the eighth and ninth centuries, India remained the primary producer of cotton goods. Spices such as cinnamon, pepper, ginger, sandalwood, cardamom, and cumin were also major export products.

Foreign Trade   Agriculture, of course, was not the only source of wealth in India. Since ancient times, the subcontinent had served as a major entrepôt for trade between the Middle East and the Pacific basin, as well as the source of other goods shipped throughout the known world. Although civil strife and piracy, heavy taxation of the business community by local rulers to finance their fratricidal wars, and increased customs duties between principalities may have contributed to a decline in internal trade, the level of foreign trade remained high, particularly in the Dravidian-speaking kingdoms in the south and along the northwestern coast, which were located along the traditional trade routes to the Middle East and the Mediterranean Sea. Much of this foreign trade was carried on by wealthy Hindu castes with close ties to the royal courts. But there were other participants as well, including such non-Hindu minorities as the Muslims, the Jews, the Parsis (PAR-seez), and the Jains. The Parsis, expatriates from Persia who practiced the Zoroastrian religion, dominated banking and the textile industry in the cities bordering the Rann of Kutch (RUN of KUTCH). Later they would become a major economic force in the modern city of Mumbai (Bombay). The Jains became prominent in trade and manufacturing even though their faith emphasized simplicity and the rejection of materialism.

According to early European travelers, merchants often lived quite well. One Portuguese observer described the "Moorish" population in Bengal as follows:

> They have girdles of cloth, and over them silk scarves; they carry in their girdles daggers garnished with silver and gold, according to the rank of the person who carries them; on their fingers many rings set with rich jewels, and cotton turbans on their heads. They are luxurious, eat well and spend freely, and have many other extravagances as well. They bathe often in great tanks which they have in their houses. Everyone has three or four wives or as many as he can maintain. They keep them carefully shut up, and treat them very well, giving them great store of gold, silver and apparel of fine silk.[6]

The Indian Economy: Promise Unfulfilled?   Outside these relatively small, specialized trading communities, most manufacturing and commerce were in the hands of petty traders and artisans, who were generally limited to local markets. This failure to build on the promise of antiquity has led some historians to ask why India failed to produce an expansion of commerce and growth of cities similar to the developments that began in Europe during the High Middle Ages or even in China during the Song Dynasty. Some have pointed to the traditionally low status of artisans and merchants in Indian society, symbolized by the comment in the *Arthasastra* that merchants were "thieves that are not called by the name of thief."[7] Yet commercial activities were frowned on in many areas in Europe throughout the Middle Ages, a fact that did not prevent the emergence of capitalist societies in much of the West.

Another factor may have been the monopoly on foreign trade held by the government in many areas of India. More important, perhaps, was the impact of the class and caste system, which reduced the ability of entrepreneurs to expand their activities and have dealings with other members of the commercial and manufacturing community. Successful artisans, for example, normally could not set up as merchants to market their products, nor could merchants compete for buyers outside their normal area of operations. The complex interlocking relationships among the various classes in a given region were a powerful factor inhibiting the development of a thriving commercial sector in medieval India.

Science and Technology   Still, Indian thinkers played an important role during this period in promoting knowledge of the sciences throughout the Eurasian world. One example is the fifth-century astronomer Aryabhata (AHR-yuh-BAH-tuh), who accurately calculated the value of pi and measured the length of the solar year at slightly more than 365 days. Indian writings on astronomy, mathematics, and medicine were influential elsewhere in the region, while, the Indian system of numbers, including the concept of zero, was introduced into the Middle East and ultimately replaced the Roman numerals then in use in medieval Europe.

The Wonder of Indian Culture   The era between the Mauryas and the Mughals in India was a period of cultural evolution as Indian writers and artists built on the literary and artistic achievements of their predecessors. This is not to say, however, that Indian culture rested on its ancient laurels. To the contrary, it was an era of tremendous innovation in all fields of creative endeavor.

Art and Architecture   At the end of antiquity, the primary forms of religious architecture were the Buddhist cave temples and monasteries. The next millennium witnessed the evolution of religious architecture from underground cavity to monumental structure.

The twenty-eight caves of Ajanta (uh-JUHN-tuh) in the Deccan Plateau are among India's greatest artistic achievements. They are as impressive for their sculptures and paintings as for their architecture. Except for a few examples from the second century B.C.E., most of the caves were carved out of solid rock over an incredibly short period of eighteen years, from 460 to 478 C.E. In contrast to the early unadorned temple halls, these caves were exuberantly decorated with ornate pillars, friezes, beamed ceilings, and statues of the Buddha and bodhisattvas. Several caves served as monasteries, which by then had been transformed from simple holes in the wall to large complexes with living apartments, halls, and shrines to the Buddha. Other temples, such as the one at Ellora (eh-LOR-uh), were carved directly out of the mountains.

All of the inner surfaces of the caves, including the ceilings, sculptures, walls, door frames, and pillars, were painted in vivid colors. Perhaps best known are the wall paintings, which illustrate the various lives and incarnations of the Buddha. These paintings are in an admirable state of preservation, making it possible to reconstruct the customs, dress, house interiors, and physical characteristics of the peoples of fifth-century India. Similar rock paintings focusing on secular subjects can be found at Sigiriya (see-gee-REE-uh), a fifth-century royal palace on the island of Sri Lanka. As a defensive measure, the palace was located on top of a gigantic volcanic rock.

Among the most impressive rock carvings in southern India are the cave temples at Mamallapuram (also known as Mahabalipuram), south of the modern city of Chennai (Madras). The sculpture, called *Descent of the Ganges River*, depicts the role played by Shiva in intercepting the heavenly waters of the Ganges and allowing them to fall gently on the earth. Mamallapuram also boasts an eighth-century shore temple, which is one of the earliest surviving freestanding structures in the subcontinent.

From the eighth century until the time of the Mughals, Indian architects built a multitude of magnificent Hindu temples, now constructed exclusively aboveground. Each temple consisted of a central shrine surmounted by a sizable tower, a hall for worshipers, a vestibule, and a porch, all set in a rectangular courtyard that might also contain other minor shrines. Temples became progressively more ornate until the eleventh century, when sculpture began to dominate the structure. The towers became higher and the temple complexes more intricate, some becoming virtual walled compounds set one within the other and resembling small towns.

Among the best examples of temple art are those in the eastern state of Orissa (uh-RIH-suh). The Sun Temple at Konarak (KUH-nar-ek), standing at the edge of the sea and covered with intricate carvings, is generally considered the masterpiece of its genre. Although now in ruins, the Sun Temple still boasts some of India's most memorable sculptures. Especially renowned are the twelve pairs of carved wheels, each 10 feet high, representing the twelve signs of the zodiac.

The greatest example of medieval Hindu temple art, however, is probably Khajuraho (khah-joo-RAH-hoh). Of the original eighty-five temples, dating from the tenth century, twenty-five remain standing today. All of the towers are buttressed at various levels on the sides, giving the whole a sense of unity and creating a vertical movement similar to Mount Kailasa (ky-LAH-suh) in the Himalayas, sacred to Hindus. Everywhere the viewer is entertained by voluptuous temple dancers bringing life to the massive structures. One is removing a thorn from her foot, another is applying eye makeup, and yet another is wringing out her hair.

In the Deccan Plateau, a different style prevailed. The southern temple style was marked by massive oblong stone towers, some 200 feet high. The towers were often covered with a profusion of sculpted figures and were visible for miles. The walls surrounding the temple complex were also surmounted with impressive gate towers, known as *gopuras* (GOH-pur-uhz). Craftsmen in the southern states also won plaudits for the high quality of their bronze statues, many of them portraying Indian deities such as Shiva and Vishnu and designed for use in Hindu religious rituals and ceremonies. Unlike the famous ritual bronzes of ancient China, Indian bronze work relied on the "lost-wax" method.

Literature   During this period, Indian authors produced a prodigious number of written works, both religious and secular. Indian religious poetry was written in Sanskrit and also in the languages of southern India. As Hinduism was transformed from a contemplative to a more devotional religion, its poetry became more ardent and erotic and prompted a sense of divine ecstasy. Much of the religious verse extolled the lives and heroic acts of Shiva, Vishnu, Rama, and Krishna by repeating the same themes over and over. In the eighth century, a tradition of poet-saints inspired by intense mystical devotion to a particular deity emerged in southern India. Many were women who sought to escape the drudgery of domestic toil

Dancing Shiva. *From the tenth to the twelfth centuries C.E., the southern kingdom of Chola excelled in the use of the lost-wax technique to make portable bronze statues of Hindu gods. Bathed, clothed, and decorated with flowers, these Chola bronzes were then paraded in religious ceremonies. One of the most numerous and iconic of these bronze deities was the dancing Shiva. As shown here, the statue portrays Shiva performing a cosmic dance in which he simultaneously creates and destroys the universe. While his upper right hand creates the cosmos, his upper left hand reduces it in flames. With his right foot, Shiva crushes the back of the dwarf of ignorance. Shiva's dancing statues visually convey to his followers the message of his power and compassion.*

© William J. Duiker

through an imagined sexual union with the god-lover. Such was the case for this twelfth-century mystic whose poem expresses her sensuous joy in the physical-mystical union with her god:

> *It was like a stream*
> *running into the dry bed*
> *of a lake,*
> *like rain pouring on plants*
> *parched to sticks.*
> *It was like this world's pleasure*
> *and the way to the other,*
> *both walking towards me.*
> *Seeing the feet of the master,*
> *O lord white as jasmine*
> *I was made worthwhile.*[8]

The great secular literature of traditional India was also written in Sanskrit in the form of poetry, drama, and prose. Some of the best medieval Indian poetry is found in single-stanza poems, which create an entire emotional scene in just a few lines. Witness this poem by the poet Amaru (am-uh-ROO):

> We'll see what comes of it, I thought,
>   and I hardened my heart against her.
> What, won't the villain speak to me? She
>   thought, flying into a rage.
> And there we stood, sedulously refusing to look one
>   another in the face,
> Until at last I managed an unconvincing laugh,
>   and her tears robbed me of my resolution.[9]

One of India's most famous authors was Kalidasa (kah-lee-DAH-suh), who lived during the Gupta dynasty. Although little is known of him, including his dates, he probably wrote for the court of Chandragupta II (r. 375–415). Even today, Kalidasa's hundred-verse creation *The Cloud Messenger* remains one of the most popular Sanskrit poems.

In addition to being a poet, Kalidasa was also a great dramatist. He wrote three plays, all dramatic romances that blend the erotic with the heroic and the comic. *Shakuntala*, perhaps the best-known play in all Indian literature, tells the story of a king who, while out hunting, falls in love with the maiden Shakuntala. He asks her to marry him and offers her a ring of betrothal but is suddenly recalled to his kingdom on urgent business. Shakuntala, who is pregnant, goes to him, but the king has been cursed by a hermit and no longer recognizes her. With the help of the gods, the king eventually recalls their love and is reunited with Shakuntala and their son.

Kalidasa was one of the greatest Indian dramatists, but he was by no means the only one. Sanskrit plays typically contained one to ten acts. They were performed in theaters in the palaces or in court temples by troupes of actors of both sexes who were trained and supported by the royal family. The plots were usually taken from Indian legends of gods and kings. No scenery or props were used, but costumes and makeup were elaborate. The theaters had to be small because much of the drama was conveyed through intricate gestures and dance conventions. There were many different positions for various parts of the body, including one hundred for the hands alone.

Like poetry, prose developed in India from the Vedic period. The use of prose was well established by the sixth and seventh centuries C.E. This is truly astonishing considering that the novel did not appear until the tenth century in Japan and until the seventeenth century in Europe. One of the greatest masters of Sanskrit prose was Dandin (DUN-din), who lived during the seventh century. In *The Ten Princes*, he created a fantastic and exciting world that fuses history and fiction. His keen powers of observation, details of low life, and humor give his writing considerable vitality.

Music   Another area of Indian creativity that developed during this era was music. Ancient Indian music had come from the chanting of the Vedic hymns and thus had a strong metaphysical and spiritual flavor. The actual physical vibrations of music (*nada*) were believed to be related to the spiritual world. An off-key or sloppy rendition of a sacred text could upset the harmony and balance of the entire universe.

In form, Indian classical music is based on a scale, called a *raga* (RAH-guh). There are dozens, if not hundreds, of separate scales, which are grouped into separate categories depending on the time of day during which they are to be performed. The performers use a stringed instrument called a *sitar* (si-TAHR) and various types of wind instruments and drums. The performers select a basic *raga* and then are free to improvise the melodic structure and rhythm. A good performer never performs a particular *raga* the same way twice. As with jazz music in the West, the audience is concerned not so much with faithful reproduction as with the performer's creativity.

THE GOLDEN REGION: EARLY SOUTHEAST ASIA

Between China and India lies the region that today is called Southeast Asia. It has two major components: a mainland region extending southward from the Chinese border down to the tip of the Malay Peninsula and an extensive archipelago, most of which is part of present-day Indonesia and the Philippines. Travel among the islands and toward regions to the west, north, and east was not difficult, so Southeast Asia has historically served as a vast land bridge for the movement of peoples between China, the Indian subcontinent, and the more than 25,000 islands of the South Pacific. The first arrival of humans probably appeared as long as 40,000 years ago, as part of the initial exodus of *Homo sapiens* from Africa. The final destination for some of these peoples was Australia, where their descendants, known today as aborigines, still live.

Mainland Southeast Asia consists of several north-south mountain ranges, separated by river valleys that run in a southerly or southeasterly direction. Several groups of migrants came down the valleys from China in search of new homelands. One of the earliest were **Malayo-Polynesian** (muh-LAY-oh-pah-leh-NEE-zhun) speakers who originated on the island of Taiwan or the southeastern coast of China. Most of them settled in the southern part of the Southeast Asian mainland or on the islands to the south. Then came the Thai (TY) from southwestern China and the Burmese from the Tibetan highlands. Once in Southeast Asia, most of these migrants settled in the fertile deltas of the rivers—the Irrawaddy (ir-uh-WAH-dee) and the Salween (SAL-ween) in Burma, the Chao Phraya (chow PRY-uh) in Thailand, and the Red River and the Mekong (MAY-kahng) in Vietnam—or in lowland areas on the islands to the south.

Although the river valleys facilitated north-south travel on the Southeast Asian mainland, movement between east and west was relatively difficult. The mountains are densely forested and infested with malaria-carrying mosquitoes. Consequently, the lowland peoples in the river valleys were often isolated from each other and had only limited contacts with the upland peoples in the mountains. These geographic barriers may help explain why mainland Southeast Asia is one of the few regions in Asia that was never unified under a single government. Communication among peoples living in the Malay Peninsula and the southern islands, however, was relatively easy.

Given Southeast Asia's location between China and India, it is not surprising that both civilizations influenced developments in the region. In 111 B.C.E., northern Vietnam was conquered by the Han dynasty and remained under Chinese control for more than a millennium. The Indian states never exerted much political control over Southeast Asia, but their influence was pervasive nevertheless. The first contacts had taken place by the fourth century B.C.E., when Indian merchants began sailing to Southeast Asia; they were soon followed by Buddhist and Hindu missionaries. Indian influence can be seen in many aspects of Southeast Asian culture, from political institutions to religion, architecture, language, and literature.

Paddy Fields and Spices: The States of Southeast Asia

The traditional states of Southeast Asia can generally be divided between agricultural societies and trading societies. The distinction between farming and trade was a product of the environment. The agricultural societies—notably, Vietnam, Angkor (AN-kor) in what is now Cambodia, and the Burmese state of Pagan (puh-GAHN)—were situated in fertile river deltas that were conducive to the development of a wet rice economy. As in India and China, the cultivation of wet rice led to an expanding population and eventually to the formation of states. Although all produced some goods for regional markets, none was tempted to turn to commerce as the prime source of national income. In fact, none was situated astride the main trade routes that crisscrossed the region. Trading societies in the Indonesian archipelago such as Srivijaya and Majapahit, however, were actively involved in the regional trade network from an early time.

The Mainland States   One exception to this general rule was the kingdom of Funan (FOO-nan), which arose in the fertile valley of the lower Mekong River in the second century C.E. At that time, much of the regional trade between India and the South China Sea moved across the narrow neck of the Malay Peninsula. With access to copper, tin, and iron, as well as a variety of tropical agricultural products, Funan played an active role in this process, and Oc Eo (ohk-EEOH), on the Gulf of Thailand, became one of the primary commercial ports in the region. Funan declined in the fifth century when trade began to pass through the Strait of Malacca (muh-LAK-uh) and was eventually replaced by the agricultural state of Chenla (CHEEN-luh) and then, three hundred years later, by the great kingdom of Angkor.

Angkor was the most powerful state to emerge in mainland Southeast Asia before the sixteenth century. The remains of its capital city, Angkor Thom (AN-kor TOHM), give a sense of the magnificence of Angkor civilization. The city formed a square 2 miles on each side. Its massive stone walls were several feet thick and were surrounded by a moat. Four main gates led into the city, which at its height had a substantial population. Recent archaeological evidence suggests that much of the population resided in suburban areas outside the extensive city wall. Like its predecessor, the wealth of Angkor was based primarily on the cultivation of wet rice, which had been introduced to the Mekong River valley from China in the third millennium B.C.E. Other products were honey, textiles, fish, and salt. By the fourteenth century, however, Angkor had begun to decline, a product of incessant wars with its neighbors and the silting up of its irrigation system, and in 1432, Angkor Thom was destroyed by the Thai, who had migrated into the region from southwestern China in the thirteenth century and established their capital at Ayuthaya (ah-yoo-TY-yuh), in lower Thailand, in 1351.

As the Thai expanded southward, however, their main competition came from the west, where the Burmese peoples had formed their own agricultural society in the valleys of the Salween and Irrawaddy Rivers. Like the Thai, they were relatively recent arrivals in the area, having migrated southward from the highlands of Tibet beginning in the seventh century C.E. After subjugating weaker societies already living in the area, in the eleventh century they founded the first great Burmese state, the kingdom of Pagan. Like the Thai, they quickly converted to Buddhism and adopted Indian political institutions and culture. For a while, they were a major force in the western part of Southeast Asia, but attacks from the Mongols in the late thirteenth century weakened

MAP 9.6 Southeast Asia in the Thirteenth Century

This map shows the major states that arose in Southeast Asia after the year 1000 C.E. Some, such as Angkor and Dai Viet, were predominantly agricultural. Others, such as Srivijaya and Champa, were commercial.

Pagan, and the resulting vacuum may have benefited the Thai as they moved into areas occupied by Burmese migrants in the Chao Phraya Valley.

The Malay World   In the Malay Peninsula and the Indonesian archipelago, a different pattern emerged. For centuries, this area had been linked to regional trade networks, and much of its wealth had come from the export of tropical products to China, India, and the Middle East. The vast majority of the inhabitants of the region were Malayo-Polynesian-speaking peoples, who, as mentioned earlier, spread from their original homeland in southeastern China into island Southeast Asia and even to more distant locations in the South Pacific, including Tahiti, Hawaii, and Easter Island.

Eventually, the islands of the Indonesian archipelago gave rise to two of the region's most notable trading societies—Srivijaya (sree-vih-JAH-yuh) and Majapahit (mah-jah-PAH-hit). Both were major participants in what might be called the "spice road," a maritime equivalent of the Silk Road on the Asian mainland. As the wealth of the Arab empire in the Middle East and then of continental Europe increased, so did the demand for the products of Southeast Asia. Merchant fleets from India and the Arabian peninsula sailed to the Indonesian islands to buy cloves, pepper, nutmeg, cinnamon, precious woods, and other exotic products coveted by the wealthy. In the eighth century, Srivijaya, which had been established along the eastern coast of Sumatra around 670, became a powerful commercial state that dominated the trade passing through the Strait of Malacca, at that time the most convenient route from East Asia into the Indian Ocean. The rulers of Srivijaya had helped bring the route to prominence by controlling the pirates who had previously plagued shipping in the strait. Another inducement was Srivijaya's capital at Palembang (pah-lem-BAHNG), a deepwater port where sailors could wait out the monsoon season before making their return voyage. In 1025, however, Chola, one of the kingdoms of southern India and a commercial rival of Srivijaya, inflicted a devastating defeat on the island kingdom. Although Srivijaya survived, it was unable to regain its former dominance, in part because the main trade route had shifted to the east, through the Strait of Sunda (SOON-duh) and directly out into the Indian Ocean. In the late thirteenth century, this shift in trade patterns led to the founding of the new kingdom of Majapahit on the island of Java. In the mid-fourteenth century, Majapahit succeeded in uniting most of the archipelago and perhaps even part of the Southeast Asian mainland under its rule.

The Role of India   Indian influence was evident in all of these societies to various degrees. Based on models from the Dravidian kingdoms of southern India, Southeast Asian kings were believed to possess special godlike qualities that set them apart from ordinary people. In some societies such as Angkor, the most prominent royal advisers constituted a *brahmin* class on the Indian model. In Pagan and Angkor, some division of the population into separate classes based on occupation and ethnic background seems to have occurred, although these divisions do not seem to have developed the rigidity of the Indian class system.

India also supplied Southeast Asians with a writing system. The societies of the region had no written scripts for their spoken languages before the arrival of the Indian merchants and missionaries. Indian phonetic symbols were borrowed and used to record the spoken language. Initially, Southeast Asian literature was written in the Indian Sanskrit but eventually came to be written in the local languages. At the same time, Southeast Asian authors borrowed popular Indian themes, such as stories from the Buddhist scriptures and tales from the Ramayana.

A popular form of entertainment among the common people, the *wayang kulit* (WAH-yahng KOO-lit), or shadow play, may have come originally from India or possibly China, but it became a distinctive art form in Java and other islands of the Indonesian archipelago. In a shadow play, flat leather puppets were manipulated behind an illuminated screen while the narrator recited tales from the Indian classics. The plays were often accompanied by a gamelan (GA-muh-lan), an orchestra composed primarily of percussion instruments such as gongs and drums that apparently originated in Java.

Daily Life   Because of the diversity of ethnic backgrounds, religions, and cultures, making generalizations about daily life in Southeast Asia during the early historical period is difficult. Nevertheless, it appears that societies in the region did not always apply the social distinctions that prevailed in India. For example, although the local population, as elsewhere, was divided according to a variety of economic functions, the dividing lines between classes were not as rigid and imbued with religious significance as they were in the Indian subcontinent.

Social Structures Still, traditional societies in Southeast Asia had some clearly hierarchical characteristics. At the top of the social ladder were the hereditary aristocrats, who monopolized both political power and economic wealth and enjoyed a borrowed aura of charisma by virtue of their proximity to the ruler. Most aristocrats lived in the major cities, which were the main source of power, wealth, and foreign influence. Beyond the major cities lived the mass of the population, composed of farmers, fishers, artisans, and merchants. In most Southeast Asian societies, the vast majority were probably rice farmers, living at a bare level of subsistence and paying heavy rents or taxes to a landlord or a local ruler.

The average Southeast Asian peasant was not actively engaged in commerce except as a consumer of various necessities. But accounts by foreign visitors indicate that in the Malay world, some were involved in growing or mining products for export, such as tropical food products, precious woods, tin, and precious gems. Most of the regional trade was carried on by local merchants, who purchased products from local growers and then transported them to the major port cities. During the early state-building era, roads were few and relatively primitive, so most of the trade was transported by small boats down rivers to the major ports along the coast. There the goods were loaded onto larger ships for delivery outside the region. Growers of export goods in areas near the coast were thus indirectly involved in the regional trade network but received few economic benefits from the relationship.

As we might expect from an area of such ethnic and cultural diversity, social structures differed significantly from country to country. In the Indianized states on the mainland, the tradition of a hereditary tribal aristocracy was probably accentuated by the Hindu practice of dividing the population into separate classes, called *varna* in imitation of the Indian model. In Angkor and Pagan, for example, the divisions were based on occupation or ethnic background. Some people were considered free subjects of the king, although there may have been legal restrictions against changing occupations. Others, however, may have been indentured to an employer. Each community was under a chieftain, who was in turn subordinated to a higher official responsible for passing on the tax revenues of each group to the central government.

In the kingdoms in the Malay Peninsula and the Indonesian archipelago, social relations were generally less formal. Most of the people in the region, whether farmers, fishers, or artisans, lived in small *kampongs* (KAHM-pahngs) (Malay for "villages") in wooden houses built on stilts to avoid flooding during the monsoon season. Some of the farmers were probably sharecroppers who paid a part of their harvest to a landlord, who was often a member of the aristocracy. But in other areas, the tradition of free farming was strong. In some cases, some of the poorer land belonged to the village as a collective unit and was assigned for use by the neediest families.

Chinese Traders in the Philippines

INTERACTION & EXCHANGE

From early times, the peoples living in the islands south of the East Asian mainland played an active role in the regional trade network between the Chinese coast and the Indian Ocean. This excerpt from a thirteenth-century Chinese account describes the nature of the commercial exchanges that took place between Chinese merchants and the indigenous population in the Philippine Islands. The author of the account, Chau Ju-kua, was a superintendent of trade in South China. His description of the indigenous peoples in the Philippines is one of the few sources on such communities before the arrival of European ships in the sixteenth century.

A Description of Barbarian Peoples

The country of Ma-i [Philippine archipelago] is to the north of P'o-ni [Borneo]. Over a thousand families are settled together along both banks of a creek (or, gully). The natives cover themselves with a sheet of cotton cloth, or hide the lower part of the body with a loincloth.

There are bronze images of gods, of unknown origin, scattered about in the grassy wilderness. Pirates seldom come to this country.

When trading ships enter the anchorage, they stop in front of the officials' place, for that is the place for bartering of the country. After a ship has been boarded, the natives mix freely with the ship's folk. The chiefs are in the habit of using white umbrellas, for which reason the traders offer them as gifts.

The custom of the trade is for the savage traders to assemble in crowds and carry the goods away with them in baskets; and, even if one cannot at first know them, and can but slowly distinguish the men who remove the goods, there will yet be no loss. The savage traders will after this carry these goods on to other islands for barter, and, as a rule, it takes them as much as eight or nine months till they return, when they repay the traders on shipboard with what they have obtained (for the goods). Some, however, do not return within the proper term, for which reason vessels trading with Ma-i are the latest in reaching home....

The products of the country consist of yellow wax, cotton, pearls, tortoise-shell, medicinal betel-nuts and *yü-ta* cloth [abaca textiles]; and (the foreign) traders

Women and the Family The women of Southeast Asia during this era have been described as the most fortunate in the world. Although most women worked side by side with men in the fields, as in Africa they often played an active role in trading activities. Not only did this lead to a higher literacy rate among women than among their male counterparts, but it also allowed them more financial independence than their counterparts in China and India, a fact that was noticed by the Chinese traveler Zhou Daguan (JOE dah-GWAHN) at the end of the thirteenth century: "In Cambodia it is the women who take charge of trade. For this reason a Chinese arriving in the country loses no time in getting himself a mate, for he will find her commercial instincts a great asset."[10]

Although, as elsewhere, warfare was normally part of the male domain, women sometimes played a role as bodyguards as well. According to Zhou Daguan, barter for these porcelain, trade-gold, iron censers, lead, coloured glass beads, and iron needles....

The San-sü (or "Three Islands"), belong to the Ma-i; their names are Kia-ma-yen (Calamián Island Group between Mindoro and Palawan), Pa-lau-yu (Palawan), and Pa-ki-nung (Busuanga Island, largest of the Calamián Islands), and each has its own tribes scattered over the islands. When ships arrive there, the natives come out to trade with them; the generic name (of these islands) is San-sü.

Their local customs are about the same as those of Ma-i. Each tribe consists of about a thousand families. The country contains many lofty ridges, and ranges of cliffs rise steep as the walls of a house.

The natives build wattled huts perched in lofty and dangerous spots, and since the hills contain no springs, the women may be seen carrying on their heads two or three jars one above the other in which they fetch water from the streams, and with their burdens mount the hills with the same ease as if they were walking on level ground....

Whenever foreign traders arrive at any of the settlements, they live on board ship before venturing to go on shore, their ships being moored in mid-stream, announcing their presence to the natives by beating drums. Upon this the savage traders race for the ship in small boats, carrying cotton, yellow wax, native cloth, cocoanut-heart mats, which they offer for barter. If the prices (of goods they may wish to purchase) cannot be agreed upon, the chief of the (local) traders must go in person, in order to come to an understanding, which being reached the natives are offered presents of silk umbrellas, porcelain, and rattan baskets; but the foreigners still retain on board one or two (natives) as hostages. After that they go on shore to traffic, which being ended they return the hostages. A ship will not remain at anchor longer than three or four days, after which it proceeds to another place; for the savage settlements along the coast of San-sü are not connected by a common jurisdiction (i.e., are all independent).

Q *How does the trading process take place in this account? How does each side seek to guarantee satisfaction?*

Source: From *Chau Ju-kua, His Work on the Chinese and Arab Trade in the Twelfth and Thirteenth Centuries, entitled Chu-fan-chi*, trans. F. Hirth and W. W. Rockhill (St. Petersburg: Printing Office of the Imperial Academy of Sciences, 1911), pp. 159–162.

women were used to protect the royal family in Angkor, as well as in kingdoms located on the islands of Java and Sumatra. While there is no evidence that such female units ever engaged in battle, they did give rise to wondrous tales of "amazon" warriors in the writings of foreign travelers such as the fourteenth-century Muslim adventurer Ibn Battuta.

One reason for the enhanced status of women in traditional Southeast Asia is that the nuclear family was more common than the joint family system prevalent in China and the Indian subcontinent. Throughout the region, wealth in marriage was passed from the male to the female, in contrast to the dowry system applied in China and India. In most societies, virginity was usually not a valued commodity in brokering a marriage, and divorce proceedings could be initiated by either party. Still, most marriages were monogamous, and marital fidelity was taken seriously.

The relative availability of cultivable land in the region may help explain the absence of joint families. Joint families under patriarchal leadership tend to be found in areas where land is scarce and individual families must work together to conserve resources and maximize income. With the exception of a few crowded river valleys, few areas in Southeast Asia had a high population density per acre of cultivable land. Throughout most of the area, water was plentiful, and the land was relatively fertile. In parts of Indonesia, much of the diet could be supplied by the bountiful produce of wild fruit trees—bananas, coconuts, mangoes, and a variety of other tropical fruits.

World of the Spirits: Religious Belief

Indian religions also had a profound effect on Southeast Asia. Traditional religious beliefs in the region took the familiar form of spirit worship and animism that we have seen in other cultures. Southeast Asians believed that spirits dwelled in the mountains, rivers, streams, and other sacred places in their environment. Mountains were probably particularly sacred, since they were considered to be the abode of ancestral spirits, the place to which the souls of all the departed would retire after death.

When Hindu and Buddhist ideas began to penetrate the area early in the first millennium C.E., they exerted a strong appeal among local elites. Not only did the new doctrines offer a more convincing explanation of the nature of the cosmos, but they also provided local rulers with a means of enhancing their prestige and power and conferred an aura of legitimacy on their relations with their subjects. In the Javanese kingdoms and in Angkor, Hindu gods such as Vishnu and Shiva provided a new and more sophisticated veneer for existing beliefs in nature deities and ancestral spirits. In Angkor, the king's duties included performing sacred rituals on the mountain in the capital city; in time, the ritual became a state cult uniting Hindu gods with local nature deities and ancestral spirits in a complex pantheon.

This state cult, financed by the royal court, eventually led to the construction of temples throughout the country. Many of these temples housed thousands of priests and retainers and amassed great wealth, including vast estates farmed by local peasants. It has been estimated that there were as many as 300,000 priests in Angkor at the height of its power. This vast wealth, which was often exempt from taxes, may be one explanation for Angkor's gradual decline in the thirteenth and fourteenth centuries. Initially, the spread of Hindu and Buddhist doctrines was essentially an elite phenomenon. Although the common people participated in the state cult and helped construct the temples, they did not give up their traditional beliefs in local deities and ancestral spirits. A major transformation began in the eleventh century, however, when Theravada Buddhism began to penetrate the mainland kingdom of Pagan from the island of Sri Lanka. From Pagan, it spread rapidly to other areas in Southeast Asia and eventually became the religion of the masses throughout the mainland west of the Annamite Mountains.

Theravada's appeal to the peoples of Southeast Asia is reminiscent of the original attraction of Buddhist thought centuries earlier on the Indian subcontinent. By teaching that individuals could seek Nirvana through their own actions rather than through the intercession of the ruler or a priest, Theravada was more accessible to the masses than the state cults promoted by the rulers. During the next centuries, Theravada gradually undermined the influence of state-supported religions and became the dominant faith in several mainland societies, including Burma,

The Spread of Buddhism in Southeast Asia

RELIGION & PHILOSOPHY

Like Fa Xian and Xuan Zang, I-tsing (635–713) was a Chinese monk who traveled to India in order to study Buddhist teachings. En route home after two decades in South Asia, he stopped at a number of ports in Southeast Asia, including Bhoga (today's Palembang) on the Indonesian island of Sumatra. As this passage indicates, Buddhism had already established a firm beachhead in the region, since many of the local elites had adopted the faith, presumably as a result of contacts with other Buddhist pilgrims and traders from the South Asian subcontinent. Other parts of the region had converted to Brahmanism. Later, both faiths would be replaced by Islam and Christianity.

A Record of the Buddhist Religion as Practised in India and the Malay Archipelago

This [East India] is the place where we embark when returning to China. Sailing from here two months in the south-east direction we come to Ka-cha [Acheh]. By this time a ship from Bhoga [Palembang] will have arrived there. This is generally in the first or second month of the year. But those who go to the Simhala Island [Ceylon] must sail in the south-west direction. They say that the island is 700 yoganas off. We stay in Ka-cha till winter, then start on board ship for the south, and we come after a month to a country of Malayau, which has now become Bhoga; there are many states (under it). The time of arrival is generally in the first or second month. We stay there till the middle of summer and we

sail to the north; in about a month we reach Kwang-fu (**Kwang-tung**). The first half of the year will be passed by this time.

When we are helped by the power of our (former) good actions, the journey everywhere is as easy and enjoyable as if we went through a market, but, on the other hand, when we have not much influence of Karma, we are often exposed to danger as if (a young one) in a reclining nest. I have thus shortly described the route and the way home, hoping that the wise may still expand their knowledge by hearing more.

Many kings and chieftains in the islands of the Southern Ocean admire and believe (Buddhism), and their hearts are set upon accumulating good actions. In the fortified city of Bhoga Buddhist priests number more than 1,000, whose minds are bent on learning and good practices. They investigate and study all the subjects that exist just as in the Middle Kingdom (Madhya-desa, India); the rules and ceremonies are not at all different. If a Chinese priest wishes to go to the West in order to hear (lectures) and read (the original), he had better stay here one or two years and practice the proper rules and then proceed to Central India.

Q *Does the author of this account appear to believe that the majority of the population in Acheh consists of fervent disciples of the Buddhist faith? Why or why not?*

Source: From I-tsing, A Record of the Buddhist Religion as Practised in India and the Malay Archipelago, trans. J. Takakusu (Oxford: Clarendon, 1896), pp. xxxiv–xxxv.

Thailand, Laos, and Cambodia. In the process, however, it was gradually appropriated by local rulers, who portrayed themselves as "immanent Buddhas," higher than ordinary mortals on the scale of human existence.

Theravada did not penetrate far into the Malay Peninsula or the Indonesian island chain, perhaps because it entered Southeast Asia through Burma farther to the north. But the Malay world found its own popular alternative to state religions when Islam began to enter the area in the thirteenth and fourteenth centuries. Because Islam's expansion into Southeast Asia took place for the most part after 1500, its emergence as a major force in the region will be discussed later in this book.

Not surprisingly, Indian influence extended to the Buddhist and Hindu temples of Southeast Asia. Temple architecture reflecting Gupta or southern Indian styles began to appear in Southeast Asia during the first centuries C.E. Most famous is the Buddhist temple at Borobudur (boh-roh-buh-DOOR), in central Java. Begun in the late eighth century at the behest of a king of Sailendra (SY-len-druh) (an agricultural kingdom based in eastern Java), Borobudur is a massive stupa with nine terraces. Sculpted on the sides of each terrace are bas-reliefs depicting the nine stages in the life of Siddhartha Gautama, from childhood to his final release from the chain of human existence. Surmounted by hollow bell-like towers containing representations of the Buddha and capped by a single stupa, the structure dominates the landscape for miles around.

The Temple of Borobudur. *The colossal pyramid temple at Borobudur, on the island of Java, is one of the greatest Buddhist monuments. Constructed in the eighth century C.E., it depicts the path to spiritual enlightenment in stone. Sculptures and relief portrayals of the life of the Buddha at the lower level depict the world of desire. At higher elevations, they give way to empty bell towers (see inset) and culminate at the summit with an empty and closed stupa, signifying the state of Nirvana. Shortly after it was built, Borobudur was abandoned when a new ruler switched his allegiance to Hinduism and ordered the erection of the Hindu temple of Prambanan nearby. Buried for a thousand years under volcanic ash and jungle, Borobudur was rediscovered in the nineteenth century and has recently been restored to its former splendor.*

Second only to Borobudur in technical excellence and even more massive in size are the ruins of the old capital city of Angkor Thom. The temple of Angkor Wat (AN-kor WAHT) is the most famous and arguably the most beautiful of all the existing structures at Angkor Thom. Built on the model of the legendary Mount Meru (the home of the gods in Hindu tradition), it combines Indian architectural techniques with native inspiration in a structure of impressive delicacy and grace.

In existence for more than six hundred years, Angkor Thom serves as a bridge between the Hindu and Buddhist architectural styles. The last of its great temples, known as the Bayon (BAY-on), followed the earlier Hindu model but was topped with sculpted towers containing four-sided representations of a bodhisattva, searching, it is said, for souls to save. Shortly after the Bayon was built, Theravada Buddhist societies in Burma and Thailand began to create a new Buddhist architecture based on the concept of a massive stupa surmounted by a spire. Most famous, perhaps, is the Shwedagon (SCHWEE-da-gahn) Pagoda in Yangon (YAN-gon) (Rangoon), capital of modern Myanmar (Burma), which is covered with gold leaf contributed by devout Buddhists from around the country.

Expansion into the Pacific   One of the great maritime feats of human history was the penetration of the islands of the Pacific Ocean by Malayo-Polynesian-speaking peoples. By 2000 B.C.E., these seafarers had migrated as far as the Bismarck Archipelago, northeast of the island of New Guinea, where they encountered Melanesian peoples whose ancestors had taken part in the first wave of human settlement into the region 30,000 years previously.

From there, the Polynesian peoples—as they are now familiarly known—continued their explorations eastward in large sailing canoes up to 100 feet long that carried more than forty people and many of their food staples, such as chickens, chili peppers, and a tuber called taro, the source of poi. Stopping in Fiji, Samoa, and the Cook Islands during the first millennium C.E., their descendants pressed onward, eventually reaching Tahiti, Hawaii, and even Easter Island, one of the most remote sites of human habitation in the world. Eventually, one group of Polynesians, now known as the Maori (MAU-ree), sailed southwestward from the island of Rarotonga and settled in New Zealand, off the coast of Australia. The final frontier of human settlement had been breached.

CHRONOLOGIES

MEDIEVAL INDIA	
c. 150 B.C.E.–c. 200 C.E.	Kushan kingdom
320–600s	Gupta dynasty
r. 320–c. 335	Chandragupta I
r. 335–375	Samudragupta
r. 375–415	Chandragupta II
c. 406	Arrival of Fa Xian in India
Seventh century	First Buddhist temples at Ellora
630–643	Travels of Xuan Zang in India

c. 711	Conquest of Sind by Arab armies
997–1030	Reign of Mahmud of Ghazni
1206–1527	Delhi sultanate
1221	Mongol invasion of northern India
1398	Invasion of Tamerlane

EARLY SOUTHEAST ASIA

111 B.C.E.	Chinese conquest of Vietnam
c. seventh century C.E.	Arrival of Burmese peoples
c. 670	Formation of Srivijaya
c. eighth century	Construction of Borobudur
c. ninth century	Creation of Angkor kingdom
c. thirteenth century	Thai migrations into Southeast Asia
1292	Rise of Majapahit empire
1432	Fall of Angkor kingdom

 MindTap™

MindTap is a fully online, highly personalized learning experience built upon Cengage Learning content. MindTap combines student learning tools—readings, multimedia, activities, and assessments—into a singular Learning Path that guides students through their course.

10

THE FLOWERING OF
TRADITIONAL CHINA

Detail of a Chinese scroll, Going up the River at the Spring Festival

---

CHAPTER OUTLINE

• China After the Han • China Reunified: The Sui, the Tang, and the Song • Explosion in Central Asia: The Mongol Empire • The Ming Dynasty • In Search of the Way • The Apogee of Chinese Culture

CHINA AFTER THE HAN

After the collapse of the Han dynasty at the beginning of the third century C.E., China fell into an extended period of division and civil war. Taking advantage of the absence of organized government in China, nomadic forces from the Gobi Desert penetrated south of the Great Wall and established their own rule over northern China. In the Yangzi Valley and farther to the south, native Chinese rule was maintained, but constant civil war and instability led later historians to refer to the period as the "era of the six dynasties."

The collapse of the Han Empire had a marked effect on the Chinese psyche. The Confucian principles that emphasized hard work, the subordination of the individual to community interests, and belief in the essentially rational order of the universe came under severe challenge, and many Chinese began to turn to more messianic creeds that emphasized the supernatural or the promise of earthly or heavenly salvation. Intellectuals began to reject the stuffy moralism and complacency of State Confucianism and sought emotional satisfaction in hedonistic pursuits or philosophical Daoism.

Eccentric behavior and a preference for philosophical Daoism became a common response to a corrupt age. A group of writers known as the "seven sages of the bamboo forest" exemplified the period. Among the best known was the poet Liu Ling (lyoo LING), whose odd behavior is described in this oft-quoted passage:

> Liu Ling was an inveterate drinker and indulged himself to the full. Sometimes he stripped off his clothes and sat in his room stark naked. Some men saw him and rebuked him. Liu Ling said, "Heaven and earth are my dwelling, and my house is my trousers. Why are you all coming into my trousers?"[1]

But neither popular beliefs in the supernatural nor philosophical Daoism could satisfy deeper emotional needs or provide solace in time of sorrow or the hope of a better life in the hereafter. Buddhism filled that gap.

Buddhism was brought to China in the first or second century C.E., probably by missionaries and merchants traveling over the Silk Road. The concept of rebirth was probably unfamiliar to most Chinese, and the intellectual hairsplitting that often accompanied discussion of the Buddha's message in India was too esoteric for Chinese tastes. Still, in the difficult years surrounding the decline of the Han dynasty, Buddhist ideas, especially those of the Mahayana school, began to find adherents among intellectuals and ordinary people alike. As Buddhism increased in popularity, it was frequently attacked by supporters of Confucianism and Daoism for its foreign origins. Some even claimed that Siddhartha Gautama had been a disciple of Lao Tzu. But such sniping did not halt the progress of Buddhism, and eventually the new faith was assimilated into Chinese culture, assisted by the efforts of such tireless advocates as the missionaries Fa Xian and Xuan Zang and the support of ruling elites in both northern and southern China.

CHINA REUNIFIED: THE SUI, THE TANG, AND THE SONG

After nearly four centuries of internal division, China was unified once again in 581 when Yang Jian (yahng JEE-YEN), a member of a respected aristocratic family in northern China, founded a new dynasty, known as the Sui (SWAY) (581–618). Yang Jian, who is also known by his reign title of Sui Wendi (SWAY wen-DEE), established his capital at the historic metropolis of Chang'an (CHENG-AHN) and began to extend his authority throughout the heartland of China.

The Sui Dynasty   Like his predecessors, the new emperor sought to create a unifying ideology for the state to enhance its efficiency. But where Liu Bang, the founder of the Han dynasty, had adopted Confucianism as the official doctrine to hold the empire together, Yang Jian turned to Daoism and Buddhism. He founded monasteries for both doctrines in the capital and appointed Buddhist monks to key positions as political advisers.

Yang Jian was a builder as well as a conqueror, ordering the construction of a new canal from the capital to the confluence of the Wei and Yellow Rivers nearly 100 miles to the east. His son, Emperor Sui Yangdi (SWAY yahng-DEE), continued the process, and the 1,400-mile-long Grand Canal, linking the two great rivers of China, the Yellow and the Yangzi, was completed during his reign. The new canal facilitated the shipment of grain and other commodities from the rice-rich southern provinces to the densely populated north. The canal also served other purposes, such as speeding communications between the two regions and permitting the rapid dispatch of troops to troubled provinces. Sui Yangdi also used the canal as an imperial highway for inspecting his empire.

The Grand Canal.
Built over centuries, the Grand Canal is one of the engineering wonders of the world and a crucial conduit for carrying goods between northern and southern China. In this stylized painting, "dragon boats" carry the emperor and his retinue on an inspection tour of the canal and its adjacent territories.

One imperial procession from the capital to the central Yangzi region was described as follows:

> The emperor caused to be built dragon boats, ... red battle cruisers, multi-decked transports, lesser vessels of bamboo slats. Boatmen hired from all the waterways ... pulled the vessels by ropes of green silk on the imperial progress to Chiang-tu [Yangzhou]. The emperor rode in the dragon boat, and civil and military officials of the fifth grade and above rode in the multi-decked transports; those of the ninth grade and above were given the vessels of yellow bamboo. The boats followed one another poop to prow for more than 200 leagues [about 65 miles]. The prefectures and counties through which they passed were ordered to prepare to offer provisions. Those who made bountiful arrangements were given an additional office or title; those who fell short were given punishments up to the death penalty.[2]

Despite such efforts to project the majesty of the imperial personage, the Sui dynasty came to an end immediately after Sui Yangdi's death. The Sui emperor was a tyrannical ruler, and his expensive military campaigns aroused widespread unrest. After his return from a failed campaign against Korea in 618, the emperor was murdered in his palace. One of his generals, Li Yuan (lee YWAHN), took advantage of the instability that ensued and declared the foundation of a new dynasty, known as the Tang (TAHNG). Building on the successes of its predecessor, the Tang lasted for three hundred years, until 907.

The Tang Dynasty   Li Yuan ruled for a brief period and then was elbowed aside by his son, who assumed the reign title Tang Taizong (tahng ty-ZOONG). Under his vigorous leadership, the Tang launched a program of internal renewal and external expansion that would make it one of the greatest dynasties in the long history of China. The northwest was pacified and given the name of Xinjiang, or "new region." After a long conflict with Tibet, Chinese control was extended for the first time over that vast and desolate plateau north of the Himalaya Mountains. The southern provinces below the Yangzi were fully assimilated into the Chinese Empire, and the imperial court established commercial and diplomatic relations with the states of Southeast Asia. With reason, China now claimed to be the foremost power in East Asia, and the emperor demanded fealty and tribute from all his fellow rulers beyond the frontier. Korea accepted tribute status and attempted to adopt the Chinese model, and the Japanese dispatched official missions to China to learn more about its customs and institutions.

Finally, the Tang Dynasty witnessed a flowering of Chinese culture. Many modern observers feel that the era represents the apogee of Chinese creativity in poetry and sculpture. One reason for this explosion of culture was the influence of Buddhism, which affected art, literature, and philosophy, as well as religion and politics. Monasteries sprang up throughout China, and Buddhist monks served as advisers at the Tang imperial court. The city of Chang'an, now restored to the glory it had known as the capital of the Han dynasty, once again became the seat of the empire. With a population estimated at nearly 2 million, it was possibly the greatest city in the world of its time. The city was filled with temples and palaces, and its markets teemed with goods from all over the known world.

But the Tang, like the Han, sowed the seeds of their own destruction. Tang rulers could not prevent the rise of internal forces that would ultimately weaken

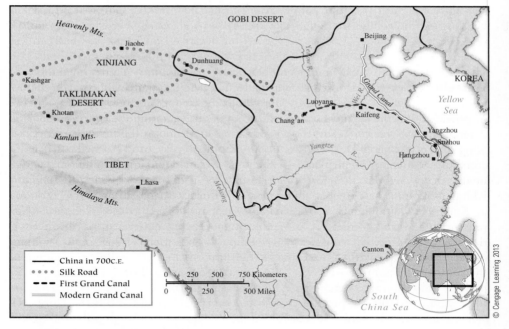

MAP 10.1 China Under the Tang

The era of the Tang Dynasty was one of the greatest periods in the long history of China. Tang influence spread from heartland China into neighboring regions, including Central and Southeast Asia.

the dynasty and bring it to an end. Two ubiquitous problems were court intrigues and official corruption. Xuanzong (shyahn-ZOONG) (r. 712–756), one of the great Tang emperors and a renowned patron of the arts, was dominated in later life by one of his favorite concubines, the beautiful Yang Guifei (yahng gway-FAY). One of her protégés, the military adventurer An Lushan (ahn loo-SHAHN), launched a rebellion in 755 and briefly seized the capital of Chang'an. The revolt was eventually suppressed, and Yang Guifei, who is viewed as one of the great villains of Chinese history, was put to death. But Xuanzong, and indeed the Tang Dynasty, never fully recovered from the catastrophe. The loss of power by the central government led to chronic instability along the northern and western frontiers, where local military commanders ruled virtually without central government interference. Climatologists also speculate that a prolonged drought that affected much of the world may have played a role in the decline of the dynasty. It was an eerie repetition of the final decades of the Han.

The end finally came in the early tenth century, when border troubles with northern nomadic peoples called the Khitan (KEE-tan) increased, leading to the final collapse of the dynasty in 907. The Tang had followed the classic Chinese strategy of "using a barbarian to oppose a barbarian" by allying with a trading people called the Uighurs (WEE-gurz), a Turkic-speaking people who had taken over many of the caravan routes along the Silk Road, against their old rivals.

But then another nomadic people called the Kirghiz (keer-GEEZ) defeated the Uighurs and turned on the Tang government in its moment of weakness and overthrew it.

The Song Dynasty

China slipped once again into disunity. This time, the period of foreign invasion and division was much shorter. In 960, a new dynasty, known as the Song (SOONG) (960–1279), rose to power. From the start, however, the Song rulers encountered more problems in defending their territory than their predecessors. Although the founding emperor, Song Taizu (soong ty-DZOO), was able to co-opt many of the powerful military commanders whose rivalry had brought the Tang Dynasty to an end, he was unable to reconquer the northwestern part of the country from the nomadic Khitan peoples. The emperor therefore established his capital farther to the east, at Kaifeng, where the Grand Canal intersected the Yellow River. Later, when pressures from the nomads in the north increased, the court was forced to move the capital even farther south, to Hangzhou (HAHNG-joe), on the coast just south of the Yangzi River delta; the emperors who ruled from Hangzhou are known as the southern Song (1127–1279). The Song also lost control over Tibet. Despite its political and military weaknesses, the dynasty nevertheless ruled during a period of economic expansion, prosperity, and cultural achievement and is therefore considered among the more successful Chinese dynasties. The population of the empire had risen to an estimated 40 million people, slightly more than that of the continent of Europe.

Yet the Song were never able to surmount the external challenge from the north, and that failure eventually brought about the end of the dynasty. During its final decades, the Song rulers were forced to pay tribute to the Jurchen (roor-ZHEN) peoples from Manchuria (man-CHUR-ee-uh). In the early thirteenth century, the Song, ignoring precedent and the fate of the Tang, formed an alliance with the Mongols, a new and obscure nomadic people from the Gobi Desert. As under the Tang, the decision proved to be a disaster. Within a few years, the Mongols had become a much more serious threat to China than the Jurchen. After defeating the Jurchen, the Mongols turned their attention to the Song, advancing on Chinese territory from both the north and the west. By this time, the Song empire had been weakened by internal factionalism and a loss of tax revenues. After a series of river battles and sieges marked by the use of catapults and gunpowder, the Song were defeated, and the conquerors announced the creation of a new Yuan (Mongol) dynasty. Ironically, the Mongols had first learned about gunpowder from the Chinese.

Political Structures: The Triumph of Confucianism

During the nearly seven hundred years from the Sui to the end of the Song, a mature political system based on principles originally established during the Qin and Han Dynasties gradually emerged in China. After the Tang Dynasty's brief flirtation with Buddhism, State Confucianism became the ideological cement that held the system together. The development of this system took several centuries, and it did not reach its height until the period of the Song Dynasty.

Equal Opportunity in China: The Civil Service Examination   At the apex of the government hierarchy was the **Grand Council**, assisted by a secretariat and a chancellery; it included representatives from all three authorities—civil, military, and censorate. Under the Grand Council was the Department of State Affairs, composed of ministries responsible for justice, military affairs, personnel, public works, revenue, and rites (ritual). This department was in effect the equivalent of a modern cabinet.

The Tang Dynasty adopted the practice of selecting some officials through periodic civil service examinations. The effectiveness of this merit system was limited, however, because the examination was administered only in the capital city and because the process was dominated by the great aristocratic clans, who had mastered the technique of preparing candidates for the exams. According to one source, fully one-third of those who succeeded on the imperial examinations during the Tang era came from the great families.

The Song were more successful at limiting aristocratic control over the bureaucracy, in part because the power of the nobility had been irreparably weakened during the final years of the Tang Dynasty and did not recover during the interregnum that followed its collapse.

One way of strengthening the power of the central administration was to make the civil service examination system the primary route to an official career. To reduce the power of the noble families, relatives of individuals serving in the imperial court, as well as eunuchs, were prohibited from taking the examinations. But if the Song rulers' objective was to make the bureaucracy more subservient to the court, they may have been disappointed. The rising professionalism of the bureaucracy, which numbered about ten thousand in the imperial capital, with an equal number at the local level, provided it with an esprit de corps and an influence that sometimes enabled it to resist the whims of individual emperors.

Under the Song, the examination system attained the form that it would retain in later centuries. In general, three levels of examinations were administered. The first was a qualifying examination given annually at the provincial capital. Candidates who succeeded in this first stage were normally not given positions in the bureaucracy except at the local level. Many stopped at this level and accepted positions as village teachers to train other candidates. Those who wished to secure an official position could take a second examination given at the capital every three years. Some went on to take the final examination, which was given in the imperial palace once every three years. Those who passed were eligible for high positions in the central bureaucracy or for appointments as district magistrates.

During the early Tang, the examinations included questions on Buddhist and Daoist as well as Confucian texts, but by Song times, examinations were based entirely on the Confucian classics. Candidates were expected to memorize passages and to be able to define the moral lessons they contained. The system guaranteed that successful candidates—and therefore officials—would have received a full dose of Confucian political and social ethics. Whether they followed those ethics, of course, was another matter. Some students brought crib notes into the examination hall (one enterprising candidate concealed an entire Confucian text in the lining of his cloak). For those candidates who succeeded,

Choosing the Best and Brightest

POLITICS &
GOVERNMENT

Wang Anshi (WAHNG anh-SHEE) (1021–1086) was a prominent government official in Song Dynasty China. As a senior adviser at court, he sought to implement a series of reforms designed to improve the operations of the Chinese state, and thus improve the well-being of the population. One key tenet of his program was to appoint honest and competent officials to key positions in the bureaucracy. In the great tradition of Chinese statecraft, Wang agreed with the proposition that it was good men, and not just laws, that created the best civil society. Current practice, however, placed primary emphasis on the ability of candidates to memorize passages from the ancient classics. In his view, what was more important was for candidates to understand the general principles of governing and behavior, principles that could be gleaned from the writings of ancient times without the need for rote memorization.

Memorial to Emperor Renzong (1058)

The most urgent need of the present time is to secure capable men. Only when we can produce a large number of capable men in the empire will it be possible to select a sufficient number of persons qualified to serve in the government. And only when we get capable men in the government will there be no difficulty in assessing what may be done, in view of the time and circumstances, and in consideration of the human distress that may be occasioned, gradually to change the decadent laws of the empire in order to approach the ideas of the ancient kings. The empire today is the same as the empire of the ancient kings. There were numerous capable men in their times. Why is there a dearth of such men today? It is because, as has been said, we do not train and cultivate men in the proper way....

What is the way to select officials? The ancient kings selected men only from the local villages and through the local schools. The people were asked to recommend those they considered to be virtuous and able, sending up their nominations to the court, which investigated each one. Only if the men recommended proved truly virtuous and able would they be appointed to official posts commensurate with their individual virtue and ability. Investigation of them did not mean that a ruler relied only upon his own keenness

official arrogance, bureaucratic infighting, corruption, and legalistic interpretations of government regulations were as prevalent in medieval China as in bureaucracies the world over.

The Song authorities tried to open up the system to provide an equal opportunity to the poor as well as to the affluent. Training academies were set up at the provincial and district levels. Without such academies, only individuals fortunate enough to receive training in the classics in family-run schools would have had the expertise to pass the examinations. Still, in most years, the majority of candidates came from the landed gentry, nonaristocratic landowners who controlled much of the wealth in the countryside. Because the gentry prized education and became the of sight and hearing or that he took the word of one man alone.... Having inquired into his actions and utterances, they then tested him in government affairs. What was meant by "investigation" was just that—to test them in government affairs....

Today, although we have schools in each prefecture and district, they amount to no more than school buildings. There are no officers of instruction and guidance; nothing is done to train and develop human talent. Only in the Imperial Academy are officers of instruction and guidance to be found, and even they are not selected with care. The affairs of the court, rites and music, punishment and correction have no place in the schools, and the students pay no attention to them, considering that rites and music, punishment and correction are the business of officials, not something they ought to know about. What is taught to students consists merely of textual exegesis [of the classics].

That, however, was not the way men were taught in ancient times. In recent years, teaching has been based on the essays required for the civil service examinations, but this kind of essay cannot be learned without resorting to extensive memorization and strenuous study, upon which students must spend their efforts the whole day long. Such proficiency as they attain is at best of no use in the government of the empire, and at most the empire can make no use of them....

In addition, candidates are examined in such fields as the Nine Classics, the Five Classics, specialization [in one classic], and the study of law. The court has already become concerned over the uselessness of this type of knowledge and has stressed the need for an understanding of general principles [as set forth in the classics].... When we consider the men selected through "understanding of the classics," however, it is still those who memorize, recite, and have some knowledge of literary composition who are able to pass the examination, while those who can apply them [the classics] to the government of the empire are not always brought in through this kind of selection.

Q *Does Wang Anshi cite examples from ancient times to strengthen his complaint about the current nature of training for a career in officialdom? Do his criticisms have relevance for our own day?*

Source: From *Sources of Chinese Tradition*, Vol. 1, 2nd ed., by William Theodore de Bary and Irene Bloom, pp. 612–616. Copyright © 1999 Columbia University Press. Reprinted with permission of the publisher.

primary upholders of the Confucian tradition, they were often called the **scholar-gentry**.

Despite such weaknesses, the civil service examination system was an impressive achievement for its day and probably provided a more efficient government and more opportunity for upward mobility than were found in any other civilization of its time. Most Western governments, for example, began to recruit officials on the basis of merit only in the nineteenth century. Furthermore, by regulating the content of the examinations, the system helped provide China with a cultural uniformity lacking in empires elsewhere in Asia.

The court also attempted to curb official misbehavior through the censorate. Specially trained officials known as censors were assigned to investigate possible

Action or Inaction: An Ideological Dispute in Medieval China

RELIGION &
PHILOSOPHY

During the interregnum between the fall of the Han dynasty in 220 C.E. and the rise of the Tang four hundred years later, Daoist critics lampooned the hypocrisy of the "Confucian gentleman" and the Master's emphasis on ritual and the maintenance of proper relations among individuals in society. In the first selection, a third-century Daoist launches an attack on the pompous and hypocritical Confucian gentleman who feigns high moral principles while secretly engaging in corrupt and licentious behavior.

By the eighth century, the tables had turned. In the second selection, Han Yu **(hahn YOO)** (768–824), a key figure in the emergence of Neo-Confucian thought as the official ideology of the state, responds to such remarks with a withering analysis of the dangers of "doing nothing"—a clear reference to the famous Daoist doctrine of "inaction."

Biography of a Great Man

What the world calls a gentleman [*chuntzu*] is someone who is solely concerned with moral law [*fa*], and cultivates exclusively the rules of propriety [*ft*]. His hand holds the emblem of jade [authority]; his foot follows the straight line of the rule. He likes to think that his actions set a permanent example; he likes to think that his words are everlasting models. In his youth, he has a reputation in the villages of his locality; in his later years, he is well known in the neighboring districts. Upward, he aspires to the dignity of the Three Dukes; downward, he does not disdain the post of governor of the nine provinces.

Have you ever seen the lice that inhabit a pair of trousers? They jump into the depths of the seams, hiding themselves in the cotton wadding, and believe they have a pleasant place to live. Walking, they do not risk going beyond the edge of the seam; moving, they are careful not to emerge from the trouser leg; and they think they have kept to the rules of etiquette. But when the trousers are ironed, the flames invade the hills, the fire spreads, the villages are set on fire and the towns burned down; then the lice that inhabit the trousers cannot escape.

What difference is there between the gentleman who lives within a narrow world and the lice that inhabit trouser legs?

Han Yu, *Essentials of the Moral Way*

In ancient times men confronted many dangers. But sages arose who taught

cases of official wrongdoing and report directly to the court. The censorate was supposed to be independent of outside pressures to ensure that its members would feel free to report wrongdoing wherever it occurred. In practice, censors who displeased high court officials were often removed or even subjected to more serious forms of punishment, which reduced the effectiveness of the system.

them the way to live and to grow together. They served as rulers and as teachers. They drove out reptiles and wild beasts and had the people settle the central lands. The people were cold, and they clothed them; hungry, and they fed them. Because the people dwelt in trees and fell to the ground, dwelt in caves and became ill, the sages built houses for them.

They fashioned crafts so the people could provide themselves with implements. They made trade to link together those who had and those who had not and medicine to save them from premature death. They taught the people to bury and make sacrifices [to the dead] to enlarge their sense of gratitude and love. They gave rites to set order and precedence, music to vent melancholy, government to direct idleness, and punishments to weed out intransigence. When the people cheated each other, the sages invented tallies and seals, weights and measures to make them honest. When they attacked each other, they fashioned walls and towns, armor and weapons for them to defend themselves. So when dangers came, they prepared the people; and when calamity arose, they defended the people.

But now the Daoists maintain:

> Till the sages are dead,
> theft will not end ...
> so break the measures, smash the
> scales,
> and the people will not contend.

These are thoughtless remarks indeed, for humankind would have died out long ago if there had been no sages in antiquity. Men have neither feathers nor fur, neither scales nor shells to ward off heat and cold, neither talons nor fangs to fight for food....

But now the Daoists advocate "doing nothing" as in high antiquity. Such is akin to criticizing a man who wears furs in winter by asserting that it is easier to make linen, or akin to criticizing a man who eats when he is hungry by asserting that it is easier to take a drink....

This being so, what can be done? Block them or nothing will flow; stop them or nothing will move. Make humans of these people, burn their books, make homes of their dwellings, make clear the way of the former kings to guide them, and "the widowers, the widows, the orphans, the childless, and the diseased all shall have care." This can be done.

Q *How might the author of the first selection have responded to Han Yu's arguments? Which author appears to make the better case for his chosen ideological preference?*

Sources: Excerpt from *Sources of Chinese Tradition*, Vol. 1, 2nd ed., by William Theodore de Bary and Irene Bloom, pp. 570–573. Copyright © 1999 by Columbia University Press. Reprinted with permission of the publisher. From *Chinese Civilization and Bureaucracy*, by Etienne Balasz. Copyright © 1964 by Yale University Press.

Local Government The Song Dynasty maintained the local government institutions that it had inherited from its predecessors. At the base of the government pyramid was the district (or county), governed by a magistrate. The magistrate, assisted by his staff of three or four officials and several other menial employees, was responsible for maintaining law and order and collecting taxes within his jurisdiction. A district could exceed 100,000 people. Below the district was the basic unit of Chinese government, the village. Because villages were so numerous in China, the central government did not appoint an official at that level and allowed the villages to administer themselves. Village government was normally in the hands of a council of elders, most often assisted by a chief. The council, usually composed of the heads of influential families in the village, maintained the local irrigation and transportation network, adjudicated local disputes, organized and maintained a militia, and assisted in collecting taxes (usually paid in grain) and delivering them to the district magistrate.

As a rule, most Chinese had little involvement with government matters. When they had to deal with the government, they almost always turned to their village officials. Although the district magistrate was empowered to settle local civil disputes, most villagers preferred to resolve problems among themselves. It was expected that the magistrate and his staff would supplement their income by charging for such services, a practice that reduced the costs of the central government but also provided an opportunity for bribes, a problem that continued to plague the Chinese bureaucracy down to modern times.

The Economy   During the long period between the Sui and the Song, the Chinese economy, like the government, grew considerably in size and complexity. China was still an agricultural society, but major changes were taking place within the economy and the social structure. The urban sector of the economy was becoming increasingly important, new social classes were beginning to appear, and the economic focus of the empire was beginning to shift from the Yellow River valley in the north to the Yangzi River valley in the center—a process that was encouraged both by the expansion of cultivation in the Yangzi delta and by the control exerted over the north by nomadic peoples during the Song.

Land Reform   The economic revival began shortly after the rise of the Tang. During the long period of internal division, land had become concentrated in the hands of noble families, and most peasants were reduced to serfdom or slavery. The early Tang tried to reduce the power of the landed nobility and maximize tax revenues by adopting the ancient "well-field" system, in which land was allocated to farmers for life in return for an annual tax payment and three weeks of conscript labor.

At first, the new system was vigorously enforced and led to increased rural prosperity and government revenue. But eventually, the rich and the politically influential, including some of the largest Buddhist monasteries, learned to manipulate the system for their own benefit and accumulated huge tracts of land. The growing population, bolstered by a rise in food production and the extended period of social stability, also put steady pressure on the system. Finally, the government abandoned the effort to equalize landholdings and returned the land to private hands while attempting to prevent inequalities through the tax system. The failure to resolve the land problem—along with the climatic changes mentioned earlier—contributed to the fall of the Tang Dynasty in the early tenth century, although the reversion of farmlands to private hands did result in more efficient production in some instances as well as an expansion of the long-distance trade in food products.

The Song tried to resolve the land problem by returning to the successful programs of the early Tang and reducing the power of the wealthy landed aristocrats. During the late eleventh century, the reformist official Wang Anshi (1021–1086) attempted to limit the size of landholdings through progressive land taxes and provided cheap credit to poor farmers to help them avoid bankruptcy. His reforms met with some success, but other developments probably contributed more to the general agricultural prosperity under the Song. These included the opening of new lands in the Yangzi River valley, improvements in irrigation techniques such as the chain pump (a circular chain of square pallets on a treadmill that enabled farmers to lift considerable amounts of water or mud to a higher level), and the introduction of a new strain of quick-growing rice from Southeast Asia, which permitted farmers in warmer regions to plant and harvest two crops each year. It was during the Song Dynasty that rice became the main food crop for the Chinese people.

An Increase in Manufacturing   Major changes also took place in the Chinese urban economy, which witnessed significant growth in manufacturing and trade. This process began under the Tang Dynasty, but it was not entirely a product of deliberate state policy. In fact, early Tang rulers shared some of the traditional prejudice against commercial activities that had been prevalent under the Han and enacted a number of regulations that restricted trade and industry. As under the Han, the state maintained monopolies over key commodities such as salt.

Despite the restrictive policies of the state, the manufacturing sector grew steadily larger and more complex, helped by several new technological developments. During the Tang, the Chinese mastered the art of manufacturing steel by mixing cast iron and wrought iron. The blast furnace was heated to a high temperature by burning coal, which had been used as a fuel in China from about the fourth century C.E. The resulting product was used in the manufacture of swords, sickles, and even suits of armor. By the eleventh century, more than 35,000 tons of steel were being produced annually. The introduction of cotton from India offered new opportunities in textile production. Gunpowder was invented by the Chinese during the Tang Dynasty and used primarily for explosives and a primitive flamethrower; it reached the West via the Arabs in the twelfth century.

The Expansion of Commerce   The nature of trade was also changing. In the past, most long-distance trade had been undertaken by state monopolies. By the time of the Song, private commerce was being actively encouraged, and many merchants engaged in shipping as well as in wholesale and retail trade. The construction of the Grand Canal, as well as the expansion of the road system under the Tang, facilitated a dramatic increase in the regional trade network. Guilds began to appear, along with a new money economy. Paper currency began to be used in the eighth and ninth centuries. Credit (at first called "flying money") also made its first appearance during the Tang. With the increased circulation of paper money, banking began to develop as merchants found that strings of copper coins were too cumbersome for their increasingly complex operations. Unfortunately, early issues of paper currency were not backed by metal coinage and led to price

COMPARATIVE ESSAY

The Spread of Technology

SCIENCE & TECHNOLOGY

From the invention of stone tools and the discovery of fire to the introduction of agriculture and the writing system, mastery of technology has been a driving force in the history of human evolution. But why do some human societies appear to be much more advanced in their use of technology than others? People living on the island of New Guinea, for example, began cultivating local crops like taro and bananas as early as ten thousand years ago but never took the next steps toward creating a complex society until the arrival of Europeans many millennia later. Advanced societies had begun to emerge in the Western Hemisphere during the classical era, but none had discovered the use of the wheel or the smelting of metals for tool making. Writing was in its infancy there.

Technological advances appear to take place for two reasons: need and opportunity. Farming peoples throughout the world needed to control the flow of water, so in areas where water was scarce or unevenly distributed, they learned to practice irrigation to make resources available throughout the region. Peoples living in the Pacific Ocean learned how to read the stars and the ocean currents in order to navigate from island to island. Sometimes, however, opportunity strikes by accident (as in the legendary story of the Chinese princess who dropped a silkworm cocoon in her cup of hot tea, thereby initiating a series of discoveries that resulted in the manufacture of silk) or when new technology is introduced from a neighboring region (as when the discovery of tin in Anatolia launched the Bronze Age throughout the Middle East).

The most important factor enabling societies to keep abreast of the latest advances in technology, it would appear, is participation in the global trade and communications network. In this respect, the relative ease of communications between the Mediterranean Sea and the Indus River valley represented a major advantage for the Abbasid Empire, as the peoples living there had rapid access to all the resources and technological advances in that part of the world. China was more isolated from other major civilizations by distance, but with its size and high level of cultural achievement, it was almost a continent in itself and was able to communicate with countries to the west via the Silk Road and the South China Sea.

Societies that were not linked to this vast network were at an enormous disadvantage in keeping up with new developments in technology. The peoples of New Guinea, at the far end of the Indonesian islands, had little or no contact with the outside world. In the Western Hemisphere, a trade network did begin to take shape between societies in the Andes and their counterparts in Mesoamerica. But because of difficulties in communication, contacts were more intermittent. As a result, technological developments taking place in distant Eurasia did not reach the Americas until the arrival of the conquistadors.

Q *In what ways did China contribute to the spread of technology and ideas throughout the world during the period from the Sui dynasty to the beginning of the Ming Dynasty? How did China benefit from the process?*

inflation. Equally useful, if more prosaic, was the invention of the abacus, an early form of calculator that simplified the computations needed for commercial transactions.

The Silk Road   Long-distance trade, both overland and by sea, expanded under the Tang and the Song. Trade with countries and peoples to the west had been carried on for centuries, but it had declined dramatically between the fourth and sixth centuries C.E. as a result of the collapse of the Han and Roman Empires. It began to revive with the rise of the Tang and the simultaneous unification of much of the Middle East under the Arabs. During the Tang era, the route that we call the Silk Road reached its zenith. Along the Silk Road to China came raw hides, furs, and horses. Chinese aristocrats, their appetite for material consumption stimulated by the affluence of Chinese society during much of the Tang and Song periods, were fascinated by the exotic goods and the flora and fauna of the desert and the tropical lands of the South Seas. Much of the trade was carried by the Turkic-speaking Uighurs or Iranian-speaking Sogdians (SAHG-dee-unz) from Central Asia. During the Tang, Uighur caravans of two-humped Bactrian camels (a hardy variety native to Iran and regions to the northeast) carried goods back and forth between China and the countries of South Asia and the Middle East.

In actuality, the Silk Road was composed of a number of separate routes. The first to be used, probably because of the jade found in the mountains south of Khotan (koh-TAHN), ran along the southern rim of the Taklimakan (tah-kluh-muh-KAHN) Desert via Kashgar (KASH-gahr) and thence through the Pamir (pah-MEER) Mountains into Bactria. The first Buddhist missionaries traveled this route between India and China. Eventually, however, this area began to dry up, and traders were forced to seek other routes. From a climatic standpoint, the best route for the Silk Road was to the north of the Tian Shan (TEE-en SHAHN) (Heavenly Mountains), where moisture-laden northwesterly winds created pastures where animals could graze. But the area was frequently infested by bandits who preyed on unwary travelers. Most caravans therefore followed the southern route, which passed along the northern fringes of the Taklimakan Desert to Kashgar and down into northwestern India. Travelers avoided the direct route through the desert (in the Uighur language, the name means "go in and you won't come out") and trudged from oasis to oasis along the southern slopes of the Tian Shan following a route littered by animal bones. The oases were created by the water runoff from winter snows in the mountains and dried up in the searing heat of the desert summer.

The eastern terminus of the Silk Road was the city of Chang'an, perhaps the wealthiest city in the world during the Tang era. The city's days as China's foremost metropolis were numbered, however. Chronic droughts throughout the region made it more and more difficult to supply the city with food, and the growing power of Turkic-speaking peoples such as the Uighurs in the hinterlands made the city increasingly vulnerable to attack by rebel forces. During the later Tang, the imperial court was periodically shifted to the old secondary capital of Luoyang (LWOH-yahng). The Song Dynasty, a product of the steady drift of the national center of gravity toward the south, was forced to abandon Chang'an altogether as a historic symbol of imperial greatness.

The Maritime Route   The Silk Road was so hazardous that shipping goods by sea became increasingly popular. China had long been engaged in sea trade with other countries in the region, but most of the commerce was originally in the hands of Korean, Japanese, Southeast Asian, or Middle Eastern merchants. Under the Song, however, Chinese maritime trade was stimulated by the invention of the compass and technical improvements in shipbuilding such as the widespread use of the sternpost rudder and the lug sail (which enabled ships to sail close to the wind). If the observations of Marco Polo, an Italian merchant who traveled to China in the late thirteenth century and then served as an official at the court of Khubilai Khan (KOO-blah KAHN), can be believed, by the thirteenth century, Chinese junks had as many as four masts and could carry several hundred men, many more than contemporary ships in the West. The Chinese governor of Canton in the early twelfth century remarked:

> According to the government regulations concerning sea-going ships, the larger ones can carry several hundred men, and the smaller ones may have more than a hundred men on board.... The ships' pilots are acquainted with the configuration of the coasts; at night they steer by the stars, and in the daytime by the Sun. In dark weather they look at the south-pointing needle. They also use a line a hundred feet long with a hook at the end, which they let down to take samples of mud from the sea-bottom; by its appearance and smell they can determine their whereabouts.[3]

A wide variety of goods passed through Chinese ports. The Chinese exported tea, silk, and porcelain to the countries beyond the South China Sea, receiving exotic woods, precious stones, cotton from India, and various tropical goods in exchange. Seaports on the southern China coast exported sweet oranges, lemons, and peaches in return for grapes, walnuts, and pomegranates. The major port of exit in southern China was Canton (also known as Guangzhou), where an estimated 100,000 merchants lived. Their activities were controlled by an imperial commissioner sent from the capital.

Some of this trade was a product of the tribute system, which the Chinese rulers used as an element of their foreign policy. The Chinese viewed the outside world as they viewed their own society—in a hierarchical manner. Rulers of smaller countries along the periphery were viewed as "younger brothers" of the Chinese emperor and owed fealty to him. Foreign rulers who accepted the relationship were required to pay tribute and to promise not to harbor enemies of the Chinese Empire. But the foreign rulers also benefited from the relationship. Not only did it confer legitimacy on them, but they often received magnificent gifts from their "elder brother" as a reward for good behavior. Merchants from their countries also gained access to the vast Chinese market.

Society in Traditional China   These political and economic changes affected Chinese society in several ways during the Tang and Song era. For one thing, it became much more complex. Whereas previously China had been almost exclusively rural, with a small urban class of merchants, artisans, and workers almost entirely dependent on the state, the cities had now grown into an important, if statistically still insignificant, part of the population. Urban life, too, had changed. Cities were no longer primarily administrative centers dominated by officials and their families but now included a much broader mix of officials, merchants, artisans, peddlers, and entertainers. Unlike European cities, however, Chinese cities did not possess special privileges that protected their residents from the rapacity of the central government.

In the countryside, equally significant changes were taking place as the relatively rigid demarcation between the landed aristocracy and the mass of the rural population gave way to a more complex mixture of landed gentry, free farmers, sharecroppers, and landless laborers. There was also a class of "base people," consisting of actors, butchers, and prostitutes, who possessed only limited legal rights and were not permitted to take the civil service examination.

The Rise of the Gentry   Under the early Tang, powerful noble families not only possessed a significant part of the national wealth, but also dominated high positions in the imperial government, just as they had at the end of the Han dynasty four hundred years earlier. Some Tang rulers, notably Empress Wu Zhao (woo ZHOW) in the late seventh century, sought to limit the power of the great families by recruiting officials through the civil service examinations, but in the end it was the expansion of regional power—often under non-Chinese military governors—after the An Lushan revolt that sounded the death knell to the aristocratic system.

Perhaps the most significant development during the Song Dynasty was the rise of the landed gentry as the most influential force in Chinese society. The gentry class controlled much of the wealth in the rural areas and, under the Song, produced the majority of the candidates for the bureaucracy. By virtue of their possession of land and specialized knowledge of the Confucian classics, the gentry had replaced the aristocracy as the political and economic elite of Chinese society. Unlike the aristocracy, however, the gentry did not form an exclusive class separated by the accident of birth from the remainder of the population. Upward and downward mobility between the scholar-gentry class and the remainder of the population was not uncommon and may have been a key factor in the stability and longevity of the system. A position in the bureaucracy opened the doors to wealth and prestige for the individual and his family, but it was no guarantee of success, and the fortunes of individual families might experience a rapid rise and fall. The soaring ambitions and arrogance of China's landed gentry are vividly described in the following wish list set in poetry by a young bridegroom of the Tang Dynasty:

> *Chinese slaves to take charge of treasury and barn,*
> *Foreign slaves to take care of my cattle and sheep.*
> *Strong-legged slaves to run by saddle and stirrup when I ride,*
> *Powerful slaves to till the fields with might and main,*
> *Handsome slaves to play the harp and hand the wine;*
> *Slim-waisted slaves to sing me songs, and dance;*
> *Dwarfs to hold the candle by my dining-couch.*[4]

For affluent Chinese in this era, life offered many more pleasures than had been available to their forebears. As a result of increased contacts with the outside world brought about as the result of the rise of the Silk Road and the new maritime routes, the country was much more cosmopolitan than it had been in previous centuries. There were new forms of entertainment, such as playing cards and chess (brought from India, although an early form had been invented in China during the Zhou dynasty); new forms of transportation, such as the paddle-wheel boat and horseback riding (made possible by the introduction of the stirrup); better means of communication (block printing was first invented in the eighth century C.E.); and new tastes for the palate introduced from lands beyond the frontier. Tables and chairs, as well as chopsticks (known in China as "fast ones"), came into common usage in the home during the Song era. Tea had been introduced from the Burmese frontier by monks as early as the Han dynasty, and brandy and other concentrated spirits produced by the distillation of alcohol made their appearance in the seventh century. Tea began to emerge as a national drink and took on ritual significance among intellectuals, poets, and Buddhist monks who believed that it could stimulate the brain cells and focus the mind.

Village and Family   The vast majority of the Chinese people still lived off the land in villages ranging in size from a few dozen residents to several thousand. A farmer's life was bounded by his village. Although many communities were connected to the outside world by roads or rivers, most Chinese rarely left the confines of their native village except for an occasional visit to a nearby market town. This isolation was psychological as well as physical, for most Chinese identified with their immediate environment and had difficulty envisioning themselves living beyond the bamboo hedges or mud walls that marked the limit of their horizon.

An even more basic unit than the village in the lives of most Chinese, of course, was the family. The ideal was the joint family with at least three generations under one roof. Because rice farming was heavily labor-intensive, the tradition of the joint family was especially prevalent in the south. When a son married, he was expected to bring his new wife back to live in his parents' home. Often the parents added a new wing to the house for the new family. Women who did not marry remained in the home where they grew up.

Chinese village architecture reflected these traditions. Most family dwellings were simple, consisting of one or at most two rooms. They were usually constructed of dried mud, stone, or brick, depending on available materials and the prosperity of the family. Roofs were of thatch or tile, and the floors were usually of packed dirt. Large houses were often built in a square around an inner courtyard, thus guaranteeing privacy from the outside world.

Within the family unit, the eldest male theoretically ruled as an autocrat. He was responsible for presiding over ancestral rites at an altar, usually in the main room of the house. He had traditional legal rights over his wife, and if she did not provide him with a male heir, he was permitted to take a second wife. She, however, had no recourse to divorce. As the old saying went, "Marry a chicken, follow the chicken; marry a dog, follow the dog." Wealthy Chinese might keep concubines, who lived in a separate room in the house and sometimes competed with the legal wife for precedence.

In accordance with Confucian tradition, children were expected, above all, to obey their parents, who not only determined their children's careers but also selected their marriage partners. Filial piety was viewed as an absolute moral good, above virtually all other moral obligations. Even today, duty to one's parents is considered important in traditional Chinese families, and the tombstones of deceased Chinese are often decorated with tile paintings depicting the filial acts that they performed during their lifetime.

Women in Tang China   The tradition of male superiority continued from ancient times into the medieval era, especially under the southern Song when it was reinforced by Neo-Confucianism. Female children were considered less desirable than males because they could not undertake heavy work in the fields or carry on the family traditions. Women were not permitted to take the civil service examinations. Poor families often sold their daughters to wealthy villagers to serve as concubines, and female infanticide was not uncommon in times of famine to ensure that there would be food for the remainder of the family. Concubines had few legal rights; female domestic servants, even fewer.

On the surface, conditions improved for women in China during the era of Tang rule, in that a number of court ladies were active in politics, and several were prominent in the entertainment world. Nevertheless, it is doubtful that such limited achievements among the elite trickled down to the mass population. In any event, any progress in women's rights was reversed under the Song, when Chinese social customs began to reflect a more rigid interpretation of Confucian orthodoxy. During the Song era, two new practices emerged that changed the equation for women seeking to obtain a successful marriage contract. First, a new form of dowry appeared. Whereas previously the prospective husband offered the bride's family a bride price, now the bride's parents were expected to pay the groom's family a dowry. With the prosperity that characterized Chinese society during much of the Song era, affluent parents sought to buy a satisfactory husband for their daughter, preferably one with a higher social standing and good prospects for an official career.

A second source of marital bait during the Song period was the promise of a bride with tiny bound feet. The process of **foot binding**, carried out on girls aged five to thirteen, was excruciatingly painful, as it bent and compressed the foot to half its normal size by imprisoning it in restrictive bandages. But the procedure was often performed by ambitious mothers intent on assuring that their daughters would have the best possible prospects for marriage. A zealous mother would also want her daughter to have a competitive edge in dealing with the other wives and concubines of her future husband. Bound feet represented submissiveness and self-discipline, two of the required attributes of an ideal Confucian wife.

Throughout northern China, foot binding became common under the Song for women of all social classes. It was less widespread in southern China, where the cultivation of wet rice could not be carried out with bandaged feet; there it tended to be limited to the scholar-gentry class. Still, most Chinese women with bound feet contributed to the labor force to supplement the family income. Tattooing the body was also not uncommon, in contrast to earlier times, when it had only been applied to criminals as a means of identification and humiliation.

As in most traditional cultures, there were exceptions to the low status of women in Chinese society. Women had substantial property rights and retained control over their dowries even after divorce or the death of the husband. Women were actively involved in commerce, especially in the major cities, where they ran restaurants and guesthouses, or served as owners or clerks of textile shops catering

Proper Etiquette in Tang Dynasty China

FAMILY & SOCIETY

During the Tang Dynasty (618–907), standards for female behavior became highly ritualized, as Confucian social norms, originally codified by the female historian Ban Zhao (Bahn-ZHOW) several hundred years earlier, were applied with increasing rigor. Song Ruozhao (Song Rwo-ZHOW) the daughter of a senior court official, was appointed by Emperor Dezong (Duh-DZONG) (r. 779–805) to instruct the royal princesses in proper etiquette. It was perhaps in this capacity that she—or her older sister Ruohua (Rwo-HWAH)—wrote the influential *Analects for Women*, an instructional pamphlet designed to provide guidance for women in the proper behavior to adopt in various forms of activity.

In some cases, the advice is almost laughingly specific, as when the hostess is instructed to adjust her clothing, place her hands up her sleeves, and walk slowly to the door where, with lowered voice, she invites the guest inside her house. The pamphlet apparently remained in print until the Qing (Ching) Dynasty in the nineteenth century.

Song Ruozhao, *Analects for Women*

Establishing Oneself as a Person

To be a woman, you must first learn how to establish yourself as a person. The way to do this is simply by working hard to establish one's purity and chastity. By purity, one keeps one's self undefiled; by chastity, one preserves one's honor.

When walking, don't turn your head; when talking, don't open your mouth wide; when sitting, don't move your knees; when standing, don't rustle your skirts; when happy, don't exult with loud laughter; when angry, don't raise your voice. The inner and outer quarters are distinct; the sexes should be segregated. Don't peer over the outer wall or go beyond the outer courtyard. If you have to go outside, cover your face; if you peep outside, conceal yourself as much as possible. Do not be on familiar terms with men outside the family; have nothing to do with women of bad character. Establish your proper self so as to become a [true] human being....

to female customers. Wives were frequently an influential force in the home, often handling the accounts and taking primary responsibility for raising the children. Some were active in politics. The outstanding example was Wu Zhao (c. 625–c. 706), popularly known as Empress Wu. Selected by Emperor Tang Taizong as a concubine, after his death she rose to a position of supreme power at court. At first, she was content to rule through her sons, but in 690, she declared herself empress of China. To bolster her claim of legitimacy, she cited a Buddhist *sutra* to the effect that a woman would rule the world seven hundred years after the death of Siddhartha Gautama. For her presumption, she has been vilified by later Chinese historians, but she was actually a quite capable ruler, strengthening the civil service examination system and initiating the process of selecting graduates of the examinations for the highest positions in government. During her last years, she reportedly fell under the influence of courtiers and was deposed in 705, when she was probably around eighty.

Ritual Decorum: Learning Proper Etiquette

To be a woman one must learn the rules of ritual decorum. When you expect a female guest, carefully clean and arrange the furniture and tea implements. When she arrives, take time to adjust your clothing, and then, with light steps and your hands drawn up in your sleeves, walk slowly to the door and with lowered voice, invite her in. Ask after her health and how her family is doing. Be attentive to what she says. After chatting in a leisurely way, serve the tea. When she leaves, send her off in a proper manner....

If you are invited to someone's house, understand your female duties and help with the preparation of the tea. After having talked for a time, rise to leave. Don't overstay your welcome. If your hostess presses you to stay longer to share a meal, conduct yourself with propriety. Don't drink so much that your face turns red and you get sloppy in the handling of your chopsticks. Take your leave before all the food is gone and before you forget your manners....

Serving a Husband

Women leave their families to marry, and the husband is the master of the household [they marry into].... The husband is to be firm, the wife soft; conjugal affections follow from this. While at home, the two of you should treat each other with the formality and reserve of a guest. Listen carefully to and obey whatever your husband tells you. If he does something wrong, gently correct him. Don't be like those women who not only do not correct their husbands but actually lead them into indecent ways.... Don't imitate those shrewish wives who love to clash head on with their husbands all the time. Take care of your husband's clothing so that he is never cold in winter, and of his meals so that he never gets thin and sickly from not being fed enough. As a couple, you and your husband share the bitter and the sweet, poverty and riches. In life you share the same bed; in death the same grave....

Q *Is any of the advice contained in this passage relevant as proper etiquette today? If so, which advice? If not, why?*

Source: From *Nu Sishu*, 1854 Japanese edition, cited in William Theodore de Bary and Irene Bloom (eds.), *Sources of Chinese Tradition*, Vol. 1, 2nd ed. (New York: Columbia University Press, 1999), pp. 827–831.

EXPLOSION IN CENTRAL ASIA: THE MONGOL EMPIRE

The Mongols, who succeeded the Song as the rulers of China in the late thirteenth century, rose to power in Asia with stunning rapidity. In the 1160s when Genghis Khan (JING-uss *or* GENG-uss KAHN) (also known as Chinggis Khan), the founder of Mongol greatness, was born, the Mongols were a relatively obscure pastoral people in the area of modern-day Outer Mongolia. Like most of the nomadic peoples in the region, they were organized loosely into clans and tribes and even lacked a common name for themselves. Rivalry among the various tribes over pastureland, livestock, and booty was intense and increased at the end of the twelfth century as a result of a growing population and the consequent overgrazing of pastures. Since they had no source of subsistence besides their herds, the Mongols were, in the words of one historian, in a "state of stress."

This challenge was met by the great Mongol chieftain Genghis Khan (c. 1162–1227), whose original name was Temuchin (TEM-yuh-jin) (or Temujin). When Temuchin was still a child, his father, an impoverished noble of his tribe, was murdered by a rival, and the boy was forced to seek refuge in the wilderness. Described by one historian as tall, adroit, and vigorous, young Temuchin gradually unified the Mongol tribes through his prowess and the power of his personality. In 1206, he was elected Genghis Khan ("universal ruler") at a massive tribal meeting in the Gobi Desert. From that time on, he devoted himself to military pursuits. Mongol nomads were now forced to pay taxes and were subject to military conscription. "Man's highest joy," Genghis Khan reportedly remarked, "is in victory: to conquer one's enemies, to pursue them, to deprive them of their possessions, to make their beloved weep, to ride on their horses, and to embrace their wives and daughters."[5]

The army that Genghis Khan unleashed on the world was not exceptionally large—totaling less than 130,000 in 1227, at a time when the total Mongol population numbered between 1 million and 2 million. But their mastery of military tactics set the Mongols apart from their rivals. Their tireless flying columns of mounted warriors surrounded their enemies and harassed them like cattle, luring them into pursuit and then ambushing them with flank attacks. John Plano Carpini (PLAN-oh car-PEE-nee), a contemporary Franciscan friar, remarked:

> As soon as they discover the enemy they charge and each one unleashes three or four arrows. If they see that they can't break him, they retreat in order to entice the enemy

The Art Archive at Art Resource, NY

The Destruction of Baghdad by the Mongols. *In 1258, the Mongols attacked the city of Baghdad and brought an end to the Abbasid caliphate, which had prospered for nearly four centuries. Their treatment of the local population was brutal. Cities were razed to the ground, while dams and other irrigation works were destroyed, reducing the people to starvation. In this fourteenth-century miniature, Mongol cavalrymen are seen attacking the troops of the last of the Baghdad caliphs. Two decades later, Mongol warriors defeated the armies of the Song and established the Yuan dynasty in China in 1279.*

to pursue, thus luring him into an ambush prepared in advance.... Their military stratagems are numerous. At the moment of an enemy cavalry attack, they place prisoners and foreign auxiliaries in the forefront of their own position, while positioning the bulk of their own troops on the right and left wings to envelop the adversary, thus giving the enemy the impression that they are more numerous than in reality.[6]

In the years after the election of Temuchin as universal ruler, the Mongols defeated tribal groups to their west and then turned their attention to the non-Chinese kingdoms of northern China. There they discovered that their adversaries were armed with a weapon called a fire-lance, an early form of flamethrower. Gunpowder had been invented in China during the late Tang period, and by the early thirteenth century, a fire-lance had been developed that could spew out flames and projectiles a distance of 30 or 40 yards, inflicting considerable damage on the enemy. The following account of a battle in the 1230s between Mongol forces and the army of the state of Jin in northern China describes the effects of this weapon:

> On the fifth day of the fifth month they sacrificed to Heaven, secretly prepared fire-lances, and embarked 450 Chin soldiers outside the south gate.... During the night they killed the enemy guards outside the dikes, and reached the Wang family temple....
> Kuan-Nu divided his small craft into squadrons of five, seven and ten boats, which came out from behind the defenses and caught the Mongols both from front and rear, using the fire-spouting lances. The Mongols could not stand up to this and fled, losing more than 3500 men drowned. Finally their stockades were burnt, and our force returned.[7]

Before the end of the thirteenth century, the fire-lance had evolved into the much more effective handgun and cannon. These inventions came too late to save China from the Mongols, however, and were transmitted to Europe by the early fourteenth century by foreigners employed by the Mongol rulers of China.

While some Mongol armies were engaged in the conquest of northern China, others traveled farther afield and advanced as far as central Europe. Only the death of Genghis Khan in 1227 may have prevented an all-out Mongol attack on western Europe. In 1231, the Mongols attacked Persia and then defeated the Abbasids at Baghdad in 1258. Mongol forces attacked the Song from the west in the 1260s and finally defeated the remnants of the Song navy in 1279. Once again, as had occurred after the fall of the Han dynasty, the heartland of China was placed under alien rule.

By then, the Mongol Empire was quite different from what it had been under its founder. Prior to the conquests of Genghis Khan, the Mongols had been purely nomadic. They spent their winters in the southern plains, where they found suitable pastures for their cattle, and traveled north in the summer to wooded areas where the water was sufficient. They lived in round, felt-covered tents (called yurts), which were lightly constructed so that they could be easily transported. For food, the Mongols depended on milk and meat from their herds and game from hunting.

To administer the new empire, Genghis Khan had set up a capital city at Karakorum (khah-rah-KOR-um), in present-day Outer Mongolia, but prohibited his fellow Mongols from practicing sedentary occupations or living in cities. But under his successors, the Mongols began to adapt to their conquered areas. As one khan remarked, quoting his Chinese adviser, "Although you inherited the Chinese

Empire on horseback, you cannot rule it from that position." Mongol aristocrats began to enter administrative positions, while commoners took up sedentary occupations as farmers or merchants.[8]

The territorial nature of the empire also changed. Following tribal custom, at the death of the ruling khan, the territory was distributed among his heirs. The once-united empire of Genghis Khan was thus divided into several separate **khanates** (KHAH-nayts), each under the autonomous rule of one of his sons by his principal wife. One of his sons was awarded the khanate of Chaghadai (chag-huh-DY) in Central Asia with its capital at Samarkand; another ruled Persia from the conquered city of Baghdad; a third took charge of the khanate of Kipchak (KIP-chahk), commonly known as the Golden Horde. But it was one of his grandsons, named Khubilai Khan (1215–1294), who completed the conquest of the Song and established a new Chinese dynasty, called the Yuan (from a phrase in the *Book of Changes* referring to the "original creative force" of the universe). Khubilai moved the capital of China northward from Hangzhou to Khanbaliq ("city of the khan"), which was located on a major trunk route from the Great Wall to the plains of northern China. Later the city would be known by the Chinese name Beijing (bay-ZHING), or Peking (pee-KING) ("northern capital").

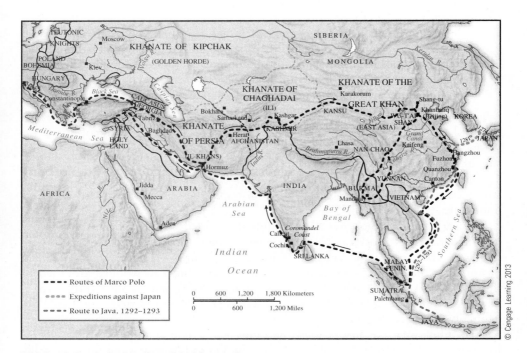

© Cengage Learning 2013

MAP 10.2 Asia Under the Mongols

This map traces the expansion of Mongol power throughout Eurasia in the thirteenth century. After the death of Genghis Khan in 1227, the empire was divided into four separate khanates.

Mongol Rule in China

At first, China's new rulers exhibited impressive vitality. Under the leadership of the talented Khubilai Khan, the Yuan continued to flex their muscles by attempting to expand their empire. Mongol armies advanced into the Red River valley and reconquered Vietnam, which had declared its independence after the fall of the Tang three hundred years earlier. Mongol fleets were launched against Malay kingdoms in Java and Sumatra and also against the islands of Japan. Only the expedition against Vietnam succeeded, however, and even that success was temporary. The Vietnamese counterattacked and eventually drove the Mongols back across the border. The attempted conquest of Japan was even more disastrous, as a massive storm destroyed the Mongol fleet, killing thousands. Yuan rulers belatedly discovered that familiar tactics such as cavalry charges and siege warfare were less effective in distant lands composed of unfamiliar terrain.

The Mongols had more success in governing China. After a failed attempt to administer their conquest as they had ruled their own tribal society (some advisers reportedly even suggested that the plowed fields be transformed into pastures), Mongol rulers adapted to the Chinese political system and made use of local talents in the bureaucracy. The tripartite division of the administration into civilian, military, and censorate was retained, as were the six ministries. The civil service system, which had been abolished in the north in 1237 and in the south forty years later, was revived in the early fourteenth century. The state cult of Confucius was also restored, although Khubilai Khan himself remained a Buddhist.

But there were some key differences. Culturally, the Mongols were nothing like the Chinese and remained a separate class with their own laws. The highest positions in the bureaucracy were usually staffed by Mongols. Although some leading Mongols followed their ruler in converting to Buddhism, most commoners retained their traditional religion. Even those who adopted Buddhism chose the Lamaist (LAH-muh-ist) variety from Tibet, which emphasized divination and magic.

Despite these differences, the Mongols were able to rule China for nearly a century. The people of the north, after all, were used to foreign rule, and although those living farther to the south may have resented their alien conquerors, they probably came to respect the stability, unity, and economic prosperity that the Mongols initially brought to China, where they continued the relatively tolerant economic policies of the southern Song. By bringing much of the Eurasian landmass under a single rule, they encouraged long-distance trade, particularly along the Silk Road, now dominated by Muslim merchants from Central Asia. To promote trade, the Grand Canal was extended from the Yellow River to the capital. Adjacent to the canal, a paved highway was constructed that extended all the way from the Song capital of Hangzhou to its Mongol counterpart at Khanbaliq.

The capital was a magnificent city. According to the Italian merchant Marco Polo, who resided there during the reign of Khubilai Khan, it was 24 miles in diameter and surrounded by thick walls of earth penetrated by a dozen massive gates. He described the old Song capital of Hangzhou as a noble city where "so many pleasures may be found that one fancies himself to be in Paradise."

Ironically, while many of their subjects prospered, the Mongols themselves often did not. Burdened by low wages and heavy military obligations that left them little time for their herds, many Mongol warriors became so impoverished

FILM & HISTORY

The Adventures of Marco Polo (1938) and Marco Polo (2007)

The famous story of Marco Polo's trip to East Asia in the late thirteenth century has sparked the imagination of Western readers ever since. The son of an Italian merchant from Venice, Polo set off for China in 1270 and did not come back for twenty-four years, traveling east via the Silk Road and returning by sea across the Indian Ocean. Captured by the Genoese in 1298 and tossed into prison, he recounted his experiences to a professional writer known as Rusticello of Pisa. Copies of the resulting book, originally titled *Description of the World*, were soon circulating throughout Europe, and one even found its way into the baggage of Christopher Columbus, who used it as a source for information on the eastern lands he sought during his own travels. Marco Polo's adventures have appeared in numerous languages, thrilling readers around the world, and filmmakers have done their part, producing feature films about his exploits for modern audiences.

But did Marco Polo actually visit China, or was the book an elaborate hoax? In recent years, some historians have expressed doubts about the veracity of his account. Frances Wood, author of *Did Marco Polo Go to China?* (1996), provoked a lively debate in the halls of academe with her suggestion that he may simply have related tales that he had heard from contemporaries.

Such reservations aside, filmmakers have long been fascinated by Marco Polo's story. The first Hollywood production, *The Adventures of Marco Polo* (1938), starred the prewar screen idol Gary Cooper, with Basil Rathbone as his evil nemesis in China. Like many film epics of the era, it was highly entertaining but was not historically accurate, and it used Western actors in all the main parts. The most recent version, a Hallmark Channel production called *Marco Polo*, appeared in 2007 and starred the young American actor Ian Somerhalder in the title role. The film is a reasonably faithful rendition of the book, with stirring battle scenes, the predictable "cast of thousands," and a somewhat unlikely love interest between Polo and a Mongolian princess thrown

that they were forced to sell their sons and daughters into slavery. In the end, the Yuan fell victim to the same fate that had afflicted other powerful dynasties in China. In fact, it was one of the shortest-lived of the great dynasties, lasting less than a century. Excessive spending on foreign conquest, inadequate tax revenues, factionalism and corruption at court and in the bureaucracy, and growing internal instability, brought about in part by a famine in central China in the 1340s, all contributed to the dynasty's demise. Khubilai Khan's successors lacked his administrative genius, and by the middle of the next century, the Yuan dynasty in China, like the Mongol khanates elsewhere in Central Asia, had begun to decline rapidly.

The immediate instrument of Mongol defeat was Zhu Yuanzhang (JOO yoo-wen-JAHNG), the son of a poor peasant in the lower Yangzi Valley. After losing most of his family in the famine of the 1340s, Zhu became an itinerant monk and then the leader of a gang of bandits. In the 1360s, unrest spread throughout the in. Although the lead character is not particularly convincing in the title role—after two grueling decades in Asia, he still bears a striking resemblance to a teenage surfing idol—the producers should be credited for their efforts to portray China as the most advanced civilization of its day. A number of Chinese inventions then unknown in Europe, such as paper money, explosives, and the compass, make their appearance in the film. Emperor Khubilai Khan (played by the veteran actor Brian Dennehy) does not project an imperial presence, however, and is unconvincing when he says that he would prefer someone who can speak the truth to power.

Scene from Adventures of Marco Polo *(1938). Marco Polo (Gary Cooper, gesturing on the right) confers with Kaidu (Alan Hale), leader of the Mongols.*

country, and after defeating a number of rivals, Zhu put an end to the disintegrating Yuan regime and declared the foundation of the new Ming (MING) ("bright") Dynasty (1369–1644).

The Mongols'
Place in History   The Mongols were the last, and arguably the greatest, of the nomadic peoples who came thundering out of the steppes of Central Asia, pillaging and conquering the territories of their adversaries. What caused this extraordinary burst of energy, and why were the Mongols so much more successful than their predecessors? Historians are divided. Some have suggested that drought and overpopulation may have depleted the available pasture on the steppes, yet another example of the unseen impact of environmental changes on human history. Others have cited the ambition and genius of Genghis Khan, who was able to arouse a sense of personal loyalty unusual in a

society where commitments were ordinarily of a tribal nature. Still others point to his reliance on the organizational unit known as the *ordos* (OR-dohz), described by the historian Samuel Adshead as "a system of restructuring tribes into decimal units whose top level of leadership was organized on bureaucratic lines."[9] Although the *ordos* system had been used by the Xiongnu and other nomadic peoples before them, the Mongols applied it to create disciplined military units that were especially effective against the relatively freewheeling tactics of their rivals on the steppes and devastating against the relatively immobile armies of the sedentary states in their path. Once organized, the Mongols used their superior horsemanship and blitzkrieg tactics effectively, while taking advantage of divisions within the enemy ranks and borrowing more advanced military technology.

Once in power, however, the Mongols' underlying weaknesses eventually proved fatal. Unlike some of their predecessors, the Mongols had difficulty making the transition from the nomadic life of the steppes to the sedentary life of the villages, and their unwieldy system of royal succession led to instability in their leadership ranks. Still, although the Mongol era was just a brief interlude in the long sweep of human history, it was rich in consequences.

The Mongols: A Reputation Undeserved?   The era of Mongol expansion has usually been portrayed as a tragic period in human history. The Mongols' conquests resulted in widespread death and suffering throughout the world. Nations and empires were humbled, cities destroyed, and irrigation systems laid waste. Then, just when the ravages of the era appeared to come to an end, bubonic plague, probably carried by lice hidden in the saddlebags of Mongol horsemen, decimated the population of Europe and the Middle East. Some regions lost as much as one-third of their population to massacre or starvation.

Few modern historians would dispute the brutality that characterized Mongol expansion. But some now point out that beyond the legacy of death and destruction, the Mongols also brought an era of widespread peace, known as the *Pax Mongolica* (PAKS *or* PAHKS mahn-GOH-lik-uh), to much of the Eurasian supercontinent and inaugurated what one scholar has described as "the idea of the unified conceptualization of the globe," creating a "basic information circuit" that spread commodities, ideas, and inventions from one end of the Eurasian supercontinent to the other. That being said, there is no denying that the Mongol invasions resulted in widespread suffering and misfortune to millions of people in their path. If there was a Mongol peace, it was, for many, the peace of death. In any event, such conditions were not destined to last.

THE MING DYNASTY

The Ming inaugurated a new era of greatness in Chinese history. Under a series of strong rulers, China extended its rule into Mongolia and Central Asia. The Ming even briefly reconquered Vietnam, which, after a thousand years of Chinese rule, had reclaimed its independence following the collapse of the Tang Dynasty in the tenth century. Along the northern frontier, the Emperor Yongle (YOONG-luh) (r. 1402–1424) strengthened the Great Wall and pacified the nomadic tribes that had troubled China in previous centuries. A tributary relationship was established with the Yi (YEE) Dynasty in Korea.

The internal achievements of the Ming were equally impressive. When they replaced the Mongols in the fourteenth century, the Ming turned to traditional Confucian institutions as a means of ruling their vast empire. These included the six ministries at the apex of the bureaucracy, the use of the civil service examinations to select members of the bureaucracy, and the division of the empire into provinces, districts, and counties. As before, Chinese villages were relatively autonomous, and local councils of elders continued to be responsible for adjudicating disputes, initiating local construction and irrigation projects, mustering a militia, and assessing and collecting taxes.

The society that was governed by this vast hierarchy of officials was a far cry from the predominantly agrarian society that had been ruled by the Han. In the burgeoning cities near the coast and along the Yangzi River valley, factories and workshops were vastly increasing the variety and output of their manufactured goods. The population had doubled, and new crops had been introduced, greatly expanding the food output of the empire.

The Voyages of Zheng He   In 1405, in a splendid display of Chinese maritime might, Emperor Yongle sent a fleet of Chinese trading ships under the eunuch admiral Zheng He (JEHNG-huh) through the Strait of Malacca and out into the Indian Ocean. There they traveled as far west as the east coast of Africa, stopping on the way at ports in South Asia. The size of the fleet was impressive: nearly 28,000 sailors on sixty-two ships, some of them junks larger by far than any other oceangoing vessels the world had yet seen (although the actual size of the larger ships is in dispute). China seemed about to become a direct participant in the vast trade network that extended as far west as the Atlantic Ocean, thereby culminating the process of opening China to the wider world that had begun with the Tang Dynasty.

Why the expeditions were undertaken has been a matter of some debate. Some historians assume that economic profit was the main reason. Others point to Yongle's native curiosity and note that the expedition—and the six others that followed it—returned not only with goods and a plethora of information about the outside world but also with some items unknown in China (the emperor was especially intrigued by the giraffes brought back from East Africa and placed them in the imperial zoo, where they were identified by soothsayers with the coming of good government). Others speculate that the emperor was seeking to ascertain the truth of rumors that his immediate predecessor, Emperor Jianwen (jee-AHN-wen) (1398–1402), had escaped to Southeast Asia to live in exile.

Whatever the case, the voyages resulted in a dramatic increase in Chinese knowledge about the world and the nature of ocean travel. They also brought massive profits for their sponsors, including individuals connected with Admiral Zheng He at court. This aroused resentment among conservatives within the bureaucracy, some of whom viewed commercial activities with a characteristic measure of Confucian disdain. One commented that an end to the voyages would provide the Chinese people with a respite "so that they can devote themselves to husbandry [agriculture] and schooling."

Shortly after Yongle's death, the voyages were discontinued, never to be revived. The decision had long-term consequences and in the eyes of many modern historians marks a turning inward of the Chinese state, away from commerce and toward a more traditional emphasis on agriculture, away from the exotic lands to the south and toward the heartland of the country in the Yellow River valley.

Ironically, the move toward the Yellow River had been initiated by Yongle himself when he had decided to move the Ming capital from Nanjing (nahn-JING), in central China, where the ships were built and the voyages launched, back to Beijing, where official eyes were firmly focused on the threat from beyond the Great Wall to the north. As a means of reducing that threat, Yongle ordered the resettlement of thousands of families from the fertile Yangzi Valley. The emperor presumably had not intended to set forces in motion that would divert the country from its contacts with the external world. After all, he had been the driving force behind Zheng He's voyages. But the end result was a shift in the balance of power from central China, where it had been since the southern Song Dynasty, back to northern China, where it had originated and would remain for the rest of the Ming era. China would not look outward again for more than four centuries.

Why Were Zheng He's Voyages Abandoned? Why the Ming government discontinued Zheng He's explorations and turned its attention back to domestic concerns has long been a quandary. Was it simply a consequence of court intrigues or the replacement of one emperor by another, or were deeper issues involved? Some scholars speculate that the real purpose of the voyages was not economic gain, but "power projection," and that when local rulers throughout the South Seas had been sufficiently intimidated to accept a tributary relationship with their "elder brother" in China, the voyages—which had been prohibitively expensive—were no longer necessary. On balance, it seems likely that the voyages were discontinued as the result of internal politics and the inordinate cost of the program.

One recent theory that has gained wide attention and spurred scholarly debate contends that the Chinese fleets did not limit their explorations to the Indian Ocean but actually circled the earth and discovered the existence of the Western Hemisphere. Although that theory has won few scholarly adherents, the voyages, and their abrupt discontinuance, remain one of the most fascinating enigmas in the history of China.

IN SEARCH OF THE WAY

By the time of the Sui dynasty, Buddhism and Daoism had emerged as major rivals of Confucianism as the ruling ideology of the state. But during the last half of the Tang Dynasty, Confucianism revived and once again became dominant at court, a position it would retain to the end of the dynastic period in the early twentieth century. Buddhist and Daoist beliefs, however, remained popular at the local level.

The Rise and Decline of Buddhism and Daoism As noted earlier, Buddhism arrived in China with merchants from India and found its first adherents among the merchant community and intellectuals intrigued by the new ideas. During the chaotic centuries following the collapse of the Han dynasty, Buddhism and Daoism appealed to those who were searching for more emotional and spiritual satisfaction than Confucianism could provide. Both faiths reached beyond the common people and found support among the ruling classes as well. The capital of Chang'an even had a small Christian church after Christianity was introduced to China by Syrian merchants in the sixth century C.E.

The Sinification of Buddhism   As Buddhism attracted more followers, it began to take on Chinese characteristics and divided into a number of separate sects. Some, like the **Chan** (Zen in Japanese) sect, called for mind training and a strict regimen as a means of seeking enlightenment, a technique that reflected Daoist ideas and appealed to many intellectuals. Others, like the **Pure Land** sect, stressed the role of devotion, an approach that was more appealing to ordinary Chinese, who lacked the time and inclination for strict monastic discipline. Still others were mystical sects, like **Tantrism** (TUHN-tri-zem), which emphasized the importance of magical symbols and ritual in seeking a preferred way to enlightenment. Some Buddhist groups, like their Daoist counterparts, had political objectives. The **White Lotus** sect, founded in 1133, often adopted the form of a rebel movement, seeking political reform or the overthrow of a dynasty and forecasting a new era when a "savior Buddha" would come to earth to herald the advent of a new age. Most believers, however, assimilated Buddhism into their daily lives, where it joined Confucian ideology and spirit worship as an element in the highly eclectic and tolerant Chinese worldview.

The burgeoning popularity of Buddhism continued into the early years of the Tang Dynasty. Early Tang rulers lent their support to the Buddhist monasteries that had been established throughout the country. Buddhist scriptures were regularly included in the civil service examinations, and Buddhist and Daoist advisers replaced shamans and Confucian scholar-officials as advisers at court. But ultimately, Buddhism and Daoism lost favor at court and were increasingly subjected to official persecution. Part of the reason was xenophobia. Envious Daoists and Confucianists made a point of criticizing the foreign origins of Buddhist doctrines, which one prominent Confucian scholar characterized as nothing but "silly relics." To deflect such criticism, Buddhists attempted to make the doctrine more Chinese, equating the Indian concept of *dharma* (law) with the Chinese concept of *Dao* (the Way). Emperor Tang Taizong ordered the Buddhist monk Xuan Zang to translate Lao Tzu's classic, *The Way of the Dao*, into Sanskrit, reportedly to show visitors from India that China had its own equivalent to the Buddhist scriptures. But another reason for this change of heart may have been financial. The great Buddhist monasteries had accumulated thousands of acres of land and serfs that were exempt from paying taxes to the state. Such wealth contributed to the corruption of the monks and other Buddhist officials and in turn aroused popular resentment and official disapproval. As the state attempted to eliminate the great landholdings of the aristocracy, the large monasteries also attracted its attention. During the later Tang, countless temples and monasteries were destroyed, and more than 100,000 monks were compelled to leave the monasteries and return to secular life.

Buddhism Under Threat   There were probably deeper cultural and ideological reasons for the growing antagonism between Buddhism and the state. By preaching the illusory nature of the material world, Buddhism was denying the very essence of Confucian teachings—the necessity for filial piety and hard work. By encouraging young Chinese to abandon their rice fields and seek refuge and wisdom in the monasteries, Buddhism was undermining the foundation stones of Chinese society—the family unit and the work ethic. In the final analysis, Buddhism was incompatible with the activist element in Chinese society, an orientation that was most effectively expressed by State Confucianism. In the competition with Confucianism for support by the state, Buddhism, like Daoism, was almost certain to lose, at least in the more this-worldly, secure, and prosperous milieu of Tang and Song China. The two doctrines continued to win converts at the local level, but official support ceased. In the meantime, Buddhism was under attack in Central Asia as well. In the eighth century, the Uighur kingdom adopted **Manichaeanism** (ma-nuh-KEE-uh-nizm), an offshoot of the ancient Zoroastrian religion with some influence from Christianity. Manichaeanism spread rapidly throughout the area and may have been a reason for the European belief that a Christian king (the legendary Prester John) ruled somewhere in Asia. By the tenth century, however, Islam was beginning to move east along the Silk Road, posing a severe threat to both Manichaean and Buddhist centers in the area. As its lifeline to the Indian subcontinent along the Silk Road was severed, Chinese Buddhism lost access to its spiritual roots and became increasingly subject to the pull of indigenous intellectual and social currents.

Neo-Confucianism: Into the vacuum left by the decline of Buddhism and
The Investigation Daoism stepped a revived Confucianism. As during the
of Things Han dynasty, the teachings of "master Kung" were used to
buttress the power and majesty of the state. The emperor continued to be seen as an intermediary between Heaven and earth, while his legitimacy was based not on the hereditary principle but on his talent and virtue, a central component of Confucian doctrine since the era of the "hundred schools" of philosophy in ancient times.

At the same time, however, it was a new form of Confucianism that had been significantly altered by its competition with Buddhist and Daoist teachings. Challenged by Buddhist and Daoist ideas about the nature of the universe, Confucian thinkers began to flesh out the spare metaphysical structure of classical Confucian doctrine with a set of sophisticated theories about the nature of the cosmos and humans' place in it. Although the origins of this effort can be traced to the early Tang period, it reached fruition during the intellectually prolific Song Dynasty, when it became the dominant ideology of the state.

The fundamental purpose of **Neo-Confucianism**, as the new doctrine was called, was to unite the metaphysical speculations of Buddhism and Daoism with the pragmatic Confucian approach to society. In response to Buddhism and Daoism, Neo-Confucianism maintained that the world is real, not illusory, and that fulfillment comes from participation, not withdrawal.

The primary contributor to this intellectual effort was the philosopher Zhu Xi (JOO SHEE). Raised during the southern Song era, Zhu Xi accepted the division of the world into a material world and a transcendent world, called by Neo-Confucianists the **Supreme Ultimate**, or *Tai Ji* (TY JEE). The Supreme Ultimate was roughly equivalent to the *Dao*, or Way, in classical Confucian philosophy.

To Zhu Xi, this Supreme Ultimate was a set of abstract principles governed by the law of *yin* and *yang* and the five elements.

Human beings served as a link between the two halves of this bifurcated universe. Although human beings live in the material world, each individual has an identity that is linked with the Supreme Ultimate, and the goal of individual action is to transcend the material world in a Buddhist sense to achieve an essential identity with the Supreme Ultimate. According to Zhu Xi and his followers, the means of transcending the material world is self-cultivation, which is achieved by the "investigation of things."

The School of Mind   During the remainder of the Song Dynasty and into the early years of the Ming, Zhu Xi's ideas became the central core of Confucian ideology and a favorite source of questions for the civil service examinations. But during the mid-Ming era, his ideas came under attack from a Confucian scholar named Wang Yangming (WAHNG yahng-MING). Wang and his supporters disagreed with Zhu Xi's focus on learning through an investigation of the outside world and asserted that the correct way to transcend the material world was through an understanding of self. According to this so-called **School of Mind**, the mind and the universe were a single unit. Knowledge was thus intuitive rather than empirical and was obtained through internal self-searching rather than through an investigation of the outside world. The debate is reminiscent of a similar disagreement between followers of the ancient Greek philosophers Plato and Aristotle. Plato had argued that all knowledge comes from within, while Aristotle argued that knowledge resulted from an examination of the external world. Wang Yangming's ideas attracted many followers during the Ming Dynasty, and the school briefly rivaled that of Zhu Xi in popularity among Confucian scholars. Nevertheless, it never won official acceptance, probably because it was too much like Buddhism in denying the importance of a life of participation and social action.

For the average Chinese, of course, an instinctive faith in the existence of household deities or nature spirits continued to take precedence over the intellectual ruminations of Buddhist monks or Confucian scholars. But a prevailing belief in the concept of *karma* and possible rebirth in a next life was one important legacy of the Buddhist connection, while a new manifestation of the Confucian concept of hierarchy was the village god—often believed to live in a prominent tree in the vicinity—who protected the community from wandering evil spirits.

THE APOGEE OF CHINESE CULTURE

The period between the Tang and the Ming Dynasties was in many ways the great age of achievement in Chinese literature and art. Enriched by Buddhist and Daoist images and themes, Chinese poetry and painting reached the pinnacle of their creativity. Porcelain emerged as the highest form of Chinese ceramics, and sculpture flourished under the influence of styles imported from India and Central Asia.

Literature   The development of Chinese literature was stimulated by two technological innovations: the invention of paper during the Han dynasty and the invention of woodblock printing during the Tang. At first, paper was used for clothing, wrapping material, toilet tissue, and even armor, but by the first century B.C.E., it was being used for writing as well.

In the seventh century C.E., the Chinese developed the technique of carving an entire page of text into a wooden block, inking it, and then pressing it onto a sheet of paper. Ordinarily, a text was printed on a long sheet of paper like a scroll. Then the paper was folded and stitched together to form a book. The earliest printed book known today is a Buddhist text published in 868 C.E.; it is more than 16 feet long. Although the Chinese eventually developed movable type as well, block printing continued to be used until relatively modern times because of the large number of Chinese characters needed to produce a lengthy text. Even with printing, books remained too expensive for most Chinese, but they did help popularize all forms of literary writing among the educated elite. Although literature was primarily a male occupation, a few women achieved prominence as a result of their creative prowess.

During the post-Han era, historical writing and essays continued to be favorite forms of literary activity. Each dynasty produced an official dynastic history of its predecessor to elucidate sober maxims about the qualities of good and evil in human nature, and local gazetteers added to the general knowledge about the various regions. Encyclopedias brought together in a single location information and documents about all aspects of Chinese life.

The Importance of Poetry   But it was in poetry, above all, that Chinese from the Tang to the Ming Dynasties most effectively expressed their literary talents. Chinese poems celebrated the beauty of nature, the changes of the seasons, and the joys of friendship and drink; others expressed sorrow at the brevity of life, old age, and parting. Given the frequency of imperial banishment and the requirement that officials serve away from their home district (an official means of preventing nepotism), it is little wonder that separation was an important theme. Love poems existed but were neither as intense as Western verse nor as sensual as Indian poetry.

The nature of the Chinese language imposed certain characteristics on Chinese poetry, the first being compactness. The most popular forms were four-line and eight-line poems, with five or seven words in each line. Because Chinese grammar does not rely on case or gender and makes no distinction between verb tenses, five-character Chinese poems were not only brief but often cryptic and ambiguous.

Two eighth-century Tang poets, Li Bo (LEE BOH), sometimes known as Li Bai or Li Taibo, and Du Fu, symbolized the genius of the era as well as the two most popular styles. Li Bo was a free spirit. His writing often centered on nature and shifted easily between moods of revelry and melancholy. One of his best-known poems is "Drinking Alone in Moonlight".

Where Li Bo was a carefree Daoist, Du Fu was a sober Confucian. His poems often dealt with historical issues or ethical themes, befitting a scholar-official living during the chaotic times of the late Tang. Many of his works reflect a concern with social injustice and the plight of the unfortunate rarely to be found in the writings of his contemporaries. Neither the poetry nor the prose of the great writers of the Tang and Song Dynasties was written for or ever reached the majority of the Chinese population. The millions of Chinese peasants and artisans living in rural villages and market towns acquired their knowledge of Chinese history, Confucian moralisms, and even Buddhist scripture from stories, plays, and songs passed down by storytellers, wandering minstrels, and itinerant monks in a rich oral tradition. One exception is the popular poem "Song of Lasting Pain" by the Tang poet Bo Ju-yi (BOH joo-YEE) (772–846), whose poignant portrayal of the emperor's consort Yang Guifei resonates among Chinese readers down to the present day.

Popular Culture   By the Song Dynasty, China had 60 million people, 1 million in Hangzhou alone. With the growth of cities came an increased demand for popular entertainment. Although the Tang Dynasty had imposed a curfew on urban residents, the Song did not. The city gates and bridges were closed at dark, but food stalls and entertainment continued through the night. At fairgrounds throughout the year, one could find comedians, musicians, boxers, fencers, wrestlers, acrobats, puppets and marionettes, shadow plays, and especially storytellers. Many of these arts had come from India centuries before and were now the favorite forms of amusement of the Chinese people.

The Chinese Novel   During the Yuan dynasty, new forms of literary creativity, including popular theater and the novel, began to appear. The two most famous novels were *Romance of the Three Kingdoms* and *Tale of the Marshes*. The former had been told orally for centuries, appearing in written form during the Song as a scriptbook for storytellers. It was first printed in 1321 but was not published for mass consumption until 1522. Each new edition was altered in some way, making the final edition a composite effort of generations of the Chinese imagination. The plot recounts the power struggle that took place among competing groups after the fall of the Han dynasty. Packed with court intrigues, descriptions of peasant life, and gripping battles, *Romance of the Three Kingdoms* stands as a magnificent epic, China's counterpart to the Mahabharata.

   Tale of the Marshes is an often violent tale of outlaw heroes who at the end of the northern Song banded together to oppose government taxes and official oppression. They rob those in power in order to share with the poor. *Tale of the Marshes* is the first prose fiction that describes the daily ordeal of ordinary Chinese people in their own language. Unlike the picaresque novel in the West, *Tale of the Marshes* does not limit itself to the exploits of one hero, offering instead 108 different story lines. This multitude of plots is a natural outgrowth of the tradition of the professional storyteller, who attempts to keep the audience's attention by recounting as many adventures as the market will bear.

Art   Although painting flourished in China under the Han and
                       reached a level of artistic excellence under the Tang, little remains from those periods. The painting of the Song and the Yuan, however, is considered the apogee of painting in traditional China.

   Like literature, Chinese painting found part of its inspiration in Buddhist and Daoist sources. Some of the best surviving examples of the Tang period are the Buddhist wall paintings in the caves at Dunhuang (doon-HWAHNG), in Central Asia. These paintings were commissioned by Buddhist merchants who stopped at Dunhuang and, while awaiting permission to enter China, wished to give thanks for surviving the rigors of the Silk Road. The entrances to the caves were filled with stones after the tenth century, when Muslim zealots began to destroy Buddhist images throughout Central Asia, and have only recently been uncovered. Like the few surviving Tang scroll paintings, these wall paintings display a love of color and refinement that are reminiscent of styles in India and Persia.

Daoism ultimately had a greater influence than Buddhism on Chinese painting. From early times, Chinese artists removed themselves to the mountains to write and paint and find the *Dao*, or Way, in nature. In the fifth century, one Chinese painter, too old to travel, began to paint mountain scenes from memory and announced that depicting nature could function as a substitute for contemplating nature itself. Painting, he said, could be the means of realizing the *Dao*. This explains in part the emphasis on nature in traditional Chinese painting. The word for *landscape* in Chinese means "mountain-water," and the Daoist search for balance between earth and water, hard and soft, *yang* and *yin*, is at play in the tradition of Chinese painting. To enhance the effect, poems were added to the paintings, underscoring the fusion of the visual and the verbal in Chinese art. Many artists were proficient in both media, the poem inspiring the painting and vice versa.

To represent the totality of nature, Chinese artists attempted to reveal the quintessential forms of the landscape. Rather than depicting the actual realistic shape of a specific mountain, they tried to portray the "idea" of a mountain. Empty spaces were left in the paintings because in the Daoist vision, one cannot know the whole truth. Daoist influence was also evident in the tendency to portray human beings as insignificant in the midst of nature. In contrast to the focus on the human body and personality in Western art, Chinese art presented people as tiny figures fishing in a small boat, meditating on a cliff, or wandering up a hillside trail, coexisting with but not dominating nature.

The Chinese displayed their paintings on long scrolls of silk or paper that were attached to a wooden cylindrical bar at the bottom. Varying in length from 3 to 20 feet, the paintings were unfolded slowly so that the eye could enjoy each segment, one after the other, beginning at the bottom with water or a village and moving upward into the hills to the mountain peaks and the sky.

By the tenth century, some Chinese painters began to eliminate color from their paintings, preferring the challenge of capturing the distilled essence of the landscape in washes of black ink on white silk. Borrowing from calligraphy, traditionally a sophisticated and revered art, they emphasized the brush stroke and created black-and-white landscapes characterized by a gravity of mood and dominated by overpowering mountains. Other artists turned toward more expressionist and experimental painting. These so-called literati artists were scholars and administrators, highly educated and adept at music, poetry, and painting. For them, the purpose of painting was not representation but expression. No longer did painters wish to evoke the feeling of wandering in nature. Rather, they tried to reveal to the viewer their own mind and feelings. Like many Western painters in the nineteenth and twentieth centuries, many of these artists were misunderstood by the public and painted only for themselves and one another.

Second only to painting in creativity was the field of ceramics, notably the manufacture of porcelain. Made of fine clay baked at unusually high temperatures in a kiln, porcelain was first produced during the period after the fall of the Han and became popular during the Tang era. During the Song, porcelain came into its own. Most renowned perhaps are the celadons (SEH-luh-dahnz), in a delicate gray-green, but Song artists also excelled in other colors and techniques. As in painting, Song delicacy and grace contrasted with the bold and often crude styles popular under the Tang. The translucency of Chinese porcelain resulted from a technique that did not reach Europe until the eighteenth century. During the Yuan and the Ming, new styles appeared. Most notable is the cobalt blue-and-white porcelain usually identified with the Ming Dynasty, which actually originated during the Yuan. The Ming also produced a multicolored porcelain—often in green, yellow, and red—covered with exotic designs.

CHRONOLOGY

MEDIEVAL CHINA

c. **first century** C.E.	Arrival of Buddhism in China
220 C.E.	Fall of the Han dynasty
581–618	Sui dynasty
618–907	Tang Dynasty
700s	Li Bo and Du Fu
712–756	Emperor Xuanzong
960–1279	Song Dynasty
1021–1086	Wang Anshi
1127–1279	Southern Song Dynasty
c. 1162–1227	Life of Genghis Khan
1279	Mongol conquest of China
1260–1294	Reign of Khubilai Khan
1368	Fall of the Yuan dynasty
1369–1644	Ming Dynasty

MindTap is a fully online, highly personalized learning experience built upon Cengage Learning content. MindTap combines student learning tools—readings, multimedia, activities, and assessments—into a singular Learning Path that guides students through their course.

11

THE EAST ASIAN RIMLANDS: EARLY JAPAN, KOREA, AND VIETNAM

The Jade Mountain Temple on Returned Sword Lake, Hanoi

© William J. Duiker

CHAPTER OUTLINE

• Japan: Land of the Rising Sun • Korea: Bridge to the East • Vietnam: The Smaller Dragon

JAPAN: LAND OF THE RISING SUN

Geography accounts for many of the historical differences between Chinese and Japanese society. Whereas China is a continental civilization, Japan is an island country. It consists of four main islands: Hokkaido (hoh-KY-doh) in the north, the main island of Honshu (hahn-SHOO) in the center, and the two smaller islands of Kyushu (KYOO-shoo) and Shikoku (shee-KOH-koo) in the southwest. Its total land area is about 146,000 square miles, about the size of the state of Montana. Japan's main islands are at approximately the same latitude as the eastern seaboard of the United States.

Like the eastern United States, Japan is blessed with a temperate climate. It is slightly warmer on the east coast, which is washed by the Pacific Current sweeping up from the south, and has a number of natural harbors that provide protection from the winds and high waves of the Pacific Ocean. As a consequence, in recent times, the majority of the Japanese people have tended to live along the east coast, especially in the flat plains surrounding the cities of Tokyo (TOH-kee-oh), Osaka (oh-SAH-kuh), and Kyoto (KYOH-toh). In these favorable environmental conditions, Japanese farmers have been able to harvest two crops of rice annually since early times.

By no means, however, is Japan an agricultural paradise. Like China, much of the country is mountainous, with only about 20 percent of the total land area suitable for cultivation. These mountains are of volcanic origin, since the Japanese islands are located at the juncture of the Asian and Pacific tectonic plates. This location is both an advantage and a disadvantage. Volcanic soils are extremely fertile, which helps explain the exceptionally high productivity of Japanese farmers. At the same time, the area is prone to earthquakes, such as the famous quake of 1923, which destroyed almost the entire city of Tokyo. In 2011, a massive earthquake

MAP 11.1 Early Japan

This map shows key cities in Japan during the early development of the Japanese state.

slightly offshore triggered a tsunami that devastated large areas along the eastern coast of northern Honshu island.

The fact that Japan is an island country has had a significant impact on Japanese history. As we have seen, the continental character of Chinese civilization, with its constant threat of invasion from the north, had a number of consequences for Chinese history. One effect was to make the Chinese more sensitive to the preservation of their culture from destruction at the hands of non-Chinese invaders. As one fourth-century C.E. Chinese ruler remarked when he was forced to move his capital southward under pressure from nomadic incursions, "The King takes All Under Heaven as his home."[1] Proud of their own considerable cultural achievements and their dominant position throughout the region, the Chinese have traditionally been reluctant to dilute the purity of their culture with foreign innovations. Culture more than race is a determinant of the Chinese sense of identity.

By contrast, the island character of Japan probably had the effect of strengthening the Japanese sense of ethnic and cultural distinctiveness. Although the Japanese view of themselves as the most ethnically homogeneous people in East Asia may not be entirely accurate (the modern Japanese probably represent a mix of peoples, much like their neighbors on the continent), their sense of racial and cultural homogeneity has enabled them to import ideas from abroad without worrying that the borrowings will destroy the uniqueness of their own culture.

A Gift from the Gods: Prehistoric Japan

According to an ancient legend recorded in historical chronicles written in the eighth century C.E., the islands of Japan were formed as a result of the marriage of the god Izanagi (ee-zah-NAH-gee) and the goddess Izanami (ee-zah-NAH-mee). After giving birth to Japan, Izanami gave birth to a sun goddess whose name was Amaterasu (ah-mah-teh-RAH-soo). A descendant of Amaterasu later descended to earth and became the founder of the Japanese nation. This Japanese creation myth is reminiscent of similar beliefs in other ancient societies, which often saw themselves as the product of a union of deities. What is interesting about the Japanese version is that it has survived into modern times as an explanation for the uniqueness of the Japanese people and the divinity of the Japanese emperor, who is still believed by some Japanese to be a direct descendant of the sun goddess Amaterasu.

Modern scholars have a more prosaic explanation for the origins of Japanese civilization. According to archaeological evidence, the Japanese islands have been occupied by human beings for at least 100,000 years. The earliest known Neolithic inhabitants, known as the Jomon (JOH-mahn) people (named for the cord pattern of their pottery), lived in the islands as early as 8000 B.C.E. They lived by hunting, fishing, and food gathering.

Agriculture may have appeared in Japan sometime during the first millennium B.C.E., although some archaeologists believe that the Jomon people had learned to cultivate some food crops considerably earlier than that. By about 400 B.C.E., rice cultivation had been introduced, probably by immigrants from the mainland by way of the Korean peninsula. Until recently, historians believed that these immigrants drove out the existing inhabitants of the area and gave rise to the emerging Yayoi (yah-YOH-ee) culture (named for the site near Tokyo where pottery from the period was found). It is now thought, however, that Yayoi culture was a product of a mixture between the Jomon people and the new arrivals, enriched by imports such as wet rice agriculture, which had been brought by the immigrants from the mainland. In any event, it seems clear that the Yayoi peoples were the ancestors of the vast majority of present-day Japanese.

At first, the Yayoi lived primarily on the southern island of Kyushu, but eventually they moved northward onto the main island of Honshu, conquering, assimilating, or driving out the previous inhabitants of the area, some of whose descendants, known as the Ainu (Y-nyoo), still live in the northern islands. Finally, in the first centuries C.E., the Yayoi settled in the Yamato (YAH-mah-toh) plain in the vicinity of the modern cities of Osaka and Kyoto. Japanese legend recounts the story of a "divine warrior," Jimmu (JIH-moo), who led his people eastward from the island of Kyushu to establish a kingdom in the Yamato plain.

In central Honshu, the Yayoi set up a tribal society based on a number of clans, called **uji** (oo-JEE). Each *uji* was ruled by a hereditary chieftain, who provided protection to the local population in return for a proportion of the annual harvest. The population itself was divided between a small aristocratic class and the majority, composed of rice farmers, artisans, and other household servants of the aristocrats. Yayoi society was highly decentralized, although eventually the chieftain of the dominant clan in the Yamato region, who claimed to be descended from the sun goddess Amaterasu, achieved a kind of titular primacy. There is no evidence, however, of a central ruler equivalent in power to the Chinese rulers of the Shang and the Zhou eras.

The Rise of the Japanese State   Although the Japanese had been aware of China for centuries, they paid relatively little attention to their more advanced neighbor until the early seventh century, when the rise of the centralized and expansionistic Tang Dynasty presented a challenge. When the Tang Dynasty began to meddle in the affairs of the Korean peninsula, Yamato rulers sought to deal with the potential threat in two ways. First, they sought alliances with the Korean states. Second, they attempted to centralize their authority so that they could mount a more effective resistance in the event of a Chinese invasion. The key figure in this effort was Shotoku Taishi (shoh-TOH-koo ty-EE-shee) (572–622), a leading aristocrat in one of the dominant clans in the Yamato region. Prince Shotoku sent missions to the Tang capital of Chang'an to learn about the political institutions already in use in the relatively centralized Tang kingdom.

Emulating the Chinese Model   Shotoku Taishi then launched a series of reforms to create a new system based roughly on the Chinese model. In the so-called seventeen-article constitution, he called for the creation of a centralized government under a supreme ruler and a merit system for selecting and ranking public officials. His objective was to limit the powers of the hereditary nobility and enhance the prestige and authority of the Yamato ruler, who claimed divine status and was now emerging as the symbol of the unique character of the Japanese nation. In reality, there is evidence that places the origins of the Yamato clan on the Korean peninsula.

After Shotoku Taishi's death in 622, his successors continued to introduce reforms to make the government more efficient. In the series of so-called **Taika**

MAP 11.2 Japan's Relations with China and Korea

This map shows the Japanese islands at the time of the Yamato state. Maritime routes taken by Japanese traders and missionaries to China are indicated.

reforms—*taika* (TY-kuh) means "great change"—that began in the mid-seventh century, the Grand Council of State was established, presiding over a cabinet of eight ministries. To the traditional six ministries of Tang China were added ministers representing the central secretariat and the imperial household. Official communications were to be based on the Chinese written language. The territory of Japan was divided into administrative districts on the Chinese pattern. The rural village, composed ideally of fifty households, was the basic unit of government. The village chief was responsible for "the maintenance of the household registers, the assigning of the sowing of crops and the cultivation of mulberry trees, the prevention of offenses, and the requisitioning of taxes and forced labor." A law code was introduced, and a new tax system was established; now all farmland technically belonged to the state, so taxes were paid directly to the central government rather than through the local nobility, as had previously been the case.

As a result of their new acquaintance with China, the Japanese also developed a strong interest in Buddhism. Some of the first Japanese to travel to China during this period were Buddhist pilgrims hoping to learn more about the exciting new doctrine and bring back scriptures. By the seventh century C.E., Buddhism had become quite popular among the aristocrats, who endowed wealthy monasteries that became active in Japanese politics. At first, the new faith did not penetrate to the masses, but eventually, popular sects such as the Pure Land sect, an import from China, won many adherents among the common people.

The Nara Period   Initial efforts to build a new state modeled roughly after the Tang state were successful. After Shotoku Taishi's death in 622, political influence fell into the hands of the powerful Fujiwara (foo-jee-WAH-rah) clan, which managed to marry into the ruling family and continue the reforms Shotoku had begun. In 710, a new capital, laid out on a grid similar to the great Tang city of Chang'an, was established at Nara (NAH-rah), on the eastern edge of the Yamato plain. The Yamato ruler began to use the title "son of Heaven" in the Chinese fashion. In deference to the belief in the ruling family's divine character, the mandate remained in perpetuity in the imperial house rather than being bestowed on an individual who was selected by heaven because of his talent and virtue, as was the case in China.

Had these reforms succeeded, Japan might have followed the Chinese pattern and developed a centralized bureaucratic government. But as time passed, the central government proved unable to curb the power of the aristocracy. Unlike the situation in Tang China, the civil service examinations in Japan were not open to commoners but were restricted to individuals of noble birth. Leading officials were awarded large tracts of land, and they and other powerful families were able to keep the taxes from the lands for themselves. Increasingly starved for revenue, the central government steadily lost power and influence.

The Heian Period   The influence of powerful Buddhist monasteries in the city of Nara soon became oppressive, and in 794, the emperor moved the capital to his family's original power base at nearby Heian (hay-AHN), on the site of present-day Kyoto. Like its predecessor, the new capital was laid out in the now familiar Chang'an checkerboard pattern, but on a larger scale than at Nara. Now increasingly self-confident, the rulers ceased to emulate the Tang and sent no more missions to Chang'an. At Heian, the emperor—as the royal line descended from the sun goddess was now styled—continued to rule in name, but actual power was in the hands of the Fujiwara clan, which had managed through intermarriage to link its fortunes closely with the imperial family. A senior member of the clan began to serve as regent (in practice, the chief executive of the government) for the emperor.

What was occurring was a return to the decentralization that had existed prior to Shotoku Taishi. The central government's attempts to impose taxes directly on the rice lands failed, and rural areas came under the control of powerful families whose wealth was based on the ownership of tax-exempt farmland called *shoen* (SHOH-en). To avoid paying taxes, peasants would often surrender their lands to a local aristocrat, who would then allow the peasants to cultivate the lands in return for the payment of rent. To obtain protection from government officials, these local aristocrats might in turn grant title of their lands to a more powerful aristocrat with influence at court. In return, these individuals would receive inheritable rights to a portion of the income from the estate.

With the decline of central power at Heian, local aristocrats tended to take justice into their own hands and increasingly used military force to protect their interests. A new class of military retainers called the **samurai** (SAM-uh-ry) emerged whose purpose was to protect the security and property of their patron. They frequently drew their leaders from disappointed aristocratic office seekers, who thus

COMPARATIVE ESSAY

Feudal Orders Around the World

POLITICS & GOVERNMENT

When we use the word *feudalism*, we usually think of European knights on horseback clad in armor and wielding a sword and lance. Between 800 and 1500, however, a form of social organization that modern historians have called feudalism developed in different parts of the world. Historians use the term to refer to a decentralized political order in which local lords owed loyalty and provided military service to a king or more powerful lord. In Europe, a feudal order based on lords and vassals arose between 800 and 900 and flourished for the next four hundred years.

In Japan, a feudal order much like that found in Europe developed between 800 and 1500. By the end of the ninth century, powerful nobles in the countryside, while owing a loose loyalty to the Japanese emperor, began to exercise political and legal power in their own extensive lands. To protect their property and security, these nobles retained samurai, warriors who owed loyalty to the nobles and provided military service for them. Like knights in Europe, the samurai followed a warrior code and fought on horseback, clad in armor, but they carried a sword and bow and arrow rather than a sword and lance.

In some respects, the political relationships among the Indian states beginning in the fifth century took on the character of the feudal relationships that emerged in Europe in the Middle Ages. Like medieval European lords, local Indian rajas were technically vassals of the king, but unlike the European situation, the relationship was not a contractual one. Still, the Indian model became highly complex, with vassals characterized as "inner" or "outer," depending on their physical or political proximity to the king, and vassals described as "greater" or "lesser," depending on their power and influence. As in Europe, the vassals themselves often had vassals.

In the Valley of Mexico between 1300 and 1500, the Aztecs developed a political system that bore some similarities to the Japanese, Indian, and European feudal orders. Although the Aztec king was a powerful, authoritarian ruler, the local rulers of lands outside the capital city were allowed considerable freedom. They did pay tribute to the king, however, and also provided him with military forces. Weapons differed from those used in Europe and Japan: Aztec warriors were armed with sharp knives made of stone and spears of wood fitted with razor-sharp blades cut from stone.

began to occupy a prestigious position in local society, where they often served an administrative as well as a military function. The samurai lived a life of simplicity and self-sacrifice and were expected to maintain an intense and unquestioning loyalty to their lord. Bonds of loyalty were also quite strong among members of the samurai class, and homosexuality was common. Like the knights of medieval Europe, the samurai fought on horseback (although a samurai carried a sword and a bow and arrows rather than lance and shield) and were supposed to live by a strict warrior code, known in Japan as **Bushido** (BOO-shee-doh), or "way of the warrior." As time went on, they became a major force and almost a surrogate government in much of the Japanese countryside.

Samurai. *During the Kamakura period, painters began to depict the adventures of the new warrior class. Here is an imposing mounted samurai warrior, the Japanese equivalent of the medieval knight in fief-holding Europe. Like his European counterpart, the samurai was supposed to live by a strict moral code and was expected to maintain an unquestioning loyalty to his liege lord. Above all, a samurai's life was one of simplicity and self-sacrifice.*

Q *What were the key characteristics of the political order we know as feudalism?*   *To what degree can Japanese conditions be considered "feudal"?*

The Kamakura Shogunate and After   By the end of the twelfth century, as rivalries among noble families led to almost constant civil war, centralizing forces again asserted themselves. This time the instrument was a powerful noble from a warrior clan named Minamoto Yoritomo (mee-nah-MOH-toh yoh-ree-TOH-moh) (1142–1199), who defeated several rivals and set up his power base on the Kamakura (kah-mah-KOO-rah) peninsula, south of the modern city of Tokyo. To strengthen the state, he created a more centralized government—the *bakufu* (buh-KOO-foo *or* bah-KOO-fuh) or "tent government"—under a powerful military leader known as the **shogun** (SHOH-gun) (general). The shogun attempted to increase the powers of the central government while reducing rival aristocratic clans to vassal status.

This **shogunate system**, in which the emperor was the titular authority while the shogun exercised actual power, served as the political system in Japan until the second half of the nineteenth century.

The shogunate (SHOH-gun-ut *or* SHOH-gun-ayt) system worked effectively, and it was fortunate that it did, because during the next century, Japan faced the most serious challenge it had confronted yet. The Mongols, who had destroyed the Song Dynasty in China, were now attempting to assert their hegemony throughout all of Asia. In 1266, Emperor Khubilai Khan demanded tribute from Japan. When the Japanese refused, he invaded with an army of more than 30,000 troops. Bad weather and difficult conditions forced a retreat, but the Mongols tried again in 1281. An army nearly 150,000 strong landed on the northern coast of Kyushu. The Japanese were able to contain them for two months until virtually the entire Mongol fleet was destroyed by a massive typhoon—a "divine wind," or *kamikaze* (kah-mi-KAH-zee). Japan would not face a foreign invader again until American forces landed on the Japanese islands in the summer of 1945.

Resistance to the Mongols had put a heavy strain on the system, however, and in 1333, the Kamakura Shogunate was overthrown by a coalition of powerful clans. A new shogun, supplied by the Ashikaga (ah-shee-KAH-guh) family, arose in Kyoto and attempted to continue the shogunate system. But the Ashikaga were unable to restore the centralized power of their predecessors. With the central government reduced to a shell, the power of the local landed aristocracy increased to an unprecedented degree. Heads of great noble families, now called **daimyo** (DYM-yoh) ("great names"), controlled vast landed estates that owed no taxes to the government or to the court in Kyoto. As clan rivalries continued, the daimyo relied increasingly on the samurai for protection, and political power came into the hands of a loose coalition of noble families.

By the end of the fifteenth century, Japan was again close to anarchy. A disastrous civil conflict known as the Onin War (1467–1477) led to the virtual destruction of the capital city of Kyoto and the disintegration of the shogunate. With the disappearance of central authority, powerful aristocrats in rural areas now seized total control over large territories and ruled as independent lords. Territorial rivalries and claims of precedence led to almost constant warfare in this period of "warring states," as it is called (in obvious parallel with a similar era during the Zhou dynasty in China). The trend back toward central authority did not begin until the last quarter of the sixteenth century.

Was Japan a Feudal Society?   That question has aroused vigorous debate among historians in recent years. Few would dispute that political, social, and economic conditions in Japan were similar in a number of respects to those in medieval Europe, where the term was first applied. But some European historians worry that the term *feudalism* has been overused; they argue that it should be narrowly defined, based on conditions that existed in Europe during a specific time period.

For the student of world history, the term obviously has some comparative value, in that the broad political and economic conditions that are normally considered to be characteristic of a feudal society can be found in a number of areas around the world. Still, it is important to remember that, under the surface, there were often profound differences between one "feudal" society and another. With that in mind, the term can be a highly useful teaching tool for world historians.

Economic and Social Structures

From the time the Yayoi culture was first established on the Japanese islands, Japan was a predominantly agrarian society. Although Japan lacked the spacious valleys and deltas of the river valley societies, its inhabitants were able to take advantage of their limited amount of tillable land and plentiful rainfall to create a society based on the cultivation of wet rice.

Trade and Manufacturing

As in China, commerce was slow to develop as an independent force in Japan. During ancient times, each *uji* had a local artisan class, composed of weavers, carpenters, and ironworkers, but trade was essentially local and was regulated by the local clan leaders. With the rise of the Yamato state, a money economy gradually began to develop, but most internal trade was still conducted through barter until the twelfth century, when metal coins introduced from China became more popular.

Trade and manufacturing began to develop more rapidly during the Kamakura period, with the appearance of quarterly markets in the larger towns and the emergence of such industries as paper, iron casting, and porcelain. Foreign trade, mainly with Korea and China, began during the eleventh century. Japan exported raw materials, paintings, swords, and other manufactured items in return for silk, porcelain, books, and copper cash. Some Japanese traders were so aggressive in pressing their interests that authorities in China and Korea attempted to limit the number of Japanese commercial missions that could visit each year. Such restrictions were often ignored, however, and encouraged some Japanese traders to turn to piracy.

Significantly, manufacturing and commerce developed rapidly during the more decentralized period of the Ashikaga Shogunate and the era of the warring states, perhaps because of the rapid growth in the wealth and autonomy of local daimyo families. Market towns, now operating on a full money economy, began to appear, and local manufacturers formed guilds to protect their mutual interests. Sometimes local peasants would bring homemade goods, such as silk or hemp clothing, household items, or food, to sell at the markets. In general, however, trade and manufacturing remained under the control of the local daimyo, who would often provide tax breaks to local guilds in return for other benefits. Although Japan remained a primarily agricultural society, it was on the verge of a major advance in manufacturing.

Daily Life

One of the first descriptions of the life of the Japanese people comes from a Chinese dynastic history from the third century C.E. It describes lords and peasants living in an agricultural society that was based on the cultivation of wet rice. Laws had been enacted to punish offenders, local trade was conducted in markets, and government granaries stored the grain that was paid as taxes.

Life for the common people probably changed very little over the next several hundred years. Most were peasants, who worked on land owned by their lord or, in some cases, by the state or by Buddhist monasteries. By no means, however, were all peasants equal either economically or socially. Although in ancient times, all land was owned by the state and peasants working the land were taxed at an equal rate depending on the nature of the crop, after the Yamato era, variations began to develop. At the top were local officials, who were often well-to-do peasants. They were responsible for organizing collective labor services and collecting tax grain from the peasants and were in turn exempt from such obligations themselves.

The majority of the peasants were under the authority of these local officials. In general, peasants were free to dispose of their harvest as they saw fit after paying their tax quota, but in practical terms, their freedom was limited. Those who were unable to pay the tax sank to the level of **genin** (GAY-nin), or landless laborers, who could be bought and sold by their proprietors like slaves along with the land on which they worked. Some fled to escape such a fate and attempted to survive by clearing plots of land in the mountains or by becoming bandits.

In addition to the *genin*, the bottom of the social scale was occupied by the **eta** (AY-tuh), a class of hereditary slaves who, like the outcastes in India, were responsible for what were considered degrading occupations, such as curing leather and burying the dead. The origins of the *eta* are not entirely clear, but they probably were descendants of prisoners of war, criminals, or mountain dwellers who were not related to the dominant Yamato peoples. As we shall see, the *eta* are still a distinctive part of Japanese society, and although their full legal rights are guaranteed under the current constitution, discrimination against them is not uncommon.

Daily life for ordinary people in early Japan resembled that of their counterparts throughout much of Asia. The vast majority lived in small villages, several of which normally made up a single *shoen*. Housing was simple. Most lived in small two-room houses of timber, mud, or thatch, with dirt floors covered by straw or woven mats—the origin, perhaps, of the well-known *tatami* (tuh-TAH-mee), or woven-mat floor, of more modern times. Their diet consisted of rice (if some was left after the payment of the grain tax), wild grasses, millet, roots, and some fish and birds. Life must have been difficult at best; as one eighth-century poet lamented:

> Here I lie on straw
> Spread on bare earth,
> With my parents at my pillow,
> My wife and children at my feet,
> All huddled in grief and tears.
> No fire sends up smoke
> At the cooking place,
> And in the cauldron
> A spider spins its web.[2]

The Role of Women   Evidence about the relations between men and women in early Japan presents a mixed picture. The Chinese dynastic history reports that "in their meetings and daily living, there is no distinction between... men and women." It notes that a woman "adept in the ways of shamanism" had briefly ruled Japan in the third century C.E. But it also remarks that polygyny was common, with nobles normally having four or five wives and commoners two or three.[3] An eighth-century law code guaranteed the inheritance rights of women, and wives abandoned by their husbands were permitted to obtain a divorce and remarry. A husband could divorce his wife if she did not produce a male child, committed adultery, disobeyed her in-laws, talked too much, engaged in theft, was jealous, or had a serious illness.[4]

When Buddhism was introduced, women were initially relegated to a subordinate position in the new faith. Although they were permitted to take up monastic life—many widows entered a monastery at the death of their husbands—they were not permitted to visit Buddhist holy places, nor were they even (in the accepted wisdom) equal with men in the afterlife. One Buddhist commentary from the late thirteenth century said that a woman could not attain enlightenment because "her sin is grievous, and so she is not allowed to enter the lofty palace of the great Brahma, nor to look upon the clouds which hover over his ministers and people."[5] Other Buddhist scholars were more egalitarian: "Learning the Law of Buddha and achieving release from illusion have nothing to do with whether one happens to be a man or a woman."[6] Such views ultimately prevailed, and women were eventually allowed to participate fully in Buddhist activities in medieval Japan.

Although women did not possess the full legal and social rights of their male counterparts, they played an active role at various levels of Japanese society. Aristocratic women were prominent at court, and some, such as the author known as Lady Murasaki (978–c. 1016), won renown for their artistic or literary talents. Though few commoners could aspire to such prominence, women often appear in the scroll paintings of the period along with men, doing the spring planting, threshing and hulling the rice, and acting as carriers, peddlers, salespersons, and entertainers.

In Search of the Pure Land: Religion in Early Japan   In Japan, as elsewhere, religious belief began with the worship of nature spirits. Early Japanese worshiped spirits called **_kami_** (KAH-mi) who resided in trees, rivers and streams, and mountains. They also believed in ancestral spirits present in the atmosphere. In Japan, these beliefs eventually evolved into a kind of state religion called **Shinto** (SHIN-toh) (the Sacred Way or Way of the Gods) that is still practiced today. Shinto still serves as an ideological and emotional force that knits the Japanese into a single people and nation.

Shinto does not have a complex metaphysical superstructure or an elaborate moral code. It does require certain ritual acts, usually undertaken at a shrine, and a process of purification, which may have originated in primitive concerns about death, childbirth, illness, and menstruation. This traditional concern about physical purity may help explain the strong Japanese concern for personal cleanliness and the practice of denying women entrance to the holy places.

Another feature of Shinto is its stress on the beauty of nature and the importance of nature itself in Japanese life. Shinto shrines are usually located in places of exceptional beauty and are often dedicated to a nearby physical feature. As time passed, such primitive beliefs contributed to the characteristic Japanese love

Seduction of the Akashi Lady

Out of the Japanese tradition of female introspective prose appeared one of the world's truly great novels, *The Tale of Genji*, written around the year 1000 by the diarist and court author Murasaki Shikibu (MOO-rah-SAH-kee SHEE-kee-boo), known as Lady Murasaki. The novel has influenced Japanese writing for more than a thousand years and even today is revered for its artistic refinement and sensitivity. A panoramic portrayal of court life in tenth-century Japan, it traces the life and loves of the courtier Genji as he strives to retain the favor of those in power while simultaneously pursuing his cult of love and beauty. The remarkable character of Genji is revealed to the reader through myriad psychological observations. In this excerpt, Genji has just seduced a lady at court and now feels misgivings at having betrayed his child bride. A *koto* is a Japanese stringed instrument similar to a zither.

Lady Murasaki, *The Tale of Genji*

A curtain string brushed against a koto, to tell him that she had been passing a quiet evening at her music.

"And will you not play for me on the koto of which I have heard so much?" ...

This lady had not been prepared for an incursion and could not cope with it. She fled to an inner room. How she could have contrived to bar it he could not tell, but it was very firmly barred indeed. Though he did not exactly force his way through, it is not to be imagined that he left matters as they were. Delicate, slender—she was almost too beautiful. Pleasure was mingled with pity at the thought that he was imposing himself upon her. She was even more pleasing than reports from afar had had her. The autumn night, usually so long, was over in a trice. Not wishing to be seen, he hurried out, leaving affectionate assurances behind.

Genji called in secret from time to time. The two houses being some distance apart, he feared being seen by fishers, who were known to relish a good rumor, and sometimes several days would elapse between his visits....

Genji dreaded having Murasaki [his bride] learn of the affair. He still loved her more than anyone, and he did not want her to make even joking reference to it. She was a quiet, docile lady, but she had more than once been unhappy with him. Why, for the sake of brief pleasure, had he caused her pain? He wished it were all his to do over again. The sight of the Akashi lady only brought new longing for the other lady.

He got off a more earnest and affectionate letter than usual, at the end of which he said: "I am in anguish at the thought that, because of foolish occurrences for which I have been responsible but have had little heart, I might appear in a guise distasteful to you. There has been a strange, fleeting encounter. That I should volunteer this story will make you see, I hope, how little I wish to have secrets from you. Let the gods be my judges."

It was but the fisherman's brush
with the salty sea pine.
Followed by a tide of tears of
longing.

Her reply was gentle and unreproachful, and at the end of it she said: "That you should have deigned to tell me a dreamlike story which you could not keep to yourself calls to mind numbers of earlier instances."

Naive of me, perhaps; yet we did
make our vows.
And now see the waves that wash
the Mountain of Waiting!

It was the one note of reproach in a quiet, undemanding letter. He found it hard to put down, and for some nights he stayed away from the house in the hills.

Q *Why does this thousand-year-old passage still resonate with readers today?*

Source: From *The Tale of the Genji* by Lady Murasaki, translated by Edward G. Seidensticker, copyright © 1976 by Edward G. Seidensticker (New York: Alfred A. Knopf).

of nature. In this sense, early Shinto beliefs have been incorporated into the lives of all Japanese.

In time, Shinto evolved into a state doctrine that was linked with belief in the divinity of the emperor and the sacredness of the Japanese nation. A national shrine was established at Ise (EE-say), north of the early capital of Nara, where the emperor annually paid tribute to the sun goddess. But although Shinto had evolved well beyond its primitive origins, like its counterparts elsewhere, it could not satisfy all the religious and emotional needs of the Japanese people. For those needs, the Japanese turned to Buddhism.

As we have seen, Buddhism was introduced into Japan from China during the sixth century C.E. and had begun to spread beyond the court to the general population by the eighth century. As in China, most Japanese saw no contradiction between worshiping both the Buddha and their local nature gods (*kami*), many of whom were considered later manifestations of the Buddha. Most of the Buddhist sects that had achieved popularity in China were established in Japan, and many of them attracted powerful patrons at court. Great monasteries were built that competed in wealth and influence with the noble families that had traditionally ruled the country.

Perhaps the two most influential Buddhist sects were the **Pure Land** (in Japanese, Jodo) sect and **Zen** (in Chinese, Chan or Ch'an). The Pure Land sect, which taught that devotion alone could lead to enlightenment and release, was very popular among the common people, for whom monastic life was one of the few routes to upward mobility. Among the aristocracy, the most influential school was Zen, which exerted a significant impact on Japanese life and culture during the era of the warring states. With its emphasis on austerity, self-discipline, and communion with nature, Zen complemented many traditional beliefs in Japanese society and became an important component of the samurai warrior's code.

In Zen teachings, there were various ways to achieve enlightenment—*satori* (suh-TAWR-ee) in Japanese. Some stressed that it could be achieved suddenly. One monk, for example, reportedly achieved *satori* by listening to the sound of a bamboo stick striking against roof tiles; another did so by carefully watching the opening of peach blossoms in the spring. But other practitioners, sometimes called adepts, said that enlightenment could come only through studying the scriptures and arduous self-discipline, known as *zazen* (ZAH-ZEN), or "seated Zen." Seated Zen involved a lengthy process of meditation that cleansed the mind of all thoughts so that it could concentrate on the essential.

Sources of Traditional Japanese Culture   Nowhere is the Japanese genius for blending indigenous and imported elements into an effective whole better demonstrated than in the national culture. In such widely diverse fields as art, architecture, sculpture, and literature, the Japanese from early times showed an impressive ability to borrow selectively from abroad without destroying essential native elements.

Growing contact with China during the rise of the Yamato state stimulated Japanese artists. Missions sent to China and Korea during the seventh and eighth centuries returned with examples of Tang literature, sculpture, and painting, all of which influenced the Japanese.

Literature   Borrowing from Chinese models was somewhat complicated, however, since the early Japanese had no system for recording their own spoken language and initially adopted the Chinese pictographic language for writing. The challenge was complicated by the fact that spoken Japanese is not part of the Sino-Tibetan family of languages. But resourceful Japanese soon adapted the Chinese written characters so that they could be used for recording the Japanese language. In some cases, Chinese characters were given Japanese pronunciations. But Chinese characters ordinarily could not be used to record Japanese words, which normally contain more than one syllable. Sometimes the Japanese simply used Chinese characters as phonetic symbols that were combined to form Japanese words. Later they simplified the characters into phonetic symbols that were used alongside Chinese characters. This hybrid system continues to be used today.

At first, most educated Japanese preferred to write in Chinese, and a court literature—consisting of essays, poetry, and official histories—appeared in the classical Chinese language. But spoken Japanese never totally disappeared among the educated classes and eventually became the instrument of a unique literature. With the lessening of Chinese cultural influence in the tenth century, Japanese verse resurfaced. Between the tenth and fifteenth centuries, twenty imperial anthologies of poetry were compiled. Initially, they were written primarily by courtiers, but with the fall of the Heian court and the rise of the warrior and merchant classes, all literate segments of society began to produce poetry.

Japanese poetry is unique. It expresses its themes in a simple form, a characteristic stemming from traditional Japanese aesthetics, Zen religion, and the language itself. The aim of the Japanese poet was to create a mood, perhaps the melancholic effect of gently falling cherry blossoms or leaves. With a few specific references, the poet suggested a whole world, just as Zen Buddhism sought enlightenment from a sudden perception. Poets often alluded to earlier poems by repeating their images with small changes, a technique that was viewed not as plagiarism but as an elaboration on the meaning of the earlier poem.

By the fourteenth century, the technique of the "linked verse" had become the most popular form of Japanese poetry. Known as *haiku* (HY-koo), it is composed of seventeen syllables divided into lines of five, seven, and five syllables, respectively. The poems usually focused on images from nature and the mutability of life. Often the poetry was written by several individuals alternately composing verses and linking them together into long sequences of hundreds and even thousands of lines. The following example, by three poets named Sogi (SOH-gee), Shohaku (shoh-HAH-koo), and Socho (SOH-choh), is one of the most famous of the period:

Snow clinging to slope,   Sogi
    On mist-enshrouded mountains
    At evening time.

In the distance flows   Shohaku
    Through plum-scented villages.

Willows cluster   Socho
    In the river breeze
    As spring appears.[7]

Poetry served a unique function at the Heian court, where it was the initial means of communication between lovers. By custom, aristocratic women were isolated from all contact with men outside their immediate family and spent their days hidden behind screens. Some amused themselves by writing poetry. When courtship began, poetic exchanges were the only means a woman had to attract her prospective lover, who would be enticed solely by her poetic art.

During the Heian period, male courtiers wrote in Chinese, believing that Chinese civilization was superior and worthy of emulation. Like the Chinese, they viewed prose fiction as "vulgar gossip." Nevertheless, from the ninth century to the twelfth, Japanese women were prolific writers of prose fiction in Japanese. Excluded from school, they learned to read and write at home and wrote diaries and stories to pass the time. Some of the most talented women were invited to court as authors in residence.

In the increasingly pessimistic world of the warring states of Kamakura (1185–1333), Japanese novels typically focused on a solitary figure who is aloof from the refinements of the court and faces battle and possibly death. Another genre, that of the heroic war tale, came out of the new warrior class. These works described the military exploits of warriors, coupled with an overwhelming sense of sadness and loneliness.

The famous classical Japanese drama known as *No* (NOH) also originated during this period. *No* developed out of a variety of entertainment forms, such as dancing and juggling, that were part of the native tradition or had been imported from China and other regions of Asia. The plots were normally based on stories from Japanese history or legend. Eventually, *No* evolved into a highly stylized drama in which the performers wore masks and danced to the accompaniment of instrumental music. Like much of Japanese culture, *No* was restrained, graceful, and refined.

Art and Architecture   In art and architecture, as in literature, the Japanese pursued their interest in beauty, simplicity, and nature. To some degree, Japanese artists and architects were influenced by Chinese forms. As they became familiar with Chinese architecture, Japanese rulers and aristocrats tried to emulate the splendor of Tang civilization and began constructing their palaces and temples in Chinese style.

During the Heian period (794–1185), the search for beauty was reflected in various art forms, such as narrative hand scrolls, screens, sliding door panels, fans, and lacquer decoration. As in the case of literature, nature themes dominated—seashore scenes, a spring rain, moon and mist, flowering wisteria and cherry blossoms. All were intended to evoke an emotional response on the part of the viewer. Japanese painting suggested the frail beauty of nature by presenting it on a smaller scale. The majestic mountain in a Chinese painting became a more intimate Japanese landscape with rolling hills and a rice field. Faces were rarely shown, and human drama was indicated by a woman lying prostrate or hiding her face in her sleeve. Tension was shown by two people talking at a great distance or with their backs to one another.

During the Kamakura period (1185–1333), the hand scroll with its physical realism and action-packed paintings of the new warrior class achieved great popularity. Reflecting these chaotic times, the art of portraiture flourished, and a scroll would include a full gallery of warriors and holy men in starkly realistic detail, including such unflattering features as stubble, worry lines on a forehead, and crooked teeth. Japanese sculptors also produced naturalistic wooden statues of generals, nobles, and saints. By far the most distinctive were the fierce heavenly "guardian kings," who still intimidate the viewer today.

Zen Buddhism, an import from China in the thirteenth century, also influenced Japanese aesthetics. With its emphasis on immediate enlightenment without recourse to intellectual analysis and elaborate ritual, Zen reinforced the Japanese predilection for simplicity and self-discipline. During this era, Zen philosophy found expression in the Japanese garden, the tea ceremony, the art of flower arranging, pottery and ceramics, and miniature plant display—the famous **bonsai** (bon-SY), literally "pot scenery."

Landscapes served as an important means of expression in both Japanese art and architecture. Japanese gardens were initially modeled on Chinese examples. Early court texts during the Heian period emphasized the importance of including a stream or pond when creating a garden. The landscape surrounding the fourteenth-century Golden Pavilion in Kyoto displays a harmony of garden, water, and architecture that makes it one of the treasures of the world. Because of the shortage of water in the city, later gardens concentrated on rock composition, using white pebbles to represent water.

Like the Japanese garden, the tea ceremony represents the fusion of Zen and aesthetics. Developed in the fifteenth century, it was practiced in a simple room devoid of external ornament except for a *tatami* floor, sliding doors, and an alcove with a writing desk and asymmetrical shelves. The participants could therefore focus completely on the activity of pouring and drinking tea. "Tea and Zen have the same flavor" goes the Japanese saying. Considered the ultimate symbol of spiritual deliverance, the tea ceremony continues to have great aesthetic value and moral significance today as well as in traditional times.

Japan and the Chinese Model   Few major societies in Asia have been as isolated as Japan. Cut off from the mainland by 120 miles of frequently turbulent ocean, the Japanese had only minimal contact with the outside world during most of their early development.

Whether or not this isolation was ultimately beneficial to Japanese society cannot be determined. On the one hand, lack of knowledge of developments taking place elsewhere probably delayed the process of change in Japan. On the other hand, the Japanese were spared the destructive invasions that afflicted other ancient civilizations. Certainly, once the Japanese became acquainted with Chinese culture at the height of the Tang era, they were quick to take advantage of the opportunity. In the space of a few decades, the young state adopted many aspects of Chinese society and culture and thereby introduced major changes into Japanese life.

Nevertheless, Japanese political institutions failed to follow all aspects of the Chinese pattern. Despite Prince Shotoku's effort to make effective use of the imperial traditions of Tang China, the decentralizing forces in Japanese society remained dominant throughout the period under discussion in this chapter. Adoption of the Confucian civil service examination did not lead to a breakdown of Japanese social divisions; instead, the examination was administered in a manner that preserved and strengthened them. Although Buddhist and Daoist doctrines made a significant

In the Garden

© William J. Duiker

© William J. Duiker

RELIGION & PHILOSOPHY

In traditional China and Japan, gardens were meant to free the observer's mind from mundane concerns, offering spiritual refreshment in the quiet of nature. Chinese gardens were designed to reconstruct an orderly microcosm of nature, where the harassed Confucian official could find spiritual renewal. Wandering through constantly changing perspectives of ponds, trees, rocks, and pavilions, he could imagine himself immersed in a monumental landscape. In the garden in Suzhou at the top, the rocks represent towering mountains to suggest a Daoist sense of withdrawal and eternity, reducing the viewer to a tiny speck in the grand flow of life.

In Japan, the traditional garden reflected the Zen Buddhist philosophy of simplicity, restraint, allusion, and tranquility. In the garden in the bottom, at the Ryoanji (RYOH-ahn-jee) temple in Kyoto, the rocks are meant to suggest mountains rising from a sea of pebbles. Such gardens served as an aid to meditation, inspiring the viewer to join with comrades in composing "linked verse."

Q *How do gardens in traditional China and Japan differ in form and purpose from gardens in Western societies? Why do you think this is the case?*

contribution to Japanese religious practices, Shinto beliefs continued to play a major role in shaping the Japanese worldview.

Why Japan did not follow the Chinese road to centralized authority has been a subject of debate among historians. Some argue that the answer lies in differing cultural traditions, while others suggest that Chinese institutions and values were introduced too rapidly to be assimilated effectively by Japanese society. One factor may have been the absence of a foreign threat (except for the brief incursion by the Mongols). A recent view holds that diseases (such as smallpox and measles) imported inadvertently from China led to a marked decline in the population of the islands, reducing food output and preventing the population from coalescing in more compact urban centers.

In any event, Japan was not the only society in Asia to assimilate ideas from abroad while at the same time preserving customs and institutions inherited from the past. Across the Sea of Japan to the west and several thousand miles to the southwest, other Asian peoples were embarked on a similar journey. We now turn to their experience.

Korea: Bridge to the East

Few of the societies on the periphery of China have been as directly influenced by the Chinese model as Korea. The relationship between China and Korea has frequently been characterized by tension and conflict, however, and Koreans have often resented what they perceive to be Chinese chauvinism and arrogance.

A graphic example of this attitude has occurred in recent years as officials and historians in both countries have presented differing interpretations of the early history of the Korean people. The Korean peninsula was probably first settled by Altaic-speaking fishing and hunting peoples from neighboring Manchuria during the Neolithic Age. Because the area, which is slightly larger than the state of Minnesota, is relatively mountainous (only about one-fifth of the peninsula is adaptable to cultivation), farming was apparently not practiced until about 2000 B.C.E. At that time, the peoples living in the area began to form organized communities.

It is this period that gives rise to disagreement. In 2004, Chinese official sources claimed that the first organized kingdom in the area, known as Koguryo (koh-GOOR-yoh) (37 B.C.E.–668 C.E.), occupied a wide swath of Manchuria as well as the northern section of the Korean peninsula and was thus an integral part of Chinese history. Korean scholars, basing their contentions on a combination of legend and scattered historical evidence, countered that the first kingdom established on the peninsula, known as Gojoseon (goh-joh-SHAWN), was created by the ruler Dangun (dan-GOON) in 2333 B.C.E., and that both he and his subjects in the surrounding area were ethnically Korean. It was at that time, these scholars maintain, that the Bronze Age got under way in northeastern Asia.

Although this dispute has not yet been resolved, most scholars today do agree that in 109 B.C.E., the northern part of the peninsula came under direct Chinese influence. During the next several generations, the area was ruled by the Han dynasty, which divided the territory into provinces and introduced Chinese institutions. With the decline of the Han in the third century C.E., power gradually shifted to local leaders, who drove out the

Chinese administrators but continued to absorb Chinese cultural influences. Eventually, three separate kingdoms emerged on the peninsula: Koguryo in the north, Paekche (bayk-JEE) in the southwest, and Silla (SIL-uh) in the southeast.

The Three Kingdoms   From the fourth to the seventh centuries, the three kingdoms were bitter rivals for influence and territory on the peninsula. At the same time, all began to adopt Chinese political and cultural institutions. Koguryo was the first among the kingdoms to introduce Buddhism in the late fourth century C.E. The first Confucian academy on the peninsula was established in the capital at Pyongyang (pyahng-YANG). All three kingdoms also appear to have accepted a tributary relationship with one or another of the squabbling states that emerged in China after the fall of the Han. The kingdom of Silla, less exposed than its two rivals to Chinese influence, was at first the weakest of the three, but eventually it emerged as the dominant power on the peninsula. To pacify the haughty Chinese, who continued to claim a degree of suzerainty with the kingdoms on the peninsula, Silla accepted tributary status under the Tang Dynasty. In the meantime, any remaining Japanese colonies in the south were eliminated.

With the country unified for the first time, the rulers of Silla attempted to use Chinese political institutions and ideology to forge a centralized state. As the state religion, Buddhism grew in popularity, and Korean monks followed the paths of their Japanese counterparts on journeys to Buddhist sites in China. Chinese architecture and art became dominant in the capital at Kyongju (KEE-yahng-joo) and other urban centers, and the written Chinese language became the official means of legal communication. But powerful aristocratic families, long dominant in the southeastern part of the peninsula, were still influential at court. They were able to prevent the adoption of the Tang civil service examination system and resisted the distribution of manorial lands to the poor. But squabbling among noble families steadily increased, and after the assassination of the king of Silla in 780, civil war erupted.

The Rise of the Koryo Dynasty   In the early tenth century, a new dynasty called Koryo (KAWR-yoh) (the root of the modern name of the country in English) arose in the north. The new kingdom adopted Chinese political institutions in an effort to strengthen its power and unify its territory. The civil service examination system was introduced in 958, but as in Japan, the bureaucracy continued to be dominated by influential aristocratic families.

The Koryo Dynasty remained in power for four hundred years, protected from invasion by the absence of a strong dynasty in neighboring China. Under the Koryo, industry and commerce slowly began to develop, but as in China, agriculture was the prime source of wealth. In theory, all land was the property of the king, but in actuality, noble families controlled their holdings. The lands were worked by peasants who were subject to burdens similar to those of European serfs. At the bottom of society was a class of **chonmin** (CHAWN-min), or "base people," composed of slaves, artisans, and other specialized workers.

From a cultural perspective, the Koryo era was one of high achievement. Buddhist monasteries, run by sects introduced from China, including Pure Land and Zen, controlled vast territories, while their monks served as royal advisers at court. At first, Buddhist themes dominated in Korean art and sculpture, and the entire Tripitaka (tri-pih-TAH-kah) (the "three baskets," or sections, of the Buddhist canon) was printed using wooden blocks. Eventually, however, with the appearance of landscape painting and porcelain, Confucian themes began to predominate.

Under the Mongols   Like its predecessor in Silla, the kingdom of Koryo was unable to overcome the power of the nobility and the absence of a reliable tax base. In the thirteenth century, the Mongols seized the northern part of the country and assimilated it into the Yuan empire. The weakened kingdom of Koryo became a tributary of the great khan in Khanbaliq.

The era of Mongol rule was one of profound suffering for the Korean people, especially the thousands of peasants and artisans who were compelled to perform conscript labor to help build the ships in preparation for Khubilai Khan's invasion of Japan. On the positive side, the Mongols introduced many new ideas and technology from China and farther afield. The Koryo dynasty had managed to survive, but only by accepting Mongol authority, and when the power of the Mongols declined, the kingdom declined with it. With the rise to power of the Ming in China, Koryo collapsed, and power was seized by the military commander Yi Song-gye (YEE-song-YEE), who declared the founding of the new Choson (also known as Yi [YEE]) Dynasty in 1392. Once again, the Korean people were in charge of their own destiny.

Always aware of potential threats emanating from more powerful neighbors, the Choson kingdom was actively interested in events taking place elsewhere in the region and was quick to follow up on technological advances taking place in China. Koreans were among the first to adopt the new invention of block printing, and Korean cartographers hastened to draw up regional and world maps based on Chinese originals. The famous "Kangnido" world map, produced in Korea in 1402, is considered to be the second oldest surviving map drawn up in Asia.

Vietnam: The Smaller Dragon

While the Korean people were attempting to establish their own identity in the shadow of the powerful Chinese Empire, the peoples of Vietnam, on China's southern frontier, were seeking to do the same. The Vietnamese (known as the Yueh in Chinese, from the peoples of that name inhabiting the southeastern coast of mainland China) began to practice irrigated agriculture in the flooded regions of the Red River Delta at an early date and entered the Bronze Age sometime during the second millennium B.C.E. By about 200 B.C.E., a young state had begun to form in the area but immediately encountered the expanding power of the Qin dynasty. The Vietnamese were not easy to subdue, however, and the collapse of the Qin temporarily enabled them to preserve their independence. Nevertheless, a century later, they were absorbed into the Han Empire.

At first, the Han were satisfied to rule the delta as an autonomous region under the administration of the local landed aristocracy. But Chinese taxes were oppressive, and in 39 C.E., a revolt led by the Trung sisters (widows of local nobles who had been executed by the Chinese) briefly brought Han rule to an end. The Chinese soon suppressed the rebellion, however, and began to rule the area directly through officials dispatched from China. The first Chinese officials to serve in the region became

A Plea to the New Emperor

POLITICS & GOVERNMENT

Like many other societies in premodern East and Southeast Asia, the kingdom of Vietnam regularly paid tribute to the imperial court in China. The arrangement was often beneficial to both sides, as the tributary states received a form of international recognition from the relationship, as well as trading privileges in the massive Chinese market. China, for its part, assured itself that neighboring areas would not harbor dissident elements hostile to its own security.

In this document, contained in a historical chronicle written by Le Tac (LAY-tac) in the fourteenth century, a claimant to the Vietnamese throne seeks recognition in 1295 from the new emperor of the Yuan (Mongol) dynasty in China. Note how the Vietnamese ruler stresses his hope that the new emperor in Beijing, Timur Khan, will adopt a policy of peace and friendship with his southern neighbor. Timur's predecessor, the great Khubilai Khan, had sent Chinese troops to invade Vietnam a few years previously in a bid to place the country back under Chinese rule.

Le Tac, *Essay on Annam*

The Dragon flies in the heavens; new life has come to the Golden Throne. Many embassies have flocked to the Palace to express their sincere congratulations.

One man has ascended the Throne and ten thousand kingdoms are at peace. In great awe I observe that, under His Imperial Majesty's rule, peace and culture flourish within the Empire. His benevolence and virtue permeate the lands beyond the sea as they do at home. Always faithful to the kingly way, He embraces with the same kindness far lands and near. He lays aside military concerns and promotes cultural achievements. He restrains the ardor of his troops and puts an end to all combat. He enlarges His own indulgence and benevolence. He illuminates the virtue and merit of His Ancestors. The sound of thunder has ceased; it has changed into a rain of Imperial blessings. His investiture of tributary kings has been granted with a heavenly generosity. For the people it is a true rebirth, for the Universe a true springtime. I and my people happily live in peace and rejoice to hear the news of His ascendance to the Throne. My glances are directed toward the Northern sky; my heart also turns toward the extreme North, toward the Imperial Dwelling. From this country so remote in the South which I govern, I wish and desire that the longevity of the Emperor may be as great as the mountains of the South are high.

Q *What message does the new ruler of Vietnam seem to be sending to his counterpart in Beijing? Why does he feel that this message is important in the mutual relations between the two countries?*

Source: From Le Tac, An-nam chi-luoc (Hue, University of Hue, 1961), p. 126 [Vietnamese version]; pp. 83–84 [Chinese version]. English translation by T. B. Lam. The translated document appears in Benda and Larkin, *The World of Southeast Asia* (New York: Harper & Row, 1967). pp. 148–149.

exasperated at the uncultured ways of the locals, who wandered around "naked without shame."[8] In time, however, these foreign officials began to intermarry with the local nobility and form a Sino-Vietnamese ruling class who, though trained in Chinese culture, began to identify with the cause of Vietnamese autonomy.

For nearly a thousand years, the Vietnamese were exposed to the art, architecture, literature, philosophy, and written language of China as the Chinese attempted to integrate the area culturally as well as politically and administratively into their empire. It was a classic example of the Chinese effort to introduce advanced Confucian civilization to the "backward peoples" along the perimeter. To all intents and purposes, the Red River Delta, then known to the Chinese as the "pacified South," or Annam (ahn-NAHM), became a part of China.

The Rise of Great Viet   Despite Chinese efforts to assimilate Vietnam, the Vietnamese sense of ethnic and cultural identity proved inextinguishable, and in 939, the Vietnamese took advantage of the collapse of the Tang Dynasty in China to overthrow Chinese rule.

The new Vietnamese state, which called itself Dai Viet (dy VEE-et) (Great Viet), became a dynamic new force on the Southeast Asian mainland. As the population of the Red River Delta expanded, Dai Viet soon came into conflict with Champa (CHAHM-puh), its neighbor to the south. Located along the central coast of modern Vietnam, Champa was a trading society based on Indian cultural traditons that had been established earlier in 192 C.E. Over the next several centuries, the two states fought on numerous occasions. Finally, in 1471, Dai Viet succeeded in conquering Champa. The Vietnamese then resumed their march southward, establishing agricultural settlements in the newly conquered territory. By the seventeenth century, the Vietnamese had reached the Gulf of Siam.

The Vietnamese faced an even more serious challenge from the north. The Song Dynasty in China, beset with its own problems on the northern frontier, eventually accepted the Dai Viet ruler's offer of tribute status, but later dynasties attempted to reintegrate the Red River delta into the Chinese Empire. The first effort was made in the late thirteenth century by the Mongols, who attempted on two occasions to conquer the Vietnamese. After a series of bloody battles, during which the Vietnamese displayed an impressive capacity for guerrilla warfare, the invaders were driven out. A little over a century later, the Ming Dynasty tried again, and for twenty years Vietnam was once more under Chinese rule. In 1428, the Vietnamese evicted the Chinese again, but the experience had contributed to the strong sense of Vietnamese identity.

The Chinese Legacy   Despite their stubborn resistance to Chinese rule, after the restoration of independence in the tenth century, Vietnamese rulers quickly discovered the convenience of the Confucian model in administering a river valley society and therefore attempted to follow Chinese practice in forming their own state. The ruler styled himself an emperor like his counterpart to the north (although he prudently termed himself a king in his direct dealings with the Chinese court), adopted Chinese court rituals, claimed the mandate of Heaven, and arrogated to himself the same authority and privileges in his dealings with his subjects. But unlike a Chinese emperor, who had no particular symbolic role as defender of the Chinese people or Chinese culture, a Vietnamese monarch was viewed, above all, as the symbol and defender of Vietnamese independence.

Like their Chinese counterparts, Vietnamese rulers fought to preserve their authority from the challenges of powerful aristocratic families and turned to the

Chinese bureaucratic model, including civil service examinations, as a means of doing so. Under the pressure of strong monarchs, the concept of merit eventually took hold, and the power of the landed aristocracy was weakened if not entirely broken. The Vietnamese adopted much of the Chinese administrative structure, including the six ministries, the censorate, and the various levels of provincial and local administration.

Another aspect of the Chinese legacy was the spread of Buddhist, Daoist, and Confucian ideas, which supplemented the traditional belief in nature spirits. Buddhist precepts became popular among the local population, who integrated the new faith into their existing belief system by founding Buddhist temples dedicated to the local village deity in the hope of guaranteeing an abundant harvest. Upper-class Vietnamese educated in the Confucian classics tended to follow the more agnostic Confucian doctrine, but some joined Buddhist monasteries. Daoism also flourished at all levels of society and, as in China, provided a structure for animistic beliefs and practices that still predominated at the village level.

During the early period of independence, Vietnamese culture also borrowed liberally from its larger neighbor. Educated Vietnamese tried their hand at Chinese poetry, wrote dynastic histories in the Chinese style, and followed Chinese models in sculpture, architecture, and porcelain. Many of the notable buildings of the medieval period, such as the Temple of Literature and the famous One-Pillar Pagoda in Hanoi, are classic examples of Chinese architecture.

But there were signs that Vietnamese creativity would eventually transcend the bounds of Chinese cultural norms. Although most classical writing was undertaken in literary Chinese, the only form of literary expression deemed suitable by Confucian conservatives, an adaptation of Chinese written characters, called **chu nom** (CHOO nahm) ("southern characters"), was devised to provide a written system for spoken Vietnamese. In use by the early ninth century, it eventually began to be used for the composition of essays and poetry in the Vietnamese language. Such pioneering efforts would lead in later centuries to the emergence of a vigorous national literature totally independent of Chinese forms.

Society and Family Life　　Vietnamese social institutions and customs were also strongly influenced by those of China. As in China, the introduction of a Confucian system and the adoption of civil service examinations undermined the role of the old landed aristocrats and led eventually to their replacement by the scholar-gentry class. Also as in China, the examinations were open to most males, regardless of family background, which opened the door to a degree of social mobility unknown in most of the other states in the region. Candidates for the bureaucracy read many of the same Confucian classics and absorbed the same ethical principles as their counterparts in China. At the same time, they were also exposed to the classic works of Vietnamese history, which strengthened their sense that Vietnam was a distinct culture similar to, but separate from, that of China.

The vast majority of the Vietnamese people, however, were peasants. Most were small landholders or sharecroppers who rented their plots from wealthier farmers, but large estates were rare due to the systematic efforts of the central government to prevent the rise of a powerful local landed elite.

Family life in Vietnam was similar in many respects to that in China. The Confucian concept of family took hold during the period of Chinese rule, along with the related concepts of filial piety and gender inequality. Perhaps the most striking difference between family traditions in China and Vietnam was that Vietnamese women possessed more rights both in practice and by law. Since ancient times, wives had been permitted to own property and initiate divorce proceedings. One consequence of Chinese rule was a growing emphasis on male dominance, but the tradition of women's rights was never totally extinguished and was legally recognized in a law code promulgated in 1460.

Moreover, Vietnam had a strong historical tradition associating heroic women with the defense of the homeland. The Trung sisters were the first but by no means the only example. In the following passage, a Vietnamese historian of the eighteenth century recounts their story:

> The imperial court was far away; local officials were greedy and oppressive. At that time the country of one hundred sons was the country of the women of Lord To. The ladies [the Trung sisters] used the female arts against their irreconcilable foe; skirts and hairpins sang of patriotic righteousness, uttered a solemn oath at the inner door of the ladies' quarters, expelled the governor, and seized the capital.... Were they not grand heroines? ... Our two ladies brought forward an army of all the people, and, establishing a royal court that settled affairs in the territories of the sixty-five strongholds, shook their skirts over the Hundred Yueh [the Vietnamese people].[9]

CHRONOLOGIES

FORMATION OF THE JAPANESE STATE

572–622	Shotoku Taishi
Mid-seventh century	Era of Taika reforms
710–784	Nara period
794–1185	Heian (Kyoto) period
978–c. 1016	Murasaki Shikibu
1142–1199	Minamoto Yoritomo
1185–1333	Kamakura Shogunate
Late thirteenth century	Mongol invasions
1333–1600	Ashikaga period
1467–1477	Onin War

EARLY KOREA AND VIETNAM

c. 2333 B.C.E.	Foundation of Gojoseon state in Korea
Second and first centuries B.C.E.	Chinese conquest of Korea and Vietnam
39 C.E.	Trung Sisters' Revolt
192	Founding of Champa
300s–600s	Era of Three Kingdoms in Korea
939	Restoration of Vietnamese independence

1257–1285	Mongol invasions of Korea and Vietnam
1392	Founding of Choson (Yi) Dynasty in Korea
1471	Vietnamese conquest of Champa

MindTap is a fully online, highly personalized learning experience built upon Cengage Learning content. MindTap combines student learning tools—readings, multimedia, activities, and assessments—into a singular Learning Path that guides students through their course.

12

THE MAKING OF EUROPE

The coronation of Charlemagne by Pope Leo III, as depicted in a medieval French manuscript

---

CHAPTER OUTLINE

• The Emergence of Europe in the Early Middle Ages • Europe in the High Middle Ages • Medieval Europe and the World

THE EMERGENCE OF EUROPE IN THE EARLY MIDDLE AGES

China descended into political chaos and civil wars after the end of the Han Empire, and it was almost four hundred years before a new imperial dynasty established political order. Similarly, after the collapse of the Western Roman Empire in the fifth century, it would also take hundreds of years to establish a new society.

The New Germanic Kingdoms The Germanic peoples were an important component of the new European civilization. Already by the third century C.E., they had begun to move into the lands of the Roman Empire. As imperial authority vanished in the fifth century, a number of German kings set up new states. By 500, the Western Roman Empire had been replaced politically by a series of states ruled by German kings.

The fusion of Romans and Germans took different forms in the various Germanic kingdoms. The kingdom of the Ostrogoths (AHSS-truh-gahths) in Italy managed to preserve the Roman tradition of government. After establishing his control over Italy, the Ostrogothic king Theodoric (thee-AHD-uh-rik) (493–526) kept the entire structure of imperial Roman government, although he used separate systems of rule for Romans and Ostrogoths. The Roman population of Italy lived under Roman law administered by Roman officials. The Ostrogoths were governed by their own customs and their own officials.

Like the kingdom of the Ostrogoths in Italy, the kingdom of the Visigoths (VIZ-uh-gahths) in Spain inherited and continued to maintain much of the Roman structure of government. In both states, the Roman population was allowed to maintain Roman institutions while being largely excluded from power as a Germanic warrior caste came to dominate the considerably larger native population. Over a period of time, the Visigoths and the native peoples began to fuse together.

Roman influence was weaker in Britain. When the Roman armies abandoned Britain at the beginning of the fifth century, the Angles and Saxons, Germanic tribes from Denmark and northern Germany, moved in and settled there. Eventually, these peoples succeeded in carving out small kingdoms throughout the island, Kent in southeast England being one of them.

The Kingdom of the Franks One of the most prominent German states on the European continent was the kingdom of the Franks. The establishment of a Frankish kingdom was the work of Clovis (KLOH-viss) (c. 482–511), a member of the Merovingian (meh-ruh-VIN-jee-un) dynasty who became a Catholic Christian around 500. He was not the first German king to convert to Christianity, but the others had joined the Arian (AR-ee-un) sect of Christianity, a group who believed that Jesus had been human and thus not truly God. The Christian church in Rome, which had become known as the Roman Catholic Church, regarded the Arians as heretics, people who believed in teachings different from the official church doctrine. To Catholics, Jesus was human, but of the "same substance" as God and therefore also truly God. Clovis found that his conversion to Catholic Christianity gained him the support of the Roman Catholic Church, which was only too eager to obtain the friendship of a major Germanic ruler who was a Catholic Christian.

MAP 12.1 The Germanic Kingdoms of the Old Western Empire

Germanic tribes filled the power vacuum caused by the demise of the Western Roman Empire, founding states that blended elements of Germanic customs and laws with those of Roman culture, including large-scale conversions to Christianity. The Franks established the most durable of these Germanic states.

By 510, Clovis had established a powerful new Frankish kingdom stretching from the Pyrenees in the west to German lands in the east (modern France and western Germany). After Clovis's death, however, his sons divided his newly created kingdom, as was the Frankish custom. During the sixth and seventh centuries, the once-united Frankish kingdom came to be divided into three major areas:

Neustria (NOO-stree-uh), in northern Gaul; Austrasia (awss-TRAY-zhuh), consisting of the ancient Frankish lands on both sides of the Rhine; and the former kingdom of Burgundy.

The Society of the Germanic Peoples   As Germans and Romans intermarried and began to form a new society, some of the social customs of the Germanic peoples came to play an important role. The crucial social bond among the Germanic peoples was the family, especially the extended family of husbands, wives, children, brothers, sisters, cousins, and grandparents. The German family structure was quite simple. Males were dominant and made all the important decisions. A woman obeyed her father until she married and then fell under the legal domination of her husband. For most women in the new Germanic kingdoms, their legal status reflected the material conditions of their lives. Most women had life expectancies of only thirty or forty years, and perhaps 15 percent of women died in their childbearing years, no doubt due to complications associated with childbirth. For most women, life consisted of domestic labor: providing food and clothing for the household, caring for the children, and assisting with farming chores.

The German conception of family affected the way Germanic law treated the problem of crime and punishment. In the Roman system, as in our own, a crime such as murder was considered an offense against society or the state and was handled by a court that heard evidence and arrived at a decision. Germanic law was personal. An injury to one person by another could lead to a blood feud in which the family of the injured party took revenge on the family of the wrongdoer. Feuds could involve savage acts of revenge, such as hacking off hands or feet or gouging out eyes. Because this system could easily get out of control, an alternative system arose that made use of a fine called **wergeld** (WUR-geld), which was paid by a wrongdoer to the family of the person injured or killed. *Wergeld*, which literally means "man money," was the value of a person in monetary terms. That value varied considerably according to social status. An offense against a nobleman, for example, cost considerably more than one against a freeman or a slave.

Germanic law also provided a means of determining guilt or innocence: the ordeal. The ordeal was based on the idea of divine intervention: divine forces (whether pagan or Christian) would not allow an innocent person to be harmed.

The Role of the Christian Church   By the end of the fourth century, Christianity had become the predominant religion of the Roman Empire. As the official Roman state disintegrated, the Christian church played an increasingly important role in the growth of the new European civilization.

The Organization of the Church   By the fourth century, the Christian church had developed a system of government. A bishop, whose area of jurisdiction was known as a bishopric, or **diocese**, headed the Christian community in each city; the bishoprics of each Roman province were joined together under the direction of an archbishop. The bishops of four great cities—Rome, Jerusalem, Alexandria, and Antioch—held positions of special power in church affairs because the churches in these cities all asserted that they had been founded by the original apostles sent out by Jesus. Soon, however, one of them—the bishop of Rome—claimed that he was the sole leader of the western Christian church. According to church tradition, Jesus had given the keys to the kingdom of heaven to Peter, who was considered the chief apostle and the first bishop of Rome. Subsequent bishops of Rome were considered Peter's successors and came to be known as popes (from the Latin word *papa*, meaning "father"). By the sixth century, the popes had been successful in extending papal authority over the Christian church in the west and converting the pagan peoples of Germanic Europe. Their primary instrument of conversion was the monastic movement.

The Monks and Their Missions   A **monk** (in Latin, *monachus*, meaning "one who lives alone") was a man who sought to live a life divorced from the world, cut off from ordinary human society, in order to pursue an ideal of total dedication to God. As the monastic ideal spread, a new form of **monasticism** based on living together in a community soon became the dominant form. Saint Benedict (c. 480–c. 543), who founded a monastic house for which he wrote a set of rules, established the basic form of monastic life in the western Christian church.

Benedict's rules divided each day into a series of activities, with primary emphasis on prayer and manual labor. Physical work of some kind was required of all monks for several hours a day because idleness was "the enemy of the soul." At the very heart of community practice was prayer, the proper "work of God." Although this included private meditation and reading, all monks gathered together seven times during the day for common prayer and chanting of psalms. The Benedictine life was a communal one. Monks ate, worked, slept, and worshiped together.

Each Benedictine monastery was strictly ruled by an **abbot**, or "father" of the monastery, who had complete authority over his fellow monks. Unquestioning obedience to the will of the abbot was expected of every monk. Each Benedictine monastery held lands that enabled it to be a self-sustaining community, isolated from and independent of the world surrounding it. Within the monastery, however, monks were to fulfill their vow of poverty: "Let all things be common to all, as it is written, lest anyone should say that anything is his own."[1] Only men could be monks, but women, called **nuns**, also began to withdraw from the world to dedicate themselves to God.

Monasticism played an indispensable role in early medieval civilization. Monks became the new heroes of Christian civilization, and their dedication to God became the highest ideal of Christian life. They were the social workers of their communities: monks provided schools for the young, hospitality for travelers, and hospitals for the sick. Monks also copied Latin works and passed on the legacy of the ancient world to the new European civilization. Monasteries became centers of learning wherever they were located, and monks worked to spread Christianity to all of Europe.

Women played an important role in the monastic missionary movement and the conversion of the Germanic kingdoms. Some served as **abbesses** (an abbess was the head of a monastery for nuns, known as a convent); many abbesses came from aristocratic families, especially in Anglo-Saxon England. In the kingdom of Northumbria, for example, Saint Hilda founded the monastery of Whitby in 657. As abbess, she was responsible for making learning an important part of the life of the monastery.

Saint Benedict. *Benedict was the author of a set of rules that was instrumental in the development of monastic groups in the Catholic Church. In this sixth-century Latin manuscript miniature, an abbot is shown offering codes and possessions to Saint Benedict.*

Charlemagne and the Carolingians

During the seventh and eighth centuries, as the kings of the Frankish kingdom gradually lost their power, the mayors of the palace—the chief officers of the king's household—assumed more control of the kingdom. One of these mayors, Pepin (PEP-in or pay-PANH), finally took the logical step of assuming the kingship of the Frankish state for himself and his family. Upon his death in 768, his son came to the throne of the Frankish kingdom.

This new king was the dynamic and powerful ruler known to history as Charles the Great (768–814), or Charlemagne (SHAR-luh-mayn) (from the Latin for Charles the Great, *Carolus Magnus*). He was determined and decisive, intelligent and inquisitive, a strong statesman, and a pious Christian. Although unable to read or write himself, he was a wise patron of learning. In a series of military campaigns, he greatly expanded the territory he had inherited and created what came to be known as the Carolingian (kar-uh-LIN-jun) Empire. At its height, Charlemagne's empire covered much of western and central Europe; not until the time of Napoleon in the nineteenth century would an empire of its size be seen again in Europe.

Charlemagne continued the efforts of his father in organizing the Carolingian kingdom. Besides his household staff, Charlemagne's administration of the empire depended on the use of counts as the king's chief representatives in local areas. As an important check on the power of the counts, Charlemagne established the *missi dominici* (MISS-ee doh-MIN-i-chee) ("messengers of the lord king"), two men who were sent out to local districts to ensure that the counts were executing the king's wishes. They had the power to remove counts if they were abusing their power, thus making the *missi* an important instrument in bolstering royal power.

What Was the Significance of Charlemagne?   As Charlemagne's power grew, so did his prestige as the most powerful Christian ruler of what one monk called the "kingdom of Europe." In 800, Charlemagne acquired a new title: emperor of the Romans. The significance of this imperial coronation has been much debated by historians. We are not even sure if the pope or Charlemagne initiated the idea when they met in the summer of 799 in Paderborn in German lands or whether Charles was pleased or displeased.

In any case, Charlemagne's coronation as Roman emperor demonstrated the strength, even after three hundred years, of the concept of an enduring Roman Empire. More important, it symbolized the fusion of Roman, Christian, and Germanic elements. Did this fusion constitute the foundations of European civilization? A Germanic king had been crowned emperor of the Romans by the spiritual leader of western Christendom. Charlemagne had created an empire that stretched from the North Sea to Italy and from the Atlantic Ocean to the Danube River. This differed significantly from the Roman Empire, which encompassed much of the Mediterranean world. Had a new civilization emerged? And should Charlemagne be regarded, as one of his biographers has argued, as the "father of Europe"?[2]

Other historians argue that there was only a weak sense of community in Europe before 1000. As one has stated, "Europe was not born in the early Middle Ages.... There was no common European culture, and certainly not any Europe-wide economy."[3]

The World of Lords and Vassals   The Carolingian Empire began to disintegrate soon after Charlemagne's death in 814, and less than thirty years later, in 843, it was divided among his grandsons into three major sections: the western Frankish lands, which formed the core of the eventual kingdom of France; the eastern lands, which eventually became Germany; and a "middle kingdom" extending from the North Sea to the Mediterranean. The territories of the middle kingdom became a source of incessant struggle between the other two Frankish rulers and their heirs. At the same time, powerful nobles gained even more dominance in their local territories while the Carolingian rulers fought each other, and incursions by outsiders into various parts of the Carolingian world furthered the process of disintegration.

Invasions of the Ninth and Tenth Centuries   In the ninth and tenth centuries, western Europe was beset by a wave of invasions. Muslims attacked the southern coasts of Europe and sent raiding parties into southern France. The Magyars (MAG-yarz), a people from western Asia, moved into central Europe at the end of the ninth century and settled on the plains of Hungary, launching forays from there into western Europe. Finally crushed at the Battle of Lechfeld (LEK-feld) in Germany in 955, the Magyars converted to Christianity, settled down, and established the kingdom of Hungary.

The most far-reaching attacks of the time came from the Northmen or Norsemen of Scandinavia, also known to us as the Vikings. The Vikings were warriors whose love of adventure and search for booty and new avenues of trade may have spurred them to invade other areas of Europe. Viking ships were the best of the period. Long and narrow with beautifully carved arched prows, the Viking "dragon ships" each carried about fifty men. Their shallow draft enabled them to sail up European rivers and attack places at some distance inland. In the ninth century, Vikings sacked villages and towns, destroyed churches, and easily defeated small local armies. Viking attacks were terrifying, and many a clergyman pleaded with his parishioners to change their behavior and appease God's anger to avert the attacks, as in this sermon by an English archbishop in 1014:

> Things have not gone well now for a long time at home or abroad, but there has been devastation and persecution in every district again and again, and the English have been for a long time now completely defeated and too greatly disheartened through God's anger; and the pirates [Vikings] so strong with God's consent that often in battle one puts to flight ten, and sometimes less, sometimes more, all because of our sins.... We pay them continually and they humiliate us daily; they ravage and they burn, plunder, and rob and carry on board; and lo, what else is there in all these events except God's anger clear and visible over this people?[4]

By the middle of the ninth century, the Norsemen had begun to build winter settlements in different areas of Europe. By 850, groups from Norway had settled in Ireland, and Danes occupied northeastern England by 878. Beginning in 911, the ruler of the western Frankish lands gave one band of Vikings land at the mouth of the Seine (SEN) River, a territory that came to be known as Normandy. This policy of settling the Vikings and converting them to Christianity was a deliberate one; by their conversion to Christianity, the Vikings were soon made a part of European civilization.

The Development of Fief-Holding   The disintegration of central authority in the Carolingian world and the invasions by Muslims, Magyars, and Vikings led to the emergence of a new type of relationship between free individuals. When governments ceased to be able to defend their subjects, it became important to find some powerful lord who could offer protection in return for service. The contract sworn between a lord and his subordinate (known as a **vassal**) is the basis of a form of social organization that modern historians called *feudalism*. But feudalism was never a cohesive system, and many historians today prefer to avoid using the term.

With the breakdown of royal governments, powerful nobles took control of large areas of land. They needed men to fight for them, so the practice arose of giving grants of land to vassals who in return would fight for their lord. The Frankish army had originally consisted of foot soldiers, dressed in coats of mail and armed with swords. But in the eighth century, larger horses began to be used, along with the stirrup, which was introduced by nomadic horsemen from Asia. Earlier, horsemen had been throwers of spears. Now they wore armor in the form of coats of mail (the larger horse could carry the weight) and wielded long lances that enabled them to act as battering rams (the stirrups kept them on their horses). For almost five hundred years, heavily armored cavalry, or *knights*, as they were called, dominated warfare in Europe. The knights came to have the greatest social prestige and formed the backbone of the European aristocracy.

Of course, it was expensive to have a horse, armor, and weapons. It also took time and much practice to learn to wield these instruments skillfully from horseback. Consequently, a lord who wanted men to fight for him had to grant each vassal a piece of land that provided for the support of the vassal and his family. In return for the land, the vassal provided his lord with his fighting skills. Each needed the other. In the society of the Early Middle Ages, where there was little trade and wealth was based primarily on land, land became the most important gift a lord could give to a vassal in return for his loyalty and military service.

By the ninth century, the grant of land made to a vassal had become known as a **fief** (FEEF). A fief was a piece of land held from the lord by a vassal in return for military service, but vassals who held such grants of land came to exercise rights of jurisdiction or political and legal authority within these fiefs. As the Carolingian world disintegrated politically under the impact of internal dissension and invasions, an increasing number of powerful lords arose who were now responsible for keeping order.

The Practice of Fief-Holding   Fief-holding also became increasingly complicated with the development of **subinfeudation** (sub-in-fyoo-DAY-shun). The vassals of a king, who were themselves great lords, might also have vassals who would owe them military service in return for a grant of land taken from their estates. Those vassals, in turn, might likewise have vassals, who at such a level would be simple knights with barely enough land to provide their equipment. The lord-vassal relationship, then, bound together both greater and lesser landowners. At all levels, the lord-vassal relationship was always an honorable relationship between free men and did not imply any sense of servitude.

Fief-holding came to be characterized by a set of practices that determined the relationship between a lord and his vassal. The major obligation of a vassal to his lord was to perform military service, usually about forty days a year. A vassal was also required to appear at his lord's court when summoned to give advice to the lord. He might also be asked to sit in judgment in a legal case, since the important vassals of a lord were peers and only they could judge each other. Finally, vassals were also responsible for aids, or financial payments to the lord on a number of occasions, including the knighting of the lord's eldest son, the marriage of his eldest daughter, and the ransom of the lord's person if he were captured.

In turn, a lord had responsibilities toward his vassals. His major obligation was to protect his vassal, either by defending him militarily or by taking his side in a court of law. The lord was also responsible for the maintenance of the vassal, usually by granting him a fief.

The Manorial System   The landholding class of nobles and knights contained a military elite whose ability to function as warriors depended on having the leisure time to pursue the arts of war. Landed estates, located on the fiefs given to a vassal

MAP 12.2 A Typical Manor

The manorial system created small, tightly knit communities in which peasants were economically and physically bound to their lord. Crops were rotated, with roughly one-third of the fields lying fallow (untilled) at any one time, which helped replenish soil nutrients.

by his lord and worked by a dependent peasant class, provided the economic sustenance that made this way of life possible. A **manor** was an agricultural estate operated by a lord and worked by peasants. Although a large class of free peasants continued to exist, increasing numbers of free peasants became **serfs**, who were bound to the land and required to provide labor services, pay rents, and be subject to the lord's jurisdiction. By the ninth century, probably 60 percent of the population of western Europe had become serfs.

Labor services involved working the lord's **demesne** (duh-MAYN *or* duh-MEEN), the land retained by the lord, which might consist of one-third to one-half of the cultivated lands scattered throughout the manor. The rest would be used by the peasants for themselves. Building barns and digging ditches were also part of the labor services. Serfs usually worked about three days a week for their lord and paid rents by giving the lord a share of every product they raised.

Serfs were legally bound to the lord's lands and could not leave without his permission. Although free to marry, serfs could not marry anyone outside their manor without the lord's approval. Moreover, lords sometimes exercised public rights or political authority on their lands, which gave them the right to try peasants in their own courts.

EUROPE IN THE HIGH MIDDLE AGES

The new European civilization that had emerged in the Early Middle Ages began to flourish in the High Middle Ages (1000–1300). New agricultural practices that increased the food supply spurred commercial and urban expansion. Both lords and vassals recovered from the invasions and internal dissension of the Early Middle Ages, and medieval kings began to exert a centralizing authority. The recovery of the Catholic Church made it a forceful presence in every area of life. The High Middle Ages also gave birth to a cultural revival.

Land and People   In the Early Middle Ages, Europe had a relatively small population of about 38 million, but in the High Middle Ages, the number of people nearly doubled to 74 million. What accounted for this dramatic increase? For one thing, conditions in Europe were more settled and more peaceful after the invasions of the Early Middle Ages had ended. For another, agricultural production surged after 1000.

The New Agriculture   During the High Middle Ages, Europeans began to farm in new ways. An improvement in climate resulted in better growing conditions, but an important factor in increasing food production was the expansion of cultivated or arable land, accomplished by clearing forested areas. Peasants of the eleventh and twelfth centuries cut down trees and drained swamps until by the thirteenth century, Europeans had more acreage available for farming than at any time before or since.

Technological changes also furthered the development of farming. The Middle Ages saw an explosion of laborsaving devices, many of which were made from iron, which was mined in different areas of Europe. Iron was used to make scythes, axes, and hoes for use on farms as well as saws, hammers, and nails for building purposes. Iron was crucial in making the *carruca* (kuh-ROO-kuh), a heavy, wheeled plow with an iron plowshare pulled by teams of horses, which could turn over the heavy clay soil north of the Alps.

Besides using horsepower, the High Middle Ages harnessed the power of water and wind to do jobs formerly done by human or animal power. Although the watermill had been invented as early as the second century B.C.E., it did not come into widespread use until the High Middle Ages. Located along streams, watermills were used to grind grain into flour. Often dams were constructed to increase the waterpower. The development of the cam enabled millwrights to mechanize entire industries; waterpower was used in certain phases of cloth production and to run trip-hammers for the working of metals. The Chinese had made use of the cam in operating trip-hammers for hulling rice by the third century C.E. but apparently had not extended its use to other industries.

Where rivers were unavailable or not easily dammed, Europeans developed windmills to use the power of the wind. Historians are uncertain whether windmills were imported into Europe (they were invented in Persia) or designed independently by Europeans. In either case, by the end of the twelfth century, they were beginning to dot the European landscape. The watermill and windmill were the most important devices for the harnessing of power before the invention of the steam engine in the eighteenth century.

The shift from a two-field to a three-field system also contributed to the increase in food production. In the Early Middle Ages, peasants had planted one field while another of equal size was allowed to lie fallow (untilled) to regain its fertility. Now estates were divided into three parts. One field was planted in the fall with winter grains, such as rye and wheat, while spring grains, such as oats or barley, and

COMPARATIVE ILLUSTRATION

The New Agriculture in the Medieval World

EARTH &
ENVIRONMENT

New agricultural methods and techniques in the Middle Ages enabled peasants in both Europe and China to increase food production. This general improvement in diet was a factor in supporting noticeably larger populations in both areas. A thirteenth-century illustration (top image) shows a group of English peasants harvesting grain. Overseeing their work is a bailiff, or manager, who supervised the work of the peasants. A thirteenth-century painting (bottom image) shows Chinese peasants harvesting rice, which became the staple food in China.

Q *How important were staple foods (such as wheat and rice) to the diet and health of people in Europe and China during the Middle Ages?*

The Art Archive at Art Resource, NY

The Art Archive at Art Resource, NY

vegetables, such as peas or beans, were planted in the second field. The third was allowed to lie fallow. By rotating the use of the fields, only one-third rather than one-half of the land lay fallow at any time. The rotation of crops also kept the soil from being exhausted so quickly, and more crops could now be grown.

Daily Life of the Peasantry　The lifestyle of the peasants was quite simple. Their cottages were built with wood frames with walls made of laths or sticks; the spaces between the laths were stuffed with straw and rubble and then plastered over with clay. Roofs were often thatched with reeds or straw. The houses of poorer peasants consisted of a single room, but others had at least two rooms—a main room for cooking, eating, and other activities and another room for sleeping.

Peasant women occupied an important but difficult position in manorial society. As mothers, they were expected to carry and bear their children, as well as provide for their socialization and religious training. Peasant women also bore responsibility for doing the spinning and weaving that provided the household's clothes, tending the family's vegetable garden and chickens, and providing the meals. A woman's ability to manage the household might determine whether a peasant family would starve or survive in difficult times. At the same time, peasant women often worked with men in the fields, especially at harvest time. Indeed, as one historian has noted, peasant marriage was an "economic partnership" in which both husbands and wives contributed their own distinctive labor.

Though simple, a peasant's daily diet was adequate when food was available. The staple of the peasant diet, and the medieval diet in general, was bread. Women made the dough for the bread at home and then brought their loaves to be baked in community ovens, which were owned by the lord of the manor. Peasant bread was highly nutritious, containing not only wheat and rye but also barley, millet, and oats, giving it a dark appearance and a very heavy, hard texture. Bread was supplemented by numerous vegetables from the household gardens, cheese from cow's or goat's milk, nuts and berries from woodlands, and fruits, such as apples, pears, and cherries. Chickens provided eggs and sometimes meat.

The Nobility of the Middle Ages　In the High Middle Ages, European society, like that of Japan during the same period, was dominated by men whose chief concern was warfare. Like the Japanese samurai, many Western nobles loved war. As one nobleman wrote:

And well I like to hear the call of "Help" and see the wounded fall
Loudly for mercy praying,
And see the dead, both great and small,
Pierced by sharp spearheads one and all.[5]

The men of war were the lords and vassals of medieval society.

The lords were the kings, dukes, counts, barons, and viscounts (and even bishops and archbishops) who had extensive landholdings and wielded considerable political influence. They formed an **aristocracy** or nobility of people who held real political, economic, and social power. Both the great lords and ordinary knights were warriors, and the institution of knighthood united them. But there were also social divisions among them based on extremes of wealth and landholdings.

In the eleventh and twelfth centuries, under the influence of the church, an ideal of civilized behavior called **chivalry** (SHIV-uhl-ree) gradually evolved among the nobility. Chivalry represented a code of ethics that knights were supposed to uphold. In addition to defending the church and the defenseless, knights were expected to treat captives as honored guests instead of throwing them in dungeons. Chivalry also implied that knights should fight only for glory, but the ideals of chivalry were not always taken seriously.

Although aristocratic women could legally hold property, most women remained under the control of men—their fathers until they married and their husbands after that. Nevertheless, these women had many opportunities for playing important roles. Because the lord was often away at war or at court, the lady of the castle had to manage the estate. Households could include large numbers of officials and servants, so this was no small responsibility. Maintaining the financial accounts alone took considerable financial knowledge. The lady of the castle was also responsible for overseeing the food supply and maintaining all the other supplies needed for the smooth operation of the household.

Although women were expected to be subservient to their husbands, there were many strong women who advised and sometimes even dominated their husbands. Perhaps the most famous was Eleanor of Aquitaine (c. 1122–1204). Married to King Louis VII of France, Eleanor accompanied her husband on a crusade, but her alleged affair with her uncle during the crusade led Louis to have their marriage annulled. Eleanor then married Henry, duke of Normandy and count of Anjou (AHN-zhoo), who became King Henry II of England (1154–1189). She took an active role in politics, even assisting her sons in rebelling against Henry in 1173 and 1174.

The New World of Trade and Cities

Medieval Europe was overwhelmingly agrarian, with most people living in small villages. In the eleventh and twelfth centuries, however, new elements were introduced that began to transform the economic foundation of European civilization: a revival of trade, the emergence of specialized craftspeople and artisans, and the growth and development of towns.

The Revival of Trade

The revival of trade was a gradual process. During the chaotic conditions of the Early Middle Ages, large-scale trade had declined in western Europe except for Byzantine contacts with Italy and the Jewish traders who moved back and forth between the Muslim and Christian worlds. By the end of the tenth century, however, people were emerging in Europe with both the skills and the products for commercial activity. Cities in Italy took the lead in this revival of trade. Venice, for example, emerged as a town by the end of the eighth century, developed a mercantile fleet, and by the end of the tenth century had become the chief western trading center for Byzantine and Islamic commerce.

While the northern Italian cities were busy trading in the Mediterranean, the towns of Flanders were doing likewise in northern Europe. Flanders, the area along the coast of present-day Belgium and northern France, was known for its high-quality woolen cloth. The location of Flanders made it an ideal center for the traders of northern Europe. Merchants from England, Scandinavia, France, and Germany converged there to trade their goods for woolen cloth. Flanders prospered

FILM & HISTORY

The Lion in Winter (1968)

Directed by Anthony Harvey, *The Lion in Winter* is based on a play by James Goldman, who also wrote the script for the movie and won an Oscar for best adapted screenplay for it. The action takes place in a castle in Chinon, France, over the Christmas holidays in 1183. The setting is realistic: medieval castles had dirt floors covered with rushes, under which lay, according to one observer, "an ancient collection of grease, fragments, bones, excrement of dogs and cats, and everything that is nasty." The powerful but world-weary King Henry II (Peter O'Toole), ruler of England and a number of French lands (the "Angevin Empire"), wants to establish his legacy and plans a Christmas gathering to decide which of his sons should succeed him. He favors his overindulged youngest son John (Nigel Terry), but he is opposed by his strong-willed and estranged wife, Eleanor of Aquitaine (Katharine Hepburn). She has been imprisoned by the king for leading a rebellion against him but has been temporarily freed for the holidays. Eleanor favors their son Richard (Anthony Hopkins), the most military minded of the brothers. The middle brother, Geoffrey (John Castle), is not a candidate but manipulates the other brothers to gain his own advantage. All three sons are portrayed as treacherous and traitorous, and Henry is distrustful of them. At one point, he threatens to imprison and even kill his sons; marry his mistress Alais (Jane Merrow), who is also the sister of the king of France; and have a new family to replace them.

In contemporary terms, Henry and Eleanor are an unhappily married couple, and their family is acutely dysfunctional. Sparks fly as family members plot against each other, using intentionally cruel comments and sarcastic responses to wound each other as much as possible. When Eleanor says to Henry, "What would you have me do? Give up? Give in?" he responds, "Give me a little peace." To which Eleanor replies, "A little? Why so modest? How about eternal peace? Now there's a thought." At one point, John responds to bad news about his chances for the throne with "Poor John. Who says poor John? Don't everybody sob at once. My God, if I went up in flames, there's not a living soul who'd pee on me to put the fire out!" His brother Richard replies, "Let's strike a flint and see." Henry can also be cruel to his sons: "You're not mine! We're not connected! I deny you! None of you will get my crown. I leave you nothing, and I wish you plague!"

In developing this well-written, imaginative re-creation of a royal family's hapless Christmas gathering, James Goldman had a great deal of material to use. Henry II was one of the most powerful

in the eleventh and twelfth centuries, and such Flemish towns as Bruges (BROOZH) and Ghent (GENT) became centers of the medieval cloth trade.

By the twelfth century, a regular exchange of goods had developed between Flanders and Italy, the two major centers of northern and southern European trade. To encourage this trade, the counts of Champagne in northern France began to hold a series of six fairs annually in the chief towns of their territory. At these fairs, northern merchants brought the furs, woolen cloth, tin, and honey of northern Europe and exchanged them for the cloth and swords of northern Italy and the silks, sugar, and spices of the East.

monarchs of his day, and Eleanor of Aquitaine was one of the most powerful women. She had first been queen of France, but that marriage was annulled. Next she married Henry, who was then count of Anjou, and became queen of England when he became king in 1154. During their stormy marriage, Eleanor and Henry had five sons and three daughters. She is supposed to have murdered Rosamond, one of her husband's mistresses, and aided her sons in a rebellion against their father in 1173, causing Henry to distrust his sons ever after. But Henry struck back, imprisoning Eleanor for sixteen years. After his death, however, Eleanor returned to Aquitaine and lived on to play an influential role in the reigns of her two sons, Richard and John, who succeeded their father.

Eleanor of Aquitaine (Katharine Hepburn) and Henry II (Peter O'Toole) at dinner in Henry's castle in Chinon, France.

The Kobal Collection at Art Resource, NY

As trade increased, both gold and silver came to be in demand at fairs and trading markets of all kinds. Slowly, a money economy began to emerge. New trading companies and banking firms were set up to manage the exchange and sale of goods. New techniques, including double-entry bookkeeping, commercial contracts, and insurance, also appeared to facilitate the expansion of businesses. All of these new practices were part of a commercial revolution based on the growth of **capitalism**, an economic system in which commerce and industry are controlled by private owners who invest in trade and goods in order to make profits.

Two Views of Trade and Merchants

INTERACTION & EXCHANGE

The revival of trade in Europe was a gradual process, but by the High Middle Ages, it had begun to expand dramatically. During the medieval period, trade already flourished in other parts of the world, especially in the Islamic world and in China. Nevertheless, many people in these societies, including rulers, nobles, and religious leaders, had some reservations about the success of merchants. The first selection is taken from an account of the life of Godric, a twelfth-century European merchant who became a saint. The second selection is from the *Prolegomena*, the first part of a universal history written by Ibn Khaldun, a Muslim historian who traveled widely in the Muslim world in the fourteenth century.

Life of Saint Godric

At first, he lived as a peddler for four years in Lincolnshire, going on foot and carrying the smallest wares; then he traveled abroad, first to St. Andrews in Scotland and then for the first time to Rome. On his return, having formed a familiar friendship with certain other young men who were eager for merchandise, he began to launch upon bolder courses, and to coast frequently by sea to the foreign lands that lay around him. Thus, sailing often to and fro between Scotland and Britain, he traded in many divers wares and, amid these occupations, learned much worldly wisdom....

Thus aspiring ever higher and higher, and yearning upward with his whole heart, at length his great labors and cares bore much fruit of worldly gain. For he labored not only as a merchant but also as a shipman ... to Denmark and to Flanders and Scotland; in all which lands he found certain rare, and therefore more precious, wares, which he carried to other parts wherein he knew them to be least familiar, and coveted by the inhabitants beyond the price of gold itself; wherefore he exchanged these wares for others coveted by men of other lands; and thus he chaffered [traded] most freely and assiduously. Hence he made great profit in all his bargains, and gathered much wealth in the sweat of his brow; for he sold dear in one place the wares which he had bought elsewhere at a small price.

Trade Outside Europe   In the High Middle Ages, Italian merchants became even more daring in their trade activities. They established trading posts in Cairo, Damascus, and a number of Black Sea ports, where they acquired spices, silks, jewelry, dyestuffs, and other goods brought by Muslim merchants from India, China, and Southeast Asia.

The spread of the Mongol Empire in the thirteenth century also opened the door to Italian merchants in the markets of Central Asia, India, and China. As nomads who relied on trade with settled communities, the Mongols maintained safe trade routes for merchants moving through their lands. Two Venetian merchants, the brothers Niccolò and Maffeo Polo, began to travel in the Mongol Empire around 1260.

And now he had lived sixteen years as a merchant, and began to think of spending on charity, to God's honor and service, the goods which he had so laboriously acquired. He therefore took the cross as a pilgrim to Jerusalem.... [When he had returned to England] Godric, that he might follow Christ the more freely, sold all his possessions and distributed them among the poor [and began to live the life of a hermit].

Ibn Khaldun, *Prolegomena*

As for trade, although it be a natural means of livelihood, yet most of the methods it employs are tricks aimed at making a profit by securing the difference between the buying and selling prices, and by appropriating the surplus. This is why [religious] Law allows the use of such methods, which, although they come under the heading of gambling, yet do not constitute the taking without return of other people's goods....

Should their standard of living, however, rise, so that they begin to enjoy more than the bare necessities, the effect will be to breed in them a desire for repose and tranquility. They will therefore cooperate to secure superfluities; their food and clothing will increase in quantity and refinement; they will enlarge their houses and plan their towns for defense. A further improvement in their conditions will lead to habits of luxury, resulting in extreme refinement in cooking and the preparation of food; in choosing rich clothing of the finest silk; in raising lofty mansions and castles and furnishing them luxuriously, and so on. At this stage the crafts develop and reach their height. Lofty castles and mansions are built and decorated sumptuously, water is drawn to them and a great diversity takes place in the way of dress, furniture, vessels, and household equipment. Such are the townsmen, who earn their living in industry or trade.

Q *What did the biographer of Godric and Ibn Khaldun see as valuable in mercantile activity? What reservations did they have about trade? How are the two perspectives alike? How are they different, and how do you explain the differences? What generalizations can you make about Christian and Muslim attitudes toward trade?*

Sources: Life of Saint Godric from Reginald of Durham, "Life of St. Godric," in G. G. Coulton, ed., *Social Life in Britain from the Conquest to the Reformation* (Cambridge: Cambridge University Press, 1918), pp. 415–420. From *An Arab Philosophy of History*, ed. and trans. by Charles Issawi. New York: Darwin Press, 1987.

The creation of the Crusader states in Syria and Palestine in the twelfth and thirteenth centuries (discussed later in this chapter) was especially favorable to Italian merchants. In return for taking the Crusaders to the east, Italian merchant fleets received trading concessions in Syria and Palestine. Venice, for example, which profited the most from this trade, was given a quarter, soon known as "a little Venice in the east," in Tyre on the coast of what is now Lebanon. Such quarters here and in other cities soon became bases for carrying on lucrative trade.

The Growth of Cities The revival of trade led to a revival of cities. Towns had greatly declined in the Early Middle Ages, especially in Europe north of the Alps. Old Roman cities continued to exist but had dwindled in size and population. With the revival of trade, merchants began to settle in these old cities, followed by craftspeople or artisans, people who on manors or elsewhere had developed skills and now saw an opportunity to ply their trade and make goods that could be sold by the merchants. In the course of the eleventh and twelfth centuries, the old Roman cities came alive with new populations and growth.

Beginning in the late tenth century, many new cities or towns were also founded, particularly in northern Europe. Usually, a group of merchants established a settlement near some fortified stronghold, such as a castle or monastery. (This explains why so many place names in Europe end in *borough, burgh, burg*, or *bourg*, all of which mean "fortress" or "walled enclosure.") Castles were particularly favored because they were generally located along trade routes; the lords of the castle also offered protection. If the settlement prospered and expanded, new walls were built to protect it.

Although lords wanted to treat towns and townspeople as they would their vassals and serfs, cities had totally different needs and a different perspective. Townspeople needed mobility to trade. Consequently, these merchants and artisans (who came to be called *burghers* or *bourgeois*, from the same root as *borough* and *burg*) needed their own unique laws to meet their requirements and were willing to pay for them. In many instances, lords and kings saw that they could also make money and were willing to sell to the townspeople the liberties they were beginning to demand, including the right to bequeath goods and sell property, freedom from any military obligation to the lord, and written urban laws that guaranteed their freedom. Some towns also obtained the right to govern themselves by choosing their own officials and administering their own courts of law.

Where townspeople experienced difficulties in obtaining privileges, they often swore an oath, forming an association called a **commune**, and resorted to force against their lay or ecclesiastical lords. Communes made their first appearance in northern Italy, in towns that were governed by their bishops, whom the emperors used as their chief administrators. In the eleventh century, city residents swore communal associations with the bishops' noble vassals and overthrew the authority of the bishops by force. Communes took over the rights of government and created new offices for self-rule. Although communes were also sworn in northern Europe, townspeople did not have the support of rural nobles, and revolts against lay lords were usually suppressed. When they succeeded, communes received the right to choose their own officials and run their own cities. Unlike the towns in Italy, however, where the decline of the emperor's authority ensured that the northern Italian cities could function as self-governing republics, towns in France and England, like their counterparts in the Islamic and Chinese empires, did not become independent city-states but remained ultimately subject to royal authority.

Medieval cities in Europe, then, possessed varying degrees of self-government, depending on the amount of control retained over them by the lord or king in whose territory they were located. Nevertheless, all towns, regardless of the degree of outside control, evolved institutions of government for running the affairs of the community. Only males who were born in the city or had lived there for a specific length of time could be citizens. In many cities, these citizens elected members of a city council who served as judges and city officials and passed laws.

Medieval cities remained relatively small in comparison with either ancient or modern cities. A large trading city might have about 5,000 inhabitants. By 1200,

COMPARATIVE ESSAY

Cities in the Medieval World

INTERACTION
& EXCHANGE

The exchange of goods between societies was a feature of both the ancient and medieval worlds. Trade routes crisscrossed the lands of the medieval world, and with increased trade came the growth of cities. In Europe, towns had dwindled after the collapse of the Western Roman Empire, but with the revival of trade in the eleventh and twelfth centuries, the cities came back to life. This revival occurred first in the old Roman cities, but soon new cities arose as merchants and artisans sought additional centers for their activities. As cities grew, so did the number of fortified houses, town halls, and churches whose towers punctuated the urban European skyline. Nevertheless, in the Middle Ages, cities in western Europe, especially north of the Alps, remained relatively small. Even the larger cities of Italy, with populations of 100,000, seemed insignificant in comparison with Constantinople and the great cities of the Middle East and China.

With a population of possibly 300,000 people, Constantinople, the capital city of the Byzantine Empire, was the largest city in Europe in the Early and High Middle Ages, and until the twelfth century, it was Europe's greatest commercial center, important for the exchange of goods between West and East. In addition to palaces, cathedrals, and monastic buildings, Constantinople also had numerous gardens and orchards that occupied large areas inside its fortified walls. Despite the extensive open and cultivated spaces, the city was not self-sufficient and relied on imports of food under close government direction.

As trade flourished in the Islamic world, cities prospered. When the Abbasids were in power, Baghdad, with a population close to 700,000, was probably the largest city in the empire and one of the greatest

cities in the world. After the rise of the Fatimids in Egypt, however, the focus of trade shifted to Cairo. Islamic cities had a distinctive physical appearance. Usually, the most impressive urban buildings were the palaces for the caliphs or the local governors and the great mosques for worship. There were also public buildings with fountains and secluded courtyards, public baths, and bazaars. The bazaar, a covered market, was a crucial part of every Muslim settlement and an important trading center where goods from throughout the known world were available. Food prepared for sale at the market was carefully supervised. A rule in one Muslim city stated, "Grilled meats should only be made with fresh meat and not with meat coming from a sick animal and bought for its cheapness." The merchants were among the greatest beneficiaries of the growth of cities in the Islamic world.

During the medieval period, cities in China were the largest in the world. The southern port of Hangzhou had at least a million residents by 1000, and a number of other cities, including Chang'an and Kaifeng, may also have reached that size. Chinese cities were known for their broad canals and wide, tree-lined streets. They were no longer administrative centers dominated by officials and their families but now included a broader mix of officials, merchants, artisans, and entertainers. The prosperity of Chinese cities was well known. Marco Polo, in describing Hangzhou to unbelieving Europeans in the late thirteenth century, said, "So many pleasures can be found that one fancies himself to be in Paradise."

Q *Based on a comparison of these medieval cities, which of these civilizations do you think was the most advanced? Why?*

London was the largest city in England with 30,000 people. On the Continent north of the Alps, only a few urban centers of commerce, such as Bruges and Ghent, had populations close to 40,000. Italian cities tended to be larger, with Venice, Florence, Genoa, Milan, and Naples numbering almost 100,000. Even the largest European city, however, seemed small beside the Byzantine capital of Constantinople or the Arab cities of Damascus, Baghdad, and Cairo.

Daily Life in the Medieval City   Medieval towns were surrounded by stone walls that were expensive to build, so the space within was precious. Consequently, most medieval cities featured narrow, winding streets with houses crowded against each other and second and third stories extending out over the streets. Because dwellings were built mostly of wood before the fourteenth century and candles and wood fires were used for light and heat, fire was a constant threat. Medieval cities burned rapidly once a fire started.

Most of the people who lived in cities were merchants involved in trade and artisans engaged in manufacturing a wide range of products, such as cloth, metalwork, shoes, and leather goods. Generally, merchants and artisans had their own sections within a city. The merchant area included warehouses, inns, and taverns. Artisan sections were usually divided along craft lines. From the twelfth century on, craftspeople began to organize themselves into **guilds**, and by the thirteenth century, there were individual guilds for virtually every craft. Each craft had its own street where its activity was pursued.

The physical environment of medieval cities was not pleasant. They were dirty and smelled of animal and human wastes deposited in backyard privies or on the streets. The rivers near most cities were polluted with wastes, especially from the tanning and butchering industries. Because of the pollution, cities did not use the rivers for drinking water but relied instead on wells.

Private and public baths also existed in medieval towns. Paris, for example, had thirty-two public baths for men and women. City laws did not allow lepers and people with "bad reputations" to use them. This did not, however, prevent public baths from being known for permissiveness due to public nudity. One contemporary commented on what occurred in public bathhouses: "Shameful things. Men make a point of staying all night in the public baths and women at the break of day come in and through 'ignorance' find themselves in the men's rooms."[6]

In medieval cities, women, in addition to supervising the household, purchasing food and preparing meals, raising the children, and managing the family finances, were also often expected to help their husbands in their trades. Some women also developed their own trades, such as brewing ale or making glass, to earn extra money. When some master craftspeople died, their widows even carried on their trades. Some women in medieval towns were thus able to lead lives of considerable independence and made important contributions to the market economy. Nevertheless, women often made less than men and faced obstacles that kept them from more rewarding opportunities. For example, women in textile production usually were given the most menial jobs. Many were forced to become domestic servants and given room and board in return for cooking, cleaning, and other domestic services.

Pollution in a Medieval City

EARTH & ENVIRONMENT

Environmental pollution is not new. Medieval cities and towns had their own problems with filthy living conditions. This excerpt is taken from an order sent by the king of England to the town of Boutham, a suburb of York, which was then being used by the king as his headquarters in a war with the Scots. It demands rectification of the town's pitiful physical conditions.

The King's Command to Boutham

To the bailiffs of the abbot of St. Mary's, York, at Boutham. Whereas it is sufficiently evident that the pavement of the said town of Boutham is so very greatly broke up that all and singular passing and going through that town sustain immoderate damages and grievances, and in addition the air is so corrupted and infected by the pigsties situated in the king's highways and in the lanes of that town and by the swine feeding and frequently wandering about in the streets and lanes and by dung and dunghills and many other foul things placed in the streets and lanes, that great repugnance overtakes the king's ministers staying in that town and also others there dwelling and passing through; the advantage of more wholesome air is impeded; the state of men is grievously injured, and other unbearable inconveniences and many other injuries are known to proceed from such corruption, to the nuisance of the king's ministers aforesaid and of others there dwelling and passing through, and to the peril of their lives.... The king, being unwilling longer to tolerate such great and unbearable defects there, orders the bailiffs to cause the pavement to be suitably repaired within their liberty before All Saints next, and to cause the pigsties, aforesaid streets and lanes to be cleansed from all dung and dunghills, and to cause proclamation to be made throughout their bailiwick forbidding any one, under pain of grievous forfeiture, to cause or permit their swine to feed or wander outside his house in the king's streets or the lanes aforesaid.

Q *What does the king's command to Boutham illustrate about the physical environment of medieval cities? What factors or human habits contributed to the degradation of the medieval urban environment?*

Source: From *English Historical Documents III*, H. Rothwell, ed. (London: Methuen, 1975).

Evolution of the European Kingdoms

The recovery and growth of European civilization in the High Middle Ages also affected the state. Although lords and vassals seemed forever mired in endless petty conflicts, some medieval kings inaugurated the process of developing new kinds of monarchical states that were based on the centralization of power rather than the decentralized political order that was characteristic of fief-holding. By the thirteenth century, European monarchs were solidifying their governmental institutions in pursuit of greater power.

England in the High Middle Ages   In late September 1066, an army of heavily armed knights under William of Normandy landed on the coast of England, and a few weeks later, on October 14, they soundly defeated King Harold and his

Anglo-Saxon foot soldiers in the Battle of Hastings. William (1066–1087) was crowned king of England at Christmastime in London and promptly began a process of combining Anglo-Saxon and Norman institutions that would change England forever. Many of the Norman knights were given parcels of land that they held as fiefs from the new English king. William made all nobles swear an oath of loyalty to him as sole ruler of England and insisted that all people owed loyalty to the king. The Normans also took over existing Anglo-Saxon institutions, such as the office of sheriff. William took a census and more fully developed the system of taxation and royal courts begun by the Anglo-Saxon kings of the tenth and eleventh centuries. All in all, William of Normandy established a strong, centralized monarchy.

The Norman Conquest had numerous repercussions. Because the new king of England was still the duke of Normandy, he was both a king (of England) and at the same time a vassal to a king (of France), but a vassal who was now far more powerful than his lord. This connection with France kept England heavily involved in European affairs throughout the High Middle Ages.

In the twelfth century, the power of the English monarchy was greatly enlarged during the reign of Henry II (1154–1189;). The new king was particularly successful in strengthening the power of the royal courts. Henry expanded the number of criminal cases to be tried in the king's court and also devised means for taking property cases from local courts to the royal courts. Henry's goals were clear: expanding the power of the royal courts increased the king's power and, of course, brought revenues into his coffers. Moreover, since the royal courts were now found throughout England, a body of **common law** (law that was common to the whole kingdom) began to replace the different law codes that often varied from place to place.

Henry was less successful at imposing royal control over the church and became involved in a famous struggle between church and state. Henry claimed the right to punish clergymen in the royal courts, but Thomas à Becket, as archbishop of Canterbury, the highest-ranking English cleric, claimed that only church courts could try clerics. Attempts at compromise failed, and the angry king publicly expressed the desire to be rid of Becket: "Who will free me of this priest?" he screamed. Four knights took the challenge, went to Canterbury, and murdered the archbishop in the cathedral. Faced with public outrage, Henry was forced to allow the right of appeal from English church courts to the papal court.

Many English nobles came to resent the growth of the king's power and rose in rebellion during the reign of King John (1199–1216). At Runnymede in 1215, John was forced to accept Magna Carta (Great Charter) guaranteeing feudal liberties. Feudal custom had always recognized that the relationship between king and vassals was based on mutual rights and obligations. Magna Carta gave written recognition to that fact and was used in later years to support the idea that a monarch's power was limited.

During the reign of Edward I (1272–1307), an institution of great importance in the development of representative government—the English Parliament—emerged. Originally, the word *parliament* was applied to meetings of the king's Great Council, in which the greater barons and chief prelates of the church met with the king's judges and principal advisers to deal with judicial affairs. But needing money, in 1295 Edward invited two knights from every county and two residents from each town to meet with the Great Council to consent to new taxes. This was the first Parliament.

Thus, the English Parliament came to be composed of two knights from every county and two burgesses from every borough as well as the barons and ecclesiastical lords. Eventually, the barons and church lords formed the House of Lords; the knights and burgesses, the House of Commons. The Parliaments of Edward I approved taxes, discussed politics, passed laws, and handled judicial business. The law of the realm was beginning to be determined not by the king alone but by the king in consultation with representatives of various groups that constituted the community.

Growth of the French Kingdom   The Carolingian Empire had been divided into three major sections in 843. The western Frankish lands formed the core of the eventual kingdom of France. In 987, after the death of the last Carolingian king, the western Frankish nobles chose Hugh Capet (YOO ka-PAY) as the new king, thus establishing the Capetian (kuh-PEE-shun) dynasty of French kings. Although they carried the title of kings, the Capetians had little real power. They controlled as the royal domain only the lands around Paris known as the Île-de-France (EEL-duh-fronhss). As kings of France, the Capetians were formally the overlords of the great lords of France, such as the dukes of Normandy, Brittany, Burgundy, and Aquitaine. In reality, however, many of the dukes were considerably more powerful than the Capetian kings. All in all, it would take the Capetian dynasty hundreds of years to create a truly centralized monarchical authority in France.

The reign of King Philip II Augustus (1180–1223) was an important turning point in the growth of the French monarchy. Philip II waged war against the Plantagenet (plan-TAJ-uh-net) rulers of England, who also ruled the French territories of Normandy, Maine, Anjou, and Aquitaine, and was successful in gaining control of most of these territories, thereby enlarging the power of the French monarchy. To administer justice and collect royal revenues in his new territories, Philip appointed new royal officials, thus inaugurating a French royal bureaucracy in the thirteenth century.

Capetian rulers after Philip II continued to add lands to the royal domain. Philip IV the Fair (1285–1314) was especially effective in strengthening the French monarchy. He reinforced the royal bureaucracy and also brought a French parliament into being by asking representatives of the three estates, or classes—the clergy (First Estate), the nobles (Second Estate), and the townspeople (Third Estate)—to meet with him. They did so in 1302, inaugurating the Estates-General, the first French parliament, although it had little real power. By the end of the thirteenth century, France was the largest, wealthiest, and best-governed monarchical state in Europe.

Christian Reconquest: The Iberian Kingdoms   Much of Spain had been part of the Islamic world since the eighth century. From the tenth century, however, the most noticeable feature of Spanish history was the weakening of Muslim power and the beginning of a Christian reconquest that lasted until the final expulsion of the Muslims at the end of the fifteenth century.

MAP 12.3   Europe in the High Middle Ages

Although the nobility dominated much of European society in the High Middle Ages, kings began the process of extending their power in more effective ways, creating the monarchies that would form the European states.

A number of small Christian kingdoms were established in northern Spain in the eleventh century, and within a hundred years, they had been consolidated into the Christian kingdoms of Castile (ka-STEEL), Navarre, Aragon, and Portugal, which first emerged as a separate kingdom in 1139. The southern half of Spain still remained under the control of the Muslims.

But in the thirteenth century, Aragon, Castile, and Portugal made significant conquests of Muslim territory. The Muslims remained ensconced only in the kingdom of Granada in the southeast of the Iberian peninsula, which remained an independent Muslim state until its final conquest by the forces of Ferdinand and Isabella of Aragon and Castile in 1492.

The Spanish kingdoms followed no consistent policy in their treatment of the conquered Muslim population. In Aragon, Muslim farmers continued to work the land but were forced to pay very high rents. In Castile, King Alfonso X (1252–1284), who called himself the "King of Three Religions," encouraged the continued development of a cosmopolitan culture shared by Christians, Jews, and Muslims.

The Lands of the Holy Roman Empire   In the tenth century, the powerful dukes of the Saxons became kings of the eastern Frankish kingdom (or Germany, as it came to be called). The best known of the Saxon kings of Germany was Otto I

(936–973), who intervened in Italian politics and for his efforts was crowned emperor of the Romans by the pope in 962, reviving a title that had not been used since the time of Charlemagne.

In the eleventh century, German kings created a strong monarchy and a powerful empire by leading armies into Italy. To strengthen their grip, they relied on their ability to control the church and select bishops, whom they could then use as royal administrators. But the struggle between church and state during the reign of Henry IV (1056–1106) weakened the king's ability to use church officials in this way. The German kings also tried to bolster their power by using their position as emperors to exploit the resources of Italy. But this strategy tended to backfire; many a German king lost armies in Italy in pursuit of a dream of empire, and no German dynasty demonstrates this better than the Hohenstaufens (hoh-en-SHTOW-fens).

The two most famous members of the Hohenstaufen dynasty, Frederick I Barbarossa (bar-buh-ROH-suh) (1152–1190) and Frederick II (1212–1250), tried to create a new kind of empire. Previous German kings had focused on building a strong German kingdom, but Frederick I planned to get his chief revenues from Italy as the center of a "holy empire," as he called it (hence the name *Holy Roman Empire*). But his attempt to conquer northern Italy ran into severe problems. The pope opposed him, fearful that the emperor wanted to absorb Rome and the Papal States into his empire. The cities of northern Italy, which had become used to their freedom, were also unwilling to be Frederick's subjects. An alliance of these northern Italian cities, with the support of the pope, defeated the emperor's forces in 1176.

The main goal of Frederick II was the establishment of a strong centralized state in Italy dominated by the kingdom in Sicily, which he had inherited from his mother. Frederick's major task was to gain control of northern Italy. In the attempt, however, he became involved in a deadly conflict with the popes, who feared that a single ruler of northern and southern Italy would mean the end of papal power in the center of the peninsula. Furthermore, the northern Italian cities were unwilling to give up their freedom. Frederick nevertheless waged a long and bitter struggle, winning many battles but ultimately losing the war.

The struggle between popes and emperors had dire consequences for the Holy Roman Empire. By spending their time fighting in Italy, the German emperors left Germany in the hands of powerful German lords who ignored the emperor and created their own independent kingdoms. This ensured that the German monarchy would remain weak and incapable of establishing a centralized monarchical state; thus, the German Holy Roman Emperor had no real power over either Germany or Italy. Unlike France and England, neither Germany nor Italy had a centralized national monarchy in the Middle Ages. Both of these regions consisted of many small, independent states, a situation that changed little until the nineteenth century.

The Slavic Peoples of Central and Eastern Europe   The Slavs were originally a single people in central Europe, but they gradually divided into three major groups: western, southern, and eastern. The western Slavs eventually formed the Polish and Bohemian kingdoms. German Christian missionaries converted both the Czechs in

Bohemia and the Slavs in Poland by the tenth century. German Christians also converted the non-Slavic kingdom of Hungary, which emerged after the Magyars settled down after their defeat in 955. The Poles, Czechs, and Hungarians all accepted Catholic or western Christianity and became closely tied to the Roman Catholic Church and its Latin culture.

The southern and eastern Slavic populations took a different path: the Slavic peoples of Moravia were converted to the Orthodox Christianity of the Byzantine Empire by two Byzantine missionary brothers, Cyril and Methodius, who began their activities in 863. The southern Slavic peoples included the Croats, Serbs, and Bulgarians. For the most part, they too embraced Eastern Orthodoxy, although the Croats came to accept the Roman Catholic faith. The adoption of Eastern Orthodoxy by the Serbs and Bulgarians tied their cultural life to the Byzantine state.

The eastern Slavic peoples, from whom the modern Russians and Ukrainians are descended, had settled in the territory of present-day Ukraine and European Russia. There, beginning in the late eighth century, they began to encounter

MAP 12.4   The Migrations of the Slavs

Originally from east-central Europe, the Slavic people broke into three groups. The western Slavs converted to Catholic Christianity, while most of the eastern and southern Slavs, under the influence of the Byzantine Empire, embraced the Eastern Orthodox faith.

Swedish Vikings who moved down the extensive network of rivers into the lands of the eastern Slavs in search of booty and new trade routes. These Vikings built trading settlements and eventually came to dominate the native peoples, who called them "the Rus" (ROOSS *or* ROOSH), from which the name Russia is derived.

The Development of Russia: Impact of the Mongols   A Viking leader named Oleg (c. 873–913) settled in Kiev (KEE-yev) at the beginning of the tenth century and founded the Rus state known as the principality of Kiev. His successors extended their control over the eastern Slavs and expanded the territory of Kiev until it included the area between the Baltic and Black Seas and the Danube and Volga Rivers. By marrying Slavic wives, the Viking ruling class was gradually assimilated into the Slavic population.

The growth of the principality of Kiev attracted religious missionaries, especially from the Byzantine Empire. One Rus ruler, Vladimir (VLAD-ih-meer) (c. 980–1015), married the Byzantine emperor's sister and in 987 officially accepted Christianity for himself and his people. By the end of the tenth century, Byzantine Christianity had become the model for Russian religious life.

The Kievan Rus state prospered and reached its high point in the first half of the eleventh century. But civil wars and new invasions by Asian nomads caused the principality of Kiev to collapse, and its sack by north Russian princes in 1169 brought an end to the first Russian state, which had remained closely tied to the Byzantine Empire, not to Europe. In the thirteenth century, the Mongols conquered Russia and cut it off even more from Europe.

The Mongols had exploded onto the scene in the thirteenth century, moving east into China and west into the Middle East and central Europe. Although they conquered Russia, they were not numerous enough to settle the vast Russian lands. They occupied only part of Russia but required Russian princes to pay tribute to them. One Russian prince soon emerged as more powerful than the others. Alexander Nevsky (NYEF-skee), prince of Novgorod (NAHV-guh-rahd), defeated a German invading army in northwestern Russia in 1242. His cooperation with the Mongols won him their favor. The khan, leader of the western part of the Mongol Empire, rewarded Alexander Nevsky with the title of grand-prince, enabling his descendants to become the princes of Moscow and eventually leaders of all Russia.

Christianity and Medieval Civilization   Christianity was an integral part of the fabric of European society and the consciousness of Europe. Papal directives affected the actions of kings and princes alike, and Christian teachings and practices touched the lives of all Europeans.

Reform of the Papacy   Since the fifth century, the popes of the Catholic Church had reigned supreme over church affairs. They had also come to exercise control over the territories in central Italy that came to be known as the Papal States, which kept the popes involved in political matters, often at the expense of their spiritual obligations. At the same time, the church became increasingly entangled in the evolving feudal relationships. High officials of the church, such as bishops and abbots, came to hold their offices as fiefs from nobles. As vassals, they were obliged to carry out the usual duties, including military service. Of course, lords assumed the right to choose their vassals and thus came to appoint bishops and abbots. Because lords often chose their vassals from other noble families for political reasons, these bishops and abbots were often worldly figures who cared little about their spiritual responsibilities.

By the eleventh century, church leaders realized the need to free the church from the interference of lords in the appointment of church officials. **Lay investiture** was the practice by which secular rulers both chose nominees to church offices and invested them with (bestowed on them) the symbols of their office. Pope Gregory VII (1073–1085) decided to fight this practice. Gregory claimed that he, as pope, was God's "vicar on earth" and that the pope's authority extended over all of Christendom, including its rulers. In 1075, he issued a decree forbidding high-ranking clerics from receiving their investiture from lay leaders.

Gregory soon found himself in conflict with the German king over his actions. King Henry IV was also a determined man who had appointed high-ranking clerics, especially bishops, as his vassals in order to use them as administrators. Henry had no intention of obeying a decree that challenged the very heart of his administration.

The struggle between Henry IV and Gregory VII, which is known as the Investiture Controversy, was one of the great conflicts between church and state in the High Middle Ages. It dragged on until a new German king and a new pope reached a compromise in 1122 called the Concordat of Worms (kun-KOR-dat of WURMZ *or* VORMPS). Under this agreement, church officials first elected a bishop in Germany. After election, the nominee paid homage to the king as his lord, who then invested him with the symbols of temporal office. A representative of the pope, however, then invested the new bishop with the symbols of his spiritual office.

The Church Supreme: The Papal Monarchy   The popes of the twelfth century did not abandon the reform ideals of Pope Gregory VII, but they were more inclined to consolidate their power and build a strong administrative system. During the papacy of Pope Innocent III (1198–1216), the Catholic Church reached the height of its power. At the beginning of his pontificate, in a letter to a priest, the pope made a clear statement of his views on papal supremacy:

> As God, the creator of the universe, set two great lights in the firmament of heaven, the greater light to rule the day, and the lesser light to rule the night, so He set two great dignities in the firmament of the universal church, … the greater to rule the day, that is, souls, and the lesser to rule the night, that is, bodies. These dignities are the papal authority and the royal power. And just as the moon gets her light from the sun, and is inferior to the sun … so the royal power gets the splendor of its dignity from the papal authority.[7]

Innocent III's actions were those of a man who believed that he, as pope, was the supreme judge of European affairs. To achieve his political ends, he did not hesitate to use the spiritual weapons at his command, especially the **interdict**, which forbade priests to dispense the **sacraments** of the church in the hope that the people, deprived of the comforts of religion, would exert pressure against their ruler. Apparently, Pope Innocent's interdicts worked: for example, one of them forced the king of France, Philip Augustus, to take back his wife and queen after Philip had tried to have his marriage annulled.

New Religious Orders and New Spiritual Ideals   Between 1050 and 1150, a wave of religious enthusiasm seized Europe, leading to a spectacular growth in the number of monasteries and the emergence of new monastic orders. Most important was the Cistercian (sis-TUR-shun) order, founded in 1098 by a group of monks dissatisfied with the moral degeneration and lack of strict discipline at their own Benedictine monastery. The Cistercians were strict. They ate a simple diet and possessed only a single robe apiece. More time for prayer and manual labor was provided by shortening the number of hours spent at religious services. The Cistercians played a major role in developing a new, activist spiritual model for twelfth-century Europe. A Benedictine monk often spent hours in prayer to honor God. The Cistercian ideal had a different emphasis: "Arise, soldier of Christ, arise! Get up off the ground and return to the battle from which you have fled! Fight more boldly after your flight, and triumph in glory!"[8] These were the words of Saint Bernard of Clairvaux (klayr-VOH) (1090–1153), who more than any other person embodied the new spiritual ideal of Cistercian monasticism.

Women were also actively involved in the spiritual movements of the age. The number of women joining religious houses grew dramatically in the High Middle Ages. Most nuns were from the ranks of the landed aristocracy. Convents were convenient for families unable or unwilling to find husbands for their daughters and for aristocratic women who did not wish to marry. Female intellectuals found them a haven for their activities. Most of the learned women of the Middle Ages were nuns.

In the thirteenth century, two new religious orders emerged that had a profound impact on the lives of ordinary people. Like their founder, Saint Francis of Assisi (uh-SEE-zee) (1182–1226), the Franciscans lived among the people, preaching repentance and aiding the poor. Their calls for a return to the simplicity and poverty of the early church, reinforced by their own example, were especially effective and made them very popular.

The Dominican order arose out of the desire of a Spanish priest, Dominic de Guzmán (DAH-muh-nik duh gooz-MAHN) (1170–1221), to defend church teachings from **heresy**—beliefs contrary to official church doctrine. Unlike Francis, Dominic was an intellectual who was appalled by the growth of heresy. He came to believe that a new religious order of men who lived lives of poverty but were learned and capable of preaching effectively would best be able to attack heresy. The Dominicans became especially well known for their roles as the inquisitors of the papal Inquisition.

The Holy Office, as the papal Inquisition was formally called, was a court established by the church to find and try heretics. Anyone accused of heresy who refused to confess was considered guilty and was turned over to the state for execution. So were relapsed heretics—those who confessed, did penance, and then reverted to heresy again. Most heretics, however, were put in prison or made to do various forms of penance. To the Christians of the thirteenth century, who believed that there was only one path to salvation, heresy was a crime against

God and against humanity. In their minds, force should be used to save souls from damnation.

Popular Religion in the High Middle Ages   We have witnessed the actions of popes, bishops, and monks. But what of ordinary clergy and laypeople? What were their religious hopes and fears? What were their spiritual aspirations?

The sacraments of the Catholic Church ensured that the church was an integral part of people's lives, from birth to death. There were (and still are) seven sacraments, administered only by the clergy. Sacraments, such as baptism and the Eucharist (YOO-kuh-rest) (the Lord's Supper), were viewed as outward symbols of an inward grace and were considered imperative for a Christian's salvation. Therefore, the clergy were seen to have a key role in the attainment of salvation.

Other church practices were also important to ordinary people. Saints were seen as men and women who, through their holiness, had achieved a special position in heaven, enabling them to act as intercessors with God. The saints' ability to protect poor souls enabled them to take on great importance at the popular level. Jesus's apostles were, of course, recognized throughout Europe as saints, but there were also numerous local saints who were of special significance to a single area. New cults developed rapidly, especially in the intense religious atmosphere of the eleventh and twelfth centuries. The English, for example, introduced Saint Nicholas, the patron saint of children, who is known today as Santa Claus.

In the High Middle Ages, the Virgin Mary, the mother of Jesus, occupied the foremost position among the saints. Mary was viewed as the most important mediator with her son, Jesus, the judge of all sinners. Moreover, from the eleventh century on, a fascination with Mary as Jesus's human mother became more evident. A sign of Mary's importance was the growing number of churches all over Europe that were dedicated to her in the twelfth and thirteenth centuries.

Emphasis on the role of the saints was closely tied to the use of relics, which also increased noticeably in the High Middle Ages. Relics were usually the bones of saints or objects intimately connected to saints that were considered worthy of veneration by the faithful. A twelfth-century English monk began his description of the abbey's relics by saying that "there is kept there a thing more precious than gold, ... the right arm of St. Oswald.... This we have seen with our own eyes and have kissed, and have handled with our own hands.... There are kept here also part of his ribs and of the soil on which he fell."[9] The monk went on to list additional relics possessed by the abbey, including two pieces of Jesus's swaddling clothes, pieces of Jesus's manger, and part of the five loaves of bread with which Jesus fed five thousand people. Because the holiness of the saint was considered to be inherent in his relics, these objects were believed to be capable of healing people or producing other miracles.

The Culture of the High Middle Ages   The High Middle Ages was a time of extraordinary intellectual and artistic vitality. It witnessed the birth of universities and a building spree that left Europe bedecked with churches and cathedrals.

The Rise of Universities   The university as we know it—with faculty, students, and degrees—was a product of the High Middle Ages. The word *university* is derived from the Latin word *universitas* (yoo-nee-VAYR-see-tahss), meaning a corporation or guild, and referred to either a corporation of teachers or a corporation of students. Medieval universities were educational guilds or corporations that produced educated and trained individuals.

The first European university appeared in Bologna (boh-LOHN-yuh), Italy, where a great teacher named Irnerius (1088–1125), who taught Roman law, attracted students from all over Europe. Most of them were laymen, usually older individuals who were administrators for kings and princes and were eager to learn more about law so that they could apply it in their own jobs. To protect themselves, students at Bologna formed a guild or *universitas*, which was recognized by Emperor Frederick Barbarossa and given a charter in 1158. Kings, popes, and princes soon competed to found new universities, and by the end of the Middle Ages, there were eighty universities in Europe, most of them in England, France, Italy, and Germany.

University students (all men—women did not attend universities in the Middle Ages) began their studies with the traditional **liberal arts** curriculum, which consisted of grammar, rhetoric, logic, arithmetic, geometry, music, and astronomy. Teaching was done by the lecture method. The word *lecture* is derived from the Latin verb for "read." Before the development of the printing press in the fifteenth century, books were expensive and few students could afford them, so teachers read from a basic text (such as a collection of laws if the subject was law) and then added their explanations. No exams were given after a series of lectures, but when a student applied for a degree, he was given a comprehensive oral examination by a committee of teachers. The exam was taken after a four- or six-year period of study. The first degree a student could earn was a bachelor of arts; later he might receive a master of arts degree.

After completing the liberal arts curriculum, a student could go on to study law, medicine, or theology. This last was the most highly regarded subject at the medieval university. The study of any of these three disciplines could take a decade or more. A student who passed his final oral examinations was granted a doctor's degree, which officially enabled him to teach his subject. Students who received degrees from medieval universities could pursue other careers besides teaching that proved to be much more lucrative. A law degree was necessary for those who wished to serve as advisers to kings and princes. The growing administrative bureaucracies of popes and kings also demanded a supply of clerks with a university education who could keep records and draw up official documents. Universities provided the teachers, administrators, lawyers, and doctors for medieval society.

Development of Scholasticism   The importance of Christianity in medieval society made it certain that theology would play a central role in the European intellectual world. Theology, the formal study of religion, was "queen of the sciences" in the new universities.

Beginning in the eleventh century, the effort to apply reason or logical analysis to the church's basic theological doctrines had a significant impact on the study of theology. The philosophical and theological system of the medieval schools is known as **scholasticism** (skoh-LAS-tih-sizm). Scholasticism tried to reconcile faith and reason, to demonstrate that what was accepted on faith was in harmony with what could be learned by reason.

The overriding task of scholasticism was to harmonize Christian teachings with the work of the Greek philosopher Aristotle. In the twelfth century, due largely to the work of Muslim and Jewish scholars in Spain, western Europe was introduced to a large number of Greek scientific and philosophical works, including the works of Aristotle. But Aristotle's works threw many theologians into consternation. Aristotle was so highly regarded that he was called "the philosopher," yet he had arrived at his conclusions by rational thought, not by faith, and some of his doctrines contradicted the teachings of the church. The most famous attempt to reconcile Aristotle and the doctrines of Christianity was that of Saint Thomas Aquinas (uh-KWY-nuss).

Aquinas (1225–1274) is best known for his *Summa Theologica* (SOO-muh tay-oh-LAH-jee-kuh) (*Summa of Theology*—a summa was a compendium of knowledge that attempted to bring together all the received learning of the preceding centuries on a given subject). Aquinas's masterpiece was organized according to the dialectical method of the scholastics. Aquinas first posed a question, cited sources that offered opposing opinions on the question, and then resolved the matter by arriving at his own conclusions. In this fashion, Aquinas raised and discussed some six hundred articles.

Aquinas's reputation derives from his masterful attempt to reconcile faith and reason. He took it for granted that there were truths derived by reason and truths derived by faith. He was certain, however, that the two truths could not be in conflict. The natural mind, unaided by faith, could arrive at truths concerning the physical universe. Without the help of God's grace, however, reason alone could not grasp spiritual truths, such as the Trinity (the manifestation of God in three separate yet identical persons—Father, Son, and Holy Spirit) or the Incarnation (Jesus's simultaneous identity as God and human).

Romanesque Architecture   The eleventh and twelfth centuries witnessed an explosion of building, both private and public. The construction of castles and churches absorbed most of the surplus resources of medieval society and at the same time reflected its basic preoccupations, God and warfare. The churches were by far the most conspicuous of the public buildings.

The cathedrals of the eleventh and twelfth centuries were built in the **Romanesque** (roh-man-ESK) style, prominent examples of which can be found in Germany, France, and Spain. Romanesque churches were normally built in the basilica shape used in the construction of churches in the Late Roman Empire. Basilicas were rectangular churches with flat wooden roofs. Romanesque builders made a significant innovation by replacing the flat wooden roof with a long, round stone vault called a barrel vault (or a cross vault where two barrel vaults intersected). Although barrel and cross vaults were technically difficult to create, they were considered aesthetically more pleasing than flat wooden roofs and were also less apt to catch fire.

Because stone roofs were extremely heavy, Romanesque churches required massive pillars and walls to hold them up. This left little space for windows, and

Romanesque churches were correspondingly dark on the inside. Their massive walls and pillars gave Romanesque churches a sense of solidity and almost the impression of a fortress.

The Gothic Cathedral   Begun in the twelfth century and brought to perfection in the thirteenth, the **Gothic** cathedral remains one of the greatest artistic triumphs of the High Middle Ages. Soaring skyward, as if to reach heaven, it was a fitting symbol for medieval people's preoccupation with God.

Two fundamental innovations of the twelfth century made Gothic cathedrals possible. The combination of ribbed vaults and pointed arches replaced the barrel vaults of Romanesque churches and enabled builders to make Gothic churches higher than Romanesque ones. The use of pointed arches and ribbed vaults created an impression of upward movement, a sense of weightless upward thrust that implied the energy of God. Another technical innovation, the flying buttress, a heavy arched pier of stone built onto the outside of the walls, made it possible to distribute the weight of the church's vaulted ceilings outward and down and thus eliminate the heavy walls used in Romanesque churches to hold the weight of the massive barrel vaults. Thus, Gothic cathedrals could be built with thin walls containing magnificent stained-glass windows, which created a play of light inside that varied with the sun at different times of the day. The extensive use of colored light in Gothic cathedrals was not accidental but was executed by people who believed that natural light was a symbol of the divine light of God.

The first fully Gothic church was the abbey of Saint-Denis (san-duh-NEE) near Paris, inspired by its famous Abbot Suger (soo-ZHAYR) (1122–1151) and built between 1140 and 1150. By the mid-thirteenth century, French Gothic architecture, most brilliantly executed in cathedrals in Paris (Notre-Dame), Reims, Amiens, and Chartres, had spread to virtually all of Europe.

A Gothic cathedral was the work of the entire community. All classes contributed to its construction. Master masons, who were both architects and engineers, designed them, and stonemasons and other craftspeople were paid a daily wage and provided the skilled labor to build them. A Gothic cathedral symbolized the chief preoccupation of a medieval Christian community, its dedication to a spiritual ideal. As we have observed before, the largest buildings of an era reflect the values of its society. The Gothic cathedral, with its towers soaring toward heaven, gave witness to an age when a spiritual impulse underlay most aspects of its existence.

MEDIEVAL EUROPE AND THE WORLD

As it developed, European civilization remained largely confined to its home continent, although Europe was never completely isolated. Some Europeans, especially merchants, had contacts with parts of Asia and Africa. The goods of those lands made their way into medieval castles, and the works of Muslim philosophers were read in medieval universities. The Vikings were also daring explorers. After 860, they sailed westward in their long ships across the North Atlantic Ocean, reaching Iceland in 874. Erik the Red, a Viking exiled from Iceland, traveled even farther west and discovered Greenland in 985. Some Vikings even reached North America, landing in Newfoundland, the only known Viking site in North America, but it proved to be short-lived as Viking expansion drew to a close by the tenth century. Only at the end of the eleventh century did Europeans begin their first concerted attempt to expand beyond the frontiers of Europe by conquering the land of Palestine.

The First Crusades   The crusades were based on the idea of a holy war against infidels (unbelievers). Christian wrath against Muslims had already found some expression in the attempt to wrest Spain from the Moors and the success of the Normans in reclaiming Sicily. At the end of the eleventh century, Christian Europe found itself with a glorious opportunity to go after the Muslims when the Byzantine emperor, Alexius I, asked Pope Urban II for help against the Seljuk Turks. The pope saw this as a chance to rally the warriors of Europe for the liberation of Jerusalem and the Holy Land of Palestine from the infidels. The Holy City of Jerusalem had long been the focus of Christian pilgrimages. At the Council of Clermont in southern France toward the end of 1095, Urban challenged Christians to take up their weapons and join in a holy war to recover the Holy Land. The pope promised remission of sins: "All who die by the way, whether by land or by sea, or in battle against the pagans, shall have immediate remission of sins. This I grant them through the power of God with which I am invested."[10] The enthusiastic crowd cried out in response: "It is the will of God, it is the will of God."

The initial response to Urban's speech reveals how appealing many people found this combined call to military arms and religious fervor. A self-appointed leader, Peter the Hermit, who preached of his visions of the Holy City of Jerusalem, convinced a large mob, most of them poor and many of them peasants, to undertake a crusade to liberate the city. One person who encountered Peter described him in these words: "Outdoors he wore a woolen tunic, which revealed his ankles, and above it a hood; he wore a cloak to cover his upper body, a bit of his arms, but his feet were bare. He drank wine and ate fish, but scarcely ever ate bread. This man, partly because of his reputation, partly because of his preaching, [assembled] a very large army."[11]

This "Peasant's Crusade" or "Crusade of the Poor" consisted of a ragtag rabble that moved through the Balkans, terrorizing natives and looting for their food and supplies. Their misplaced religious enthusiasm led to another tragic by-product as well, the persecution of the Jews, long pictured by the church as the murderers of Christ. As a contemporary chronicler described it, "They persecuted the hated race of the Jews wherever they were found." Two bands of peasant crusaders, led by Peter the Hermit, managed to reach Constantinople. The Byzantine emperor wisely shipped them over to Asia Minor, where the Turks massacred the undisciplined and poorly armed mob.

Pope Urban II did not share the wishful thinking of the peasant crusaders but was more inclined to trust knights who had been well trained in the art of war. Three organized crusading bands of noble warriors, most of them French, made their way eastward. The crusading army probably numbered several thousand cavalry and as many as ten thousand infantry. After the capture of Antioch in 1098, much of the crusading host proceeded down the Palestinian coast, evading the well-defended coastal cities, and reached Jerusalem in June 1099. After a five-week siege, the Holy City was taken amid a horrible massacre of the inhabitants—men, women, and children.

After further conquest of Palestinian lands, the crusaders ignored the wishes of the Byzantine emperor and organized four Latin crusader states. Because the crusader kingdoms were surrounded by Muslims hostile to them, they grew increasingly dependent on the Italian commercial cities for supplies from Europe. Some Italian cities, such as Genoa, Pisa, and especially Venice, grew rich and powerful in the process.

But it was not easy for the crusader kingdoms to maintain themselves. Already by the 1120s, the Muslims had begun to strike back. The fall of one of the Latin kingdoms in 1144 led to renewed calls for another crusade, especially from the monastic firebrand Saint Bernard of Clairvaux. He exclaimed, "Now, on account of our sins, the enemies of the cross have begun to show their faces.... What are you doing, you servants of the cross? Will you throw to the dogs that which is most holy? Will you cast pearls before swine?"[12] Bernard even managed to enlist two powerful rulers, but their Second Crusade proved to be a total failure.

The Third Crusade was a reaction to the fall of the Holy City of Jerusalem in 1187 to the Muslim forces under Saladin. Now all of Christendom was ablaze with calls for a new crusade. Three major monarchs agreed to lead their forces in person: Emperor Frederick Barbarossa of Germany, Richard I the Lionhearted of England (1189–1199), and Philip II Augustus, king of France. Some of the crusaders finally arrived in the Holy Land by 1189 only to encounter problems. Frederick Barbarossa drowned while swimming in a local river, and his army quickly disintegrated. The English and French arrived by sea and met with success against the coastal cities, where they had the support of their fleets, but when they moved inland, they failed miserably. Eventually, after Philip went home, Richard the Lionhearted negotiated a settlement whereby Saladin agreed to allow Christian pilgrims free access to Jerusalem.

The Later Crusades
After the death of Saladin in 1193, Pope Innocent III initiated the Fourth Crusade. On its way east, the crusading army became involved in a dispute over the succession to the Byzantine throne. The Venetian leaders of the Fourth Crusade saw an opportunity to neutralize their greatest commercial competitor, the Byzantine Empire. Diverted to Constantinople, the crusaders sacked the great capital city of Byzantium in 1204 and set up the new Latin Empire of Constantinople. Not until 1261 did a Byzantine army recapture Constantinople. In the meantime, additional crusades were undertaken to reconquer the Holy Land. All of them were largely disasters, and by the end of the thirteenth century, the European military effort to capture Palestine was recognized as a complete failure.

What Were the Effects of the Crusades?
Whether the crusades had much effect on European civilization is debatable. The only visible remains are the European castles that began to incorporate features adopted from fortresses that the crusaders observed in the east. Although there may have been some broadening of perspective from the exchange between two cultures, the interaction of Christian Europe with the Muslim world was actually both more intense and more meaningful in Spain and Sicily than in the Holy Land.

Did the crusades help stabilize European society by removing large numbers of young warriors who would have fought each other in Europe? Some historians think so and believe that Western monarchs established their control more easily as a result. There is no doubt that the crusades did contribute to the economic growth of the Italian port cities, especially Genoa, Pisa, and Venice. But it is important to remember that the growing wealth and population of twelfth-century Europe had made the crusades possible in the first place. The crusades may have enhanced the revival of trade, but they certainly did not cause it. Even without the crusades, Italian merchants would have pursued new trade contacts with the Eastern world.

Did the crusades have side effects that would haunt European society for generations? Some historians have argued that the crusades might be considered a "Christian holy war," whose memories still trouble the relationship between the Muslim world and the West today. Other historians argue that the early crusaders were motivated as much by economic and political reasons as religious ones.

Another possible side effect is more apparent. The first widespread attacks on the Jews began with the crusades. As some Christians argued, to undertake holy wars against infidel Muslims while the "murderers of Christ" ran free at home was unthinkable. With the crusades, the massacre of Jews became a regular feature of medieval European life.

CHRONOLOGIES
THE EUROPEAN KINGDOMS

England

1066	Norman Conquest
1066–1087	William the Conqueror
1154–1189	Henry II
1199–1216	John
1215	Magna Carta
1272–1307	Edward I
1295	First Parliament

France

1180–1223	Philip II Augustus
1285–1314	Philip IV
1302	First Estates-General

Germany and the Holy Roman Empire

936–973	Otto I
1056–1106	Henry IV
1152–1190	Frederick I
1176	Northern Italian cities defeat Frederick
1212–1250	Frederick II

The Eastern World

c. 1220–1263	Alexander Nevsky, prince of Novgorod
1230s	Mongol conquest of Russia

THE CRUSADES

1095	Pope Urban II's call for a crusade at Clermont
1096–1099	First Crusade
1147–1149	Second Crusade
1187	Saladin's conquest of Jerusalem
1189–1192	Third Crusade
1204	Fourth Crusade—sack of Constantinople
1204–1261	Latin Empire of Constantinople

MindTap is a fully online, highly personalized learning experience built upon Cengage Learning content. MindTap combines student learning tools—readings, multimedia, activities, and assessments—into a singular Learning Path that guides students through their course.

13

THE BYZANTINE EMPIRE AND CRISIS AND RECOVERY IN THE WEST

Scala/Art Resource, NY

Justinian and Theodora

CHAPTER OUTLINE

• From Eastern Roman to Byzantine Empire • The Zenith of Byzantine Civilization (750–1025) • The Decline and Fall of the Byzantine Empire (1025–1453) • The Crises of the Fourteenth Century in the West • Recovery: The Renaissance

FROM EASTERN ROMAN TO BYZANTINE EMPIRE

As noted earlier, the Western and Eastern parts of the Roman Empire began to drift apart in the fourth century. As the Germanic peoples moved into the Western part of the empire and established various kingdoms over the course of the fifth century, the Late Roman Empire in the East solidified and prospered.

Constantinople, the imperial capital, viewed itself not only as the center of a world empire but also as a special Christian city. The inhabitants believed that the city was under the protection of God and the Virgin Mary. One thirteenth-century Byzantine said: "About our city you shall know: until the end she will fear no nation whatsoever, for no one will entrap or capture her, not by any means, for she has been given to the Mother of God and no one will snatch her out of Her hands. Many nations will break their horns against her walls and withdraw with shame."[1] The Byzantines saw their state as a Christian empire.

The Reign of Justinian (527–565)

In the sixth century, the empire in the East came under the control of one of its most remarkable rulers, the emperor Justinian (juh-STIN-ee-un). As the nephew and heir of the previous emperor, Justinian had been well trained in imperial administration. He was determined to reestablish the Roman Empire in the entire Mediterranean world and began his attempt to reconquer the West in 533.

Justinian's army under Belisarius (bell-uh-SAH-ree-uss), probably the best general of the late Roman world, presented a formidable force. Belisarius sailed to North Africa and quickly defeated the Vandals in two major battles. From North Africa, he led his forces onto the Italian peninsula after occupying Sicily in 535. But it was not until 552 that the Ostrogoths were finally defeated. The struggle devastated Italy, which suffered more from Justinian's reconquest than from all of the previous barbarian invasions.

Justinian has long been criticized for overextending his resources and bankrupting the empire. Historians now think, however, that a devastating plague in 542 and long-term economic factors were far more damaging to the Eastern Roman Empire than Justinian's conquests. Before he died, Justinian appeared to have achieved his goals. He had restored the imperial Mediterranean world; his empire included Italy, part of Spain, North Africa, Asia Minor, Palestine, and Syria. But the conquest of the Western empire proved fleeting. Only three years after Justinian's death, another Germanic people, the Lombards, entered Italy. Although the Eastern empire maintained the fiction of Italy as a province, its forces were limited to small pockets here and there.

The Codification of Roman Law

Though his conquests proved short-lived, Justinian made a lasting contribution to Western civilization through his codification of Roman law. The Eastern empire was heir to a vast quantity of materials connected to the development of Roman law. These included laws passed by the senate and assemblies, legal commentaries of jurists, decisions of praetors, and the edicts of emperors. Justinian had been well trained in imperial government and was thoroughly acquainted with Roman law. He wished to codify and simplify this mass of materials.

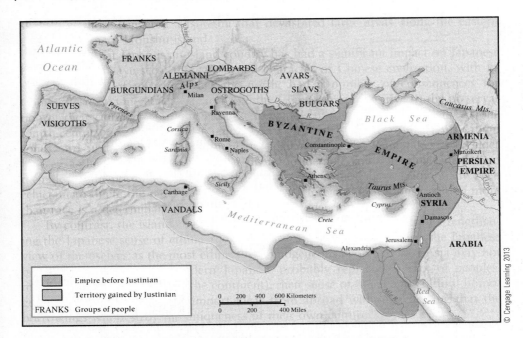

MAP 13.1 The Eastern Roman Empire in the Time of Justinian

The Eastern Roman emperor Justinian briefly restored much of the Mediterranean portion of the old Roman Empire. His general, Belisarius, conquered the Vandals in North Africa quite easily but wrested Italy from the Ostrogoths only after a long and devastating struggle.

To accomplish his goal, Justinian authorized the jurist Trebonian to make a systematic compilation of imperial edicts. The result was the Code of Law, the first part of the *Corpus Iuris Civilis* (KOR-pus YOOR-iss SIV-i-liss) (Body of Civil Law), completed in 529. Four years later, two other parts of the *Corpus* appeared: the *Digest*, a compendium of writings of Roman jurists, and the *Institutes*, a brief summary of the chief principles of Roman law that could be used as a textbook. The fourth part of the *Corpus* was the *Novels*, a compilation of the most important new edicts issued during Justinian's reign.

Justinian's codification of Roman law became the basis of imperial law in the Byzantine Empire until its end in 1453. More important, however, since it was written in Latin (it was, in fact, the last product of Eastern Roman culture to be written in Latin, which was soon replaced by Greek), it was also eventually used in the West and in fact became the basis of the legal system of all of continental Europe.

The Empress Theodora Theodora (thee-uh-DOR-uh) was the daughter of the "keeper of bears" for the games at Constantinople, who died when Theodora was a child. Theodora followed in her mother's footsteps by becoming an actress, which at that time was considered a lower-class activity. Often actresses also worked as prostitutes, and Theodora was no exception. At the age of twenty-five, she met Justinian, who was forty. His uncle, the emperor Justin, had to change the law to allow an aristocratic senator to marry a woman who had been an actress. After his uncle died in 527, Justinian became emperor and Theodora empress, a remarkable achievement for a woman from the lower classes.

Justinian and Theodora were close and loving companions. She also influenced her husband in both church and state affairs. A strong-willed and intelligent woman, she proved especially valuable in 532, when her steely resolve during the Nika Revolt convinced Justinian to fight and crush the protesters rather than to flee. Theodora also helped establish a number of churches and monasteries, including a convent for former prostitutes.

The Emperor's Building Program   After the riots destroyed much of Constantinople, Justinian rebuilt the city and gave it the appearance it would keep for almost a thousand years. Earlier, Emperor Theodosius (thee-uh-DOH-shuss) II (408–450) had constructed an enormous defensive wall to protect the capital on its land side. The city was dominated by an immense palace complex, a huge arena known as the Hippodrome, and hundreds of churches. No residential district was particularly fashionable; palaces, tenements, and slums ranged alongside one another. Justinian added many new buildings. His public works projects included roads, bridges,

MAP 13.2   Constantinople

In the Middle Ages, Constantinople was the largest European city and a nexus of trade between East and West. Emperor Justinian oversaw a massive building program that produced important architectural monuments such as Hagia Sophia.

walls, public baths, law courts, and colossal underground reservoirs to hold the city's water supply. He also built hospitals, schools, monasteries, and churches. Churches were his special passion, and in Constantinople he built or rebuilt thirty-four of them. His greatest achievement was the famous Hagia Sophia (HAG-ee-uh soh-FEE-uh), the Church of the Holy Wisdom.

Completed in 537, Hagia Sophia was designed by two Greek scientists who departed radically from the simple, flat-roofed basilica of Western architecture. The center of Hagia Sophia consisted of four huge piers crowned by an enormous dome, which seemed to be floating in space. This effect was emphasized by Procopius (pruh-KOH-pee-uss), the court historian, who at Justinian's request wrote a treatise on the emperor's building projects: "From the lightness of the building, it does not appear to rest upon a solid foundation, but to cover the place beneath as though it were suspended from heaven by the fabled golden chain." In part, this impression was created by putting forty-two windows around the base of the dome, which allowed an incredible play of light within the cathedral. Light served to remind the worshipers of God; as Procopius commented:

> Whoever enters there to worship perceives at once that it is not by any human strength or skill, but by the favor of God that this work has been perfected; his mind rises sublime to commune with God, feeling that He cannot be far off, but must especially love to dwell in the place which He has chosen; and this takes place not only when a man sees it for the first time, but it always makes the same impression upon him, as though he had never beheld it before.[2]

As darkness is illuminated by invisible light, so too, it was believed, the world is illuminated by invisible spirit.

The royal palace complex, Hagia Sophia, and the Hippodrome were the three greatest buildings in Constantinople. This last was a huge amphitheater, constructed of brick covered by marble, holding as many as 60,000 spectators. Although gladiator fights were held there, the main events were the chariot races; twenty-four would usually be presented in one day. The citizens of Constantinople were passionate fans of chariot racing. Successful charioteers were acclaimed as heroes and honored with public statues. Crowds in the Hippodrome also took on political significance. Being a member of the two chief factions of charioteers—the Blues or the Greens—was the only real outlet for political expression. Even emperors had to be aware of their demands and attitudes: the loss of a race in the Hippodrome frequently resulted in bloody riots that could threaten the emperor's power.

A New Kind of Empire

Justinian's accomplishments had been spectacular, but when he died, he left the Eastern Roman Empire with serious problems: too much distant territory to protect, an empty treasury, a smaller population after a devastating plague, and renewed threats to the frontiers. The seventh century proved to be an important turning point in the history of the empire.

Problems of the Seventh Century

In the first half of the century, during the reign of Heraclius (he-ruh-KLY-uss *or* huh-RAK-lee-uss) (610–641), the empire faced attacks from the Persians to the East and the Slavs to the north. A new system of defense was put in place, using a new and larger administrative unit, the *theme*, which combined civilian and military offices in the hands of the same person. Thus, the civil governor was also the military leader of the area. Although this innovation helped the empire survive, it also fostered an increased militarization of the empire. By the mid-seventh century, it had become apparent that a restored Mediterranean empire was simply beyond the resources of the Eastern empire, which now increasingly turned its back on the Latin West. A renewed series of external threats in the second half of the seventh century strengthened this development.

The most serious challenge to the empire was the rise of Islam, which unified the Arab tribes and created a powerful new force that swept through the region. The defeat of an Eastern Roman army near the Yarmuk River in 636 meant the loss of the provinces of Syria and Palestine. The Arabs also moved into the old Persian Empire and conquered it. An Arab attempt to besiege Constantinople that began in 674 failed, in large part due to the use of Greek fire against the Arab fleets. Greek fire was a petroleum-based compound containing quicklime and sulfur. Because it would burn under water, the Byzantines created the equivalent of modern flamethrowers by using tubes to blow Greek fire onto wooden ships, with frightening effect. Arabs and Eastern Roman forces now faced each other along a frontier in southern Asia Minor.

Problems also arose along the northern frontier, especially in the Balkans, where an Asiatic people known as the Bulgars had arrived earlier in the sixth century. In 679, the Bulgars defeated the Eastern Roman forces and took possession of the lower Danube valley, setting up a strong Bulgarian kingdom.

By the beginning of the eighth century, the Eastern Roman Empire was greatly diminished in size, consisting only of a portion of the Balkans and Asia Minor. It was now an Eastern Mediterranean state. These external challenges had important internal repercussions as well. By the eighth century, the Eastern Roman Empire had been transformed into what historians call the Byzantine Empire, a civilization with its own unique character that would last until 1453 (Constantinople was built on the site of an older city named Byzantium—hence the name *Byzantine*).

The Byzantine Empire in the Eighth Century The Byzantine Empire was a Greek state. Justinian's *Corpus Iuris Civilis* had been the last official work published in Latin. Increasingly, Latin fell into disuse as Greek became not only the common language of the Byzantine Empire but its official language as well.

The Byzantine Empire was also a Christian state, built on a faith in Jesus that was shared in a profound way by almost all its citizens. An enormous amount of artistic talent was poured into the construction of churches, church ceremonies, and church decoration. Spiritual principles deeply permeated Byzantine art. The importance of religion to the Byzantines explains why theological disputes took on an exaggerated form. The most famous of these disputes, the so-called iconoclastic controversy, threatened the stability of the empire in the first half of the eighth century.

Beginning in the sixth century, the use of religious images, especially in the form of icons or pictures of sacred figures, became so widespread that charges of idolatry, the worship of images, began to be heard. The use of images or icons

COMPARATIVE ILLUSTRATION

Religious Imagery in the Medieval World

RELIGION & PHILOSOPHY

The Middle Ages was a golden age of religious art, reflecting the important role of religion itself in medieval society. These illustrations show different aspects of medieval religious imagery. Byzantine art was deeply

Erich Lessing/Art Resource, NY

had been justified by the argument that icons were not worshiped but were simply used to help illiterate people understand their religion. This argument failed to stop the **iconoclasts,** as the opponents of icons were called.

Iconoclasm was not unique to the Byzantine Empire. In the neighboring Islamic empire, religious art did not include any physical representations of Muhammad. Iconoclasm would also play a role among some of the new religious groups that emerged in the Protestant Reformation in sixteenth-century Europe.

religious, as was especially evident in icons. In the middle is an icon of the Virgin and Child (Mary and Jesus) from the monastery of Saint Catherine at Mount Sinai in Egypt dating to around the year 600. Painted on wood, this icon shows the enthroned Virgin and Child between Saints Theodore and George with two angels behind them looking upward to a beam of light containing the hand of God. The figures are not realistic; the goal of the icon was to bridge the gap between the divine and the outer material world. Artists in the Muslim world faced a different challenge—Muslims warned against imitating God by creating pictures of living beings, thus effectively prohibiting the representation of humans, especially Muhammad. Islamic religious artists therefore used decorative motifs based on geometric patterns and the Arabic script. The scriptural panel in the bottom illustration is an artistic presentation of a verse from the Qur'an, thus blending the spiritual and artistic spheres.

Q *How is the importance of religious imagery in the Middle Ages evident in these illustrations?*

Vanni Archive/ Art Resource, NY

Beginning in 730, the Byzantine emperor Leo III (717–741) outlawed the use of icons. Strong resistance ensued, especially from monks. Leo also used the iconoclastic controversy to add to the prestige of the patriarch of Constantinople, the highest church official in the East and second in dignity only to the bishop of Rome. The Roman popes were opposed to the iconoclastic edicts, and their opposition created considerable dissension between the popes and the Byzantine emperors. Late in the eighth century, the Byzantine rulers reversed their stand on the use of images, but not before considerable damage had been done to the unity of the Christian church.

Although the final separation between Roman Catholicism and Greek Orthodoxy (as the Christian church in the Byzantine Empire was called) did not occur until 1054, the iconoclastic controversy was important in moving both sides in that direction.

The Byzantine Emperor   The emperor occupied a crucial position in the Byzantine state. Portrayed as chosen by God, the Byzantine emperor was crowned in elaborate sacred ceremonies, and his subjects were expected to prostrate themselves in his presence. The wives of the emperors also played significant roles in the court rituals that upheld imperial authority.

The importance of court ritual is apparent in the *Book of Ceremonies*, a tenth-century compendium of imperial ceremonies and court rituals. Court ritual could be very complicated and included a variety of activities. Everyday rituals included the daily opening of the imperial palace: imperial officials, all arranged in order of rank, waited until the palace doors were officially opened; then they marched into the palace in a procession. A similar ceremony was held for the opening of the palace in the afternoon. In addition to these regular daily ceremonies, special ceremonies involving specific rituals were held on many occasions, including the emperor's birthday, the promotion of officials, imperial marriages, and commemorations of important military battles. The emperor was also required to participate in the ceremonies held regularly in the churches on important saints' days and during church festivals.

The power of the Byzantine emperor was considered absolute and was limited in practice only by assassination. A rather unusual ruling class assisted the emperors. Civil servants and high churchmen essentially stemmed from the same ranks of the urban society of Constantinople. They received the same education and often followed the same careers in civil service until they went their separate ways into church and government offices. A strong bureaucracy was one of the most basic features of the Byzantine Empire.

The Byzantine Empire was characterized by what might be called a permanent war economy. Byzantine emperors maintained the late Roman policy of state regulation of economic affairs. Of course, this practice was easy to justify: the survival of the empire depended on careful shepherding of economic resources and the maintenance of the army. Thus, the state encouraged agricultural production, regulated the guilds or corporations responsible for industrial production and the various stages of manufacturing, and controlled commerce by making trade in grain and silk, the two most valuable products, government monopolies.

In addition, because of their many foreign enemies, Byzantine emperors spent considerable energy on war and preparation for war. Manuals on war, providing instruction in the ways of fighting, were a common type of Byzantine literature. Byzantine armies, often led by the emperors, were well trained and equipped with the latest weapons. The Byzantines, however, often preferred to secure their goals through diplomacy rather than fighting. Our word *byzantine*—often defined as "extremely complicated" or "carried on by underhanded methods"—stems from the complex and crafty instructions that Byzantine rulers sent to their envoys.

Because the emperor appointed the patriarch, he also exercised control over both church and state. The Byzantines believed that God had commanded their state to preserve the true faith, Orthodox Christianity. Emperor, clergy, and civic officials were all bound together in service to this ideal. It can be said that spiritual values truly held the Byzantine state together.

By 750, it was apparent that two of Rome's heirs, the Germanic kingdoms and the Byzantine Empire, were moving in different directions. Nevertheless, Byzantine influence on the Western world was significant. The images of a Roman imperial state that continued to haunt the West lived on in Byzantium. As noted, the legal system of the West came to owe much to Justinian's codification of Roman law. In addition, the Byzantine Empire served in part as a buffer state, protecting the West for a long time from incursions from the East.

Intellectual Life   The intellectual life of the Byzantine Empire was greatly influenced by the traditions of Classical civilization. Scholars actively strived to preserve the works of the ancient Greeks and based a great deal of their own literature on Classical models. Although the Byzantines produced a substantial body of literature, much of it was of a very practical nature, focusing on legal, military, and administrative matters. The most outstanding literary achievements of the empire's early centuries, however, were historical and religious works. Many of the latter were theological treatises, often of an extremely combative nature because of the intense theological controversies. More popular were biographies of saints, which traced the adventures of religious figures who after many struggles achieved a life of virtue.

The empire's best-known historian was Procopius (c. 500–c. 562), court historian during the reign of Justinian. Procopius served as secretary to the great general Belisarius and accompanied him on his wars on behalf of Justinian. Procopius's best historical work, the *Wars*, is a firsthand account of Justinian's wars of reconquest in the Western Mediterranean and his wars against the Persians in the East. Deliberately modeled after the work of his hero, the Greek historian Thucydides, Procopius's narrative features vivid descriptions of battle scenes, clear judgment, and noteworthy objectivity.

Life in Constantinople: The Importance of Trade   With a population in the hundreds of thousands, Constantinople was the largest city in Europe during the Middle Ages. Until the twelfth century, Constantinople was also Europe's greatest commercial center. The city was the chief entrepôt for the exchange of products between West and East, and trade formed the basis for its fabulous prosperity. Foreign merchants, however, largely carried on this trade. As one contemporary said:

> All sorts of merchants come here from the land of Babylon, from … Persia, Media, and all the sovereignty of the land of Egypt, from the lands of Canaan, and from the empire of Russia, from Hungaria, Khazaria [the Caspian region], and the land of Lombardy and Sepharad [Spain]. It is a busy city, and merchants come to it from every country by sea or land, and there is none like it in the world except Baghdad, the great city of Islam.[3]

Highly desired in Europe were the products of the East: silk from China, spices from Southeast Asia and India, jewelry and ivory from India (used by artisans for church items), wheat and furs from southern Russia, and flax and honey from the

Balkans. Many of these Eastern goods were then shipped to the Mediterranean area and northern Europe. Despite the Germanic incursions, trade with Europe did not entirely end.

Moreover, imported raw materials were used in Constantinople for local industries. During Justinian's reign, two Christian monks smuggled silkworms from China to begin a silk industry. The state had a monopoly on the production of silk cloth, and the workshops themselves were housed in Constantinople's royal palace complex. European demand for silk cloth made it the city's most lucrative product. It is interesting to note that the upper classes, including emperors and empresses, were not discouraged from making money through trade and manufacturing. Indeed, one empress even manufactured perfumes in her bedroom.

The Zenith of Byzantine Civilization (750–1025)

In the seventh and eighth centuries, the Byzantine Empire lost much of its territory to Slavs, Bulgars, and Muslims. By 750, the empire consisted only of Asia Minor, some lands in the Balkans, and the southern coast of Italy. Although Byzantium was beset with internal dissension and invasions in the ninth century, it was able to deal with them and not only endured but even expanded, reaching its high point in the tenth century, which some historians have called the golden age of Byzantine civilization.

The Beginning of a Revival   During the reign of Michael III (842–867), the Byzantine Empire began to experience a revival. Iconoclasm was finally abolished in 843, and reforms were made in education, church life, the military, and the peasant economy. There was a noticeable intellectual renewal. But the empire was still plagued by persistent problems. The Bulgars mounted new attacks, and the Arabs continued to harass the periphery. Moreover, a new religious dispute with political repercussions erupted over differences between the pope as leader of the Western Christian church and the patriarch of Constantinople as leader of the Eastern Christian church. Patriarch Photius (FOH-shuss) condemned the pope as a heretic for accepting a revised form of the Nicene Creed stating that the Holy Spirit proceeded from the Father and the Son instead of from the Father alone. A council of Eastern bishops followed Photius's wishes and excommunicated the pope, creating the so-called Photian schism. Although the differences were later papered over, this controversy inserted a greater wedge between the Eastern and Western Christian churches.

The Macedonian Dynasty   The problems that arose during Michael's reign were effectively dealt with by a new Dynasty of Byzantine emperors known as the Macedonians (867–1056). The founder of the Dynasty, Basil I (867–886), was a Macedonian of uncertain background who came to Constantinople to improve his lot in life. After impressing Emperor Michael III with his wrestling skills, he married the emperor's mistress and was made co-emperor. One year later, he arranged the murder of Michael and then became sole ruler, establishing a Dynasty that would last almost two hundred years.

The Macedonian Dynasty managed to hold off Byzantium's external enemies and reestablish domestic order. Supported by the church, the emperors thought of the Byzantine Empire as a continuation of the Christian Roman Empire of late antiquity. Although for diplomatic reasons they occasionally recognized the imperial titles of earlier Western emperors, such as Charlemagne and Otto I, they still regarded them as little more than barbarian parvenus.

Economic and Religious Policies   The Macedonian emperors could boast of a remarkable number of achievements in the late ninth and tenth centuries. They worked to strengthen the position of the free farmers, who felt threatened by the attempts of landed aristocrats to expand their estates at the farmers' expense. The emperors were well aware that the free farmers made up the rank and file of the Byzantine cavalry and provided the military strength of the empire. Nevertheless, despite their efforts, the Macedonian emperors found that it was not easy to control the power of the landed nobles, and many free farmers continued to lose their lands to the nobles.

The Macedonian emperors also fostered a burst of economic prosperity by expanding trade relations with Western Europe, especially by selling silks and metalwork, and the city of Constantinople flourished. Foreign visitors continued to be astounded by its size, wealth, and physical surroundings. To Western Europeans, it was the stuff of legends and fables.

In this period of prosperity, Byzantine cultural influence expanded due to the active missionary efforts of Eastern Byzantine Christians. Eastern Orthodox Christianity was spread to Eastern European peoples, such as the Bulgars and Serbs. Perhaps the greatest missionary success occurred when the prince of Kiev in Russia converted to Christianity in 987. From the end of the tenth century on, Byzantine Christianity became the model for Russian religious life, just as Byzantine imperial ideals came to influence the outward forms of Russian political life.

Political and Military Achievements   Under the Macedonian rulers, Byzantium enjoyed a strong civil service, talented emperors, and military advances. Well-educated, competent aristocrats from Constantinople staffed the Byzantine civil service and oversaw the collection of taxes, domestic administration, and foreign policy. At the same time, the Macedonian Dynasty produced some truly outstanding emperors skilled in administration and law, including Leo VI and Constantine VII. Leo VI (886–912), known as Leo the Wise, was an accomplished scholar who composed works on politics and theology, systematized rules for regulating both trade and court officials, and arranged for a new codification of all Byzantine law. Constantine VII (945–959) wrote a detailed treatise on foreign policy to instruct his officials, as well as his son, on running the empire wisely. Constantine also worked to reduce the tax burden on the peasants.

In the tenth century, competent emperors combined with a number of talented generals to mobilize the empire's military resources and take the offensive. Especially important was Basil II (976–1025), who campaigned regularly against the Bulgars. Although his first campaign was a failure, he continued his efforts until he defeated the Bulgars and annexed Bulgaria to the empire. After his final victory over the Bulgars in 1014, Basil blinded 14,000 Bulgar captives before allowing them to return to their homes. The Byzantines went on to add the islands of Crete and Cyprus to the empire and to defeat the Muslim forces in Syria, expanding the empire to the upper Euphrates. By the end of Basil's reign in 1025, the Byzantine Empire was the largest it had been since the beginning of the seventh century.

Women in the Byzantine Empire   In Byzantium, as in European society, women were regarded as inferior to men and, at times, even considered to be the instrument of the devil. In general, women were expected to remain at home. They could leave to shop, visit parents, and take part in civic celebrations, but they were supposed to wear veils on these occasions.

Women were generally expected to fulfill three major functions: to marry and bear children, to maintain the household, and to weave clothes for their families. Thus, a good wife was seen as a special gift to her husband. Contrary to these ideal female roles, some women in the Byzantine world worked outside the home as artisans and sellers, especially of foodstuffs, in the markets of Constantinople. Others served as midwives, bakers, cooks, and dancers, although some dancers also worked as prostitutes.

Upper-class women had greater opportunities to play important roles in the empire. Some aristocratic wives funded the establishment of monasteries, occupied important positions at court, and patronized the arts. Imperial wives could exercise considerable political power as regents for their sons; some even became empresses in their own right. Irene, for example, served as regent for her son until 797 when she blinded and deposed him; she then ruled in her own right until she was overthrown in 802.

THE DECLINE AND FALL OF THE BYZANTINE EMPIRE (1025–1453)

The Macedonian Dynasty of the tenth and eleventh centuries had restored much of the power of the Byzantine Empire; its incompetent successors, however, reversed most of the gains.

New Challenges and New Responses   After the Macedonian Dynasty was extinguished in 1056, the empire was beset by internal struggles for power between ambitious military leaders and aristocratic families who bought the support of the great landowners of Anatolia by allowing them greater control over their peasants. This policy was self-destructive, however, because the peasant-warrior was an important source of military strength in the Byzantine state. By the middle of the eleventh century, the Byzantine army began to decline; with fewer peasant recruits, military leaders also began to rely more on mercenaries.

A Christian Schism   The growing division between the Roman Catholic Church of the West and the Eastern Orthodox Church of the Byzantine Empire also weakened the Byzantine state. The Eastern Orthodox Church was unwilling to accept the pope's claim that he was the sole head of the Christian church. This dispute reached a climax in 1054 when Pope Leo IX and Patriarch Michael Cerularius (sayr-yuh-LAR-ee-uss), head of the Byzantine church, formally excommunicated each other, initiating a schism between the two branches of Christianity that has not been healed to this day.

Islam and the Seljuk Turks   The Byzantine Empire faced external threats to its security as well. In the West, the Normans were menacing the remaining Byzantine possessions in Italy. A much greater threat, however, came from the world of Islam. By the mid-tenth century, the Islamic empire led by the Abbasid caliphate in Baghdad was disintegrating. An attempt was made around that time to unify the Islamic world under the direction of a Shi'ite Dynasty known as the Fatimids. Originating in North Africa, they conquered Egypt and founded the new city of Cairo as their capital. In establishing a Shi'ite caliphate, they became rivals to the Sunni caliphate of Baghdad and divided the Islamic world.

The Fatimid Dynasty prospered and soon surpassed the Abbasid caliphate as the dynamic center of Islam. Benefiting from their position in the heart of the Nile Delta, the Fatimids played a major role in the regional trade passing from the Mediterranean to the Red Sea and beyond. They were tolerant in matters of religion and created a strong army by using nonnative peoples as mercenaries. One of these peoples, the Seljuk Turks, soon posed a threat to the Fatimids themselves.

A nomadic people from Central Asia, the Seljuk Turks had been converted to Islam. As their numbers increased, they moved into the Eastern provinces of the Abbasid Empire, and in 1055 they captured Baghdad and occupied the rest of the empire. When they moved into Asia Minor—the heartland of the Byzantine Empire and its main source of food and manpower—the Byzantines were forced to react. Emperor Romanus IV led an army of recruits and mercenaries into Asia Minor in 1071 and met Turkish forces at Manzikert (MANZ-ih-kurt), where the Byzantines were soundly defeated. Seljuk Turks then went on to occupy much of Anatolia, where many peasants, already disgusted by their exploitation at the hands of Byzantine landowners, readily accepted Turkish control.

A New Dynasty   After the loss at Manzikert, factional fighting erupted over the imperial title until Alexius Comnenus (kahm-NEE-nuss) (1081–1118) seized the throne and established a Dynasty that breathed new life into the Byzantine Empire. Under Alexius, the Byzantines were victorious on the Greek Adriatic coast against the Normans, defeated their enemies in the Balkans, and stopped the Turks in Anatolia. In the twelfth century, the Byzantine Empire experienced a cultural revival and a period of prosperity, fueled by an expansion of trade. The era was also marked by the increased importance of aristocratic families, especially those from a military background. In fact, Alexius's power was built on an alliance of the Comnenus family with other aristocratic families. But both the Comneni Dynasty and the revival of the twelfth century were ultimately threatened by Byzantium's encounters with crusaders from the West.

Impact of the Crusades   Lacking the resources to undertake additional campaigns against the Turks, Emperor Alexius turned to the West for military assistance and asked Pope Urban II for help against the Seljuk Turks. Instead of the military aid the emperor had expected, the pope set in motion the First Crusade, a decision that created enormous difficulties for the Byzantines. To pursue the goal of liberating Palestine from the Muslims, Western crusading armies would have to go through Byzantine lands to reach their objective. Alexius, and especially his daughter, Anna Comnena (who was also the Byzantine Empire's only female historian), were fearful that "to all appearances they were on pilgrimage; in reality they planned to dethrone Alexius and seize the capital."[4]

The Byzantines became cautious; Alexius requested that the military leaders of the First Crusade take an oath of loyalty to him and promise that any territory they conquered would be under Byzantine control. The crusaders ignored the emperor's wishes, and after conquering Antioch, Jerusalem, and additional Palestinian lands, they organized the four crusading states of Edessa, Antioch, Tripoli, and Jerusalem. The Byzantines now had to worry not only about the Turks in Anatolia but also about Westerners in the crusading states. The Second and Third crusades posed similar difficulties for the Byzantine emperors.

With the crusades, the Byzantine Empire also became better acquainted with Westerners and Western customs. In the mid-twelfth century, the Byzantine emperor Manuel I (1140–1183) introduced the Western practice of knightly jousting to the Byzantine aristocracy. The Byzantine emperors also conferred trading concessions on the Italian city-states of Venice, Pisa, and Genoa, and in the course of the century, probably 60,000 Western Europeans came to live in Constantinople. But the presence of Westerners and Western practices also led to a growing hostility. Byzantine writers began to denounce Western attitudes, and Westerners often expressed jealousy of Constantinople's wealth. In 1171, Emperor Manuel I expelled the Venetians and seized their goods and ships, arousing in Venice a desire for revenge that was no doubt a factor in the disastrous Fourth Crusade in 1204.

The Latin Empire of Constantinople   After the death of Saladin in 1193, Pope Innocent III launched the Fourth Crusade. Judging the moment auspicious, Innocent encouraged the nobility of Europe to don the crusader's mantle. The Venetians agreed to transport the crusaders to the East but diverted them from the Holy Land by persuading them to first capture Zara, a Christian port on the Dalmatian coast. The crusading army thus became enmeshed in Byzantine politics.

At the start of the thirteenth century, the Byzantine Empire was experiencing yet another struggle for the imperial throne. One contender, Alexius, son of the overthrown Emperor Isaac II, appealed to the crusaders in Zara for assistance, offering to pay them 200,000 marks in silver (the Venetians were getting 85,000 as a transport fee) and to reconcile the Eastern Orthodox Church with the Roman Catholic Church. The crusade leaders now diverted their forces to Constantinople. When the crusading army arrived, the deposed Isaac II was reestablished with his son, Alexius IV, as co-emperor. Unfortunately, the emperors were unable to pay the promised sum. Relations between the crusaders and the Byzantines deteriorated, leading to an attack on Constantinople by the crusaders in the spring of 1204. On April 12, they stormed and sacked the city. Christian crusaders took gold, silver, jewelry, and precious furs, while the Catholic clergy accompanying the crusaders stole as many relics as they could find.

The Byzantine Empire now disintegrated into a series of petty states ruled by crusading barons and Byzantine princes. The chief state was the new Latin Empire of Constantinople led by Count Baldwin of Flanders as emperor. The Venetians seized the island of Crete and assumed control of Constantinople's trade. Why had the Western crusaders succeeded so easily when Persians, Bulgars, and Arabs had failed for centuries to conquer Constantinople? Although the crusaders were no doubt motivated by greed and a lust for conquest, they were also convinced that they were acting in God's cause. After all, a Catholic patriarch (a Venetian) had now been installed in Constantinople, and the reconciliation of Eastern Orthodoxy with Catholic Christianity had been accomplished. Nor should we overlook the military superiority of the French warriors and the superb organizational skills of the Venetians; together, they formed a powerful and highly effective union.

Revival of the Byzantine Empire   Although he protested the diversion of the crusade from the Holy Land, Pope Innocent III belatedly accepted as "God's work" the conversion of Greek Byzantium to Latin Christianity. Some have argued that Innocent did realize, however, that the use of force to reunite the churches virtually guaranteed the failure of any permanent reunion. All too soon, this proved correct. The West was unable to maintain the Latin Empire, for the Western rulers of the newly created principalities were soon engrossed in fighting each other. Some parts of the Byzantine Empire had managed to survive under Byzantine princes. In 1259, Michael Paleologus (pay-lee-AWL-uh-guss), a Greek military leader, took control of the kingdom of Nicaea in Western Asia Minor, led a Byzantine army to recapture Constantinople two years later, and then established a new Byzantine Dynasty, the Paleologi.

The Byzantine Empire had been saved, but it was no longer a Mediterranean power. The restored empire was a badly truncated entity, consisting of the city of Constantinople and its surrounding territory, some lands in Asia Minor, and part of Thessalonica. It was surrounded by enemies—Bulgarians, Mongols, Turks, and Westerners, especially the resentful Venetians. And there was still internal opposition to Michael VIII. But the emperor survived and began a badly needed restoration of Constantinople.

Even in its reduced size, the empire limped along for another 190 years, and Constantinople remained an active economic center. Scholars continued to study the classics, and new churches and monasteries were built. Yet civil strife persisted as rival claimants struggled over the throne, and enemies continued to multiply. The threat from the Turks finally doomed the aged empire.

The Ottoman Turks and the Fall of Constantinople   Beginning in northeastern Asia Minor in the thirteenth century, the Ottoman Turks spread rapidly, seizing the lands of the Seljuk Turks and the Byzantine Empire. In 1345, they bypassed Constantinople and pushed into the Balkans. Under Sultan Murad (moo-RAHD), Ottoman forces moved through Bulgaria and into the lands of the Serbs; in 1389, at the Battle of Kosovo (KAWSS-suh-voh), Ottoman forces defeated the Serbs. By the beginning of the fifteenth century, the Byzantine Empire had been reduced to little more than Constantinople, now surrounded on all sides by the Ottomans. When Mehmet (meh-MET) II

Erich Lessing/Art Resource, NY

The Fall of Constantinople. *Few events in the history of the Ottoman Empire are more dramatic than the conquest of Constantinople in 1453. Although the Venetian painter Palma Giovane did not witness the conquest itself, he tried to capture the drama in his opulent reconstruction of the first attack by the Turks on the legendary city. This painting was one of a series done for the Doge's Palace in Venice.*

came to the throne in 1451 at the age of only nineteen, he was determined to capture Constantinople and complete the demise of the Byzantine Empire.

The siege began in April when Mehmet moved his army—probably about 80,000 men—within striking distance of the 13-mile-long land walls along the Western edge of the city. The pope and the Italian city-states of Venice and Genoa promised aid, but most of it was too little and too late. The city probably had 6,000 to 8,000 soldiers mobilized for its defense. On April 2, Emperor Constantine XI (1449–1453), the last Byzantine emperor, ordered that a floating chain or boom be stretched across the Golden Horn, the inlet that forms the city's harbor, to prevent a naval attack from the north. Mehmet's forces, however, took control of the tip of the peninsula north of the Golden Horn and then pulled their ships overland across the peninsula from the Bosporus and placed them into the water behind the chains. The Ottoman fleet in the Horn built a pontoon bridge and set up artillery, forcing the Byzantines to defend the city on all sides.

The Ottomans' main attack, however, came against the land walls. On April 6, the artillery onslaught began. The Ottoman invaders had a distinct advantage with their cannons. One of them, constructed by a Hungarian engineer, had a 26-foot barrel that fired stone balls weighing 1,200 pounds. It took 60 oxen and 2,000 men to pull the great cannon into position. On May 29, Mehmet decided on a final assault, focused against the areas where the walls had been breached. When Ottoman forces broke into the city, the emperor became one of the first casualties. Irregular Ottoman forces began to loot the city before regular troops were able to stop them. About 4,000 defenders were killed, and thousands of the inhabitants were sold into slavery. Early in the afternoon, Mehmet II rode into the city, exalted the power of Allah from the pulpit in the cathedral of Hagia Sophia, and ordered that it be converted into a mosque. He soon began rebuilding the city as the capital of the Ottoman Empire. The Byzantine Empire had come to an end.

THE CRISES OF THE FOURTEENTH CENTURY IN THE WEST

At the beginning of the fourteenth century, changes in global weather patterns ushered in what has been called a "little ice age." Shortened growing seasons and disastrous weather conditions, including heavy storms and constant rain, led to widespread famine and hunger. Soon an even greater catastrophe struck.

The Black Death: From Asia to Europe   In the mid-fourteenth century, a disaster known as the **Black Death** struck in Asia, North Africa, and Europe. Bubonic plague was the most common and most important form of plague in the diffusion of the Black Death and was spread by black rats infested with fleas who were host to the deadly bacterium *Yersinia pestis* (yur-SIN-ee-uh PES-tiss).

Role of the Mongols   This great plague originated in Asia. After disappearing from Europe and the Middle East in the Middle Ages, bubonic plague continued to haunt areas of southwestern China. In the early 1300s, rats accompanying Mongol troops spread the plague into central China and by 1331 to northeastern China. In one province near Beijing, it was reported that 90 percent of the population died. Overall, China's population may have declined from 120 million in the mid-1300s to 80 million by 1400.

In the thirteenth century, the Mongols had brought much of the Eurasian landmass under a single rule, which in turn facilitated long-distance trade, particularly along the Silk Road, now dominated by Muslim merchants from Central Asia. The spread of people and goods throughout this Eurasian landmass also facilitated the spread of the plague.

In the 1330s, the plague had spread to Central Asia; by 1339 it had reached Samarkand, a caravan stop on the Silk Road. From Central Asia, trading caravans brought the plague to Caffa, on the Black Sea, in 1346 and to Constantinople by the following year. Its arrival in the Byzantine Empire was noted in a work by Emperor John VI, who lost a son: "Upon arrival in Constantinople she [the empress] found Andronikos, the youngest born, dead from the invading plague, which ... attacked almost all the sea coasts of the world and killed most of their people."[5] By 1348, the plague had spread to Egypt and also to Mecca, Damascus, and other parts of the Middle East. The Muslim historian Ibn Khaldun (IB-un kahl-DOON), writing in the fourteenth century, commented, "Civilization in the East and West was visited by a destructive plague which devastated nations and caused

COMPARATIVE ESSAY

The Role of Disease in History

INTERACTION & EXCHANGE

When Hernán Cortés and his fellow conquistadors arrived in Mesoamerica in 1519, the local inhabitants were frightened of the horses and the firearms that accompanied the Spaniards. What they did not know was that the most dangerous enemies brought by these strange new arrivals were invisible—the disease-bearing microbes that would soon kill them by the millions.

Diseases have been the scourge of animal species since the dawn of prehistory, making the lives of human beings, in the words of the English philosopher Thomas Hobbes, "nasty, brutish, and short." With the increasing sophistication of forensic evidence, archaeologists today are able to determine from recently discovered human remains that our immediate ancestors were plagued by such familiar ailments as anemia, arthritis, tuberculosis, and malaria.

With the explosive growth of the human population brought about by the agricultural revolution, the problems posed by the presence of disease intensified. As people began to congregate in villages and cities, bacteria settled in their piles of refuse and were carried by lice in their clothing. The domestication of animals made humans more vulnerable to diseases carried by their livestock. As population density increased, the danger of widespread epidemics increased with it.

As time went on, succeeding generations gradually developed partial or complete immunity to many of these diseases, which became chronic rather than fatal to their victims, as occurred with malaria in parts of Africa, for example, and chickenpox in the Americas. But when a disease was introduced to a particular society that had not previously been exposed to it, the consequences were often devastating. The most dramatic example was the famous Black Death, the plague that ravaged Europe and China during the fourteenth century, killing one-fourth to one-half of the inhabitants in the affected regions (and even greater numbers in certain areas). Smallpox had the same impact in the Americas after the arrival of Christopher Columbus, and malaria was fatal to many Europeans on their arrival in West Africa. How were these diseases transmitted? In most instances, they followed the trade routes. Such was the case with the Black Death, which was initially carried by fleas living in the saddlebags of Mongol warriors as they advanced toward Europe in the thirteenth and fourteenth centuries and thereafter by rats in the holds of cargo ships. Smallpox and other diseases were brought to the Americas by the conquistadors. Epidemics, then, are a price that humans pay for having developed the network of rapid communication that has accompanied the evolution of human society.

Q *What role has disease played in human history?*

populations to vanish. It swallowed up many of the good things of civilization and wiped them out."[6] Egypt was particularly devastated by the plague; it has been estimated that the population of Egypt did not return to its pre-1347 level until the nineteenth century.

The Black Death in Europe   The Black Death of the mid-fourteenth century was the most devastating natural disaster in European history, ravaging Europe's population and causing economic, social, political, and cultural upheaval. Contemporary chroniclers lamented that parents attempted to flee, abandoning their children; one related the words of a child left behind: "Oh father, why have you abandoned me? ... Mother where have you gone?"[7]

The plague reached Europe in October 1347 when Genoese merchants brought it from Caffa to the island of Sicily off the coast of Italy. One contemporary wrote, "As it happened, among those who escaped from Caffa by boat, there were a few sailors who had been infected with the poisonous disease. Some boats were bound for Genoa, others went to Venice and other Christian areas. When the sailors reached these places and mixed with the people there, it was as if they had brought evil spirits with them."[8] The plague quickly spread to southern Italy and then to southern France by the end of the year. Diffusion of the Black Death followed commercial trade routes. In 1348, it spread through Spain, France, and the Low Countries and into Germany. By the end of that year, it had moved to England. By the

MAP 13.3 Spread of the Black Death

The plague entered Europe through Sicily in 1347 and within three years had killed between one-quarter and one-half of the population. Outbreaks continued into the early eighteenth century, and the European population took two hundred years to return to the level it had reached before the Black Death.

© Cengage Learning 2013

end of the next, the plague had reached northern Europe and Scandinavia. Eastern Europe and Russia were affected by 1351.

Mortality figures for the Black Death were incredibly high. Especially hard hit were Italy's crowded cities, where 50 to 60 percent of the people died. One citizen of Florence wrote, "A great many breathed their last in the public streets, day and night; a large number perished in their homes, and it was only by the stench of their decaying bodies that they proclaimed their deaths to their neighbors. Everywhere the city was teeming with corpses."[9] In England and Germany, entire villages simply disappeared. It has been estimated that out of a total European population of 75 million, as many as 38 million people may have died of the plague between 1347 and 1351.

As contemporaries attempted to explain the Black Death and mitigate its harshness, some turned to extreme sorts of behavior. Many believed that the plague either had been sent by God as a punishment for humans' sins or had been caused by the devil. Some, known as flagellants (FLAJ-uh-lunts), resorted to extreme measures to gain God's forgiveness. Groups of flagellants, both men and women, wandered from town to town, flogging each other with whips to beg the forgiveness of God whom they believed had sent the plague to punish humans for their sinful ways. One contemporary chronicler described a flagellant procession:

> The penitents went about, coming first out of Germany. They were men who did public penance and scourged themselves with whips of hard knotted leather with little iron spikes. Some made themselves bleed very badly between the shoulder blades and some foolish women had cloths ready to catch the blood and smear it on their eyes, saying it was miraculous blood. While they were doing penance, they sang very mournful songs about the nativity and the passion of Our Lord. The object of this penance was to put a stop to the mortality, for in that time ... at least a third of all the people in the world died.[10]

The flagellants attracted attention and created mass hysteria wherever they went. The Catholic Church, however, became alarmed when flagellant groups began to kill Jews and attack clergy who opposed them. Pope Clement VI condemned the flagellants in October 1349 and urged the public authorities to crush them. By the end of 1350, most of the flagellant movement had been destroyed.

An outbreak of virulent anti-Semitism also accompanied the Black Death. Jews were accused of causing the plague by poisoning town wells. The worst **pogroms** (POH-grums) (massacres) against this minority were carried out in Germany, where more than sixty major Jewish communities had been exterminated by 1351. Many Jews fled Eastward to Russia and especially to Poland, where the king offered them protection. Eastern Europe became home to large Jewish communities.

Economic Dislocation and Social Upheaval   The deaths of so many people in the fourteenth century had severe economic consequences. Trade declined, and some industries suffered greatly. Florence's woolen industry, one of the giants, had produced 70,000 to 80,000 pieces of cloth in 1338; in 1378, it was yielding only 24,000 pieces.

Both peasants and noble landlords were also affected. A shortage of workers caused a dramatic rise in the price of labor, while the decline in the number of people lowered the demand for food, resulting in falling prices. Landlords were now paying more for labor at the same time that their rental income was declining. Concurrently, the decline in the number of peasants after the Black Death made it easier for some to convert their labor services to rent, thus freeing them from serfdom. But there were limits to how much the peasants could advance. They faced the same economic hurdles as the lords, who also attempted to impose wage restrictions and reinstate old forms of labor service. New governmental taxes also hurt. Peasant complaints became widespread and soon gave rise to rural revolts.

The English Peasants' Revolt of 1381 was the most prominent. The immediate cause of the revolt was the monarchy's attempt to raise revenues by imposing a poll tax, a flat charge on each adult member of the population. Peasants in Eastern England refused to pay the tax and expelled the collectors forcibly from their villages. Rebellion spread as peasants burned down the manor houses of aristocrats, lawyers, and government officials. Soon, however, the young king, Richard II (1377–1399), with the assistance of aristocrats, arrested hundreds of the rebels and ended the revolt. The poll tax was eliminated, however, and in the end most of the rebels were pardoned.

Although the peasant revolts sometimes resulted in short-term gains for the participants, the uprisings were relatively easily crushed and their gains quickly lost. Accustomed to ruling, the established classes easily combined and stifled dissent. Nevertheless, the revolts of the fourteenth century had introduced a new element to European life; henceforth, social unrest would be a characteristic of European history.

Political Instability   Famine, plague, economic turmoil, and social upheaval were not the only problems of the fourteenth century. War and political instability must also be added to the list. And of all the struggles that ensued, the Hundred Years' War was the most violent.

The Hundred Years' War   In the thirteenth century, England still held one small possession in France known as the duchy of Gascony. As duke of Gascony, the English king pledged loyalty as a vassal to the French king, but when King Philip VI of France (1328–1350) seized Gascony in 1337, the duke of Gascony—King Edward III of England (1327–1377)—declared war on Philip.

The war began in a burst of knightly enthusiasm. The French army of 1337 still relied largely on heavily armed noble cavalrymen, who looked with contempt on foot soldiers and crossbowmen, whom they regarded as social inferiors. The English, too, used heavily armed cavalry, but they relied even more on large numbers of paid foot soldiers. Armed with pikes, many of these soldiers had also adopted the longbow, invented by the Welsh. The longbow had a longer range and greater speed of fire than the crossbow.

The first major battle of the war occurred in 1346 at Crécy (kray-SEE), just south of Flanders. The larger French army followed no battle plan but simply attacked the English lines in a disorderly fashion. The arrows of the English archers decimated the French cavalry. As the chronicler Froissart (frwah-SAR) described it, "The English [with their longbows] continued to shoot into the thickest part of the crowd, wasting none of their arrows. They impaled or wounded horses and riders, who fell to the ground in great distress, unable to get up again without the help of several men."[11] It was a stunning victory for the English and the foot soldier.

The Battle of Crécy was not decisive, however. The English simply did not possess the resources to subjugate all of France, but they continued to try. The English king, Henry V (1413–1422), was especially eager to achieve victory. At the Battle of Agincourt (AH-zhen-koor) in 1415, the heavy, armor-plated French knights attempted to attack across a field turned to mud by heavy rain; the result was a disastrous French defeat and the death of 1,500 French nobles. The English had become the masters of northern France.

The seemingly hopeless French cause fell into the hands of the dauphin (DAH-fin or doh-FAN) Charles, the heir to the throne, who governed the southern two-thirds of French lands. Charles's cause seemed doomed until a French peasant woman quite unexpectedly saved the timid monarch. Born in 1412, the daughter of well-to-do peasants, Joan of Arc was a deeply religious person who came to believe that her favorite saints had commanded her to free France. In February 1429, Joan made her way to the dauphin's court and persuaded Charles to allow her to accompany a French army to Orléans (or-lay-AHN). Apparently inspired by the faith of the peasant girl known as "the Maid of Orléans," the French armies found new confidence in themselves and liberated the city. Joan had brought the war to a decisive turning point.

But she did not live to see the war concluded. Captured in 1430, Joan was turned over by the English to the Inquisition, which tried her on charges of witchcraft. In the fifteenth century, spiritual visions were thought to be inspired by either God or the devil. Joan was condemned to death as a heretic and burned at the stake in 1431.

Joan of Arc's accomplishments proved decisive. Although the war dragged on for another two decades, defeats of English armies in Normandy and Aquitaine led to French victory by 1453. Important to the French success was the use of the cannon, a new weapon made possible by the invention of gunpowder. The Chinese had invented gunpower in the tenth century and devised a simple cannon by the thirteenth. The Mongols greatly improved this technology, developing more accurate cannons and cannonballs; both spread to the Middle East in the thirteenth century and to Europe by the fourteenth. The use of gunpowder eventually brought drastic changes to European warfare by making castles, city walls, and armored knights obsolete.

Political Disintegration   By the fourteenth century, the feudal order had begun to break down. With money from taxes, kings could now hire professional soldiers, who tended to be more reliable than feudal knights anyway. Fourteenth-century kings had their own problems as well. Many dynasties in Europe were unable to produce male heirs, while the founders of new dynasties had to fight for their positions as factions of nobles, trying to gain advantages for themselves, supported opposing candidates. Rulers encountered financial problems too. Hiring professional soldiers left them always short of cash, adding yet another element of uncertainty and confusion to fourteenth-century politics.

The Decline of the Church   The papacy of the Roman Catholic Church reached the height of its power in the thirteenth century. But crises in the fourteenth century led to a serious decline for the church. By that time, the monarchies of Europe were no longer willing to accept papal claims of temporal supremacy, as is evident in the struggle between Pope Boniface VIII (1294–1303) and King Philip IV (1285–1314) of France. In his desire to acquire new revenues, Philip claimed the right to tax the clergy of France, but Boniface VIII insisted that the clergy of any state could not pay taxes to their secular ruler without the pope's consent. In no uncertain terms he argued that popes were supreme over both the church and the state.

Philip IV refused to accept the pope's position and sent a small contingent of French forces to capture Boniface and bring him back to France for trial. The pope escaped but soon died from the shock of his experience. To ensure his position and avoid any future papal threat, Philip IV engineered the election of a Frenchman, Clement V (1305–1314), as pope. Using the excuse of turbulence in the city of Rome, the new pope took up residence in Avignon (ah-veen-YOHN) on the East bank of the Rhone River.

From 1305 to 1377, the popes resided in Avignon, leading to an increase in antipapal sentiment. The city of Rome was the traditional capital of the universal church. The pope was the bishop of Rome, and it was unseemly that the head of the Catholic Church should reside in Avignon instead of Rome. Moreover, the splendor in which the pope and cardinals were living in Avignon led to highly vocal criticism of both clergy and papacy. At last, Pope Gregory XI (1370–1378), perceiving the disastrous decline in papal prestige, returned to Rome in 1377.

The Great Schism and Cries for Reform   Gregory XI died in Rome the spring after his return. When the college of cardinals met to elect a new pope, the citizens of Rome, fearful that the French majority would choose another Frenchman who would move the papacy back to Avignon, threatened that the cardinals would not leave Rome alive unless they elected a Roman or an Italian as pope. Wisely, the terrified cardinals duly elected the Italian archbishop of Bari as Pope Urban VI (1378–1389). Five months later, a group of dissenting cardinals—the French ones—declared Urban's election invalid and chose one of their number, a Frenchman, who took the title of Clement VII and promptly returned to Avignon. Because Urban remained in Rome, there were now two popes, beginning a crisis that has been called the Great Schism of the church.

The Great Schism divided Europe. France and its allies supported the pope in Avignon, whereas France's enemy England and its allies supported the pope in Rome. The Great Schism was also damaging to the faith of Christian believers. The pope was widely believed to be the true leader of Christendom; when both lines of popes denounced the other as the Antichrist, people's faith in the papacy and the church was undermined.

Meanwhile, the crises in the Catholic Church produced cries for reform. The Great Schism led large numbers of churchmen to take up the theory of **conciliarism**, or the belief that only a general council of the church, and not the pope, could bring reform to the church in its "head and members." These cries for change finally led to a church council that met at Constance in Switzerland in 1417. After the competing popes resigned or were deposed, a new pope was elected who was acceptable to all parties.

Although the Council of Constance ended the Great Schism, the council's efforts to reform the church were less successful. By the mid-fifteenth century, the papacy had reasserted its authority and ended the conciliar movement. At the same time, however, as a result of these crises, the church had lost much of its temporal power. Even worse, the papacy and the church had also lost much of their moral prestige.

RECOVERY: THE RENAISSANCE

People who lived in Italy between 1350 and 1550 or so believed that they were witnessing a rebirth of Classical antiquity—the world of the Greeks and Romans. To them, this marked a new age, which historians later called the **Renaissance** (French for "rebirth") and viewed as a distinct period of European history, which began in Italy and then spread to the rest of Europe.

Renaissance Italy was largely an urban society. The city-states became the centers of Italian political, economic, and social life. Within this new urban society, a secular spirit emerged as increasing wealth created new possibilities for the enjoyment of worldly things.

The Renaissance was also an age of recovery from the disasters of the fourteenth century, including the Black Death, political disorder, and economic recession. In pursuing that recovery, Italian intellectuals became intensely interested in the glories of their own past, the Greco-Roman culture of antiquity.

A new view of human beings emerged as people in the Italian Renaissance began to emphasize individual ability. The fifteenth-century Florentine architect Leon Battista Alberti (LAY-un buh-TEESS-tuh al-BAYR-tee) expressed the new philosophy succinctly: "Men can do all things if they will."[12] This high regard for human worth and for individual potentiality gave rise to a new social ideal of the well-rounded personality or "universal person"—*l'uomo universale* (LWOH-moh OO-nee-ver-SAH-lay)—who was capable of achievements in many areas of life.

The Intellectual Renaissance   The emergence and growth of individualism and secularism as characteristics of the Italian Renaissance are most noticeable in the intellectual and artistic realms. The most important literary movement associated with the Renaissance was humanism.

Renaissance humanism was an intellectual movement based on the study of the classics, the literary works of Greece and Rome. Humanists studied the liberal arts—grammar, rhetoric, poetry, moral philosophy or ethics, and history—all based on the writings of ancient Greek and Roman authors. We call these subjects the humanities.

Petrarch (PEE-trark *or* PET-trark) (1304–1374), who has often been called the father of Italian Renaissance humanism, did more than any other individual in the fourteenth century to foster its development. Petrarch sought to find forgotten Latin manuscripts and set in motion a ransacking of monastic libraries throughout Europe. He also began the humanist emphasis on the use of pure Classical Latin. Humanists used the works of Cicero as a model for prose and those of Virgil for poetry. As Petrarch said, "Christ is my God; Cicero is the prince of the language."

In Florence, the humanist movement took a new direction at the beginning of the fifteenth century. Fourteenth-century humanists such as Petrarch had described the intellectual life as one of solitude. They rejected family and a life of action in the community. Now, however, the humanists who worked as secretaries for the city council of Florence took a new interest in civic life. They came to believe that it was the duty of an intellectual to live an active life for one's state. Humanists came to believe that their study of the humanities should be put to the service of the state. It is no accident that humanists served as secretaries in Italian city-states or at courts of princes or popes.

Also evident in the humanism of the first half of the fifteenth century was a growing interest in Classical Greek civilization. One of the first Italian humanists to gain a thorough knowledge of Greek was Leonardo Bruni (leh-ah-NAHR-doh BROO-nee), who became an enthusiastic pupil of the Byzantine scholar Manuel Chrysoloras (man-WEL kriss-uh-LAHR-uss), who taught in Florence from 1396 to 1400.

Was There a Renaissance for Women?   Historians have disagreed over the benefits of the Renaissance for women. Some maintain that during the Middle Ages upper-class women in particular had greater freedom to satisfy their emotional needs, whereas upper-class women in the Renaissance experienced a contraction of both social and personal options as they became even more subject to male authority. Other historians have argued that although conditions remained bleak for most women, some women, especially those in courtly, religious, and intellectual environments, found ways to develop a new sense of themselves as women. This may be especially true of women who were educated in the humanist fashion and went on to establish literary careers.

Isotta Nogarola (ee-ZAHT-uh noh-guh-ROH-luh), born to a noble family in Verona, mastered Latin and wrote numerous letters and treatises that brought her praise from male Italian intellectuals. Cassandra Fedele (FAY-duh-lee) of Venice, who learned both Latin and Greek from humanist tutors hired by her family, became prominent in Venice for her public recitations of orations. Laura Cereta (say-REE-tuh) was educated in Latin by her father, a physician from Brescia. Laura defended the ability of women to pursue scholarly pursuits.

The Artistic Renaissance   Renaissance artists sought to imitate nature in their works of art. Their search for naturalism became an end in itself: to persuade onlookers of the reality of the object or event they were portraying. At the same time, the new artistic standards reflected the new attitude of mind in which human beings became the focus of attention, the "center and measure of all things," as one artist proclaimed.

The frescoes by Masaccio (muh-ZAH-choh) (1401–1428) in Florence have long been regarded as the first masterpieces of Early Renaissance art. With his use of monumental figures, a more realistic relationship between figures and landscape,

A Woman's Defense of Learning

As a young woman, Laura Cereta was proud of her learning, but she was condemned by a male world that found it unseemly for women to be scholars. One monk said to her father, "She gives herself to things unworthy of her—namely, the classics." Before being silenced, Laura Cereta wrote a series of letters, including one to a male critic who had argued that her work was so good it could not have been written by a woman.

Laura Cereta, *Defense of the Liberal Instruction of Women*

Your complaints are hurting my ears, for you say publicly and quite openly that you are not only surprised but pained that I am said to show this extraordinary intellect of the sort one would have thought nature would give to the most learned of men—as if you had reached the conclusion, on the facts of the case, that a similar girl had seldom been seen among the peoples of the world. You are wrong on both counts....

I would remain silent, believe me, if you, with your longstanding hostile and envious attitude towards me, had learned to attack me alone.... But I am angry and my disgust overflows. Why should the condition of our sex be shamed by your little attacks? Because of this, a mind thirsting for revenge is set afire.... My cause itself is worthy: I am impelled to show what great glory that noble lineage which I carry in my own breasts has won for virtue and literature—a lineage that knowledge, the bearer of honors, has exalted in every age....

My point is that your mouth has grown foul because you keep it sealed so that no arguments can come of it that might enable you to admit that nature imparts one freedom to all human beings equally—to learn. But the question of my exceptionality remains. And here choice alone, since it is the arbiter of character, is the distinguishing factor. For some women worry about the styling of their hair, the elegance of their clothes, and the pearls and other jewelry they wear

and the visual representation of the laws of perspective, a new realistic style of painting was born. Onlookers became aware of a world of reality that appeared to be a continuation of their own.

This new Renaissance style was absorbed and modified by other Florentine painters in the fifteenth century. Especially important were two major developments. One emphasized the technical side of painting—understanding the laws of perspective and the geometrical organization of outdoor space and light. The second development was the investigation of movement and anatomical structure. The realistic portrayal of the human nude became one of the foremost preoccupations of Italian Renaissance artists.

A new style in architecture also emerged when Filippo Brunelleschi (fee-LEE-poh BROO-nuh-LESS-kee) (1377–1446), inspired by Roman models, created an interior in the Church of San Lorenzo in Florence that was very different from that of the great medieval cathedrals. San Lorenzo's Classical columns, rounded arches, and coffered ceiling created an environment that did not overwhelm the worshipers physically and psychologically, as Gothic cathedrals did, but comforted them as a space created to fit human, not divine, measurements. Like on their fingers. Others love to say cute little things, to hide their feelings behind a mask of tranquility, to indulge in dancing, and lead pet dogs around on a leash. For all I care, other women can long for parties with carefully appointed tables, for the peace of mind of sleep, or they can yearn to deface with paint the pretty face they see reflected in their mirrors. But those women for whom the quest for the good represents a higher value restrain their young spirits and ponder better plans. They harden their bodies with sobriety and toil, they control their tongues, they carefully monitor what they hear, they ready their minds for all-night vigils, and they rouse their minds for the contemplation of probity in the case of harmful literature. For knowledge is not given as a gift but by study. For a mind free, keen, and unyielding in the face of hard work always rises to the good, and the desire for learning grows in depth and breadth....

My goodness towards men isn't always rewarded, and you may imagine in your disdain for women that I alone marvel at the felicitousness of having talent.... Do not think, most despicable of men, that I might believe I have fallen out of favor with Jove. I am a scholar and a pupil who has been lulled to sleep by the meager fire of a mind too humble. I have been too much burned, and my injured mind has accumulated too much passion; for tormenting itself with the defending of our sex, my mind sighs, conscious of its obligation. For all things—those deeply rooted inside us as well as those outside us—are being laid at the door of our sex.

Q *How did Cereta explain her intellectual interests and accomplishments? Why were Renaissance women rarely taken seriously when they sought educational opportunities and recognition for their intellectual talents? Were any of those factors unique to the Renaissance era?*

Source: Laura Cereta, "To Biblio Semproni" from *The Collected Letters of a Renaissance Feminist*, ed. and trans. Diana Robin (Chicago, 1997), pp. 74–80 © 1997 The University of Chicago Press. Reprinted by permission of The University of Chicago Press.

painters and sculptors, Renaissance architects sought to reflect a human-centered world.

By the end of the fifteenth century, Italian artists had mastered the new techniques for scientific observation of the world around them and were now ready to move into new forms of creative expression. This marked the shift to the High Renaissance, which was dominated by the work of three artistic giants, Leonardo da Vinci (leh-ah-NAHR-doh dah VEEN-chee) (1452–1519), Raphael (RAFF-ee-ul) (1483–1520), and Michelangelo (my-kuh-LAN-juh-loh) (1475–1564). Leonardo carried on the fifteenth-century experimental tradition by studying everything and even dissecting human bodies in order to see how nature worked. But Leonardo stressed the need to advance beyond such realism and initiated the High Renaissance's preoccupation with the idealization of nature, an attempt to generalize from realistic portrayal to an ideal form.

At twenty-five, Raphael was already regarded as one of Italy's best painters. He was acclaimed for his numerous madonnas, in which he attempted to achieve an ideal of beauty far surpassing human standards. He is well known for his frescoes in the Vatican Palace, which reveal a world of balance, harmony, and order—the underlying principles of the art of Classical Greece and Rome.

Michelangelo, an accomplished painter, sculptor, and architect, was fiercely driven by a desire to create, and he worked with great passion and energy on a remarkable number of projects. Michelangelo was influenced by Neoplatonism, especially evident in his figures on the ceiling of the Sistine Chapel. These muscular figures reveal an ideal type of human being with perfect proportions. In good Neoplatonic fashion, their beauty is meant to be a reflection of divine beauty; the more beautiful the body, the more God-like the figure. Another manifestation of Michelangelo's search for ideal beauty was his *David*, a colossal marble statue commissioned by the government of Florence in 1501 and completed in 1504.

The State in the Renaissance   In the second half of the fifteenth century, attempts were made to reestablish the centralized power of monarchical governments after the political disasters of the fourteenth century. Some historians called these states the "new monarchies," especially those of France, England, and Spain.

MAP 13.4 Europe in the Second Half of the Fifteenth Century

By the second half of the fifteenth century, monarchs in Western Europe, particularly France, Spain, and England, had begun the process of modern state building. With varying success, they reined in the power of the church and nobles, increased their ability to levy taxes, and established effective government bureaucracies.

The Italian States   The Italian states provided the earliest examples of state building in the fifteenth century. During the Middle Ages, Italy had failed to develop a centralized territorial state, and by the fifteenth century, five major powers dominated the Italian peninsula: the duchy of Milan, the republics of Florence and Venice, the Papal States, and the kingdom of Naples.

Milan, Florence, and Venice proved especially adept at building strong, centralized states. Under a series of dukes, Milan became a highly centralized territorial state in which the rulers devised systems of taxation that generated enormous revenues for the government. The maritime republic of Venice remained an extremely stable political entity governed by a small oligarchy of merchant-aristocrats. Its commercial empire brought in vast revenues and gave it the status of an international power. In Florence, Cosimo de' Medici (KAH-zee-moh duh MED-ih-chee) took control of the merchant oligarchy in 1434. Through lavish patronage and careful courting of political allies, he and his family dominated the city at a time when Florence was the center of the cultural Renaissance.

As strong as these Italian states became, they still could not compete with the powerful monarchical states to the north and West. Beginning in 1494, Italy became a battlefield for the great power struggle between the French and Spanish monarchies, a conflict that led to Spanish domination of Italy in the sixteenth century.

Machiavelli and Political Power in the Renaissance   No one gave better expression to the Renaissance preoccupation with political power than Niccolò Machiavelli (nee-koh-LOH mahk-ee-uh-VEL-ee) (1469–1527), an Italian who wrote *The Prince* (1513), one of the most influential works on political power in the Western world. Machiavelli's major concerns in *The Prince* were the acquisition, maintenance, and expansion of political power as the means to restore and maintain order. In the Middle Ages, many political theorists stressed the ethical side of a prince's activity—how a ruler ought to behave based on Christian moral principles. Machiavelli bluntly contradicted this approach: "For the gap between how people actually behave and how they ought to behave is so great that anyone who ignores everyday reality in order to live up to an ideal will soon discover he had been taught how to destroy himself, not how to preserve himself."[13] Machiavelli considered his approach far more realistic than that of his medieval forebears. He maintained that political activity should not be restricted by moral considerations. The prince acts on behalf of the state and for the sake of the state must be willing to let his conscience sleep. Machiavelli was among the first Western thinkers to abandon morality as the basis for the analysis of political activity.

Western Europe   The Hundred Years' War left France prostrate. But it had also engendered a certain degree of French national feeling toward a common enemy that the kings could use to reestablish monarchical power. The development of a French territorial state was greatly advanced by King Louis XI (1461–1483), known as the Spider because of his wily and devious ways. Louis strengthened the use of the *taille* (TY)—an annual direct tax usually on land or property—as a

The Renaissance Prince: The Views of Machiavelli and Erasmus

POLITICS & GOVERNMENT

At the beginning of the sixteenth century, two writers produced very different views of political power and how a ruler should conduct affairs of state. In this selection from Chapter 17 of *The Prince*, Machiavelli analyzes whether it is better for a ruler to be loved than to be feared. Three years later, the Dutch intellectual Erasmus, leader of the Christian humanists, also wrote a treatise on political power, entitled *Education of a Christian Prince*. As is evident in this excerpt from his treatise, Erasmus followed in the footsteps of medieval theorists regarding power by insisting that a true prince should think only of his moral obligations to the people he rules.

Machiavelli, *The Prince* (1513)

This leads us to a question that is in dispute: Is it better to be loved than feared, or vice versa? My reply is one ought to be both loved and feared; but, since it is difficult to accomplish both at the same time, I maintain it is much safer to be feared than loved, if you have to do without one of the two. For of men one can, in general, say this: They are ungrateful, fickle, deceptive and deceiving, avoiders of danger, eager to gain. As long as you serve their interests, they are devoted to you.... But as soon as you need help, they turn against you. Any ruler who relies simply on their promises and makes no other preparations, will be destroyed. For you will find that those whose support you buy, who do not rally to you because they admire your strength of character and nobility of soul, these are people you pay for, but they are never yours, and in the end you cannot get the benefit of your investment. Men are less nervous of offending someone who makes himself lovable, than someone who makes himself frightening. For love attaches men by ties of obligation, which, since men are wicked, they break whenever their interests are at stake. But fear restrains men because they are afraid of punishment, and this fear never leaves them. Still, a ruler should make himself feared in such a way that, if he does not inspire love, at least he does not provoke hatred. For it is perfectly possible to be

permanent tax imposed by royal authority, giving him a sound, regular source of income, which created the foundations of a strong French monarchy.

The Hundred Years' War had also strongly affected the English. The cost of the war in its final years and the losses to the labor force strained the English economy. At the end of the war, England faced even greater turmoil when a civil war, known as the War of the Roses, erupted and aristocratic factions fought over the monarchy until 1485, when Henry Tudor established a new Dynasty.

As the first Tudor king, Henry VII (1485–1509) worked to establish a strong monarchical government. Henry ended the petty wars of the nobility by abolishing their private armies. He was also very thrifty. By not overburdening the nobility and the middle class with taxes, Henry won their favor, and they provided him much support.

feared and not hated. You will only be hated if you seize the property or the women of your subjects and citizens. Whenever you have to kill someone, make sure that you have a suitable excuse and an obvious reason; but, above all else, keep your hands off other people's property; for men are quicker to forget the death of their father than the loss of their inheritance....

Erasmus, *Education of a Christian Prince* (1516)

A good prince ... is a living likeness of God, who is at once good and powerful. His goodness makes him want to help all; his power makes him able to do so. On the other hand, an evil prince, who is like a plague to his country, is the incarnation of the devil, who has great power joined with his wickedness. All his resources to the very last, he uses for the undoing of the human race....

[A good prince is one] who holds the life of each individual dearer than his own; who works and strives night and day for just one end—to be the best he can for everyone; with whom rewards are ready for all good men ... for so much does he want to be of real help to his people, without thought of recompense, that if necessary he would not hesitate to look out for their welfare at great risk to himself; who considers his wealth to lie in the advantage of his country; who is ever on the watch so that everyone else may sleep deeply; who grants no leisure to himself so that he may spend his life in the peace of his country; who worries himself with continual cares so that his subjects may have peace and quiet.... He does everything and allows everything that will bring everlasting peace to his country, for he realizes that war is the source of all misfortunes to the state.

Q *What does Machiavelli have to say about being loved rather than feared? How does this view contrast with that of Erasmus on the characteristics of a good ruler? Which viewpoint do you consider more modern? Why? Which viewpoint do you think is correct? Why?*

Sources: Machiavelli, The Prince (1513). From *The Prince* by Machiavelli, translated by David Wootton, pp. 51–52. Copyright © 1995 by Hackett Publishing Company, Inc. Erasmus, Education of a Christian Prince (1516). From *The Education of a Christian Prince*, by Erasmus, translated by L. K. Born. Copyright © 1936 by Columbia University Press.

Spain, too, experienced the growth of a strong national monarchy by the end of the fifteenth century. During the Middle Ages, several independent Christian kingdoms had emerged in the course of the long reconquest of the Iberian Peninsula from the Muslims. Two of the strongest were Aragon and Castile. The marriage of Isabella of Castile (1474–1504) and Ferdinand of Aragon (1479–1516) in 1469 was a major step toward unifying Spain. The two rulers worked to strengthen royal control of government. They filled the royal council, which supervised the administration of the government, with middle-class lawyers. Trained in Roman law, these officials operated on the belief that the monarchy embodied the power of the state. Ferdinand and Isabella also reorganized the military forces of Spain, making the new Spanish army the best in Europe by the sixteenth century.

Central and Eastern Europe   Unlike France, England, and Spain, the Holy Roman Empire failed to develop a strong monarchical authority. The failure of the German emperors in the thirteenth century ended any chance of centralized authority, and Germany became a land of hundreds of virtually independent states. After 1438, the position of Holy Roman Emperor was held by members of the Habsburg (HAPS-burg) Dynasty. Having gradually acquired a number of possessions along the Danube, known collectively as Austria, the house of Habsburg had become one of the wealthiest landholders in the empire and by the mid-fifteenth century had begun to play an important role in European affairs.

In Eastern Europe, rulers struggled to achieve the centralization of the territorial states. Religious differences troubled the area as Roman Catholics, Eastern Orthodox Christians, and other groups, including the Mongols, confronted each other. In Poland, the nobles gained the upper hand and established the right to elect their kings, a policy that drastically weakened royal authority.

Since the thirteenth century, Russia had been under the domination of the Mongols. Gradually, the princes of Moscow rose to prominence by using their close relationship to the Mongol khans to increase their wealth and expand their possessions. During the reign of the great Prince Ivan III (1462–1505), a new Russian state was born. Ivan annexed other Russian principalities and took advantage of dissension among the Mongols to throw off their yoke by 1480.

CHRONOLOGIES

THE EASTERN ROMAN/BYZANTINE EMPIRE TO 750	
529–533	Justinian codifies Roman law
535–552	Reconquest of Italy by Justinian
537	Completion of Hagia Sophia
610–641	Attacks on the empire in the reign of Heraclius
636	Arab defeat of the Byzantines at Yarmuk
679	Defeat by the Bulgars; losses in the Balkans
717–741	Leo III and iconoclasm

THE BYZANTINE EMPIRE, 750–1453	
842–867	Revival under Michael III
867–1056	Macedonian Dynasty
867–886	Basil I
886–912	Leo VI
945–959	Constantine VII
976–1025	Basil II

1054	Schism between Eastern Orthodox Church and Roman Catholic Church
1071	Turkish defeat of the Byzantines at Manzikert
1081–1118	Revival under Alexius Comnenus
1140–1183	Manuel Comnenus
1204–1261	Latin Empire of Constantinople
1261	Revival of Byzantine Empire
1389	Turkish defeat of Serbs at Kosovo
1449–1453	Constantine XI, the last Byzantine emperor
1453	Fall of the empire

 MindTap™

MindTap is a fully online, highly personalized learning experience built upon Cengage Learning content. MindTap combines student learning tools—readings, multimedia, activities, and assessments—into a singular Learning Path that guides students through their course.

Part Three

The Emergence of New World Patterns (1500–1800)

CHAPTER 14
New Encounters: The Creation of a World Market

CHAPTER 15
Europe Transformed: Reform and State Building

CHAPTER 16
The Muslim Empires

CHAPTER 17
The East Asian World

CHAPTER 18
The West on the Eve of a New World Order

Historians often refer to the period from the sixteenth through the eighteenth centuries as the early modern era. During these years, several factors were at work that created the conditions of our own time.

From a global perspective, perhaps the most noteworthy event of the period was the extension of the maritime trade network throughout the entire populated world. Traders from the Middle East had spearheaded the process with their voyages to East Asia and southern Africa in the first millennium C.E., and the Chinese had followed suit with Zheng He's groundbreaking voyages to India and East Africa. Then, at the end of the fifteenth century, a resurgent Europe suddenly exploded onto the world scene when the Portuguese discovered a maritime route to the East and the Spanish opened up European contacts with the peoples in the Western Hemisphere. Although the Europeans were late to the game, they were quick learners, and over the next three centuries they gradually managed to dominate shipping on international trade routes.

Some contemporary historians argue that it was this sudden burst of energy from Europe that created the first truly global economic network. Although it is true that European explorers were responsible for opening up communications with the vast new world of the Americas, other historians note that it was the rise of the Arab empire in the Middle East and the Mongol expansion a few centuries later that played the greatest role in creating a widespread communications network that enabled goods and ideas to travel from one end of the Eurasian supercontinent to the other.

Whatever the truth of this debate, there are still many reasons for considering the end of the fifteenth century to be a crucial date in world history. In the first place, it marked the end of the long isolation of the Western Hemisphere from the rest of the inhabited world. In so doing, it led to the creation of the first truly global network of ideas and commodities, which would introduce plants, ideas, and (unfortunately) new diseases to all humanity. Second, the period gave birth to a stunning increase in trade and manufacturing that stimulated major economic changes not only in Europe but in other parts of the world as well.

The period from 1500 to 1800, then, was an incubation period for the modern world and the launching pad for an era of Western domination that would reach fruition in the nineteenth century. To understand why the West emerged as the leading force in the world at that time, it is necessary to grasp what factors were at work in Europe and why they were absent in other major civilizations around the globe.

Historians have identified improvements in navigation, shipbuilding, and weaponry that took place in Europe in the early modern era as essential elements in the Age of Exploration. As we have seen, many of these technological advances were based on earlier discoveries that had taken place elsewhere—in China, India, and the Middle East—and had then been brought to Europe on Muslim ships or along the trade routes through Central Asia. But it was the capacity and the desire of the Europeans to enhance their wealth and power by making practical use of the discoveries of others that was the significant factor in the equation and enabled them to dominate international sea lanes and create vast colonial empires in the Western Hemisphere.

European expansion was not fueled solely by economic considerations, however. As in the rise of Islam in the seventh and eighth centuries, religion played a major role in motivating the European Age of Exploration in the early modern era. Although Christianity was by no means a new faith in the sixteenth century (as Islam had been at the moment of Arab expansion), the world of Christendom was in the midst of a major period of conflict with the forces of Islam, a rivalry that had been exacerbated by the conquest of the Byzantine Empire by the Ottoman Turks in 1453.

Although the claims of Portuguese and Spanish adventurers that their activities were motivated primarily by a desire to bring the word of God to non-Christian peoples certainly included a considerable measure of self-delusion and hypocrisy, there seems no reason to doubt that religious motives played a meaningful part in the European Age of Exploration. Religious motives were perhaps less evident in the activities of the non-Catholic powers that entered the competition beginning in the seventeenth century. English and Dutch merchants and officials were more inclined to be motivated purely by the pursuit of economic profit.

While Europe was on the cusp of a dynamic era of political, economic, and cultural expansion, conditions in other parts of the world were less conducive to these economic and political developments. In China, a centralized monarchy was smugly confident of its superiority to all potential rivals and continued to rely on a prosperous agricultural sector as the economic foundation of the empire. In Japan, the powerful Tokugawa Shogunate seized power at the beginning of the seventeenth century, and the era of peace and stability that ensued saw an increase in manufacturing and commercial activity. But Japanese elites, after initially expressing interest in the outside world, abruptly shut the door on European trade and ideas in an effort to protect the "land of the gods" from external contamination.

In the societies of India and the Middle East, commerce and manufacturing had played a vital role since the emergence of the Indian Ocean trade network in the first centuries C.E. But beginning in the eleventh century, the area had suffered through an extended period of political instability, marked by invasions by nomadic peoples from Central Asia. The violence of the period and the local rulers' lack of experience in promoting maritime commerce severely depressed urban manufacturing and trade.

In the early modern era, then, Europe was best placed to take advantage of the technological innovations that had become increasingly available. Whereas other regions were still beset by internal obstacles or had deliberately turned inward to seek their destiny, Europe now turned outward to seek a new and dominant position in the world. This does not imply, however, that significant changes were not taking place in other parts of the world as well, and many of these changes had relatively little to do with the situation in the West. As we shall see, the impact of European expansion on the rest of the world was still limited at the end of the eighteenth century. Although European political authority was firmly established in a few key areas, such as the Spice Islands and Latin America, traditional societies remained relatively intact in most regions of Africa and Asia. And processes at work in these societies were often operating independently of events in Europe and would later give birth to forces that acted to restrict or shape the Western impact. One of these forces was the progressive emergence of centralized states, some of them built on the concept of ethnic unity.

14

NEW ENCOUNTERS: THE CREATION OF A WORLD MARKET

CALECHVT CELEBERRI-
MVM INDIÆ EMPORIVM.

Mary Evans Picture Library/The Image Works

The port of Calicut, India, in the mid-1500s

CHAPTER OUTLINE

• An Age of Exploration and Expansion • The Portuguese Maritime Empire • The Conquest of the "New World" • Africa in Transition • Southeast Asia in the Era of the Spice Trade

---

AN AGE OF EXPLORATION AND EXPANSION

Western historians have customarily regarded the voyage of Vasco da Gama as a crucial step in the opening of trade routes to the East. In the sense that the voyage was a harbinger of future European participation in the spice trade, this view undoubtedly has merit. In fact, however, the Indian Ocean had been a busy thoroughfare for centuries. The spice trade had been carried on by sea in the region since the days of the legendary Queen of Sheba, and Arab dhows, Indian sailing ships, and Chinese junks had sailed throughout the area in search of cloves and nutmeg and other precious items since the Tang Dynasty.

Islam and the Spice Trade   By the fourteenth century, a growing portion of the spice trade was being transported in Muslim ships sailing from ports in India or the Middle East. Muslims, either Arabs or Indian converts, had taken part in the Indian Ocean trade for centuries, and by the thirteenth century, Islam had established a presence in seaports on the islands of Sumatra and Java and was gradually moving inland. In 1292, the Venetian traveler Marco Polo observed that Muslims were engaging in missionary activity in northern Sumatra: "This kingdom is so much frequented by the Saracen merchants that they have converted the natives to the Law of Mahomet—I mean the townspeople only, for the hill people live for all the world like beasts, and eat human flesh, as well as other kinds of flesh, clean or unclean."[1]

But the major impetus for the spread of Islam in Southeast Asia came in the early fifteenth century, with the foundation of a new sultanate at Malacca (muh-LAK-uh), on the strait that today bears the same name. The founder was Paramesvara (pahr-uh-muss-VAHR-uh), a vassal of the Hindu state of Majapahit (mah-jah-PAH-hit) on Java, whose original base of operations had been at Palembang (pah-lem-BAHNG), on the island of Sumatra. In 1390, he had moved his base to Tumasik (tuh-MAH-sik) (modern Singapore), at the tip of the Malay Peninsula, hoping to enhance his ability to play a role in the commerce passing through the region. Under pressure from the expanding power of the Thai state of Ayuthaya (ah-yoo-TY-yuh) in the early fifteenth century, Paramesvara moved once again to Malacca. The latter's potential strategic importance was confirmed in the sixteenth century by a visitor from Portugal, who noted that Malacca "is a city that was made for commerce; ... the trade and commerce between the different nations for a thousand leagues on every hand must come to Malacca."[2]

Shortly after its founding, Malacca was visited by a Chinese fleet under the command of Admiral Zheng He. To protect his patrimony from local rivals, Paramesvara agreed to become a tributary of the Chinese empire and cemented the new relationship by making an official visit to the Ming imperial court in Beijing. He also converted to Islam, undoubtedly with a view to enhancing Malacca's ability to participate in the trade that passed through the strait, much of which was dominated by Muslim merchants. Blessed by its fortunate location, within a few years, Malacca had become the leading economic power in the region and helped promote the spread of Islam to trading ports throughout the islands of Southeast Asia, including Java, Borneo, Sulawesi (soo-lah-WAY-see), and the Philippines. Adoption of the Muslim faith was eased by the popularity of Sufism, a brand of Islam that expressed a marked tolerance for mysticism and local religious beliefs.

The Spread of Islam in West Africa   In the meantime, Muslim commercial and religious influence continued to expand south of the Sahara into the Niger River valley in West Africa. The area had been penetrated by traders from across the Sahara since ancient times, and contacts undoubtedly increased after the establishment of Muslim control over the Mediterranean coastal regions. Muslim traders—first Arabs and later African converts—crossed the desert carrying Islamic values, political culture, and legal traditions along with their goods. The early stage of state formation had culminated with the kingdom of Mali, symbolized by the renowned Mansa Musa, whose pilgrimage to Mecca in the fourteenth century had left an indelible impression on observers.

The Empire of Songhai   With the decline of Mali in the late fifteenth century, a new power eventually appeared: the empire of Songhai (song-GY). The founder of Songhai was Sonni Ali (Sonni the Great), a local chieftain from Gao, a major trading entrepôt (ON-truh-poh) on the Niger River east of Timbuktu. After seizing power in 1464, he set out to destroy the remnants of the Mali Empire and restore the formidable empire of his predecessors. Rumored to possess magical powers, Sonni Ali was criticized by Muslim scholars for supporting traditional religious practices, but under his rule, Songhai emerged as a major trading state in the region. When he died in 1492, his son ascended to the throne but was deposed

MAP 14.1 The Songhai Empire

Songhai was the last of the great states to dominate the Niger River valley prior to the European takeover in the nineteenth century.

shortly thereafter by one of his military commanders, who seized power as king under the name Askia Mohammed (r. 1493–1528).

Under the new ruler, a fervent Muslim, Songhai increasingly relied on Islamic institutions and ideology to strengthen national unity and centralize its authority. Askia Mohammed himself embarked on a pilgrimage to Mecca and was recognized by the caliph of Cairo as the Muslim ruler of the Niger River valley. On his return from Mecca, he tried to revive Timbuktu as a major center of Islamic learning but had less success in converting his predominantly animist subjects. He did preside over a significant increase in trans-Saharan trade in gold, salt, and slaves, which provided a steady source of income to Songhai and other states in the region. Gold, the source of which was located south of the city of Jenne, was used as the local currency, as well as cowrie shells from the Indian Ocean. Despite the efforts of Askia Mohammed and his successors, however, centrifugal forces within Songhai, brought on by rivalries at court, chronic drought, and bouts of the plague, led to civil disorder and eventually led to its breakup. The end came in 1591, when Moroccan forces armed with firearms conquered the city of Gao in a bid to gain control over the gold trade in the region. At that point, the city of Timbuktu, and the trade route that had enabled its rise, began a long period of decline, as other forces began to make their entrance into the region.

A New Player: Europe　For almost a millennium, the Catholic states of Europe had largely been confined to the western part of that continent. Their one major attempt to expand beyond those frontiers— the crusades—ultimately had failed. Of course, Europe had never completely lost contact with the outside world. With the revival of trade in the later Middle Ages, European merchants began to travel more frequently to Africa and Asia, much of it driven by a voracious appetite for the spices of the Orient. Nevertheless, their over-all contacts with other parts of the world remained limited until the fifteenth century, when Europeans began to embark on a remarkable series of overseas journeys. What caused European seafarers to undertake such dangerous voyages to the ends of the earth? Two famous early travelers to the lands of the East help to provide us with an explanation.

The Motives　Europeans had long been entranced by legends depicting exotic lands of great riches and magic beyond the rising sun. Such visions had lured the Polos of Venice on their journeys to the fabled Orient. Economic motives had been temporarily derailed by the Mongol conquests, but they revived after the Mongol threat to Europe had begun to recede, and Italian merchants from Genoa and Venice took an active part in the spice trade that passed through the Indian Ocean en route to the Caribbean. Access to the riches of the East was interrupted in the fifteenth century, however, by the Ottoman takeover of the Eastern Mediterranean. Spices and other precious goods from Asia continued to be transported to Europe via Arab intermediaries but were outrageously expensive. Adventurous Europeans did not hesitate to express their desire to share in the wealth. As one Spanish conquista-dor (kahn-KEESS-tuh-dor) explained, he and his kind went to the Americas to "serve God and His Majesty, to give light to those who were in darkness, and to grow rich, as all men desire to do."[3]

That statement alludes to another major reason for the overseas voyages—religious zeal. John Plano Carpini, the Franciscan friar dispatched in 1245 by the Vatican to the Mongol capital at Karakorum, had initiated the process by appealing to his hosts to convert to the Christian faith. Two centuries later, that crusading mentality reasserted itself in Portugal and Spain, where conflict with regional Muslim powers had intensified religious rivalries. Contemporaries of Prince Henry the Navigator of Portugal, an outspoken advocate of European expansion, said that he was motivated by his zeal to spread the Christian message to pagan peoples beyond the confines of Europe. Although most scholars believe that the religious motive was secondary to economic considerations, it would be foolish to overlook the genuine desire on the part of both explorers and conquistadors, let alone missionaries, to convert the heathen to Christianity. Hernán Cortés (hayr-NAHN kor-TAYSS *or* kor-TEZ), the conqueror of Mexico, asked his Spanish rulers if it was not their duty to ensure that the native Mexicans were "introduced into and instructed in the holy Catholic faith."[4] Thus spiritual and secular motives were closely intertwined in the sixteenth century. No doubt dreams of personal grandeur and glory, along with intellectual curiosity and a spirit of adventure, also played a role in European expansion.

The Means If "God, glory, and gold" were the primary motives, what made the voyages possible? Perhaps first and foremost, by the end of the fifteenth century, European states had achieved a level of knowledge and technology that enabled them to carry out ambitious ocean voyages well beyond the confines of continental Europe. Although the highly schematic and symbolic maps popular in the medieval era were of little help to sailors, detailed charts made by medieval navigators and mathematicians in the thirteenth and fourteenth centuries, known as **portolani** (pohr-tuh-LAH-nee), were more useful. With details on coastal contours, distances between ports (thus the name), and compass readings, they proved of great value for voyages in European waters. But because the *portolani* were drawn on a flat surface and took no account of the curvature of the earth, they were of little use for longer overseas voyages. Only when seafarers began to venture beyond the coasts of Europe did they begin to accumulate information about the actual shape of the earth and how to measure it. By the end of the fifteenth century, cartography had developed to the point that Europeans possessed fairly accurate maps of the known world.

In addition, Europeans had developed remarkably seaworthy ships as well as new navigational techniques. European shipbuilders had mastered the use of the sternpost rudder, an import from China (previous rudders had been located on the right side of the vessel), and had learned how to combine the use of lateen sails (commonly used in the Indian Ocean) with the square rig familiar in northern European waters. With these innovations, they could construct **caravels** (KER-uh-velz), ships mobile enough to sail against the wind and engage in naval warfare and also large enough to be armed with heavy cannons and carry a substantial amount of goods over long distances. Previously, sailors had used a quadrant and their knowledge of the position of the polestar to ascertain their latitude. Below the equator, however, this technique was useless. Only with the assistance of new navigational aids such as the compass (a Chinese invention) and the astrolabe, an astronomical instrument reportedly developed from ancient Greek examples by Arab sailors, were they able to explore the high seas with confidence.

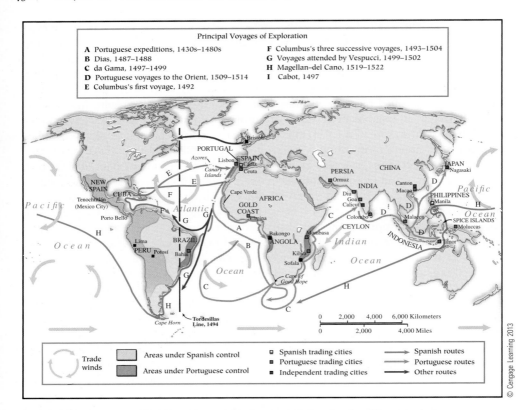

Principal Voyages of Exploration

A Portuguese expeditions, 1430s–1480s
B Dias, 1487–1488
C da Gama, 1497–1499
D Portuguese voyages to the Orient, 1509–1514
E Columbus's first voyage, 1492

F Columbus's three successive voyages, 1493–1504
G Voyages attended by Vespucci, 1499–1502
H Magellan–del Cano, 1519–1522
I Cabot, 1497

MAP 14.2 European Voyages and Possessions in the Sixteenth and Seventeenth Centuries

This map indicates the most important voyages launched by Europeans during their momentous Age of Exploration in the sixteenth and seventeenth centuries.

A final spur to exploration was the growing knowledge of the wind patterns in the Atlantic Ocean. The first European fleets sailing southward along the coast of West Africa had found their efforts to return hindered by the strong winds that blew steadily from the north along the coast. During the mid-fifteenth century, however, sailors had learned to tack out into the ocean, where they were able to catch westerly winds in the vicinity of the Azores that brought them back to the coast of western Europe. Christopher Columbus used this technique in his voyages to the Americas, and others relied on their new knowledge of the winds to round the continent of Africa in search of spices.

THE PORTUGUESE MARITIME EMPIRE

Portugal took the lead when it began exploring the western coast of Africa under the sponsorship of Prince Henry the Navigator (1394–1460). Henry had three objectives: acquiring new trade opportunities for his kingdom (especially in the gold trade with West Africa), weakening the Muslim states in Spain and West Africa, and extending Christianity. In 1419, he founded a school for navigators on the southwestern coast of Portugal. Shortly thereafter, Portuguese fleets began probing southward along the western coast of Africa in search of gold, which had for centuries been carried northward from its source south of the Sahara. In 1441, Portuguese ships reached the Senegal River, just north of Cape Verde. They found no gold but brought home a cargo of black Africans, most of whom were sold as slaves to wealthy buyers elsewhere in Europe. Within a few years, about a thousand slaves a year were shipped from the area back to Lisbon. Although obtaining slaves had not been one of their original motives for exploring the west coast of Africa, the Portuguese had inadvertently found a way to circumvent the traditional trans-Saharan slave route from Central Africa to the Mediterranean.

Continuing southward, in 1471 the Portuguese discovered a source of gold along the southern coast of the hump of West Africa (an area that would henceforth be known to Europeans as the Gold Coast). A few years later, they established contact with the inland state of Benin, north of the Gold Coast. To facilitate trade in gold, ivory, and slaves (not all slaves were brought back to Lisbon; some were bartered to local merchants for gold), the Portuguese leased land from local rulers and built stone forts along the coast. Trade was slow to develop at first, however, because the Portuguese initially did not have many products that appealed to potential African buyers.

En Route to India

Hearing reports of a route to India around the southern tip of Africa, Portuguese sea captains continued their probing. A few years later, contacts were established with the kingdom of Kongo, near the mouth of the Congo River. Then, in 1487, Bartolomeu Dias (bar-toh-loh-MAY-oo DEE-uhs) took advantage of westerly winds in the South Atlantic to round the Cape of Good Hope, but fearing a mutiny from his crew, he returned home without continuing further. Ten years later, a fleet under the command of Vasco da Gama rounded the cape and stopped at several ports controlled by Muslim merchants along the coast of East Africa, including Sofala, Kilwa, and Mombasa. Then, having located a Muslim navigator who was familiar with seafaring in the region, da Gama's fleet crossed the Arabian Sea and arrived off the port of Calicut, on the southwestern coast of India, on May 18, 1498. The Portuguese crown had sponsored da Gama's voyage with the clear objective of destroying the Muslim monopoly over the spice trade, a monopoly that had been intensified by the Ottoman conquest of Constantinople in 1453. Calicut was a major entrepôt on the long route from the Spice Islands to the Mediterranean Sea, but the ill-informed Europeans believed it was the source of the spices themselves. Purchasing as much in the way of spices as his ships could carry, after three months in India, da Gama set out for home. Although he lost two ships along the way, the remaining vessels returned to Europe with their holds filled with ginger and cinnamon, a cargo that earned the investors a profit of several thousand percent.

The Search for the Source of Spices

During the next years, the Portuguese set out to gain control of the spice trade. In 1510, Admiral Afonso de Albuquerque (ah-FAHN-soh day AL-buh-kur-kee) established his headquarters at Goa (GOH-uh), on the western coast of India south of present-day Mumbai, formerly called Bombay. Over the next few years, they

The Portuguese Conquest of Malacca

INTERACTION & EXCHANGE

In 1511, a Portuguese fleet led by Afonso de Albuquerque attacked the Muslim sultanate at Malacca, on the west coast of the Malay Peninsula. Occupation of the port gave the Portuguese control over the strategic Strait of Malacca and the route to the Spice Islands. In this passage, Albuquerque tells his men the reasons for the attack. Note that he sees control of Malacca as a way to reduce the power of the Muslim world. The relevance of economic wealth to military power continues to underlie conflicts among nations today. The Pacific War in the 1940s, for example, began as a result of a conflict over control of the rich resources of Southeast Asia.

The Commentaries of the Great Afonso de Albuquerque, Second Viceroy of India

Although there be many reasons which I could allege in favor of our taking this city and building a fortress therein to maintain possession of it, two only will I mention to you, on this occasion....

The first is the great service which we shall perform to Our Lord in casting the Moors out of this country.... If we can only achieve the task before us, it will result in the Moors resigning India altogether to our rule, for the greater part of them—or perhaps all of them—live upon the trade of this country and are become great and rich, and lords of extensive treasures.... For when we were committing ourselves to the business of cruising in the Straits [of the

Red Sea], where the King of Portugal had often ordered me to go (for it was there that His Highness considered we could cut down the commerce which the Moors of Cairo, of Mecca, and of Judah, carry on with these parts), Our Lord for his service thought right to lead us hither, for when Malacca is taken the places on the Straits must be shut up, and they will never more be able to introduce their spiceries into those places.

And the other reason is the additional service which we shall render to the King D. Manuel in taking this city, because it is the headquarters of all the spiceries and drugs which the Moors carry every year hence to the Straits without our being able to prevent them from so doing; but if we deprive them of this their ancient market there, there does not remain for them a single port, nor a single situation, so commodious in the whole of these parts, where they can carry on their trade in these things.... I hold it as very certain that if we take this trade of Malacca away out of their hands, Cairo and Mecca are entirely ruined, and to Venice will no spiceries be conveyed except that which her merchants go and buy in Portugal.

Q *What reasons does the author advance to justify his decision to launch an attack on Malacca? How might the ruler of Malacca respond to these reasons?*

Source: From The Commentaries of the Great Afonso Dalboquerque, Second Viceroy of India, trans. Walter de Gray Birch (London: Printed for the Hakluyt Society, 1880), Vol. III, pp. 116–118.

---

established a series of fortresses and trading posts along the coasts of western India and East Africa in a bid to dominate the trade network of the Indian Ocean. From these ports, the Portuguese raided Arab shippers, provoking the following comment from an Arab source: "[The Portuguese] took about seven vessels, killing those on board and making some prisoner. This was their first action, may God curse them."[5] In 1511, Albuquerque attacked Malacca itself.

For Albuquerque, control of Malacca would serve two purposes. It could help destroy the Arab spice trade network by blocking passage through the Strait of Malacca, and it could also provide the Portuguese with a way station en route to the Spice Islands (known today as the Moluccas) and other points east. After a short but bloody battle, the Portuguese seized the city and put the local Arab population to the sword. They then proceeded to erect the normal accoutrements of the day—a fort, a "factory" (warehouse), and a church.

From Malacca, the Portuguese launched expeditions farther east, to China in 1514 and the Moluccas (muh-LUHK-uhz). There they signed a treaty with a local sultan for the purchase and export of cloves to the European market. Within a few years, they had managed to seize control of much of the spice trade from Muslim traders and had garnered substantial profits for the Portuguese monarchy.

Why were the Portuguese so successful? Basically, it was a matter of guns and seamanship. The first Portuguese fleet to arrive in Indian waters was relatively modest in size. It consisted of three ships and twenty guns, a force sufficient for self-defense and intimidation but not for serious military operations. Most sixteenth-century Portuguese fleets were more heavily armed and were capable of inflicting severe defeats if necessary on local naval and land forces. The Portuguese by no means possessed a monopoly on the use of firearms and explosives, but their highly maneuverable, light ships enabled them to maintain their distance while bombarding the enemy with their powerful cannons. Such tactics gave them a military superiority over lightly armed rivals that they were able to exploit until the arrival of other European forces several decades later.

New Rivals Enter the Scene   Portugal's efforts to dominate the spice trade network were never totally successful, however. After some early disastrous defeats at sea, Muslim rivals sought to recover the initiative, harassing Portuguese fleets from seaports on the Arabian peninsula and the coast of Africa and thereby preventing the latter from obtaining a monopoly on trade within the region. For their part, the Portuguese lacked both the numbers and the wealth to overcome local resistance and colonize the Asian regions. Moreover, their massive investments in ships and laborers for their empire (hundreds of ships and hundreds of thousands of workers in shipyards and overseas bases) proved very costly. Disease, shipwrecks, and battles took a heavy toll. The empire was simply too large and Portugal too small to maintain it, and by the end of the sixteenth century, the Portuguese were being severely challenged by European rivals.

The Spanish   First on the scene was Spain. Queen Isabella of Spain had already signaled her intent to enter the competition in 1492 when she sponsored the voyage of Christopher Columbus into the Atlantic Ocean in search of a westward route to the Indies. That led to a dispute between the two Iberian nations over the rights to newly conquered territories. In 1494, in an effort to head off potential conflict between the two countries, the Treaty of Tordesillas (tor-day-SEE-yass) divided the newly discovered world into separate Portuguese and Spanish spheres of influence. Thereafter, the route east around the Cape of Good Hope was reserved for the Portuguese, while the route across the Atlantic (except for the eastern hump of South America) was assigned to Spain.

Columbus's later voyages eventually convinced influential figures at the Spanish court that the lands he had reached were not the Indies but an unknown land that possessed its own attractions. Still seeking a route to the Spice Islands, in 1519 Spain dispatched a fleet under the command of the Portuguese adventurer Ferdinand Magellan that sailed around the southern tip of South America, proceeded across the Pacific Ocean, and landed on the island of Cebu in the Philippine Islands. Although Magellan and some forty of his crew were killed there in a skirmish with the local population, one of the two remaining ships sailed on to Tidor, in the Moluccas, and thence around the world via the Cape of Good Hope. In the words of a contemporary historian, having completed the first circumference of the earth, they arrived in Cádiz "with precious cargo and fifteen men surviving out of a fleet of five sail."[6]

As it turned out, the Spanish, who were increasingly preoccupied with the territories newly discovered by Columbus, could not follow up on Magellan's accomplishment, and in 1529 they sold their rights in Tidor to the Portuguese. But Magellan's voyage was not a total loss to the Spanish, who soon managed to consolidate their control over the Philippines and transformed it into a major way station in the carrying trade across the Pacific. Spanish galleons learned to follow the Pacific trade winds by carrying silk and other luxury from China to Acapulco in exchange for silver from the mines of Mexico.

The English and the Dutch   The primary threat to the Portuguese toehold in Southeast Asia came from the English and the Dutch. In 1591, the first English expedition to the Indies through the Indian Ocean arrived in London with a cargo of pepper. Nine years later, a private joint-stock company, the East India Company, was founded to provide a stable source of capital for future voyages. In 1608, an English fleet landed at Surat (SOOR-et), on the northwestern coast of India. Trade with Southeast Asia soon followed.

The Dutch, bitter trade rivals to the English, were equally determined to show the flag in the region. Seven years after the first Dutch fleet arrived in India in 1595, the Dutch East India Company (Vereenigde Oost-Indische Compagnie, or VOC) was established under government sponsorship and began to compete actively for access to the spice trade. In 1611, a Dutch fleet made history by sailing directly east on the "roaring forties" (the powerful westerly winds circling the globe at that southern latitude) from South Africa to the Indonesian archipelago. In 1641, the Dutch seized the entrepôt of Malacca, one of the linchpins of Portugal's trading empire in Asia.

THE CONQUEST OF THE "NEW WORLD"

Although the Portuguese had successfully defeated their Spanish rivals in obtaining access to the spice trade in the Indies, the latter, aided by their greater resources, were on the verge of establishing a far grander overseas empire.

The Voyages An important figure in the history of Spanish exploration was an Italian from Genoa, Christopher Columbus (1451–1506). Like many knowledgeable Europeans, Columbus was aware that the world was round, but he was also convinced that the circumference of the earth was smaller than some of his contemporaries believed. He therefore argued that Asia could easily be reached by sailing due west instead of eastward around Africa. After his plan was rejected by the Portuguese, he persuaded Queen Isabella of Castile to finance his exploratory expedition, which left Spain in early August 1492 and reached land somewhere in the islands of the Bahamas five weeks later. For the next few weeks, his three ships explored the coastline of Cuba and the northern shores of the neighboring island of Hispaniola (his-puhn-YOH-luh *or* ees-pahn-YAH-luh). Columbus believed that he had reached Asia and in three subsequent voyages (1493, 1498, and 1502) sought in vain to find a route through the outer islands to the Asian mainland. In his four voyages, Columbus reached all the major islands of the Caribbean, which he called the Indies, as well as Honduras in Central America.

Although Columbus clung for the rest of his life to his belief that he had reached Asia, other navigators realized that he had discovered a new frontier altogether and joined the race to what Europeans began to call the "New World." A Venetian seafarer, John Cabot, explored the New England coastline of the Americas under a license from King Henry VII of England. The continent of South America was discovered accidentally by the Portuguese sea captain Pedro Cabral (PAY-droh kuh-BRAHL) in 1500. Amerigo Vespucci (ahm-ay-REE-goh vess-POO-chee), a Florentine, accompanied several of Cabral's voyages and wrote a series of letters describing the geography of the lands he observed. The publication of these letters led eventually to the use of the name "America" (after Amerigo) for the new lands.

The Conquests The newly discovered territories that Europeans referred to as the New World actually contained flourishing civilizations populated by millions of people. But the Americas were new to the Europeans, who quickly saw opportunities for conquest and exploitation. With Portugal clearly in the lead in the race to exploit the riches of the Indies, the importance of these lands was magnified in the minds of the Spanish, especially those who saw a chance to win fame and fortune for themselves and their families.

The Spanish **conquistadors**, as they were called, were a hardy lot of mostly upper-class individuals motivated by a typical sixteenth-century blend of glory, greed, and religious zeal. Their superior weapons, organizational skills, and determination brought them incredible success in their new environment. In 1519, a Spanish expedition under the command of Hernán Cortés landed at Veracruz, on the Gulf of Mexico. Marching to Tenochtitlán (teh-nahch-teet-LAHN) at the head of a small contingent of troops, Cortés received a friendly welcome from the Aztec monarch Moctezuma Xocoyotzin (mahk-tuh-ZOO-muh shoh-koh-YAHT-seen) (often called Montezuma), who initially believed his visitor was a representative of Quetzalcoatl (KWET-sul-koh-AHT-ul), the legendary and godlike feathered serpent of the Amerindian peoples. The king and his subjects were astounded to see men on

COMPARATIVE ILLUSTRATION

The Spaniards Conquer a New World

The perspective that the Spanish brought to their arrival in
the Americas was quite different from that of the indigenous

peoples. In the European painting below,
the encounter was a peaceful one, and the
upturned eyes of Columbus and his fellow voyagers imply that their motives

North Wind/North Wind Picture Archives

horseback, for the horse had disappeared from the Americas at least ten thousand
years earlier.

But tensions soon erupted between the Spaniards and the Aztecs, provoked in
part by demands by Cortés that the Aztecs renounce their native beliefs and accept
Christianity. When the Spanish took Moctezuma hostage and began to destroy
Aztec religious shrines, the local population revolted and drove the invaders from
the city. Receiving assistance from the Aztec tribute state of Tlaxcallan (tuh-
lah-SKAH-lahn), Cortés managed to fight his way back into the city. Meanwhile,
the Aztecs were beginning to suffer the first effects of the diseases brought by the
Europeans, which would eventually wipe out the majority of the local population.
In a battle that to many Aztecs must have seemed to symbolize the dying of the legendary fifth sun, the Aztecs were finally vanquished. Within months, their magnificent city and its temples, believed by the conquerors to be the work of Satan, had
been destroyed.

were spiritual rather than material. The above image, drawn by an Aztec artist, expresses a dramatically different point of view, as the Spanish invaders, assisted by their Indian allies, use superior weapons against the bows and arrows of their adversaries to bring about the conquest of Mexico.

Q *What does the Aztec painting presented here show the viewer about the nature of the conflict between the two contending armies?*

A similar fate awaited the powerful Inka Empire in South America. Between 1531 and 1536, another expedition, led by a hardened and somewhat corrupt soldier, Francisco Pizarro (frahn-CHESS-koh puh-ZAHR-oh) (1470–1541), destroyed Inka power high in the Peruvian Andes. The Spanish conquests were undoubtedly facilitated by the prior arrival of European diseases, which had decimated the local population. Although it took another three decades before the western part of Latin America was brought under Spanish control, already by 1535, the Spanish had created a system of colonial administration that made the New World—at least in European eyes—an extension of the old.

The Portuguese in Brazil   Although the Spanish had taken the lead in planting their flag in the Western Hemisphere, they were not alone. After the Portuguese sea captain Pedro Cabral inadvertently discovered the eastern coast of Latin America in 1500 while en route to the Indies, the Portuguese crown established the colony of Brazil in the area, basing its claim on the Treaty of Tordesillas, which had allocated that territory to the Portuguese sphere of influence. Like their Spanish rivals, the Portuguese initially viewed their new colony as a source of gold and silver, but they soon discovered that profits could be made in other ways as well. A formal administrative system was instituted in Brazil in 1549, and Portuguese migrants arrived to establish plantations to produce sugar, coffee, and other tropical products for export to Europe.

Governing the Empires   While Portugal set out to strengthen its control over Brazil, Spain began to construct a colonial empire that included Central America, most of South America, and parts of North America. Within the lands of Central and South America, a new civilization arose that we have come to call Latin America.

Latin America rapidly became a multiracial society. Already by 1501, Spanish rulers allowed intermarriage between Europeans and the inhabitants of the Americas, whom the Europeans called Indians. Their offspring became known as **mestizos** (mess-TEE-zohz). In addition, over a period of three centuries, possibly as many as 8 million African slaves were brought to Spanish and Portuguese America to work the plantations that were established. **Mulattoes** (muh-LAH-tohz)—the offspring of Africans and whites—joined mestizos and descendants of whites, Africans, and local Indians to produce a unique multiracial society in Latin America.

The State and the Church in Colonial Latin America   Although the colonial empires of Portuguese Brazil and Spanish America lasted more than three hundred years, the difficulties of communication and travel between the Americas and Europe made it virtually impossible for the home-country monarchs to provide close regulation of their empires. This left colonial officials in Latin America with much autonomy in implementing imperial policies. Nevertheless, the Iberians tried to keep the most important posts of colonial government in the hands of Europeans.

To rule their American empires, the kings of Spain and Portugal appointed **viceroys**, who ruled over a bureaucracy staffed primarily by Europeans, known as *peninsulares*. The first Spanish viceroyalty was established for New Spain (Mexico) in 1535. Another was organized in Peru in 1543, and later two additional ones—New Granada and La Plata—were added. Viceroyalties were in turn subdivided into smaller units, where **creoles**—American-born descendants of Europeans—often held prominent positions.

From the beginning, Spanish and Portuguese rulers were determined to convert the indigenous peoples of the Western Hemisphere to Christianity. Catholic missionaries fanned out to different parts of the Spanish Empire, where they brought Indians together into villages where they could be converted to Christianity, taught a trade, and encouraged to grow crops. The Catholic Church also built hospitals, orphanages, and schools to instruct Indian students in the rudiments of reading, writing, and arithmetic.

Exploiting the Riches of the Americas   The most vital task for administrators in the Americas was to enable the home countries to profit economically from their colonies in Latin America. The chief source of wealth, in the minds of European

MAP 14.3 Latin America from c. 1500 to 1750

From the sixteenth century, Latin America was largely the colonial preserve of the Spanish, although Portugal dominated Brazil. The Latin American colonies supplied the Spanish and Portuguese with gold, silver, sugar, tobacco, cotton, and animal hides.

immigrants, came from the abundant supplies of gold and silver, and they sought the precious metals wherever they went in the Americas. One Aztec observer commented that the Spanish conquerors "longed and lusted for gold. Their bodies swelled with greed, and their hunger was ravenous; they hungered like pigs for that

FILM & HISTORY

The Mission (1986)

Directed by Roland Joffé, *The Mission* examines religion, politics, and colonialism in Europe and South America in the mid-eighteenth century. The movie begins with a flashback as Cardinal Altamirano (Ray McAnally) is dictating a letter to the pope to discuss the fate of the Jesuit missions in Paraguay. (The Jesuits were members of the Society of Jesus, a Roman Catholic religious order that was founded in the sixteenth century.) He begins by describing the establishment of a new Jesuit mission (San Carlos) in Spanish territory in the borderlands of Paraguay and Brazil. Father Gabriel (Jeremy Irons) has been able to win over the Guaraní Indians and create a community based on communal livelihood and property (private property has been abolished). The mission includes dwellings for the Guaraní and a church where they can practice their new faith by learning the Gospel and singing hymns. This small band of Jesuits is joined by Rodrigo Mendozo (Robert De Niro), who has been a slave trader dealing in Indians and now seeks to atone for killing his brother in a fit of jealous rage by joining the community at San Carlos. Won over to Father Gabriel's perspective, he also becomes a member of the Jesuit order.

Cardinal Altamirano now travels to South America, sent by a pope anxious to appease the Portuguese monarch over the activities of the Jesuits. Portuguese settlers in Brazil are eager to use the local people as slaves and to confiscate their communal lands and property. In 1750, when Spain agrees to turn over the Guaraní territory in Paraguay to Portugal, the settlers seize their opportunity. Although the cardinal visits a number of missions, including San Carlos, and obviously approves of their accomplishments, his hands are tied by the Portuguese king, who is threatening to disband the Jesuit order if the missions are not closed. The cardinal acquiesces, and Portuguese troops are sent to take over the missions. Although Rodrigo and the other Jesuits join the Guaraní in fighting the Portuguese while Father Gabriel remains nonviolent, all are massacred. The cardinal returns to Europe, dismayed by the murderous activities of the Portuguese but hopeful that the Jesuit order will be spared. All is in vain, however, as the Catholic monarchs of Europe expel the Jesuits from their countries and pressure Pope Clement XIV into disbanding the Jesuit order in 1773.

In its approach to the destruction of the Jesuit missions, *The Mission* clearly exalts the dedication of the Jesuit order and praises its devotion to the welfare of the

gold."[7] Rich silver deposits were found and exploited in Mexico and in southern Peru (modern Bolivia). When the mines at Potosí (poh-toh-SEE) in Peru were opened in 1545, the value of precious metals imported into Europe quadrupled. It has been estimated that between 1503 and 1650, some 16 million kilograms (17,500 tons) of silver and 185,000 kilograms (200 tons) of gold entered the port of Seville in Spain.

Although the pursuit of gold and silver offered prospects of fantastic financial rewards, agriculture ultimately proved to be a more abiding source of prosperity for Latin America. The American colonies became sources of raw materials for Spain

Indians. The movie ends with a small group of Guaraní children, now all orphans, picking up a few remnants of debris in their destroyed mission and moving off down the river back into the wilderness to escape enslavement. The final words on the screen illuminate the movie's message about the activities of the Europeans who destroyed the local civilizations in their conquest of the Americas: "The Indians of South America are still engaged in a struggle to defend their land and their culture. Many of the priests who, inspired by faith and love, continue to support the rights of the Indians, do so with their lives," a reference to the ongoing struggle in Latin America against the regimes that continue to oppress the landless masses.

The Jesuit missionary Father Gabriel (Jeremy Irons) with the Guaraní Indians of Paraguay before their slaughter by Portuguese troops.

Warner Brothers/Everett Collection

and Portugal as sugar, tobacco, chocolate, precious woods, animal hides, and a number of other natural products made their way to Europe. In turn, the mother countries supplied their colonists with manufactured goods. Both Spain and Portugal closely regulated the trade of their American colonies to keep others out, but the English and the French eventually became too powerful to be excluded from this lucrative Latin American market.

To produce these goods, colonial authorities initially tried to rely on local sources of human labor. Spanish policy toward the Indians was a combination of confusion, misguided paternalism, and cruel exploitation. Confusion arose over

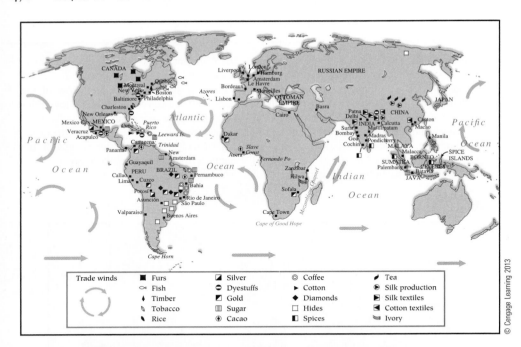

MAP 14.4 Patterns of World Trade Between 1500 and 1800

This map shows the major products that were traded by European merchants throughout the world during the era of European exploration.

the nature of the Indians. Queen Isabella declared the Indians to be subjects of Castile and instituted the ***encomienda* system**, under which European settlers received grants of land and could collect tribute from the indigenous peoples and use them as laborers. In return, the holders of an ***encomienda*** (en-koh-MYEN-duh) were supposed to protect the Indians and supervise their spiritual and material needs. In practice, this meant that the settlers were free to implement the system as they pleased. Three thousand miles from Spain, Spanish settlers largely ignored their government and brutally used the Indians to pursue their own economic interests. Indians were put to work on sugar plantations and in the lucrative gold and silver mines.

Forced labor, starvation, and especially disease took a fearful toll on Indian lives. With little or no natural resistance to European diseases, the Indians were ravaged by smallpox, measles, and typhus brought by the explorers and the conquistadors. Although scholarly estimates vary drastically, a reasonable guess is that at least half of the local population in some areas died of European diseases. On Hispaniola alone, out of an initial population of 100,000 when Columbus arrived in 1493, only 300 Indians survived by 1570. In 1542, largely in response to the publications of Bartolomé de Las Casas (bahr-toh-loh-MAY day lahs KAH-sahs), a Dominican monk who championed the Indians, the government abolished the *encomienda* system and provided more protection for the Indians. By then, however, the indigenous population had been decimated by disease, causing the Spanish—and eventually the Portuguese as well—to import African slaves to replace the Indians in the sugar fields.

The Competi-
tion Intensifies
The success of the Spanish and the Portuguese in exploiting the riches of the Americas soon attracted competition from other European trading states. In 1607, after an abortive effort to establish a base near Cape Hatteras had failed, the English set up its first permanent settlement at Jamestown, near the Chesapeake Bay. Within a few years, other European states had followed suit, and by the end of the seventeenth century, they had occupied much of the eastern seaboard of North America.

But the major area of competition was in South America and the Caribbean islands, where the lure of profits from the sugar trade was difficult to resist. The Dutch formed their own West India Company in 1621 to compete with Spanish and Portuguese interests and briefly took control of the sugar plantations on the east coast of Brazil. The French and the English focused their efforts on the Caribbean, where their privateers preyed on Spanish galleons carrying silver from the Americas back to Seville. They also competed actively for control of several of the Caribbean islands, where sugar plantations were producing fabulous profits for their new European owners. A number of the islands in the region shifted control several times over the course of the seventeenth and eighteenth centuries.

Christopher
Columbus: Hero
or Villain?
For centuries, the explorer Christopher Columbus has generally been viewed by most observers in a positive light. By discovering the Western Hemisphere, he opened up the world and laid the foundations for the modern global economy. Recently, however, some historians have begun to challenge the prevailing image of Columbus as a heroic figure in world history and view him instead as a symbol of European colonial repression and a prime mover in the virtual extinction of the peoples and cultures of the Americas.

Certainly, they have a point. As we have seen, the immediate consequences of Columbus's voyages were tragic for countless peoples in the Western Hemisphere. And as historical studies have shown, Columbus, who was himself not an entirely sympathetic figure, viewed the indigenous peoples that he encountered with condescension, describing them to his sponsors as naïve innocents who could be exploited for the purpose of bringing wealth and power to Spain. As a consequence, his men frequently treated the local population brutally.

But is it fair to blame Columbus for possessing many of the character traits and prejudices common to his era? To do so is to demand that an individual transcend the limitations of his time and adopt the values of another generation several hundred years into the future—something that few, if any, would be able to achieve. Perhaps it is better to note simply that Columbus and his contemporaries showed relatively little understanding and sympathy for the cultural values of peoples who lived beyond the borders of their own civilization, a limitation that would probably apply to one degree or another to all generations, including our own. Whether Columbus was a hero or a

OPPOSING VIEWPOINTS

The March of Civilization

As Europeans began to explore new parts of the world in the fifteenth century, they were convinced that it was their duty to introduce civilized ways to the heathen peoples they encountered. This attitude is reflected in the first selection, which describes the Spanish captain Vasco Núñez de Balboa (BAHS-koh NOON-yez day bal-BOH-uh) in 1513, when from a hill on the Isthmus of Panama he first laid eyes on the Pacific Ocean.

Bartolomé de Las Casas (1474–1566) was a Dominican monk who participated in the conquest of Cuba and received land and Indians in return for his efforts. But in 1514, he underwent a radical transformation that led him to believe that the Indians had been cruelly mistreated by his fellow Spaniards. He spent the remaining years of his life fighting for the Indians. The second selection is taken from his most influential work, *Brevísima Relación de la Destrucción de las Indias*, known to English readers as *The Tears of the Indians*. This work was largely responsible for the reputation of the Spanish conquistadors as cruel and murderous fanatics.

Gonzalo Fernández de Ovieda, *Historia General y Natural de las Indias*

On Tuesday, the twenty-fifth of September of the year 1513, at ten o'clock in the morning, Captain Vasco Núñez, having gone ahead of his company, climbed a hill with a bare summit, and from the top of this hill saw the South Sea. Of all the Christians in his company, he was the first to see it. He turned back toward his people, full of joy, lifting his hands and his eyes to Heaven, praising Jesus Christ and his glorious Mother the Virgin, Our Lady. Then he fell upon his knees on the ground and gave great thanks to God for the mercy He had shown him, in allowing him to discover that sea, and thereby to render so great a service to God and to the most serene Catholic Kings of Castile, our sovereigns....

And he told all the people with him to kneel also, to give the same thanks to God, and to beg Him fervently to allow them to see and discover the secrets and great riches of that sea and coast, for the greater glory and increase of the Christian faith, for the conversion of the Indians, natives of those

villain will remain a matter of debate. That he and his contemporaries played a key role in the emergence of the modern world is a matter on which there can be no doubt.

AFRICA IN TRANSITION

Although the primary objective of the Portuguese in rounding the Cape of Good Hope was to find a sea route to the Spice Islands, they soon discovered that profits were to be made en route, along the eastern coast of Africa.

The Portuguese in Africa

In the early sixteenth century, a Portuguese fleet commanded by Francisco de Almeida (fran-CHESS-koh duh ahl-MAY-duh) seized a number of East African port cities, including Kilwa, southern regions, and for the fame and prosperity of the royal throne of Castile and of its sovereigns present and to come. All the people cheerfully and willingly did as they were bidden; and the Captain made them fell a big tree and make from it a tall cross, which they erected in that same place, at the top of the hill from which the South Sea had first been seen.

Bartolomé de Las Casas, *The Tears of the Indians*

There is nothing more detestable or more cruel than the tyranny which the Spaniards use toward the Indians for the getting of pearl. Surely the infernal torments cannot much exceed the anguish that they endure, by reason of that way of cruelty; for they put them under water some four or five ells deep, where they are forced without any liberty of respiration, to gather up the shells wherein the Pearls are; sometimes they come up again with nets full of shells to take breath, but if they stay any while to rest themselves, immediately comes a hangman row'd in a little boat, who as soon as he hath well beaten them, drags them again to their labor. Their food is nothing but filth, and the very same that contains the Pearl, with small portion of that bread which that Country affords; in the first whereof there is little nourishment; and as for the latter, it is made with great difficulty, besides that they have not enough of that neither for sustenance; they lie upon the ground in fetters, lest they should run away; and many times they are drown'd in this labor, and are never seen again till they swim upon the top of the waves; oftentimes they also are devoured by certain sea monsters, that are frequent in those seas. Consider whether this hard usage of the poor creatures be consistent with the precepts which God commands concerning charity to our neighbor....

Q *Can the sentiments expressed by Vasco Núñez be reconciled with the treatment accorded to the Indians as described by Las Casas? Which selection do you think better describes the behavior of the Spaniards in the Americas? Compare the treatment of the Indians described here with the treatment of African slaves.*

Source: From *The Age of Reconnaissance* by J. H. Parry (International Thomson Publishing, 1969), pp. 233–234. From *The Tears of the Indians*, Bartolomé de Las Casas. Copyright © 1970 by The John Lilburne Company Publishers.

Sofala, and Mombasa, and built forts along the coast in an effort to control the trade in the area. Above all, the Portuguese wanted to monopolize the trade in gold, which was mined in the hills along the upper Zambezi River and then shipped to Sofala on the coast. For centuries, the gold trade had been monopolized by local Bantu-speaking Shona peoples at Zimbabwe. In the fifteenth century, it had come under the control of a Shona dynasty known as the Mwene Mutapa (MWAY-nay moo-TAH-puh).

The Mwene Mutapa had originally controlled the region south of the Zambezi River and may have been the builders of the impressive city known today as Great Zimbabwe, but sometime in the fifteenth century, they moved northeastward to the valley of the Zambezi. Here they encountered the arriving Portuguese, who had begun to move inland to gain access to the lucrative gold trade and had established

COMPARATIVE ESSAY

The Columbian Exchange

INTERACTION & EXCHANGE

In the Western world, the discovery of the Americas has traditionally been viewed in a largely positive sense, as the first step in a process that expanded the global trade network and eventually led to increased economic well-being and the spread of civilization throughout the world. In recent years, however, that view has come under sharp attack from some observers, who point out that for the peoples of the Americas, the primary legacy of the European conquest was not improved living standards but harsh colonial exploitation and the spread of pestilential diseases that devastated local populations.

Certainly, the record of the European conquistadors leaves much to be desired, and the voyages of Columbus were not of universal benefit to his contemporaries or to later generations. They not only resulted in the destruction of vibrant civilizations in the Americas but also led ultimately to the enslavement of millions of Africans, who were separated from their families and shipped to a far-off world in deplorable, inhuman conditions.

But to focus solely on the evils committed in the name of exploration and civilization misses a larger point and obscures the long-term ramifications of the events taking place. The age of European expansion that began in the fifteenth century was only the latest in a series of population movements that included the spread of nomadic peoples across Central Asia and the expansion of Islam out of the Middle East after the death of the prophet Muhammad. In fact, the migration of peoples in search of a better livelihood has been a central theme in the evolution of the human race since the dawn of prehistory. Virtually all of the migrations involved acts of unimaginable cruelty and the forcible displacement of peoples and societies.

In retrospect, it seems clear that the consequences of such broad population movements are too complex to be summed up in moral or ideological simplifications. The Mongol invasions and the expansion

ports on the Zambezi River. The Portuguese opened treaty relations with the Mwene Mutapa, and Jesuit priests were eventually posted to the court in 1561. At first, the Mwene Mutapa found the Europeans useful as an ally against local rivals, but by the end of the sixteenth century, the Portuguese had established a protectorate and forced the local ruler to grant title to large tracts of land to European officials and private individuals living in the area. Eventually, those lands would be integrated into the colony of Mozambique. The Portuguese, however, lacked the personnel and the capital to dominate local trade, and in the late seventeenth century, a vassal of the Mwene Mutapa succeeded in driving them from the plateau; his descendants maintained control of the area for the next two hundred years.

North of the Zambezi River, Bantu-speaking peoples were coming under pressure not only from the Portuguese but also from pastoralists migrating southward from the southern Sudan. The latter were frequently aggressive and began to occupy the rift valley and parts of the lake district that had previously of Islam are two examples of movements that brought benefits as well as costs for the peoples who were affected. By the same token, the European conquest of the Americas not only brought the destruction of cultures and dangerous new diseases but also initiated the exchange of plant and animal species that have ultimately fed millions and been of widespread benefit to peoples throughout the globe. The introduction of the horse, the cow, and various grain crops vastly increased food production in the Americas. The cultivation of corn, manioc, and the potato, all of them products of the Western Hemisphere, has had the same effect in Asia, Africa, and Europe. The **Columbian Exchange**, as it is sometimes labeled, has had far-reaching consequences that transcend facile moral judgments.

The opening of the Americas had other long-term ramifications as well. The importation of vast amounts of gold and silver fueled a price revolution that for years distorted the Spanish economy. At the same time, the increase in liquid capital due to this expansion was a crucial factor in the growth of commercial capitalism that set the stage for the global economy of the modern era. Some have even suggested that the precious metals that flowed into the treasuries of major European trading states may have helped finance the Industrial Revolution that is now spreading rapidly throughout the modern world.

Viewed in that context, the Columbian Exchange, whatever its moral failings, ultimately brought benefits to peoples throughout the world. For some, the costs were high, and it can be argued that the indigenous peoples of the Americas might have better managed the transformation on their own. But the "iron law" of history operates at its own speed and does not wait for laggards. For good or ill, the Columbian Exchange marks a major stage in the transition between the traditional and the modern world.

Q *How can the costs and benefits of the Columbian Exchange be measured? What standards would you apply in attempting to measure them?*

been controlled by Bantu-speaking farmers. In some cases, the conflict between farmers and pastoralists was fairly clear-cut. In Rwanda and Burundi, immediately west of Lake Victoria, farming Hutu peoples defended their hilltop communities against roving Tutsi pastoralists occupying the surrounding lowlands.

The Dutch in South Africa   The first Europeans to settle in southern Africa were the Dutch. After an unsuccessful attempt to seize the Portuguese settlement on the island of Mozambique off the East African coast, in 1652 the Dutch set up a way station at the Cape of Good Hope to serve as a base for their fleets en route to the East Indies. At first, the new settlement was intended simply to provide food and other provisions to Dutch ships, but eventually it developed into a permanent colony. Dutch farmers, known as **Boers** and speaking a Dutch dialect that evolved into Afrikaans, began to settle in the sparsely occupied areas outside the city of Cape Town. The temperate climate and the absence of tropical diseases made the territory near the cape almost the only land south of the Sahara that the Europeans found suitable for habitation.

The Dutch, like their chief rivals, the English and the French, also took advantage of the decline of the Songhai Empire to become active in the West African trade in the mid-sixteenth century, encroaching particularly on the Portuguese spheres of influence. During the mid-seventeenth century, the Dutch seized a number of Portuguese forts along the West African coast while at the same time taking over the bulk of the Portuguese trade across the Indian Ocean.

The Slave Trade   The European exploration of the African coastline had little immediate significance for most peoples living in the interior of the continent, except for a few who engaged in direct or indirect trade with the foreigners. But for peoples living on or near the coast, the impact was often great indeed. As the trade in slaves increased during the sixteenth, seventeenth, and eighteenth centuries, thousands and then millions of men, women, and even children were removed from their homes and forcibly exported to plantations in the Western Hemisphere.

The Arrival of the Europeans   There were different forms of slavery in Africa before the arrival of the Europeans. For centuries, slaves—often captives seized in battle or in raids between neighboring villages—had been used in many African societies as agricultural laborers, household servants, or concubines. Many served as domestic servants or as wageless workers for the local ruler, and some were permitted to purchase their freedom under certain conditions. After the expansion of Islam south of the Sahara in the eighth century, a vigorous traffic in slaves developed, as Arab merchants traded for slaves along routes snaking across the Sahara or up the Nile River Valley. Under Askia Mohammad and his successors, Songhai became active in the process, launching raids in non-Muslim areas and selling their captives to Arab merchants for shipment to the Middle East, where they were put to use as domestic servants or as workers on plantations throughout the region. Slavery also existed in many European countries, where a few slaves from Africa or Slavic-speaking peoples captured in war in the regions near the Black Sea (the English word *slave* derives from "Slav") were used for domestic purposes or as agricultural workers in the lands adjacent to the Mediterranean. Merchants from Genoa routinely traded captives that had been seized along the coast of the Black Sea to their Arab counterparts in return for spices.

With the arrival of the Europeans in Africa in the fifteenth century, the African slave trade changed dramatically, although the change did not occur immediately. At first, the Portuguese simply replaced European slaves with African ones. During the second half of the fifteenth century, about a thousand slaves were taken to Portugal each year; the vast majority were apparently destined to serve as domestic servants for affluent families throughout Europe. But the discovery of the Western Hemisphere in the 1490s and the subsequent planting of sugarcane in South America and on the islands of the Caribbean changed the situation dramatically.

Cane sugar was native to Indonesia and had first been introduced to Europeans from the Middle East during the crusades. By the fifteenth century, sugar cane was grown (often by slaves from Africa or the region of the Black Sea) in modest amounts on the islands of Cyprus and Sicily and in the southern regions of the Iberian Peninsula. But when the Ottoman Empire seized much of the eastern Mediterranean, the Europeans needed to seek out new areas suitable for cultivation. In 1490, the Portuguese established sugar plantations worked by African laborers at São Tomé, an island off the central coast of Africa. Demand increased as sugar gradually replaced honey as a sweetener, especially in northern Europe.

But the primary impetus to the sugar industry came from the colonization of the Americas. During the sixteenth century, plantations were established along the eastern coast of Brazil and on several islands in the Caribbean. Because the cultivation of cane sugar is an arduous process demanding both skill and large quantities of labor, the new plantations required more workers than could be provided by the importation of Europeans (mostly prisoners) or by the Indian population in the Americas, many of whom rapidly died of diseases imported from Europe and Africa. Since the climate and soil of much of West Africa were not especially conducive to the cultivation of sugar (cane sugar requires access to ample water and a frost-free environment), African slaves began to be shipped to Brazil and the Caribbean to work on the plantations. The first were sent from Portugal, but in 1518, a Spanish ship carried the first boatload of African slaves directly from Africa to the Americas.

The Middle Passage   During the next two centuries, the trade in slaves increased by massive proportions. An estimated 275,000 enslaved Africans were exported to other countries during the sixteenth century, more than two-thirds of them to the Americas. The total climbed beyond a million in the seventeenth century and jumped to 6 million in the eighteenth century, when the trade spread from West and Central Africa to East Africa. Even during the nineteenth century, when Great Britain and a number of other European countries attempted to end the slave trade, nearly 2 million humans were exported. It has been estimated that altogether as many as 10 million African slaves were transported to the Americas between the early sixteenth and the late nineteenth centuries. As many as 2 million were exported to other areas during the same period.

One reason for these astonishing numbers, of course, was the tragically high death rate. In what is often called the **Middle Passage**, the arduous voyage from Africa to the Americas, losses were frequently appalling. Although figures on the number of slaves who died on the journey are almost entirely speculative, during the first shipments, up to one-third of the human cargo may have died of disease or malnourishment. Even among crew members, mortality rates were sometimes as high as one in four. Later merchants became more efficient and reduced losses to about 10 percent. Still, the future slaves were treated inhumanely, chained together in the holds of ships reeking with the stench of human waste and diseases carried by vermin.

Slavery in the Americas   Ironically, African slaves who survived the brutal voyage fared somewhat better than whites after their arrival. Mortality rates for

MAP 14.5   The Slave Trade

Beginning in the sixteenth century, the trade in African slaves to the Americas became a major source of profit to European merchants. This map traces the routes taken by slave-trading ships, as well as the territories and ports of call of European powers in the seventeenth century.

Europeans in the West Indies were ten to twenty times higher than in Europe, and death rates for those newly arrived in the islands averaged more than 125 per 1,000 annually. But the figure for Africans, many of whom had developed at least a partial immunity to yellow fever, was only about 30 per 1,000.

The reason for the staggering death rates was clearly more than maltreatment, although that was certainly a factor. As we have seen, the transmission of diseases from one continent to another brought high death rates among those lacking immunity. African slaves were somewhat less susceptible to European diseases than the American Indian populations. Indeed, they seem to have possessed a degree of immunity, perhaps because their ancestors had developed antibodies to diseases common to the Old World from the centuries of contact via the trans-Saharan trade. The Africans would not have had immunity to native American diseases, however.

The mortality rates were higher for immigrants than for individuals born in the Americas, who as children gradually developed at least a partial immunity to many diseases. Death rates for native-born slaves tended to be significantly lower than for recent arrivals, which raises the question of why the slave population did not begin to rise after the initial impact of settlement had worn off. The answer appears to be a matter of economics. In the first place, only half as many women were enslaved as men, birthrates for women living in slavery were low, and infant mortality was high. In the second place, as long as the price of slaves was low, many slave owners in the West Indies apparently believed that purchasing a new slave was less expensive than raising a child from birth to working age at adolescence. After the price of slaves began to rise during the eighteenth century, plantation owners started to devote more efforts to replenishing the supply of workers by natural methods.

One of the lesser-known facts about slavery in the Americas is that many Africans did not accept their brutal life on the sugar, cotton, and tobacco plantations and escaped into the wilderness where they set up so-called "maroon" communities safe from control of the European colonial authorities. The most successful such efforts were in Brazil and on the island of Jamaica, where camps for escaped slaves, known as **maroons**, survived for decades carrying out an existence independent of colonial authority. In some cases, maroon communities even won recognition from the local colonial authorities in return for agreeing to return recently escaped slaves to their European masters.

Sources of Slaves   For the most part, Europeans obtained their slaves by traditional means, purchasing them from local African merchants at the infamous slave markets in exchange for gold, guns, or other European manufactured goods such as textiles, copper, or iron utensils. The "third leg" of this so-called **Triangular Trade** took place when slave owners in the Americas paid for their slaves with sugar or its by-products (such as rum and molasses) exported to buyers in Europe. At first, local slave traders obtained their supply from nearby regions, but as demand increased, they had to move further inland to find their victims. In a few cases, local rulers became concerned about the impact of the slave trade on the political and social well-being of their societies. As a general rule, however, the local monarchs viewed the slave trade as a source of income, and many launched forays against defenseless villages in search of unsuspecting victims.

Historians once thought that Europeans controlled the terms of the slave trade and were thus able to obtain victims at bargain prices. Recently, however, it has become clear that African intermediaries—private merchants, local elites, and trading state monopolies—were very active in the process and were often able to dictate the price, volume, and availability of slaves to European purchasers. The majority of the slaves sold to European buyers were males; females, who were in great demand in Africa and on the trans-Saharan trade, tended to be reserved for those markets. The slave merchants were often paid in various types of imported goods, including East Asian textiles (highly desired for their bright colors and durability), furniture, and other manufactured products. Until the end of the seventeenth century, the Portuguese preferred gold to slaves and would sometimes pay for the gold by selling slaves to African kingdoms that were short of labor. In fact, not until the beginning of the eighteenth century did slaves surpass gold and ivory as the continent's leading exports.

The Effects of the Slave Trade   The effects of the slave trade varied from area to area. It might be assumed that apart from the tragic effects on the lives of individual victims and their families, the practice would have led to the depopulation of vast areas of the continent. This did occur in some areas, notably in modern Angola, south of the mouth of the Congo River, and in thinly populated regions in East Africa, but it was less true in West Africa. There high birthrates were often able to counterbalance the loss of able-bodied adults, and the introduction of new crops from the Americas, such as maize, peanuts, and manioc, led to an increase in food production that made it possible to support a larger population. One of the many cruel ironies of history is that while the institution of slavery was a tragedy for many, it benefited others.

Still, there is no denying the reality that from a moral point of view, the slave trade represented a tragic loss for millions of Africans, not only for the individual victims but also for their families. One of the more poignant aspects of the trade is that as many as 20 percent of those sold to European slavers were children, a statistic that may be partly explained by the fact that many European countries enacted regulations that permitted more children than adults to be transported aboard the ships.

Beyond the effects on individual Africans and their families, the slave trade also had a corrosive impact on the structure of society as a whole. Another consequence of the arrival of the Europeans was the introduction of firearms into the African continent. As the European demand for slaves steadily increased, African slave traders began to use their newly purchased guns to raid neighboring villages in search of captives, initiating a chain of violence that rapidly extended into the interior and created a climate of fear and insecurity throughout the region. Old polities were undermined, and new regimes ruled by rapacious "merchant princes" began to proliferate on the coast.

How did Europeans justify cruelty of such epidemic proportions? In some cases, they rationalized that slave traders were only carrying on a tradition that had existed for centuries throughout the Mediterranean and African world. In others, they eased their consciences by noting that slaves brought from Africa would now be exposed to the Christian faith and would be able to replace American Indian workers, many of whom were considered too physically fragile for the heavy human labor involved in cutting sugarcane.

Political and Social Structures in a Changing Continent

Of course, the Western economic penetration of Africa had other dislocating effects. As in other parts of the non-Western world, the importation of manufactured goods from Europe undermined the foundations of local cottage industries and impoverished countless families. The demand for slaves and the introduction of firearms intensified political instability and civil strife. At the same time, the impact of the Europeans should not be exaggerated. Only in a few isolated areas, such as South Africa and Mozambique, were permanent European settlements established. Elsewhere, at the insistence of African rulers and merchants, European influence generally did not penetrate beyond the coastal regions.

Nevertheless, inland areas were often affected by events taking place elsewhere. In the western Sahara, for example, the diversion of trade routes toward the coast led to the weakening of the old Songhai trading empire and its eventual conquest by a vigorous new Moroccan dynasty in the late sixteenth century. Morocco had long hoped to expand its influence into the Sahara in order to seize control over the commerce in gold and salt, and in 1590, Moroccan forces defeated Songhai's army at Gao, on the Niger River, and then occupied the great caravan center of Timbuktu. Even after the departure of the invaders, Songhai was beyond recovery, and the next two centuries were marked by ongoing strife between divergent states and intense competition between Muslims in the cities and towns and adherents of traditional African religions in rural areas.

European influence had a more direct impact along the coast of West Africa, especially in the vicinity of European forts such as Dakar and Sierra Leone, but no European colonies were established there before 1800. Most of the numerous African states in the area from Cape Verde to the delta of the Niger River were sufficiently strong to resist Western encroachments, and they often allied with each other to force European purchasers to respect their monopoly over trading operations. Some, like the powerful Ashanti kingdom, established in 1680 on the Gold Coast, profited substantially from the rise in seaborne commerce. Some states, particularly along the so-called Slave Coast, in what is now Benin and Togo, or in the densely populated Niger River delta, took an active part in the slave trade. The demands of slavery and the temptations of economic profit, however, also contributed to the increase in conflict among the states in the area.

This was especially true in the region of the Congo River, where Portuguese activities eventually led to the splintering of the state of Kongo and two centuries of rivalry and internal strife among the successor states in the area. A similar pattern developed in East Africa, where Portuguese activities led to the decline and eventual collapse of the Mwene Mutapa. Northward along the coast, in present-day Kenya and Tanzania, African rulers, assisted by Arab forces from Oman and Muscat in the Arabian peninsula, expelled the Portuguese from Mombasa in 1698. Swahili culture now regained some of the dynamism it had possessed before the arrival of Vasco da Gama and his successors. But with much shipping now diverted southward to the route around the Cape of Good Hope, the commerce of the area never completely recovered and was increasingly dependent on the export of slaves and ivory obtained through contacts with African states in the interior.

SOUTHEAST ASIA IN THE ERA OF THE SPICE TRADE

As we noted earlier, Southeast Asia was affected in various ways by the expansion of the global trade network that began to accelerate in the early fifteenth century with the arrival of Chinese fleets under the command of Admiral Zheng He. Although the Chinese presence soon receded, that of Islam, introduced by merchants from India and the Middle East, now began to make serious inroads, notably in the Malay Peninsula and in coastal regions in the Indonesian archipelago. In 1511, however, the seizure of the Malaccan sultanate by a Portuguese fleet introduced a new threat into the region, while inaugurating a period of intense conflict among various European competitors for access to the spice trade.

At first, the rulers of most of the local states in the region were able to fend off these challenges and maintain their independence. However, the reprieve was only temporary.

The Arrival of the West   Where the Portuguese trod, others soon followed. By the early seventeenth century, the Dutch, English, and French had begun to join the scramble for rights to the lucrative spice trade. Within a short time, the Dutch appeared to have the advantage. Formed in 1602, the aggressive and well-financed Dutch East India Company (Vereenigde Oost-Indische Compagnie, or VOC) possessed ten times the capital of the English East India Company and not only succeeded in elbowing its rivals out of the spice trade but also had begun to consolidate political and military control over the area. On the island of Java, where they established a fort at Batavia (today's Jakarta) in 1619, the Dutch found that it was necessary to bring the inland regions under their control to protect their position on the coast. Rather than establishing a formal colony, however, they tried to rule as much as possible through the local landed aristocracy. On Java and the neighboring island of Sumatra, the VOC established pepper plantations, which soon produced massive profits for Dutch merchants in Amsterdam. Elsewhere they attempted to monopolize the clove trade by limiting cultivation of the crop to one island. By the end of the eighteenth century, the Dutch had succeeded in bringing almost the entire Indonesian archipelago under their control.

The arrival of the Europeans had somewhat less impact on mainland Southeast Asia, where cohesive monarchies in Burma (modern Myanmar), Thailand, and Vietnam resisted foreign encroachment. In addition, the coveted spices did not thrive on the mainland, so the Europeans' efforts there were far less intense than in the islands. The Portuguese did establish limited trade relations with several mainland states, including the Thai kingdom at Ayuthaya, Burma, Vietnam, and the remnants of the old Angkor kingdom in Cambodia. By the early seventeenth century, other European nations had followed and had begun to compete actively for trade and missionary privileges. As was the case elsewhere, the Europeans soon became involved in local factional disputes as a means of obtaining political and economic advantages. In Burma, the English and the French supported rival groups in the internal struggles of the monarchy until a new dynasty emerged and threw the foreigners out. A similar process took place at Ayuthaya, which survived the pressure from the Europeans but was eventually destroyed by a Burmese army in 1767.

In Vietnam, the arrival of Western merchants and missionaries coincided with a period of internal conflict among ruling groups in the country. After their arrival in the mid-seventeenth century, the European powers characteristically began to intervene in local politics, with the Portuguese and the Dutch supporting rival factions. By the end of the century, when it became clear that economic opportunities were limited, most European states abandoned their trading stations in the area. French missionaries attempted to remain, but their efforts were hampered by the local authorities, who viewed the Catholic insistence that converts give their primary loyalty to the pope as a threat to the legal status and prestige of the Vietnamese emperor.

**State and
Society in
Precolonial
Southeast Asia**
Between 1500 and 1800, Southeast Asia experienced the last flowering of traditional culture before the advent of European rule in the nineteenth century. Although the coming of the Europeans had an immediate and direct impact in some areas, notably the Philippines and parts of the Malay world, in most areas Western influence was still relatively limited. Europeans occasionally dabbled in local politics and modified regional trade patterns, but they generally were not a decisive factor in the evolution of local political or social systems.

Nevertheless, Southeast Asian societies were changing in several subtle ways—in their trade patterns, their means of livelihood, and their religious beliefs. In some ways, these changes accentuated the differences between individual states in the region. Yet beneath these differences was an underlying commonality of life for most people. Despite the diversity of cultures and religious beliefs in the area, Southeast Asians were in most respects closer to each other than they were to peoples outside the region. For the most part, the states and peoples of Southeast Asia were still in control of their own destiny.

Religion and Kingship   During the early modern era, both Buddhism and Islam became well established in Southeast Asia, although Christianity began to attract some converts, especially in port cities directly occupied by Europeans, such as Malacca and Batavia, and in the Philippines. Buddhism was dominant in lowland areas on the mainland, from Burma to Vietnam. At first, Muslim influence was felt mainly on the Malay Peninsula and along the northern coasts of Java and Sumatra, where local merchants encountered their Muslim counterparts from foreign lands on a regular basis. At the same time, traditional religious beliefs continued to survive, especially in inland areas, where the local populations either ignored the new doctrines or integrated them into their traditional forms of spirit worship. Buddhists in rural Burma and Thailand, for example, might also believe in nature spirits. On Java and Sumatra, where Islam was slow to penetrate into the interior, the result was a division between devout Muslims in the cities and essentially animist peasants in the rural villages.

Both Buddhism and Islam brought other changes in their train—temple education for Buddhists and schools for Islamic scholars and new religious and moral restrictions on human behavior such as refraining from eating pork and drinking wine for Muslims (though some foreign Muslims complained that the latter rule was not always followed). Because Islam discouraged the traditional tattooing of the body, Muslim converts turned to the technique of decorating textiles called *batik* (buh-TEEK).

Buddhism and Islam also helped shape Southeast Asian political institutions. As the political systems began to mature, they evolved into four main types: Buddhist kings, Javanese kings, Islamic sultans, and Vietnamese emperors. In each case, institutions and concepts imported from abroad were adapted to local circumstances.

The Buddhist style of kingship took shape between the eleventh and the fifteenth centuries as Theravada Buddhism spread throughout the area. It became the predominant political system in the Buddhist states of mainland Southeast Asia—Burma, Ayuthaya, Laos, and Cambodia. Perhaps the most prominent feature of the Buddhist model was the godlike character of the monarch, who was considered by virtue of his *karma* to be innately superior to other human beings and served as a link between human society and the cosmos. Court rituals stressed the sacred nature of the monarch, and even the palace was modeled after the symbolic design of the Hindu universe. In its center was an architectural rendering of sacred Mount Meru, the legendary home of the gods.

The Javanese model was a blend of Buddhist and Islamic political traditions. Like their mainland counterparts, Javanese monarchs possessed a sacred quality and maintained the balance between the sacred and the material world, but as Islam penetrated the Indonesian islands in the fifteenth and sixteenth centuries, the monarchs began to lose their semidivine quality.

The Islamic model was found mainly on the Malay Peninsula and along the coast of the Indonesian archipelago. In this pattern, the head of state was a sultan, who was viewed as a mortal, although he still possessed some magical qualities. The sultan served as a defender of the faith and staffed his bureaucracy mainly with aristocrats, but he also frequently relied on the Muslim community of scholars—the *ulama*—and was expected, at least in theory, to rule according to the *Shari'a*.

Economy and Society During the early period of European penetration, the economy of most Southeast Asian societies was based on agriculture, as it had been for thousands of years. Still, by the sixteenth century, commerce was beginning to affect daily life, especially in the cities that were beginning to proliferate along the coasts or on navigable rivers. In part, this was because agriculture itself was becoming more commercialized as cash crops like sugar and spices replaced subsistence farming of rice or other cereals in some areas.

Regional and interregional trade were already expanding before the coming of the Europeans. The central geographic location of Southeast Asia enabled it to become a focal point in a widespread trading network. Spices, of course, were the mainstay of the interregional trade, but other products were exchanged as well. The region exported tin (mined in Malaya since the tenth century), copper, gold, tropical fruits and other agricultural products, cloth, gems, and luxury goods in exchange for manufactured goods, ceramics, and high-quality textiles such as silk from China. Although on balance the region was an importer of manufactured goods, it produced some high-quality goods of its own. The ceramics of Vietnam and Thailand, though not made with the high-temperature firing techniques used in China, were still of good quality. The Portuguese traveler Duarte Barbosa (DWAR-tay bar-BOH-suh) observed that the Javanese were skilled cabinetmakers, weapons manufacturers, shipbuilders, and locksmiths. The royal courts were both the main producers and the primary consumers of luxury goods, most of which were produced by highly skilled slaves in the employ of the court.

In general, Southeast Asians probably enjoyed a somewhat higher living standard than their contemporaries elsewhere in Asia, and hunger was not a widespread problem. Several factors help explain this relative prosperity. In the first place, the region has been blessed with a salubrious climate. The uniformly high temperatures and the abundant rainfall enable farmers to grow two or even three crops each year. Second, although the soil in some areas is poor, the alluvial deltas on the mainland are fertile, and the volcanoes of Sumatra and Java periodically spew forth rich volcanic ash that renews the mineral resources of the soil on both islands. Finally, most of Southeast Asia was relatively thinly populated. According to one estimate, the population of the entire region in 1600 was about 20 million, or about 14 persons per square mile, well below levels elsewhere in Asia. Only in a few areas such as the Red River delta in northern Vietnam was overpopulation a serious problem.

CHRONOLOGIES

SPANISH AND PORTUGUESE ACTIVITIES IN THE AMERICAS

1492	Christopher Columbus's first voyage to the Americas
1500	Portuguese fleet arrives in Brazil
1502–1504	Columbus's last voyages
1519–1522	Spanish conquest of Mexico
1531–1536	Francisco Pizarro's conquest of the Inkas
1535	Viceroyalty of New Spain established
1549	Formal colonial administrative system established in Brazil

THE PENETRATION OF AFRICA

1394–1460	Life of Prince Henry the Navigator
1441	Portuguese ships reach the Senegal River
1487	Bartolomeu Dias sails around the tip of Africa
1518	First boatload of slaves to the Americas
1652	Dutch way station established at the Cape of Good Hope
1680	Ashanti kingdom established in West Africa
1698	Portuguese expelled from Mombasa

THE SPICE TRADE

1498	Vasco da Gama lands at Calicut in southwestern India
1510	Albuquerque establishes base at Goa

1511	Portuguese seize Malacca
1514	Portuguese ships land in southern China
1519–1522	Magellan's voyage around the world
1600	English East India Company established
1602	Dutch East India Company established
1608	English arrive at Surat in northwestern India
1619	Dutch fort established at Batavia
1641	Dutch seize Malacca from the Portuguese
1767	Burmese sack of Ayuthaya

 MindTap™

MindTap is a fully online, highly personalized learning experience built upon Cengage Learning content. MindTap combines student learning tools—readings, multimedia, activities, and assessments—into a singular Learning Path that guides students through their course.

15

EUROPE TRANSFORMED: REFORM AND STATE BUILDING

A nineteenth-century engraving showing Luther before the Diet of Worms

Art Resource, NY

CHAPTER OUTLINE

• The Reformation of the Sixteenth Century • Europe in Crisis, 1560–1650
  • Response to Crisis: The Practice of Absolutism • England and Limited
Monarchy • The Flourishing of European Culture

THE REFORMATION OF THE SIXTEENTH CENTURY

The **Protestant Reformation** is the name given to the religious reform movement that divided the Western Christian church into Catholic and Protestant groups. Although the Reformation began with Martin Luther in the early sixteenth century, several earlier developments had set the stage for religious change.

Background to the Reformation   Changes in the fifteenth century—the age of the Renaissance—helped prepare the way for the dramatic upheavals in sixteenth-century Europe.

The Growth of State Power   In the first half of the fifteenth century, European states had continued the disintegrative patterns of the previous century. In the second half of that century, however, recovery had set in, and attempts had been made to reestablish the centralized power of monarchical governments. To characterize the results, some historians have used the label "Renaissance states"; others have spoken of the "**new monarchies**," especially those of France, England, and Spain at the end of the fifteenth century.

What was new about these Renaissance monarchs was their concentration of royal authority, their attempts to suppress the nobility, their efforts to control the church in their lands, and their desire to obtain new sources of revenue in order to increase royal power and enhance the military forces at their disposal. Like the rulers of fifteenth-century Italian states, the Renaissance monarchs were often crafty men obsessed with the acquisition and expansion of political power. Of course, none of these characteristics was entirely new; a number of medieval monarchs, especially in the thirteenth century, had exhibited them. Nevertheless, the Renaissance period marks a significant expansion of centralized royal authority and a new preoccupation with the acquisition, maintenance, and expansion of political power.

Social Changes in the Renaissance   Social changes in the fifteenth century also helped to create an environment in which the Reformation of the sixteenth century could occur. After the severe economic reversals and social upheavals of the fourteenth century, the European economy gradually recovered as manufacturing and trade increased in volume. The Italians and especially the Venetians expanded their wealthy commercial empire, rivaled only by the increasingly powerful Hanseatic (han-see-AT-ik) League, a commercial and military alliance of north German coastal towns. Not until the sixteenth century, when overseas discoveries gave new importance to the states facing the Atlantic, did the Italian city-states begin to suffer from the competitive advantages of the more powerful national territorial states.

Society in the Middle Ages was divided into three estates: the clergy, or First Estate, whose preeminence was grounded in the belief that people should be guided to spiritual ends; the nobility, or Second Estate, whose privileges rested on the principle that nobles provided security and justice for society; and the peasants and inhabitants of the towns and cities, the Third Estate. Although this social order continued into the Renaissance, some changes also became evident.

Throughout much of Europe, the landholding nobles faced declining real incomes during most of the fourteenth and fifteenth centuries. Many members of the old nobility survived, however, and new blood also infused their ranks. In 1500, the nobles, old and new, who constituted between 2 and 3 percent of the population in most countries, still dominated society, as they had in the Middle Ages, holding important political posts and serving as advisers to the king.

Except in the heavily urban areas of northern Italy and Flanders, peasants made up the overwhelming mass of the Third Estate—they constituted 85 to 90 percent of the total European population. Serfdom had decreased as the manorial system continued its decline. Increasingly, the labor dues owed by peasants to their lord were converted into rents paid in money. By 1500, especially in western Europe, more and more peasants were becoming legally free. At the same time, peasants in many areas resented their social superiors and sought to keep a greater share of the benefits from their labor. In the sixteenth century, the grievances of peasants, especially in Germany, led many of them to support religious reform movements.

Inhabitants of towns and cities, originally merchants and artisans, constituted the remainder of the Third Estate. But by the fifteenth century, the Renaissance town or city had become more complex. At the top of urban society were the patricians, whose wealth from capitalistic enterprises in trade, industry, and banking enabled them to dominate their urban communities economically, socially, and politically. Below them were the petty burghers—the shopkeepers, artisans, guild-masters, and guildsmen—who were largely concerned with providing goods and services for local consumption. Below these two groups were the propertyless workers earning pitiful wages and the unemployed, living squalid and miserable lives. These poor city-dwellers made up 30 to 40 percent of the urban population. The pitiful conditions of the lower groups in urban society often led them to support calls for radical religious reform in the sixteenth century.

The Impact of Printing   The Renaissance witnessed the development of printing, which made an immediate impact on European intellectual life and thought. Printing from hand-carved wooden blocks had been done in the West since the twelfth century and in China even before that. What was new in the fifteenth century in Europe was multiple printing with movable metal type. The development of printing from movable type was a gradual process that culminated sometime between 1445 and 1450; Johannes Gutenberg (yoh-HAH-nuss GOO-ten-bayrk) of Mainz (MYNTS) played an important role in bringing the process to completion. Gutenberg's Bible, completed in 1455 or 1456, was the first true book produced from movable type.

By 1500, there were more than a thousand printers in Europe, who collectively had published almost 40,000 titles (between 8 million and 10 million copies). Probably half of these books were religious—Bibles and biblical commentaries, books of devotion, and sermons. Next in importance were the Latin and Greek classics, medieval grammars, legal handbooks, and works on philosophy.

The printing of books encouraged scholarly research and the desire to attain knowledge. Printing also stimulated the development of an ever-expanding lay reading public, a development that had an enormous impact on European society. Indeed, without the printing press, the new religious ideas of the Reformation would not have spread as rapidly as they did in the sixteenth century. Moreover, printing allowed European civilization to compete for the first time with the civilization of China.

Prelude to Reformation   During the second half of the fifteenth century, the new Classical learning of the Italian Renaissance spread to the European countries north of the Alps and spawned a movement called **Christian humanism** or **northern Renaissance humanism**, whose major goal was the reform of Christianity. The Christian humanists believed in the ability of human beings to reason and improve themselves and thought that through education in the sources of Classical, and especially Christian, antiquity, they could instill an inner piety or an inward religious feeling that would bring about a reform of the church and society. To change society, they must first change the human beings who compose it.

The most influential of all the Christian humanists was Desiderius Erasmus (dez-i-DEER-ee-uss i-RAZZ-mus) (1466–1536), who formulated and popularized the reform program of Christian humanism. He called his conception of religion "the philosophy of Christ," by which he meant that Christianity should be a guiding philosophy for the direction of daily life rather than the system of dogmatic beliefs and practices that the medieval church seemed to stress. In other words, he emphasized inner piety and de-emphasized the external forms of religion (such as the sacraments, pilgrimages, fasts, and relics). To Erasmus, the reform of the church meant spreading an understanding of the philosophy of Jesus, providing enlightened education in the sources of early Christianity, and criticizing the abuses in the church. No doubt his work helped prepare the way for the Reformation; as contemporaries proclaimed, "Erasmus laid the egg that Luther hatched."

Church and Religion on the Eve of the Reformation   Corruption in the Catholic Church was another factor that led people to want reform. Between 1450 and 1520, a series of popes—called the Renaissance popes—failed to meet the church's spiritual needs. The popes were supposed to be the spiritual leaders of the Catholic Church, but as rulers of the Papal States, they were all too often involved in worldly concerns. Julius II (1503–1513), the fiery "warrior-pope," personally led armies against his enemies, much to the disgust of pious Christians, who thought the pope's role was to serve as a spiritual leader. As one intellectual wrote, "How, O bishop standing in the room of the Apostles, dare you teach the people the things that pertain to war?" Many high church officials were also concerned with accumulating wealth and used their church offices as opportunities to advance their careers and their fortunes, and many ordinary parish priests seemed ignorant of their spiritual duties.

While the leaders of the church were failing to meet their responsibilities, ordinary people were clamoring for meaningful religious expression and certainty of salvation. As a result, for some the process of salvation became almost mechanical. As more and more people sought certainty of salvation through veneration of relics (bones or other objects intimately associated with the saints), collections of **relics** grew. Frederick the Wise, elector (one of the seven German princes who chose the Holy Roman Emperor) of Saxony and Martin Luther's prince, had amassed nearly 19,000 relics to which were attached **indulgences** that could reduce a person's time in purgatory by nearly 2 million years. (An indulgence is a remission, after death, of all or part of the punishment due to sin.) Other people sought certainty of salvation in more spiritual terms by participating in the popular mystical movement known as the Modern Devotion, which downplayed religious dogma and stressed the need to follow the teachings of Jesus.

What is striking about the revival of religious piety in the fifteenth century—whether expressed through such external forces as the veneration of relics and the buying of indulgences or the mystical path—was its adherence to the orthodox beliefs and practices of the Catholic Church. The agitation for certainty of salvation and spiritual peace occurred within the framework of the "holy mother Church." But disillusionment grew as the devout experienced the clergy's inability to live up to their expectations. The deepening of religious life, especially in the second half of the fifteenth century, found little echo among the worldly-wise clergy, and this environment helps explain the tremendous and immediate impact of Luther's ideas.

Martin Luther and the Reformation in Germany
Martin Luther (1483–1546) was a monk and a professor at the University of Wittenberg (VIT-ten-bayrk), where he lectured on the Bible. Probably sometime between 1513 and 1516, through his study of the Bible, he arrived at an answer to a problem—the assurance of salvation—that had disturbed him since his entry into the monastery.

Catholic doctrine had emphasized that both faith and good works were required for a Christian to achieve personal salvation. In Luther's eyes, human beings, weak and powerless in the sight of an almighty God, could never do enough good works to merit salvation. Through his study of the Bible, Luther came to believe that humans are saved not through their good works but through faith in the promises of God, made possible by the sacrifice of Jesus on the cross. This doctrine of salvation, or justification by grace through faith alone, became the primary doctrine of the Protestant Reformation (**justification by faith** is the act by which a person is made deserving of salvation). Because Luther had arrived at this doctrine from his study of the Bible, the Bible became for Luther, as for all other Protestants, the chief guide to religious truth.

Luther did not see himself as a rebel, but he was greatly upset by the widespread selling of indulgences. Especially offensive in his eyes was the monk Johann Tetzel, who hawked indulgences with the slogan "As soon as the coin in the coffer [money box] rings, the soul from purgatory springs." Greatly angered, in 1517 he issued a stunning indictment of the abuses in the sale of indulgences, known as the Ninety-Five Theses. Thousands of copies were printed and quickly spread to all parts of Germany.

By 1520, Luther had begun to move toward a more definite break with the Catholic Church and called on the German princes to overthrow the papacy in Germany and establish a reformed German church. Through all his calls for change, Luther expounded more and more on his new doctrine of salvation. It is faith alone, he said, not good works, that justifies and brings salvation through Christ.

Unable to accept Luther's ideas, the church excommunicated him in January 1521. He was also summoned to appear before the Reichstag (RYKHSS-tahk) (imperial diet) of the Holy Roman Empire, convened by the newly elected Emperor Charles V (1519–1556). Ordered to recant the heresies he had espoused, Luther refused and made the famous reply that became the battle cry of the Reformation:

> Unless I am convicted by Scripture and plain reason—I do not accept the authority of popes and councils, for they have contradicted each other—my conscience is captive to the Word of God. I cannot and I will not recant anything, for to go against conscience is neither right nor safe. Here I stand, I cannot do otherwise. God help me. Amen.[1]

Members of the Reichstag were outraged and demanded that Luther be arrested and delivered to the emperor. But Luther's ruler, Elector Frederick of Saxony, stepped in and protected him.

During the next few years, Luther's movement began to grow and spread. As it made an impact on the common people, it also created new challenges. This was especially true of the Peasants' War that erupted in 1524. Social discontent created by their pitiful conditions became entangled with religious revolt as the German peasants looked to Martin Luther for support. But when the peasants took up arms and revolted against their landlords, Luther turned against them and called on the German princes, who in Luther's eyes were ordained by God to maintain peace and order, to crush the rebels. By May 1525, the German princes had ruthlessly suppressed the peasant hordes. By this time, Luther found himself dependent on the state authorities for the growth of his reformed church.

Luther now succeeded in gaining the support of many of the rulers of the three hundred or so German states that made up the Holy Roman Empire. These rulers quickly took control of the churches in their territories. The Lutheran churches in Germany (and later in Scandinavia) became territorial or state churches in which the state supervised the affairs of the church. As part of the development of these state-dominated churches, Luther also instituted new religious services to replace the Catholic Mass. These focused on reading the Bible, preaching the word of God, and singing hymns. Following his own denunciation of clerical celibacy, Luther married a former nun, Katherina von Bora, in 1525. His union provided a model of married and family life for the new Protestant minister.

Politics and Religion in the German Reformation   From its very beginning, the fate of Luther's movement was closely tied to political affairs. In 1519, Charles I, king of Spain and the grandson of Emperor Maximilian, was elected Holy Roman Emperor as Charles V. Charles V ruled over an immense empire, consisting of Spain and its overseas possessions, the traditional Austrian Habsburg lands, Bohemia, Hungary, the Low Countries, and the kingdom of Naples in southern Italy. Politically, Charles wanted to maintain his enormous empire; religiously, he hoped to preserve the unity of his empire in the Catholic faith. A number of problems, however, kept him preoccupied and cost him both his dream and his health.

Moreover, the internal political situation in the Holy Roman Empire was not in Charles's favor. Although all the German states owed loyalty to the emperor, during the Middle Ages these states had become quite independent of imperial authority. By the time Charles V was able to bring military forces to Germany in 1546, Lutheranism had become well established and the Lutheran princes were well organized. Unable to defeat them, Charles was forced to negotiate a truce. An end to religious warfare in Germany came in 1555 with the Peace of Augsburg (OUKS-boork). The division of Christianity was formally acknowledged; Lutheran states were to have the same legal rights as Catholic states. Although the German states were now free to choose between Catholicism and Lutheranism, the peace settlement did not recognize the principle of religious toleration for individuals. The right of each German ruler to determine the religion of his subjects was accepted, but not the right of the subjects to choose their own religion. With the Peace of Augsburg, what had at first been merely feared was now certain: the ideal of Christian unity was forever lost. The rapid spread of new Protestant groups made this a certainty.

The Spread of the Protestant Reformation   Switzerland was home to two major Reformation movements, Zwinglianism and Calvinism. Ulrich Zwingli (OOL-rikh TSFING-lee) (1484–1531) was ordained a priest in 1506 and accepted an appointment as a cathedral priest in the Great Minster of Zürich (ZOOR-ik *or* TSIH-rikh) in 1518. Zwingli's preaching of the Gospel caused such unrest that in 1523 the city council held a public disputation (debate) in the town hall. Zwingli's party was accorded the victory, and over the next two years, evangelical reforms were promulgated in Zürich by a city council strongly influenced by Zwingli. Relics and images were abolished; all paintings and decorations were removed from the churches and replaced by whitewashed walls. The Mass was replaced by a new liturgy consisting of Scripture reading, prayer, and sermons. Monasticism, pilgrimages, the veneration of saints, clerical celibacy, and the pope's authority were all abolished as remnants of papal Christianity.

As his movement began to spread to other cities in Switzerland, Zwingli sought an alliance with Martin Luther and the German reformers. Although both the German and the Swiss reformers realized the need for unity to defend against the opposition of the Catholic authorities, they were unable to agree on the interpretation of the Lord's Supper, the sacrament of Communion. Zwingli believed that the scriptural words "This is my body, this is my blood" should be taken figuratively, not literally, and refused to accept Luther's insistence on the real presence of the body and blood of Jesus "in, with, and under the bread and wine." In October 1531, war erupted between the Swiss Protestant and Catholic states. Zürich's army was routed, and Zwingli was found wounded on the battlefield. His enemies killed him, cut up his body, burned the pieces, and scattered the ashes. The leadership of Swiss Protestantism now passed to John Calvin, the systematic theologian and organizer of the Protestant movement.

Calvin and Calvinism   John Calvin (1509–1564) was educated in his native France, but after converting to Protestantism, he was forced to flee to the safety of Switzerland. In 1536, he published the first edition of the *Institutes of the*

A Reformation Debate: Conflict at Marburg

RELIGION & PHILOSOPHY

Debates played a crucial role in the Reformation period. They were a primary instrument for introducing the Reformation in innumerable cities as well as a means of resolving differences among like-minded Protestant groups. This selection contains an excerpt from the vivacious and often brutal debate between Luther and Zwingli over the sacrament of the Lord's Supper at Marburg in 1529. The two protagonists failed to reach agreement.

The Marburg Colloquy, 1529

THE HESSIAN CHANCELLOR FEIGE: My gracious prince and lord [Landgrave Philip of Hesse] has summoned you for the express and urgent purpose of settling the dispute over the sacrament of the Lord's Supper.... Let everyone on both sides present his arguments in a spirit of moderation.... Now then, Doctor Luther, you may proceed.

LUTHER: Noble prince, gracious lord! Undoubtedly the colloquy is well intentioned.... Although I have no intention of changing my mind, which is firmly made up, I will nevertheless present the grounds of my belief and show where the others are in error.... Your basic contentions are these: In the last analysis you wish to prove that a body cannot be in two places at once, and you produce arguments about the unlimited body which are based on natural reason. I do not question how Christ can be God and man and how the two natures can be joined. For God is more powerful than all our ideas, and we must submit to his word.

Prove that Christ's body is not there where the Scripture says, "This is my body!" Rational proofs I will not listen to.... It is God who commands, "Take, eat, this is my body." I request, therefore, valid scriptural proof to the contrary.

ZWINGLI: I insist that the words of the Lord's Supper must be figurative. This is ever apparent, and even required by

Christian Religion, a masterful synthesis of Protestant thought that immediately secured his reputation as one of the new leaders of Protestantism.

On most important doctrines, Calvin stood very close to Luther. He adhered to the doctrine of justification by faith alone to explain how humans achieved salvation. But Calvin also placed much emphasis on the absolute sovereignty or allpowerful nature of God—what Calvin called the "power, grace, and glory of God." One of the ideas derived from his emphasis on the absolute sovereignty of God—**predestination**—gave a unique cast to Calvin's teachings. This "eternal decree," as Calvin called it, meant that God had predestined some people to be saved (the elect) and others to be damned (the reprobate). According to Calvin, "He has once for all determined, both whom He would admit to salvation, and whom He would condemn to destruction."[2] Although Calvin stressed that there could be no absolute certainty of salvation, his followers did not always make this distinction. The practical psychological effect of predestination was to give later the article of faith: "taken up into heaven, seated at the right hand of the Father." Otherwise, it would be absurd to look for him in the Lord's Supper at the same time that Christ is telling us that he is in heaven. One and the same body cannot possibly be in different places....

LUTHER: I call upon you as before: your basic contentions are shaky. Give way, and give glory to God!

ZWINGLI: And we call upon you to give glory to God and to quit begging the question! The issue at stake is this: Where is the proof of your position? I am willing to consider your words carefully—no harm meant! You're trying to outwit me.... You'll have to sing another tune.

LUTHER: You're being obnoxious.

ZWINGLI: (excitedly) Don't you believe that Christ was attempting in John 6 to help those who did not understand?

LUTHER: You're trying to dominate things! You insist on passing judgment! Leave that to someone else! ... It is your point that must be proved, not mine. But let us stop this sort of thing. It serves no purpose.

ZWINGLI: It certainly does! It is for you to prove that the passage in John 6 speaks of a physical repast.

LUTHER: You express yourself poorly and make about as much progress as a cane standing in a corner. You're going nowhere.

ZWINGLI: No, no, no! This is the passage that will break your neck!

LUTHER: Don't be so sure of yourself. Necks don't break this way. You're in Hesse, not Switzerland.

Q *How did the positions of Zwingli and Luther on the sacrament of the Lord's Supper differ? What was the purpose of this debate? Based on this example, why did many Reformation debates lead to further hostility rather than compromise and unity between religious and sectarian opponents? What implications did this have for the future of the Protestant Reformation?*

Source: "The Marburg Colloquy," edited by Donald Ziegler, from *Great Debates of the Reformation*, ed. Donald Ziegler, copyright © 1969 by Donald Ziegler.

Calvinists an unshakable conviction that they were doing God's work on earth, making Calvinism a dynamic and activist faith.

In 1536, Calvin began working to reform the city of Geneva. He was able to fashion a tightly organized church order that employed both clergy and laymen in the service of the church. The Consistory, a special body for enforcing moral discipline, functioned as a court to oversee the moral life, daily behavior, and doctrinal orthodoxy of Genevans and to admonish and correct deviants. Citizens in Geneva were punished for such varied "crimes" as dancing, singing obscene songs, drunkenness, swearing, and playing cards.

Calvin's success in Geneva enabled the city to become a vibrant center of Protestantism. Following Calvin's lead, missionaries trained in Geneva were sent to all parts of Europe. Calvinism became established in France, the Netherlands, Scotland, and central and eastern Europe, and by the mid-sixteenth century, Calvin's Geneva stood as the fortress of the Reformation.

The English Reformation   The English Reformation was rooted in politics, not religion. King Henry VIII (1509–1547) had a strong desire to divorce his first wife, Catherine of Aragon, with whom he had a daughter, Mary, but no male heir. The king wanted to marry Anne Boleyn (BUH-lin *or* buh-LIN), with whom he had fallen in love. Impatient with the pope's unwillingness to grant him an annulment of his marriage, Henry turned to England's own church courts. As archbishop of Canterbury and head of the highest church court in England, Thomas Cranmer ruled in May 1533 that the king's marriage to Catherine was "absolutely void." At the beginning of June, Anne was crowned queen, and three months later, a child was born; much to the king's disappointment, the baby was a girl (the future Queen Elizabeth I).

In 1534, at Henry's request, Parliament moved to finalize the break of the Church of England with Rome. The Act of Supremacy of 1534 declared that the king was "the only supreme head on earth of the Church of England," a position that gave him control of doctrine, clerical appointments, and discipline. Although Henry VIII had broken with the papacy, little change occurred in matters of doctrine, theology, and ceremony. Some of his supporters, including Archbishop Cranmer, sought a religious reformation as well as an administrative one, but Henry was unyielding. But he died in 1547 and was succeeded by his son, the underage and sickly Edward VI (1547–1553), and during Edward's reign, Cranmer and others inclined toward Protestant doctrines were able to move the Church of England (or Anglican Church) in a more Protestant direction. New acts of Parliament gave the clergy the right to marry and created a new Protestant church service.

Edward VI was succeeded by Mary (1553–1558), a Catholic who attempted to return England to Catholicism. Her actions aroused much anger, however, especially when "bloody Mary" burned more than three hundred Protestant heretics. By the end of Mary's reign, England was more Protestant than it had been at the beginning.

The Anabaptists   The Anabaptists were the radical reformers of the Protestant Reformation. To Anabaptists, the true Christian church was a voluntary association of believers who had undergone spiritual rebirth and had then been baptized into the church. Anabaptists advocated adult rather than infant baptism. They also wanted to return to the practices and spirit of early Christianity and considered all believers to be equal. Each church chose its own minister, who might be any member of the community since all Christians were considered priests (though women were often excluded).

Finally, unlike the Catholics and other Protestants, most Anabaptists believed in the complete separation of church and state. Government was to be excluded from the realm of religion and could not exercise political jurisdiction over real Christians. Anabaptists refused to hold political office or bear arms because many took the commandment "Thou shall not kill" literally. Their political beliefs as much as their religious beliefs caused the Anabaptists to be regarded as dangerous radicals who threatened the very fabric of sixteenth-century society. Indeed, the chief thing Protestants and Catholics could agree on was the need to persecute Anabaptists.

The Social Impact of the Protestant Reformation

The Protestants were especially important in developing a new view of the family. Because Protestantism had eliminated any idea of special holiness for celibacy and had abolished both monasticism and a celibate clergy, the family could be placed at the center of human life, and a new stress on "mutual love between man and wife" could be extolled.

But were doctrine and reality the same? Most often, reality reflected the traditional roles of husband as the ruler and wife as the obedient servant whose chief duty was to please her husband. Luther stated it clearly:

> The rule remains with the husband, and the wife is compelled to obey him by God's command. He rules the home and the state, wages war, defends his possessions, tills the soil, builds, plants, etc. The woman on the other hand is like a nail driven into the wall ... so the wife should stay at home and look after the affairs of the household, as one who has been deprived of the ability of administering those affairs that are outside and that concern the state. She does not go beyond her most personal duties.[3]

Obedience to her husband was not a wife's only role; her other important duty was to bear children. To Calvin and Luther, this function of women was part of the divine plan, and for most Protestant women, family life was their only destiny. Overall, the Protestant Reformation did not noticeably alter women's subordinate place in society.

The Catholic Reformation

By the mid-sixteenth century, Lutheranism had become established in Germany and Scandinavia and Calvinism in Scotland, Switzerland, France, the Netherlands, and eastern Europe. In England, the split from Rome had resulted in the creation of a national church. The situation in Europe did not look particularly favorable for the Roman Catholic Church.

Catholic Reformation or Counter-Reformation?

There is no doubt that the Catholic Church underwent a revitalization in the sixteenth century. But was this reformation a **Catholic Reformation** or a Counter-Reformation? Some historians prefer the term *Counter-Reformation* to focus on the aspects that were a direct reaction against the Protestant movement. Historians who prefer the term *Catholic Reformation* point out that elements of reform were already present in the Catholic Church at the end of the fifteenth century and the beginning of the sixteenth century. Especially noticeable were the calls for reform from the religious orders of the Franciscans, Dominicans, and Augustinians. Members of these groups put particular emphasis on preaching to laypeople. Another example was the Oratory of Divine Love, first organized in Italy in 1497 as an informal group of clergy and laymen who worked to foster reform by emphasizing personal spiritual development and outward acts of charity. The Oratory's members included a Spanish archbishop, Cardinal Ximenes (khee-MAY-ness), who was especially active in using Christian humanism to reform the church in Spain.

No doubt, both positions on the nature of the reformation of the Catholic Church contain elements of truth. The Catholic Reformation revived the best features of medieval Catholicism and then adjusted them to meet new conditions, as is most apparent in the emergence of a new mysticism, closely tied to the traditions

COMPARATIVE ESSAY

Marriage in the Early Modern World

Marriage is an ancient institution. In China, myths about the beginnings of Chinese civilization maintained that the rite of marriage began with the primordial couple Fuxi and Nugun and that marriage actually preceded such discoveries as fire, farming, and medicine. In the early modern world, family and marriage were inseparable and were at the center of all civilizations.

In the early modern period, the family was still at the heart of Europe's social organization. For the most part, people viewed the family in traditional terms, as a patriarchal institution in which the husband dominated his wife and children. The upper classes in particular thought of the family as a "house," an association whose collective interests were more important than those of its individual members. Parents (especially the fathers) generally selected marriage partners for their children, based on the interests of the family. When the son of a French noble asked about his upcoming marriage, his father responded, "Mind your own business." Details were worked out well in advance, sometimes when children were only two or three years old, and were set out in a legally binding contract. An important negotiating point was the size of the dowry, money presented by the bride's family to the groom upon marriage. The dowry could be a large sum, and all families were expected to provide dowries for their daughters.

Arranged marriages were not unique to Europe but were common throughout the world. In China, marriages were normally arranged for the benefit of the family, often by a go-between, and the groom and bride were usually not consulted. Frequently, they did not meet until the marriage ceremony. Love was obviously not a reason for marriage and in fact was often viewed as a detriment because it could distract the married couple from their responsibility to the larger family unit. In Japan too, marriages were arranged, often by the heads of dominant families in rural areas, and the new wife moved in with the family of her husband. In India, not only were marriages arranged, but it was not uncommon for women to be married before the age of ten. In colonial Latin America, parents selected marriage partners for their children and often chose a dwelling for the couple as well. In many areas, before members of the lower classes could marry, they had to offer gifts to the powerful noble landowners in the region and obtain their permission. These nobles often refused to allow women to marry in order to keep them as servants.

Arranged marriages were the logical result of a social system in which men dominated and women's primary role was to bear children, manage the household, and work in the field. Not until the nineteenth century did a feminist movement emerge in Europe to improve the rights of women. By the beginning of the twentieth century, that movement had spread to other parts of the world. The New Culture Movement in China, for example, advocated the free choice of spouses. Although the trend throughout the world is toward allowing people to choose their mates, in some areas, especially in rural communities, families remain active in choosing marriage partners.

Q *In what ways were marriage practices similar in the West and the East during the early modern period? Were there any significant differences?*

MAP 15.1   Catholics and Protestants in Europe by 1560

The Reformation continued to evolve beyond the basic split of the Lutherans from the Catholics. Several Protestant sects broke away from the teachings of Martin Luther, each with a separate creed and different ways of worship. In England, Henry VIII broke with the Catholic Church for political and dynastic reasons.

of Catholic piety, and the revival of monasticism through the regeneration of older religious orders and the founding of new orders.

The Society of Jesus   Of all the new religious orders, the most important was the Society of Jesus, known as the Jesuits, founded by a Spanish nobleman, Ignatius of Loyola (if-NAY-schuss of loi-OH-luh) (1491–1556). Loyola brought together a small group of individuals who were recognized as a religious order by the pope in 1540. The new order was grounded on the principles of absolute obedience to the papacy, a strict hierarchical order for the society, the use of education to achieve its goals, and a dedication to engage in "conflict for God." A special vow of absolute obedience to the pope made the Jesuits an important instrument for papal policy. Jesuit missionaries proved singularly successful in restoring Catholicism to parts of Germany and eastern Europe.

Another prominent Jesuit activity was the propagation of the Catholic faith among non-Christians. Francis Xavier (ZAY-vee-ur) (1506–1552), one of the original members of the Society of Jesus, carried the message of Catholic Christianity to the East. After attracting tens of thousands of converts in India, he traveled to Malacca and the Moluccas before finally reaching Japan in 1549. He spoke highly of the Japanese: "They are a people of excellent morals—good in general and not malicious."[4] Thousands of Japanese, especially in the southernmost islands, became Christians. In 1552, Xavier set out for China but died of fever before he reached the mainland.

Although conversion efforts in Japan proved short-lived, Jesuit activity in China, especially that of the Italian Matteo Ricci (ma-TAY-oh REE-chee), was more long-lasting. Recognizing the Chinese pride in their own culture, the Jesuits attempted to draw parallels between Christian and Confucian concepts and to show the similarities between Christian morality and Confucian ethics. For their part, the missionaries were much impressed with many aspects of Chinese civilization, and reports of their experiences heightened European curiosity about this great society on the other side of the world.

A Reformed Papacy   A reformed papacy was another important factor in the development of the Catholic Reformation. The involvement of Renaissance popes in dubious finances and Italian political and military affairs had created numerous sources of corruption. It took the jolt of the Protestant Reformation to bring about serious reform. Pope Paul III (1534–1549) perceived the need for change and took the audacious step of appointing a reform commission to ascertain the church's ills. The commission's report in 1537 blamed the church's problems on the corrupt policies of popes and cardinals. Paul III also formally recognized the Jesuits and summoned the Council of Trent.

The Council of Trent   In March 1545, a group of high church officials met in the city of Trent on the border between Germany and Italy and initiated the Council of Trent, which met intermittently from 1545 to 1563 in three major sessions. The final decrees of the Council of Trent reaffirmed traditional Catholic teachings in opposition to Protestant beliefs. Scripture and tradition were affirmed as equal authorities in religious matters; only the church could interpret Scripture. Both faith and good works were declared necessary for salvation. Belief in purgatory and in the use of indulgences was strengthened, although the selling of indulgences was prohibited.

After the Council of Trent, the Roman Catholic Church possessed a clear body of doctrine and a unified structure under the acknowledged supremacy of the popes. Although the Roman Catholic Church had become one Christian denomination among many, the church entered a new phase of its history with a spirit of confidence.

EUROPE IN CRISIS, 1560–1650

Between 1560 and 1650, Europe experienced religious wars, revolutions and constitutional crises, economic and social disintegration, and a witchcraft craze. It was truly an age of crisis.

Politics and the Wars of Religion in the Sixteenth Century   By 1560, Calvinism and Catholicism had become activist religions dedicated to spreading the word of God as they interpreted it. Although their struggle for the minds and hearts of Europeans was at the heart of the religious wars of the sixteenth century, economic, social, and political forces also played important roles in these conflicts.

The French Wars of Religion (1562–1598)   Religion was central to the French civil wars of the sixteenth century. The growth of Calvinism had led to persecution by the French kings, but the latter did little to stop the spread of Calvinism. Huguenots (**HYOO-guh-nots**), as the French Calvinists were called, constituted only about 7 percent of the population, but 40 to 50 percent of the French nobility became Huguenots, including the house of Bourbon (**boor-BOHN**), which stood next to the Valois (**val-WAH**) in the royal line of succession. The conversion of so many nobles made the Huguenots a potentially dangerous political threat to monarchical power. Still, the Calvinist minority was greatly outnumbered by the Catholic majority, and the Valois monarchy was staunchly Catholic.

The religious issue was not the only factor that contributed to the French civil wars. Towns and provinces, which had long resisted the growing power of monarchical centralization, were only too willing to join a revolt against the monarchy. So were the nobles, and the fact that so many of them were Calvinists created an important base of opposition to the crown.

For thirty years, battles raged in France between Catholic and Calvinist parties. Finally, in 1589, Henry of Navarre, the political leader of the Huguenots and a member of the Bourbon Dynasty, succeeded to the throne as Henry IV (1589–1610). Realizing, however, that he would never be accepted by Catholic France, Henry converted to Catholicism. With his coronation in 1594, the Wars of Religion had finally come to an end. The Edict of Nantes (**NAHNT**) in 1598 solved the religious problem by acknowledging Catholicism as the official religion of France while guaranteeing the Huguenots the right to worship and to enjoy all political privileges, including the holding of public offices.

Philip II and Militant Catholicism   The greatest advocate of militant Catholicism in the second half of the sixteenth century was King Philip II of Spain (1556–1598), the son and heir of Charles V. Philip's reign ushered in an age of Spanish greatness, both politically and culturally. Philip had inherited from his father Spain, the Netherlands, and possessions in Italy and the Americas. To strengthen his control, Philip insisted on strict conformity to Catholicism and strong monarchical authority. Achieving the latter was not an easy task, because each of the lands of his empire had its own structure of government.

The Catholic faith was crucial to the Spanish people and their ruler. Driven by a heritage of crusading fervor, Spain saw itself as a nation of people chosen by God to save Catholic Christianity from the Protestant heretics. Philip II, the "most Catholic king," became the champion of Catholicism throughout Europe. Spain's leadership of a "holy league" against Turkish encroachments in the Mediterranean resulted in a stunning victory over the Turkish fleet in the Battle of Lepanto (LEH-pahn-toh *or* LIH-pan-toh) in 1571. But Philip's problems with the Netherlands and the English Queen Elizabeth led to his greatest misfortunes.

Philip's attempt to strengthen his control in the Spanish Netherlands, which consisted of seventeen provinces (modern Netherlands and Belgium), soon led to a revolt. The nobles, who stood to lose the most politically, strongly opposed Philip's efforts. Religion also became a major catalyst for rebellion when Philip attempted to crush Calvinism. Violence erupted in 1566, and the revolt became organized, especially in the northern provinces, where the Dutch, under the leadership of William of Nassau, the prince of Orange, offered growing resistance. The struggle dragged on for decades until 1609, when a twelve-year truce ended the war, virtually recognizing the independence of the northern provinces. These seven northern provinces, which called themselves the United Provinces of the Netherlands, became the core of the modern Dutch state.

To most Europeans at the beginning of the seventeenth century, Spain still seemed the greatest power of the age, but the reality was quite different. The Spanish treasury was empty, the armed forces were obsolescent, and the government was inefficient. Spain continued to play the role of a great power, but real power had shifted to England.

The England of Elizabeth   When Elizabeth Tudor, the daughter of Henry VIII and Anne Boleyn, ascended the throne in 1558, England was home to fewer than 4 million people. Yet during her reign (1558–1603), the small island kingdom became the leader of the Protestant nations of Europe and laid the foundations for a world empire.

Intelligent, cautious, and self-confident, Elizabeth moved quickly to solve the difficult religious problem she inherited from her half-sister, Queen Mary. Elizabeth's religious policy was based on moderation and compromise. She repealed the Catholic laws of Mary's reign, and a new Act of Supremacy designated Elizabeth as "the only supreme governor" of both church and state. The Church

Queen Elizabeth I: "I Have the Heart of a King"

POLITICS & GOVERNMENT

Queen Elizabeth I ruled England from 1558 to 1603 with a consummate skill that contemporaries considered unusual in a woman. Though shrewd and paternalistic, Elizabeth's power, like that of other sixteenth-century monarchs, depended on the favor of her people. When England was faced with the threat of an invasion by the armada of Philip II, Elizabeth sought to rally her troops with a speech in Tilbury, a town on the Thames River. This selection is taken from her speech.

Queen Elizabeth I, Speech at Tilbury

My loving people, we have been persuaded by some, that are careful of our safety, to take heed how we commit ourselves to armed multitudes, for fear of treachery; but I assure you, I do not desire to live to distrust my faithful and loving people. Let tyrants fear; I have always so behaved myself that, under God, I have placed my chiefest strength and safeguard in the loyal hearts and good will of my subjects. And therefore I am come amongst you at this time, not as for my recreation or sport, but being resolved, in the midst and heat of the battle, to live or dies amongst you all; to lay down, for my God, and for my kingdom, and for my people, my honor and my blood, even the dust. I know I have but the body of a weak and feeble woman; but I have the heart of a king, and of a king of England, too; and think foul scorn that Parma or Spain, or any prince of Europe, should dare to invade the borders of my realms: to which, rather than any dishonor should grow by me, I myself will take up arms; I myself will be your general, judge, and rewarder of every one of your virtues in the field. I know already, by your forwardness, that you have deserved rewards and crowns; and we do assure you, on the word of a prince, they shall be duly paid you. In the mean my lieutenant general shall be in my stead, than whom never princes commanded a more noble and worthy subject; not doubting by your obedience to my general, by your concern in the camp and by your valor in the field, we shall shortly have a famous victory over the enemies of my God, of my kingdom, and of my people.

Q *What qualities evident in Elizabeth's speech would have endeared her to her listeners? How was her popularity connected to the events of the late sixteenth century?*

Source: From Elizabeth I's Speech at Tillbury in 1588 to the troops.

of England under Elizabeth was basically Protestant, but it was of a moderate bent that kept most people satisfied.

Elizabeth proved as adept in government and foreign policy as in religious affairs. Assisted by competent officials, she handled Parliament with much skill. Caution and moderation also dictated Elizabeth's foreign policy. Nevertheless, Elizabeth was gradually drawn into conflict with Spain. Having resisted for years the idea of invading England as too impractical, Philip II of Spain was finally persuaded to do so by advisers who assured him that the people of England would rise against their queen when the Spaniards arrived. A successful invasion of England would mean the overthrow of heresy and the return of England to Catholicism.

Philip ordered preparations for a fleet of warships, the *armada*, to spearhead the invasion of England.

The armada was a disaster. The Spanish fleet that finally set sail had neither the ships nor the manpower that Philip had planned to send. Battered by a number of encounters with the English, the Spanish fleet sailed back to Spain by a northward route around Scotland and Ireland, where it was further pounded by storms. Although the English and Spanish would continue their war for another sixteen years, the defeat of the armada guaranteed for the time being that England would remain a Protestant country.

Economic and Social Crises   The period of European history from 1560 to 1650 witnessed severe economic and social crises as well as political upheaval. Economic contraction began to be evident in some parts of Europe by the 1620s. In the 1630s and 1640s, as imports of silver from the Americas declined, economic recession intensified, especially in the Mediterranean area. Once the industrial and financial center of Europe in the age of the Renaissance, Italy was now becoming an economic backwater.

Population Decline   Population trends of the sixteenth and seventeenth centuries also reveal Europe's worsening conditions. The population of Europe increased from 60 million in 1500 to 85 million by 1600, the first major recovery of the European population since the devastation of the Black Death in the mid-fourteenth century. By 1650, however, records indicate that the population had declined, especially in central and southern Europe. Europe's longtime adversaries—war, famine, and plague—continued to affect population levels. After the middle of the sixteenth century, another "little ice age," when average temperatures fell, reduced harvests and led to food shortages. Europe's problems created social tensions, some of which became manifested in an obsession with witches.

Witchcraft Mania   Hysteria over witchcraft affected the lives of many Europeans in the sixteenth and seventeenth centuries. Perhaps more than 100,000 people were prosecuted throughout Europe on charges of witchcraft. As more and more people were brought to trial, the fear of witches, as well as the fear of being accused of witchcraft, escalated to frightening levels.

Common people—usually those who were poor and without property—were more likely to be accused of witchcraft. Indeed, where lists are available, those mentioned most often are milkmaids, peasant women, and servant girls. In the witchcraft trials of the sixteenth and seventeenth centuries, more than 75 percent of the accused were women, most of them single or widowed and many over fifty years old.

That women should be the chief victims of witchcraft trials was hardly accidental. Nicholas Rémy (nee-koh-LAH ray-MEE), a witchcraft judge in France in the 1590s, found it "not unreasonable that this scum of humanity, i.e., witches, should be drawn chiefly from the feminine sex." To another judge, it came as no surprise that witches would confess to sexual experiences with Satan: "The Devil uses them so, because he knows that women love carnal pleasures, and he means to bind them to his allegiance by such agreeable provocations."[5]

By the mid-seventeenth century, the witchcraft hysteria had begun to subside. As governments grew stronger, fewer magistrates were willing to accept the unsettling and divisive conditions generated by the trials of witches. Moreover, by the end of the seventeenth century and the beginning of the eighteenth, more and more people were questioning their old attitudes toward religion and found it especially contrary to reason to believe in the old view of a world haunted by evil spirits.

Economic Trends in the Seventeenth Century   In the course of the seventeenth century, new economic trends also emerged. **Mercantilism** is the name historians apply to the economic practices of the seventeenth century. According to the mercantilists, the prosperity of a nation depended on a plentiful supply of bullion (gold and silver). For this reason, it was desirable to achieve a favorable balance of trade in which goods exported were of greater value than those imported, promoting an influx of gold and silver payments that would increase the quantity of bullion. Furthermore, to encourage exports, governments should stimulate and protect export industries and trade by granting trade monopolies, encouraging investment in new industries through subsidies, importing foreign artisans, and improving transportation systems by building roads, bridges, and canals. By imposing high tariffs on foreign goods, they could reduce imports and prevent them from competing with domestic industries. Colonies were also deemed valuable as sources of raw materials and markets for finished goods.

Mercantilist theory on the role of colonies was matched in practice by Europe's overseas expansion. With the development of colonies and trading posts in the Americas and the East, Europeans embarked on an adventure in international commerce in the seventeenth century. Although some historians speak of a nascent world economy, we should remember that local, regional, and intra-European trade still predominated. At the end of the seventeenth century, for example, English imports totaled 360,000 tons, but only 5,000 tons came from the East Indies. What made the transoceanic trade rewarding, however, was not the volume but the value of its goods. Dutch, English, and French merchants were bringing back products that were still consumed largely by the wealthy but were beginning to make their way into the lives of artisans and merchants. Pepper and spices from the Indies, West Indian and Brazilian sugar, and Asian coffee and tea were becoming more readily available to European consumers.

The commercial expansion of the sixteenth and seventeenth centuries was made easier by new forms of commercial organization, especially the **joint-stock company**. Individuals bought shares in a company and received dividends on their investment while a board of directors ran the company and made the important business decisions. The return on investments could be spectacular. During its first ten years, investors received 30 percent annually on their money from the Dutch East India Company, which opened the Spice Islands and Southeast Asia to Dutch activity. The joint-stock company made it easier to raise large amounts of capital for world trading ventures.

Despite the growth of commercial capitalism, most of the European economy still depended on an agricultural system that had experienced few changes since the thirteenth century. At least 80 percent of Europeans still worked on the land. Almost all of the peasants in western Europe were free of serfdom, although many still owed a variety of feudal dues to the nobility. Despite the expanding markets and rising prices, European peasants saw little or no improvement in their lot as they faced increased rents and fees and higher taxes imposed by the state.

Seventeenth-Century Crises: Revolution and War   During the first half of the seventeenth century, a series of rebellions and civil wars rocked the domestic stability of many European governments. A devastating war that affected much of Europe also added to the sense of crisis.

The Thirty Years' War (1618–1648)   The Thirty Years' War began in 1618 in the Germanic lands of the Holy Roman Empire as a struggle between Catholic forces, led by the Habsburg Holy Roman Emperors, and Protestant—primarily Calvinist—nobles in Bohemia who rebelled against Habsburg authority. What began as a struggle over religious issues soon became a wider conflict perpetuated by political motivations as both minor and major European powers—Denmark, Sweden, France, and Spain—entered the war. The competition for European leadership

© Cengage Learning 2013

MAP 15.2 Europe in the Seventeenth Century

This map shows Europe at the time of the Thirty Years' War (1618–1648). Although the struggle began in Bohemia and much of the fighting took place in the Germanic lands of the Holy Roman Empire, the conflict became a Europe-wide struggle.

between the Bourbon dynasty of France and the Habsburg dynasties of Spain and the Holy Roman Empire was an especially important factor. Nevertheless, most of the battles were fought on German soil.

The war in Germany was officially ended in 1648 by the Peace of Westphalia, which proclaimed that all German states, including the Calvinist ones, were free to determine their own religion. The major contenders gained new territories, and France emerged as the dominant nation in Europe. The more than three hundred entities that made up the Holy Roman Empire were recognized as independent states, and each was given the power to conduct its own foreign policy; this brought an end to the Holy Roman Empire and ensured German disunity for another two hundred years. The Peace of Westphalia made it clear that political motives, not religious convictions, had become the guiding force in public affairs.

Was There a Military Revolution?   By the seventeenth century, war played an increasingly important role in European affairs. Military power was considered essential to a ruler's reputation and power; thus, the pressure to build an effective military machine was intense. Some historians believe that the changes that occurred in the science of warfare between 1560 and 1650 warranted the title of military revolution.

Medieval warfare, with its mounted knights and supplementary archers, had been transformed in the Renaissance by the employment of infantry armed with pikes and halberds (long-handled weapons combining an axe with a spike) and arranged in massed rectangles known as squadrons or battalions. The use of firearms required adjustments to the size and shape of the massed infantry and made the cavalry less effective.

It was Gustavus Adolphus (goo-STAY-vus uh-DAHL-fuss), the king of Sweden (1611–1632), who developed the first standing army of conscripts, notable for the flexibility of its tactics. The infantry brigades of Gustavus's army were composed of equal numbers of musketeers and pikemen, standing six men deep. They employed the salvo, in which all rows of the infantry fired at once instead of row by row. These salvos of fire, which cut up the massed ranks of the opposing infantry squadrons, were followed by a pike charge, giving the infantry a primarily offensive deployment. Gustavus also used his cavalry in a more mobile fashion. After shooting a pistol volley, they charged the enemy with their swords. Additional flexibility was obtained by using lighter artillery pieces that were more easily moved during battle. All of these innovations required coordination, careful training, and better discipline, forcing rulers to move away from undisciplined mercenary forces. Naturally, the success of Gustavus Adolphus led to imitation.

Some historians have questioned the use of the phrase "military revolution" to describe the military changes from 1560 to 1660, arguing instead that military developments were gradual. In any case, for the rest of the seventeenth century, warfare continued to change. Standing armies, based partly on conscription, grew ever larger and more expensive. Standing armies necessitated better-disciplined and better-trained soldiers and led to the education of officers in military schools. Armies also introduced the use of linear rather than square formations to provide greater flexibility and mobility in tactics. There was also an increased use of fire-arms as the musket with attached bayonet increasingly replaced the pike in the ranks of the infantry. A naval arms race in the seventeenth century led to more and bigger warships or capital ships known as "ships of the line."

Larger armies and navies could be maintained only by levying heavier taxes, making war a greater economic burden and an ever more important part of the early modern European state. The creation of large bureaucracies to super-vise the military resources of the state led to growth in the power of state governments.

RESPONSE TO CRISIS: THE PRACTICE OF ABSOLUTISM

Many people responded to the crises of the seventeenth century by searching for order. An increase in monarchical power became an obvious means for achieving stability. The result was what historians have called absolutism or absolute monar-chy, in which the sovereign power or ultimate authority in the state rested in the hands of a king who claimed to rule by divine right—the idea that kings received their power from God and were responsible to no one but God. Late-sixteenth-century political theorists believed that sovereign power consisted of the authority to make laws, levy taxes, administer justice, control the state's administra-tive system, and determine foreign policy.

France Under   France during the reign of Louis XIV (1643–1715) has tradi-
Louis XIV   tionally been regarded as the best example of the practice of
                     absolute or **divine-right monarchy** in the seventeenth cen-
tury. French culture, language, and manners reached into all levels of European society. French diplomacy and wars overwhelmed the political affairs of western and central Europe. The court of Louis XIV seemed to be imitated everywhere in Europe.

Political Institutions   One of the keys to Louis's power was his control of the cen-tral policy-making machinery of government because it was part of his own court and household. The royal court, located in the magnificent palace at Versailles (vayr-SY), outside Paris, served three purposes simultaneously: it was the personal household of the king, the location of central governmental machinery, and the place where powerful subjects came to find favors and offices for themselves and their clients. The greatest danger to Louis's personal rule came from the very high nobles and princes of the blood (the royal princes), who considered it their natural function to assert the policy-making role of royal ministers. Louis eliminated this threat by removing them from the royal council, the chief administrative body of the king, and enticing them to his court, where he could keep them preoccupied with court life and out of politics. Instead of the high nobility and royal princes, Louis relied for his ministers on nobles who came from relatively new aristocratic families. His ministers were expected to be subservient: "I had no intention of shar-ing my authority with them," Louis said.

Court life at Versailles itself became highly ritualized with Louis at the center of it all. The king had little privacy; only when he visited his wife or mother or mistress was he free of the noble courtiers who swarmed about the palace. Most daily ceremonies were carefully staged, including those attending Louis's rising from bed, dining, praying, attending Mass, and going to bed. A mob of nobles aspired to assist the king in carrying out these solemn activities. It was considered a great honor for a noble to be chosen to hand the king his shirt while dressing. Court etiquette was also a complex matter. Nobles and royal princes were arranged in an elaborate order of seniority and expected to follow certain rules of precedence. Who could sit down and on what kind of chair was a subject of much debate.

Louis's domination of his ministers and secretaries gave him control of the central policy-making machinery of government and thus authority over the traditional areas of monarchical power: the formulation of foreign policy, the making of war and peace, the assertion of the secular power of the crown against any religious authority, and the ability to levy taxes to fulfill these functions. Louis had considerably less success with the internal administration of the kingdom, however. The traditional groups and institutions of French society—the nobles, officials, town councils, guilds, and representative estates in some provinces—were simply too powerful for the king to have direct control over the lives of his subjects. As a result, control of the provinces and the people was achieved largely by bribing the individuals responsible for carrying out the king's policies.

The Economy and the Military The cost of building palaces, maintaining his court, and pursuing his wars made finances a crucial issue for Louis XIV. He was most fortunate in having the services of Jean-Baptiste Colbert (ZHAHN-bap-TEEST kohl-BAYR) (1619–1683) as his controller general of finances. Colbert sought to increase the wealth and power of France through general adherence to mercantilism, which advocated government intervention in economic activities for the benefit of the state. To decrease imports and increase exports, Colbert granted subsidies to individuals who established new industries. To improve communications and the transportation of goods internally, he built roads and canals. To decrease imports directly, Colbert raised tariffs on foreign goods.

The increase in royal power that Louis pursued led the king to develop a professional army numbering 100,000 men in peacetime and 400,000 in time of war. To achieve the prestige and military glory befitting an absolute king as well as to ensure the domination of his Bourbon dynasty over European affairs, Louis waged four wars between 1667 and 1713. His ambitions roused much of Europe to form coalitions against him to prevent the certain destruction of the European balance of power by Bourbon hegemony. Although Louis added some territory to France's northeastern frontier and established a member of his own Bourbon dynasty on the throne of Spain, he also left France impoverished and surrounded by enemies.

Absolutism in Central and Eastern Europe During the seventeenth century, a development of great importance for the modern Western world took place with the appearance in central and eastern Europe of three new powers: Prussia, Austria, and Russia.

COMPARATIVE ILLUSTRATION

Sun Kings, West and East

POLITICS & GOVERNMENT

At the end of the seventeenth century, two powerful rulers held sway in kingdoms that dominated the affairs of the regions around them. Both rulers saw themselves as favored by divine authority—Louis XIV of France as a divine-right monarch and Kangxi (GANG-zhee) of China as possessing the mandate of Heaven. Thus, both rulers saw themselves not as divine beings but as divinely ordained beings whose job was to govern organized societies. In the photo below, Louis, who ruled France from 1643 to 1715, is seen in a portrait by Hyacinthe Rigaud (ee-ah-SANT ree-GOH) that captures the king's sense of

RMN-Grand Palais/Art Resource, NY

Prussia Frederick William the Great Elector (1640–1688) laid the foundation for the Prussian state. Realizing that the land he had inherited, known as Brandenburg-Prussia, was a small, open territory with no natural frontiers for defense, Frederick William built an army of 40,000 men, making it the fourth largest in Europe. To sustain the army, Frederick William established the General War Commissariat to

Hu Weibiao/Panorama/The Image Works

royal dignity and grandeur. One person at court said of the king: "Louis XIV's vanity was without limit or restraint." At the top, Kangxi, who ruled China from 1661 to 1722, is seen in a portrait that shows him seated in majesty on his imperial throne. A dedicated ruler, Kangxi once wrote, "One act of negligence may cause sorrow all through the country, and one moment of negligence may result in trouble for hundreds and thousands of generations."

Q *Although these rulers practiced very different religions, why did they justify their powers in such a similar fashion?*

levy taxes for the army and oversee its growth. The Commissariat soon evolved into an agency for civil government as well. The new bureaucratic machine became the elector's chief instrument to govern the state. Many of its officials were members of the Prussian landed aristocracy, the Junkers (YOONG-kers), who also served as officers in the all-important army.

In 1701, Frederick William's son Frederick officially gained the title of king. Elector Frederick III became King Frederick I, and Brandenburg-Prussia simply Prussia. In the eighteenth century, Prussia emerged as a great power in Europe.

Austria   The Austrian Habsburgs had long played a significant role in European politics as Holy Roman Emperors. By the end of the Thirty Years' War, the Habsburg hopes of creating an empire in Germany had been dashed. In the seventeenth century, the house of Austria created a new empire in eastern and southeastern Europe.

The nucleus of the new Austrian Empire remained the traditional Austrian hereditary possessions: Lower and Upper Austria, Carinthia, Carniola, Styria, and Tyrol. To these had been added the kingdom of Bohemia and parts of northwestern Hungary. After the defeat of the Turks in 1687, Austria took control of all of Hungary, Transylvania, Croatia, and Slovenia, thus establishing the Austrian Empire in southeastern Europe. By the beginning of the eighteenth century, the house of Austria had assembled an empire of considerable size.

The Austrian monarchy, however, never became a highly centralized, absolutist state, primarily because it contained so many different national groups. The Austrian Empire remained a collection of territories held together by the Habsburg emperor, who was archduke of Austria, king of Bohemia, and king of Hungary. Each of these regions, however, had its own laws and political life.

From Muscovy to Russia   A new Russian state had emerged in the fifteenth century under the leadership of the principality of Muscovy and its grand dukes. In the sixteenth century, Ivan IV (1533–1584) became the first ruler to take the title of *tsar* (the Russian word for "Caesar"). Ivan expanded the territories of Russia eastward and crushed the power of the Russian nobility. He was known as Ivan the Terrible because of his ruthless deeds, among them stabbing his son to death in a heated argument. When Ivan's dynasty came to an end in 1598, fifteen years of anarchy ensued until the Zemsky Sobor (ZEM-skee suh-BOR), or national assembly, chose Michael Romanov (ROH-muh-nahf) as the new tsar, establishing a dynasty that lasted more than four hundred years. One of its most prominent members was Peter the Great.

Peter the Great (1689–1725) was an unusual character. A strong man towering 6 feet 9 inches tall, Peter enjoyed low humor—belching contests and crude jokes—and vicious punishments, including floggings, impalings, and roastings. Peter got a firsthand view of the West when he made a trip there in 1697–1698 and returned to Russia with a firm determination to westernize Russia. He was especially eager to borrow European technology in order to create the army and navy he needed to make Russia a great power.

As could be expected, one of his first priorities was the reorganization of the army and the creation of a navy. Employing both Russians and Europeans as officers, he conscripted peasants for twenty-five-year stints of service to build a standing army of 210,000 men and at the same time formed the first navy Russia had ever had.

To impose the rule of the central government more effectively throughout the land, Peter divided Russia into provinces. Although he hoped to create a "police state," by which he meant a well-ordered community governed in accordance with law, few of his bureaucrats shared his concept of loyalty to the state. Peter hoped to evoke a sense of civic duty among his people, but his own forceful personality created an atmosphere of fear that prevented any such sentiment.

The object of Peter's domestic reforms was to make Russia into a great state and military power. His primary goal was to "open a window to the west," meaning an ice-free port easily accessible to Europe. This could only be achieved on the Baltic, but at that time, the Baltic coast was controlled by Sweden, the most important power in northern Europe. A long and hard-fought war with Sweden won Peter the lands he sought. In 1703, Peter began the construction of a new city, Saint Petersburg, his window to the west and a symbol that Russia was looking westward to Europe. By the time Peter died in 1725, Russia had become a great military power and an important European state.

ENGLAND AND LIMITED MONARCHY

Not all states were absolutist in the seventeenth century. One of the most prominent examples of resistance to absolute monarchy came in England, where king and Parliament struggled to determine the roles each should play in governing England.

Conflict Between King and Parliament With the death of the childless Queen Elizabeth I in 1603, the Tudor dynasty became extinct, and the Stuart line of rulers was inaugurated with the accession to the throne of Elizabeth's cousin, King James VI of Scotland, who became James I (1603–1625) of England. James espoused the divine right of kings, a viewpoint that alienated Parliament, which had grown accustomed under the Tudors to act on the premise that monarch and Parliament together ruled England as a "balanced polity." Then, too, the **Puritans**—Protestants within the Anglican Church who, inspired by Calvinist theology, wished to eliminate every trace of Roman Catholicism from the Church of England—were alienated by the king's strong defense of the Anglican Church. Many of England's gentry, mostly well-to-do landowners, had become Puritans and formed an important and substantial part of the House of Commons, the lower house of Parliament. It was not wise to alienate these men.

The conflict that had begun during the reign of James came to a head during the reign of his son Charles I (1625–1649). Like his father, Charles believed in divine-right monarchy, and religious differences also added to the hostility between Charles I and Parliament. The king's attempt to impose more ritual on the Anglican Church struck the Puritans as a return to Catholic practices. When Charles tried to force the Puritans to accept his religious policies, thousands of them went off to the "howling wildernesses" of America.

Civil War and Commonwealth Grievances mounted until England finally slipped into a civil war (1642–1648) won by the parliamentary forces, due largely to the New Model Army of Oliver Cromwell, the only real military genius of the war. The New Model Army was composed primarily of more extreme Puritans known as the Independents, who, in typical Calvinist fashion, believed they were doing battle for God. As Cromwell wrote in one of his military reports, "Sir, this is none other but the hand of God; and to Him alone belongs the glory." We might give some credit to Cromwell; his soldiers were well trained in the new military tactics of the seventeenth century.

After the execution of Charles I on January 30, 1649, Parliament abolished the monarchy and the House of Lords and proclaimed England a republic or commonwealth. But Cromwell and his army, unable to work effectively with Parliament, dispersed it by force and established a military dictatorship. After Cromwell's death in 1658, the army decided that military rule was no longer feasible and restored the monarchy in the person of Charles II, the son of Charles I.

Restoration and a Glorious Revolution   Charles was sympathetic to Catholicism, and Parliament's suspicions were aroused in 1672 when Charles took the audacious step of issuing the Declaration of Indulgence, which suspended the laws that Parliament had passed against Catholics and Puritans after the restoration of the monarchy. Parliament forced the king to suspend the declaration.

The accession of James II (1685–1688) to the crown virtually guaranteed a new constitutional crisis for England. An open and devout Catholic, his attempt to further Catholic interests made religion once more a primary cause of conflict between king and Parliament. James named Catholics to high positions in the government, army, navy, and universities. Parliamentary outcries against James's policies stopped short of rebellion because members knew that he was an old man and that his successors were his Protestant daughters Mary and Anne, born to his first wife. But on June 10, 1688, a son was born to James II's second wife, also a Catholic. Suddenly, the specter of a Catholic hereditary monarchy loomed large. A group of prominent English noblemen invited the Dutch chief executive, William of Orange, husband of James's daughter Mary, to invade England. William and Mary raised an army and invaded England while James, his wife, and their infant son fled to France. With little bloodshed, England had undergone its "Glorious Revolution."

In January 1689, Parliament offered the throne to William and Mary, who accepted it along with the provisions of a bill of rights. The Bill of Rights affirmed Parliament's right to make laws and levy taxes. The rights of citizens to keep arms and have a jury trial were also confirmed. By deposing one king and establishing another, Parliament had destroyed the divine-right theory of kingship (William was, after all, king by grace of Parliament, not God) and asserted its right to participate in the government. Parliament did not have complete control of the government, but it now had the right to participate in affairs of state. Over the next century, it would gradually prove to be the real authority in the English system of **limited (constitutional) monarchy**.

THE FLOURISHING OF EUROPEAN CULTURE

Despite religious wars and the growth of absolutism, European culture continued to flourish. The era was blessed with a number of prominent artists and writers.

Art: The Baroque

The artistic movement known as the **Baroque** (buh-ROHK) dominated the Western artistic world for a century and a half. The Baroque began in Italy in the last quarter of the sixteenth century and spread to the rest of Europe and Latin America. Baroque artists sought to harmonize the Classical ideals of Renaissance art with the spiritual feelings of the sixteenth-century religious revival. In large part, Baroque art and architecture reflected the search for power that was characteristic of much of the seventeenth century. Baroque churches and palaces featured richly ornamented facades, sweeping staircases, and an overall splendor meant to impress people. Kings and princes wanted not only their subjects but also other kings and princes to be in awe of their power.

Baroque painting was known for its use of dramatic effects to arouse the emotions. This style was especially evident in the works of Peter Paul Rubens (1577–1640) of Flanders, a prolific artist and an important figure in the spread of the Baroque from Italy to other parts of Europe. In his artistic masterpieces, bodies in violent motion, heavily fleshed nudes, a dramatic use of light and shadow, and rich sensuous pigments converge to express highly intense emotions.

Gian Lorenzo Bernini, *Ecstasy of Saint Theresa.* *One of the great artists of the Baroque period was the Italian sculptor and architect Gian Lorenzo Bernini. The* Ecstasy of Saint Theresa, *created for the Cornaro Chapel in the Church of Santa Maria della Vittoria in Rome, was one of Bernini's most famous sculptures. Bernini sought to convey visually Theresa's mystical experience when, according to her description, an angel pierced her heart repeatedly with a golden arrow.*

Perhaps the greatest figure of the Baroque was the Italian architect and sculptor Gian Lorenzo Bernini (JAHN loh-RENT-zoh bur-NEE-nee) (1598–1680), who completed Saint Peter's Basilica at the Vatican and designed the vast colonnade enclosing the piazza in front of it. Action, exuberance, profusion, and dramatic effects mark the work of Bernini in the interior of Saint Peter's, where his *Throne of Saint Peter* hovers in midair, held by the hands of the four great doctors of the Catholic Church. Above the chair, rays of golden light drive a mass of clouds and angels toward the spectator. In his most striking sculptural work, the *Ecstasy of Saint Theresa*, Bernini depicts a moment of mystical experience in the life of the sixteenth-century Spanish saint. The elegant draperies and the expression on her face create a sensuously real portrayal of physical ecstasy.

Art: Dutch Realism

A brilliant flowering of Dutch painting paralleled the supremacy of Dutch commerce in the seventeenth century. Wealthy patricians and burghers of Dutch urban society commissioned works of art for their guild halls, town halls, and private dwellings. The subject matter of many Dutch paintings reflected the interests of this bourgeois society: portraits of themselves, group portraits of their military companies and guilds, landscapes, seascapes, genre scenes, still lifes, and the interiors of their residences. Unlike Baroque artists, Dutch painters were primarily interested in the realistic portrayal of secular everyday life.

This interest in painting scenes of everyday life is evident in the work of Judith Leyster (LESS-tur) (c. 1609–1660), who established her own independent painting career, a remarkable achievement for a woman in seventeenth-century Europe. Leyster became the first female member of the painters' Guild of Saint Luke in Haarlem, which enabled her to set up her own workshop and take on three male pupils. Musicians playing their instruments, women sewing, children laughing while playing games, and actors performing all form the subject matter of Leyster's portrayals of everyday Dutch life.

A Golden Age of Literature in England

In England, writing for the stage reached new heights between 1580 and 1640. The golden age of English literature is often called the Elizabethan era because much of the English cultural flowering occurred during Elizabeth's reign. Elizabethan literature exhibits the exuberance and pride associated with English exploits at the time. Of all the forms of Elizabethan literature, none expressed the energy and intellectual versatility of the era better than drama. And no dramatist is more famous or more accomplished than William Shakespeare (1564–1614).

Shakespeare was a "complete man of the theater." Although best known for writing plays, he was also an actor and a shareholder in the chief acting company of the time, the Lord Chamberlain's Company, which played in various London theaters. Shakespeare is to this day hailed as a genius. A master of the English language, he imbued its words with power and majesty. And his technical proficiency was matched by incredible insight into human psychology. Whether writing tragedies or comedies, Shakespeare exhibited a remarkable understanding of the human condition.

CHRONOLOGIES

KEY EVENTS OF THE REFORMATION ERA

1517	Luther's Ninety-Five Theses
1521	Excommunication of Luther
1534	Act of Supremacy in England
1534–1549	Pontificate of Paul III
1536	John Calvin's *Institutes of the Christian Religion*
1540	Society of Jesus (Jesuits) recognized as a religious order
1545–1563	Council of Trent
1555	Peace of Augsburg

EUROPE IN CRISIS, 1560–1650: KEY EVENTS

1556–1598	Reign of Philip II
1562–1598	French Wars of Religion
1566	Outbreak of revolt in the Netherlands
1588	Defeat of the Spanish armada
1598	Edict of Nantes
1609–1621	Truce between Spain and the Netherlands
1618–1648	Thirty Years' War
1648	Peace of Westphalia

ABSOLUTE AND LIMITED MONARCHY

France	
1643–1715	Louis XIV
Brandenburg-Prussia	
1640–1688	Frederick William the Great Elector
1688–1713	Elector Frederick III (King Frederick I)
Russia	
1533–1584	Ivan IV the Terrible
1689–1725	Peter the Great
1697–1698	First trip to the West
1703	Construction of Saint Petersburg begins
England	
1642–1648	Civil wars
1649–1653	Commonwealth

1660–1685	Charles II
1672	Declaration of Indulgence
1685–1688	James II
1688	Glorious Revolution
1689	Bill of Rights

MindTap is a fully online, highly personalized learning experience built upon Cengage Learning content. MindTap combines student learning tools—readings, multimedia, activities, and assessments—into a singular Learning Path that guides students through their course.

16

THE MUSLIM EMPIRES

Turks fight Christians at the Battle of Mohács

The Art Archive/Topkapi Museum, Istanbul/Gianni Dagli Orti

CHAPTER OUTLINE

- The Ottoman Empire • The Safavids • The Grandeur of the Mughals

THE OTTOMAN EMPIRE

The Ottoman Turks were among the Turkic-speaking nomadic peoples who had spread westward from Central Asia in the ninth, tenth, and eleventh centuries. The first to appear in the Middle East were the Seljuk Turks, who initially attempted to revive the declining Abbasid caliphate in Baghdad. Later they established themselves in the Anatolian peninsula as the successors to the Byzantine Empire. Turks served as warriors or administrators, while the peasants who tilled the farmland were mainly Greek.

The Rise of the Ottoman Turks   In the late thirteenth century, a new group of Turks under the tribal leader Osman (os-MAHN) (r. 1280–1326) began to consolidate power in the northwestern corner of the Anatolian peninsula. That land had been given to them by the Seljuk rulers as a reward for helping drive out the Mongols in the late thirteenth century. At first, the Osman Turks were relatively peaceful and engaged in pastoral pursuits, but as the Seljuk empire began to crumble in the early fourteenth century, the Osman Turks began to expand and founded the Osmanli (os-MAHN-lee) dynasty, with its capital at Bursa (BURR-suh). The Osmanlis later came to be known as the Ottomans.

A key advantage for the Ottomans was their location in the northwestern corner of the peninsula. From there they were able to expand westward and eventually take over the Bosporus and the Dardanelles, between the Mediterranean and the Black Seas. The Byzantine Empire, of course, had controlled the area for centuries, serving as a buffer between the Muslim Middle East and the Latin West. The Byzantines, however, had been severely weakened by the sack of Constantinople in the Fourth Crusade in 1204 and the occupation of much of the empire by western Europeans for the next half century. In 1345, Ottoman forces under their leader Orkhan (or-KHAHN) I (r. 1326–1360) crossed the Bosporus for the first time to support a usurper against the Byzantine emperor in Constantinople. Setting up their first European base at Gallipoli (gah-LIP-poh-lee) at the Mediterranean entrance to the Dardanelles, Turkish forces expanded gradually into the Balkans and allied with fractious Serbian and Bulgar forces against the Byzantines. In these unstable conditions, the Ottomans gradually established permanent settlements throughout the area, where Turkish provincial governors, called **beys** (BAYS) (from the Turkish *beg*, "knight"), collected taxes from the local Slavic peasants after driving out the previous landlords. The Ottoman leader now began to claim the title of **sultan** (SUL-tun) or sovereign of his domain.

In 1360, Orkhan was succeeded by his son Murad (moo-RAHD) I, who consolidated Ottoman power in the Balkans, set up a capital at Edirne (eh-DEER-nay), and gradually reduced the Byzantine emperor to a vassal. Murad did not initially attempt to conquer Constantinople because his forces were composed mostly of the traditional Turkish cavalry and lacked the ability to breach the strong walls of the city. Instead, he began to build up a strong military administration based on the recruitment of Christians into an elite guard. Called **janissaries** (JAN-nih-say-reez) (from the Turkish *yeni cheri*, "new troops"), they were recruited from the local Christian population in the Balkans and then converted to Islam and trained as foot soldiers or administrators. One of the major advantages of the janissaries was

MAP 16.1   The Ottoman Empire

This map shows the territorial growth of the Ottoman Empire from the eve of the conquest of Constantinople in 1453 to the end of the seventeenth century, when a defeat at the hands of Austria led to the loss of a substantial portion of central Europe.

that they were directly subordinated to the sultanate and therefore owed their loyalty to the person of the sultan. Other military forces were organized by the beys and were thus loyal to their local tribal leaders.

The janissary corps also represented a response to changes in warfare. As the knowledge of firearms spread in the late fourteenth century, the Turks began to master the new technology, including siege cannons and muskets. The traditional nomadic cavalry charge was now outmoded and was superseded by infantry forces armed with muskets. Thus, the janissaries provided a well-armed infantry that served both as an elite guard to protect the palace and as a means of extending Turkish control in the Balkans. With his new forces, Murad defeated the Serbs at the famous Battle of Kosovo (KAWSS-suh-voh) in 1389 and ended Serbian hegemony in the area.

Expansion of the Empire   Under Murad's successor, Bayazid (by-uh-ZEED) I (r. 1389–1402), the Ottomans advanced northward, annexed Bulgaria, and slaughtered the French cavalry at a major battle on the Danube. A defeat at Ankara (AN-kuh-ruh) at the hands of the Mongol

COMPARATIVE ESSAY

The Changing Face of War

SCIENCE & TECHNOLOGY

"War," as the renowned French historian Fernand Braudel once observed, "has always been a matter of arms and techniques. Improved techniques can radically alter the course of events." Braudel's remark was directed to the situation in the Mediterranean region during the sixteenth century, when the adoption of artillery changed the face of warfare and gave enormous advantages to the countries—such as the Ottoman Empire—that stood at the head of the new technological revolution in firearms. But it can just as easily be applied to the present day, when potential adversaries possess weapons capable of reaching across oceans and continents.

One crucial aspect of military superiority, of course, lies in the nature of weaponry. From the invention of the bow and arrow to the advent of the atomic era, the possession of superior instruments of war has provided a distinct advantage against a poorly armed enemy. It was at least partly the possession of bronze weapons, for example, that enabled the invading Hyksos to conquer Egypt during the second millennium B.C.E.

Mobility is another factor of vital importance. During the second millennium B.C.E., horse-drawn chariots revolutionized the art of war from the Mediterranean Sea to the Yellow River valley in northern China. Later, the invention of the stirrup enabled mounted warriors to shoot arrows from horseback, a technique applied with great effect by the Mongols as they devastated civilizations across the Eurasian supercontinent.

To protect themselves from marauding warriors, settled societies began to erect massive walls around their cities and fortresses. That in turn led to the invention of siege weapons like the catapult and the battering ram. The Mongols allegedly even came up with an early form of chemical warfare, hurling human bodies infected with the plague into the bastions of their enemies.

The invention of explosives launched the next great revolution in warfare. First used as a weapon of war by the Tang Dynasty in China, explosives were brought to the West by the Turks, who used them with great effectiveness in the fifteenth century against the Byzantine Empire. But the Europeans quickly mastered the new technology and took it to new heights, inventing handheld firearms and mounting iron cannons on their warships. The latter represented a significant advantage to European fleets as they

warrior Tamerlane in 1402 proved to be only a temporary setback. When Mehmet (meh-MET) II (r. 1451–1481) succeeded to the throne, he was determined to capture Constantinople. Already in control of the Dardanelles, he ordered the construction of a major fortress on the Bosporus just north of the city, which put the Turks in a position to strangle the Byzantines.

The Fall of Constantinople   The last Byzantine emperor desperately called for help from the Europeans, but only the Genoese came to his defense. With 80,000 troops ranged against only 6,000 to 8,000 defenders, Mehmet laid siege to Constantinople in 1453. In their attack on the city, the Turks made use of massive cannons with 26-foot barrels that could launch stone balls weighing up to 1,200 pounds each. The Byzantines stretched heavy chains across the Golden

Roman troops defeating Celtic warriors; from the Great Altar of Pergamum.

began to compete with rivals for control of the Indian and Pacific Oceans.

The twentieth century saw revolutionary new developments in the art of warfare, from armed vehicles to airplanes to nuclear arms. But as weapons grow ever more fearsome, they are more dangerous to use, resulting in the paradox of the Vietnam War, when lightly armed Viet Cong guerrilla units were able to fight the world's mightiest army to a virtual standstill. As the Chinese military strategist Sun Tzu had long ago observed, victory in war often goes to the smartest, not the strongest.

Q *Why were the Europeans, rather than other peoples, able to make effective use of firearms to expand their influence throughout the world?*

Horn, the inlet that forms the city's harbor, to prevent a naval attack from the north and prepared to make their final stand behind the 13-mile-long wall along the western edge of the city. But Mehmet's forces seized the tip of the peninsula north of the Golden Horn and then dragged their ships overland across the peninsula from the Bosporus and put them into the water behind the chains. Finally, the walls were breached; the Byzantine emperor died in the final battle. Mehmet II, standing before the palace of the emperor, paused to reflect on the passing nature of human glory. But it was not long before he and the Ottomans were again on the march.

The Advance into Western Asia and Africa   With their new capital at Constantinople, eventually renamed Istanbul, the Ottoman Turks had become a dominant

The Fall of Constantinople

POLITICS &
GOVERNMENT

Few events in the history of the Ottoman Empire are more dramatic than the conquest of Constantinople in 1453. In this excerpt, the conquest is described by Kritovoulos, a Greek who later served in the Ottoman administration. Although the author did not witness the conquest itself, he was apparently well informed about the event and provides us with a vivid description.

Kritovoulos, *Life of Mehmed the Conqueror*

[H]e [the Sultan] led them himself. And they, with a shout on the run and with a fearsome yell, went on ahead of the Sultan, pressing on up to the palisade. After a long and bitter struggle they hurled back the Romans [Byzantines] from there and climbed by force up the palisade. They dashed some of their foe down into the ditch between the great wall and the palisade, which was deep and hard to get out of, and they killed them there. The rest they drove back to the gate.

He had opened this gate in the great wall, so as to go easily over to the palisade. Now there was a great struggle there and great slaughter among those stationed there, for they were attacked by the heavy infantry and not a few others in irregular formation, who had been attracted from many points by the shouting. There the Emperor Constantine [Constantine XI Palaeologus], with all who were with him, fell in gallant combat.

The heavy infantry were already streaming through the little gate into the City, and others had rushed in through the breach in the great wall. Then all the rest of the army, with a rush and a roar, poured in brilliantly and scattered all over the City. And the Sultan stood before the great wall, where the standard also was and the ensigns, and watched the proceedings. The day was already breaking....

The soldiers fell on them [the citizens] with anger and great wrath. For one thing, they were actuated by the hardships of the siege. For another, some foolish people had hurled taunts and curses at them from the battlements all through the siege. Now, in general they killed so as to frighten all the City, and to terrorize and enslave all by the slaughter.

When they had had enough of murder, and the City was reduced to slavery, some of the troops turned to the mansions of the mighty, by bands and companies and divisions, for plunder and spoil. Others went to the robbing of churches, and others dispersed to the simple homes of the common people, stealing, robbing, plundering, killing, insulting, taking and enslaving men, women, and children, old and young, priests, monks—in short, every age and class....

After this the Sultan entered the City and looked about to see its great size, its situation, its grandeur and beauty, its teeming population, its loveliness, and the costliness of its churches and public buildings and of the private houses and community houses and those of the officials.... When he saw what a large number had been killed, and the ruin of the buildings, and the wholesale ruin and destruction of the City, he was filled with compassion and repented not a little at the destruction and plundering. Tears fell from his eyes as he groaned deeply and passionately: "What a city we have given over to plunder and destruction."

Q *What strategy did the Turkish forces use to seize the city of Constantinople? Compare this description of the capture of Constantinople to the description of its capture 250 years earlier. What are the similarities? What are the differences?*

Source: From Kritovoulos, *Life of Mehmed the Conqueror*, trans. Charles T. Riggs. © 1954 Princeton University Press. © renewed 1982 Princeton University Press.

force in the Balkans and the Anatolian peninsula. They now began to advance to the east against the Shi'ite kingdom of the Safavids (sah-FAH-weeds) in Persia, which had been promoting rebellion among the Anatolian tribal population and disrupting Turkish trade through the Middle East. After defeating the Safavids at a major battle in 1514, Emperor Selim (seh-LEEM) I (r. 1512–1520) consolidated Turkish control over Mesopotamia and then turned his attention to the Mamluks (MAM-looks) in Egypt, who had failed to support the Ottomans in their struggle against the Safavids. The Mamluks were defeated in Syria in 1516; Cairo fell a year later. Now controlling several of the holy cities of Islam, including Jerusalem, Mecca, and Medina, Selim declared himself the new caliph, or successor to Muhammad. During the next few years, Turkish armies and fleets advanced westward along the African coast, occupying Tripoli, Tunis, and Algeria and eventually penetrating almost to the Strait of Gibraltar. In their advance, the invaders had taken advantage of the progressive disintegration of the Nasrid (NAS-rid) dynasty in Morocco, which had been in decline for decades and had lost its last foothold on the European continent when Granada fell to Spain in 1492.

The impact of Turkish rule on the peoples of North Africa was relatively light. Like their predecessors, the Turks were Muslims, and they preferred where possible to administer their conquered regions through local rulers. The central government utilized appointed **pashas** (PAH-shuz) who were directly responsible to Istanbul; the pashas collected taxes, paying a fixed percentage as tribute to the central government, and maintained law and order. The Turks ruled from coastal cities such as Algiers, Tunis, and Tripoli and made no attempt to control the interior beyond maintaining the trade routes through the Sahara to the commercial centers along the Niger River. Meanwhile, local pirates along the Barbary Coast—the northern coast of Africa from Egypt to the Atlantic Ocean—competed with their Christian rivals in raiding the shipping that passed through the Mediterranean.

By the seventeenth century, the links between the imperial court in Istanbul and its appointed representatives in the Turkish regencies in North Africa had begun to weaken. Some of the pashas were dethroned by local elites, while others, such as the bey of Tunis, became hereditary rulers. Even Egypt, whose agricultural wealth and control over the route to the Red Sea made it the most important country in the area to the Turks, gradually became autonomous under a new official class of janissaries. Many of them became wealthy landowners by exploiting their official positions and collecting tax revenues far in excess of what they had to remit to Istanbul. In the early eighteenth century, the Mamluks returned to power, although the Turkish government managed to retain some control by means of a viceroy appointed from Istanbul.

Turkish Expansion in Europe   After their conquest of Constantinople in 1453, the Ottoman Turks tried to complete their conquest of the Balkans, where they had been established since the fourteenth century. Although they were successful in taking the Romanian territory of Wallachia (wah-LAY-kee-uh) in 1476, the resistance of the Hungarians initially kept the Turks from advancing up the Danube valley. From 1480 to 1520, internal problems and the need to consolidate their eastern frontiers kept the Turks from any further attacks on Europe.

Suleyman (SOO-lay-mahn) I the Magnificent (r. 1520–1566), however, brought the Turks back to Europe's attention. Advancing up the Danube, the Turks seized

Belgrade in 1521 and won a major victory over the Hungarians at the Battle of Mohács (MOH-hach) on the Danube in 1526. Subsequently, the Turks overran most of Hungary, moved into Austria, and advanced as far as Vienna, where they were finally repulsed in 1529. At the same time, they extended their power into the western Mediterranean and threatened to turn it into a Turkish lake until a large Turkish fleet was destroyed by the Spanish at Lepanto in 1571. Despite the defeat, the Turks continued to hold nominal suzerainty over the southern shores of the Mediterranean. One year after Lepanto, the Turks reconstituted their fleet and seized the island of Cyprus. Responding to the joy expressed in Europe over the naval victory at Lepanto, the **grand vizier** (veh-ZEER) (Turkish *vezir*), or chief minister, in Constantinople remarked to the Venetian ambassador, "There is a big difference between our loss and yours. In taking Cyprus, we have cut off one of your arms. In sinking our fleet you only shaved our beard. A lost arm cannot be replaced, but a shorn beard grows back quickly to its prior magnificence."[1]

Although Christians in Europe frequently called for new Crusades against the "infidel" Turks, by the beginning of the seventeenth century the Ottoman Empire was being treated like any other European power by European rulers seeking alliances and trade concessions. During the first half of the seventeenth century, the Ottoman Empire was viewed as a "sleeping giant." Involved in domestic bloodletting and heavily threatened by a challenge from Persia, the Ottomans were content with the status quo in eastern Europe. But under a new line of grand viziers in the second half of the seventeenth century, the Ottoman Empire again took the offensive. By mid-1683, the Ottomans had marched through the Hungarian plain and once again laid siege to Vienna. Repulsed by a mixed army of Austrians, Poles, Bavarians, and Saxons, the Turks retreated and were pushed out of Hungary by a new European coalition. Although they retained the core of their empire, the Ottoman Turks would never again be a threat to Europe and, by the end of the seventeenth and the eighteenth centuries, they faced new challenges from the ever-expanding Austrian Empire in southeastern Europe and the new Russian giant to the north.

The Nature of Turkish Rule

Like other Muslim empires in Persia and India, the Ottoman political system was the result of the evolution of tribal institutions into a sedentary empire. At the apex of the Ottoman system was the sultan, who was the supreme authority in both a political and a military sense. The origins of this system can be traced back to the bey, who was only a tribal leader, a first among equals, who could claim loyalty from his chiefs so long as he could provide booty and grazing lands for his subordinates. Disputes were settled by tribal law; Muslim law was secondary. Tribal leaders collected taxes—or booty—from areas under their control and sent one-fifth on to the bey. Both administrative and military power were centralized under the bey, and the capital was wherever the bey and his administration happened to be.

The Role of the Sultan But the rise of empire brought about changes and an adaptation to Byzantine traditions of rule much as Abbasid political practices had been affected by Persian monarchical tradition at an earlier time in Baghdad. The status and prestige of the sultan now increased relative to the subordinate tribal leaders, and the position took on the trappings of imperial rule. Court rituals were inherited from the Byzantines and Persians, and a centralized administrative system was adopted that increasingly isolated the sultan in his palace. The position of the sultan was hereditary, with a son, although not necessarily the eldest, always succeeding the father. This practice led to chronic succession struggles upon the death of individual sultans, and the losers were often executed (strangled with a silk bowstring) or later imprisoned. Potential heirs to the throne were assigned as provincial governors to provide them with experience.

The Harem   The heart of the sultan's power was in the Topkapi (tahp-KAH-pee) Palace in the center of Istanbul. Topkapi (meaning "cannon gate") was constructed in 1459 by Mehmet II and served as an administrative center as well as the private residence of the sultan and his family. Eventually, it had a staff of 20,000 employees. The private domain of the sultan was called the **harem** ("sacred place"). Here he resided with his concubines. Normally, a sultan did not marry but chose several concubines as his favorites; they were accorded this status after they gave birth to sons. When a son became a sultan, his mother became known as the queen mother and served as adviser to the throne. This tradition, initiated by the influential wife of Suleyman the Magnificent, often resulted in considerable authority for the queen mother in affairs of state.

Like the janissaries, members of the harem were often of slave origin and formed an elite element in Ottoman society. Since the enslavement of Muslims was forbidden, slaves were taken among non-Islamic peoples. Some concubines were prisoners selected for the position, while others were purchased or offered to the sultan as gifts. They were then trained and educated like the janissaries in a system called ***devshirme*** (dev-SHEER-may) ("collection"). *Devshirme* had originated in the practice of requiring local clan leaders to provide prisoners to the sultan as part of their tax obligation. Talented males were given special training for eventual placement in military or administrative positions, while their female counterparts were trained for service in the harem, with instruction in reading, the Qur'an, sewing and embroidery, and musical performance. They were ranked according to their status, and some were permitted to leave the harem to marry officials. If they were later divorced, they were sometimes allowed to return to the harem.

Unique to the Ottoman Empire from the fifteenth century onward was the exclusive use of slaves to reproduce its royal heirs. Contrary to myth, few of the women of the imperial harem were used for sexual purposes, as the majority were relatives of the sultan's extended family—sisters, daughters, widowed mothers, and in-laws, with their own personal slaves and entourages. Contemporary European observers compared the atmosphere in the Topkapi harem to a Christian nunnery, with its hierarchical organization, enforced chastity, and rule of silence.

Because of their proximity to the sultan, the women of the harem often wielded so much political power that the era has been called the "sultanate of women." Queen mothers administered the imperial household and engaged in diplomatic relations with other countries while controlling the marital alliances of their daughters with senior civilian and military officials or members of other royal families in the region. One princess was married seven separate times from the age of two after her previous husbands died either in battle or by execution.

Administration of the Government   The sultan ruled through an imperial council that met four days a week and was chaired by the grand vizier. The sultan often attended behind a screen, whence he could privately indicate his desires to the grand vizier. The latter presided over the imperial bureaucracy. Like the palace guard, the bureaucrats were not an exclusive group but were chosen at least partly by merit from a palace school for training officials. Most officials were Muslims by birth, but some talented janissaries became senior members of the bureaucracy, and almost all the later grand viziers came from the *devshirme* system.

Local administration during the imperial period was a product of Turkish tribal tradition and was similar in some respects to fief-holding in Europe. The empire was divided into provinces and districts governed by officials who, like their tribal predecessors, combined both civil and military functions. They were assisted by bureaucrats trained in the palace school in Istanbul. Senior officials were assigned land in fief by the sultan and were then responsible for collecting taxes and supplying armies to the empire. These lands were then farmed out to the local cavalry elite called the **sipahis** (suh-PAH-heez), who obtained their salaries by exacting a tax from all peasants in their fiefdoms. These local officials were not hereditary aristocrats, but sons often inherited their fathers' landholdings, and the vast majority were descendants of the beys who had formed the tribal elites before the imperial period.

Religion and Society in the Ottoman World   Like most Turkic-speaking peoples in the Anatolian peninsula and throughout the Middle East, the Ottoman ruling elites were Sunni Muslims. Ottoman sultans had claimed the title of caliph ("defender of the faith") since the early sixteenth century and thus were theoretically responsible for guiding the flock and maintaining Islamic law, the *Shari'a*. In practice, the sultan assigned these duties to a supreme religious authority, who administered the law and maintained a system of schools for educating Muslims.

Islamic law and customs were applied to all Muslims in the empire. Although most Turkic-speaking people were Sunni Muslims, some communities were attracted to Sufism or other heterodox doctrines. The government tolerated such activities as long as their practitioners remained loyal to the empire, but in the early sixteenth century, unrest among these groups—some of whom converted to the Shi'ite version of Islam—outraged the conservative *ulama* and eventually led to war against the Safavids.

The Treatment of Minorities   Non-Muslims—mostly Orthodox Christians (Greeks and Slavs), Jews, and Armenian Christians—formed a significant minority within the empire, which treated them with relative tolerance. Non-Muslims were compelled to pay a head tax (as compensation for their exemption from military service), and they were permitted to practice their religion or convert to Islam (people who were already Muslim were prohibited from adopting another faith). Most of the population in European areas of the empire remained Christian, but in some places, such as the Balkan territory now known as Bosnia and Herzegovina, substantial numbers converted to Islam.

Each religious group within the empire was organized as an administrative unit called a **millet** (mi-LET) ("nation" or "community"). Each group, including the

Muslims themselves, had its own patriarch, priest, or grand rabbi who dealt as an intermediary with the government and administered the community according to its own laws. The leaders of the individual *millets* were responsible to the sultan and his officials for the behavior of the subjects under their care and collected taxes for transmission to the government. Each *millet* established its own system of justice, set its own educational policies, and provided welfare for the needy.

Nomadic peoples were placed in a separate *millet* and were subject to their own regulations and laws. They were divided into the traditional nomadic classifications of tribes, clans, and "tents" (individual families) and were governed by their hereditary chiefs, the beys. As we have seen, the beys were responsible for administration and for collecting taxes for the state.

Social Classes   The subjects of the Ottoman Empire were also divided by occupation and place of residence. In addition to the ruling class, there were four main occupational groups: peasants, artisans, merchants, and pastoral peoples. The first three were classified as "urban" residents. Peasants tilled land that was leased to them by the state (ultimate ownership of all land resided with the sultan), but the land was deeded to them, so they were able to pass it on to their heirs. They were not allowed to sell the land and thus in practice were forced to remain on the soil. Taxes were based on the amount of land the peasants possessed and were paid to the local sipahis, who held the district in fief.

Artisans were organized according to craft guilds. Each guild, headed by a council of elders, was responsible not only for dealing with the governmental authorities but also for providing financial services, social security, and training for its members. Outside the ruling elite, merchants were the most privileged class in Ottoman society. They were largely exempt from government regulations and taxes and were therefore able in many cases to amass large fortunes. Charging interest was technically illegal under Islamic law, but the rules were often ignored in practice. In the absence of regulations, merchants often established monopolies and charged high prices, which caused them to be bitterly resented by other subjects of the empire.

The Position of Women   Technically, women in the Ottoman Empire were subject to the same restrictions that afflicted their counterparts in other Muslim societies, but their position was ameliorated to some degree by a variety of factors. In the first place, non-Muslims were subject to the laws and customs of their own religions; thus, Orthodox Christian, Armenian Christian, and Jewish women were spared some of the restrictions applied to their Muslim sisters (although they were then subject to restrictions imposed by their own faith). In the second place, Islamic laws as applied in the Ottoman Empire defined the legal position of women comparatively tolerantly. Women were permitted to own and inherit property, including their dowries. They could not be forced into marriage and in certain cases were permitted to seek a divorce. As we have seen, women often exercised considerable influence in the palace and in a few instances even served as senior officials, such as governors of provinces. The relatively tolerant attitude toward women in Ottoman-held territories has been ascribed by some to Turkish tribal traditions, which took a more egalitarian view of gender roles than the sedentary societies of the region did.

The Ottoman Empire Under Challenge

The Ottoman Empire reached its zenith under Suleyman the Magnificent, often known as Suleyman Kanuni, or "the law-giver," who launched the conquest of Hungary. But Suleyman also sowed the seeds of later difficulties for his successors. He executed his two most able sons on suspicion of factionalism and was succeeded by Selim II (the Sot, or "the drunken sultan"), the only surviving son and a disaster as ruler.

By the late seventeenth century, the expansionist tendencies of earlier eras had largely disappeared, although the first loss of imperial territory did not occur until 1699, at the Treaty of Karlowitz (KARL-oh-vits), when the Ottomans lost substantial territories in central Europe. Apparently, a number of factors were involved. In the first place, the administrative system inherited from the tribal period began to break down. Although the *devshirme* system of training officials continued to function, *devshirme* graduates were now permitted to marry and inherit property and to enroll their sons in the palace corps. Thus, they were gradually transformed from a meritocratic administrative elite into a privileged and often degenerate hereditary caste. Local administrators were corrupted and taxes rose as the central bureaucracy lost its links with rural areas. The imperial treasury was depleted by constant wars, and transport and communications were neglected. Interest in science and technology, once a hallmark of the Arab empire, had not kept up with developments in Europe. In addition, the empire was increasingly beset by economic difficulties, caused by the diversion of trade routes away from the eastern Mediterranean and the price inflation brought about by the influx of cheap American silver.

Ottoman society was by no means isolated from the outside world. Sophisticated officials and merchants began to mimic the habits and lifestyles of their European counterparts, dressing in the European fashion, purchasing Western furniture and art objects, and ignoring Muslim strictures against the consumption of alcohol and sexual activities outside marriage. During the sixteenth and early seventeenth centuries, coffee and tobacco were introduced into polite Ottoman society, and cafés for the consumption of both began to appear in the major cities. Such behavior aroused concern in some quarters. One sultan in the early seventeenth century issued a decree prohibiting the consumption of both coffee and tobacco, arguing (correctly, no doubt) that many cafés were nests of antigovernment intrigue. He even began to wander incognito through the streets of Istanbul at night. Any of his subjects detected in immoral or illegal acts were summarily executed and their bodies left on the streets as an example to others.

One of the key weaknesses in Ottoman society after the seventeenth century was that the ruling family lost much of its vitality. Whereas the first sultans reigned twenty-seven years on average, later ones averaged only thirteen years, and the laws of succession appeared to operate against the stability of the state. The throne routinely went to the oldest surviving male, while his rivals were kept secluded in a latticed cage and thus had no governmental experience if they succeeded to rule. Later sultans also became less involved in government, and more power flowed to the office of the grand vizier, called the **Sublime Porte** (PORT), or to eunuchs and members of the harem. Palace intrigue increased as a result.

The Ottoman Empire: A Civilization in Decline?

Over the years, many observers have interpreted the conditions described in the previous section as clear signs that the Ottoman Empire was entering a period of decline, a long slide that ultimately resulted in the collapse of the sultanate in the early twentieth century. Recently, however, some historians—undoubtedly inspired by the desire to discredit the traditional Eurocentric view of history—have taken issue with this paradigm, maintaining that in many respects the empire remained relatively healthy up to the twentieth century and had actually begun to reform itself when World War I broke out in 1914. The debate perhaps hinges more on semantics than on the interpretation of relevant facts. Although some Ottoman rulers made significant efforts during the nineteenth century to initiate reforms in the system, the results were relatively meager, and when war broke out in 1914, the old empire had fallen significantly behind its European counterparts in meeting the challenges of the new century. In that respect, as we shall see, it was hardly alone.

Ottoman Art

The Ottoman sultans were enthusiastic patrons of the arts and maintained large ateliers of artisans and artists, primarily at the Topkapi Palace in Istanbul but also in other important cities of the vast empire. The period from Mehmet II in the fifteenth century to the early eighteenth century witnessed a flourishing of pottery, rugs, silk and other textiles, jewelry, arms and armor, and calligraphy. All adorned the palaces of the new rulers, testifying to their opulence and exquisite taste. The artists came from all parts of the realm and beyond. Besides Turks, there were Persians, Greeks, Armenians, Hungarians, and Italians, all vying for the esteem and generous rewards of the sultans and fearing that losing favor might mean losing their heads! In the second half of the sixteenth century, Istanbul alone listed more than 150 craft guilds, ample proof of the artistic activity of the era.

Architecture

By far the greatest contribution of the Ottoman Empire to world art was its architecture, especially the magnificent mosques of the second half of the sixteenth century. Traditionally, prayer halls in mosques were subdivided by numerous pillars that supported small individual domes, creating a private, forestlike atmosphere. The Turks, however, modeled their new mosques on the open floor plan of the Byzantine church of Hagia Sophia (completed in 537), which had been turned into a mosque by Mehmet II, and began to push the pillars toward the outer wall to create a prayer hall with an uninterrupted central area under one large dome. With this plan, large numbers of believers could worship in unison in accordance with Muslim preference. By the mid-sixteenth century, the greatest of all Ottoman architects, Sinan (si-NAHN), began erecting the first of his eighty-one mosques with an uncluttered prayer area. Each was topped by an imposing dome, and often, as at Edirne, the entire building was framed with four towering narrow minarets. By emphasizing its vertical lines, the minarets camouflaged the massive stone bulk of the structure and gave it a feeling of incredible lightness. These four graceful minarets would find new expression sixty years later in India's white marble Taj Mahal.

The lightness of the exterior was reinforced in the mosque's interior by the soaring height of the dome and the numerous windows. Added to this were delicate plasterwork and tile decoration that transformed the mosque into a monumental oasis of spirituality, opulence, and power. Sinan's masterpieces, such as the Suleymaniye

COMPARATIVE ILLUSTRATION

Hagia Sophia and the Suleymaniye Mosque

ART & IDEAS

The magnificent mosques built under the patronage of Suleyman the Magnificent are a great legacy of the Ottoman Empire and a fitting supplement to Hagia Sophia, the cathedral built by the Byzantine emperor Justinian in the sixth century C.E. Towering under a central dome, these mosques seem to defy gravity and, like European Gothic cathedrals, convey a sense of weightlessness. The Suleymaniye Mosque (top photo), constructed in the mid-sixteenth century on a design by the great architect Sinan, borrowed many elements from its great predecessor (bottom photo) and today is one of the most impressive and most graceful in Istanbul. A far cry from the seventh-century desert mosques constructed of palm trunks, the Ottoman mosques stand among the architectural wonders of the world.

Q *How would you compare the mosques built by the architect Sinan and his successors with the Gothic cathedrals that were being built at the same time in Europe? What do you think accounts for the differences?*

Fergus O'Brien/The Image Bank/Getty Images

© William J. Duiker

(soo-lay-MAHN-ee-eh) and the Blue Mosque of Istanbul, were always part of a large socioreligious compound that included a library, school, hospital, mausoleums, and even bazaars, all of equally magnificent construction.

Earlier, the thirteenth-century Seljuk Turks of Anatolia had created beautiful tile decorations with two-color mosaics. Now Ottoman artists invented a new glazed tile art with painted flowers and geometrical designs in brilliant blue, green, yellow, and their own secret "tomato red." Entire walls, both interior and exterior, were covered with the painted tiles, which adorned palaces as well as mosques. Produced at Iznik (the old Nicaea), the distinctive tiles and pottery were in great demand; the city's ateliers boasted more than three hundred artisans in the late sixteenth century.

Textiles   The sixteenth century also witnessed the flourishing of textiles and rugs. The Byzantine emperor Justinian had introduced the cultivation of silkworms to the West in the sixth century, and the silk industry resurfaced under the Ottomans. Its capital was at Bursa, where factories produced silks for wall hangings, soft covers, and especially court costumes. Perhaps even more famous than Turkish silk are the rugs. But whereas silks were produced under the patronage of the sultans, rugs were a peasant industry. Each village boasted its own distinctive design and color scheme for the rugs it produced.

THE SAFAVIDS

After the collapse of the empire of Tamerlane in the early fifteenth century, the area extending from Persia into Central Asia lapsed into anarchy. The Uzbeks (ooz-BEKS), Turkic-speaking peoples from Central Asia, were the chief political and military force in the area. From their capital at Bokhara (boh-KAHR-uh *or* boo-KAH-ruh), they maintained a semblance of control over the fluid tribal alignments until the emergence of the Safavid Dynasty in Persia at the beginning of the sixteenth century.

The Rise of the Safavids   The Safavid Dynasty was founded by Shah Ismail (IS-mah-eel) (r. 1487–1524), a descendant of Sheikh Safi al-Din (SAH-fee ul-DIN) (hence the name *Safavid*), who traced his origins to Ali, the fourth *imam* of the Muslim faith. In the early fourteenth century, Safi had been the leader of a community of Turkic-speaking people in Azerbaijan, near the Caspian Sea. Safi's community was one of many Sufi mystical religious groups throughout the area. In time, the doctrine spread among nomadic groups throughout the Middle East and was transformed into the more activist Shi'ite faith. Its adherents were known as "red heads" because of their distinctive red cap with twelve folds, meant to symbolize allegiance to the twelve *imams* of the Shi'ite faith.

In 1501, Ismail seized much of the lands of modern Iran and Iraq and proclaimed himself shah of a new Persian state. Baghdad was subdued in 1508, as were the Uzbeks in Bokhara shortly thereafter. Ismail now sent Shi'ite preachers into Anatolia to proselytize and promote rebellion among Turkish tribal peoples in the Ottoman Empire. In retaliation, the Ottoman sultan, Selim I, advanced against the Safavids in Persia and won a major battle near Tabriz (tah-BREEZ) in 1514. But Selim could not maintain control of the area, and Ismail regained Tabriz a few years later.

The Ottomans returned to the attack in the 1580s and forced the new Safavid shah, Abbas (uh-BAHS) I (r. 1587–1629), to sign a punitive peace in which he acceded to the loss of much territory. The capital was subsequently moved from Tabriz in the northwest to Isfahan (is-fah-HAHN) in the south. Still, it was under Shah Abbas that the Safavids reached the zenith of their glory. He established a system similar to the janissaries in Turkey to train administrators to replace the traditional warrior elite. He also used the period of peace to strengthen his army, now armed with modern weapons, and in the early seventeenth century, he attempted to regain the lost territories. Although he had some initial success, war resumed in the 1620s, and a lasting peace was not achieved until 1638.

Collapse of the Dynasty   Abbas the Great had managed to strengthen the dynasty significantly, and for a time after his death in 1629, it remained stable and vigorous. But succession conflicts plagued the dynasty. Partly as a result, the power of the more militant Shi'ites began to increase at court and in Safavid society at large. The intellectual freedom that had characterized the empire at its height was curtailed under the pressure of religious orthodoxy, and Iranian women, who had enjoyed considerable freedom and influence during the early empire, were forced to withdraw into seclusion and behind the veil. Meanwhile, attempts to suppress the religious beliefs of minorities led to increased popular unrest. In the early eighteenth century, Afghan warriors took advantage of local revolts to seize the capital of Isfahan, forcing the remnants of the Safavid ruling family to retreat to Azerbaijan, their original homeland. As the Ottomans seized territories along the western border, the empire finally collapsed

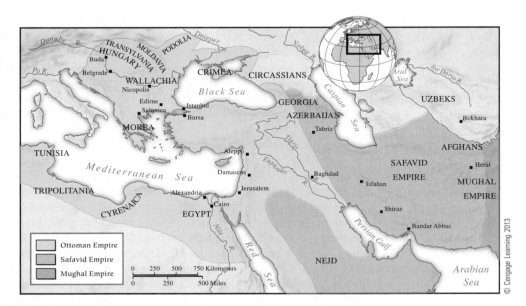

MAP 16.2 The Ottoman and Safavid Empires, c. 1683

During the seventeenth century, the Ottoman and Safavid Empires contested vigorously for hegemony in the eastern Mediterranean and the Middle East. This map shows the territories controlled by each state in the late seventeenth century.

in 1723. Eventually, order was restored by the military adventurer Nadir Shah Afshar (NAH-der shah ahf-SHAR), who launched an extended series of campaigns that restored the country's borders and even occupied the Mughal capital of Delhi. After his death, the Zand dynasty ruled until the end of the eighteenth century.

Safavid Politics and Society   Like the Ottoman Empire, Persia under the Safavids was a mixed society. The Safavids had come to power with the support of nomadic Turkic-speaking tribal groups, and leading elements from those groups retained considerable influence within the empire. But the majority of the population were Iranian, descendants of migrating peoples who had arrived in the area in the first millennium B.C.E.; most of them were farmers or townspeople, with attitudes inherited from the relatively sophisticated and urbanized culture of pre-Safavid Iran. Faced with the problem of integrating unruly Turkic-speaking tribal peoples with the sedentary Persian-speaking population of the urban areas, the Safavids used the Shi'ite faith as a unifying force. The shah himself acquired an almost divine quality and claimed to be the spiritual leader of all Islam. Shi'ism was declared the state religion.

Although there was a landed aristocracy, aristocratic power and influence were firmly controlled by strong-minded shahs, who confiscated aristocratic estates when possible and brought them under the control of the crown. Appointment to senior positions in the bureaucracy was by merit rather than birth. To avoid encouraging competition between Turkish and non-Turkish elements, Shah Abbas I hired a number of foreigners from neighboring countries for positions in his government.

The Safavid shahs took a direct interest in the economy and actively engaged in commercial and manufacturing activities, although there was also a large and affluent urban bourgeoisie. Like the Ottoman sultan, one shah regularly traveled the city streets incognito to check on the honesty of his subjects. When he discovered that a baker and a butcher were overcharging for their products, he had the baker cooked in his own oven and the butcher roasted on a spit. Although the road system was said to be quite poor, most goods traveled by caravan. The government provided accommodations for weary travelers and, at least in times of strong rulers, kept the roads relatively clear of thieves and bandits.

At its height, Safavid Iran was a worthy successor of the great Persian empires of the past, although it was probably not as wealthy as its neighbors to the east and west, the Mughals and the Ottomans. Hemmed in by the seapower of the Europeans to the south and by the land power of the Ottomans to the west, the Safavids had no navy and were forced to divert overland trade with Europe through southern Russia to avoid an Ottoman blockade. Still, the brocades, carpets, and leather goods of Persia were highly prized throughout the world. A school of philosophy that sought truth in a fusion of rationalist and intuitive methods flourished in the sixteenth and seventeenth centuries, and Safavid science, medicine, and mathematics were the equal of other societies in the region.

Safavid Art and Literature   Persia witnessed an extraordinary flowering of the arts during the reign of Shah Abbas I. His new capital, Isfahan, was a grandiose planned city with wide visual perspectives and a sense of order almost unique in the region. Shah Abbas ordered his architects to position his palaces, mosques, and bazaars around a massive rectangular polo ground. Much of the original city is still in good condition and remains the gem of modern Iran. The immense mosques are richly decorated with elaborate blue tiles. The palaces are delicate structures with unusual slender wooden columns. These architectural wonders of Isfahan epitomize the grandeur, delicacy, and color that defined the Safavid golden age. To adorn the splendid buildings, Safavid artisans created imaginative metalwork, tile decorations, and original and delicate glass vessels. The ceramics of the period, imitating Chinese prototypes of celadon or blue-and-white Ming design, largely ignored traditional Persian designs.

The greatest area of productivity, however, was in textiles. Silk weaving based on new techniques became a national industry. The silks depicted birds, animals, and flowers in a brilliant mass of color with silver and gold threads. Above all, carpet weaving flourished, stimulated by the great demand for Persian carpets in the West. Still highly prized all over the world, these seventeenth-century carpets reflect the grandeur and artistry of the Safavid Dynasty.

The long tradition of Persian painting continued into the Safavid era, but changed dramatically in two ways during the second half of the sixteenth century. First, taking advantage of the growing official toleration of portraiture, painters began to highlight the inner character of their subjects. Second, since royal patronage was not always forthcoming, artists sought to attract a larger audience by producing individual paintings that promoted their own distinctive styles and proudly bore their own signature.

THE GRANDEUR OF THE MUGHALS

In retrospect, the period from the sixteenth to eighteenth centuries can be viewed both as a high point of traditional culture in India and as the first stage of perhaps its biggest challenge. The era began with the creation of one of the subcontinent's greatest empires, that of the Mughals (MOO-guls). Mughal rulers, although foreigners and Muslims like many of their immediate predecessors, nevertheless brought India to a peak of political power and cultural achievement. For the first time since the Mauryan dynasty, the entire subcontinent was united under a single government, with a common culture, at least on the surface, that inspired admiration and envy throughout the region.

Babur: Founder of the Mughal Dynasty   When the Portuguese fleet led by Vasco da Gama arrived at the port of Calicut in the spring of 1498, the Indian subcontinent was still divided into a number of Hindu and Muslim kingdoms. But it was on the verge of a new era of unity that would be brought about by a foreign dynasty called the Mughals. Like so many other rulers of northern India, the founders of the Mughal Empire were not natives of India but came from the mountainous region north of the Ganges River. The founder of the dynasty, known to history as Babur (BAH-burr) (1483–1530), had an illustrious pedigree. His father was descended from the great Asian conqueror Tamerlane, his mother from the Mongol conqueror Genghis Khan.

Babur had inherited a fragment of Tamerlane's empire in an upland valley of the Syr Darya (SEER DAHR-yuh) River. Driven south by the rising power of the

Uzbeks and then the Safavid Dynasty in Persia, Babur and his warriors seized Kabul in 1504 and, thirteen years later, crossed the Khyber Pass into India.

Following a pattern that we have seen before, Babur began his rise to power by offering to help an ailing dynasty against its opponents. Although his own forces were far less numerous than those of his adversaries, he possessed advanced weapons, including artillery, and used them to great effect. His use of mobile cavalry was particularly successful against his enemy's massed forces supplemented by mounted elephants. In 1526, with only 12,000 troops against an enemy force nearly ten times that size, Babur captured Delhi (DEL-ee) and established his power in the plains of northern India. Over the next several years, he continued his conquests in northern India until his death in 1530 at the age of forty-seven.

Babur's success was due in part to his vigor and his charismatic personality, which earned him the undying loyalty of his followers. His son and successor, Humayun (hoo-MY-yoon) (r. 1530–1556), was, in the words of one British historian, "intelligent but lazy." Whether or not this is a fair characterization, Humayun clearly lacked the will to consolidate his father's conquests and the personality to inspire loyalty among his subjects. In 1540, he was forced to flee to Persia, where he lived in exile for sixteen years. Finally, with the aid of the Safavid shah of Persia, he returned to India and reconquered Delhi in 1555 but died the following year in a household accident, reportedly from injuries suffered in a fall after smoking a pipeful of opium.

Humayun was succeeded by his son Akbar (AK-bar) (r. 1556–1605). Born while his father was living in exile, Akbar was only fourteen when he mounted the throne. Illiterate but highly intelligent and industrious, Akbar set out to extend his domain, then limited to the Punjab (puhn-JAHB) and the upper Ganges River valley. "A monarch," he remarked, "should be ever intent on conquest, otherwise his neighbors rise in arms against him. The army should be exercised in warfare, lest from want of training they become self-indulgent."[2] By the end of his life, he had brought Mughal rule to most of the subcontinent, from the Himalaya Mountains to the Godavari (goh-DAH-vuh-ree) River in central India and from Kashmir to the mouths of the Brahmaputra (brah-muh-POO-truh) and the Ganges. In so doing, Akbar had created the greatest Indian empire since the Mauryan dynasty nearly two thousand years earlier.

Akbar and Indo-Muslim Civilization   Although Akbar was probably the greatest of the conquering Mughal monarchs, like his famous predecessor Ashoka, he is best known for the humane character of his rule. Above all, he accepted the diversity of Indian society and took steps to reconcile his Muslim and Hindu subjects.

Religion and the State   Though raised an orthodox Muslim, Akbar had been exposed to other beliefs during his childhood and had little patience with the pedantic views of Muslim scholars at court. As emperor, he displayed a keen interest in other religions, not only tolerating Hindu practices in his own domains but also welcoming the expression of Christian views by his Jesuit advisers. Akbar put his policy of religious tolerance into practice by taking a Hindu princess as one of his wives, and the success of this marriage may well have had an effect on his

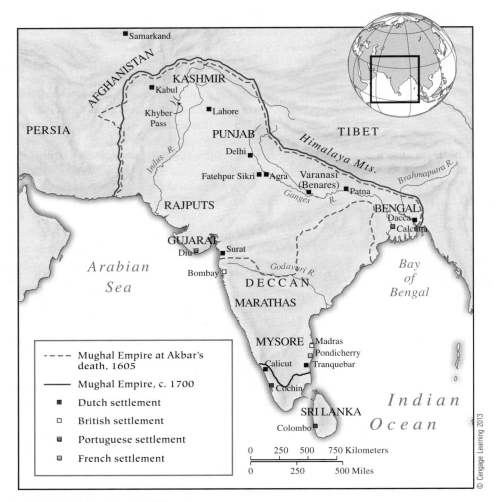

MAP 16.3 The Mughal Empire

This map shows the expansion of the Mughal Empire from the death of Akbar in 1605 to the reign of Aurangzeb at the end of the seventeenth century.

religious convictions. He patronized classical Indian arts and architecture and abolished many of the restrictions faced by Hindus in a Muslim-dominated society.

During his later years, Akbar became steadily more hostile to Islam. To the dismay of many Muslims at court, he sponsored a new form of worship called the Divine Faith (*Din-i-Ilahi*), which combined characteristics of several religions with a central belief in the infallibility of all decisions reached by the emperor. Some historians have maintained that Akbar totally abandoned Islam and adopted a Persian model of imperial divinity. But others have pointed out that the emperor was claiming only divine guidance, not divine status, and suggest that the new ideology was designed to cement the loyalty of officials to the person of the monarch. Whatever the case, the new faith aroused deep hostility in Muslim circles and vanished rapidly after his death.

Administrative Reforms Akbar also extended his innovations to the imperial administration. The empire was divided into provinces, and the administration of each province was modeled after the central government, with separate departments for military, financial, commercial, and legal affairs. Senior officials in each department reported directly to their counterparts in the capital city of Agra.

Although the upper ranks of the government continued to be dominated by nonnative Muslims, a substantial proportion of lower-ranking officials were Hindus, and a few Hindus were appointed to positions of importance. At first, most officials were paid salaries, but later they were ordinarily assigned sections of agricultural land for their temporary use; they kept a portion of the taxes paid by the local peasants in lieu of a salary. These local officials, known as **zamindars** (zuh-meen-DAHRZ), were expected to forward the rest of the taxes from the lands under their control to the central government, which also derived much of its revenue from the exploitation of substantial crown lands. *Zamindars* often recruited a number of military and civilian retainers and accumulated considerable power in their localities.

The same tolerance that marked Akbar's attitude toward religion and administration extended to the Mughal legal system. While Muslims were subject to the Islamic codes (the *Shari'a*), Hindu law (the *Dharmashastra*) applied to areas settled by Hindus, who after 1579 were no longer required to pay the unpopular *jizya* (JIZ-yuh), or poll tax on non-Muslims. Punishments for crime were relatively mild, at least by the standards of the day, and justice was administered in a relatively impartial and efficient manner.

A Harmonious Society A key element in Akbar's vision of the ideal social order was the concept of harmony, meaning that each individual and group within the empire would play their assigned role and contribute to the welfare of society as a whole. This concept of social harmony was based in part on his vision of a world shaped by the laws of Islam as transmitted by Muhammad *(Shari'a)*, but it also corresponded to the deep-seated indigenous belief in the importance of class hierarchy, as expressed in the Indian class and caste system. In its overall conception, it bears a clear resemblance to the social structure adopted by the Mughals' contemporaries to the west, the Ottoman Empire.

Overall, Akbar's reign was a time of peace and prosperity. Although all Indian peasants were required to pay about one-third of their annual harvest to the state through the *zamindars*, in general the system was applied fairly, and when drought struck in the 1590s, the taxes were reduced or even suspended altogether. Thanks to a long period of relative peace and political stability, commerce and manufacturing flourished. Foreign trade, in particular, thrived as Indian goods, notably textiles, tropical food products, spices, and precious stones, were exported in exchange for gold and silver. Tariffs on imports were low. Much of the foreign commerce was handled by Arab traders, since the Indians, like their Mughal rulers, did not care for travel by sea. Internal trade, however, was dominated by large merchant castes, which also were active in banking and handicrafts.

Akbar's Successors   Akbar died in 1605 and was succeeded by his son Jahangir (juh-HAHN-geer) (r. 1605–1628). During the early years of his reign, Jahangir continued to strengthen central control over the vast empire. Eventually, however, his grip began to weaken (according to his memoirs, he "only wanted a bottle of wine and a piece of meat to make merry"), and the court fell under the influence of one of his wives, the Persian-born Nur Jahan (NOOR juh-HAHN). The empress took advantage of her position to enrich her own family and arranged for her niece Mumtaz Mahal (MOOM-tahz muh-HAHL) to marry her husband's third son and ultimate successor, Shah Jahan (r. 1628–1657). When Shah Jahan succeeded to the throne, he quickly demonstrated the single-minded quality of his grandfather (albeit in a much more brutal manner), ordering the assassination of all of his rivals in order to secure his position.

The Reign of Shah Jahan   During a reign of three decades, Shah Jahan maintained the system established by his predecessors while expanding the boundaries of the empire by successful campaigns in the Deccan Plateau and against Samarkand, north of the Hindu Kush. But Shah Jahan's rule was marred by his failure to deal with the growing domestic problems. He had inherited a nearly empty treasury because of Empress Nur Jahan's penchant for luxury and ambitious charity projects. Though the majority of his subjects lived in grinding poverty, Shah Jahan's frequent military campaigns and expensive building projects put a heavy strain on the imperial finances and compelled him to raise taxes. At the same time, the government did little to improve rural conditions. In a country where transport was primitive (it often took three months to travel the 600 miles between Patna, in the middle of the Ganges River valley, and Delhi) and drought conditions frequent, the dynasty made few efforts to increase agricultural efficiency or to improve the roads or the irrigation network, although a grand trunk road was eventually constructed between the capital Agra (AH-gruh) and Lahore (luh-HOHR), a growing city several hundred miles to the northwest. A Dutch merchant in Gujarat (goo-juh-RAHT) described conditions during a famine in the mid-seventeenth century:

> As the famine increased, men abandoned towns and villages and wandered helplessly. It was easy to recognize their condition: eyes sunk deep in head, lips pale and covered with slime, the skin hard, with the bones showing through, the belly nothing but a pouch hanging down empty, knuckles and kneecaps showing prominently. One would cry and howl for hunger, while another lay stretched on the ground dying in misery; wherever you went, you saw nothing but corpses.[3]

In 1648, Shah Jahan moved his capital from Agra to Delhi and built the famous Red Fort in his new capital city. But he is best known for the Taj Mahal (tahj muh-HAHL) in Agra, widely considered to be the most beautiful building in India, if not in the entire world. The story is a romantic one—that the Taj was built by the emperor in memory of his wife Mumtaz Mahal, who had died giving birth to her thirteenth child at the age of thirty-nine. But the reality has a less attractive side: the expense of the building, which employed 20,000 masons over twenty years, forced the government to raise agricultural taxes, further impoverishing many Indian peasants.

The Rule of Aurangzeb   Succession struggles returned to haunt the dynasty in the mid-1650s when Shah Jahan's illness led to a struggle for power between his sons Dara Shikoh (DA-ruh SHIH-koh) and Aurangzeb (ow-rang-ZEB). Dara Shikoh was described by his contemporaries as progressive and humane, although possessed of a violent temper and a strong sense of mysticism. But he apparently lacked political acumen and was outmaneuvered by Aurangzeb (r. 1658–1707), who had Dara Shikoh put to death and then imprisoned his father in the fort at Agra.

Aurangzeb is one of the most controversial individuals in the history of India. A man of high principle, he attempted to eliminate many of what he considered India's social evils, prohibiting the immolation of widows on their husband's funeral pyre (*sati*), the castration of eunuchs, and the exaction of illegal taxes. With less success, he tried to forbid gambling, drinking, and prostitution. But Aurangzeb, a devout and somewhat doctrinaire Muslim, also adopted a number of measures that reversed the policies of religious tolerance established by his predecessors. The building of new Hindu temples was prohibited, and the Hindu poll tax was restored. Forced conversions to Islam were resumed, and non-Muslims were driven from the court. Aurangzeb's heavy-handed religious policies led to considerable domestic unrest and to a revival of Hindu fervor during the last years of his reign. A number of revolts also broke out against imperial authority.

The Shadows Lengthen   During the eighteenth century, Mughal power was threatened from both within and without. Fueled by the growing power and autonomy of the local gentry and merchants, rebellious groups in provinces throughout the empire, from the Deccan to the Punjab, began to reassert local authority and reduce the power of the Mughal emperor to that of a "tinsel sovereign." Increasingly divided, India was vulnerable to attack from abroad. In 1739, Delhi was sacked by the Persians, who left it in ashes and carried off its splendid Peacock Throne.

A number of obvious reasons for the virtual collapse of the Mughal Empire can be identified, including the draining of the imperial treasury and the decline in competence of the Mughal rulers. By 1700, the Europeans, who at first were no more than an irritant, had begun to seize control of regional trade routes and to meddle in the internal politics of the subcontinent.

It should be noted, however, that even at its height under Akbar, the empire was less a centralized state than a loosely knit collection of heterogeneous principalities held together by the authority of the throne, which tried to combine Persian concepts of kingship with the Indian tradition of decentralized power. Decline set in when centrifugal forces gradually began to predominate over centripetal ones.

Ironically, one element in this process was the very success of the system, which led to the rapid expansion of wealth and autonomous power at the local level. As local elites increased their wealth and influence, they became less willing to accept the authority and financial demands from Delhi. The reassertion of Muslim orthodoxy under Aurangzeb and his successors simply exacerbated the problem by irritating many of the emperor's Hindu subjects. This process was hastened by the growing European military and economic presence along the periphery of the empire.

The Impact of European Power in India   As we have seen, the first Europeans to arrive were the Portuguese. Although they sought to establish a virtual monopoly over regional trade in the Indian Ocean, they did not seek to penetrate the interior of the subcontinent but focused on establishing way stations en route to China and the Spice Islands. The situation changed at the end of the sixteenth century when the English and the Dutch entered the scene. Soon both powers were in active competition with Portugal and with each other for trading privileges in the region.

Penetration of the new market was not easy for the Europeans because they initially had little to offer their hosts, who had been conducting a thriving trade with peoples throughout the Indian Ocean regional market for centuries. As a result, European merchants focused on taking part in the carrying trade between one Asian port and another. The Portuguese, for example, carried high-quality textile goods from India to Africa in exchange for gold from the mines in Zimbabwe. With their profits, they paid for spices to be transported back to Europe. Eventually, goods such as textiles and spices were paid for with gold and silver bullion mined in Latin America.

The experience of the English was a prime example. When in 1608 the first English fleet arrived at Surat (SOOR-et), a thriving port on the northwestern coast of India, the English request for trading privileges was rejected by Emperor Jahangir, at the suggestion of the Portuguese advisers already in residence at the imperial court. Needing lightweight Indian cloth to trade for spices in the East Indies, the English persisted, and in 1616, they were finally permitted to install their own ambassador at the imperial court in Agra. Three years later, the first English factory, or warehouse, was established at Surat.

During the next several decades, the English presence in India steadily increased as Mughal power waned. By mid-century, additional English trading posts had been established at Bombay ("good bay" in Portuguese) on the west coast of the peninsula, at Fort William (now the great city of Calcutta, recently renamed Kolkata) on the Hoogly River near the Bay of Bengal, and at Madras (muh-DRAS or muh-DRAHS) (now Chennai) on the southeastern coast. From there, English ships carried high-quality Indian-made cotton goods back home to the British Isles, where they began to compete effectively with locally produced woolen products, or to the East Indies, where they were bartered for spices to be shipped back to England.

English success in India attracted rivals, including the Dutch and the French. The Dutch eventually abandoned their interests in India to concentrate on the spice trade, but the French were more persistent and seized Madras in 1746. For a brief period, the French competed successfully for trade privileges with the British, but the military genius of Sir Robert Clive (CLYV), an aggressive British administrator and empire builder who eventually became the chief representative of the East India Company in the subcontinent, combined with the refusal of the French government to provide financial support for French actions in India eventually left the latter with only a fort at Pondicherry (pon-dir-CHEH-ree) and a handful of other tiny enclaves on the southeastern coast.

In the meantime, Clive began to consolidate British control in Bengal (ben-GAHL), where the local Indian ruler had attacked Fort William and

OPPOSING VIEWPOINTS

The Capture of Port Hoogly

INTERACTION & EXCHANGE

In 1632, the Mughal ruler, Shah Jahan, ordered an attack on the city of Hoogly (HOOG-lee), a fortified Portuguese trading post on the northeastern coast of India. For the Portuguese, who had profited from half a century of triangular trade between India, China, and various countries in the Middle East and Southeast Asia, the loss of Hoogly at the hands of the Mughals hastened the decline of their influence in the region. Presented here are two contemporary versions of the battle. The first, from the *Padshahnama* (pad-shah-NAHM-uh) (*Book of Kings*), relates the course of events from the Mughal point of view. The second account is by John Cabral, a Jesuit missionary who was resident in Hoogly at the time.

The *Padshahnama*

During the reign of the Bengalis, a group of Frankish [European] merchants ... settled in a place one *kos* from Satgaon ... and, on the pretext that they needed a place for trading, they received permission from the Bengalis to construct a few edifices. Over time, due to the indifference of the governors of Bengal, many Franks gathered there and built dwellings of the utmost splendor and strength, fortified with cannons, guns, and other instruments of war. It was not long before it became a large settlement and was named Hoogly.... The Franks' ships trafficked at this port, and commerce was established, causing the market at the port of Satgaon to slump.... Of the peasants of those places, they converted some to Christianity by force and others through greed and sent them off to Europe in their ships....

Since the improper actions of the Christians of Hoogly Port toward the Muslims was accurately reflected in the mirror of the mind of the Emperor before his accession to the throne, when the imperial banners cast their shadows over Bengal, and inasmuch as he was always inclined to propagate the true religion and eliminate infidelity, it was decided that when he gained control over this region he would eradicate the corruption of these abominators from the realm.

John Cabral, *Travels of Sebastian Manrique, 1629–1649*

Hugli continued at peace all the time of the great King Jahangir. For, as this Prince, by what he showed, was more attached to Christ than to Mohammad and was a Moor in name and dress only.... Sultan Khurram was in everything unlike his father, especially as regards the latter's leaning towards Christianity.... He declared himself the mortal enemy of the Christian name and the restorer of the law of Mohammad.... He sent a *firman* [order] to the Viceroy of Bengal, commanding him without reply or delay, to march upon the Bandel of Hugli and put it to fire and the sword. He added that, in doing so, he would render a signal service to God, to Mohammad, and to him....

Consequently, on a Friday, September 24, 1632.... all the people [the Portuguese] embarked with the utmost secrecy.... Learning what was going on, and wishing to be able to boast that they had taken Hugli by storm, they [the imperialists] made a general attack on the Bandel by Saturday noon. They began by setting fire to a mine, but lost in it more men than we. Finally, however, they were masters of the Bandel.

Q *How do these two accounts of the Battle of Hoogly differ? Is there any way to reconcile the two into a single narrative?*

Sources: From *King of the World: A Mughal Manuscript from the Royal Library, Windsor Castle*, trans. by Wheeler Thackston, text by Milo Cleveland Beach and Ebba Koch (London: Thames and Hudson, 1997), p. 59.

imprisoned the local British population in the infamous Black Hole of Calcutta (an underground prison for holding the prisoners, many of whom died in captivity). In 1757, a small British force numbering about three thousand defeated a Mughal-led army over ten times that size in the Battle of Plassey. As part of the spoils of victory, the British East India Company exacted from the now-decrepit Mughal court the authority to collect taxes from extensive lands in the area surrounding Calcutta. Less than ten years later, British forces seized the reigning Mughal emperor in a skirmish at Buxar (buk-SAHR), and the British began to consolidate their economic and administrative control over Indian territory through the surrogate power of the now powerless Mughal court.

To officials of the East India Company, the expansion of their authority into the interior of the subcontinent probably seemed like a simple commercial decision, a move designed to seek guaranteed revenues to pay for the increasingly expensive military operations in India. To historians, it marks a major step in the gradual transfer of all of the Indian subcontinent to the British East India Company and later, in 1858, to the British crown. The process was more haphazard than deliberate. Under a new governor general, Warren Hastings, the British attempted to consolidate areas under their control and defeat such rivals as the rising Hindu Marathas (muh-RAH-tuhz), who exploited the decline of the Mughals to expand their own territories in Maharashtra (mah-huh-RAHSH-truh).

The Economic Consequences of Conquest   The British East India Company's takeover of vast landholdings, notably in the eastern Indian states of Orissa (uh-RIH-suh) and Bengal, may have been a windfall for enterprising British officials, but it had serious consequences for the Indian economy. In the first place, it resulted in the transfer of capital from the local Indian aristocracy to company officials, most of whom sent their profits back to Britain. Second, it eventually hastened the destruction of India's once healthy textile industry. At first, exports of high-quality Indian cotton goods skyrocketed, as the attractive local muslins and colorful calicoes began to replace the traditional woolen garments previously in fashion in Europe. Eventually, however, rising costs for imported Indian textiles, combined with stiff resistance from the woolen industry, produced dramatic changes in British textile production. Imports of cheap raw cotton from fields newly planted in the Americas, combined with revolutionary new inventions in the spinning and weaving process, transformed the British Isles during the eighteenth century into the center of global textile production. Inexpensive British machine-made textiles were now imported duty-free into India to compete against local goods, many of which were produced on hand looms in Indian villages, thus putting millions out of work.

Finally, British expansion in India hurt the peasants. As the British took over the administration of the land tax, they began to apply British law, which allowed the lands of those unable to pay the tax to be confiscated. In the 1770s, a series of famines led to the death of an estimated one-third of the population in the areas under company administration. The British government attempted

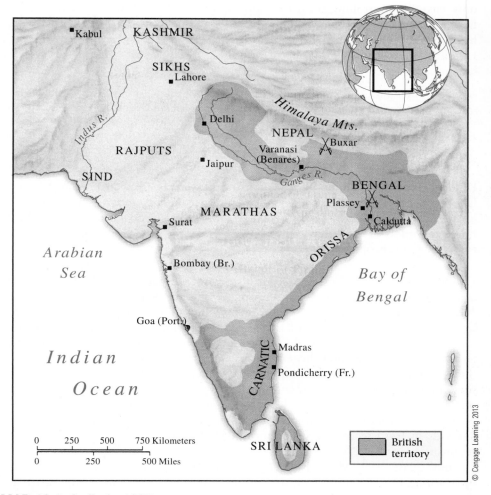

MAP 16.4   India in 1805

By the early nineteenth century, much of the Indian subcontinent had fallen under British domination.

to resolve the problem by assigning tax lands to the local revenue collectors (*zamindars*) in the hope of transforming them into English-style rural gentry, but many collectors themselves fell into bankruptcy and sold their lands to absentee bankers while the now landless peasants remained in abject poverty. It was hardly an auspicious beginning to "civilized" British rule.

Resistance to the British   As a result of such conditions, Britain's rise to power in India did not go unchallenged. Although Mughal authority was by now virtually moribund, local forces took matters into their own hands. Astute Indian commanders avoided pitched battles with the well-armed British troops but harassed and ambushed them in the manner of guerrillas in our time. Said Haidar Ali (HY-dur AH-lee), one of Britain's primary rivals for control in southern India:

> You will in time understand my mode of warfare. Shall I risk my cavalry which cost a thousand rupees each horse, against your cannon ball which cost two pice? No! I will march your troops until their legs swell to the size of their bodies. You shall not have a blade of grass, nor a drop of water. I will hear of you every time your drum beats, but you shall not know where I am once a month. I will give your army battle, but it must be when I please, and not when you choose.[4]

Unfortunately for India, not all its commanders were as astute as Haidar Ali. In the last years of the eighteenth century, when the East India Company's authority came into the capable hands of Lord Cornwallis and his successor, Lord Mornington, the future marquess of Wellesley, the stage was set for the final consolidation of British rule over the subcontinent.

The Mughal Dynasty: A "Gunpowder Empire"?

To some recent historians, the success of the Mughals, like that of the Ottomans and the Safavids, was due to their mastery of the techniques of modern warfare, especially the use of firearms. In this view, firearms played a central role in the ability of all three empires to overcome their rivals and rise to regional hegemony. Accordingly, some scholars have labeled them "gunpowder empires." Although technical prowess in the art of warfare was undoubtedly a key element in their success, we should not forget that other factors, such as dynamic leadership, political acumen, and the possession of an ardent following motivated by religious zeal (at least in the case of the Safavids in Iran) were equally important in their drive to power and ability to retain it.

In the case of the Mughals, the "gunpowder empire" thesis has been challenged by historian Douglas Streusand, who argues that the Mughals used "the carrot and the stick" to extend their authority, relying not just on heavy artillery but also on other forms of siege warfare and the offer of negotiations. Once in power, the Mughals created an empire that appeared highly centralized from the outside but was actually a collection of semiautonomous principalities ruled by provincial elites and linked together by the overarching majesty of the Mughal emperor—and not simply by the barrel of a gun. Even today, many Indians regard Akbar as the country's greatest ruler, a tribute not only to his military success but also to the humane policies adopted during his reign.

Society Under the Mughals: A Synthesis of Cultures

The Mughals were the last of the great traditional Indian dynasties. Like so many of their predecessors since the fall of the Guptas nearly a thousand years before, the Mughals were Muslims. But like the Ottoman Turks, the best Mughal rulers did not simply impose Islamic institutions and beliefs on the predominantly Hindu population; they combined Muslim with Hindu and even Persian concepts and cultural values in a unique social and cultural synthesis that even today seems to epitomize the greatness of Indian civilization. The new faith of Sikhism, founded in the early sixteenth century in an effort to blend both faiths, undoubtedly benefited from the mood of syncretism promoted by the Mughal court.

To be sure, Hindus sometimes attempted to defend themselves and their religious practices against the efforts of some Mughal monarchs to impose the Islamic religion and Islamic mores on the indigenous population. In some cases, despite official prohibitions, Hindu men forcibly married Muslim women and then converted them to the native faith, while converts to Islam normally lost all of their inheritance rights within the Indian family. Government orders to destroy Hindu temples were often ignored by local officials, sometimes as the result of bribery or intimidation. Although the founding emperor Babur expressed little admiration for the country he had subjected to his rule, ultimately Indian practices had an influence on the Mughal elites, as many Mughal chieftains married Indian women and adopted Indian forms of dress.

In some areas, Emperor Akbar's tireless effort to bring about a blend of Middle Eastern and South Asian religious and cultural values paid rich dividends, as substantial numbers of Indians decided to convert to the Muslim faith during the centuries of Mughal rule. Some were undoubtedly attracted to the egalitarian characteristics of Islam, but others found that the mystical and devotional qualities promoted by Sufi missionaries corresponded to similar traditions among the local population. This was especially true in Bengal, on the eastern edge of the Indian subcontinent, where Hindu practices were not as well established and where forms of religious devotionalism had long been popular among the population.

The Economy   Although much of the local population in the subcontinent lived in the grip of grinding poverty, punctuated by occasional periods of widespread famine, the first centuries of Mughal rule were in some respects a period of relative prosperity for the region. India was a leading participant in the growing foreign trade that crisscrossed the Indian Ocean from the Red Sea and the Persian Gulf to the Strait of Malacca and the Indonesian archipelago. High-quality cloth from India was especially prized, and the country's textile industry made it, in the words of one historian, "the industrial workshop of the world."

Long-term stability led to increasing commercialization and the spread of wealth to new groups within Indian society. The Mughal era saw the emergence of an affluent landed gentry and a prosperous merchant class. Members of prestigious castes from the pre-Mughal period reaped many of the benefits of the increasing wealth, but some of these changes transcended caste boundaries and led to the emergence of new groups who achieved status and wealth on the basis of economic achievement rather than traditional kinship ties. During the late eighteenth century, this economic prosperity was shaken by the decline of the Mughal Empire and the increasing European presence. But many prominent Indians reacted by establishing commercial relationships with the foreigners. For a time, such relationships often worked to the Indians' benefit. Later, as we shall see, they would have cause to regret the arrangement.

The Position of Women   Deciding whether Mughal rule had much effect on the lives of ordinary Indians is somewhat problematic. The treatment of women is a good example. Women had traditionally played an active role in Mongol tribal society—many actually fought on the battlefield alongside the men—and Babur and his successors often relied on the women in their families for political advice. Women from aristocratic families were often awarded honorific titles, received salaries, and were permitted to own land and engage in business. Women at court sometimes received an education, and Emperor Akbar reportedly established a girls' school at Fatehpur Sikri to provide teachers for his own daughters. Aristocratic women often expressed their creative talents by writing poetry, painting, or playing music. Women of all castes were adept at spinning thread, either for their own use or to sell to weavers to augment the family income. Weaving was carried out in the home by all members of the families of the weaving subcaste. They sold simple cloth to local villages and fine cotton, silk, and wool to the Mughal court. By Akbar's reign, the textile manufacturing was of such high quality and so well established that India sold cloth to much of the world: Arabia, the coast of East Africa, Egypt, Southeast Asia, and Europe.

To a certain degree, these Mughal attitudes toward women may have had an impact on Indian society. Women were allowed to inherit land, and some even possessed *zamindar* rights. Women from mercantile castes sometimes took an active role in business activities. At the same time, however, as Muslims, the Mughals subjected women to certain restrictions under Islamic law. On the whole, these Mughal practices coincided with and even accentuated existing tendencies in Indian society. The Muslim practice of isolating women and preventing them from associating with men outside the home (*purdah*) was adopted by many upper-class Hindus as a means of enhancing their status or protecting their women from unwelcome advances by Muslims in positions of authority. In other ways, Hindu practices were unaffected. The custom of *sati* continued to be practiced despite efforts by the Mughals to abolish it, and child marriage (most women were betrothed before the age of ten) remained common. Women were still instructed to obey their husbands without question and to remain chaste.

Mughal Culture   The era of the Mughals was one of synthesis in culture as well as in politics and religion. The Mughals combined Islamic themes with Persian and indigenous motifs to produce a unique style that enriched and embellished Indian art and culture. The Mughal emperors were zealous patrons of the arts and enticed painters, poets, and artisans from as far away as the Mediterranean. Apparently, the generosity of the Mughals made it difficult to refuse a trip to India. It was said that they would reward a poet with his weight in gold.

Architecture Undoubtedly, the Mughals' most visible achievement was in architecture. Here they integrated Persian and Indian styles in a new and sometimes breathtakingly beautiful form best symbolized by the Taj Mahal, built by the emperor Shah Jahan in the mid-seventeenth century. Although the human and economic cost of the Taj tarnishes the romantic legend of its construction, there is no denying the beauty of the building. It had evolved from a style that originated several decades earlier with the tomb of Humayun, which was built by his widow in Agra in 1565 during the reign of Akbar.

Humayun's mausoleum had combined Persian and Islamic motifs in a square building finished in red sandstone and topped with a dome. The style was repeated in a number of other buildings erected throughout the empire, but the Taj brought the style to perfection. Working with a model created by his Persian architect, Shah Jahan raised the dome and replaced the red sandstone with brilliant white marble. The entire exterior and interior surface is decorated with cut-stone geometric patterns, delicate black stone tracery, or intricate inlay of colored precious stones in floral and Qur'anic arabesques. The technique of creating dazzling floral mosaics of lapis lazuli, malachite, carnelian, turquoise, and mother-of-pearl may have been introduced by Italian artists at the Mughal court. Shah Jahan had intended to erect a similar building in black marble across the river for his own remains, but the plans were abandoned after he was deposed by his son Aurangzeb. Shah Jahan spent his last years imprisoned in a room in the Red Fort at Agra; from his windows, he could see the beautiful memorial to his beloved wife.

The Taj was by no means the only magnificent building erected during the Mughal era. Akbar, who, in the words of a contemporary, "dresses the work of his mind and heart in the garment of stone and clay," was the first of the great Mughal builders. His first palace at Agra, the Red Fort, was begun in 1565. A few years later, he ordered the construction of a new palace at Fatehpur Sikri, 26 miles to the west. The new palace was built in honor of a Sufi mystic who had correctly forecast the birth of a son to the emperor. In gratitude, Akbar decided to build a new capital city and palace on the site of the mystic's home. Over a period of fifteen years, from 1571 to 1586, a magnificent new city in red sandstone was constructed. Although the city was abandoned before completion and now stands almost untouched, it is a popular destination for tourists and pilgrims.

Painting The other major artistic achievement of the Mughal period was painting. Painting had never been one of the great attainments of Indian culture due in part to a technological difficulty. Paper was not introduced to India from Persia until the latter part of the fourteenth century, so traditionally painting had been done on palm leaves, which had severely hampered artistic creativity. By the fifteenth century, Indian painting had made the transition from palm leaf to paper, and the new medium eventually stimulated a burst of creativity, particularly in the genre of miniatures, or book illustrations.

As in so many other areas of endeavor, painting in Mughal India resulted from the blending of two cultures. While living in exile, Emperor Humayun had learned to admire Persian miniatures. On his return to India in 1555, he invited two Persian masters to live in his palace and introduce the technique. His successor, Akbar, appreciated the new style and popularized it with his patronage. He established a state workshop at Fatehpur Sikri for two hundred artists, mostly Hindus, who worked under the guidance of the Persian masters to create the Mughal school of painting.

The "Akbar style" combined Persian with Indian motifs, such as the use of extended space and the portrayal of humans engaged in physical action, characteristics not usually seen in Persian art. Akbar also apparently encouraged the imitation of European art forms, including the portrayal of Christian subjects, the use of perspective, lifelike portraits, and the shading of colors in the Renaissance style. The depiction of the human figure in Mughal painting outraged orthodox Muslims at court, but Akbar argued that the painter, "in sketching anything that has life ... must come to feel that he cannot bestow individuality upon his work, and is thus forced to think of God, the Giver of Life, and will thus increase in knowledge."[5]

Painting during Akbar's reign followed the trend toward realism and historical narrative that had originated in the Ottoman Empire. For example, Akbar had the illustrated *Book of Akbar* made to record his military exploits and court activities. Many of the paintings of Akbar's life portray him in action in the real world. After his death, his son and grandson continued the patronage of the arts.

Literature The development of Indian literature was held back by the absence of printing, which was not introduced until the end of the Mughal era. Literary works were inscribed by calligraphers, and one historian has estimated that the library of Agra contained more than 24,000 volumes. Poetry, in particular, flourished under the Mughals, who established poets laureate at court. Poems were written in the Persian style and in the Persian language. In fact, Persian became the official language of the court until the sack of Delhi in 1739. At the time, the Indians' anger at their conquerors led them to adopt Urdu as the new language for the court and for poetry. By that time, Indian verse on the Persian model had already lost its original vitality and simplicity and had become more artificial in the manner of court literature everywhere.

Another aspect of the long Mughal reign was a Hindu revival of devotional literature, much of it dedicated to Krishna and Rama. The retelling of the Ramayana in the vernacular, beginning in the southern Tamil languages in the eleventh century and spreading slowly northward, culminated in the sixteenth-century Hindi version by the great poet Tulsidas (tool-see-DAHSS) (1532–1623). His *Ramcaritmanas* (RAM-kah-rit-MAH-nuz) presents the devotional story with a deified Rama and Sita. Tulsidas's genius was in combining the conflicting cults of Vishnu and Shiva into a unified and overwhelming love for the divine, which he expressed in some of the most moving of all Indian poetry. The *Ramcaritmanas* has eclipsed its two-thousand-year-old Sanskrit ancestor in popularity and even became the basis of an Indian television series in the late 1980s.

CHRONOLOGIES

THE OTTOMAN EMPIRE

1280–1326	Reign of Osman I
1345	Ottoman Turks cross the Bosporus
1360	Murad I consolidates Turkish power in the Balkans
1389	Ottomans defeat the Serbian army at Kosovo
1402	Tamerlane defeats the Ottoman army at Ankara
1451–1481	Reign of Mehmet II the Conqueror
1453	Turkish conquest of Constantinople
1516–1517	Turks defeat the Mamluks in Syria and seize Cairo
1520–1566	Reign of Suleyman I the Magnificent
1526	Defeat of the Hungarians at Battle of Mohács
1529	Defeat of the Turks at Vienna
1571	Battle of Lepanto
1683	Second siege of Vienna

THE SAFAVIDS

1501	Ismail seizes lands of present-day Iran and Iraq and becomes shah of Persia
1508	Ismail conquers Baghdad and defeats the Uzbeks
1587–1629	Reign of Shah Abbas I
1638	Truce achieved between Ottomans and Safavids
1723	Collapse of the Safavid Empire

THE MUGHAL ERA

1498	Arrival of Vasco da Gama at Calicut
1526	Babur seizes Delhi
1530	Death of Babur
1555	Humayun recovers throne in Delhi
1556	Death of Humayun and accession of Akbar
1605	Death of Akbar and accession of Jahangir

1608	Arrival of English at Surat
1616	English embassy to Agra
1628–1657	Reign of Emperor Shah Jahan
1639	Foundation of English factory at Madras
1658	Aurangzeb succeeds to the throne
1707	Death of Aurangzeb
1739	Sack of Delhi by the Persians
1746	French capture Madras
1757	Battle of Plassey

 MindTap is a fully online, highly personalized learning experience built upon Cengage Learning content. MindTap combines student learning tools—readings, multimedia, activities, and assessments—into a singular Learning Path that guides students through their course.

17

THE EAST ASIAN WORLD

Emperor Kangxi

CHAPTER OUTLINE

• China at Its Apex • Changing China • Tokugawa Japan • Korea and Vietnam

CHINA AT ITS APEX

In 1514, a Portuguese fleet dropped anchor off the coast of China, just south of the Pearl River estuary and present-day Hong Kong. It was the first direct contact between the Chinese Empire and the West since the arrival of the Venetian adventurer Marco Polo two centuries earlier, and it opened an era that would eventually change the face of China and, indeed, all the world.

The Later Ming   Marco Polo had reported on the magnificence of China after visiting Beijing (bay-ZHING) during the reign of Khubilai Khan, the great Mongol ruler. By the time the Portuguese fleet arrived off the coast of China, of course, the Mongol Empire had long since disintegrated. It had gradually weakened after the death of Khubilai Khan and was finally overthrown in 1368 by a massive peasant rebellion under the leadership of Zhu Yuanzhang (JOO yoo-wen-JAHNG), who had declared himself the founding emperor of a new Ming (Bright) Dynasty (1369–1644), with his capital at Nanjing (nahn-JING) in central China.

As we have seen, the Ming inaugurated a period of territorial expansion westward into Central Asia and southward into Vietnam while consolidating control over China's vast heartland. It had also embarked on a brief era of maritime expansion, when the admiral Zheng He (JEHNG-huh) led a series of voyages that spread Chinese influence far into the Indian Ocean. In 1433, however, those voyages were suddenly discontinued, as the dynasty turned its attention to domestic concerns. To underline the new policy, Emperor Yongle (YOONG-luh) transplanted his capital to Beijing, where he ordered the construction of a new imperial home—known as the Imperial City—on the grounds of Khubilai's old palace under the Yuan dynasty.

First Contacts with the West   Despite the Ming's retreat from active participation in maritime trade, when the Portuguese arrived in 1514, China was in command of a vast empire that stretched from the steppes of Central Asia to the China Sea, from the Gobi Desert to the tropical rain forests of Southeast Asia. From the lofty perspective of the imperial throne in Beijing, the Europeans could only have seemed like an unusually exotic form of barbarian to be inserted within the familiar framework of the tributary system, the hierarchical arrangement in which rulers of all other countries were regarded as "younger brothers" of the Son of Heaven. Indeed, the bellicose and uncultured behavior of the Portuguese initially so outraged Chinese officials that they expelled the Europeans. After further negotiations, however, Chinese officials relented and authorized the Portuguese to occupy the tiny territory of Macao (muh-KOW) as a means of retaining sporadic contacts with the Celestial Empire.

As a result, the arrival of the Portuguese did not have much impact on Chinese society. Direct trade between Europe and China was limited, and Portuguese ships became involved in the regional trade network, carrying silk from China to Japan in return for Japanese silver. Eventually, the Spanish also began to participate, using the Philippines as an anchor in the galleon trade between China and the great silver mines in the Americas.

More influential than trade, perhaps, were the ideas introduced by Christian missionaries, who first received permission to reside in China in the last quarter of the sixteenth century. Among the most active and the most effective were highly educated

Jesuits, who were familiar with European philosophical and scientific developments. Court officials were particularly impressed by the visitors' ability to predict the exact time of a solar eclipse, an event that the Chinese viewed with extreme reverence.

Recognizing the Chinese pride in their own culture, the Jesuits attempted to draw parallels between Christian and Confucian concepts (for example, they identified the Western concept of God with the Chinese character for Heaven) and to show the similarities between Christian morality and Confucian ethics. European inventions such as the clock, the prism, and various astronomical and musical instruments impressed Chinese officials, hitherto deeply imbued with a sense of the superiority of Chinese civilization, and helped Western ideas win acceptance at court. An elderly Chinese scholar expressed his wonder at the miracle of eyeglasses:

> White glass from across the Western Seas
> Is imported through Macao:
> Fashioned into lenses big as coins,
> They encompass the eyes in a double frame.
> I put them on—it suddenly becomes clear;
> I can see the very tips of things!
> And read fine print by the dim-lit window
> Just like in my youth.[1]

For their part, the missionaries were much impressed with many aspects of Chinese civilization, and reports of their experiences heightened European curiosity about this great society on the other side of the world. By the late seventeenth century, European philosophers and political thinkers had begun to praise Chinese civilization and to hold up Confucian institutions and values as a mirror to criticize their counterparts in the West.

The Ming Brought to Earth   During the late sixteenth century, the Ming began to decline as a series of weak rulers led to an era of corruption, concentration of land ownership, and ultimately peasant rebellions and tribal unrest along the northern frontier. The inflow of vast amounts of foreign silver to pay for Chinese goods led to an alarming increase in inflation. Then the arrival of the English and the Dutch, whose ships preyed on the Spanish galleon trade between Asia and the Americas, disrupted the silver trade; silver imports plummeted, severely straining the Chinese economy by raising the value of the metal relative to that of copper. Crop yields declined due to harsh weather—linked to the "little ice age" of the early seventeenth century—and the resulting scarcity made it difficult for the government to provide food in times of imminent starvation. High taxes, necessitated in part because corrupt officials siphoned off revenues, led to rural unrest and violent protests among urban workers. A folk song of the period, addressed to the "Lord of Heaven," complained:

> Old skymaster,
> You're getting on, your ears are deaf, your eyes are gone.
> Can't see people, can't hear words.
> Glory for those who kill and burn;
> For those who fast and read the scriptures,
> Starvation.
> Fall down, old master sky, how can you be so high?
> How can you be so high? Come down to earth.[2]

As always, internal problems were accompanied by disturbances along the northern frontier. Following long precedent, the Ming had attempted to pacify the frontier tribes by forging alliances with them, arranging marriages between them and the local aristocracy, and granting trade privileges. One of the alliances was with the Manchus (man-CHOOZ)—also known as the Jurchen (roor-ZHEN)—the descendants of a non-Chinese people who had briefly established a kingdom in northern China during the early thirteenth century. The Manchus, a mixed agricultural and hunting people, lived northeast of the Great Wall in the area known today as Manchuria (man-CHUR-ee-uh).

At first, the Manchus were satisfied with consolidating their territory and made little effort to extend their rule south of the Great Wall. But during the first decades of the seventeenth century, the problems of the Ming Dynasty began to come to a head. A major epidemic devastated the population in many areas of the country. The suffering brought on by the epidemic helped spark a vast peasant revolt led by the formal postal worker Li Zicheng (lee zuh-CHENG) (1604–1651). With the imperial court now increasingly preoccupied by tribal attacks along the frontier, in

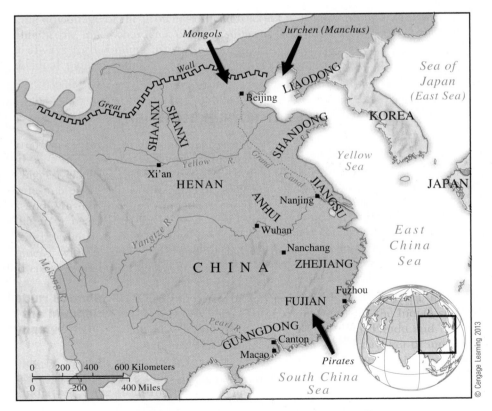

MAP 17.1   China and Its Enemies During the Late Ming Era

During the seventeenth century, the Ming Dynasty faced challenges on two fronts: from China's traditional adversaries, nomadic groups north of the Great Wall, and from new arrivals, European merchants who had begun to press for trading privileges along the southern coast.

the 1630s, Li managed to extend the revolt throughout the country, and his forces finally occupied the capital, Beijing, in 1644. The last Ming emperor committed suicide by hanging himself from a tree in the palace gardens.

But the rebels were unable to hold their conquest. Emboldened by the overthrow of the dynasty, the Manchus—now assisted by military commanders who had deserted from the Ming—managed to seize Beijing. Li Zicheng's army rapidly disintegrated, and the Manchus declared a new dynasty: the Qing (CHING) (or Pure), which lasted from 1644 until 1911. Once again, China was under foreign rule.

The Greatness of the Qing

The accession of the Manchus to power in Beijing was not universally applauded. Their ruthless policies and insensitivity to Chinese customs soon provoked resistance. Some Ming loyalists fled to Southeast Asia, but others sought to resist the new rulers from inside the country. To make it easier to identify rebels, the government ordered all Chinese to adopt Manchu dress and hairstyles. All Chinese males were to shave their foreheads and braid their hair into a queue (KYOO); those who refused were to be executed. As a popular saying put it, "Lose your hair or lose your head."[3]

But the Manchus eventually proved to be more adept at adapting to Chinese conditions than their predecessors, the Mongols. Unlike the latter, who had tried to impose their own methods of ruling, the Manchus adopted the Chinese political system (although, as we shall see, they retained their distinct position within it) and were gradually accepted by many Chinese as the legitimate rulers of the country.

Like all of China's great dynasties, the Qing was blessed with a series of strong early rulers who pacified the country, rectified many of the most obvious social and economic inequities, and restored peace and prosperity to the country. For the Ming Dynasty, these strong emperors had been Zhu Yuanzhang and Yongle; under the Qing, they would be Kangxi and Qianlong (CHAN-loong). The two Qing monarchs ruled China from the middle of the seventeenth century to the end of the eighteenth and were responsible for much of the greatness of Manchu China.

The Reign of Kangxi

Kangxi (r. 1661–1722) was arguably the greatest ruler in Chinese history. Ascending to the throne at the age of seven, he was blessed with diligence, political astuteness, and a strong character and began to take charge of Qing administration while still an adolescent. During the six decades of his reign, Kangxi not only stabilized imperial rule by pacifying the restive peoples along the northern and western frontiers but also managed to make the dynasty acceptable to the general population. As an active patron of arts and letters, he cultivated the support of scholars through a number of major projects.

During Kangxi's reign, the activities of the Western missionaries, Dominicans and Franciscans as well as Jesuits, reached their height. An intellectually curious ruler like the Mughal emperor Akbar, Kangxi was quite tolerant of the Christians, and several Jesuit missionaries became influential at court. Several hundred court officials converted to Christianity, as did an estimated 300,000 among the general population. But the Christian effort was ultimately undermined by squabbling among the Western religious orders over the Jesuit policy of accommodating local beliefs and practices in order to facilitate conversion. The Jesuits had acquiesced to the emperor's insistence that traditional Confucian rituals such as ancestor veneration were civil ceremonies and thus could be undertaken by Christian converts. Jealous Dominicans and Franciscans complained to the pope, who issued an edict ordering all missionaries and converts to conform to the official orthodoxy set forth in Europe. At first, Kangxi attempted to resolve the problem by appealing directly to the Vatican, but the pope was uncompromising. After Kangxi's death, his successor began to suppress Christian activities throughout China.

The Reign of Qianlong   Kangxi's achievements were carried on by his successors, Yongzheng (YOONG-jehng) (r. 1722–1736) and Qianlong (r. 1736–1795). Like Kangxi, Qianlong was known for his diligence, tolerance, and intellectual curiosity, and he too combined vigorous military action against the unruly tribes along the frontier with active efforts to promote economic prosperity, administrative efficiency, and scholarship and artistic excellence. The result was continued growth for the Manchu Empire throughout much of the eighteenth century.

But it was also under Qianlong that the first signs of the internal decay of the Manchu Dynasty began to appear. The clues were familiar ones. Qing military campaigns along the frontier were expensive and placed heavy demands on the imperial treasury. As the emperor aged, he became less astute in selecting his subordinates and fell under the influence of corrupt elements at court, including the notorious Manchu official Heshen (HEH-shen). Funds officially destined for military or other official use were increasingly siphoned off by Heshen or his favorites, arousing resentment among military and civilian officials.

Corruption at the center led inevitably to unrest in rural areas, where higher taxes, bureaucratic venality, and rising pressure on the land because of the growing population had produced economic hardship. In central China, discontented peasants who had recently been resettled on infertile land launched a revolt known as the White Lotus Rebellion (1796–1804). The revolt was eventually suppressed, but at great expense.

Qing Political Institutions   One reason for the success of the Manchus was their ability to adapt to their new environment. They retained the Ming political system with relatively few changes. They also tried to establish their legitimacy as China's rightful rulers by stressing their devotion to the principles of Confucianism. Emperor Kangxi ostentatiously studied the Confucian classics and issued a "sacred edict" that proclaimed to the entire empire the importance of the moral values established by "the Master."

Still, the Manchus, like the Mongols, were ethnically, linguistically, and culturally different from their subject population. The Qing attempted to cope with this reality by adopting a two-pronged strategy. One part of this strategy was aimed at protecting their distinct identity within an alien society. The Manchus, representing less than 2 percent of the entire population, were legally defined as distinct from everyone else in China. The Manchu nobles retained their aristocratic privileges, while their economic base was protected by extensive landholdings and revenues provided from the state treasury. Other Manchus were assigned farmland and organized into eight military units, called **banners**, which were stationed as separate units in various strategic positions throughout China. These "bannermen" were the primary fighting force of the empire. Ethnic Chinese were prohibited from settling in Manchuria and were still compelled to wear their hair in a queue as a sign of submission to the ruling dynasty.

At the same time that the Qing attempted to preserve their identity, they recognized the need to bring ethnic Chinese into the top ranks of imperial administration. Their solution was to create a system, known as **diarchy** (DY-ahr-kee), in which all important administrative positions were shared equally by Chinese and Manchus. Of the six members of the grand secretariat, three were Manchu and three were Chinese. Each of the six ministries had an equal number of Chinese and Manchu members, and Manchus and Chinese also shared responsibilities at the provincial level. Below the provinces, Chinese were dominant. Although the system did not work perfectly, the Manchus' willingness to share power did win the allegiance of many Chinese. Meanwhile, the Manchus themselves, despite official efforts to preserve their separate language and culture, were increasingly assimilated into Chinese civilization.

The new rulers also tinkered with the civil service examination system. In an effort to make it more equitable, quotas were established for each major ethnic group and each province to prevent the positions from being monopolized by candidates from certain provinces in central China that had traditionally produced large numbers of officials. In practice, however, the examination system probably became less equitable during the Manchu era because increasingly positions were assigned to candidates who had purchased their degree instead of competing through the system. Moreover, positions were becoming harder to obtain because their number did not rise fast enough to match the unprecedented increase in population under Qing rule.

China on the Eve of the Western Onslaught   In some ways, China was at the height of its power and glory in the mid-eighteenth century. But as we have seen, it was also during this period that the first signs of serious trouble for the Qing Dynasty began to appear.

Unfortunately for China, the decline of the Qing occurred just as China's modest relationship with the West was about to give way to a new era of military confrontation and increased pressure for trade. The first challenges came in the north, where Russian traders seeking skins and furs began to penetrate the region between Siberian Russia and Manchuria. Earlier the Ming Dynasty had attempted to deal with the Russians by the traditional method of placing them in a tributary relationship and playing them off against other non-Chinese groups in the area. But the tsar refused to play by Chinese rules. His envoys to Beijing ignored the tribute system and refused to perform the **kowtow** (the ritual of prostration and touching the forehead to the ground), the classical symbol of fealty demanded of all foreign ambassadors to the Chinese court. Formal diplomatic relations were finally established in 1689, when the Treaty of Nerchinsk (ner-CHINSK), negotiated with the aid of Jesuit missionaries resident at the Qing court, settled the boundary dispute and provided for regular trade between the two countries. Through such arrangements, the Manchus were able not only to pacify the northern frontier but also to extend their rule over Xinjiang (SHIN-jyahng) and Tibet to the west and southwest. In the meantime, tributary relations were established with such neighboring countries as Korea, Burma, Vietnam, and Ayuthaya.

Dealing with the foreigners who arrived by sea was more difficult. By the end of the seventeenth century, the English had replaced the Portuguese as the dominant force in European trade. Operating through the East India Company, which served as both a trading unit and the administrator of English territories in Asia, the English

MAP 17.2   The Qing Empire in the Eighteenth Century

The boundaries of the Chinese Empire at the height of the Qing Dynasty in the eighteenth century are shown on this map.

established their first trading post at Canton (KAN-tun) in 1699. Over the next decades, trade with China, notably the export of tea and silk to England, increased rapidly. To limit contact between Chinese and Europeans, the Qing licensed Chinese trading firms at Canton to be the exclusive conduit for trade with the West. Eventually, the Qing confined the Europeans to a small island just outside the city walls and permitted them to reside there only from October through March.

For a while, the British tolerated this system, which brought considerable profit to the East India Company and its shareholders. But by the end of the eighteenth century, the British had begun to demand that they be allowed access to other cities along the Chinese coast and that the country be opened to British manufactured goods. The British government and traders alike were restive at the uneven balance of trade between the two countries, which forced the British to ship vast amounts of silver bullion to China in exchange for its silk, porcelain, and tea. In 1793, a mission under Lord Macartney visited Beijing to press for liberalization of trade restrictions. A compromise was reached on the kowtow (Macartney was permitted to bend on one knee, as was the British custom), but Qianlong expressed no interest in British manufactured products. An exasperated Macartney compared the Chinese Empire to "an old, crazy, first-rate man-of-war" that had once awed its neighbors "merely by her bulk and appearance" but was now destined under incompetent leadership to be "dashed to pieces on the shore."[4] With his contemptuous dismissal of the British request, the emperor had inadvertently sowed the seeds for a century of humiliation.

CHANGING CHINA

During the Ming and Qing Dynasties, China remained a predominantly agricultural society; nearly 85 percent of its people were farmers. But although most Chinese still lived in rural villages, the economy was undergoing changes that led to the emergence of a vibrant and rapidly growing industrial and commercial sector. A number of cities, notably along the coast or along the major river systems, began to prosper under the impact of growing contacts between China and the outside world.

The Population Explosion   In the first place, the center of gravity was continuing to shift steadily from the north to the south. In the early centuries of Chinese civilization, the bulk of the population had been located along the Yellow River. Smaller settlements were located along the Yangzi and in the mountainous regions of the south, but the bulk of the population lived in the north. By the Song period, however, that emphasis had begun to shift drastically as a result of climatic changes, deforestation, and continuing pressure from nomads in the Gobi Desert. By the early Qing, the economic breadbasket of China was located along the Yangzi River or in the mountains to the south. One concrete indication of this shift occurred during the Ming Dynasty, when Emperor Yongle ordered the renovation of the Grand Canal to facilitate the shipment of rice from the Yangzi delta to the food-starved north.

Moreover, the population was beginning to increase rapidly. For centuries, China's population had remained within a range of 50 to 100 million, rising in times of peace and prosperity and falling in periods of foreign invasion and internal strife. During the Ming and the early Qing, however, the population increased from an estimated 70 to 80 million in 1390 to more than 300 million at the end of the eighteenth century. There were probably several reasons for this population increase: the relatively long period of peace and stability under the early Qing; the introduction of new crops from the Americas, including peanuts, sweet potatoes, and maize; and the planting of a new species of faster-growing rice from Southeast Asia.

Of course, this population increase meant much greater pressure on the land, smaller farms, and a razor-thin margin of safety in the event of a natural disaster. The imperial court attempted to deal with the problem through various means, most notably by preventing the concentration of land in the hands of wealthy landowners. Nevertheless, by the eighteenth century, almost all the land that could be irrigated was already under cultivation, and the problems of rural hunger and landlessness were becoming increasingly serious.

Seeds of Industrialization   Another change that took place during the early modern period in China was the steady growth of manufacturing and commerce. Taking advantage of the long era of peace and prosperity, merchants and manufacturers began to expand their operations beyond their immediate provinces. Commercial networks began to operate on a

European Warehouses at Canton. *Aggravated by the growing presence of foreigners in the eighteenth century, the Chinese court severely restricted the movement of European traders in China. They were permitted to live only in a compound near Canton during the seven months of the trading season and could go into the city only three times a month. In this painting, foreign flags (including, from the left, those of the United States, Sweden, Great Britain, and Holland) fly over the warehouses and residences of the foreign community while Chinese sampans and junks sit anchored in the river.*

regional and sometimes even a national basis as trade in silk, metal and wood products, porcelain, cotton goods, and cash crops like cotton and tobacco developed rapidly. Foreign trade also expanded after the Ming court in 1567 suspended its prohibition on such activities. In response, Chinese merchants began to set up extensive contacts with countries in Southeast Asia. As Chinese tea, silk, and porcelain became ever more popular in other parts of the world, the trade surplus grew as the country's exports greatly outnumbered its imports. Silver bullion, carried to the Philippines by Spanish galleons from the Americas, flooded into Chinese coffers. As the economy expanded, Chinese officials encouraged the importation of silver as a means of supplementing the inadequate supply of bronze coinage, but eventually the glut of silver in the marketplace caused price distortions that may have contributed to the fall of the Ming Dynasty.

The Qing Economy: Ready for Takeoff?   In recent years, a number of historians have suggested that because of these impressive advances, by the end of the eighteenth century China was poised to make the transition from an agricultural to a predominantly manufacturing and commercial economy—a transition that began to take place in western Europe with the onset of the Industrial Revolution at the end of the eighteenth century.

COMPARATIVE ESSAY

Population Explosion

EARTH & ENVIRONMENT

Between 1700 and 1800, Europe, China, and to a lesser degree India and the Ottoman Empire experienced a dramatic growth in population. In Europe, the population grew from 120 million people to almost 200 million by 1800; in China, from less than 200 million to more than 300 million during the same period.

Four developments in particular contributed to this population explosion. First, better growing conditions, made possible by an improvement in climate, affected wide areas of the world and enabled people to produce more food. Both China and Europe experienced warmer summers beginning in the early eighteenth century. Second, by the eighteenth century, people had begun to develop immunities to the epidemic diseases that had caused widespread loss of life between 1500 and 1700. The increase in travel by ship after 1500 had led to devastating epidemics. For example, the arrival of Europeans in Mexico introduced smallpox, measles, and chickenpox to a native population that had no immunities to European diseases. In 1500, between 11 and 20 million people lived in the area of Mexico; by 1650, only 1.5 million remained. Gradually, however, people developed resistance to these diseases.

A third factor in the population increase was the introduction of new foods. As a result of the Columbian Exchange, American food crops, such as corn, potatoes, and sweet potatoes, were transported to other parts of the world, where they became important food sources. China imported a new species of rice from Southeast Asia that had a shorter harvest cycle than existing varieties. These new foods provided additional sources of nutrition that enabled more people to live for a longer time. At the same time, land development and canal building in the eighteenth century enabled government authorities to move food supplies to areas threatened with crop failure and famine.

Finally, the use of new weapons based on gunpowder allowed states to control larger territories and ensure a new degree of order. The early rulers of the Qing Dynasty, for example, pacified the Chinese Empire and ensured a long period of peace and stability. Absolute monarchs achieved similar goals in a number of European states. Less violence resulted in fewer deaths at the same time that an increase in food supplies and a decrease in deaths from diseases were occurring, thus making possible in the eighteenth century the beginning of the world population explosion that persists to this day.

Q *What were the main reasons for the dramatic expansion in the world population during the early modern era?*

Certainly, in many respects, the Chinese economy in the mid-Qing era was as advanced as any of its counterparts around the world. China's achievements in technology over the past centuries were unsurpassed, and the population as a whole was among the most prosperous in the world. A perceptive observer at the time might well have concluded that the Manchu Empire would be highly competitive with the most advanced nations around the globe for the indefinite future.

Nevertheless, a number of factors raise doubts that China in the mid-Qing era was poised to advance rapidly into the industrial age. In the first place, the mercantile class was not as independent in China as in some European societies. Trade and manufacturing in China remained under the firm control of the state. In addition, political and social prejudices against commercial activity remained strong, and the road to success was still seen as resulting from a career in officialdom. Reflecting an ancient preference for agriculture over manufacturing and trade, the state levied heavy taxes on manufacturing and commerce while attempting to keep agricultural taxes low.

To a considerable degree, these views were shared by the population at large, as the scholar-gentry continued to dominate intellectual fashions in China throughout the early Qing period. Chinese elites in general had little interest in the natural sciences or economic activities and often viewed them as a threat to their own dominant status within Chinese society as a whole. The commercial middle class, lacking social status and an independent position in society, had little say in intellectual matters and relatively little influence at court.

At the root of such attitudes was the lingering influence of Neo-Confucianism, which remained the official state doctrine in China down to the end of the Qing Dynasty. Although the founding fathers of Neo-Confucianism had originally focused on the "investigation of things," as time passed its practitioners tended to emphasize the elucidation of moral principles rather than the expansion of scientific knowledge. Though the Chinese economy was gradually being transformed from an agricultural to a commercial and industrial giant, scholars tended to look back to antiquity, rather than to empirical science, as the prime source for knowledge of the natural world and human events. The result was an intellectual environment that valued continuity over change and tradition over innovation.

The Chinese indifference to foreign trade provides a good example. Although the early Ming emperor Yongle had expressed a strong interest in expanding Chinese contacts with the external world, his successors tended to focus on internal concerns and for a time even sought to prohibit trade with foreign countries in a bid to bring an end to the chronic pirate attacks taking place along the coast. Interest in geography and the shape of the world also declined, despite advances in map-making.

The Chinese reaction to European clock-making techniques provides an additional case study. In the early seventeenth century, the Jesuit priest Matteo Ricci introduced advanced European clocks driven by weights or springs. The emperor was fascinated and found the clocks more reliable than Chinese timekeepers, but the population at large did not adopt the Western invention. Although European timepieces became a popular novelty at court, the Chinese expressed little curiosity about the technology involved, provoking one European observer to remark that playthings like cuckoo clocks "will be received here with much greater interest than scientific instruments or *objets d'art.*"[5]

Daily Life in Qing China   Despite the changes in the economy, daily life in China under the Ming and early Qing Dynasties continued for the most part to follow traditional patterns.

The Family   Chinese society continued to be organized around the family. As in earlier periods, the ideal family unit in Qing China was the joint family, in which three or four generations lived under the same roof. When sons married, they brought their wives to live with them in their family homestead. Prosperous families would add a separate section to the house to accommodate the new family unit. Unmarried daughters would also remain in the house. Aging parents and grandparents remained under the same roof until they died and were cared for by younger members of the household. This ideal did not always correspond to reality, however, since many families did not possess sufficient land to support a large household. One historian has estimated that only about 40 percent of Chinese families actually lived in joint families.

Still, the family retained its importance in early Qing times for the same reasons as in earlier eras. As a labor-intensive society based primarily on the cultivation of rice, China needed large families to help with the harvest and to provide security for parents too old to work in the fields. Sons were especially prized, not only because they had strong backs but also because they would raise their own families under the parental roof. With few opportunities for employment outside the family, sons had little choice but to remain with their parents and help on the land. Within the family, the oldest male was in charge, and theoretically his wishes had to be obeyed by all family members. These values were reiterated in Emperor Kangxi's Sacred Edict, which listed filial piety and loyalty to the family as its first two maxims.

For many Chinese, the effects of these values were also apparent in the choice of a marriage partner. Arranged marriages were the norm, and the primary consideration in selecting a spouse was whether the union would benefit the family unit as whole. The couple usually had no say in the matter and might not even meet until the marriage ceremony. Not only were romantic feelings between the couple considered unimportant in marriage, but they were often viewed as undesirable because they could draw the attention of the husband and wife away from their primary responsibility to the larger family unit.

Although this emphasis on filial piety might seem to represent a blatant disregard for individual rights, the obligations were not all on the side of the children. The father was expected to provide support for his wife and children and, like the ruler, was supposed to treat those in his care with respect and compassion. All too often, however, the male head of the family was able to exact his privileges without performing his responsibilities in return.

Beyond the joint family was the clan, which was an extended kinship unit consisting of dozens or even hundreds of joint and nuclear families linked by a clan council of elders and a variety of other common social and religious functions. The clan served several useful purposes. Some possessed lands that could be rented out to poorer families, or richer families within the clan might provide land for the poor. Since there was no general state-supported educational system, sons of poor families might be invited to study in a school established in the home of a more prosperous relative. If the young man succeeded in becoming an official, he would be expected to provide favors and prestige for the clan as a whole.

Like joint families, clans were not universal, and millions of Chinese had none. They may have originated among the great landed families of the Tang era and managed to survive despite periodic efforts by the imperial court to weaken and destroy them. In many cases, clan solidarity was weakened by intralineage conflicts or differing levels of status and economic achievement. Nevertheless, in the early modern period, they were still an influential force at the local level and were particularly prevalent in the south.

The Role of Women   In traditional China, the role of women had always been inferior to that of men. A sixteenth-century Spanish visitor to South China observed that Chinese women were "very secluded and virtuous, and it was a very rare thing for us to see a woman in the cities and large towns, unless it was an old crone."[6] Women were more visible, he said, in rural areas, where they frequently could be seen working in the fields.

The concept of female inferiority had deep roots in Chinese history. This view was embodied in the belief that only a male could carry on sacred family rituals and that men alone had the talent to govern others. Only males could aspire to a career in government or scholarship. Within the family system, the wife was clearly subordinated to the husband. Legally, she could not divorce her husband or inherit property. The husband, however, could divorce his wife if she did not produce male heirs, or he could take a second wife as well as a concubine for his pleasure. Life was especially difficult for a widow: she had to raise her children on a single income or fight off her dead husband's greedy relatives, who would try to coerce her to remarry because, by law, they would then inherit all of her previous property and her original dowry. Female children were also less desirable because of their limited physical strength and because their parents would have to pay a dowry to the parents of their future husbands. Female children normally did not receive an education, and in times when food was in short supply, daughters might even be put to death.

Though women were clearly inferior to men in theory, this was not always the case in practice. Capable women often compensated for their legal inferiority by playing a strong role within the family. Women were often in charge of educating the children and handling the family budget. Some privileged women also received training in the Confucian classics, although their schooling was generally for a shorter time and less rigorous than that of their male counterparts. A few produced significant works of art and poetry.

All in all, however, life for women in traditional China was undoubtedly difficult. In Chinese novels, women were treated as scullery maids or love objects. They were frequently under the domination of both their husband and their mother-in-law, and in some cases the bullying was so brutal that suicide seemed to be the only way out.

Cultural Developments

During the late Ming and early Qing Dynasties, traditional culture in China reached new heights of achievement. With the rise of a wealthy urban class, the demand for art, porcelain, textiles, and literature increased dramatically.

The Rise of the Chinese Novel

During the Ming Dynasty, a new form of literature arose that eventually evolved into the modern Chinese novel. Although considered less respectable than poetry and nonfiction prose, these groundbreaking works (often written anonymously or under pseudonyms) were enormously popular, especially among well-to-do urban dwellers.

Written in a colloquial but realistic style, the new fiction produced vivid portraits of Chinese society. Many of the stories sympathized with society's downtrodden—often helpless maidens—and dealt with such crucial issues as love, money, marriage, and power. Adding to the realism were sexually explicit passages that depicted the private side of Chinese life. Readers delighted in sensuous tales that, no matter how pornographic, always professed a moral lesson; the villains were punished and the virtuous rewarded. During the more puritanical Qing era, a number of the more erotic works were censored or banned and found refuge in Japan, where several have recently been rediscovered by scholars.

A Plea for Women's Education

FAMILY & SOCIETY

As Chinese society evolved under the impact of the economic and social changes that took place during the early Qing era, the role of women in society came under increased scrutiny, and some commentators argued that women should be given an opportunity to play a more active role in society. In this essay, the career official Chen Hongmou (**Chehn HOONG-mow**) (1696–1771) takes up the case, arguing that women should no longer be cloistered in the home, but should receive an education in the classical texts like their male counterparts. Although Chen did not take issue with the traditional view that women lacked the capacity for deep intellectual thought and achievement, he maintained that an educated woman would be a better daughter, wife, and mother.

Chen Hongmou was a follower of the Song Dynasty neo-Confucian philosopher Zhu Xi (**JOO SHEE**) and an ardent advocate of seeking practical solutions to problems of governance. His writings on Chinese statecraft were highly influential during the first century of the Qing Dynasty and beyond.

Chen Hongmou, *Jiaonu yigui*

There is no uneducable person in the world. There is also no person whom it is justifiable not to educate. How then can female children alone be excepted? From the moment they grow out of infancy, they are protectively shut up deep within the women's quarters, rather than, like male children, being allowed out into the wider world, to be carefully corrected in their behavior by teachers and friends and to be cultivated by exposure to the classical literary canon. Although parents may love their daughter deeply, they give no more serious thought to her personal development than by providing her with a home,

food, and clothing. They teach her to sew, prepare her dowry, and nothing more.... This view that female children need not be educated is a violation of Principle and an affront to the Way....

Now, a woman in her parents' home is a daughter; when she leaves home she becomes a wife; when she bears children she becomes a mother. If she is a worthy daughter, she will become a worthy wife. If she is a worthy wife, she will become a worthy mother. If she is a worthy mother, she will have worthy sons and grandsons. Thus, the process of civilization begins in the women's quarters, and the fortunes of the entire household rest on the pillar of its womenfolk. Female education is a matter of the utmost importance.

Some will object: "But women who can learn to read are few. And if they do become literate, in many cases it will actually hinder their acquisition of proper female virtue." This argument fails to recognize that all women possess a degree of natural intelligence. Even if they cannot learn to master the classics and histories, they nevertheless can get a rough idea of their message.... Moreover, it is evident that in today's world there are already many women with a smattering of learning. They cling fast to the half-baked ideas they have absorbed, cherishing them till their dying day and imparting them to others. Under these circumstances, would it not be better if they [learned to] recite the classical texts in order to get their message right?

Q *What arguments does the author put forth to justify education for women in Qing China? Does he call for equal treatment of the sexes in education? If not, why not?*

Source: From *Sources of Chinese Tradition*, Vol. 2, pg. 162, by Wm. Theodore de Bary and Richard Lufrano. Copyright © 1999 Columbia University Press. Reprinted with permission of the publisher.

Gold Vase Plum, known in English translation as *The Golden Lotus*, presents a cutting exposé of the decadent aspects of late Ming society. Considered by many the first realistic social novel—preceding its European counterparts by two centuries—*The Golden Lotus* depicts the depraved life of a wealthy landlord who cruelly manipulates those around him for sex, money, and power. In a rare exception in Chinese fiction, the villain is not punished for his evil ways; justice is served instead by the misfortunes that befall his descendants.

The Dream of the Red Chamber is generally considered China's most distinguished popular novel. Published in 1791, some 150 years after *The Golden Lotus*, it tells of the tragic love of two young people caught in the financial and moral disintegration of a powerful Chinese clan. The hero and the heroine, both sensitive and spoiled, represent the inevitable decline of the Chia family and come to an equally inevitable tragic end, she in death and he in an unhappy marriage to another.

The Art of the Ming and the Qing   During the Ming and the early Qing, China produced its last outpouring of traditional artistic brilliance. Although most of the creative work was modeled on past examples, the art of this period is impressive for its technical perfection and impressive quantity.

In architecture, the most outstanding example is the Imperial City in Beijing, which, on the order of Ming emperor Yongle, was constructed on the remnants of the old imperial palace of the Yuan dynasty. His successors continued to add to the palace, but the basic design has not changed since the Ming era. Surrounded by high walls, the immense compound is divided into a maze of private apartments and offices and an imposing ceremonial quadrangle with a series of stately halls for imperial audiences and banquets. The grandiose scale, richly carved marble, spacious gardens, and graceful upturned roofs also contribute to the splendor of the "Forbidden City."

The decorative arts flourished in this period, especially intricately carved lacquerware and boldly shaped and colored cloisonné (kloi-zuh-NAY *or* KLWAH-zuh-nay), a type of enamelwork in which thin metal bands separate areas of colored enamel. Silk production reached its zenith, and the best-quality silks were highly prized in Europe, where chinoiserie (sheen-wah-zuh-REE *or* shee-nwahz-REE), as Chinese art of all kinds was called, was in vogue. Perhaps the most famous of all the achievements of the Ming era was the blue-and-white porcelain, still prized by collectors throughout the world. Of unsurpassed luminosity, this porcelain was used by Ming emperors to promote the prestige of their opulent and powerful empire. One variety caused such a sensation in the Netherlands that the Dutch began to manufacture their own blue-and-white porcelain at a new factory set up in Delft.

During the Qing Dynasty, Chinese artists produced great quantities of paintings to grace the walls of elite Chinese compounds. The commercial city of Yangzhou (YAHNG-Joh) on the Grand Canal emerged as an active artistic center. Inside the Forbidden City in Beijing, court painters worked alongside Jesuit artists and experimented with Western techniques. In general, however, European art, dismissed by some local artists as "mere craftsmanship," did not greatly influence Chinese painting at this time. Scholarly painters and the literati totally rejected foreign techniques and became obsessed with traditional Chinese styles. As a result, Qing painting became progressively more repetitive and stale. Ironically, the Qing Dynasty thus represents both the apogee of traditional Chinese art and the beginning of its decline.

TOKUGAWA JAPAN

At the end of the fifteenth century, the traditional Japanese system was at a point of near anarchy. With the decline in the authority of the Ashikaga (ah-shee-KAH-guh) Shogunate at Kyoto (KYOH-toh), clan rivalries had exploded into an era of warring states similar to the period of the same name in Zhou dynasty China. Even at the local level, power was frequently diffuse. For a typical daimyo (DYM-yoh) (great lord), the domain had become little more than a coalition of fief-holders held together by a loose allegiance to the manor lord. Prince Shotoku's dream of a united Japan seemed only a distant memory. In actuality, Japan was on the verge of an extended era of national unification and peace under the rule of its greatest shogunate, the Tokugawa.

The Three Great Unifiers The process began in the mid-sixteenth century with the emergence of three very powerful political figures: Oda Nobunaga (1568–1582), Toyotomi Hideyoshi (1582–1598), and Tokugawa Ieyasu (1598–1616). In 1568, Oda Nobunaga (OH-dah noh-buh-NAH-guh), the son of a samurai (SAM-uh-ry) and a military commander under the Ashikaga Shogunate, seized the imperial capital of Kyoto and placed the reigning shogun under his domination. During the next few years, the brutal and ambitious Nobunaga attempted to consolidate his rule throughout the central plains by defeating his rivals and suppressing the power of the Buddhist estates, but he was killed by one of his generals in 1582 before the process was complete. He was succeeded by Toyotomi Hideyoshi (toh-yoh-TOH-mee hee-day-YOH-shee), a farmer's son who had worked his way up through the ranks to become a military commander. Originally lacking a family name of his own, he eventually adopted the name Toyotomi ("abundant provider") to embellish his reputation for improving the material standards of his domain. Hideyoshi placed his capital at Osaka (oh-SAH-kuh), where he built a castle to accommodate his headquarters, and gradually extended his power outward to the southern islands of Shikoku (shee-KOH-koo) and Kyushu (KYOO-shoo). By 1590, he had persuaded most of the daimyo on the Japanese islands to accept his authority and created a national currency. Then he invaded Korea in an abortive effort to export his rule to the Asian mainland.

Despite their efforts, however, neither Nobunaga nor Hideyoshi was able to eliminate the power of the local daimyo. Both were compelled to form alliances with some daimyo in order to destroy other more powerful rivals. At the conclusion of his conquests in 1590, Toyotomi Hideyoshi could claim to be the supreme proprietor of all registered lands in areas under his authority. But he then reassigned those lands as fiefs to the local daimyo, who declared their allegiance to him. The daimyo in turn began to pacify the countryside, carrying out extensive "sword hunts" to disarm the population and attracting samurai to their service. The Japanese tradition of decentralized rule had not yet been overcome.

After Hideyoshi's death in 1598, Tokugawa Ieyasu (toh-koo-GAH-wah ee-yeh-YAH-soo), the powerful daimyo of Edo (EH-doh)—modern Tokyo—moved to fill the vacuum. Neither Hideyoshi nor Oda Nobunaga had claimed the title of shogun (SHOH-gun), but Ieyasu named himself shogun in 1603, initiating the most powerful and long-lasting of all Japanese shogunates. The Tokugawa rulers completed the restoration of central authority begun by Nobunaga and Hideyoshi and

MAP 17.3 Tokugawa Japan

This map shows the Japanese islands during the long era of the Tokugawa Shogunate. Key cities, including the shogun's capital of Edo (Tokyo), are shown.

remained in power until 1868, when a war dismantled the entire system. As a contemporary phrased it, "Oda pounds the national rice cake, Hideyoshi kneads it, and in the end Ieyasu sits down and eats it."[7]

Opening to the West

The unification of Japan took place almost simultaneously with the coming of the Europeans. Portuguese traders sailing in a Chinese junk that may have been blown off course by a typhoon had landed on the islands in 1543. Within a few years, Portuguese ships were stopping at Japanese ports on a regular basis to take part in the regional trade between Japan, China, and Southeast Asia. The first Jesuit missionary, Francis Xavier (ZAY-vee-ur), arrived in 1549.

Initially, the visitors were welcomed. Although Japanese leaders were somewhat ambivalent about establishing relations with countries in the outside world, Japanese traders were active in the regional trade network, and when the Ming court sought to prohibit all maritime trade in the 1530s, Japanese merchants countered by engaging in piracy or smuggling along the Chinese coast, despite efforts by leaders in both countries to stop them. The Europeans added a new dimension to the equation. The curious

Japanese (the Japanese were "very desirous of knowledge," said Francis Xavier) were fascinated by tobacco, clocks, spectacles, and other European goods, and local daimyo were especially interested in purchasing all types of European weapons and armaments. Oda Nobunaga and Toyotomi Hideyoshi found the new firearms helpful in defeating their enemies and unifying the islands. The effect on Japanese military architecture was particularly striking as local lords began to erect castles on the European model. Many of these castles, such as Hideyoshi's castle at Osaka, still exist today.

The missionaries also had some success. Though confused by misleading translations of sacred concepts in both cultures (Francis Xavier was notoriously poor at learning foreign languages), they converted a number of local daimyo, some of whom may have been motivated in part by the desire for commercial profits. By the end of the sixteenth century, thousands of Japanese in the southernmost islands of Kyushu and Shikoku had become Christians. One converted daimyo ceded the superb natural harbor of the modern city of Nagasaki (nah-gah-SAH-kee) to the Society of Jesus, which proceeded to use the new settlement for both missionary and trading purposes. But papal claims to the loyalty of all Japanese Christians and the European habit of intervening in local politics soon began to arouse suspicion in official circles. Missionaries added to the problem by deliberately destroying local idols and shrines and turning some temples into Christian schools or churches.

Expulsion of the Christians   Inevitably, the local authorities reacted. In 1587, Toyotomi Hideyoshi issued an edict prohibiting further Christian activities within his domains. Japan, he declared, was "the land of the Gods," and the destruction of shrines by the foreigners was "something unheard of in previous ages." To "corrupt and stir up the lower classes" to commit such sacrileges, he declared, was "outrageous."[8] The parties responsible (the Jesuits) were ordered to leave the country within twenty days. Hideyoshi was careful to distinguish missionary from trading activities, however, and merchants were permitted to continue their operations.

The Jesuits protested the expulsion, and eventually Hideyoshi relented, permitting them to continue proselytizing as long as they were discreet. But he refused to repeal the edicts, and when the aggressive activities of newly arrived Spanish Franciscans aroused his ire, he ordered the execution of nine missionaries and a number of their Japanese converts. When the missionaries continued to interfere in local politics (some even tried to incite the daimyo in the southern islands against the shogunate government in Edo), Tokugawa Ieyasu completed the process by ordering the eviction of all missionaries in 1612. The persecution of Japanese Christians intensified, leading to an abortive revolt by Christian peasants on the island of Kyushu in 1637, which was bloodily suppressed.

At first, Japanese authorities hoped to maintain commercial relations with European countries even while suppressing the Western religion, but eventually they decided to regulate foreign trade more closely and closed the two major foreign factories on the island of Hirado (heh-RAH-doh) and at Nagasaki. The sole remaining opening to the West was at the island of Deshima (deh-SHEE-muh or den-JEE-muh) in Nagasaki harbor, where in 1609 a small Dutch community was permitted to engage in limited trade with Japan (the Dutch, unlike the Portuguese and the Spanish, had not allowed missionary activities to interfere with their commercial interests). Dutch ships were permitted to dock at Nagasaki harbor only once a year and, after close inspection, were allowed to remain for two or three months. Conditions on the island of Deshima itself were quite confining: the

Dutch physician Engelbert Kaempfer complained that the Dutch lived in "almost perpetual imprisonment."[9] Nor were the Japanese free to engage in foreign trade, as the *bakufu* (buh-KOO-foo *or* bah-KOO-fuh)—the central government—sought to restrict the ability of local authorities to carry out commercial transactions with foreign merchants. A small amount of commerce took place with China and other parts of Asia, but Japanese subjects of the shogunate were forbidden to leave the country on penalty of death.

The Tokugawa "Great Peace" Once in power, the Tokugawa attempted to strengthen the system that had governed Japan for more than three hundred years. They followed precedent in ruling through the *bakufu*, composed now of a coalition of daimyo, and a council of elders. But the system was more centralized than it had been previously. Now the shogunate government played a dual role. It set national policy on behalf of the emperor in Kyoto while simultaneously governing the shogun's own domain, which included about one-quarter of the national territory as well as the three great cities of Edo, Kyoto, and Osaka. As before, the state was divided into separate territories, called domains (*han*), which were ruled by a total of about 250 individual daimyo lords. The daimyo themselves were divided into two types: the *fudai* (FOO-dy) **daimyo** (inside daimyo), who were mostly small daimyo that were directly subordinate to the shogunate, and the *tozama* (toh-ZAH-mah) **daimyo** (outside daimyo), who were larger, more independent lords that were usually more distant from the center of shogunate power in Edo.

Daimyo and Samurai In theory, the daimyo were essentially autonomous, since they were able to support themselves from taxes on their lands (the shogunate received its own revenues from its extensive landholdings). In actuality, the shogunate was able to guarantee daimyo loyalties by compelling daimyo lords to maintain two residences, one in their own domains and the other at Edo, and to leave their families in Edo as hostages for the daimyo's good behavior. Keeping up two residences also placed the Japanese nobility in a difficult economic position. Some were able to defray the high costs by concentrating on cash crops such as sugar, fish, and forestry products, but most were rice producers, and their revenues remained roughly the same throughout the period. The daimyo were also able to protect their economic interests by depriving their samurai retainers of their proprietary rights over the land and transforming them into salaried officials. The fief thus became a stipend, and the personal relationship between the daimyo and his retainers gradually gave way to a bureaucratic authority.

The Tokugawa also tinkered with the social system by limiting the size of the samurai class and reclassifying samurai who supported themselves by tilling the land as commoners. In fact, with the long period of peace brought about by Tokugawa rule, the samurai gradually ceased to be a warrior class and were required to live in the castle towns. As a gesture to their glorious past, samurai were still permitted to wear their two swords, and a rigid separation was maintained between persons of samurai status and the nonaristocratic segment of the population. The Jesuit missionary Francis Xavier observed that "on no account would a poverty-stricken gentleman marry with someone outside the gentry, even if he were given great sums to do so."[10]

Seeds of Capitalism The long period of peace under the Tokugawa Shogunate made possible a dramatic rise in commerce and manufacturing, especially in the growing cities. By the mid-eighteenth century, Edo, with a population of more than one million, was one of the largest cities in the world. The growth of trade and industry was stimulated by a rising standard of living—driven in part by technological advances in agriculture and an expansion of arable land—and the voracious appetites of the aristocrats for new products. The daimyo's need for income also contributed as many of them began to promote the sale of local goods from their domains, such as textiles, forestry products, sugar, and sake (SAH-kee) (fermented rice wine).

Most of this commercial expansion took place in the major cities and the castle towns, where the merchants and artisans lived along with the samurai, who were clustered in neighborhoods surrounding the daimyo's castle. Banking flourished, and paper money became the normal medium of exchange in commercial transactions. Merchants formed guilds not only to control market conditions but also to facilitate government oversight and the collection of taxes. Under the benign, if somewhat contemptuous, supervision of Japan's noble rulers, a Japanese merchant class gradually began to emerge from the shadows to play a significant role in the life of the Japanese nation. Some historians view the Tokugawa era as the first stage in the rise of an indigenous form of capitalism, based loosely on the Western model.

Eventually, the increased pace of industrial activity spread beyond the cities into rural areas. As in Great Britain, cotton was a major factor. Cotton had been introduced to China during the Song Dynasty and had spread to Korea and Japan shortly thereafter. Traditionally, however, cotton cloth had been too expensive for the common people, who instead wore clothing made of hemp. Imports increased during the sixteenth century, however, when cotton cloth began to be used for uniforms, matchlock fuses, and sails. Eventually, technological advances reduced the cost, and specialized communities for producing cotton cloth began to appear in the countryside and were gradually transformed into towns. By the eighteenth century, cotton had firmly replaced hemp as the cloth of choice for most Japanese.

Not everyone benefited from the economic changes of the seventeenth and eighteenth centuries, however, notably the samurai, who were barred by tradition and prejudice from commercial activities. Although some profited from their transformation into a managerial class on the daimyo domains, most still relied on their revenues from rice lands, which were often insufficient to cover their rising expenses; consequently, they fell heavily into debt. Others were released from servitude to their lord and became "masterless samurai." Occasionally, these unemployed warriors—known as *ronin* (ROH-nihn), or "wave men"—revolted or plotted against the local authorities. In one episode, made famous in song and story as "The Forty-Seven *Ronin*," the masterless samurai of a local lord who had been forced to commit suicide by a shogunate official later assassinated the official in revenge. Although their act received wide popular acclaim, the *ronin* were later forced to take their own lives.

Land Problems   The effects of economic developments on the rural population during the Tokugawa era are harder to estimate. Some farm families benefited by exploiting the growing demand for cash crops. But not all prospered. Most peasants continued to rely on rice cultivation and were whip-sawed between declining profits and rising costs and taxes (as daimyo expenses increased, land taxes often took up to 50 percent of the annual harvest). Many were forced to become tenants or to work as wage laborers on the farms of wealthy neighbors or in village industries. When rural conditions in some areas became desperate, peasant revolts erupted. According to one estimate, nearly seven thousand disturbances took place during the Tokugawa era. Peasant disturbances became a more or less routine means of protesting against rising taxes and official corruption or of demanding "benevolence" from the manor lord in times of natural disaster.

Some historians take issue with this grim picture and point out that Japanese peasants did not suffer the same level of hardship as was taking place among their counterparts in neighboring China. In the first place, an increase in the amount of land under cultivation, combined with improved agricultural technology, led to increased yields. Secondly, Japan experienced a relatively low rate of population growth during the Tokugawa era. Although the reasons for that phenomenon are not entirely clear, Honda Toshiaki (HAHN-duh toh-SHEE-ah-kee), a late-eighteenth-century demographer, ascribed the primary cause to a combination of late marriage, abortion, and infanticide. As he described the situation:

> Aware that if they have many children they will not have any property to leave them, [husbands and wives] confer and decide that rather than rear children who in later years will have great difficulty in making a decent living, it is better to take precautions before they are born and not add another mouth to feed. If they do have a child, they secretly destroy it, calling the process by the euphemism of "thinning out."[11]

Life in the Village The changes that took place during the Tokugawa era had a major impact on the lives of ordinary Japanese. In some respects, the result was an increase in the power of the central government at the village level. The shogunate increasingly relied on Confucian maxims advocating obedience and hierarchy to enhance its authority with the general population. Decrees from the *bakufu* instructed the peasants on all aspects of their lives, including their eating habits and their behavior. At the same time, the increased power of the government led to more autonomy from the local daimyo for the peasants. Villages now had more control over their local affairs and were responsible to the central government as much as to the nearby manor lord, although land taxes were still paid to the daimyo.

At the same time, the Tokugawa era saw the emergence of the nuclear family (*ie*) as the basic unit in Japanese society. In previous times, Japanese peasants had few legal rights. Most were too poor to keep their conjugal family unit intact or to pass property on to their children. Many lived at the manorial residence or worked as servants in the households of more affluent villagers. Now, with farm income on the rise, the nuclear family took on the same form as in China, although without the joint family concept. The Japanese system of inheritance was based on primogeniture (pry-moh-JEN-ih-chur). Family property was passed on to the eldest son, although younger sons often received land from their parents to set up their own families after marriage.

The Role of Women Another result of the changes under the Tokugawa was that women were somewhat more restricted than they had been previously. The rights of females were especially restricted in the samurai class, where Confucian values were highly influential. Male heads of households had broad authority over property, marriage, and divorce; wives were expected to obey their husbands on pain of death. Males often took concubines or homosexual partners, while females were expected to remain chaste. The male offspring of samurai parents studied the Confucian classics in schools established by the daimyo, while females were reared at home, where only the fortunate might receive a rudimentary training in reading and writing Chinese characters. Some women, however, became accomplished poets and painters since, in aristocratic circles, female literacy was prized for enhancing the refinement, social graces, and moral virtue of the home. Under the Tokugawa, it was the obligation of the wife in elite families to reflect her husband's rank and status through a strict code of comportment and dress.

Women were similarly at a disadvantage among the common people. Marriages were arranged, and as in China, the new wife moved in with the family of her husband. A wife who did not meet the expectations of her spouse or his family was likely to be divorced. Still, gender relations were more egalitarian than among the nobility. Women were generally valued as childbearers and homemakers, and both sexes worked in the fields. Coeducational schools were established in villages and market towns, and about one-quarter of the students were female. Poor families, however, often put infant daughters to death or sold them into prostitution and the "floating world" of entertainment. During the late Tokugawa era, peasant women became more outspoken and active in social protests and in some cases played a major role in provoking demonstrations against government exactions or exploitation by landlords or merchants.

Such attitudes toward women operated within the context of the increasingly rigid stratification of Japanese society. Deeply conservative in their social policies, the Tokugawa rulers established strict legal distinctions between the four main classes in Japan (warriors, artisans, peasants, and merchants). Intermarriage between classes was forbidden in theory, although sometimes the prohibitions were ignored in practice. Below these classes were Japan's outcasts, the *eta* (AY-tuh). Formerly, they were permitted to escape their status, at least in theory. The Tokugawa made their status hereditary and enacted severe discriminatory laws against them, regulating their place of residence, their dress, and even their hairstyles.

Tokugawa Culture   Under the Tokugawa, the tensions between the old society and the emerging new one were starkly reflected in the arena of culture. On the one hand, the classical culture, influenced by Confucian themes, Buddhist quietism, and the samurai warrior tradition, continued to flourish under the patronage of the shogunate. On the other, a vital new set of cultural values began to appear, especially in the cities. This innovative era witnessed the rise of mass entertainment and a popular literature written by and for the townspeople. With the development of woodblock printing in the early seventeenth century, literature became available to the common people, literacy levels rose, and lending libraries increased the accessibility of printed works. In contrast to the previous mood of doom and gloom, the new prose was cheerful and even frivolous, its primary aim being to divert and amuse.

The Literature of the New Middle Class   The best examples of this new urban fiction are the works of Saikaku (Sy-KAH-koo) (1642–1693), considered one of Japan's finest novelists. Saikaku's greatest novel, *Five Women Who Loved Love*, relates the amorous exploits of five women of the merchant class. Based partly on

OPPOSING VIEWPOINTS

Some Confucian Commandments

FAMILY & SOCIETY

Although the Qing Dynasty was of foreign origin, its rulers found Confucian maxims convenient for maintaining the social order. In 1670, the great emperor Kangxi issued the Sacred Edict to popularize Confucian values among the common people. The edict was read publicly at periodic intervals in every village in China and set the standard for behavior throughout the empire. Like the Qing Dynasty in China, the Tokugawa shoguns attempted to keep their subjects in line with decrees that carefully prescribed all kinds of behavior. Yet a subtle difference in tone can be detected between these two documents. Whereas Kangxi's edict tended to encourage positive behavior, the decree of the Tokugawa Shogunate focused more on actions that were prohibited or discouraged.

Kangxi's Sacred Edict

1. Esteem most highly filial piety and brotherly submission, in order to give due importance to the social relations.
2. Behave with generosity toward your kindred, in order to illustrate harmony and benignity.
3. Show that you prize moderation and economy, in order to prevent the lavish waste of your means.
4. Extirpate strange principles, in order to exalt the correct doctrine.
5. Lecture on the laws, in order to warn the ignorant and obstinate.
6. Labor diligently at your proper callings, in order to stabilize the will of the people.
7. Instruct sons and younger brothers, in order to prevent them from doing what is wrong.
8. Put a stop to false accusations, in order to preserve the honest and good.
9. Fully remit your taxes, in order to avoid being pressed for payment.
10. Remove enmity and anger, in order to show the importance due to the person and life.

real-life experiences, it broke from the Confucian ethic that stressed a wife's fidelity to her husband and portrayed women who were willing to die for love—and all but one eventually did. Despite the tragic circumstances, the tone of the novel is upbeat and sometimes comic, and the author's wry comments prevent the reader from becoming emotionally involved with the heroines' misfortunes. In addition to heterosexual novels for the merchant class, Saikaku also wrote of homosexual liaisons among the samurai.

In the theater, the rise of Kabuki (kuh-BOO-kee) threatened the long dominance of the *No* (NOH) play, replacing the somewhat restrained and elegant thematic and stylistic approach of the classical drama with a new emphasis on violence, music, and dramatic gestures. Significantly, the new drama emerged not from the rarefied world of the court but from the new world of entertainment and amusement. Its very commercial success, however, led to difficulties with the government, which periodically attempted to restrict or even suppress it. Early Kabuki was often performed by prostitutes, and shogunate officials, fearing that such activities could

Maxims for Peasant Behavior in Tokugawa Japan

1. Young people are forbidden to congregate in great numbers.

2. Entertainments unsuited to peasants, such as playing the samisen or reciting ballad dramas, are forbidden.

3. Staging sumo matches is forbidden for the next five years.

4. The edict on frugality issued by the han at the end of last year must be observed.

5. If a person has to leave the village for business or pleasure, that person must return by ten at night.

6. Father and son are forbidden to stay overnight at another person's house. An exception is to be made if it is to nurse a sick person.

7. Corvée [obligatory labor] assigned by the han must be performed faithfully.

8. Children who practice filial piety must be rewarded.

9. One must never get drunk and cause trouble for others.

10. Peasants who neglect farm work and cultivate their paddies and upland fields in a slovenly and careless fashion must be punished.

11. Fights and quarrels are forbidden in the village.

12. The deteriorating customs and morals of the village must be rectified.

13. Peasants who are suffering from poverty must be identified and helped.

14. This village has a proud history compared to other villages, but in recent years bad times have come upon us. Everyone must rise at six in the morning, cut grass, and work hard to revitalize the village.

15. The punishments to be meted out to violators of the village code and gifts to be awarded the deserving are to be decided during the last assembly meeting of the year.

Q *In what ways did Kangxi's set of commandments conform to the principles of State Confucianism? How do Kangxi's standards compare with those applied in Japan?*

Sources: From *Popular Culture in Late Imperial China* by David Johnson et al. Copyright © 1985 The Regents of the University of California. From Chi Nakane and Oishi Shinsabura, *Tokugawa Japan: The Social and Economic Antecedents of Modern Japan* (Japan, University of Tokyo, 1990), pp. 51–52. Translated by Conrad Totman. Copyright 1992 by Columbia University Press.

have a corrupting effect on the nation's morals, prohibited women from appearing on the stage; at the same time, they attempted to create a new professional class of male actors to impersonate female characters on stage. The decree had a mixed effect, however, because it encouraged homosexual activities, which had been popular among the samurai and in Buddhist monasteries since medieval times. Yet the use of male actors also promoted a greater emphasis on physical activities such as acrobatics and swordplay and furthered the evolution of Kabuki into a mature dramatic art.

In contrast to the popular literature of the Tokugawa period, poetry persevered in its more serious tradition. Although linked verse, so popular in the fourteenth and fifteenth centuries, found a more lighthearted expression in the sixteenth century, the most exquisite poetry was produced in the seventeenth century by the greatest of all Japanese poets, Basho (BAH-shoh) (1644–1694). He was concerned with the search for the meaning of existence and the poetic expression of his experience. Basho's genius lies in his sudden juxtaposition of a general or eternal

COMPARATIVE ILLUSTRATION

Popular Culture: East and West

FAMILY & SOCIETY

By the seventeenth century, a popular culture distinct from the elite culture of the nobility was beginning to emerge in the urban worlds of both the East and the West. Below is a festival scene from the pleasure district of Kyoto known as the Gion. Spectators on a balcony are enjoying a colorful parade of floats and costumed performers. The festival originated

Newark Museum/Art Resource, NY

condition with an immediate perception, a spark that instantly reveals a moment of truth. Thanks to his love of Daoism and Zen Buddhism, Basho found answers to his quest for the meaning of life in nature, and his poems are grounded in seasonal imagery. The following are among his most famous poems:

The ancient pond
A frog leaps in
The sound of the water.
On the withered branch
A crow has alighted—
The end of autumn.

His last poem, dictated to a disciple only three days before his death, succinctly expressed his frustration with the unfinished business of life:

On a journey, ailing—
my dreams roam about
on a withered moor.

Scala/Art Resource, NY

as a celebration of the passing of a deadly epidemic in medieval Japan. In the photo above is a scene from the celebration of Carnival on the Piazza Sante Croce in Florence, Italy. Carnival was a period of festivities before Lent, celebrated primarily in Roman Catholic countries. It became an occasion for indulgence in food, drink, games, and practical jokes as a prelude to the austerity of the forty-day Lenten season from Ash Wednesday to Easter.

Q *Do festivals such as these still exist in our own day? What purpose might they serve?*

Like all great artists, Basho made his poems seem effortless and simple. He speaks directly to everyone, everywhere.

Tokugawa Art   The arts also reflected the dynamism and changes in Japanese culture under the Tokugawa regime. The shogun's order that all daimyo and their families live every other year in Edo set off a burst of building as provincial rulers competed to erect the most magnificent mansion. Furthermore, the shoguns themselves constructed splendid castles adorned with sumptuous, almost ostentatious décor and furnishings. And the prosperity of the newly rising merchant class added fuel to the fire. Japanese paintings, architecture, textiles, and ceramics all flourished during this affluent era.

Court painters filled magnificent multipaneled screens with gold foil, which was also used to cover walls and even ceilings. This lavish use of gold foil mirrored the grandeur of the new Japanese rulers but also served a practical purpose: it reflected light in the dark castle rooms, where windows were kept small for defensive purposes. In contrast to the almost gaudy splendors of court painting, however, some Japanese artists of the late sixteenth century returned to the tradition of black ink wash. No longer copying the Chinese, these masterpieces expressed Japanese themes and techniques. In *Pine Forest* by Tohaku (toh-HAH-koo), a pair of six-panel screens depicting pine trees, 85 percent of the paper is left blank, suggesting mist and the quiet of an autumn dawn.

Although Japan was isolated from the Western world during much of the Tokugawa era, Japanese art was enriched by ideas from other cultures. Japanese pottery makers borrowed both techniques and designs from Korea to produce handsome ceramics. The passion for "Dutch learning" inspired Japanese to study Western medicine, astronomy, and languages and also led to experimentation with oil painting and Western ideas of perspective and the interplay of light and dark. Some painters depicted the "southern barbarians," with their strange ships and costumes, large noses, and plumed hats. Europeans desired Japanese lacquerware and metalwork, inlaid with ivory and mother-of-pearl, and especially the ceramics, which were now as highly prized as those of the Chinese.

Perhaps the most famous of all Japanese art of the Tokugawa era is the woodblock print. Genre painting, or representations of daily life, began in the sixteenth century and found its new mass-produced form in the eighteenth-century woodblock print. The now literate mercantile class was eager for illustrated texts of the amusing and bawdy tales that had circulated in oral tradition. At first, these prints were done in black and white, but later they included vibrant colors. The self-confidence of the age is dramatically captured in these prints, which represent a collective self-portrait of the late Tokugawa urban classes. Some prints depict entire city blocks filled with people, trades, and festivals, while others show the interiors of houses; thus, they provide us with excellent visual documentation of the times. Others portray the "floating world" of the entertainment quarter, with scenes of carefree revelers enjoying the pleasures of life.

One of the most renowned of the numerous block-print artists was Utamaro (OO-tah-mah-roh) (1754–1806), who painted erotic and sardonic women in everyday poses, such as walking down the street, cooking, or drying their bodies after a bath. Hokusai (HOH-kuh-sy) (1760–1849) was famous for *Thirty-Six Views of Mount Fuji*, a new and bold interpretation of the Japanese landscape. Finally, Ando Hiroshige (AHN-doh hee-roh-SHEE-gay) (1797–1858) developed the genre of the travelogue print in his *Fifty-Three Stations of the Tokaido Road*, which presented ordinary scenes of daily life, both in the country and in the cities, all enveloped in a lyrical, quiet mood.

Why did a new popular culture begin to appear in Tokugawa Japan while traditional values continued to prevail in neighboring China? One factor was the rapid growth of the cities as the main point of convergence for all the dynamic forces taking place in Japanese society. But other factors may have been at work as well. Despite the patent efforts of the Tokugawa rulers to promote traditional Confucian values, Confucian doctrine had historically occupied a relatively weak position in Japanese society. In China, the scholar-gentry class served as the defenders and propagators of traditional orthodoxy, but the samurai, who were steeped in warrior values and had little exposure to Confucian learning, did not play a similar role in Japan. Tokugawa policies also contributed. Whereas the scholar-gentry class in Qing China continued to reside in the villages, serving as members of the local council or as instructors in local schools, the samurai class in Japan was deliberately isolated from the remainder of the population by government fiat and class privilege. The result was an ideological and cultural vacuum that would eventually be filled by the growing population of merchants and artisans in the major cities.

KOREA AND VIETNAM

On the fringes of the East Asian mainland, two of China's close neighbors sought to preserve their fragile independence from the expansionistic tendencies of the powerful Ming and Qing Dynasties.

Korea: In a Dangerous Neighborhood
While Japan under the Tokugawa Shogunate moved steadily out from the shadows of the Chinese Empire by creating a unique society with its own special characteristics, the Cho-son Dynasty in Korea continued to pattern itself, at least on the surface, after the Chinese model. The dynasty had been founded by the military commander Yi Song Gye (YEE song yee) in the late fourteenth century and immedi-ately set out to establish close political and cultural relations with the Ming Dynasty. From their new capital at Seoul (SOHL), located on the Han (HAHN) River in the center of the peninsula, the Choson rulers accepted a tributary relation-ship with their powerful neighbor and engaged in the wholesale adoption of Chi-nese institutions and values. As in China, the civil service examinations tested candidates on their knowledge of the Confucian classics, and success was viewed as an essential step toward upward mobility.

There were differences, however. As in Japan, the dynasty continued to restrict entry into the bureaucracy to members of the aristocratic class, known in Korea as the *yangban* (YAHNG-ban) (or "two groups," civilian and military). At the same time, the peasantry remained in serflike conditions, working on government estates or on the manor holdings of the landed elite. A class of slaves, called chonmin (CHAWN-min), labored on government plantations or served in certain occupations, such as butchers and entertainers, considered beneath the dignity of other groups in the population.

Eventually, Korean society began to show signs of independence from Chinese orthodoxy. In the fifteenth century, a phonetic alphabet for writing the Korean spo-ken language (*hangul*) was devised. Although it was initially held in contempt by the elites and used primarily as a teaching device, eventually it became the medium for private correspondence and the publishing of fiction for a popular audience. At the same time, changes were taking place in the economy, where rising agricultural production contributed to a population increase and the appearance of a small urban industrial and commercial sector, and in society, where the long domination of the *yangban* class began to weaken. As their numbers increased and their power and influence declined, some *yangban* became merchants or even moved into the ranks of the peasantry, further blurring the distinction between the aristocratic class and the common people.

Meanwhile, the Choson Dynasty faced continual challenges to its independence from its neighbors. Throughout much of the sixteenth century, the main threat came from the north, where Manchu forces harassed Korean lands just south of the Yalu (YAH-loo) River. By the 1580s, however, the larger threat came from the east in the form of a newly united Japan. During much of the sixteenth century, leading Japanese daimyo had been involved in a protracted civil war, as Oda Nobunaga, Toyotomi Hideyoshi, and Tokugawa Ieyasu strove to solidify their control over the islands. Of the three, only Hideyoshi lusted for an empire beyond the seas. Although born to a commoner family, he harbored visions of grandeur and in the late 1580s announced plans to attack the Ming Empire. When the Korean king Sonjo (SOHN-joe) (1567–1608) refused Hideyoshi's offer of an alliance, in 1592 the latter launched an invasion of the Korean peninsula.

At first the campaign went well, and Japanese forces, wreaking death and devastation throughout the countryside, advanced as far as the Korean capital at Seoul. But eventually the Koreans, under the inspired leadership of the military commander Yi Sunshin (YEE-soon-SHIN) (1545–1598), who designed fast but heavily armed ships that could destroy the more cumbersome landing craft of the invading forces, managed to repel the attack and safeguard their independence. The respite was brief, however. By the 1630s, a new threat from the Manchus had emerged from across the northern border. A Manchu force invaded northern Korea in the 1630s and eventually compelled the Choson Dynasty to promise allegiance to the new imperial government in Beijing. Korea was relatively untouched by the arrival of European merchants and missionaries, although information about Christianity was brought to the peninsula by Koreans returning from tribute missions to China, and a small Catholic community was established there in the late eighteenth century.

Vietnam: The Perils of Empire   Vietnam—or Dai Viet (dy VEE-et), as it was known at the time—managed to avoid the fate of many of its neighbors during the seventeenth and eighteenth centuries. Isolated from the major maritime routes that passed through the region, the country was only peripherally involved in the spice trade with the West and did not suffer the humiliation of losing territory to European colonial powers. In fact, Dai Viet had followed an imperialist path of its own, defeating the trading state of Champa to the south in 1471 and imposing its suzerainty over the rump of the old Angkor empire—today known as Cambodia. The state of Dai Viet then extended from the Chinese border to the shores of the Gulf of Siam.

But expansion undermined the cultural integrity of traditional Vietnamese society, as those migrants who settled in the marshy Mekong River delta developed a "frontier spirit" far removed from the communal values long practiced in the old national heartland of the Red River valley. By the seventeenth century, a civil war had split Dai Viet into two squabbling territories in the north and south, providing European powers with the opportunity to meddle in the country's internal affairs to their own benefit. In 1802, with the assistance of a French adventurer long active in the region, a member of the southern royal family managed to reunite the country under the new Nguyen (NGWEN) dynasty, which lasted until 1945.

To placate China, the country was renamed Vietnam (South Viet), and the new imperial capital was placed in the city of Hué (HWAY), a small river port roughly equidistant from the two rich river valleys that provided the country with its chief sustenance, wet rice. The founder of the new dynasty, who took the reign title of Gia Long, fended off French efforts to promote Christianity among his subjects and sought to promote traditional Confucian values among an increasingly diverse population.

CHRONOLOGIES

CHINA DURING THE EARLY MODERN ERA

1369	Rise of the Ming Dynasty
1405–1433	Voyages of Zheng He
1514	Portuguese arrive in southern China
1601	Matteo Ricci arrives in China
1644	Li Zicheng occupies Beijing
1644	Manchus seize China
1661–1722	Reign of Kangxi
1689	Treaty of Nerchinsk
1699	First English trading post at Canton
1736–1795	Reign of Qianlong
1793	Lord Macartney's mission to China
1796–1804	White Lotus Rebellion

JAPAN AND KOREA DURING THE EARLY MODERN ERA

Fifteenth century	First phonetic alphabet in Korea
1543	Portuguese merchants arrive in Japan
1549	Francis Xavier arrives in Japan
1568–1582	Rule of Oda Nobunaga
1568	Seizure of Kyoto
1582–1598	Rule of Toyotomi Hideyoshi
1587	Edict prohibiting Christianity in Japan
1592	Japan invades Korea
1598	Death of Hideyoshi and withdrawal of the Japanese army from Korea

1598–1616	Rule of Tokugawa Ieyasu
1603	Creation of Tokugawa Shogunate
1609	Dutch granted permission to trade at Nagasaki
1612	Order evicting Christian missionaries
1630s	Yi Dynasty of Korea declares fealty to China

 MindTap is a fully online, highly personalized learning experience built upon Cengage Learning content. MindTap combines student learning tools—readings, multimedia, activities, and assessments—into a singular Learning Path that guides students through their course.

18

THE WEST ON THE EVE OF A NEW WORLD ORDER

The storming of the Bastille

CHAPTER OUTLINE

• Toward a New Heaven and a New Earth: An Intellectual Revolution in the West • Economic Changes and the Social Order • Colonial Empires and Revolution in the Americas • Toward a New Political Order and Global Conflict • The French Revolution • The Age of Napoleon

Toward a New Heaven and a New Earth: An Intellectual Revolution in the West

In the seventeenth century, a group of scientists set the Western world on a new path known as the **Scientific Revolution**, which exposed Europeans to a new way of viewing the universe and their place in it. The Scientific Revolution affected only a small number of Europe's educated elite. But in the eighteenth century, this changed dramatically as a group of intellectuals popularized the ideas of the Scientific Revolution and used them to undertake a dramatic reexamination of all aspects of life. The widespread impact of these ideas on their society has caused historians ever since to call the eighteenth century in Europe the Age of Enlightenment.

The Scientific Revolution   The Scientific Revolution ultimately challenged conceptions and beliefs about the nature of the external world that had become dominant by the Late Middle Ages.

Toward a New Heaven: A Revolution in Astronomy   The philosophers of the Middle Ages had used the ideas of Aristotle, Ptolemy (the greatest astronomer of antiquity, who lived in the second century C.E.), and Christianity to form the Ptolemaic (tahl-uh-MAY-ik) or **geocentric theory** of the universe. In this conception, the universe was seen as a series of concentric spheres with a fixed or motionless earth at its center. Composed of material substance, the earth was imperfect and constantly changing. The spheres that surrounded the earth were made of a crystalline, transparent substance and moved in circular orbits around the earth. The heavenly bodies, which in 1500 were believed to number ten, were pure orbs of light, embedded in the moving, concentric spheres. Working outward from the earth, the first eight spheres contained the moon, Mercury, Venus, the sun, Mars, Jupiter, Saturn, and the fixed stars. The ninth sphere imparted to the eighth sphere of the fixed stars its daily motion, while the tenth sphere was frequently described as the prime mover that moved itself and imparted motion to the other spheres. Beyond the tenth sphere was the Empyrean Heaven—the location of God and all the saved souls. Thus, God and the saved souls were at one end of the universe, and humans were at the center. They had power over the earth, but their real purpose was to achieve salvation.

Nicolaus Copernicus (NEE-koh-lowss kuh-PURR-nuh-kuss) (1473–1543), a native of Poland, was a mathematician who felt that Ptolemy's geocentric system failed to accord with the observed motions of the heavenly bodies and hoped that his **heliocentric (sun-centered) theory** would offer a more accurate explanation. Copernicus argued that the sun was motionless at the center of the universe. The planets revolved around the sun in the order of Mercury, Venus, the earth, Mars, Jupiter, and Saturn. The moon, however, revolved around the earth. Moreover, what appeared to be the movement of the sun around the earth was really explained by the daily rotation of the earth on its axis and the journey of the earth around the sun each year. But Copernicus did not reject the idea that the heavenly spheres moved in circular orbits.

Johannes Kepler (yoh-HAHN-us KEP-lur) (1571–1630) took the next step in destroying the geocentric conception and supporting the Copernican system.

A brilliant German mathematician and astronomer, Kepler arrived at laws of planetary motion that confirmed Copernicus's heliocentric theory. In his first law, however, he contradicted Copernicus by showing that the orbits of the planets around the sun were not circular but elliptical, with the sun at one focus of the ellipse rather than at the center.

Kepler's work destroyed the basic structure of the Ptolemaic system. People could now think in new terms of the actual paths of planets revolving around the sun in elliptical orbits. But important questions remained unanswered. For example, what were the planets made of? An Italian scientist achieved the next important breakthrough to a new cosmology by answering that question.

Galileo Galilei (gal-li-LAY-oh GAL-li-lay) (1564–1642) taught mathematics and was the first European to make systematic observations of the heavens by means of a telescope, inaugurating a new age in astronomy. Galileo turned his telescope to the skies and made a remarkable series of discoveries: mountains on the moon, four moons revolving around Jupiter, and sunspots. Galileo's observations seemed to destroy yet another aspect of the traditional cosmology in that the universe seemed to be composed of material similar to that of earth rather than a perfect and unchanging substance.

Galileo's revelations, published in *The Starry Messenger* in 1610, made Europeans aware of a new picture of the universe. But the Catholic Church condemned Copernicanism and ordered Galileo to abandon the Copernican thesis. The church attacked the Copernican system because it threatened not only Scripture but also an entire conception of the universe. The heavens were no longer a spiritual world but a world of matter.

By the 1630s and 1640s, most astronomers had come to accept the new heliocentric conception of the universe. Nevertheless, no one yet had explained motion in the universe and tied together the ideas of Copernicus, Galileo, and Kepler. This would be the work of an Englishman who has long been considered the greatest genius of the Scientific Revolution.

Isaac Newton (1642–1727) taught at Cambridge University, where he wrote his major work, *Mathematical Principles of Natural Philosophy*, known simply as the *Principia* (prin-SIP-ee-uh) by the first word of its Latin title. In the first book of the *Principia*, Newton defined the three laws of motion that govern the planetary bodies, as well as objects on earth. Crucial to his whole argument was the universal law of gravitation, which explained why the planetary bodies did not go off in straight lines but continued in elliptical orbits about the sun. In mathematical terms, Newton explained that every object in the universe is attracted to every other object by a force called gravity.

Newton had demonstrated that one mathematically proven universal law could explain all motion in the universe. At the same time, the Newtonian synthesis created a new cosmology in which the universe was seen as one huge, regulated machine that operated according to natural laws in absolute time, space, and motion. Newton's **world-machine** concept dominated the modern worldview until the twentieth century, when Albert Einstein's concept of relativity created a new picture of the universe.

Toward a New Earth: Descartes and Rationalism   The new conception of the universe contained in the cosmological revolution of the sixteenth and seventeenth

Image Select/Art Resource, NY

Medieval Conception of the Universe. *As this sixteenth-century illustration shows, the medieval cosmological view placed the earth at the center of the universe, surrounded by a series of concentric spheres. The earth was imperfect and constantly changing, whereas the heavenly bodies that surrounded it were perfect and incorruptible. Beyond the tenth and final sphere was heaven, where God and all the saved souls were located. (The circles read, from the center outward: 1. Moon, 2. Mercury, 3. Venus, 4. Sun, 5. Mars, 6. Jupiter, 7. Saturn, 8. Firmament (of the Stars), 9. Crystalline Sphere, 10. Prime Mover; and around the outside, Empyrean Heaven—Home of God and All the Elect, that is, saved souls.)*

centuries inevitably had an impact on the Western view of humankind. Nowhere is this more evident than in the work of the French philosopher René Descartes (ruh-NAY day-KART) (1596–1650). The starting point for Descartes's new system was doubt. As Descartes explained at the beginning of his most famous work, *Discourse on Method*, written in 1637, he decided to set aside all that he had learned and begin again. One fact seemed to Descartes beyond doubt—his own existence:

> I immediately became aware that while I was thus disposed to think that all was false, it was absolutely necessary that I who thus thought should be something; and noting that this truth *I think, therefore I am*, was so steadfast and so assured that the suppositions of the skeptics, to whatever extreme they might all be carried, could not avail to shake it, I concluded that I might without scruple accept it as being the first principle of the philosophy I was seeking.[1]

With this emphasis on the mind, Descartes asserted that he would accept only things that his reason said were true.

From his first postulate, Descartes deduced an additional principle, the separation of mind and matter. Descartes argued that since "the mind cannot be doubted

The Copernican System. *The Copernican system was presented in* On the Revolutions of the Heavenly Spheres, *published shortly before Copernicus's death. As shown in this illustration from the first edition of the book, Copernicus maintained that the sun was the center of the universe and that the planets, including the earth, revolved around it. Moreover, the earth rotated daily on its axis. (The circles read, from the center outward: Sun; VII. Mercury, orbit of 80 days; VI. Venus; V. Earth, with the moon, orbit of one year; IIII. Mars, orbit of 2 years; III. Jupiter, orbit of 12 years; II. Saturn, orbit of 30 years; I. Immobile Sphere of the Fixed Stars.)*

but the body and material world can, the two must be radically different." From this came an absolute dualism between mind and matter, or what has also been called **Cartesian dualism.** Using mind or human reason and its best instrument, mathematics, humans can understand the material world because it is pure mechanism, a machine that is governed by its own physical laws because it was created by God—the great geometrician.

Descartes's separation of mind and matter allowed scientists to view matter as dead or inert, as something that was totally separate from themselves and could be investigated independently by reason. The split between mind and body led Westerners to equate their identity with mind and reason rather than with the whole organism. Descartes has rightly been called the father of modern **rationalism.**

Europe, China, and Scientific Revolutions   An interesting question that arises is why the Scientific Revolution occurred in Europe and not in China. In the Middle Ages, China had been the most technologically advanced civilization in the world.

COMPARATIVE ESSAY

The Scientific Revolution

SCIENCE &
TECHNOLOGY

When Catholic missionaries arrived in China in the sixteenth century, they marveled at the sophistication of Chinese civilization and its many accomplishments, including woodblock printing and the civil service examination system. In turn, their hosts were impressed with European inventions such as the spring-driven clock and eyeglasses.

It is not surprising that visitors from the West were impressed with what they saw in China, for that country had long been at the forefront of human achievement. After the sixteenth century, however, Europe would take the lead in the advance of science and technology, a phenomenon that would ultimately bring about the Industrial Revolution and set in motion a transformation of human society.

Why did Europe suddenly become the engine for rapid change in the seventeenth and eighteenth centuries? One factor was the change in the European worldview, the shift from a metaphysical to a materialist perspective and the growing inclination among European intellectuals to question first principles. In contrast to China, where, for example, the "investigation of things" proposed by Song Dynasty thinkers had been used to analyze and confirm principles first established by Confucius and his contemporaries, empirical scientists in early modern Europe rejected received religious ideas, developed a new conception of the universe, and sought ways to improve material conditions around them.

Why were European thinkers more interested in practical applications of their discoveries than their counterparts elsewhere? No doubt the literate mercantile and propertied elites of Europe were attracted to the new science because it offered new ways to exploit resources for profit. Some of the early scientists made it easier for these groups to accept the new ideas by showing how they could be applied directly to specific industrial and technological needs. Galileo, for example, consciously sought an alliance between science and the material interests of the educated elite when he assured his listeners that the science of mechanics would be quite useful "when it becomes necessary to build bridges or other structures over water, something occurring mainly in affairs of great importance."

Finally, the political changes that were beginning to take place in Europe during this period may also have contributed. Many European states enlarged their bureaucratic machinery and consolidated their governments in order to collect the revenues and amass the armies needed to compete militarily with rivals. Political leaders desperately sought ways to enhance their wealth and power and grasped eagerly at whatever tools were available to guarantee their survival and prosperity.

Q *Why did the Scientific Revolution emerge in Europe and not in China?*

After 1500, that distinction passed to the West. Historians are not sure why. Some have contrasted the sense of order in Chinese society with the competitive spirit existing in Europe. Others have emphasized China's ideological viewpoint that favored living in harmony with nature rather than trying to dominate it. One historian has even suggested that China's civil service system drew the "best and the brightest" into government service, to the detriment of other occupations.

Background to the Enlightenment

The impetus for political and social change in the eighteenth century stemmed in part from the **Enlightenment**. The Enlightenment was a movement of intellectuals who were greatly impressed with the accomplishments of the Scientific Revolution. When they used the word *reason*—one of their favorite words—they were advocating the application of the **scientific method** to the understanding of all life. All institutions and all systems of thought were subject to the rational, scientific way of thinking if people would only free themselves from the shackles of past, worthless traditions, especially religious ones. If Isaac Newton could discover the natural laws regulating the world of nature, they too, by using reason, could find the laws that governed human society. This belief in turn led them to hope that they could make progress toward a better society than the one they had inherited. *Reason, natural law, hope, progress*—these were the buzzwords in the heady atmosphere of eighteenth-century Europe.

Major sources of inspiration for the Enlightenment were Isaac Newton and his fellow Englishman John Locke (1632–1704). Newton had contended that the world and everything in it worked like a giant machine. Enchanted by the grand design of this world-machine, the intellectuals of the Enlightenment were convinced that by following Newton's rules of reasoning, they could discover the natural laws that governed politics, economics, justice, and religion.

John Locke's theory of knowledge also made a great impact. In his *Essay Concerning Human Understanding*, written in 1690, Locke denied the existence of innate ideas and argued instead that every person was born with a *tabula rasa* (TAB-yuh-luh RAH-suh), a blank mind:

> Let us then suppose the mind to be, as we say, white paper, void of all characters, without any ideas. How comes it to be furnished? Whence comes it by that vast store which the busy and boundless fancy of man has painted on it with an almost endless variety? Whence has it all the materials of reason and knowledge? To this I answer, in one word, from experience.... Our observation, employed either about external sensible objects or about the internal operations of our minds perceived and reflected on by ourselves, is that which supplies our understanding with all the materials of thinking.[2]

By denying innate ideas, Locke's philosophy implied that people were molded by their environment, by whatever they perceived through their senses from their surrounding world. Thus, by altering the environment and subjecting people to proper influences, they could be changed and a new society created. And how should the environment be changed? Newton had paved the way: reason enabled enlightened people to discover the natural laws to which all institutions should conform.

The Philosophes and Their Ideas

The intellectuals of the Enlightenment were known by the French term *philosophes* (fee-loh-ZAHFS), although they were not all French and few were philosophers in the strict sense of the term. The **philosophes** were literary people, professors, journalists, economists, political scientists, and, above all, social reformers. They came from both the nobility and the middle class, and a few even stemmed from lower-middle-class origins. Although it was a truly international and cosmopolitan movement, the Enlightenment also enhanced the dominant role being played by French culture; Paris was its recognized capital. Most of the leaders of the Enlightenment were French. The French philosophes, in turn, affected intellectuals elsewhere and created a movement that touched the entire Western world, including the British and Spanish colonies in America. (The terms *British* and *Great Britain* came to be used after 1707 when the United Kingdom of Great Britain came into existence, uniting the governments of England and Scotland, as well as Wales, which had been joined to England previously.)

MAP 18.1   The Enlightenment in Europe

"Have the courage to use your own intelligence!" The words of the German philosopher Immanuel Kant (i-MAHN-yoo-el KAHNT) epitomize the role of the individual in using reason to understand all aspects of life—the natural world and the sphere of human nature, behavior, and institutions.

To the philosophes, the role of philosophy was not just to discuss the world but to change it. To the philosophes, reason was a scientific method, and it relied on an appeal to facts. A spirit of rational criticism was to be applied to everything, including religion and politics. Spanning almost a century, the Enlightenment evolved with each succeeding generation, becoming more radical as new thinkers built on the contributions of their predecessors. A few individuals, however, dominated the landscape so completely that we can gain insight into the core ideas of the philosophes by focusing on the three French giants—Montesquieu, Voltaire, and Diderot.

Montesquieu   Charles de Secondat (SHARL duh suh-KAHN-da), the baron de Montesquieu (MOHN-tess-kyoo) (1689–1755), came from the French nobility. His most famous work, *The Spirit of the Laws*, was published in 1748. In this comparative study of governments, Montesquieu attempted to apply the scientific method to the social and political arena to ascertain the "natural laws" governing the social and political relationships of human beings. Montesquieu distinguished three basic kinds of governments: republic, monarchy, and despotism.

Montesquieu used England as an example of monarchy, and it was his analysis of England's constitution that led to his most lasting contribution to political thought—the importance of checks and balances achieved by means of a **separation of powers**. He believed that England's system, with its separate executive, legislative, and judicial branches that served to limit and control each other, provided the greatest freedom and security for a state. The translation of his work into English two years after publication ensured that it would be read by American political leaders, who eventually incorporated its principles into the U.S. Constitution.

Voltaire   The greatest figure of the Enlightenment was François-Marie Arouet (frahn-SWAH-ma-REE ahr-WEH), known simply as Voltaire (vohl-TAYR) (1694–1778). Son of a prosperous middle-class family from Paris, he studied law, although he achieved his first success as a playwright. Voltaire was a prolific author and wrote an almost endless stream of pamphlets, novels, plays, letters, philosophical essays, and histories.

Voltaire was especially well known for his criticism of traditional religion and his strong attachment to the ideal of religious toleration. As he grew older, Voltaire became ever more strident in his denunciations. "Crush the infamous thing," he thundered repeatedly—the infamous thing being religious fanaticism, intolerance, and superstition.

Throughout his life, Voltaire championed not only religious tolerance but also **deism**, a religious outlook shared by most other philosophes. Deism was built on the Newtonian world-machine, which implied the existence of a mechanic (God) who had created the universe. To Voltaire and most other philosophes, the universe was like a clock, and God was the clockmaker who had created it, set it in motion, and allowed it to run according to its own natural laws.

Diderot   Denis Diderot (duh-NEE dee-DROH) (1713–1784) was the son of a skilled craftsman from eastern France who became a writer so that he could be free to study and read in many subjects and languages. One of Diderot's favorite topics was Christianity, which he condemned as fanatical and unreasonable. Of all religions, Christianity, he averred, was the worst, "the most absurd and the most atrocious in its dogma."

Diderot's most famous contribution to the Enlightenment was the *Encyclopedia, or Classified Dictionary of the Sciences, Arts, and Trades*, a twenty-eight-volume compendium of knowledge that he edited and referred to as the "great work of his life." Its purpose, according to Diderot, was to "change the general way of thinking." It did precisely that in becoming a major weapon of the philosophes' crusade against the old French society. The contributors included many philosophes who attacked religious intolerance and advocated a program for social, legal, and political improvements that would lead to a society that was more cosmopolitan, more tolerant, more humane, and more reasonable. The *Encyclopedia* was sold to doctors, clergymen, teachers, lawyers, and even military officers, thus spreading the ideas of the Enlightenment.

Toward a New "Science of Man"   The Enlightenment belief that Newton's scientific methods could be used to discover the natural laws underlying all areas of human life led to the emergence in the eighteenth century of what the philosophes called a "science of man," or what we would call the social sciences. In a number of areas, such as economics, politics, and education, the philosophes arrived at natural laws that they believed governed human actions.

Adam Smith (1723–1790) has been viewed as one of the founders of the modern discipline of economics. Smith believed that individuals should be free to pursue their own economic self-interest. Through the actions of these individuals, all society would ultimately benefit. Consequently, the state should in no way interrupt the free play of natural economic forces by government regulations on the economy but should leave it alone, a doctrine that subsequently became known as **laissez-faire** (less-ay-FAYR) (French for "leave it alone").

Smith allotted government only three basic functions: to protect society from invasion (via an army), defend its citizens from injustice (by means of a police force), and keep up certain public works, such as roads and canals, that private individuals could not afford.

The Later Enlightenment   By the late 1760s, a new generation of philosophes who had grown up with the worldview of the Enlightenment began to move beyond their predecessors' beliefs. Most famous was Jean-Jacques Rousseau (ZHAHNH-ZHAHK roo-SOH) (1712–1778), whose political beliefs were presented in two major works. In his *Discourse on the Origins of the Inequality of Mankind*, Rousseau argued that people had adopted laws and governors in order to preserve their private property. In the process, they had become enslaved by government. What, then, should people do to regain their freedom? In his celebrated treatise *The Social Contract*, published in 1762, Rousseau found an answer in the concept of the social contract, whereby an entire society agreed to be governed by its general will. Each individual might have a particular will contrary to the general will, but if the individual put his particular will (self-interest) above the general will, he should be forced to abide by the general will. "This means nothing less than that he will be forced to be free," said Rousseau, because the general will, being ethical and not just political, represented what the entire community ought to do.

Another influential treatise by Rousseau was his novel *Émile*, one of the Enlightenment's most important works on education. Rousseau's fundamental concern was that education should foster, rather than restrict, children's natural instincts. Rousseau's own experiences had shown him the importance of the emotions. What he sought was a balance between heart and mind, between emotion and reason.

But Rousseau did not necessarily practice what he preached. His own children were sent to orphanages, where many children died at a young age. Rousseau also viewed women as "naturally different" from men. In *Émile*, Sophie, Émile's intended wife, was educated for her role as wife and mother by learning obedience and the nurturing skills that would enable her to provide loving care for her husband and children. Not everyone in the eighteenth century agreed with Rousseau, however.

The "Woman Question" in the Enlightenment   For centuries, many male intellectuals had argued that the nature of women made them inferior to men and made male domination of women necessary and right. In the Scientific Revolution, however, some women had made notable contributions. Maria Winkelmann (VINK-ul-mahn) in Germany, for example, was an outstanding practicing astronomer. Nevertheless, when she applied for a position as assistant astronomer at the Berlin Academy, for which she was highly qualified, she was denied the post by the academy's members, who feared that hiring a woman would set a bad precedent ("mouths would gape"). Winkelmann's difficulties with the Berlin Academy were typical of the obstacles women faced in being accepted in scientific work, which was considered a male preserve.

Female thinkers in the eighteenth century disagreed with this attitude and offered suggestions for improving conditions for women. The strongest statement for the rights of women was advanced by the English writer Mary Wollstonecraft (WULL-stun-kraft) (1759–1797), viewed by many as the founder of modern European **feminism**.

In her *Vindication of the Rights of Woman*, written in 1792, Wollstonecraft pointed out two contradictions in the views of women held by such Enlightenment thinkers as Rousseau. To argue that women must obey men, she said, was contrary to the beliefs of the same individuals that a system based on the arbitrary power of monarchs over their subjects or slave owners over their slaves was wrong. The subjection of women to men was equally wrong. In addition, she argued, the Enlightenment was based on an ideal of reason innate in all human beings. If women have reason, then they should have the same rights as men to obtain an education and engage in economic and political life.

Culture in an Enlightened Age   Although the Baroque style that had dominated the seventeenth century continued to be popular, by the 1730s, a new style affecting decoration and architecture known as **Rococo** (ruh-KOH-koh) had spread throughout Europe. Unlike the Baroque, which stressed power, grandeur, and movement, Rococo emphasized grace, charm, and gentle action. Rococo rejected strict geometrical patterns and had a fondness for curves; it liked to follow the wandering lines of natural objects, such as seashells and flowers. It made much use of interlaced designs colored in gold with delicate contours and graceful arcs. Highly secular, its lightness and charm spoke of the pursuit of pleasure, happiness, and love.

Some of Rococo's appeal is evident in the work of Antoine Watteau (AHN-twahn wah-TOH) (1684–1721), whose lyrical views of aristocratic life, refined, sensual, and civilized, with gentlemen and ladies in elegant dress, revealed a world of upper-class pleasure and joy. Underneath that exterior, however, was an element of sadness as the artist revealed the fragility and transitory nature of pleasure, love, and life.

Another aspect of Rococo was that its decorative work could easily be paired with Baroque architecture. The palace at Versailles had made an enormous impact on Europe. "Keeping up with the Bourbons" became important as European rulers built grandiose palaces. While imitating Versailles in size, they were not so much modeled after the French classical style as they were after the seventeenth-century Italian Baroque, as modified by a series of brilliant German and Austrian sculptor-architects. This Baroque-Rococo architectural style typified eighteenth-century palaces and church buildings, and often the same architects designed both. This is evident in the work of one of the greatest architects of the eighteenth century, Johann Balthasar Neumann (yoh-HAHN BAHL-tuh-zahr NOI-mahn) (1687–1753). One of Neumann's masterpieces was the pilgrimage church known as the Vierzehn-heiligen (feer-tsayn-HY-li-gen) (Fourteen Saints) in southern Germany. Secular and spiritual merge in its lavish and fanciful ornamentation; light, bright colors; and elaborate, rich detail.

High Culture   Historians have grown accustomed to distinguishing between a civilization's high culture and its popular culture. **High culture** is the literary and artistic culture of the educated and wealthy ruling classes; **popular culture** is the written and unwritten culture of the masses, most of which has traditionally been passed down orally.

By the eighteenth century, the two forms were beginning to blend, owing to the expansion of both the reading public and publishing. Whereas French publishers issued 300 titles in 1750, about 1,600 were being published yearly in the 1780s. Although the majority of these titles were still intended for small groups of the educated elite, many were directed to the new reading public of the middle classes, which included women and even urban artisans.

An important aspect of the growth of publishing and reading in the eighteenth century was the development of magazines for the general public. Great Britain saw 25 different periodicals published in 1700, 103 in 1760, and 158 in 1780. Along with magazines came daily newspapers. The first was printed in London in 1702, but by 1780, thirty-seven other English towns had their own newspapers.

Popular Culture   The distinguishing characteristic of popular culture is its collective nature. Group activity was especially common in the *festival*, a broad name used to cover a variety of celebrations: community festivals in Catholic Europe that celebrated the feast day of the local patron saint; annual festivals, such as

Christmas and Easter, that went back to medieval Christianity; and the ultimate festival, Carnival, which was celebrated in the Mediterranean world of Spain, Italy, and France as well as in Germany and Austria.

Carnival began after Christmas and lasted until the start of Lent, the forty-day period of fasting and purification leading up to Easter. Because people were expected to abstain from meat, sex, and most recreations during Lent, Carnival was a time of great indulgence, when heavy consumption of food and drink was the norm. It was a time of intense sexual activity as well. Songs with double meanings that would ordinarily be considered offensive could be sung publicly at this time of year. A float of Florentine "keymakers," for example, sang this ditty to the ladies: "Our tools are fine, new and useful. We always carry them with us. They are good for anything. If you want to touch them, you can."[3]

ECONOMIC CHANGES AND THE SOCIAL ORDER

The eighteenth century in Europe witnessed the beginning of economic changes that ultimately had a strong impact on the rest of the world.

New Economic Patterns   Europe's population began to grow around 1750 and continued to increase steadily. The total European population was probably around 120 million in 1700, 140 million in 1750, and 190 million in 1790. A falling death rate was perhaps the most important reason for this population growth. Of great significance in lowering death rates was the disappearance of bubonic plague, but so was diet. More plentiful food and better transportation of food supplies led to improved nutrition and relief from devastating famines.

More plentiful food was in part a result of improvements in agricultural practices and methods in the eighteenth century, especially in Britain, parts of France, and the Low Countries. Food production increased as more land was farmed, yields per acre increased, and climate improved. Climatologists believe that the "little ice age" of the seventeenth century waned in the eighteenth, especially evident in moderate summers that provided more ideal growing conditions. Also important to the increased yields was the cultivation of new vegetables, including two important American crops, the potato and maize (Indian corn). Both had been brought to Europe from the Americas in the sixteenth century.

Textiles were the most important product of European industry in the eighteenth century. Most were still produced by master artisans in guild workshops, but in many areas, textile production was beginning to shift to the countryside where the "putting-out" or "domestic" system was used. A merchant-capitalist entrepreneur bought the raw materials, mostly wool and flax, and "put them out" to rural workers who spun the raw material into yarn and then wove it into cloth on simple looms. The capitalist entrepreneurs sold the finished product, made a profit, and used it to purchase materials to manufacture more. This system became known as the **cottage industry** because the spinners and weavers worked at spinning wheels and looms in the cottages where they lived.

In the eighteenth century, overseas trade boomed. Some historians speak of the emergence of a true global economy, pointing to the patterns of trade that

MAP 18.2 Global Trade Patterns of the European States in the Eighteenth Century

New patterns of trade interlocked Europe, Africa, the East, and the Americas. Dutch, English, French, Spanish, and Portuguese colonies had been established in North and South America, and the ships of these nations followed the trade routes across the Atlantic, Pacific, and Indian Oceans.

interlocked Europe, Africa, the East, and the Americas. In one trade pattern, gold and silver flowed into Spain from its colonial American empire. Much of this gold and silver made its way to Britain, France, and the Netherlands in return for manufactured goods. The British, French, and Dutch merchants then used their profits to buy tea, spices, silk, and cotton goods from China and India to sell in Europe. The plantations of the Western Hemisphere were another important source of trading activity. The plantations produced coffee, tobacco, sugar, and cotton, which were shipped to Europe. In a third pattern of trade, British merchant ships carried British manufactured goods to Africa, where they were traded for cargoes of slaves, which were then shipped to Virginia and paid for with tobacco, which was in turn shipped back to Britain, where it was processed and then sold in Germany for cash.

As a result of the growth in trade, historians have argued that during the eighteenth century, England and parts of northern Europe experienced a "consumer revolution," where ordinary people partook in a large increase in the consumption of consumer goods. Expensive commodities such as Chinese porcelain became more affordable as production moved to Europe by the beginning of the eighteenth century, while imports of inexpensive Indian fabric increased the sale of clothing. By the end of the eighteenth century, most ordinary families could consume former luxury goods such as tea, sugar, tobacco, furniture, cutlery and clothing.

Commercial capitalism resulted in enormous prosperity for some European countries. By 1700, Spain, Portugal, and the Dutch Republic, which had earlier monopolized overseas trade, found themselves increasingly overshadowed by France and England, which built hugely profitable colonial empires in the course of the eighteenth century. After the French lost the Seven Years' War in 1763, Britain emerged as the world's strongest overseas trading nation, and London became the world's greatest port.

European Society in the Eighteenth Century   The patterns of Europe's social organization, first established in the Middle Ages, continued well into the eighteenth century. Society was still divided into the traditional orders or estates determined by heredity.

Because society was still mostly rural in the eighteenth century, the peasantry constituted the largest social group, about 85 percent of Europe's population. There were rather wide differences within this group, however, especially between free peasants and serfs. In eastern Germany, eastern Europe, and Russia, serfs remained tied to the lands of their noble landlords. In contrast, peasants in Britain, northern Italy, the Low Countries, Spain, most of France, and some areas of western Germany were largely free.

The nobles, who constituted only 2 to 3 percent of the European population, played a dominating role in society. Being born a noble automatically guaranteed a place at the top of the social order, with all its attendant special privileges and rights. Nobles, for example, were exempt from many forms of taxation. Since medieval times, landed aristocrats had functioned as military officers, and eighteenth-century nobles held most of the important offices in the administrative machinery of state and controlled much of the life of their local districts.

Townspeople were still a distinct minority of the total population except in the Dutch Republic, Britain, and parts of Italy. At the end of the eighteenth century, about one-sixth of the French population lived in towns of two thousand people or more. The biggest city in Europe was London, with a million inhabitants; Paris was a little more than half that size.

Many cities in western and even central Europe had a long tradition of **patrician** oligarchies that continued to control their communities by dominating town and city councils. Just below the patricians stood an upper crust of the middle classes: nonnoble officeholders, financiers and bankers, merchants, wealthy *rentiers* (rahn-TYAYS) who lived off their investments, and important professionals, including lawyers. Another large urban group was the lower middle class, made up of master artisans, shopkeepers, and small traders. Below them were the laborers or working classes and a large group of unskilled workers who served as servants, maids, and cooks at pitifully low wages.

COLONIAL EMPIRES AND REVOLUTION IN THE AMERICAS

In the sixteenth century, Spain and Portugal had established large colonial empires in the Americas. Portugal continued to profit from its empire in Brazil. The Spanish also maintained an enormous South American empire, but Spain's importance as a commercial power declined rapidly in the seventeenth century because of a drop in the output of the silver mines and the poverty of the Spanish monarchy. By the beginning of the seventeenth century, both Portugal and Spain found themselves facing new challenges to their American empires from the Dutch, English, and French, who increasingly sought to create their own colonial empires in the Western Hemisphere, both within the West Indies and on the North American continent.

The West Indies   Both the French and British colonial empires in the Americas ultimately included large parts of the West Indies. The British held Barbados, Jamaica, and Bermuda, and the French possessed Saint-Dominique, Martinique, and Guadeloupe. On these tropical islands, both the British and the French used African slaves to work plantations that produced tobacco, cotton, coffee, and sugar, all products increasingly in demand in Europe.

The "sugar factories," as the sugar plantations in the Caribbean were called, played an especially prominent role. By the last two decades of the eighteenth century, Jamaica, one of Britain's most important colonies, was producing 50,000 tons of sugar annually with the slave labor of 200,000 blacks. The French colony of Saint-Dominique (later Haiti) had 500,000 slaves working on three thousand plantations during the same period. This colony produced 100,000 tons of sugar a year, but at the expense of a high death rate from the brutal treatment of the slaves. It is not surprising that Saint-Dominique saw the first successful slave uprising in 1793.

British North America   Although Spain had claimed all of North America as part of its American overseas empire, other nations largely ignored its claim, following the English argument that "prescription without possession availeth nothing." The Dutch had been among the first to establish settlements on the North American continent. Their activities began after 1609 when Henry Hudson, an English explorer hired by the Dutch, discovered the river that bears his name. Within a few years, the Dutch had established the mainland colony of New Netherland, which stretched from the mouth of the Hudson River as far north as Albany, New York. Present-day names such as Staten Island and Harlem remind us that it was the Dutch who initially settled the Hudson River valley. In the second half of the seventeenth century, competition from the English and French and years of warfare with those rivals led to the decline of the Dutch commercial empire. In 1664, the English seized the colony of New Netherland and renamed it New York.

In the meantime, the English had begun to establish their own colonies in North America. The first permanent English settlement in America was Jamestown, founded in 1607 in what is now Virginia. The settlers barely survived, making it clear that colonizing American lands was not necessarily conducive to quick profits. But the desire to practice one's own religion, combined with economic interests, could lead to successful colonization, as the Massachusetts Bay Company demonstrated. The Massachusetts colony had 4,000 settlers in its early years, but by 1660 their numbers had swelled to 40,000. By the end of the seventeenth century, the English had established control over most of the eastern seaboard of the present United States.

British North America came to consist of thirteen colonies. They were thickly populated, containing about 1.5 million people by 1750, and were also prosperous. Supposedly run by the British Board of Trade, the Royal Council, and Parliament, these thirteen colonies had legislatures that tended to act independently. Merchants in such port cities as Boston, Philadelphia, New York, and Charleston resented and resisted regulation from the British government.

Both the North American and the West Indian colonies of Britain were assigned roles in keeping with mercantilist theory. They provided raw materials for the mother country while buying the latter's manufactured goods. Navigation acts regulated what could be taken from and sold to the colonies. Theoretically, the system was supposed to provide a balance of trade favorable to the mother country.

French North America   The French also established a colonial empire in North America. In 1534, the French explorer Jacques Cartier (ZHAHK kar-TYAY) had discovered the Saint Lawrence River and laid claim to Canada as a French possession. Not until Samuel de Champlain (sa-my-ELL duh shahm-PLAN *or* SHAM-playn) established a settlement at Quebec in 1608, however, did the French take a serious interest in Canada as a colony. In 1663, Canada was made the property of the French crown and administered by a French governor like a French province.

French North America was run autocratically as a vast trading area, where valuable furs, leather, fish, and timber were acquired. The inability of the French state to persuade its people to emigrate to its Canadian possessions, however, left the territory thinly populated. In the mid-eighteenth century, there were only about 15,000 French Canadians, most of whom were hunters, trappers, missionaries, or explorers. The French also failed to provide adequate men or money for the venture, allowing their wars in Europe to take precedence over the conquest of the North American continent. Already in 1713, by the Treaty of Utrecht, the French began to cede some of their American possessions to their British rival. As a result of the Seven Years' War, they surrendered the rest of their Canadian lands to Britain in 1763.

The American Revolution   By the mid-eighteenth century, increasing trade and industry had led to a growing middle class in Britain that favored expansion of trade and world empire. These people found a spokesman in William Pitt the Elder (1708–1778), who became prime minister in 1757 and began to expand the British Empire. In North America, after the end of the Seven Years' War in 1763, Britain controlled Canada and the lands east of the Mississippi.

The Americans and the British had different conceptions of how the empire should be governed, however. In eighteenth-century Britain, the king or queen and Parliament shared power, with Parliament gradually gaining the upper hand. The monarch chose ministers who were responsible to the crown and who set policy and guided Parliament. Parliament had the power to make laws, levy taxes, pass budgets, and indirectly influence the monarch's ministers. The British envisioned that Parliament would be the supreme authority performing these functions throughout the empire. But the Americans had their own representative assemblies. They believed that neither king nor Parliament should interfere in their internal affairs and that no tax could be levied without the consent of their own assemblies. After the Seven Years' War, when British policymakers sought to obtain new revenues from the colonies to pay for British army expenses in defending the colonies, the colonists resisted. An attempt to levy new taxes by the Stamp Act of 1765 led to riots and the law's quick repeal.

Crisis followed crisis in the 1770s until 1776, when the colonists decided to declare their independence from the British Empire. On July 4, 1776, the Second Continental Congress approved a declaration of independence written by Thomas Jefferson (1743–1826). A stirring political document, the Declaration of Independence affirmed the Enlightenment's natural rights of "life, liberty, and the pursuit of happiness" and declared the colonies to be "free and independent states absolved from all allegiance to the British crown." The war for American independence had formally begun.

Of great importance to the colonies' cause was the support of foreign countries that were eager to gain revenge for earlier defeats at the hands of the British. French officers and soldiers served in the American Continental Army under George Washington (1732–1799), the commander in chief. When the British army of General Cornwallis was forced to surrender to a combined American and French army and French fleet under Washington at Yorktown in 1781, the British decided to call it quits. The Treaty of Paris, signed in 1783, recognized the independence of the American colonies and granted the Americans control of the territory from the Appalachians to the Mississippi River.

Birth of a New Nation   The thirteen American colonies had gained their independence, but a fear of concentrated power and concern for their own interests caused them to have little enthusiasm for establishing a united nation with a strong central government, and so the Articles of Confederation, ratified in 1781, did not create one. A movement for a different form of national government soon arose. In the summer of 1787, fifty-five delegates attended a convention in Philadelphia to revise the Articles of Confederation. The convention's delegates—wealthy, politically experienced, and well educated—rejected revision and decided instead to devise a new constitution.

The proposed United States Constitution established a central government distinct from and superior to the governments of the individual states. The central or federal government was divided into three branches, each with some power to check the functioning of the others. A president would serve as the chief executive with the power to execute laws, veto the legislature's acts, supervise foreign affairs, and direct military forces. Legislative power was vested in the second branch of government, a bicameral legislature composed of the Senate, elected by the state legislatures, and the House of Representatives, elected directly by the people. A supreme court and other courts "as deemed necessary" by Congress provided the third branch of government. They would enforce the Constitution as the "supreme law of the land."

The Constitution was approved by the states—by a slim margin. Important to its success was a promise to add a bill of rights to the Constitution as the new government's first piece of business. Accordingly, in March 1789, the new Congress enacted the first ten amendments to the Constitution, known ever since as the Bill of Rights. These guaranteed freedom of religion, speech, press, petition, and assembly, as well as the right to bear arms, protection against unreasonable searches and arrests, trial by jury, due process of law, and protection of property rights. Many of these rights were derived from the **natural rights** philosophy of the eighteenth-century philosophes and the American colonists. Is it any wonder that many European intellectuals saw the American Revolution as the embodiment of the Enlightenment's political dreams?

TOWARD A NEW POLITICAL ORDER AND GLOBAL CONFLICT

There is no doubt that Enlightenment thought had some impact on the political development of European states in the eighteenth century. The philosophes believed in natural rights, which were thought to be privileges that ought not to be withheld from any person. These natural rights included equality before the law, freedom of religious worship, freedom of speech and press, and the right to assemble, hold property, and seek happiness.

But how were these natural rights to be established and preserved? Most philosophes believed that people needed to be ruled by an enlightened ruler. What made rulers enlightened? They must allow religious toleration, freedom of speech and press, and the rights of private property. They must foster the arts, sciences, and education. Above all, they must obey the laws and enforce them fairly for all subjects. Only strong monarchs seemed capable of overcoming vested interests and effecting the reforms society needed. Reforms then should come from above (from absolute rulers) rather than from below (from the people).

Many historians once assumed that a new type of monarchy emerged in the later eighteenth century, which they called *enlightened despotism* or **enlightened absolutism**. Monarchs such as Frederick II of Prussia, Catherine the Great of Russia, and Joseph II of Austria supposedly followed the advice of the philosophes and ruled by enlightened principles. Recently, however, scholars have questioned the usefulness of the concept of enlightened absolutism. We can determine the extent to which it can be applied by examining the major "enlightened absolutists" of the late eighteenth century.

Prussia: The Army and the Bureaucracy   Frederick II, known as Frederick the Great (1740–1786), was one of the best-educated and most cultured monarchs of the eighteenth century. He was well versed in Enlightenment thought and even invited Voltaire to live at his court for several years. A believer in the king as the "first servant of the state," Frederick the Great was a conscientious ruler who enlarged the Prussian army (to 200,000 men) and kept a strict watch over the bureaucracy. The Prussian army, because of its size and excellent reputation, was the most important institution in the state. Its officers, who were members of the nobility or landed aristocracy, had a strong sense of service to the king or state. As Prussian nobles, they believed in duty, obedience, and sacrifice. The bureaucracy also had its own code in which the supreme values were obedience, honor, and service to the king as the highest duty.

For a time, Frederick seemed quite willing to make enlightened reforms. He abolished the use of torture except in treason and murder cases and also granted limited freedom of speech and press, as well as complete religious toleration. At the same time, however, he kept Prussia's rigid social structure and serfdom intact and avoided any additional reforms.

The Austrian Empire of the Habsburgs   The Austrian Empire had become one of the great European states by the beginning of the eighteenth century. Yet it was difficult to rule because it was a sprawling conglomerate of nationalities, languages, religions, and cultures. Empress Maria Theresa (1740–1780) managed to make administrative reforms that helped centralize the Austrian Empire, but they were done for practical reasons—to strengthen the power of the Habsburg state—and were accompanied by an enlargement and modernization of the armed forces. Maria Theresa remained staunchly conservative and was not open to the wider reform calls of the philosophes. But her successor was.

Joseph II (1780–1790) believed in the need to sweep away anything standing in the path of reason. As he said, "I have made Philosophy the lawmaker of my empire; her logical applications are going to transform Austria." Joseph's reform program was far-reaching. He abolished serfdom, abrogated the death penalty, and established the principle of equality of all before the law. Joseph carried out drastic religious reforms as well, including complete religious toleration.

Joseph's reform program proved overwhelming for Austria, however. He alienated the nobility by freeing the serfs and alienated the church by his attacks on the monastic establishment. Joseph realized his failure when he wrote the epitaph for his own gravestone: "Here lies Joseph II, who was unfortunate in everything that he undertook." His successors undid many of his reforms.

Russia Under Catherine the Great   Catherine II the Great (1762–1796) was an intelligent woman who was familiar with the works of the philosophes and seemed to favor enlightened reforms. She invited the French philosophe Diderot to Russia and, when he arrived, urged him to speak frankly "as man to man." He did, outlining a far-reaching program of political and financial reform. But Catherine was skeptical about impractical theories, which, she said, "would have turned everything in my kingdom upside

© Cengage Learning 2013

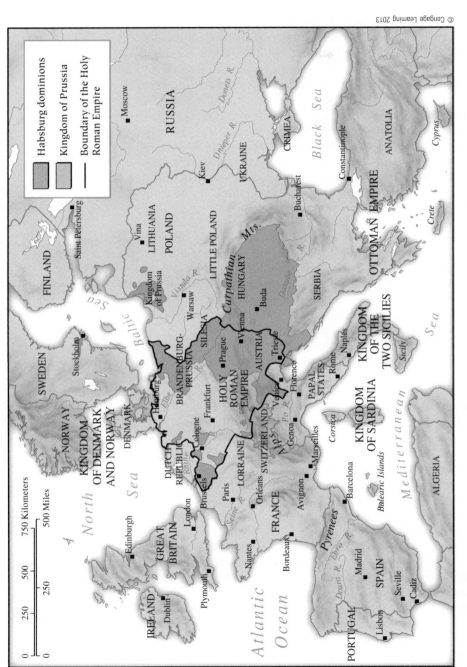

MAP 18.3 Europe in 1763

By the middle of the eighteenth century, five major powers dominated Europe—Prussia, Austria, Russia, Britain, and France. Each sought to enhance its power both domestically, through a bureaucracy that collected taxes and ran the military, and internationally, by capturing territory or preventing other powers from capturing territory.

down." She did consider the idea of a new law code that would recognize the principle of the equality of all people in the eyes of the law. But in the end she did nothing, knowing that her success depended on the support of the Russian nobility. In 1785, she gave the nobles a charter that exempted them from taxes.

Catherine's policy of favoring the landed nobility led to even worse conditions for the Russian peasants and a rebellion. Incited by an illiterate Cossack, Emelyan Pugachev (yim-yil-YAHN poo-guh-CHAHF), the rebellion began in 1773 and spread across southern Russia. But the rebellion soon faltered. Pugachev was captured, tortured, and executed. The rebellion collapsed completely, and Catherine responded with even stronger measures against the peasantry.

Above all, Catherine proved a worthy successor to Peter the Great in her policies of territorial expansion westward into Poland and southward to the Black Sea. Russia spread southward by defeating the Turks. Russian expansion westward occurred at the expense of neighboring Poland. In three partitions of Poland, Russia gained about 50 percent of Polish territory.

Enlightened Absolutism Reconsidered   Of the rulers we have discussed, only Joseph II sought truly radical changes based on Enlightenment ideas. Both Frederick II and Catherine II liked to talk about enlightened reforms, and they even attempted some. But the policies of neither seemed seriously affected by Enlightenment thought. Necessities of state and maintenance of the existing system took precedence over reform. Indeed, many historians maintain that Joseph, Frederick, and Catherine were all primarily guided by a concern for the power and well-being of their states. In the final analysis, heightened state power was used to create armies and wage wars to gain more power.

It would be foolish, however, to overlook the fact that the ability of enlightened rulers to make reforms was also limited by political and social realities. Everywhere in Europe, the hereditary aristocracy was still the most powerful class in society. Enlightened reforms were often limited to administrative and judicial measures that did not seriously undermine the powerful interests of the European nobility. As the chief beneficiaries of a system based on traditional rights and privileges for their class, they were not willing to support a political ideology that trumpeted the principle of equal rights for all. The first serious challenge to their supremacy would come in the French Revolution, an event that blew open the door to the modern world of politics.

Changing Patterns of War: Global Confrontation   The philosophes condemned war as a foolish waste of life and resources in stupid quarrels of no value to humankind. Despite their words, the rivalry among states that led to costly struggles remained unchanged in the European world of the eighteenth century. Europe consisted of a number of self-governing, individual states that were largely guided by the self-interest of the ruler. And as Frederick the Great of Prussia said, "The fundamental rule of governments is the principle of extending their territories."

By far the most dramatic confrontation occurred in the Seven Years' War. Although it began in Europe, it soon turned into a global conflict fought in Europe,

India, and North America. In Europe, the British and Prussians fought the Austrians, Russians, and French. With his superb army and military skill, Frederick the Great of Prussia was able for some time to defeat the Austrian, French, and Russian armies. Eventually, however, his forces were gradually worn down and faced utter defeat until a new Russian tsar withdrew Russian troops from the conflict. A stalemate ensued, ending the European conflict in 1763.

The struggle between Britain and France in the rest of the world had more decisive results. In India, local rulers allied with British and French troops fought a number of battles. Ultimately, the British under Robert Clive won out, not because they had better forces but because they were more persistent. By the Treaty of Paris in 1763, the French withdrew and left India to the British.

The greatest conflicts of the Seven Years' War took place in North America, where it was known as the French and Indian War. British and French rivalry led to a number of confrontations. The French had more troops in North America but less naval support. The defeat of French fleets in 1759 left the French unable to reinforce their garrisons. That year, British forces under General Wolfe defeated the French under General Montcalm on the Plains of Abraham, outside Quebec. The British went on to seize Montreal, the Great Lakes area, and the Ohio Valley. The French were forced to make peace. In the Treaty of Paris, they ceded Canada and the lands east of the Mississippi to Britain. Their ally Spain transferred Spanish Florida to British control; in return, the French gave their Louisiana territory to the Spanish. By 1763, Great Britain had become the world's greatest colonial power. The loss of France's empire was soon followed by an even greater internal upheaval.

The French Revolution

The year 1789 witnessed two far-reaching events, the beginning of a new United States of America under its revamped constitution and the eruption of the French Revolution. Compared to the American Revolution a decade earlier, the French Revolution was more complex, more violent, and far more radical in its attempt to reconstruct both a new political order and a new social order.

Background to the French Revolution   The root causes of the French Revolution must be sought in the condition of French society. Before the Revolution, France was a society grounded in privilege and inequality. Its population of 27 million was divided, as it had been since the Middle Ages, into three orders or estates.

Social Structure of the Old Regime   The First Estate consisted of the clergy and numbered about 130,000 people who owned approximately 10 percent of the land. Clergy were exempt from the *taille* (TY), France's chief tax. Clergy were also radically divided: the higher clergy, stemming from aristocratic families, shared the interests of the nobility, while the parish priests were often poor and from the class of commoners.

The Second Estate consisted of the nobility, composed of about 350,000 people who owned about 25 to 30 percent of the land. The nobility had continued to play an important and even crucial role in French society in the eighteenth century, holding many of the leading positions in the government, the military, the law courts, and the higher church offices. The nobles sought to expand their power at the expense of the monarchy and to maintain their control over positions in the military, church, and government. Moreover, the possession of privileges remained a hallmark of the nobility. Common to all nobles were tax exemptions, especially from the *taille*.

The Third Estate, or the commoners of society, constituted the overwhelming majority of the French population. They were divided by vast differences in occupation, level of education, and wealth. The peasants, who constituted 75 to 80 percent of the total population, were by far the largest segment of the Third Estate. They owned 35 to 40 percent of the land, although their landholdings varied from area to area and more than half had little or no land on which to survive. Serfdom no longer existed on any large scale in France, but French peasants still had obligations to their local landlords that they deeply resented. These "relics of feudalism," or aristocratic privileges, had survived from an earlier age and included the payment of fees for the use of village facilities, such as the flour mill, community oven, and winepress.

Another part of the Third Estate consisted of skilled craftspeople, shopkeepers, and other wage earners in the cities. In the eighteenth century, these urban groups suffered a noticeable decline in purchasing power as consumer prices rose faster than wages. Their daily struggle for survival led many of these people to play an important role in the Revolution, especially in Paris.

About 8 percent of the population, or 2.3 million people, constituted the bourgeoisie or middle class, who owned about 20 to 25 percent of the land. This group included merchants, industrialists, and bankers who controlled the resources of trade, manufacturing, and finance and benefited from the economic prosperity after 1730. The bourgeoisie also included professional people—lawyers, holders of public offices, doctors, and writers. Many members of the bourgeoisie had their own set of grievances because they were often excluded from the social and political privileges monopolized by nobles.

Moreover, the new political ideas of the Enlightenment proved attractive to both the aristocracy and the bourgeoisie. Both elites, long accustomed to a new socioeconomic reality based on wealth and economic achievement, were increasingly frustrated by a monarchical system resting on privileges and on an old and rigid social order based on the concept of estates. The opposition of these elites to the **old order** led them ultimately to take drastic action against the monarchical **old regime**. In a real sense, the Revolution had its origins in political grievances.

Other Problems Facing the French Monarchy   Although France had enjoyed fifty years of economic expansion in the first half of the eighteenth century, in the late 1780s bad harvests in 1787 and 1788 and the beginnings of a manufacturing depression had resulted in food shortages, rising prices for food and other goods, and unemployment in the cities. The number of poor, estimated at almost one-third of the population, reached crisis proportions on the eve of the Revolution.

The French monarchy seemed incapable of dealing with the new social realities. Louis XVI (1774–1792) had become king in 1774 at the age of twenty; he knew little about the operations of the French government and lacked the energy to deal decisively with state affairs. His wife, Marie Antoinette (ma-REE ahn-twahn-NET), was a spoiled Austrian princess who devoted much of her time to court intrigues. As France's crises worsened, neither Louis nor his queen seemed able to fathom the depths of despair and discontent that soon led to violent revolution.

The immediate cause of the French Revolution was the near collapse of government finances. Costly wars and royal extravagance drove French governmental expenditures ever higher. The government responded by borrowing. Poor taxation policy contributed to the high debt, with most of the monarchy's funds coming from the peasantry. Unlike Britain, where the Bank of England financed the borrowing of money at low interest rates, France had no central bank, and instead relied on private loans. By 1788, the interest on the debt alone constituted half of government spending. Financial lenders, fearful they would never be repaid, were refusing to lend additional amounts.

On the verge of a complete financial collapse, the government of Louis XVI was finally forced to call a meeting of the Estates-General, the French parliamentary body that had not met since 1614. The Estates-General consisted of representatives from the three orders of French society. In the elections for the Estates-General, the government had ruled that the Third Estate should get double representation (it did, after all, constitute 97 percent of the population). Consequently, while both the First Estate (the clergy) and the Second Estate (the nobility) had about three hundred delegates each, the Third Estate had almost six hundred representatives, most of whom were lawyers from French towns.

From Estates-General to National Assembly   The Estates-General opened at Versailles on May 5, 1789. It was troubled from the start with the question of whether voting should be by order or by head (each delegate having one vote). Traditionally, each order would vote as a group and have one vote. That meant that the First and Second Estates could outvote the Third Estate two to one. The Third Estate demanded that each deputy have one vote. With the assistance of liberal nobles and clerics, that would give the Third Estate a majority. When the First Estate declared in favor of voting by order, the Third Estate responded dramatically. On June 17, 1789, the Third Estate declared itself the "National Assembly" and decided to draw up a constitution. This was the first step in the French Revolution because the Third Estate had no legal right to act as the National Assembly. But this audacious act was soon in jeopardy, as the king sided with the First Estate and threatened to dissolve the Estates-General. Louis XVI now prepared to use force.

The common people, however, saved the Third Estate from the king's forces. On July 14, a mob of Parisians stormed the Bastille, a royal armory, and proceeded to dismantle it, brick by brick. Louis XVI was soon informed that the royal troops were unreliable. Louis's acceptance of that reality signaled the collapse of royal authority; the king could no longer enforce his will.

At the same time, popular revolts broke out throughout France, both in the cities and in the countryside. Behind the popular uprising was a growing resentment of the entire landholding system, with its fees and obligations. The fall of the Bastille and the king's apparent capitulation to the demands of the Third Estate

FILM & HISTORY

Marie Antoinette (2006)

The film *Marie Antoinette* (2006), directed by Sofia Coppola, is based on Antonia Fraser's interpretation of the early life of Marie Antoinette in her book, *Marie Antoinette: A Journey* (2001). The film begins with the marriage of Marie Antoinette (Kirsten Dunst), the daughter of Empress Maria Theresa of Austria (Marianne Faithful), to the dauphin Louis (Jason Schwartzman), the heir to the French throne. Four years later, in 1774, Marie Antoinette became queen of France; in 1793, she went to the guillotine. Although the Revolution and financial troubles of the monarchy briefly enter the film toward the end, the majority of the film focuses on the experiences of a young woman thrust into the court of Versailles where she faces increasing suspicion, frustration, and isolation.

Perhaps the best part of the film is the portrayal of court life at Versailles. The film depicts days filled with courtly ceremonies, daily mass, and attendance of the public at meals. Under intense scrutiny due to her Austrian heritage and unfamiliar with the protocol of life at Versailles, Marie Antoinette makes several early missteps. She refuses to speak to Louis XV's mistress, the comtesse du Barry (Asia Argento), because the comtesse threatens Marie Antoinette's position as the highest-ranking woman at court. Ignoring the king's mistress, however, places the young dauphine in the precarious position of appearing to insult the king.

In addition to her troubles at court, Marie Antoinette faces an even greater challenge: the need to secure her place by producing an heir to the French throne. But her young husband, whose interests include hunting, lock making, and reading, creates problems for the young couple. Their marriage is not consummated for seven years. During these years, Marie Antoinette faces increasing pressure from her mother, who has produced sixteen children while ruling the Austrian Empire. Bored but aware that she must remain chaste, the young dauphine turns to frivolous pursuits including games, plays, outings in Paris, decorating, gambling, and, above all, purchasing clothes. Marie Antoinette's desire for elaborate gowns is encouraged by her role as the tastemaker for the French court. In 1782, she commissions ninety-three gowns made of silk and other expensive fabrics. The scene of Marie Antoinette's twenty-first birthday is particularly effective in conveying how her frustration and boredom have led her to a life of frivolity and luxury. Sitting in her finery, she plays cards and eats sweets until the early hours of the morning.

After the birth of her children, the first in 1777, Marie Antoinette begins to withdraw from the scrutiny of the court.

now led peasants to take matters into their own hands. The peasant rebellions that occurred throughout France had a great impact on the National Assembly meeting at Versailles.

Destruction of the Old Regime   One of the first acts of the National Assembly was to abolish the rights of landlords and the fiscal exemptions of nobles, clergy, towns, and provinces. Three weeks later, the National Assembly adopted the Declaration of the Rights of Man and the Citizen. This charter of basic liberties proclaimed freedom and equal rights for all men and access to

Columbia/American Zoetrope/Sony/The Kobal Collection

Marie Antoinette (Kirsten Dunst) at Versailles.

In 1783, she is given the keys to the Petit Trianon, a small palace on the grounds of Versailles, where she spends most of her days. Although she is spending more time with her children and less on the frivolity of her earlier days at Versailles, her increasing estrangement from the court only worsens her reputation with the French public.

Filmed at Versailles, the film captures the grandeur and splendor of eighteenth-century royal life. But the movie did not receive favorable reviews when it opened in France, in part because of its use of contemporary music by artists such as The Cure and The Strokes and the inclusion of modern products such as Converse sneakers. Although the flurry of costumes and music can be distracting, they also convey the rebelliousness of a young woman, frustrated and bored, isolated, and yet always on display.

public office based on talent. All citizens were to have the right to take part in the legislative process. Freedom of speech and the press were coupled with the outlawing of arbitrary arrests.

The declaration also raised another important issue. Did its ideal of equal rights for "all men" also include women? Many deputies insisted that it did, provided that, as one said, "women do not hope to exercise political rights and functions." Olympe de Gouges (oh-LAMP duh GOOZH), a playwright, refused to accept this exclusion of women from political rights. Echoing the words of the official declaration, she penned the Declaration of the Rights of Woman and the Female Citizen, in

The State of French Finances

POLITICS & GOVERNMENT

In 1781, Jacques Necker (ZHAHK neh-KAIR), the assistant to Louis XVI's controller general of finance (Necker could not be named controller general due to his Swiss birth and Protestant faith), published an account of the French monarchy's finances. Although Necker denied that the monarchy was in debt and hid France's enormous interest payments, his efforts to expose the inadequacies of the monarchy's monetary policies were the first real steps toward financial reform. His efforts, however, could not prevent the financial crisis that engulfed the French monarchy.

Jacques Necker, *Preface to the King's Accounts* (1781)

Sire,

[I] offer Your Majesty ... a public account of ... the current state of His Majesty's finances....

If one examines the great credit that England enjoys and which is currently its greatest strength in the war, one should not attribute that entirely to the nature of its government; because, regardless of the authority of the monarch of France, since his interests are known always to rest on the foundation of faithfulness and justice, he could easily make all forget that he has the power to dismiss those principles; it is up to Your Majesty, with his strength of character and virtue, to make this truth felt through experience.

But another cause of the great credit of England is ... the public renown to which the status of its finances is subject. That status is presented to Parliament each year, and printed afterward; and thus all lenders have regular knowledge of the balance being maintained between revenue and expenditure, they are never troubled by suspicions and imaginary fears....

In France, a great mystery is always made of the status of the finances; or, if they are occasionally discussed, it is in the preambles of edicts and always when we want to borrow; but those words, too often the same to be true, have necessarily lost their authority and experienced men no longer believe them without the guarantee, so to speak, of the moral character of the minister of finance. It is vital to found confidence on a more solid base. I admit that, under certain circumstances, it has been possible to profit from the veil cast over the financial situation to obtain, in the midst of disorder, some mediocre credit that was not warranted; but this momentary advantage, which sustained a misleading illusion and favored the indifference of the administration, was soon followed by unhappy transactions, the memory of which lasts longer and which will take long to correct....

The sovereign of a realm like that of France can always, when he wants to do so, maintain the balance between expenditures and ordinary revenue; the diminution of the former, always seconded by the wishes of the public, is in his hands; and when circumstances require, increasing taxes is within his power; but the most dangerous, and the most unjust of resources, is to seek momentary aid with blind confidence and take loans without insuring the interest, or to raise revenues, or to economize.

Such administration, which is seductive because it postpones the moment of difficulty, only increases ills and digs itself deeper into the hole; while another kind of conduct, simpler and more frank, multiplies the means available to the Sovereign and forever protects it from any sort of injustice.

It is thus this broad view of administration on the part of His Majesty which has permitted us to offer a public account of the state of his finances; and I hope that, for the good of the realm and his power, this happy institution will not be temporary.

Q *What did Necker believe were the main differences between the French and British systems of public finance?*

Source: From Mason, *The French Revolution*, 1e. © 1999 Cengage Learning.

The Natural Rights of the French People: Two Views

POLITICS & GOVERNMENT

One of the important documents of the French Revolution, the Declaration of the Rights of Man and the Citizen, was adopted on August 26, 1789, by the National Assembly. The declaration affirmed that "men are born and remain free and equal in rights," that government must protect these natural rights, and that political power is derived from the people.

Olympe de Gouges (the pen name used by Marie Gouze) was a butcher's daughter who wrote plays and pamphlets. She argued that the Declaration of the Rights of Man and the Citizen did not apply to women and composed her own Declaration of the Rights of Woman and the Female Citizen in 1791.

Declaration of the Rights of Man and the Citizen

1. Men are born and remain free and equal in rights. Social distinctions can only be founded upon the general good.
2. The aim of all political association is the preservation of the natural and imprescriptible rights of man. These rights are liberty, property, security, and resistance to oppression.
3. The principle of all sovereignty resides essentially in the nation. No body or individual may exercise any authority which does not proceed directly from the nation.
4. Liberty consists in being able to do everything which injures no one else....
6. Law is the expression of the general will. Every citizen has a right to participate personally or through his representative in its formation. It must be the same for all, whether it protects or punishes. All citizens being equal in the eyes of the law are equally eligible to all dignities and to all public positions and occupations according to their abilities and

without distinction except that of their virtues and talents.

7. No person shall be accused, arrested, or imprisoned except in the cases and according to the forms prescribed by law....
10. No one shall be disturbed on account of his opinions, including his religious views, provided their manifestation does not disturb the public order established by law.
11. The free communication of ideas and opinions is one of the most precious of the rights of man. Every citizen may, accordingly, speak, write and print with freedom, being responsible, however, for such abuses of this freedom as shall be defined by law.
12. The security of the rights of man and of the citizen requires public military force. These forces are, therefore, established for the good of all and not for the personal advantage of those to whom they shall be entrusted....
14. All the citizens have a right to decide either personally or by their representatives as to the necessity of the public contribution, to grant this freely, to know to what uses it is put, and to fix the proportion, the mode of assessment, and of collection, and the duration of the taxes.
15. Society has the right to require of every public agent an account of his administration.
16. A society in which the observance of the law is not assured nor the separation of powers defined has no constitution at all.
17. Property being an inviolable and sacred right, no one shall be deprived thereof except where public necessity, legally determined, shall clearly demand it, and then only on condition that the owner shall have been previously and equitably indemnified.

Declaration of the Rights of Woman and the Female Citizen

Mothers, daughters, sisters and representatives of the nation demand to be constituted into a national assembly. Believing that ignorance, omission, or scorn for the rights of woman are the only causes of public misfortunes and of the corruption of governments, the women have resolved to set forth in a solemn declaration the natural, inalienable, and sacred rights of woman in order that this declaration, constantly exposed before all the members of the society, will ceaselessly remind them of their rights and duties....

Consequently, the sex that is as superior in beauty as it is in courage during the sufferings of maternity recognizes and declares in the presence and under the auspices of the Supreme Being, the following Rights of Woman and of Female Citizens.

1. Woman is born free and lives equal to man in her rights. Social distinctions can be based only on the common utility.

2. The purpose of any political association is the conservation of the natural and imprescriptible rights of woman and man; these rights are liberty, property, security, and especially resistance to oppression.

3. The principle of all sovereignty rests essentially with the nation, which is nothing but the union of woman and man; no body and no individual can exercise any authority which does not come expressly from [the nation].

4. Liberty and justice consist of restoring all that belongs to others; thus, the only limits on the exercise of the natural rights of woman are perpetual male tyranny; these limits are to be reformed by the laws of nature and reason....

6. The law must be the expression of the general will; all female and male citizens must contribute either personally or through their representatives to its formation; it must be the same for all: male and female citizens, being equal in the eyes of the law, must be equally admitted to all honors, positions, and public employment according to their capacity and without other distinctions besides those of their virtues and talents.

7. No woman is an exception; she is accused, arrested, and detained in cases determined by law. Women, like men, obey this rigorous law....

10. No one is to be disquieted for his very basic opinions; woman has the right to mount the scaffold; she must equally have the right to mount the rostrum, provided that her demonstrations do not disturb the legally established public order.

11. The free communication of thought and opinions is one of the most precious rights of woman, since that liberty assured the recognition of children by their fathers....

12. The guarantee of the rights of woman and the female citizen implies a major benefit; this guarantee must be instituted for the advantage of all, and not for the particular benefit of those to whom it is entrusted....

14. Female and male citizens have the right to verify, either by themselves or through their representatives, the necessity of the public contribution. This can only apply to women if they are granted an equal share, not only of wealth, but also of public administration, and in the determination of the proportion, the base, the collection, and the duration of the tax.

15. The collectivity of women, joined for tax purposes to the aggregate of men, has the right to demand an accounting of his administration from any public agent.

16. No society has a constitution without the guarantee of rights and the separation of powers; the constitution is null if the majority of individuals comprising the nation have not cooperated in drafting it.

17. Property belongs to both sexes whether united or separate; for each it is an inviolable and sacred right; no one can be deprived of it, since it is the true patrimony of nature, unless the legally determined public need obviously dictates it, and then only with a just and prior indemnity.

Q *What "natural rights" does the first document proclaim? To what extent was this document influenced by the writings of the philosophes? What rights for women does the second document enunciate? Given the nature and scope of the arguments in favor of natural rights and women's rights in these two documents, what key effects on European society would you attribute to the French Revolution?*

Sources: Excerpt from Thomas Carlyle, *The French Revolution: A History*, Vol. I, (George Bell and Sons, London, 1902), pp. 346–348. From *Women in Revolutionary Paris, 1789–1795: Selected Documents Translated with Notes and Commentary*. Translated with notes and commentary by Darline Gay Levy, Harriet Branson Applewhite, and Mary Durham Johnson. Copyright © 1979 by the Board of Trustees of the University of Illinois. Used with permission of the editors and the University of Illinois Press.

which she insisted that women should have all the same rights as men. The National Assembly ignored her demands.

Because the Catholic Church was seen as an important pillar of the old order, it too was reformed. Most of the lands of the church were seized. The new Civil Constitution of the Clergy was put into effect in 1790. Both bishops and priests were to be elected by the people and paid by the state. The Catholic Church, still an important institution in the life of the French people, now became an enemy of the Revolution.

By 1791, the National Assembly had completed a new constitution that established a limited constitutional monarchy. There was still a monarch (now called "king of the French"), but the new Legislative Assembly was to make the laws. The Legislative Assembly, in which sovereign power was vested, was to sit for two years and consist of 745 representatives, or deputies, chosen by an indirect system of election that preserved power in the hands of the more affluent members of society. A small group of 50,000 electors chose the deputies.

By 1791, the old order had been destroyed. The new order, however, had many opponents—Catholic priests, nobles, lower classes hurt by a rise in the cost of living, peasants who remained opposed to dues that had still not been abandoned, and political clubs like the Jacobins (JAK-uh-binz) that offered more radical solutions to France's problems. The king also made things difficult for the new government when he sought to flee France in June 1791 and almost succeeded before being recognized, captured, and brought back to Paris. In this unsettled situation, under a discredited and seemingly disloyal monarch, the new Legislative Assembly held its first session in October 1791. France's relations with the rest of Europe soon led to Louis's downfall.

On August 27, 1791, the monarchs of Austria and Prussia, fearing that revolution would spread to their countries, invited other European monarchs to use force to reestablish monarchical authority in France. The French fared badly in the initial fighting in the spring of 1792, and a frantic search for scapegoats began. As one observer noted, "Everywhere you hear the cry that the king is betraying us, the generals are betraying us, that nobody is to be trusted; ... that Paris will be taken in six weeks by the Austrians.... We are on a volcano ready to spout flames."[4] Defeats in war coupled with economic shortages in the spring led to renewed political demonstrations, especially against the king. In August 1792, radical political groups in Paris attacked the royal palace, took the king captive, and forced the Legislative Assembly to suspend the monarchy and call for a national convention, chosen on the basis of universal male suffrage, to decide on the future form of government. The French Revolution was about to enter a more radical stage.

The Radical Revolution   In September 1792, the newly elected National Convention began its sessions. Dominated by lawyers and other professionals, two-thirds of its deputies were under the age of forty-five, and almost all had gained political experience as a result of the Revolution. Almost all distrusted the king. As a result, the convention's first step on September 21 was to abolish the monarchy and establish a republic. On January 21, 1793, the king was executed, and the destruction of the old regime was complete. But the execution of the king created new enemies for the Revolution both at home and abroad.

In Paris, the local government, known as the Commune, whose leaders came from the working classes, favored radical change and put constant pressure on the convention, pushing it to ever more radical positions. Meanwhile, peasants in the west and inhabitants of the major provincial cities refused to accept the authority of the convention.

A foreign crisis also loomed large. By beginning of 1793, after the king had been put to death, most of Europe—an informal coalition of Austria, Prussia, Spain, Portugal, Britain, the Dutch Republic, and even Russia—aligned militarily against France. Grossly overextended, the French armies began to experience reverses, and by late spring, France was threatened with invasion.

A Nation in Arms   To meet these crises, the convention gave broad powers to an executive committee of twelve known as the Committee of Public Safety, which came to be dominated by Maximilien Robespierre (mak-see-meel-YENH ROHBZ-pyayr). For a twelve-month period, from 1793 to 1794, the Committee of Public Safety took control of France. To save the Republic from its foreign foes, the committee decreed a universal mobilization of the nation on August 23, 1793:

> Young men will fight, young men are called to conquer. Married men will forge arms, transport military baggage and guns and will prepare food supplies. Women, who at long last are to take their rightful place in the revolution and follow their true destiny, will forget their futile tasks: their delicate hands will work at making clothes for soldiers; they will make tents and they will extend their tender care to shelters where the

defenders of the *Patrie* [nation] will receive the help that their wounds require. Children will make lint of old cloth. It is for them that we are fighting: children, those beings destined to gather all the fruits of the revolution, will raise their pure hands toward the skies. And old men, performing their missions again, as of yore, will be guided to the public squares of the cities where they will kindle the courage of young warriors and preach the doctrines of hate for kings and the unity of the Republic.[5]

In less than a year, the French revolutionary government had raised an army of 650,000 and by 1795 had pushed the allies back across the Rhine and even conquered the Austrian Netherlands.

The French revolutionary army was an important step in the creation of modern **nationalism**. Previously, wars had been fought between governments or ruling dynasties by relatively small armies of professional soldiers. The new French army was the creation of a "people's" government; its wars were now "people's" wars. The entire nation was to be involved in the war. But when dynastic wars became people's wars, warfare increased in ferocity and lack of restraint. The wars of the French revolutionary era opened the door to the total war of the modern world.

Reign of Terror   To meet the domestic crisis, the National Convention and the Committee of Public Safety launched the "Reign of Terror." Revolutionary courts were instituted to protect the Republic from its internal enemies. In the course of nine months, 16,000 people were officially killed under the blade of the guillotine—a revolutionary device designed for the quick and efficient separation of heads from bodies.

Revolutionary armies were set up to bring recalcitrant cities and districts back under the control of the National Convention. The Committee of Public Safety decided to make an example of Lyons (LYOHNH), which had defied the authority of the National Convention. By April 1794, some 1,880 citizens of Lyons had been executed. When the guillotine proved too slow, cannon fire was used to blow condemned men into open graves. A German observed:

Whole ranges of houses, always the most handsome, burnt. The churches, convents, and all the dwellings of the former patricians were in ruins. When I came to the guillotine, the blood of those who had been executed a few hours beforehand was still running in the street.... I said to a group of [radicals] that it would be decent to clear away all this human blood. Why should it be cleared? one of them said to me. It's the blood of aristocrats and rebels. The dogs should lick it up.[6]

Equality and Slavery: Revolution in Haiti   Early in the French Revolution, the desire for equality led to a discussion of what to do about slavery. A club called Friends of the Blacks advocated the abolition of slavery, which was achieved in France in September 1791. However, French planters in the West Indies, who profited greatly from the use of slaves on their sugar plantations, opposed the abolition of slavery in the French colonies. When the National Convention came to power, the issue was revisited, and on February 4, 1794, guided by ideals of equality, the government abolished slavery in the colonies.

In one French colony, slaves had already rebelled for their freedom. In 1791, black slaves in the French sugar colony of Saint-Domingue (san doh-MAYNG) (the western third of the island of Hispaniola), inspired by the ideals of the revolution occurring in France, revolted against French plantation owners. Slaves attacked, killing plantation owners and their families and burning their buildings. White planters retaliated with equal brutality. One wealthy French settler reported, "How can we stay in a country where slaves have raised their hands against their masters?"

Eventually, leadership of the revolt was taken over by Toussaint L'Ouverture (too-SANH loo-vayr-TOOR) (1746–1803), a son of African slaves, who seized control of all of Hispaniola by 1801. Although Napoleon, the French leader, had accepted the revolutionary ideal of equality, he did not reject the reports of white planters that the massacres of white planters by slaves demonstrated the savage nature of blacks. In 1802, he reinstated slavery in the French West Indian colonies and sent an army that captured L'Ouverture, who died in a French dungeon within a year. But the French soldiers, weakened by disease, soon succumbed to the slave forces. On January 1, 1804, the western part of Hispaniola, now called Haiti, announced its freedom and became the first state in Latin America to win its independence. Despite Napoleon's efforts to the contrary, one of the French revolutionary ideals had triumphed abroad.

Reaction and the Directory   By the summer of 1794, the French had been successful on the battlefield against their foreign foes, making the Reign of Terror less necessary. But the Terror continued because Robespierre, who had become a figure of power and authority, became obsessed with purifying the body politic of all the corrupt. Many deputies in the National Convention were fearful, however, that they were not safe while Robespierre was free to act and gathered enough votes to condemn him. Robespierre was sent to the guillotine on July 28, 1794.

After the death of Robespierre, a reaction set in as more moderate middle-class leaders took control. The Reign of Terror came to a halt, and the National Convention reduced the power of the Committee of Public Safety. In addition, in August 1795 a new constitution was drafted that reflected the desire for a stability that did not sacrifice the ideals of 1789. Five directors—known as the Directory—acted as the executive authority.

Government under the Directory (1795–1799) was characterized by stagnation and corruption. The Directory faced political enemies on both the left and the right. On the right, royalists who wanted to restore the monarchy continued their agitation. On the left, radical hopes of power were revived by continuing economic problems. Battered from both sides, unable to solve the country's economic problems, and still carrying on the wars inherited from the Committee of Public Safety, the Directory increasingly relied on the military to maintain its power. This led to a coup d'état in 1799 in which a popular military general, Napoleon Bonaparte (1769–1821), seized power.

THE AGE OF NAPOLEON

Napoleon dominated both French and European history from 1799 to 1815. The coup that brought him to power occurred exactly ten years after the outbreak of the French Revolution. In a sense, Napoleon brought the Revolution to an end, but he was also its child; he even called himself the Son of the Revolution. The French Revolution had made possible his rise first in the military and then to supreme power in France. Even beyond this, Napoleon had once said, "I am the Revolution," and he never ceased to remind the French that they owed to him the preservation of all that was beneficial in the revolutionary program.

The Rise of Napoleon   Napoleon was born in Corsica in 1769, only a few months after France had annexed the island. The son of an Italian lawyer whose family stemmed from the Florentine nobility, Napoleone Buonaparte (his birth name) grew up in the countryside of Corsica, a willful and demanding child who nevertheless developed discipline, thriftiness, and loyalty to his family. His father's connections in France enabled him to study first at a school in the French town of Autun, where he learned to speak French, and then to obtain a royal scholarship to study at a military school. At that time, he changed his first name to the more French-sounding Napoleon (he did not change his last name to Bonaparte until 1796).

Napoleon's military education led to his commission as a lieutenant in 1785, although he was not well liked by his fellow officers because he was short, spoke with an Italian accent, and had little money. For the next seven years, Napoleon spent much of his time reading the works of the philosophes, especially Rousseau, and educating himself in military matters by studying the campaigns of great military leaders from the past, including Alexander the Great, Charlemagne, and Frederick the Great. The French Revolution and the European war that followed broadened his sights and presented him with new opportunities.

Napoleon rose quickly through the ranks. In 1794, at the age of only twenty-five, he was made a brigadier general by the Committee of Public Safety. Two years later, he commanded the French armies in Italy, where he won a series of victories and returned to France as a conquering hero. After a disastrous expedition to Egypt, Napoleon returned to Paris, where he participated in the coup that gave him control of France. He was only thirty years old.

After the coup of 1799, a new form of the Republic, called the Consulate, was proclaimed in which Napoleon, as first consul, controlled the entire executive authority of government. He had overwhelming influence over the legislature, appointed members of the administrative bureaucracy, commanded the army, and conducted foreign affairs. In 1802, Napoleon was made consul for life, and in 1804, he returned France to monarchy when he crowned himself Emperor Napoleon I.

Domestic Policies   One of Napoleon's first domestic policies was to establish peace with the oldest and most implacable enemy of the Revolution, the Catholic Church. In 1801, Napoleon arranged a concordat with the pope that recognized Catholicism as the religion of a majority of the French people. In return, the pope agreed not to raise the question of the church lands confiscated in the Revolution. As a result of the concordat, the Catholic Church was no longer an enemy of the French government, and Frenchmen who had acquired church lands during the Revolution were assured that they would not be stripped of them, an assurance that made them supporters of the Napoleonic regime.

Napoleon's most enduring domestic achievement was his codification of the laws. Before the Revolution, France had some three hundred local legal systems. During the Revolution, efforts were made to prepare a single code of laws for the entire nation, but it remained for Napoleon to bring the work to completion in the famous Civil Code. This preserved most of the revolutionary gains by recognizing the principle of the equality of all citizens before the law, the abolition of serfdom and feudalism, and religious toleration. Property rights were also protected.

At the same time, the Civil Code strictly curtailed the rights of some people. During the radical phase of the French Revolution, new laws had made divorce an easy process for both husbands and wives and allowed sons and daughters to inherit property equally. Napoleon's Civil Code undid these laws. Divorce was still allowed but was made more difficult for women to obtain. Women were now "less equal than men" in other ways as well. When they married, their property came under the control of their husbands.

Napoleon also developed a powerful, centralized administrative machine and worked hard to develop a bureaucracy of capable officials. Early on, the regime showed that it cared little whether the expertise of officials had been acquired in royal or revolutionary bureaucracies. Promotion, whether in civil or military offices, was to be based not on rank or birth but on ability only. This principle of a government career open to talent was, of course, what many bourgeois had wanted before the Revolution.

In his domestic policies, then, Napoleon both destroyed and preserved aspects of the Revolution. Although equality and the opening of careers to talent were retained in the law code, the creation of a new aristocracy, the strong protection accorded to property rights, and the use of conscription for the military make it clear that much equality had been lost. Liberty had been replaced by an initially benevolent despotism that grew increasingly arbitrary. Napoleon shut down sixty of France's seventy-three newspapers and insisted that all manuscripts be subjected to government scrutiny before they were published. Even the mail was opened by government police.

Napoleon's Empire   When Napoleon became consul in 1799, France was at war with a second European coalition of Russia, Great Britain, and Austria. Napoleon realized the need for a pause and made a peace treaty in 1802. But war was renewed in 1803 with Britain, which was soon joined by Austria, Russia, and Prussia in the Third Coalition. In a series of battles from 1805 to 1807, Napoleon's Grand Army defeated the Austrian, Prussian, and Russian armies, giving Napoleon the opportunity to create a new European order.

The Grand Empire   From 1807 to 1812, Napoleon was the master of Europe. His Grand Empire was composed of three major parts: the French Empire, dependent states, and allied states. Dependent states were kingdoms under the rule of

MAP 18.4 Napoleon's Grand Empire

Napoleon's Grand Army won a series of victories against Austria, Prussia, and Russia that gave the French emperor full or partial control over much of Europe by 1807.

Napoleon's relatives; these came to include Spain, the Netherlands, the kingdom of Italy, the Swiss Republic, the Grand Duchy of Warsaw, and the Confederation of the Rhine (a union of all German states except Austria and Prussia). Allied states were those defeated by Napoleon and forced to join his struggle against Britain; these included Prussia, Austria, Russia, and Sweden.

Within his empire, Napoleon sought acceptance of certain revolutionary principles, including legal equality, religious toleration, and economic freedom. In the inner core and dependent states of his Grand Empire, Napoleon tried to destroy the old order. Nobility and clergy everywhere in these states lost their special privileges. He decreed equality of opportunity with offices open to talent, equality before the law, and religious toleration. This spread of French revolutionary principles was an important factor in the development of liberal traditions in these countries.

Napoleon hoped that his Grand Empire would last for centuries; it collapsed almost as rapidly as it had been formed. As long as Britain ruled the waves, it was not subject to military attack. Napoleon hoped to invade Britain, but he could not overcome the British navy's decisive defeat of a combined French-Spanish fleet at Trafalgar in 1805. To defeat Britain, Napoleon turned to his **Continental system**. An alliance put into effect between 1806 and 1808, it attempted to prevent British goods from reaching the European continent in order to weaken Britain economically and destroy its capacity to wage war. But the Continental system failed. Allied states resented it; some began to cheat and others to resist.

Napoleon also encountered new sources of opposition. His conquests made the French hated oppressors and aroused the patriotism of the conquered peoples. A Spanish uprising against Napoleon's rule, with British support, kept a French force of 200,000 pinned down for years.

The Fall of Napoleon   The beginning of Napoleon's downfall came in 1812 with his invasion of Russia. The refusal of the Russians to remain in the Continental system left Napoleon with little choice. Although aware of the risks in invading such a huge country, he also knew that if the Russians were allowed to challenge the Continental system unopposed, others would soon follow suit. In June 1812, he led his Grand Army of more than 600,000 men into Russia. Napoleon's hopes for victory depended on quickly defeating the Russian armies, but the Russian forces retreated and refused to give battle, torching their own villages and countryside to keep Napoleon's army from finding food. When the Russians did stop to fight at Borodino, Napoleon's forces won an indecisive and costly victory. When the remaining troops of the Grand Army arrived in Moscow, they found the city ablaze. Lacking food and supplies, Napoleon abandoned Moscow late in October and made a retreat across Russia in terrible winter conditions. Only 40,000 of the original 600,000 men managed to arrive back in Poland in January 1813.

This military disaster led other European states to rise up and attack the crippled French army. Paris was captured in March 1814, and Napoleon was sent into exile on the island of Elba, off the coast of Italy. Meanwhile, the Bourbon monarchy was restored in the person of Louis XVIII, the count of Provence, brother of the executed king. (Louis XVII, son of Louis XVI, had died in prison at age ten.) Napoleon, bored on Elba, slipped back into France. When troops were sent to capture him, Napoleon opened his coat and addressed them: "Soldiers of the 5th regiment, I am your Emperor.... If there is a man among you would kill his Emperor, here I am!" No one fired a shot. Shouting "Vive l'Empereur! Vive l'Empereur!" the troops went over to his side, and Napoleon entered Paris in triumph on March 20, 1815.

The powers that had defeated him pledged once more to fight him. Having decided to strike first at his enemies, Napoleon raised yet another army and moved to attack the allied forces stationed in what is now Belgium. At Waterloo on June 18, Napoleon met a combined British and Prussian army under the duke of Wellington and suffered a bloody defeat. This time, the victorious allies exiled him to Saint Helena, a small, forsaken island in the South Atlantic. Only Napoleon's memory continued to haunt French political life.

CHRONOLOGIES

ENLIGHTENED ABSOLUTISM IN EIGHTEENTH-CENTURY EUROPE

Prussia

1740–1786	Frederick II the Great

Austrian Empire

1740–1780	Maria Theresa
1780–1790	Joseph II

Russia

1762–1796	Catherine II the Great
1773–1775	Pugachev's rebellion
1785	Charter of the Nobility

THE FRENCH REVOLUTION

May 5, 1789	Meeting of the Estates-General
June 17, 1789	Formation of the National Assembly
July 14, 1789	Fall of the Bastille
August 26, 1789	Declaration of the Rights of Man and the Citizen
July 12, 1790	Civil Constitution of the Clergy
June 20–21, 1791	Flight of the king
August 10, 1792	Attack on the royal palace
September 21, 1792	Abolition of the monarchy
January 21, 1793	Execution of the king
August 23, 1793	Universal mobilization
July 28, 1794	Execution of Robespierre
August 22, 1795	Adoption of the Constitution of 1795 and the Directory

MindTap is a fully online, highly personalized learning experience built upon Cengage Learning content. MindTap combines student learning tools—readings, multimedia, activities, and assessments—into a singular Learning Path that guides students through their course.

Notes

CHAPTER 01

1. J. M. Chauvet et al., *Dawn of Art: The Chauvet Cave* (New York, 1996), pp. 49–50.
2. Quoted in A. Kuhrt, *The Ancient Near East, c. 3000–330 B.C.* (London, 1995), vol. 1, p. 68.
3. Quoted in Michael Wood, *Legacy: The Search for Ancient Cultures* (New York, 1995), p. 34.
4. Quoted in M. Van de Mieroop, *A History of the Ancient Near East, ca. 3000–323 B.C.* (Oxford, 2004), p. 69.
5. Quoted in ibid., p. 106.
6. Quoted in T. Jacobsen, "Mesopotamia," in H. Frankfort et al., *Before Philosophy* (Baltimore, 1949), p. 139.
7. Quoted in M. Covensky, *The Ancient Near Eastern Tradition* (New York, 1966), p. 51.
8. Quoted in B. G. Trigger et al., *Ancient Egypt: A Social History* (Cambridge, 1983), p. 74.
9. Quoted in R.-M. Hagen and R. Hagen, *Egypt: People, Gods, Pharaohs* (Cologne, 2002), p. 148.
10. J. B. Pritchard, *Ancient Near Eastern Texts*, 3rd ed. (Princeton, N.J., 1969), p. 413.
11. Ibid., p. 420.
12. Psalms 137:1, 4–6.
13. Psalms 145:8–9.
14. Exodus 20:13–15.
15. Isaiah 2:4.
16. Quoted in H. W. F. Saggs, *The Might That Was Assyria* (London, 1984), p. 261.
17. Ibid., p. 262.
18. Quoted in J. M. Cook, *The Persian Empire* (New York, 1983), p. 32.
19. Herodotus, *The Persian Wars*, trans. G. Rawlinson (New York, 1942), p. 257.
20. Isaiah, 44:28, 45:1.
21. Quoted in Cook, *The Persian Empire*, p. 76.

CHAPTER 02

1. Quoted in R. Lannoy, *The Speaking Tree: A Study of Indian Culture and Society* (London, 1971), p. 318.
2. The quotation is from ibid., p. 319. Note also that the *Law of Manu* says that "punishment alone governs all created beings.... The whole world is kept in order by punishment, for a guiltless man is hard to find."
3. Strabo's *Geography*, bk. 15, quoted in M. Edwardes, *A History of India: From the Earliest Times to the Present Day* (London, 1961), p. 55.
4. Ibid., p. 54.
5. Ibid., p. 57.
6. From the *Law of Manu*, quoted in A. L. Basham, *The Wonder That Was India* (London, 1961), pp. 180–181. © 1961 Pan Macmillan, London.
7. According to historian Karen Armstrong, the gradual shift from rites to ethics was a characteristic of many belief systems during what historians call the "Axial Age" in the middle of the first millennium B.C.E., when the focus of religious belief began to shift from the priestly classes to the common people. On the Axial Age. see Chapter 4.

8. Quoted in A. K. Coomaraswamy, *Buddha and the Gospel of Buddhism* (New York, 1964), p. 34.

CHAPTER 03

1. *Book of Changes*, quoted in Chang Chi-yun, *Chinese History of Fifty Centuries*, vol. 1, *Ancient Times* (Taipei, 1962), pp. 15, 31, and 65.
2. Ibid., p. 381.
3. Quoted in E. N. Anderson, *The Food of China* (New Haven, Conn., 1988), p. 21.
4. According to Chinese tradition, the *Rites of Zhou* was written by the duke of Zhou himself near the time of the founding of the Zhou dynasty. However, modern histor- ians believe that it was written much later, perhaps as late as the fourth century B.C.E.
5. From *The Book of Songs*, quoted in S. de Grazia, ed., *Masters of Chinese Political Thought: From the Begin- nings to the Han Dynasty* (New York, 1973), pp. 40–41.
6. *Confucian Analects* (Lun Yu), ed. J. Legge (Taipei, 1963), 11:11 and 6:20. Author's translation.
7. Ibid., 15:23.
8. *Book of Rites*, sec. 9, quoted in W. T. de Bary et al., eds., *Sources of Chinese Tradition* (New York, 1960), p. 192.
9. *Confucian Analects*, 17:2.
10. *Book of Mencius* (Meng Zi), 4A:9, quoted in de Bary, *Sources of Chinese Tradition*, p. 93.
11. Quoted in ibid., p. 51.
12. M. Lewis, *The Early Chinese Empires: Qin and Han* (Cambridge, Mass., 2007), p. 31, citing *Shiji* 68, pp. 2230, 2232.
13. B. Watson, *Records of the Grand Historian of China* (New York, 1961), vol. 2, pp. 155, 160.
14. Ibid., pp. 32, 53.

15. C. Waltham, *Shu Ching: Book of History* (Chicago, 1971), p. 154.
16. Lewis, *Early Chinese Empires*, p. 85.
17. Quoted in H. A. Giles, *A History of Chinese Literature* (New York, 1923), p. 19.
18. Waley, ed., *Chinese Poems* (London, 1983), p. xx.
19. Chang Chi-yun, *Chinese History*, vol. 1, p. 183.

CHAPTER 04

1. Xenophon, *Symposium*, trans. O. J. Todd (New York, 1946), III, 5.
2. Homer, *Odyssey*, pp. 290–291.
3. Quoted in T. R. Martin, *Ancient Greece* (New Haven, Conn., 1996), p. 62.
4. Quoted in V. D. Hanson, *The Wars of the Ancient Greeks*, rev. ed. (London, 2006), p. 14.
5. These words from Plutarch are quoted in E. Fantham et al., *Women in the Classical World* (New York, 1994), p. 64.
6. Aeschylus, *The Persians*, in *The Complete Greek Tragedies*, vol. 1, ed. David Grene and Richard Lattimore (Chicago, 1959), p. 229.
7. Thucydides, *The Peloponnesian War*, trans. R. Warner (New York, 1954), p. 24.
8. Sophocles, *Oedipus the King*, trans. D. Grene (Chicago, 1959), pp. 68–69.
9. Sophocles, *Antigone*, trans. D. Taylor (London, 1986), p. 146.
10. Plato, *The Republic*, trans. F. M. Cornford (New York, 1945), pp. 178–179.
11. Quotations from Aristotle are in S. Blundell, *Women in Ancient Greece* (Cambridge, Mass., 1995), pp. 106, 186.
12. Quoted in S. B. Pomeroy et al., *Ancient Greece: A Political, Social, and Cultural History* (Oxford, 1999), p. 390.

13. Quoted in G. Shipley, *The Greek World After Alexander, 323–30 B.C.* (London, 2000), p. 304.
14. Plutarch, *Life of Marcellus*, trans. J. Dryden (New York, n.d.), p. 378.
15. Quoted in W. W. Tarn, *Hellenistic Civilization* (London, 1930), p. 324.

CHAPTER 05

1. Tacitus, *The Annals of Imperial Rome*, trans. M. Grant (Harmondsworth, England, 1964), p. 31.
2. Virgil, *The Aeneid*, trans. C. Day Lewis (Garden City, N.Y., 1952), p. 154.
3. Juvenal, *The Sixteen Satires*, trans. P. Green (New York, 1967), p. 207.
4. Quoted in C. Starr, *Past and Future in Ancient History* (Lanham, Md., 1987), pp. 38–39.
5. Matthew 7:12.
6. Mark 12:30–31.

CHAPTER 06

1. Quoted in S. Morley and G. W. Brainerd, *The Ancient Maya* (Stanford, Calif., 1983), p. 513.
2. B. Díaz, *The Conquest of New Spain* (Harmondsworth, England, 1975), p. 210.
3. Quoted in M. D. Coe, D. Snow, and E. P. Benson, *Atlas of Ancient America* (New York, 1988), p. 149.
4. G. de la Vega (El Inca), *Royal Commentaries of the Incas and General History of Peru*, pt. 1, trans. H. V. Livermore (Austin, Tex., 1966), p. 180.

CHAPTER 07

1. M. M. Pickthall, trans., *The Meaning of the Glorious Koran* (New York, 1953), p. 89.
2. Quoted in T. W. Lippman, *Understanding Islam: An Introduction to the Moslem World* (New York, 1982), p. 118.
3. F. Hirth and W. W. Rockhill, trans., *Chau Ju-kua: His Work on the Chinese and Arab Trade in the Twelfth and Thirteenth Centuries, Entitled "Chu-fan-chi"* (New York, 1966), p. 115.
4. al-Mas'udi, *The Meadows of Gold: The Abbasids*, ed. P. Lunde and C. Stone (London, 1989), p. 151.
5. Quoted in G. Wiet, *Baghdad: Metropolis of the Abassid Caliphate*, trans. S. Feiler (Norman, Okla., 1971), pp. 118–119.
6. L. Africanus, *The History and Description of Africa and of the Notable Things Therein Contained* (New York, n.d.), pp. 820–821.
7. Hirth and Rockhill, *Chau Ju-kua*, p. 116.
8. E. Yarshater, ed., *Persian Literature* (Albany, N.Y., 1988), pp. 154–159.
9. E. Rehatsek, trans., *The Gulistan or Rose Garden of Sa'di* (New York, 1964), pp. 65, 67, 71.

CHAPTER 08

1. F. Fernández-Armesto, *Civilizations* (London, 2000), pp. 66–68.
2. S. Hamdun and N. King, eds., *Ibn Battuta in Africa* (London, 1975), p. 19.
3. *The Book of Duarte Barbosa* (Nedeln, Liechtenstein, 1967), p. 28.
4. Herodotus, *The Histories*, trans. A. de Sélincourt (Baltimore, 1964), p. 307.
5. Sidi Salem Ould Elhadj, "The Pachalik arma de Tombouctou, 1591–1826," cited in M. de Villiers and S. Hirtle, *Timbuktu: The Sahara's Fabled City of Gold* (New York, 2007), p. 68.
6. C. R. Boxer, ed., *The Tragic History of the Sea, 1589–1622* (Cambridge, 1959), pp. 121–122.

7. Quoted in D. Nurse and T. Spear, *The Swahili: Reconstructing the History and Language of an African Society, 800–1500* (Philadelphia, 1985), p. 84.
8. Hamdun and King, *Ibn Battuta in Africa*, p. 47.
9. Ibid., p. 28.
10. Ibid., p. 28.
11. Ibid., p. 30.

CHAPTER 09

1. Hiuen Tsiang, *Si-Yu-Ki: Buddhist Records of the Western World*, trans. S. Beal (London, 1982), pp. 89–90.
2. "Fo-Kwo-Ki" (Travels of Fa Xian), ch. 20, p. 43, in ibid.
3. E. C. Sachau, *Alberoni's India* (London, 1914), vol. 1, p. 22.
4. Quoted in S. M. Ikram, *Muslim Civilization in India* (New York, 1964), p. 68.
5. Hiuen Tsiang, *Si-Yu-Ki*, pp. 73–74.
6. D. Barbosa, *The Book of Duarte Barbosa* (Nedeln, Liechtenstein, 1967), pp. 147–148.
7. Quoted in R. Lannoy, *The Speaking Tree: A Study of Indian Culture and Society* (London, 1971), p. 232.
8. Quoted in S. Tharu and K. Lalita, *Women Writing in India*, vol. 1 (New York, 1991), p. 77.
9. Quoted in A. L. Basham, *The Wonder That Was India* (London, 1954), p. 426.
10. Quoted in S. Hughes and B. Hughes, *Women in World History*, vol. 1 (Armonk, N.Y., 1995), p. 217.

CHAPTER 10

1. Quoted in A. F. Wright, *Buddhism in Chinese History* (Stanford, Calif., 1959), p. 30.
2. Quoted in A. F. Wright, *The Sui Dynasty* (New York, 1978), p. 180.

3. Chu-yu, *P'ing-chow Table Talks*, quoted in R. Temple, *The Genius of China: 3,000 Years of Science, Discovery, and Invention* (New York, 1986), p. 150.
4. Quoted in E. H. Schafer, *The Golden Peaches of Samarkand: A Study of T'ang Exotics* (Berkeley, Calif., 1963), p. 43.
5. Quoted in J. K. Fairbank, E. O. Reischauer, and A. M. Craig, *East Asia: Tradition and Transformation* (Boston, 1973), p. 164.
6. Quoted in R. Grousset, *L'Empire des Steppes* (Paris, 1939), p. 285.
7. Temple, *Genius of China*, pp. 242–243.
8. A. M. Khazanov, *Nomads and the Outside World* (Cambridge, 1983), p. 241.
9. S. A. M. Adshead, *China in World History* (New York, 2000), p. 132.

CHAPTER 11

1. Cited in C. Holcombe, *The Genesis of East Asia, 221 B.C.–A.D. 907* (Honolulu, 2001), p. 41.
2. Quoted in D. J. Lu, *Sources of Japanese History*, vol. 1 (New York, 1974), p. 7.
3. From "The History of Wei," quoted in ibid., p. 10.
4. From "The Law of Households," quoted in ibid., p. 32.
5. From "On the Salvation of Women," quoted in ibid., p. 127.
6. Quoted in B. Ruch, "The Other Side of Culture in Medieval Japan," in K. Yamamura, ed., *The Cambridge History of Japan*, vol. 3, *Medieval Japan* (Cambridge, 1990), p. 506.
7. Excerpt from *The Cambridge History of Japan*, Vol. III, edited by Koza Yamamura, excerpt from "A Sample of Linked Verse" by H. Paul

Verley, from p. 480. Copyright © 1990 Cambridge University Press.

8. K. W. Taylor, *The Birth of Vietnam* (Berkeley, Calif., 1983), p. 76.
9. Quoted in ibid., pp. 336–337.

CHAPTER 12

1. Quoted in N. F. Cantor, ed., *The Medieval World, 300–1300* (New York, 1963), p. 104.
2. A. Barbero, *Charlemagne: Father of a Continent*, trans. A. Cameron (Berkeley, Calif., 2004), p. 4.
3. C. Wickham, *The Inheritance of Rome: A History of Europe from 400 to 1000* (New York, 2009), p. 4.
4. Quoted in S. Keynes, "The Vikings in England, c. 790–1016," in P. Sawyer, ed., *The Oxford Illustrated History of the Vikings* (Oxford, 1997), p. 81.
5. Quoted in M. Perry, J. Peden, and T. von Laue, *Sources of the Western Tradition*, vol. 1 (Boston, 1987), p. 218.
6. Quoted in J. Gimpel, *The Medieval Machine* (Harmondsworth, England, 1977), p. 92.
7. O. J. Thatcher and E. H. McNeal, eds., *A Source Book for Medieval History* (New York, 1905), p. 208.
8. Quoted in R. H. C. Davis, *A History of Medieval Europe from Constantine to Saint Louis*, 2nd ed. (New York, 1988), p. 252.
9. Quoted in R. Brooke and C. Brooke, *Popular Religion in the Middle Ages* (London, 1984), p. 19.
10. Quoted in Thatcher and McNeal, *Source Book for Medieval History*, p. 517.
11. Quoted in T. Asbridge, *The First Crusade: A New History* (Oxford, 2004), pp. 79–80.
12. Quoted in H. E. Mayer, *The Crusades*, trans. J. Gillingham (New York, 1972), pp. 99–100.

CHAPTER 13

1. Quoted in J. Harris, *Constantinople: Capital of Byzantium* (New York, 2007), p. 40.
2. Procopius, *Buildings of Justinian* (London, 1897), pp. 9, 6–7.
3. Quoted in Harris, *Constantinople*, p. 118.
4. A. Cameron, *The Byzantines* (Oxford, 2006), p. 45.
5. Quoted in C. S. Bartsocas, "Two Fourteenth-Century Descriptions of the 'Black Death,'" *Journal of the History of Medicine* (October 1966), p. 395.
6. Quoted in M. Dols, *The Black Death in the Middle East* (Princeton, N.J., 1977), p. 270.
7. Quoted in D. J. Herlihy, *The Black Death and the Transformation of the West*, ed. S. K. Cohn Jr. (Cambridge, Mass., 1997), p. 9.
8. Quoted in R. Horrox, *The Black Death* (Manchester, England, 1994), p. 16.
9. G. Boccaccio, *The Decameron*, trans. F. Winwar (New York, 1955), p. xiii.
10. J. Froissart, *Chronicles*, ed. and trans. G. Brereton (Harmondsworth, England, 1968), p. 111.
11. Ibid., p. 89.
12. Quoted in J. Burckhardt, *The Civilization of the Renaissance in Italy*, trans. S. G. C. Middlemore (London, 1960), p. 81.
13. N. Machiavelli, *The Prince*, trans. D. Wootton (Indianapolis, Ind., 1995), p. 48.

CHAPTER 14

1. H. J. Benda and J. A. Larkin, eds., *The World of Southeast Asia: Selected Historical Readings* (New York, 1967), p. 13.
2. Parry, *European Reconnaissance*, quoting from A. Cortesão, *The*

Summa Oriental of Tomé Pires (London, 1944), vol. 2, pp. 283, 287.

3. Quoted in J. H. Parry, *The Age of Reconnaissance: Discovery, Exploration, and Settlement, 1450 to 1650* (New York, 1963), p. 33.

4. Quoted in R. B. Reed, "The Expansion of Europe," in R. DeMolen, ed., *The Meaning of the Renaissance and Reformation* (Boston, 1974), p. 308.

5. K. N. Chaudhuri, *Trade and Civilization in the Indian Ocean: An Economic History from the Rise of Islam to 1750* (Cambridge, 1985), p. 65.

6. Quoted in Parry, *Age of Reconnaissance*, pp. 176–177.

7. Quoted in M. Leon-Portilla, ed., *The Broken Spears: The Aztec Account of the Conquest of Mexico* (Boston, 1969), p. 51.

CHAPTER 15

1. Quoted in R. Bainton, *Here I Stand: A Life of Martin Luther* (New York, 1950), p. 144.

2. J. Calvin, *Institutes of the Christian Religion*, trans. J. Allen (Philadelphia, 1936), vol. 1, p. 228; vol. 2, p. 181.

3. Quoted in B. S. Anderson and J. P. Zinsser, *A History of Their Own: Women in Europe from Prehistory to the Present* (New York, 1988), vol. 1, p. 259.

4. Quoted in J. O'Malley, *The First Jesuits* (Cambridge, Mass., 1993), p. 76.

5. Quoted in J. Klaits, *Servants of Satan: The Age of Witch Hunts* (Bloomington, Ind., 1985), p. 68.

CHAPTER 16

1. Cited in Christophe Courau, "Turquie: Sublime Porte de 1'Europe," in *Historia* (October 2005), p. 15.

2. Quoted in V. A. Smith, *The Oxford History of India* (Oxford, 1967), p. 341.

3. Quoted in M. Edwardes, *A History of India: From the Earliest Times to the Present Day* (London, 1961), p. 188.

4. Quoted in ibid., p. 220.

5. Quoted in R. C. Craven, *Indian Art: A Concise History* (New York, 1976), p. 205.

CHAPTER 17

1. Quoted in R. Strassberg, *The World of K'ang Shang-jen: A Man of Letters in Early Ch'ing China* (New York, 1983), p. 275.

2. Quoted in F. Wakeman Jr., *The Great Enterprise: The Manchu Reconstruction of Imperial Order in Seventeenth-Century China* (Berkeley, Calif., 1985), p. 16.

3. L. Struve, *The Southern Ming, 1644–1662* (New Haven, Conn., 1984), p. 61.

4. J. L. Cranmer-Byng, *An Embassy to China: Lord Macartney's Journal, 1793–1794* (London, 1912), p. 340.

5. Quoted in D. J. Boorstin, *The Discoverers: A History of Man's Search to Know His World and Himself* (New York, 1983), p. 63.

6. Quoted in C. R. Boxer, ed., *South China in the Sixteenth Century* (London, 1953), p. 265.

7. Quoted in C. Nakane and S. Oishi, eds., *Tokugawa Japan* (Tokyo, 1990), p. 14.

8. Quoted in J. Elisonas, "Christianity and the Daimyo," in J. W. Hall, ed., *The Cambridge History of Japan*, vol. 4 (Cambridge, 1991), p. 360.

9. E. Kaempfer, *The History of Japan: Together with a Description of the*

Kingdom of Siam, 1690–1692, vol. 2 (Glasgow, 1906), pp. 173–174.

10. Quoted in J. H. Parry, *European Reconnaissance: Selected Documents* (New York, 1968), p. 144.

11. Quoted in D. Keene, *The Japanese Discovery of Europe, 1720–1830,* rev. ed. (Stanford, Calif., 1969), p. 114.

Chapter 18

1. R. Descartes, *Philosophical Writing,* ed. and trans. N. K. Smith (New York, 1958), pp. 118–119.

2. J. Locke, *An Essay Concerning Human Understanding* (New York, 1964), pp. 89–90.

3. Quoted in P. Burke, *Popular Culture in Early Modern Europe,* rev. ed. (New York, 1994), p. 186.

4. Quoted in W. Doyle, *The Oxford History of the French Revolution* (Oxford, 1989), p. 184.

5. Quoted in L. Gershoy, *The Era of the French Revolution* (Princeton, N.J., 1957), p. 157.

6. Quoted in Doyle, *Oxford History,* p. 254.

Chapter 19

1. Quotations in E. R. Pike, *Human Documents of the Industrial Revolution in Britain* (London, 1966), pp. 314, 343.

2. Ibid., p. 315.

3. C. Dickens, *The Old Curiosity Shop* (New York, 2000), p. 340. Originally published in 1840–1841.

4. K. Marx and F. Engels, *The Communist Manifesto* (Harmondsworth, England, 1967), p. 80. Originally published in 1848.

5. Ibid., pp. 91, 94.

6. Quoted in L. L. Snyder, ed., *Documents of German History* (New Brunswick, N.J., 1958), p. 202.

7. Quoted in S. Galai, *The Liberation Movement in Russia, 1900–1905* (Cambridge, 1973), p. 26.

Chapter 20

1. Quoted in J. C. Chasteen, *Americanos: Latin America's Struggle for Independence* (Oxford, 2008), p. 122.

2. Quoted in H. Herring, *A History of Latin America* (New York, 1961), p. 255.

3. Quoted in P. Bakewell, *A History of Latin America* (Oxford, 1997), p. 367.

4. Quoted in M. C. Eakin, *The History of Latin America: Collision of Cultures* (New York, 2007), p. 188.

5. Quoted in Bakewell, *History of Latin America,* p. 372.

6. Quoted in E. B. Burns, *Latin America: A Concise Interpretive History,* 4th ed. (Englewood Cliffs, N.J., 1986), p. 116.

7. Quoted in N. Bullock and J. Read, *The Movement for Housing Reform in Germany and France, 1840–1914* (Cambridge, 1985), p. 42.

8. W. Wordsworth, "The Tables Turned," *Poems of Wordsworth,* ed. M. Arnold (London, 1963), p. 138.

9. Quoted in A. E. E. McKenzie, *The Major Achievements of Science* (New York, 1960), vol. 1, p. 310.

10. F. von Bernhardi, *Germany and the Next War,* trans. A. H. Powles (New York, 1914), pp. 18–19.

11. Quoted in J. Rewald, *History of Impressionism* (New York, 1961), pp. 456–458.

12. Quoted in A. Higonnet, *Berthe Morisot's Images of Women* (Cambridge, Mass., 1992), p. 19.

CHAPTER 21

1. K. Pearson, *National Life from the Standpoint of Science* (London, 1905), p. 184.
2. Quoted in H. Braunschwig, *French Colonialism, 1871–1914* (London, 1961), p. 80.
3. Quoted in G. Garros, *Forceries Humaines* (Paris, 1926), p. 21.
4. Cited in B. Schwartz's review of D. Cannadine's *Ornamentalism: How the British Saw Their Empire*, in *The Atlantic*, November 2001, p. 135.
5. Quoted in R. Bartlett, ed., *The Record of American Diplomacy: Documents and Readings in the History of American Foreign Relations* (New York, 1952), p. 385.
6. Quoted in L. Roubaud, *Vietnam: La Tragédie Indochinoise* (Paris, 1926), p. 80.
7. Quoted in J. Iliffe, *Africans: The History of a Continent* (Cambridge, 1995), p. 124.
8. Quoted in T. Pakenham, *The Scramble for Africa* (New York, 1991), p. 13.
9. Quoted in ibid., p. 182, citing a letter to Queen Victoria dated August 7, 1879.
10. Quoted in P. C. W. Gutkind and I. Wallerstein, eds., *The Political Economy of Contemporary Africa* (Beverly Hills, Calif., 1976), p. 14.

CHAPTER 22

1. H. B. Morse, *The International Relations of the Chinese Empire* (London, 1910–1918), vol. 2, p. 622.

2. William Theodore de Bary and Richard Lufrano, eds., *Sources of Chinese Tradition*, 2nd ed, (New York, 1999), vol. 2, p. 252.
3. Quoted in S. Teng and J. K. Fairbank, eds., *China's Response to the West: A Documentary Survey, 1839–1923* (New York, 1970), p. 167.
4. J. K. Fairbank, A. M. Craig, and E. O. Reischauer, *East Asia: Tradition and Transformation* (Boston, 1973), p. 514.
5. Quoted in J. W. Dower, ed., *The Origins of the Modern Japanese State: Selected Writings of E. H. Norman* (New York, 1975), p. 13.
6. C. Brinton, *The Anatomy of Revolution* (New York, 1965), quoted in W. G. Beasley, *The Meiji Restoration* (Stanford, Calif., 1972), p. 423.

CHAPTER 23

1. Quoted in J. Remak, "1914–The Third Balkan War: Origin Reconsidered," *Journal of Modern History* 43 (1971), pp. 364–365.
2. Quoted in J. M. Winter, *The Experience of World War I* (New York, 1989), p. 142.
3. Quoted in Hew Strachan, *The First World War* (New York, 2004), pp. 94–95.
4. Quoted in ibid., p. 72.
5. Quoted in C. W. Reilly, ed., *Scars upon My Heart: Women's Poetry and Verse of the First World War* (London, 1981), p. 90.
6. Quoted in W. M. Mandel, *Soviet Women* (Garden City, N.Y., 1975), p. 43.
7. Quoted in M. D. Steinberg, *Voices of Revolution, 1917* (New Haven, Conn., 2001), p. 55.
8. Quoted in S. Audoin-Rouzeau and A. Becker, *14–18: Understanding*

the Great War, trans. C. Temerson (New York, 2002), p. 212.

9. Quoted in ibid., p. 213.
10. Quoted in ibid., p. 41.
11. Quoted in R. Paxton, *Europe in the Twentieth Century*, 2nd ed. (San Diego, Calif., 1985), p. 237.
12. Quoted in I. Howe, ed., *The Basic Writings of Trotsky* (London, 1963), p. 162.

CHAPTER 24

1. Speech delivered in London, September 1931, while attending the first Roundtable Conference.
2. V. I. Lenin, "The Awakening of Asia," in *The Awakening of Asia: Selected Essays* (New York, 1963–1968), p. 22.
3. Ts'ai Yüan-p'ei, "Ta Lin Ch'in-nan Han," in *Ts'ai Yüan-p'ei Hsien-sheng Ch'uan-chi* [Collected Works of Mr. Cai Yuanpei] (Taipei, 1968), pp. 1057–1058.
4. Quoted in N. R. Clifford, *Spoilt Children of Empire: Westerners in Shanghai and the Chinese Revolution of the 1920s* (Hanover, N.H., 1991), p. 93.
5. Quoted in W. T. de Bary et al., eds., *Sources of Chinese Tradition* (New York, 1963), p. 783.
6. Lu Xun, "Diary of a Madman," in *Selected Works of Lu Hsun* (Beijing, 1957), vol. 1, p. 20.

CHAPTER 25

1. Mussolini, "The Doctrine of Fascism," in A. Lyttleton, ed., *Italian Fascisms from Pareto to Gentile* (London, 1973), p. 42.
2. Quoted in A. De Grand, "Women Under Italian Fascism," *Historical Journal* 19 (1976) pp. 958–959.

3. Quoted in J. J. Spielvogel and D. Redles, *Hitler and Nazi Germany: A History*, 6th ed. (Upper Saddle River, N.J., 2010), p. 60.
4. Quoted in J. Fest, *Hitler*, trans. R. Winston and C. Winston (New York, 1974), p. 418.
5. Quoted in S. Fitzpatrick, *Everyday Stalinism—Ordinary Life in Extraordinary Times: Soviet Russia in the 1930s* (New York, 1999), p. 87.
6. A. Hitler, *Mein Kampf*, trans. R. Manheim (Boston, 1971), p. 654.
7. *Documents on German Foreign Policy* (London, 1956), Series D, vol. 7, p. 204.
8. Memorandum by John Van Antwerp MacMurray, quoted in A. Waldron, *How the Peace Was Lost: The 1935 Memorandum* (Stanford, Calif., 1992), p. 5.
9. Quoted in W. Murray and A. R. Millett, *A War to Be Won: Fighting the Second World War* (Cambridge, Mass., 2000), p. 137.
10. Quoted in A. Speer, *Spandau*, trans. R. Winston and C. Winston (New York, 1976), p. 50.
11. *Nazi Conspiracy and Aggression* (Washington, D.C., 1946), vol. 6, p. 262.
12. International Military Tribunal, *Trial of the Major War Criminals* (Nuremberg, 1947–1949), vol. 22, p. 480.
13. Quoted in R. Hilberg, *The Destruction of the European Jews*, rev. ed. (New York, 1985), vol. 1, pp. 332–333.
14. *Nazi Conspiracy and Aggression*, vol. 6, p. 789.
15. Quoted in J. Campbell, *The Experience of World War II* (New York, 1989), p. 170.
16. Quoted in C. Koonz, "Mothers in the Fatherland: Women in Nazi Germany," in R. Bridenthal and

C. Koonz, eds., *Becoming Visible: Women in European History* (Boston, 1977), p. 466.

17. Quoted in Campbell, *Experience of World War II*, p. 143.

18. Quoted in N. Graebner, *Cold War Diplomacy, 1945–1960* (Princeton, N.J., 1962), p. 117.

19. Ibid., p. 117

20. Quoted in W. Loth, *The Division of the World, 1941–1955* (New York, 1988), p. 81.

CHAPTER 26

1. Quoted in J. M. Jones, *The Fifteen Weeks (February 21–June 5, 1947)*, 2nd ed. (New York, 1964), pp. 140–141.

2. Quoted in M. Glenny, *The Balkans: Nationalism, War, and the Great Powers* (New York, 1999), pp. 543–544.

3. Cited in the *New York Review of Books*, June 9, 2011, p. 71.

4. V. Sebestyen, *Revolution 1989: The Fall of the Soviet Empire* (New York, 2009), p. 91.

CHAPTER 27

1. Quoted in V. Zubok and C. Pleshakov, *Inside the Kremlin's Cold War: From Stalin to Khrushchev* (Cambridge, Mass., 1996), p. 166.

2. N. Khrushchev, *Khrushchev Remembers*, trans. S. Talbott (Boston, 1970), p. 77.

3. Quoted in H. Smith, *The New Russians* (New York, 1990), p. 30.

4. Quoted in F. B. Tipton and R. Aldrich, *An Economic and Social History of Europe from 1939 to the Present* (Baltimore, 1987), p. 193.

5. Quoted in Smith, *New Russians*, p. 74.

6. "Report on an Investigation of the Peasant Movement in Hunan (March 1927)," in *Quotations from Chairman Mao Tse-tung* (Beijing, 1976), p. 12.

7. Quoted in S. Karnow, *Mao and China: Inside China's Cultural Revolution* (New York, 1972), p. 95.

8. Quoted from an article by Mao in the journal *Red Flag* (June 1, 1958), in S. R. Schram, *The Political Thought of Mao Tse-tung* (New York, 1963), p. 253.

9. Liang Heng and J. Shapiro, *Son of the Revolution* (New York, 1983).

10. Quoted in J. Spence, *Chinese Roundabout: Essays in History and Culture* (New York, 1992), p. 285.

CHAPTER 28

1. Quoted in W. I. Hitchcock, *The Struggle for Europe: The Turbulent History of a Divided Continent, 1945–2002* (New York, 2003), pp. 399–400.

2. D. D. Eisenhower, *The White House Years: Waging Peace, 1956–1961* (Garden City, N.Y., 1965), p. 533.

3. Quoted in T. Judt, *Postwar: A History of Europe Since 1945* (New York, 2005), p. 390.

4. Quoted in H. Scott, *Sweden's "Right to Be Human"—Sex-Role Equality: The Goal and the Reality* (London, 1982), p. 125.

5. Quoted in M. Rowe et al., *Spare Rib Reader* (Harmondsworth, England, 1982), p. 574.

6. Quoted in R. Bridenthal, "Women in the New Europe," in R. Bridenthal, S. M. Stuard, and M. E. Wiesner, eds., *Becoming Visible:*

Women in European History, 3rd ed. (Boston, 1998), pp. 564–565.

7. Quoted in Joan W. Scott, *The Politics of the Veil* (Princeton, N.J., 2009), p. 1.

8. Quoted in H. Grosshans, *The Search for Modern Europe* (Boston, 1970), p. 421.

9. Quoted in R. Maltby, ed., *Passing Parade: A History of Popular Culture in the Twentieth Century* (New York, 1989), p. 11.

in African Literature (Portsmouth, N.H., 1986), p. 103.

7. Quoted in R. R. Andersen, R. F. Seibert, and J. G. Wagner, *Politics and Change in the Middle East: Sources of Conflict and Accommodation*, 4th ed. (Englewood Cliffs, N.J., 1982), p. 51.

8. S. Sachs, "Assad Looks at Syria's Economy in Inaugural Talk," *New York Times*, July 18, 2000.

9. S. Azadi, with A. Ferrante, *Out of Iran* (London, 1987), p. 223.

CHAPTER 29

1. According to a report issued by the United Nations, life expectancy in Africa dropped dramatically in the first years of the new millennium because of the prevalence of AIDS. See C. W. Dugger, "Devastated by AIDS, Africa Sees Life Expectancy Plunge," in *The New York Times*, July 16, 2004.

2. Cited in M. Meredith, *The Fate of Africa* (New York, 2004), p. 168.

3. A. Nicol, "*A Truly Married Woman*" *and Other Stories* (London, 1965), p. 12.

4. A. Ata Aidoo, *No Sweetness Here* (New York, 1995), p. 136.

5. G. Médioni, "Stand Up, Africa!" *World Press Review*, July 2002, p. 34.

6. Ngugi Wa Thiong'o, *Decolonising the Mind: The Politics of Language*

CHAPTER 30

1. Quoted in L. Collins and D. Lapierre, *Freedom at Midnight* (New York, 1975), p. 252.

2. Quoted in Somini Sengupta, "In World's Largest Democracy, Tolerance Is a Weak Pillar," *New York Times*, October 29, 2008.

3. From Pankaj Mishra, "Impasse in India," *New York Review of Books*, June 28, 2007, p. 51.

4. For a lengthy discussion of occupation efforts to create a new Japanese culture, see I. Buruma, *Inventing Japan, 1853–1964* (New York, 2004), pp. 131–140.

5. Y. Mishima and G. Bownas, eds., *New Writing in Japan* (Harmondsworth, England, 1972), p. 16.

Index

Note: Italicized page numbers show the locations of illustrations and maps.

A

Abbasid Empire, 230–234, *231*, 240, 244, 326, 395, 520; Seljuk Turks and, 232–234, 427
Abbas I (r. 1587–1629) (Safavids), 533–535, *551*
Abbesses, 380
Abbots, 403
Abd al-Rathman (Umayyad), 236, 238
Abraham (patriarch), 35
Absolutism, 508–513, 514; in central and Eastern Europe, 509–512
Abu al-Abbas (Abbasid), 230
Abu Bakr (Muslim caliph), 226
Academies: Islamic, 244; of Plato (Athens), 133, 244
Achaemenid dynasty, 42
Achilles (Greek hero), 118
Actium, Battle of, 163
Act of Supremacy (England), 502
Adal (Muslim state), 262
Aden, 240
Admonitions for Women (Ban Zhao), 172
Adriatic Sea, 154
Adshead, Samuel (historian), 339–340
Adulis, 255
Adultery: in Egypt, 32; Hammurabi's Code on, 18
Adventures of Marco Polo, The (1938), 338–339
Aegean Sea region, 115, 117. *See also* specific countries
Aegospotami, battle at, 127
Aeneid, The (Virgil), 168
Aeolian Greeks, 118
Aeschylus, 125, 128
Afghanistan: as Bactria, 70
Africa: advance into Western Asia and, 523, 525; agriculture in, 10, 253–254; ancient, 252; architecture in, 262, 276–277; civilizations of, 251–278; culture(s) in, 274–278; East, 257–260; Europeans and, 472–481; history of, 270–271; human origins in, 7, 252; Islam in, 260–268, 455–456; Kush in, 33; land in, 252–253; lineage groups in, 260; literature in, 18–20, 277–278; migration from, 257; migration in, 258; music in, 275–276; Nile in, 20; peoples, migration of, 258; Phoenicians in, 35; political and social structures in, 480–481; Portugal and, 458; religion in, 260; slavery in, 274; slave trade and, 459, 472–480, *478*; society in, 271–274; southern, 270; states, emergence in, *268*; states in, *268*; trade in, 256–258; urban areas in, 270–272; use of name, 260; village life in, 272; women in, 272–274. *See also* Slavery; Slave trade; specific regions and locations
Afrikaans language, 478
Afterlife: in China, 82; in Egypt, 28
Against Celsus (Origen), 182
Agamemnon (king of Mycenae), 117, 118
Age of Enlightenment, 586
Age of Exploration, 454–458, 454–462, *458*; Columbian Exchange and, 474
Age of Pericles (Athens), 126–127
Agincourt, Battle of, 436
Agra (India), 539–540, *552*
Agricultural revolution, 9–10, 11, 51
Agriculture: Americas and, 192, 468–468; in Asia, 10; Assyrian, 41; in China, 10, 79, 88, 184; civilization and, 3; Harappan, 50; in India, 10; Inka, 214; in Japan, 351, 352; Mayan, 197; Middle Ages, 386, 388; Neolithic Revolution and, 9–10; plantation, 242; of Pueblo peoples, 215–216; in Roman Empire, 161, 167–168; technology and, 88; in Teotihuacán, 195; transition from hunting-gathering to farming, 11
Ahuramazda (god), 44
Ainu people, 353
Ajanta caves (India), 76, 297
Akbar (r. 1556–1605) (Mughals), 537, *551*; accession of, *551*; administrative reforms, 539; harmonious society, 539; and Indo-Muslim civilization, 537–539; reign of Shah Jahan, 540; religion and state, 537–539; rule of Aurangzeb, 541; shadows lengthen, 541; successors, 540; textile manufacturing, 548
Akhenaten (Egypt), 30
Akhetaten (city), 30
Akkad and Akkadians, 17
al-Andaluz, 236
Ala-ud-din (monarch), 289, 292

Alberti, Leon Battista, 438
al-Biruni (historian), 287
Albuquerque, Afonso de, 459–461
Alcohol: in Abbasid Empire, 232; in China, 107
Alexander Nevsky, 403
Alexander the Great, 2, 140–144; Egypt and, 31; in India, 54, 142; Judah and, 38; legacy of, 143–144
Alexander the Great Failure (biography), 144
Alexandria, bishops of, 379
Alexandria, Egypt, 141, *141,* 146, 166
Alexius I (Byzantine Empire), 234, 410
Alexius I Comnenus (Byzantine Empire), 427
Alfonso VI (Castile), 237
Alfonso X (Castile), 245, 400
Algebra, 244
Alhambra, 238, 248
Ali (Muhammad's cousin and son-in-law), 228
Allah, 220, 222, 224, 225, 227, 238, 239, 247
Alliances: Spartan, 123
al-Maghrib, 261
al-Ma'mun, 230, 232
al-Mas'udi (historian), 232, 245, 247
Almeida, Francisco de, 472
Almohads, 245
Almoravids, 238, 245
Alphabets, 51; Chinese, 111–112; Greek, 35, 118, 124; Phoenician, 35, 124; Roman, 35
Alps, 164
al-Qaeda, 234
al-Sabahh, Hasan, 234
Altaic-speaking people, 368
Amaterasu (god), 352
Amazonia, 217
Amazon River region (Amazonia), 207, 214, 217
American Revolution, 602–603
Americas, 191–218; cultures in, 207; first peoples of, 192; naming of, 463; peopling of, 192–193; slave trade and, 478; Spain and, 502; stateless societies in, 214–217; sugar industry in, 477
Amerindians, 192
Amiens, 409
Amin (Abbasid), 232
Amon-Re (god), 30
Amorites (Old Babylonians), 17
Amphitheaters: Roman, 169, 173
Anabaptists, 496
Analects (Confucius), 89, 91, 92, 112
Analects for Women (Ruohua), 332
Anatolia, 34, 233, 426–428. *See also* Turkey
Anatolian peninsula, 520, 525, 528, 533
Ancient world: writing systems in, 53
Andalusia, 229, 236–237
Andes region, 192, 207, 208, 209, 465

Angkor, 302, 482
Angkor Empire, 582
Angkor Thom, 302, 311
Angles, 377
Anglo-Saxons: Normans and, 398
Angola, 480
Animals: hunting of, 8; Neolithic, 10; in Paleolithic cave painting, 8
Ankara, 521
An Lushan (China), 317
Anna Comnena, 428
Annam, 371
Anne (England), 514
Antigonid dynasty, 144
Antigonus Gonatus, 144
Antioch: bishops of, 379; in Crusades, 410, 428
Antony, Mark, 163
Anyang, China, 81, 85, 109
Aphrodite (god), 136
Apollo (god), 136
Apostles (Christian), 406
Aquitaine: duke of, 399; in Hundred Years' war, 436. *See also* Eleanor of Aquitaine
Arab empire, 225–249
Arabesques, 249
Arabia: Rome and, 165
Arabian Nights, The, 246
Arabic numerals, 76, 244
Arabs and Arab world: art and architecture in, 247–249; Islam and, 220–249; literature in, 245–246; Portugal and, 460
Aragon, 400
Arawak people, 216–217
Archaic Age (Greece), 119
Archbishop, 379, 383, 388, 398
Arches, 169
Archimedean screw, 149
Archimedes of Syracuse, 149, 245
Architecture, 243, 247–249; Baroque, 515–516; Chinese, 316; Gothic, 409; in Greece, 130–132; Harappan, 50; Hellenistic, 148–149; in India, 73, 76; Islamic, 247–249; in Japan, 365–366; in Mughal culture, 549; in Ottoman Empire, 531, 533; Romanesque, 408–409; in Roman society, 169; in Rome, 169; in Vietnam, 373
Arete (heroic excellence), 118
Arian Christianity, 377
Aristarchus of Samos, 149
Aristocracy, 388; in China, 86, 91; in Greece, 118–119; in Japan, 355; in Rome, 161; in Vietnam, 370, 372, 373. *See also* Nobility
Aristophanes, 129
Aristotle, 133–134, 139, 408, 586
Arjuna (Indian mythology), 47
Armada (Spain), 504

Arsinoë, 148
Arthasastra (Kautilya), 54, 55, 59, 72, 296
Articles of Confederation, 602
Artillery, 507
Artisans: Aztec, 205; Neolithic, 10, 12
Art(s): Assyrian, 41; Aztec, 205; Baroque, 515–516; as characteristic of civilization, 13; in China, 108–109, 316, 347–349; Classical, 130–132; Dutch realism in, 516; in Egypt, 29; in Greece, 130–132; Harappan, 50; Hellenistic, 148–149; Islamic, 247–249; in Japan, 363, 365–366; in Korea, 369–370; Paleolithic, 8; Renaissance in, 439–442; in Rome, 169. *See also* Cave art; Culture(s); Rock architecture; specific arts
Aryabhata, 297
Aryans (India), 48, 52–63, 66, 68, 72
Asceticism, in India, 62, 63
Ashanti kingdom and people (Ghana), 260, 481, 1004
Ashikaga shogunate (Japan), 358, 359, 569
Ashoka (India), 68–70, 537; empire of, *69*, 145; stupas of, 73, 76
Ashur (Indian mythology), 41
Ashurbanipal (Assyria), 39, 41
Asia: advance into Western, 523, 525; agriculture in, 10; Black Death in, 431; European trade with, 392; Indo-European speakers in, 33; migration into Americas from, 192; trade in, 3. *See also* Middle East; specific locations
Asia Minor, 34, 42, 124, 230. *See also* specific locations
Askia Mohammed (Songhai), 460, 480
Assassins (guardians), 234
Assyrian Empire, 2, 39–41; Israelites and, 36
Astrolabe, 245
Astrology, in China, 94
Astronomy: Chavín society and, 208–209; Hellenistic, 149; in India, 76; Mayan, 199; Mesopotamian, 20; Moche, 209; Muslim, 244
Aten (god), 30
Athena (god), 131
Athens, 115, 123–124; architecture in, 131; democracy in, 124, 126, 132; empire of, 126–127; government of, 123–124, 127, 133; lifestyle in classical period, 137; male homosexuality in, 140; navy of, 125–126; Pericles in, 126–127; Persia and, 44; philosophy in, 132–134; Platonic Academy in, 244; women in, 138–139
Athletic games, in Greece, 136–137
Atlantic Ocean region: Columbus in, 461
Atman (soul), 66, 67
Attalus I and Attalid dynasty (Pergamum), 145
Attica, 115, 123

Atum (god), 27
Augsburg, Peace of, 493
Augustinians, 497
Augustus (Octavian), 163–165, *166*
Aurangzeb (r. 1658–1707) (Mughals), 541, 552; rule of, 541
Australopithecines, 6
Austrasia, 379
Austria, 512; Habsburgs in, 512. *See also* World War I
Austrian Empire: Habsburgs and, 512
Autocracy, 231
Avalokitesvara, 284
Averroës, 245
Avicenna, 244
Avignon, papacy in, 437
Axial Age, 134–135, *135*
Axum, 254–256
Ayuthaya, Thailand, 302, 458, 482, 484
Azania, 263
Azerbaijan, 534
Aztecs, 201–206, 356, 464

B

Babur (1483–1530) (founder of Mughal dynasty), 536–537, *551*
Babylon and Babylonia: Alexander the Great and, 142–143; Assyria and, 39; Chaldean, 41; Hammurabi in, 17–18; Jews in, 43
Babylonian captivity of Judah, 38
Bactria, 70, 327
Badajoz, battle at, 238
Baghdad, 230, 240, 395; destruction of, *334*; Seljuk Turks in, 427
Baghdadi, Khatib, 233
Bakufu (Japan), 357, 572, 574
Baldwin of Flanders, 429
Balearic Islands, 236
Balkans: agriculture in, 33; Bulgars in, 419; Roman control of, 164
Ball games: Aztec, 204–205; Mayan, 198; Olmec, 193–194
Baltic region, 403
Banking: medieval, 391
Banners, military units, 558
Banpo, China, 83
Bantu, 257
Bantu-speaking peoples: trade and, 473
Ban Zhao, 172, 332
Bao-jia system (China), 106
Baptism, 406
Barani, Zia-ud-din (historian), 292
Barbarian peoples, 306
Barbosa, Duarte, 484
Bard, professional storyteller, 276

Barley, 10, 11, 14
Barmakid family, 232
Baroque-Rococo style (architecture), 596
Baroque style (architecture), 595
Barrel vaults, 408, 409
Basho (1644–1694) (Japanese poet), 577–579
Basil I (Byzantine Empire), 424
Basilicas, 76, 408
Basil II (Byzantine Empire), 425
Bastille fall of, 585, 609, 623
Batavia (Jakarta), 482, 483
Baths: in European cities, 396; Roman, 169
Battalions, 507
Battle of Kosovo in 1389, 521
Battle of Lepanto, 526, 551
Battle of Mohács, 519, 526
Battle of Plassey, 544, 552
Bayazid I (r. 1389–1402) (Ottomans), 521
Bay of Naples, 167, 176
Bayon, 311
Becket, Thomas à, 398
Bedouin, 220
Beijing (China), 336, 554, 557, 568
Belgium: trade in, 389
Belisarius (Byzantine general), 416, 423
Bells in China, 113
Benares (Varanasi), 67
Benedict (Saint), and Benedictines, 380, 381, 405
Benin, 275, 459, 481
Benin sculptures, 275
Berbers, 228, 256, 261, 266
Berber tribes, 274
Berenike (city), 241
Bering Strait, migration across, 192
Bernard of Clairvaux (Saint), 405, 411
Bernini, Gian Lorenzo, 515
Beys, 520
Bhagavad Gita, 73
Bhaja (Indian rock chamber), 76
Bhakti, 285
Bible, 36; of Gutenberg, 489
"Big man" (head of village), 272
Bill of Rights: in England, 514
Birth rate: of Africans, 480
Bishops (Christian), 379, 380, 388, 394, 401, 403, 404
Bismarck Archipelago, 311
Black Death (plague), 431–434, 432–434, 433; in Byzantine Empire, 415; in Europe, 431–434, 432–434, 433
Black Hole of Calcutta, 544
Black Sea region, 403
Black Seas, 520
Blast furnace, 84, 109
Blood feud: Germanic, 379

Blue Mosque of Istanbul, 533
Blue Nile, 253
Blues (Byzantine faction), 418
Bodhi (wisdom), 67, 284
Bodhisattva, 284
Boeotia, 115
Boers, 475
Bogazköy, 34
Bohemia, 506, 512; Slavs in, 401
Bo Ju-yi (poet), 347
Bokhara, 533
Boleyn, Anne, 496
Bologna, Italy, university in, 407
Boniface VIII (Pope), 437
Bonsai, 366
Book of Akbar, 550
Book of Ceremonies (Byzantine Empire), 422
Book of History (China), 107
Book of Kings, The (Ferdowzi), 246
Book of Lords, The, 245
Book of Songs, The (China), 87, 108, 112
Books: Middle Ages, 407; printing and, 489–490
Borneo, 458
Borobudur, temple at, 310–311
Boroughs, 394, 399
Bosnia and Herzegovina, 528
Bosporus, 177
Bourbon dynasty (France), 501, 507, 509
Boys, in Sparta, 122
Brahman (god), 56, 63
Brahman (Hindu Great World Soul), 63, 64, 67
Brahmanism: Buddhism and, 67–68; Hinduism and, 63
Brahmin Class, 56, 285, 294, 304; in India, 56, 62, 63
Brandenburg-Prussia, 512
Braudel, Fernand, 522
Brazil: Dutch and, 471; Portugal and, 465–466; slavery in, 477
Britain, 599–602, 607; Germanic tribes in, 377; Rome and, 165, 377. See also England (Britain)
British colonial empires, 600
British East India Company, 462
British North America, 600–601
Brittany, duke of, 399
Bronze, 85; in China, 84, 109–110; in Egypt, 29
Bronze Age, 12, 368, 370
Bruges, 390, 396
Brunelleschi, Filippo, 440
Bruni, Leonardo, 439
Bubonic plague, 431–434
Buddha and Buddhism, 66–67, 73, 76, 134; Borobudur temple and, 310, 310;

brahmins and, 285; in China, 342–344; decline of, in India, 285–286; in India, 48, 68, 283–286; in Japan, 354, 361–363; in Korea, 369; Mahayana, 76; as religion, 283–284; in Southeast Asia, 308; spread of, 309; trade and, 241; transformation of, 283–285; in Vietnam, 373; women and, 68

Bulgars, 419; Byzantines and, 419, 424

Bullion, 505

Bureaucracy: Abbasid, 231; Aztec, 202; in Brazil, 466–471; Byzantin, 422; in France, 399; in Korea, 369; in Roman Empire, 164, 177; in Russia, 511; in Vietnam, 373. *See also* Civil service examination

Bureaucracy (Prussia), 604

Burghers, 394, 489, 516

Burgundy: duke of, 399; kingdom of, 379, 399

Burials, 6. *See also* Tombs

Burma (Myanmar), 482

Bursa, 520, 533

Burundi, 475

Bushido (way of the warrior, Japan), 356

Buxar, battle at, 544

Byblos, 35

Byzantine Empire, 414–431, 520; in 8th century, 419–422; Christianity from, 403; in Constantinople, 520; Crusades and, 410–411; decline and fall of, 426–431; Islam and, 226; Ottomans and, 429–431; religion in, 419, 425; revival of, 427; Seljuk Turks and, 427; trade in, 395, 423–424; and Western world, 428; women, 426; zenith of (750–1025), 424–426. *See also* Eastern Roman Empire; Roman Empire; specific rulers

C

Cabot, John, 463

Cabral, John, *543*

Cabral, Pedro, 463

Cacao trees, 197

Cactus Hill, Virginia, 193

Cádiz, 462

Caesar, Julius, 162, 163

Caffa, plague in, 431, 433

Cahokia, 215

Cairo, *24*, 226, 232, 240, 392, 395, 396, 400

Calakmul (city), 199

Calendar: Caesar and, 163; Mayan, 199–200; Sumerian, 20

Calicut (Kozhikode, India), 459

Caliphs and caliphate, 228; Abbasid, 230–234; of Abd al-Rathman, 236, 238; Fatimid, 427; Umayyad, 228

Calligraphy: Chinese, 111

Calpullis (Aztec kin groups), 203

Calvin, John, and Calvinism, 493–495; Anglican Church and, 513; in France, 501

Cambodia: Vietnam and, 582

Cambyses (Persian Empire), 43

Camel caravans, 256

Camels, 33

Campania, 154

Canaan, 10, 30; Hebrews and, 35, 36; Phoenicians in, 35

Canals: in China, 88; in South America, 208

Cannons, 430, 431, 436, 457, 461

Canton (China), 97, 328, 560, *562*

Cao Cao, 105

Cape Guardafui, 257

Cape Hatteras, 471

Cape of Good Hope, 459, 462, 472, 475, 481

Capet, Hugh, 399

Capetian dynasty, 399

Cape Town, 476

Cape Verde, 481

Capital (financial), 505

Capital cities: of Arab Empire, 228, 230; in China, 83, 85, 97, 105

Capitalism, 391; commercial, 391, 505

Caracalla, 165, 169

Caral, Peru, 14, 208–209, 214

Caravans, 241; along Silk Road, 167; Bedouin, 220; in Hellenistic world, 147; plague spread by, 431

Caravels, 457

Carolingian Empire, 382; France after, 399

Carpets: Middle Eastern, 249

Carpini, John Plano, 334

Carruca (plow), 386

Cartesian dualism, 589

Carthage: destruction of, 159–160; Phoenicians in, 35; Punic Wars, 159–160

Cartier, Jacques, 601

Cassava, 216

Castes: in India, 55–58

Castile, 400

Çatal Hüyük, 10

Cathedrals: Gothic, 409

Catherine, Saint: monastery of, *420*

Catherine II the Great (1762–1796) (Russia), 604, 606, *623*

Catherine of Aragon, 496

Catholic Reformation, 497, 500

Cato, 160

Cattle: in India, 63

Cavalry in China, 95

Cave art: Paleolithic, 8

Cavern of the Painted Rock, 208

Caves: in China, 106. *See also* Cave art

Celadon pottery, 110
Celadons, 349
Celestial Empire, 554
Central America: peoples and cultures of, 192–205, *207*
Central Asia: Black Death in, 431; China and, 80, 167; civilizations of, 14, 48–62; Mongols in, 333–340
Central Europe, 446; absolutism in, 509–512
Centralization: in China, 97, 184
Centuriate assembly, 158
Ceramics in China, 109, 110
Cereta, Laura, 439, 440
Chaeronea, Battle of, 140
Chaldeans, 36, 38, 39, 41
Champagne, fairs in, 390
Champa kingdom, 171, 184, 372, 582
Chan Buddhism, 363. *See also* Zen Buddhism (Japan)
Chan Chan, 210
Chandragupta, 282
Chandragupta II, 282
Chandragupta Maurya (India), 54, 55, 61, 68; Mauryan Empire of, 145
Chang'an, China, 99, 316, 395
Chan sect, 343
Chariots, 29, 81, 83, 418
Charlemagne, *376*, 381–382
Charles I (England), 514
Charles I (Spain), as Holy Roman Emperor, 492
Charles II (England), 514
Charles Martel, Arabs and, 229
Charles V (Holy Roman Empire), 492, 493, 502
Chartres, 409
Chauvet cave, 8
Chavín de Huantar, 208
Chemistry, Muslims and, 245
Chen Hongmou (1696–1771) (Qing Dynasty), 567
Chenla (state), 302
Chesapeake region: English colonies in, 471
Chiang Kai-shek (China), 106
Chiapas, 197
Chichén Itzá, *200*, 201
Child marriage: in India, 59
Children: in China, 105; in Egypt, 32; in Israel, 35; in Roman Empire, 169, 170
Chile, 208, 211, 212
Chimor kingdom, 210
Chimú people, 211
China, 2, 554–561; afterlife in, 82; agriculture in, 10, 79, 88; architecture in, 330; art of Ming and Qing, 568; arts in, 108–109, 316, 347–349; bronzes in, 84, 109–110;

Buddhism in, 314; bureaucracy in, 97; changing, 561–568; Christianity in, 557–558; cities and towns in, 395; cities in, 107; civilization in, 13–14, 79–85; civil service examination in, 319–322, 319–322; Confucianism in, 89–91, 99, 101; contact between Europeans and, 560; cultural developments, 566, 568; culture in, 108–113, 316, 345–349; daily life in Qing, 564–566; direct trade between Europe and, 554; during early modern era, *583*; economy of, 87–88, 184, 324–328, 324–332; emperor in, *510*; etiquette in, 332–333; European inventions impressed officials, 555; European warehouses at Canton, *562*; on eve of western onslaught, 559–561; expanding contact with external world, 564; expansion by, 184, 316; families in, 184, 330–331, 564–565; female inferiority in, 566; first contacts with west, 554–555; foods in, 106; foot binding and, 331; foreign affairs in, 97; foreign trade, 559–560; gender relationships in, 107–108; gentry, rise of, 329–330; government in, 81–87, 184; greatness of Qing, 557; Great Wall in, 97–98; Han Empire, 165, 171, 172–173, 178, 184–185; indifference to foreign trade, 564; iron in, 109; at its apex, 554–561; and its enemies during late Ming era, *556*; Japan and, 316, 351, 353, 354, 363, 366, 368; Korea and, 316, 368–369; land and peoples in, 79–81; land reforms in, 324–325; languages in, 111–112; later Ming, 554; lifestyle in, 106–107; literature in, 111–112, 316, 345–347; Malacca and, 454, 461; manufacturing in, 325; maritime trade in, 328; metal and metalwork in, 109–110; in mid-Qing era, 563; military in, 185; Ming brought to earth, 555–557; Mongols and, 318, 333–340; music in, 112–113; New Culture Movement in, 498; novels in, 347; painting in, 347–349; peasants in, 85, 87, 97; Period of the Warring States in, 87, 95; philosophy in, 89–95, 134; political structures in, 86–87, 96–97; population explosion, 561, *563*; population in, 184, 346; Portuguese trade, *543*; Qing economy, 562–564; Qing political institutions, 558–559; reign of Kangxi, 557–558; reign of Qianlong, 558; religion in, 89, 94, 342–345; rise of Chinese novel, 566, 568; roads in, 167; role of women, 565–566; Rome and, 184–186; Scientific Revolution in Europe and, 589–590; seeds of industrialization, 561–562; silk from, 88; society in, 83–85, 87–88, 97, 328–332; Tang Dynasty, *522*; textiles in, 325; Tibet and, 316, 318;

tombs in, 82, 83; trade in, 87, 167, 325–327; tribute system in, 316, 328, 372; urban areas in, 328; Vietnam and, 370, 372–374; villages in, 330–331; women in, 107–108, 331–332; women's education, 567; writing in, 51, 81, 85, 91, *111*, 111–112. *See also* Japan; Korea; Mao Zedong; Vietnam; World War I; specific rulers, dynasties, and empires

Chinampas, 195, 198, 203

Chinese civilization, 555, 559; early centuries of, 561

Chinese language, in Japan, 364–365

Chinese society, 554, 564, 566, 567

Chivalry, 389

Chocolate, 197

Cholas, 289

Chonmin (Korean slave class), 369, 581

Chosen people, Jews as, 38

Choson Dynasty (Korea), 581–582

Christ, Jesus, 179–181

Christian humanism, 490

Christianity: in Andalusia, 237–238; in Byzantine Empire, 415; Charlemagne and, 381–382; church organization and, 379–380; court officials converted to, 557; Crusades and, 234–235, 410–411; expulsion in Japan, 571–572; festival, 596–597; to form geocentric theory of universe, 586; Germanic kingdoms, 379–380; humanist reform of, 490; Japanese, 571; in Kiev, 403; of Magyars, 382; in Middle Ages, 403–406; missionaries, 554, *590*; Muhammad and, 222, 224–225; Pliny and Origen on, 182–183; in Portugal, 400; Protestant-Catholic division of, 493; in Roman world, 178–184; in Russia, 425; schism in, 426–427; scholasticism and, 407–408; in Slavic lands, 401; in Southeast Asia, 63; in Spain, 238, 400; spread of, 181–184; Vikings and, 383; Zoroastrianism and, 45. *See also* Conversion; Reformation; specific groups

Chrysoloras, Manuel, 439

Chu nom written characters, 373

Church and state: in Islam, 239; separation of, 496

Church(es): Christian, 181, 379–380; Constantinople, 418; Gothic, 409; Romanesque, 408–409

Church of England, 496, 513

Church of San Lorenzo (Florence), 440

Cicero, 179, 439

Cincinnatus, 155

Cistercian order, 405

Cities and towns: in Arab world, 239–242; in China, 107, 395; in Europe, 389–396; Greek polis as, 119–121; Hellenistic, 146;

in India, 49; lifestyle in, 393–396; in Middle East, 239–242; in Roman Empire, 166; Sumerian, 15–16. *See also* Villages; specific locations

Citizens and citizenship: in Athens, 126–127; in Greece, 119–120; in Rome, 157–159 164, 165, 169

City-states: Greek, 42, 119–124; Mayan, 198; in Mesopotamia, 15–18; Sumerian, 15–16

Civil Code (Napoleon), 620

Civil Constitution of the Clergy, 615, *623*

Civilization(s), 12–13; Americas, 192–217; Byzantine, 424–426; Central America, 193–205; characteristics of, 13; decline and fall of, 210; Egyptian, 20–33; emergence of, 1–3, 12–14; fall of ancient, 3; Greek, 114–151; Harappan (India), 13, 48–53, *49*; of Islam, 238–249; Mesopotamia, 14–20; Mycenaean, 117; spread to new areas, 33–39; trade and, 241; writing and, 51. *See also* Culture(s); specific civilizations

Civil law (Rome), 169

Civil service: Byzantine, 422; in China, 101

Civil service examination: China, 100; in Japan, 355, 366; in Korea, 369; in Vietnam, 373

Civil war(s): and Commonwealth, 513–514; in England, 514; in Rome, 162

Ci Wara, 275

Clans, in Japan, 353, 357, 358

Classes: Aztec, 204; in India, 55–58; in Islam, 242; in Japan, 359–360; in Korea, 369; Sumerian, 18. *See also* Estates (social orders); specific classes

Classical antiquity, 176

Classical Greece, 125–140; civilization of, 439; culture of, 128–134; lifestyle in, 137

Classical literature, 489–490

Cleisthenes (Athens), 124

Clement V (Pope), 437

Clement VI (Pope), 434

Cleopatra VII, 163

Clergy, as First Estate, 399, 488

Clermont, Council of, 410

Climate: decline of civilizations and, 210; Japan, 351; Mesopotamian, 19; Southeast Asia, 485

Clive, Robert (England), 542, 607

Cloths and clothing, Neolithic, 12

Cloud Messenger, The (Sanskrit poems), 300

Clove trade, 482

Clovis (Franks), 377, 378

Code of Hammurabi, 17–18

Code of Law (Justinian), 416

Colbert, Jean-Baptiste, 509

Colonies and colonization: Dutch, 471; French, 471; government of, 466–471; Greek,

120–121, 157; labor in, 469–470; in Latin America, 462–472; mercantilism and, 505; Phoenician, 35; in South Africa, 475–476; Spanish, 462–472

Color of skin, in Indian society, 55–56

Colosseum, 174

Columbian Exchange, 474–475

Columbus, Christopher, 192, 458, *458,* 461–463, *464,* 471–472

Comedies (Greek), 129, 148

Commerce: in China, 185, 325, 327; Dutch, 516; expansion of, 241; Harappan, 51; Hellenistic, 147; in India, 61–62; in Indian Ocean region, 241; in Japan, 359

Commercial capitalism, 391, 505, 599

Committee of Public Safety, 616, 618–619

Common law (England), 398

Common people: in Japan, 359–360; Sumerian, 15–16; witchcraft hysteria and, 504–505. *See also* Third estate

Commonwealth, in England, 513–514

Communes: in Italy, 394; in Paris, 616

Communication: in Assyrian Empire, 39; Inka, 214; in Persian Empire, 44

Comneni dynasty (Byzantine Empire), 427

Compass, 241, 457

Conciliarism, 437

Concordat of Worms, 404

Confucian Classics, 112

Confucius and Confucianism, 134, 555; Analects of, 89; in China, 89–91, 99–101, 101, 314–315, 318–322, 342; commandments, 576–577; Daoism and, 92–94, 342–343; Neo-Confucianism and, 344–345; rituals, 557–558; state cult of (China), 337; training for women, 566; values, 580–581, 583; in Vietnam, 372–374; women and, 331

Congo River valley, 269

Conquistadors, 456, 457, 463, *464,* 470, 472, 474

Constance, Council of, 438

Constantine, 177–178, 184

Constantine (Constantine XI Palaeologus), *524*

Constantine VII (Byzantine Empire), 425

Constantine XI (Byzantine Empire), 430; fall of, 429–431; sacks of, 428

Constantinople (Istanbul), 177, 395, 396, 410, 411; Arab siege of, 229, 419; in Crusades, 411; fall of, 522–523, *524;* in Fourth Crusade in 1204, 520; Latin Empire of, 411, 428–429; plague in, 431; rebuilding of, *417,* 417–418; trade in, 423–424

Constitution of the Spartans (Xenophon), 138–139

Constitution(s): in Japan, 353

Consulate, 619

Consuls, 157

Consumer revolution, Europe, 599

Continental system, 622

Convents, 380, 405. *See also* Monks and monasticism; Nuns

Conversion: to Christianity, 380, 466; to Islam, 227, 228. *See also* Missions and missionaries; specific orders and religions

Convivéncia (commingling), 236

Copán, 198

Copernican system, 586–587, *589*

Copernicus, Nicolaus (1473–1543), 586

Copper and copper industry, 12, 84

Coptic Christianity, 255, 261

Córdoba, 236; mosque at, 248

Coronations of Charlemagne, 382

Corpus Iuris Civilis (Justinian), 416, 419

Corruption, in Abbasid Empire, 232

Corsica, 156

Cortés, Hernán, 432, 457, 463–464

Cosmology: Aztec, 204

Cosmos: Chinese speculation about, 89

Cottage industry, 597

Cotton and cotton industry: Harappan, 50

Coubertin, Pierre de, 137

Council of elders, 158

Council of Five Hundred (Athens), 124

Council of the plebs, 158, 162

Councils (Christian): of Clermont, 410; Constance, 437; of Trent, 500

Counter-Reformation, 497, 500

Courts (royal): in Byzantine Empire, 422; in China, 112; at Versailles, 508. *See also* specific countries

Covenant (Jewish), 38

Crafts: after Neolithic Revolution, 12; guilds and, 396

Cranmer, Thomas, 496

Crassus, 162–163

Creation myths: Aztec religion, 205; Japanese, 352

Crécy, Battle of, 436

Creoles, 466

Crete, Egypt and, 26

Crime and criminals: Code of Hammurabi on, 17–18

Croatia, 512

Croesus (Lydia), 136

Cromwell, Oliver, 513–514

Crops: in Abbasid Empire, 231; in Americas, 193; Assyrians, 40; in China, 79, 88; Neolithic, 9

Crossbow, 435

Crusader states, 393, 411, 427–428

Crusades, 234–235, 410–411; Byzantine Empire and, 427–428; siege of Jerusalem in, 235

Cuba: Columbus in, 463
Cults: Egyptian, 27, 28; Greek religion and, 135; religious, 405
Culture(s): in Americas, 207–208, 214–217; of Andalusia, 236; Assyrian, 41; Aztec, 204–205; Chavín society and, 208; in China, 108–113, 500; developments in China, 566–568; Egyptian, 27–29; in Enlightened Age, 595–596; Greek, 124, 128–134; Harappan, 50–51; Hellenistic, 148–151; high, 596; in High Middle Ages, 406–409; in India, 72–76; Inka, 214; Islamic, 230–234, 243–249; in Japan, 352, 363–366; Maya, 197–201; Mesopotamian, 18–20; Moche, 209; Olmec, 193–194; Phoenician, 35; popular, 596–597; prehistoric period in, 352–353; in Rome, 168; society under Mughals, 546–550; in Spain, 399–400; in Teotihuacán, 195; Tokugawa Japan, 575–581; Zapotec, 194–195. See also Art(s); Intellectual thought; Religion; Society; Trade; specific peoples
Cuneiform writing, 20, 21, 51
Curriculum: in universities, 407
Cuzco, Peru, 211
Cyprus, 37; Byzantines and, 426
Cyrus the Great (Persia), 42–44

D

Dacia, 165
Da Gama, Vasco, 454, 458, 459, 481, 536
Daimyo (Japan), 358, 359, 569, 571–572
Dai Viet (Great Viet), 372, 582–583
Dakar, 481
Damascus, 228, 240, 392, 396
Dams, 386
Dangun (Korea), 368
Danibaan, 195
Danube River region, 164, 165, 177, 403, 419
Danube valley, 525–526
Dao (Way), 90, 343
Dao De Jing (The Way of the Tao), 93
Daoism (Taoism), 92–94, 314, 342–343, 578; Confucianism and, 92–94; in Vietnam, 373
Dara Shikoh (Mughals), 541
Dardanelles, 520, 522
Dar es Salaam, 264
Darius (Persia), 44, 54, 125
Darius III (Persia), 141
Dark Age, in Greece, 117–119
David (Michelangelo), 442
Davidson, Basil, 270
Dead Sea region, 10
Deccan Plateau, 52, 60
Decentralization: Japan, 355, 366

Declaration of Independence (U.S.), 602
Declaration of Indulgence (England), 514
Declaration of the Rights of Man and the Citizen (France), 613, 623
Declaration of the Rights of Woman and the Female Citizen (de Gouges), 611, 614–615, 616
Defense of the Liberal Instruction of Women (Cereta), 440
de Gouges, Olympe (France), 611, 613
Deir el Bahri: temple at, 30
Deism (religious outlook), 593
Delhi (India), 535, 537, 540–541, 550; Babur seizes, 551; Humayun recovers throne in, 551; sack by Persians, 552
Delhi sultanate, 288, 289
Delian League, 126
Delphi, oracle at, 136
Demesne, 385, 385
Democracy: in Athens, 124, 126, 132
Denmark: Vikings from, 383
Dervishes, 247
Descartes, René (1596–1650), 588
Descent of the Ganges River (sculpture), 298
Deshima Island, 571
Devi (Hindu female deity), 293
Devshirme system, 527–528, 530
Dezong (emperor), 332
Dharma (law), 54, 55, 63, 73, 90, 343
Dharmashastra (Hindu law), 539
Di (god), 83
Dialectic: of Thomas Aquinas, 408
Diamond, Jared: Guns, Germans, and Steel: The Fates of Human Societies, 11
Diarchy system, 559
Dias, Bartolomeu, 458, 459
Díaz, Bernal, 202, 204, 205
Dictators and dictatorship, 163; Caesar and, 163
Diderot (1713–1784), 593–594
Diet (food): in Athens, 137; in China, 106; in Japan, 360; in peasant society, 386. See also Food
Diet of Worms, 487
Diffusion hypothesis, 85
Digest (Justinian), 416
Diocese, 379
Diocletian, 177
Diplomacy: in Byzantine Empire, 422
Directory (1795–1799) (France), 618
Discourse on Method (Descartes), 588
Discourse on the Origins of the Inequality of Mankind (Rousseau), 594
Diseases: in Americas, 464, 470; historical role of, 432
Divination, 19

Divine Faith (Din-i-Ilahi), 538
Divine-right monarchy, 508, 513
Divinity: of kings, 16
Divorce: in Abbasid Empire, 232; in Egypt, 32; in India, 59; in Japan, 361; in Vietnam, 374
Diwan (council), 231
Domains (han), 572
Dome of the Rock, 248
Domes, 169
Domestication, of animals, 10
Dominicans, 497
Dominic de Guzmán (Saint), 405
Dorian Greeks, 118
Doryphoros (statue), 132
Double Crown (Egypt), 25
Drama: in Greece, 128–129; Hellenistic, 146; in Japan, 365; Shakespeare and, 516
Dravidian languages, 72
Dravidian people (India), 48, 52
Dream of the Red Chamber, The (novel), 568
Dualism: in Zoroastrianism, 45
Dutch, 600–601; English and, 462; exploration by, 462; realistic art by, 516; in South Africa, 475–476; and United Provinces of the Netherlands, 502
Dutch East India Company (VOC), 462, 482, 505
Dutch West India Company, 471
Dyaus (god), 62

E

Early History of Rome, The (Livy), 155
Early Middle Ages (Europe), 376, 377–385; Carolingian Empire in, 381–382; Christian church in, 379–380; Germanic kingdoms in, 377
Early modern era, 449, 450
Early Renaissance, 439–440
Early Roman Empire, 163–176
Earth, 586
East Africa, 253, 257–260, 263–265; slavery and, 480
East African Rift Valley, 253
East Asia: China and, 85
Easter Island, 210
Eastern Asia: religions, spread of, 286
Eastern Europe, 446; absolutism in, 509–512; Jews in, 434; Slavic peoples of, 401–403
Eastern Orthodox Christianity, 425, 446; schism with Catholic Church, 426–427
Eastern Roman Empire, 415, 416, 418, 419. See also Byzantine Empire; Roman Empire; Rome (ancient)
Eastern Woodlands cultures, 215
East India Company, 542, 544, 546, 559–560

Economy: in Abbasid Empire, 230; in Athens, 123; Black Death and, 434–435; in Byzantine Empire, 422, 425; changes and social order in Europe, 597–600; Chinese, 87–88, 101, 184, 324–328; consequences of conquest during European power in India, 544–545; in Egypt, 26–27; in Europe (17th century), 505–506; European expansion and, 456–457; Harappan, 50; in India, 60–62; in Japan, 359–361; in Malacca, 454; money in, 391; in Mughals, 547–548; in Qing Dynasty, 562–564; in Rome, 162, 167; in Southeast Asia, 484–485; Sumerian, 16. See also Capitalism; Industrial Revolution
Ecstasy of Saint Theresa (Bernini), 515, 516
Ecuador, 208, 211
Edessa, 428
Edict of Milan, 184
Edict of Nantes, 501
Edirne, 520, 531
Edo. see Tokyo
Education: Buddhist, 483; Islamic, 483; scholasticism and, 407–408; for women in China, 567
Edward I (England), 398
Edward III (England), 435
Edward VI (England), 496
Egalitarianism: of Islam, 242
Egypt, 1, 20–33; agriculture in, 10; Alexander the Great in, 141; art in, 29; culture of, 27–29; daily life in, 31–32; economy in, 26–27; Fatimid dynasty in, 232, 240; Greek culture and, 124; Jewish exodus from, 38; Kush and, 32; Nubia and, 32–33; Old Kingdom in, 24, 25–26; pharaohs in, 25, 26, 27; plague in, 431; Ptolemies in, 142; pyramids in, 27, 28–29, 196; religion in, 27–28; Saladin in, 235; Seljuk Turks and, 235; society in, 26–28; women in, 32, 148; writing in, 29
Eighteenth dynasty (Egypt), 29, 30
Einstein, Albert, 587
Eleanor of Aquitaine, 389–391, 391
"Elect": Calvin on, 494
Elements (Euclid), 149
Elite(s): Sumerian, 16
Elizabeth I (England), 496, 503, 513
Elliot, J. S., 238
Ellora temples, 297
El Niño, 209, 210
El Salvador, 194
Émile (Rousseau), 595
Emir, 236
Emperors: Byzantine, 422–423; Chinese, 510; Japanese, 363; Roman, 163–165. See also specific rulers
Empyrean Heaven, 586

Encomienda and encomienda system, 470
Encomienda system, 470
Encyclopedia (Diderot), 594
Engineering: Roman, 169
England (Britain): civil war in, 513–514; Elizabeth I in, 503, 513; France and, 398; golden age of literature in, 516; in High Middle Ages, 397–399; Hundred Years' War and, 435–436; limited monarchy in, 513–514; Parliament in, 398; Peasants' Revolt (1381) in, 434–435; Protestantism in, 496; Reformation in, 496; trade in, 391
Enki (god), 19
Enkidu (god), 20
Enlightened absolutism, 603, 606
Enlightenment (Buddhism), 66
Enlightenment movement: background to, 591; belief of, 594; culture in Enlightened Age, 595–596; Diderot's contribution to, 594; in Europe, 592; intellectuals of, 591; later, 594–595; philosophes and their ideas, 591–593; scientific method, 591; sources of inspiration for, 591; toward new "Science of Man," 594; woman question in, 595
Enlil (god), 19
Entrepôts, 423
Environment: Abbasid, 232; decline of civilizations and, 210; Moche and, 209
Epic literature: Greek, 118; Indian, 72–73; Roman, 168
Epic of Gilgamesh, 19, 20, 51
Epic of Son-Jara, The (poem), 277
Epicurus and Epicureanism, 150
Equality: in Islamic society, 243; Paleolithic society, 8
Erasmus, Desiderius, 490
Eratosthenes, 149
Eridu, Mesopotamia, 15
Erik the Red, 409
Essay Concerning Human Understanding (Locke), 591
Essenes, 179
Estates (social orders): in France, 399
Estates-General (France), 399
Eta (Japanese class), 360, 575
Ethiopia, 254, 255, 261–263
Etruria, 156
Etruscans, 156–157
Eucharist, 406
Euclid, 149, 245
Eunuchs in China, 98
Euphrates River region, 14, 30, 232
Euripides, 129
Europe: in 17th century, 506; Africa and, 472–481; aristocracy in, 388; Black Death in, 432–434, 433; under Charlemagne,

381–382; Christians in, 526; cities and towns in, 393–396; crises in (14th century), 431–438; crises in (1560–1650), 501–508; Crusades and, 410–411; economy in, 505–506; exploration by, 456–458; Indo-European speakers in, 33, 34; invasions of (9th and 10th centuries), 382–383; Jesuits in, 500; kingdoms in, 397–403; knights in, 384; in Middle Ages, 377–413, 400; mortality rates in West Indies, 477–478; population of, 504; Renaissance in, 438–446; in second half of the fifteenth century, 442; slave trade and, 472–480, 478; trade in, 392–393; Turkish expansion in, 525–526; Viking invasions of, 383; world and, 410–411. *See also* Christianity; Colonies and colonization; Western world; specific empires and regions
European clock-making techniques, 564
European Warehouses (Canton), 562
Europe/European: in 1763, 605; American Revolution, 602; Austrian Empire of Habsburgs, 604; background to Enlightenment, 591; birth of new nation, 602–603; British North America, 600–601; changing patterns of war, 606–607; clock-making techniques, 564; colonial empires and revolution in americas, 600–603; consumer revolution, 599; culture in Enlightened Age, 595–596; descartes and rationalism, 587–589; direct trade between China and, 554; economic changes and social order, 597–600; enlightened absolutism reconsidered, 606; Enlightenment in, 592; food and food supplies, 597; French North America, 601; global trade in eighteenth century, 598; high culture, 596; intellectual revolution in west, 586–597; inventions impressed Chinese officials, 555; later, 594–595; new economic patterns, 597, 599; patterns of social organization, 599; philosophers to praise Chinese civilization, 555; political changes in, 590; political order and global conflict in, 603–607; popular culture, 596–597; population, 597, 599–600; population explosion, 563; Prussia, 604; revolution in astronomy, 586–587; Russia under Catherine the Great, 604, 606; Scientific Revolution in China and, 586–590; society in eighteenth century, 599–600; textile production, 597; toward new "Science of Man," 594; trade pattern, 597, 599; warehouses at Canton, 562; West Indies, 600; woman question in Enlightenment, 595
Evans, Arthur, 115
Evolution, Darwinian concept of, 192
"Exchange Between Pliny and Trajan, An," 182–183

Excommunication: of Leo IX and Michael Cerularius, 427; of Luther, 492

Exodus, 35, 38; Book of, 35

Expansion, 457; by China, 184; of Islam, 229; of Russia, 512. *See also* Colonies and colonization

Exploration, 458; by Europe, 458; of New World, 463; by Portugal, 454; by Vikings, 383; voyages of, *458. See also* specific explorers and countries

Exports: African, 477

F

Faith, reason and, 408

Families: Athenian, 137–140; Aztec, 202, 203–204; in China, 83–85, 101, 184; in Egypt, 31–32; Germanic, 377; in Hammurabi's Code, 18; in India, 57–58; marriage and, 498; in peasant society, 388; in Rome, 169–170; slave, 480; in Vietnam, 373–374. *See also* Marriage

Farms and farming, 242; in Americas, 193; China and, 326; hunter-gatherer transition to, 11; in India, 61; Inka, 214; in Japan, 351; Mayan, 198; Mesolithic, 9–10; Neolithic, 10, 12; of Pueblo peoples, 215–216

Fatehpur Sikri (India), 548–550

Father of modern rationalism (Descartes, René), 589

Fathers: Hammurabi's Code on, 18; in Roman families, 170

Fatimid dynasty, 232, 427

Fa Xian (monk), 281, 282

Feminism: in Europe, 498

Ferdinand of Aragon (Spain), 445

Ferdowsi (Persian poet), 246

Fernández-Armesto, Felipe (historian), 257

Fernández de Ovieda, Gonzalo, 472

Fertile Crescent, 15

Festivals: Greek, 135, 136

Feudalism: breakdown of, 436; Catholic Church and, 403; in Japan, 358–359. *See also* Middle Ages

Fiefs and fief-holding, 384

Fifty-Three Stations of the Tokaido Road (Ando Hiroshige), 580

Filial piety, in China, 105

Finances: in Europe, 436

Fire, Paleolithic use of, 8

Firearms, 456, 461, 480; in Africa, 480

First Crusade(s), 235, 410–411, 428

First Estate, 399, 488, 607, 609

First Punic War, 159

First Triumvirate, 162

Fishing: Paleolithic, 8

Five good emperors (Rome), 165

Five Pillars of Islam, 225

Five relationships in China, 105

Five Women Who Loved Love (Saikaku), 575

Flagellants, Black Death and, 435–436

Flanders: Hundred Years' War in, 435; trade in, 389, 390

Flint, 12

Flooding: by Nile, 20, 23; by Tigris and Euphrates rivers, 14. *See also* Great Flood

Florence (Italy), 434, 439, 440, 442, 443, *579*

Food(s): in Americas, 193; in Çatal Hüyük, 10; in China, 106; cultivation of, 11; eating habits and, 242; farm technology and, 88; in Islamic world, 242; Paleolithic, 8

Foot binding, 331

Forbidden City (Beijing), 568

Forced labor: in Americas, 470

Forests: clearing, 386

Forts (Africa): Dutch seizure of, 473

Fort William, 542

Forty-Seven Ronin, The, 573

Fourth Crusade, 411, 428

France: agriculture in, 33; Britain and, 607; cave art in, 8; dominance of, 507; England and, 398; French finances, *612*; Huguenots in, 501; Hundred Years' War and, 435; kingdom in, 399; politics, 508–509; trade in, 389, 390; wars of religion in (1562–1598), 501–502. *See also* French Revolution; Gaul; World War I; specific leaders; specific wars

Franciscans, 405, 497

Francis of Assisi (Saint), 405

Franks: Arabs and, 229; kingdom of, 377–379. *See also* Charlemagne

Frederick I ("Barbarossa," Holy Roman Empire and Germany), 401

Frederick I (Prussia), 510

Frederick II (Holy Roman Empire), 401

Frederick II (Sicily), 245

Frederick the Great (1740–1786) (Prussia), 604, 606–607, *623*

Frederick the Wise (elector of Saxony), 491

Frederick William (Great Elector, Brandenburg-Prussia), 510

French and Indian War, 607

French colonial empires, 600

French colony of Saint-Dominique, The (later Haiti), 600

French monarchy, 608–609

French North America, 601

French Revolution, 607–618; background to, 607–609; destruction of old regime, 610–611, 615–616; equality and slavery, 617–618; from Estates-General to National Assembly, 609–610; nation in arms,

616–617; problems facing French monarchy, 608–609; radical Revolution, 616; reaction and Directory, 618; Reign of Terror, 617; social structure of old regime, 607–608

Frescoes, 439, 441

Friends of the Blacks, 617

Froissart (chronicler), 435

Frontiers: of China, 97–98; of Roman Empire, 164, 165–166, 177

Fudai daimyo (Japan), 572

Fujiwara clan (Japan), 355

Funan, 302

Fu Xi (Fu Hsi) (China), 79

Fu Xuan (Chinese poet), 108

G

Gabriel (angel), 221

Gaius Musonius Rufus, 172

Galen (physician), 245

Galilei, Galileo (1564–1642), 587

Galleon trade, 554

Gallipoli, 520

Gamelan (orchestra), 304

Ganesha (god), 65–66

Ganges River region, 53

Gao, 265, 481

Garamantes, 256–257

Gascony, 435

Gaugamela, battle at, 141

Gaul (France): Caesar in, 163; Neustria in, 379

Gender: in Aztec society, 203; in China, 107–108

General War Commissariat (Prussia), 510

Geneva, Calvin in, 495

Genghis Khan (Mongol), 235, 289, 333, 339–340, 536

Genin (Japanese landless laborers), 360

Genoa, 396, 411, 412; trade in, 428

Gentiles, 181

Geocentric theory of universe, 586

Geometry: Euclid and, 149; Mesopotamian, 20

Germanic languages, 33

Germanic peoples, 178; in Britain, 377; kingdoms of, 377; in Old Western Empire, 378; society of, 379

Germany, 382, 383, 400; independent states in, 446; Luther and Lutheranism in, 488, 493; Neanderthals from, 6; pogroms against Jews in, 434; Roman Empire and, 164; trade in, 389

Ghana, 260, 265–267

Ghazni (state), 287

Ghent, 390; trade in, 390

Gia Long dynasty (Vietnam), 583

Gibbon, Edward, 210

Gibraltar, Strait of, 261

Gilgamesh (legendary king), 20

Giza, pyramids of, 28–29, 196

Gladiator (film), 174

Gladiators, 173–176

Glorious Revolution (England), 514

Goa, 459

Gobi Desert, 80, 258, 318, 334, 561. *See also* Mongols

Gods and goddesses: Aztec, 204; Egyptian, 27–28; in Greece, 179; Greek, 124; in India, 62; Israelite, 38; Mayan, 198; in Roman Empire, 179; Sumerian, 16

Gojoseo kingdom, 368

Gold, 84, 505; in Africa, 266, 473; Americas, 466; in money economy, 391

Gold Coast, 459, 481. *See also* Ghana

Golden Horde, 336

Golden Horn, 430, 522–523

Golden Pavilion (Kyoto), 366

Gold Vase Plum (The Golden Lotus), 568

Good emperors (Rome), 165

Goods: in Byzantine Empire, 424. *See also* Trade

Gopuras (gate towers), 298

Gospels, 181, 183

Gothic cathedrals, 409

Government: of Athens, 123–124, 127, 133; Aztec, 202; in China, 83, 86, 95, 184, 323–324; in communes, 394; of Eastern Woodlands peoples, 215; of England, 398; feudalism and, 383; fiefs and, 383; of Greece, 121, 122; of Japan, 351; Kangxi on, 510; of Persian Empire, 42–43; of Rome, 156–159; of Russia, 511; of Song dynasty, 323–324; of Spanish and Portuguese empires, 466; of Sparta, 122; of Sumer, 16; of Vietnam, 373. *See also* Absolutism; Colonies and colonization; Law codes; Law(s); Politics; specific countries and regions

Gracchus, Gaius, 162

Gracchus, Tiberius, 162

Gracchus brothers, 162

Grain: in China, 88; Neolithic, 9; watermill for, 386. *See also* specific crops

Granada, 238, 400

Grand Canal (China), 315, *315*

Grand Council, 319

Grand Council of State (Japan), 354

Grand Empire (Napoleon), 620–622, *621*

Grand vizier, 526, 530

Granicus River, battle at, 141

Great Altar of Pergamum, *523*

Great Britain, 573. *See also* England (Britain)

Great Council (England), 398

Great flood: in Epic of Gilgamesh, 19, 20

Great King, in Persia, 43, 142

Great Peloponnesian War, 127

Great Plains region, 192, 214
Great Pyramid (Giza), 28–29
Great Schism: in Catholic church, 437–438
Great Wall (China), 97–98, 556
Great Zimbabwe, 269–270, 473
Greece, 115, *116*; alphabet in, 118, 124; Antigonid dynasty in, 144; Archaic Age in, 119; arts in, 130–132; Byzantine Empire and, 419; citizens in, 119; city-states in, 119–124; classical civilization in, 125, 439; colonization by, 120–121; culture in, 128–134; Dark Age in, 117–119; foreign influence on culture of, 124; geography of, 115; government of, 123–124; Homeric, 118; homosexuality in, 140; India and, 54; military in, 120; Minoan Crete and, 115–117; Mycenaean, 117; Persian Empire and, 42–43, 125–126; philosophy in, 132–134, 243–244; religion in, 135–137; Sparta and, 115, 122–123; trireme in, 125; tyrants in, 121; warfare in, 120. *See also* Hellenistic world
Greek fire, 419
Greek language, 33, 34, 419
Greek Orthodoxy, 422. *See also* Eastern Orthodox Christianity
Greens (Byzantine faction), 418
Gregory VII (Pope), 404
Gregory XI (Pope), 437
Guangzhou, China, 102, 328
Guan Yin, 284
"Guardian kings" (Japan), 366
Guatemala, 197, *200*
Guilds, 61, 396, 489, 509, 516
Gujarat (India), 540
Gulf of Mexico region, 463
Gunpowder, 436
Gunpowder empires, Mughals, 546
Guns, Germans, and Steel: The Fates of Human Societies (Diamond), 11
Gupta Empire (India), 282, *283*
Guru (teacher), 58
Guru Nanak, 293
Gustavus Adolphus (Sweden), 507
Gutenberg, Johannes, 489

H

Habsburg dynasty, 507, 512; Austrian Empire and, 512; in Holy Roman Empire, 446, 512
Hadith, 220, 225, 239, 249
Hadrian, 165, 185
Hagia Sophia, 418, 431, *532*
Haidar Ali, 546
Haiku poetry, 364
Haiti: revolution in, 617–618

Hajj, 225
Hall of Mirrors (Versailles), *508*
Hammurabi (Babylonia), 17
Han dynasty (China), 99–105; empire of, *103*
Han Empire (China), 165, 171, 172–173, 178, 184–185; China after, 314; decline and fall of, 314; Korea and, 370; Vietnam and, 370; women in, 172–173
Han Gaozu (Liu Bang), 99, 185
Hangul (Korean spoken language), 581
Hangzhou, China, 318, 395
Hannibal, 160
Hanoi, 350. *See also* Vietnam; Vietnam War
Hanseatic League, 488
Hanuman (India), 73
Han Wudi, 102
Han Yu, 322–323
Harappa (city), 13
Harappan civilization, 13, 48–49
Harem, 243, 527; in Egypt, 31
Harold (England), 397
Harun al-Rashid (Abbasid), 230, 232, 233, 243
Hashemite clan, 223
Hastings, Battle of, 398
Hastings, Warren, 544
Hatshepsut (Egypt), 30, 32
Hattusha, 34
Heaven, Aztec concept of, 204
Hebrew Bible, 35
Hebrews, 35. *See also* Israel; Jews and Judaism
Hegira, 223
Heian Japan, 355–356, 366
Heliocentric (sun-centered) theory, 586–587
Heliocentric view of universe, 149
Hellenistic world, 142, 144; cities and towns in, 146; culture of, 148; kingdoms of, 144, *145*; Rome and, 160; women in, 147–148
Helots, 122
Henry II (England), 389, 398
Henry IV (France), 501
Henry IV (Germany), 401, 404
Henry the Navigator (Portugal), 457, 458
Henry V (England), 436
Henry VII (England), 444, 463
Henry VIII (England), 496, *499*, 502
Heraclius (Byzantine Empire), 418
Herculaneum, 176
Heresy: of Arians, 377; Dominicans on, 405
Herodotus (historian), 43, 128, 220, 265
Hideyoshi. *see* Toyotomi Hideyoshi (1582–1598) (Japan)
Hideyoshi castle (Osaka), 571
Hierarchies in India, 55
Hieroglyphs, 29, 51; in Central America, 193; Mayan, 198, 199–200, *200*; in tomb of Ramesses I, 21

High culture, 596
High Middle Ages (Europe), 385–386; culture of, 406; kingdom in, 399; land and people in, 386, 388; trade and cities in, 392
High Renaissance, 441
Hilda (Saint), 380
Himalayan Mountains, 48
Hinayana, 284
Hindu law (the *Dharmashastra*), 539
Hindu poll tax, 541
Hindus and Hinduism, 134, 283–284, 285; architecture of, 295–296, 297–298; Buddhism and, 283–284; in India, 286–287, 536; Islam and, 292; Mughals and, 539, 547; in Southeast Asia, 308; trade and, 241
Hippodrome (Constantinople), 417, 418
Hirado Island, 571
Hiroshige, Ando (1797–1858) (Japanese artist), 580
Hispaniola, 463
Historia General y Natural de lasIndias (Fernández de Ovieda), 472
History of the Peloponnesian War (Thucydides), 128
History of the Persian Wars (Herodotus), 128
Hittites, 34, 53
Hohenstaufens, 401
Hokkaido, 351
Hokusai (1760–1849) (Japanese artist), 580
Holy league, Spain and, 502
Holy Office, 405. *See also* Inquisition
Holy Roman Empire, *506*; Habsburgs in, 512; popes and, 401; Thirty Years' War and, 506–507
Homer and Homeric Greece, 118, 135
Hominids, 6, 192
Homo erectus, 6
Homo habilis, 6
Homo sapiens, 6, 79, 192, 301; of Africa, *252*
Homosexuality: in Abbasid Empire, 232; male, in Athens, 140
Honda Toshiaki, 574
Honduras, 463
Honshu, 351, 352, 353
Hoogly, capture of Port, *543*
Hopewell culture, 215
Hopi Indians, 216
Hoplites, in Greece, 120, 125
Horatius, *153*
Horses, 33
Horus (god), 27
House of Commons (England), 399
House of Lords (England), 399, 514
Housing: in Çatal Hüyük, 10; in China, 106; in Europe, 395; Harappan, 50; in Japan, 359, 360; Mayan, 198; Paleolithic, 8; in Sumer, 16

Huang Di (China), 79
Huayna Inka, 211
Hudson, Henry, 600
Hué (Vietnam), 583
Huguenots, 501. *See also* Protestants and Protestantism
Huitzilopochtli (god), 201, 204
Hulegu (Mongols), 235
Human-heartedness. *See* Humanity
Humanism: Christian (northern Renaissance), 490; Renaissance, 438
Humanity: Confucian concept of, 90
Humans: African origins of, 7; in Americas, 192; spread of, 6–7
Human sacrifice, *191*; by Arawak, 216; Aztec, 205; Mayan, 199
Humayun (r. 1530–1556) (Mughals), 537, 550, *551*
"Hundred schools" of philosophy (China), 89–95
Hundred Years' War, 435–436
Hungary: in Austrian Empire, 512; Magyars in, 383, 402
Hunger, in Southeast Asia, 484
Huns, 178
Hunting and gathering societies: Paleolithic, 7–8; transition to farming, 9–10, 11
Husini Kubwa, 264
Hussein (Ali's second son), 230
Hutu peoples, 475
Hydaspes River, Battle of the, 142
Hyksos people, Egypt and, 29

I

Ibn Battuta (Arab traveler), 245, 264, 272, 273–274
Ibn Khaldun, 247, 431
Ice age: "little ice age" (Europe), 431, 504; Paleolithic, 8
Icons, iconoclasts, and iconoclasm, 419–420
Ideographs: in China, 111; Mayan, 199
Ideologies in China, 96
Ife, 275
Ignatius of Loyola (Saint), 500
Iliad (Homer), 118, 144
Imam, 226, 239, 533
Immortality: Mesopotamians on, 20
Immortals (Persian cavalry), 45
Imperator, 164
Imperial City, 554, 568
Incest, Hammurabi's Code on, 18
India, 1, *288*; from 1000-1200, *288*; in 1805, *545*; after Mauryan Empire, 70–72, 282–287; agriculture in, 10, 295–296; Alexander the Great in, 54, 142; ancient

period in, 47–77; Arabs and, 287–290; architecture in, 73, 76, 295–296, 297–298; arts in, 297–298; Aryans in, 52–62; Aurangzeb in, 541; Babur in, 536–537; Buddhism in, 48, 67–70, 283–286; castes in, 55–58, 293–295; classes in, 55–58, 293–295; culture in, 72–76; culture of, 297–301; daily life in, 58–60, 295–297; diversity in, 48; Dutch and, 462; economic consequences of conquest, 544–545; economy in, 60–62, 295–297; foreign trade, 547; Greece and, 54; Gupta Empire in, 282, 283; Harappan civilization in, 13; Hinduism and, 286–287; Hinduism in, 48, 286–287; impact of European power, 542, 544–546; Indo-European speakers in, 33, 34; Islam and, 48, 287–290, 292; Kushan kingdom in, 71; literature in, 72–73, 298–300; Mauryan Empire in, 54–55; Mughal culture in, 548–550; Mughal Empire in, 290; music in, 300–301; numerical system from, 244; Persian Empire and, 42, 44, 54; Portugal and, 290, 459; Portuguese trade, 543; religion in, 48, 62–72, 290–293, 290–295; resistance to British, 545–546; sciences in, 76, 297; sculpture in, 73–76; Sikhs in, 48, 293; society and culture in, 290–301; society in, 55–58; Southeast Asia and, 301–302, 304; Taj Mahal, 540; Tamerlane in, 289–290, 290; technology in, 297; trade in, 296; traditional culture in, 536; women in, 59–60, 292–293, 548. See also specific dynasties and empires
Indian Ocean region, 49, 264; commerce of, 241; Europeans trade, 542; trade in, 454
Indians (Native Americans): Spanish treatment of, 469–470. See also specific groups
Indies: Columbus and, 462–463
Individual in Renaissance, 438
Indo-European languages, 34, 52–53, 156
Indo-Europeans, 33–34, 34, 52–53, 117
Indo-European-speaking peoples, 258
Indo-Muslim civilization: administrative reforms, 539; Akbar and, 537–539; harmonious society, 539; religion and state, 537–539
Indonesia, 484; religion in, 484
Indonesian archipelago, 303–304
Indra (god), 62
Indulgences, 491
Indus River region, 13, 44, 48–49, 49. See also India
Industrialization: in China, 561–564
Industrial Revolution, 562
Industry: Greek, 121; in Roman Empire, 167–168
Infantry, 120, 507
Inka Empire, 211–214, 212

Innocent III (Pope), 238, 404, 411, 428, 429
Inquisition, 405; Joan of Arc and, 436; in Spain, 238
Institutes (Justinian), 416
Institutes of the Christian Religion (Calvin), 493–494
Instruments (music): in China, 113
Intellectual thought: in Andalusia, 236–238; in Arab world, 244–245; in Byzantine Empire, 423; as characteristic of civilization, 13; in monasteries, 380; in Renaissance, 438–439
Interdict, 404
Intermediate Period (Egypt), 25
Interregional trade, 241
Investiture Controversy, 404
Ionia and Ionians, 42, 44, 125
Iran: Persians in, 41, 42
Iranian-speaking Sogdians, 327
Ireland: Vikings in, 383
Iron and iron industry, 84; in China, 109; in Greece, 118; in High Middle Ages, 386; Hittites and, 34; in India, 53
Iroquois Indians, 215
Irrawaddy Rivers, 301, 302
Irrigation, 87, 88; in Chimor, 211; in China, 13, 87, 88; in Egypt, 23; in India, 61; in Mesopotamia, 14; in Peru, 14; in South America, 208
Isaac II (Byzantine Empire), 428
Isabella of Castile (Spain), 400, 445, 463
Isfahan, 534–535
Isis (god), 27, 151
Islam: in Andalusia, 236–238; arts and architecture of, 247–249; Byzantine Empire and, 420; civilization of, 238–249; culture of, 243–249; expansion of, 454; in India, 48; literature of, 245–247; philosophy and science in, 243–245; poetry in, 245–246; Seljuk Turks and, 427; society of, 238–239, 242–243; spice trade and, 454–455; Sufism and, 247; in West Africa, 455–456
Ismail, Shah (r. 1487–1524) (Safavids), 533, 551
Israel, ancient, 36–38
Israelites, 35–39
Issus, Battle of, 141
Italy, 154; cities in, 394; city-states in, 489; communes in, 394; Crusades and, 411; geography of, 154; Germany and, 401; Holy Roman Empire and, 401; Lombards in, 415; plague in, 433; Renaissance in, 438, 441, 443; states in, 443; trade in, 389, 390. See also Roman Empire; Roman Republic; Rome (ancient); specific wars
Ivan III (Russia), 446
Ivan IV (Russia), 512
Iznik (Nicaea), 533

J

Jacobins (club), 615
Jade, trade in, 88
Jahangir (Mughals), *543, 551*
Jains and Jainism, 68
James I (England), 513
James II (England), 514
Jamestown (America), 601
Janissaries, 520–521
Japan, 351–368; arts of, 365–366; Buddhism in, 354–355; China and, 351, 353, 354, 363, 366, 368; civil service examination in, 355, 366; constitution in, 353; cotton trade, 573; creation myth in, 352; culture of, 352; diet in, 360; during early modern era, *583–584*; early period in, 351; economy of, 359–361; fascinated by, 571; feudalism in, 358–359; government in, 353–359; Heian period in, 355–356; Korea and, *354*; language in, 364–365; law code in, 354; marriages in, 498; Mongols and, 358; Nara period in, 355; religion in, 353, 361–363; society in, 359–361; system of inheritance, 574; Tokugawa, 569–581, *570*; trade in, 359; unification of, 570; women in, 360–361, 365; Yayoi culture in, 352, 353, 359. *See also* specific wars
Jati (Indian caste), 57–58, 272, 282
Java, 454, 482, 483, 484, 485; religion in, 483
Jefferson, Thomas, 602
Jericho, 10
Jerusalem, 36; bishops of, 379; in Crusades, 235, 428; destruction by Romans, 179; siege of, 235
Jesuits, 500, 555, 557, 559, 568, 571
Jesus of Nazareth, 179–181, 222; Roman Catholic and Arian views of, 377
Jews and Judaism, 38; in Anadalusia, 237, 238; Crusades and, 410, 412; Muhammad and, 222; pogroms against, 434; Rome and, 179; in Spain, 238; trade and, 389, 392
Jianwen (emperor), 341
Jia Yi, 100
Jihad, 226
Jimmu (divine warrior, Japan), 353
Jizya, 539
Joan of Arc, 436
Joffé, Roland, 468–469
John (England), 398
John, Prester, 256
John VI (Byzantine Empire), 431
Joint-stock company, 505
Jomon people (Japan), 352, 353
Joseph II (1780–1790) of Austria, 603–604, 623

Judaea, 179
Judah, kingdom of, 36–38, *37, 179*
Julio-Claudian dynasty, 164
Julius II (Pope), 490
Junkers (Prussia), 511
Juno, 179
Jupiter Optimus Maximus, 179
Jurchen people, 318, 556
Justification by faith alone, 491, 494
Justinian (Byzantine emperor), *532, 533*
Justinian (Byzantine Empire), 244, *414, 415–418, 417, 532, 533*
Juvenal, 171

K

Ka (spiritual body, Egypt), 28
Ka'aba (Mecca), 220
Kabuki theater, 576–577
Kabul, 537
Kaempfer, Engelbert, 572
Kaifeng, China, 395
Kailasa (Mount), 298
Kalidasa, 300
Kamakura shogunate (Japan), *357,* 357–358, 359, 365
Kami (spirits), 361
Kamikaze (divine wind, Japan), 358
Kampongs (villages), 305
Kangxi (China), *553;* reign of, *557–558, 583;* sacred edict, *576*
Karakoram mountains, 48
Karakorum, 335
Karli (Indian rock chamber), 76
Karma (actions), 63, 67, 345, 484
Kashgar, 327
Kautilya (Indian philosopher), 54
Kazakhstan, 83
Kent, England: Germanic tribes in, 377
Kenya, 481
Kepler, Johannes (1571–1630), 586–587
Khadija, 221
Khajuraho, temple art, 298
Khanate of Chaghadai, 336
Khanate of Kipchak, 336
Khanates, 336
Khayyam, Omar, 246
Khitan, 317
Khoi peoples, 270
Khoisan, language, 270
Khorsabad, Assyria, 41
Khotan, 280, 327
Khubilai Khan (Mongols), 235, 328, 337, 554; Japan and, 358
Khufu (Egypt), 28
Khusrau, Amir, 289

Kiev, 403, 425

Kilwa (city), 264, 459, 472

Kings and kingdoms: Assyrian, 39–41; in Bactria, 70; in Egypt, 25–26; Frankish, 377–379, 381–383, 400; Germanic, 377–379; Hellenistic, 144–151; in India, 54; in Israel, 36–38; in Korea, 369; in Mahabharata, 73; Mayan, 198; Persian, 42–44; Sumerian, 16, 17; vassals and, 383; in Vietnam, 370–372. *See also* Monarchs and monarchies; specific rulers and kingdoms

Kinship groups: Aztec, 203. *See also* Families

Kirghiz, 318

Knights, 384, 388, 389, 397–399, 410, 436

Knossus, 115

Koguryo kingdom (Korea), 368, 369

Kongo, 459, 481

Korea, 368–370; arts in, 369–370; Buddhism in, 369; China and, 353, 368–369; civil service examination in, 369; in dangerous neighborhood, 581–582; during early modern era, *583–584*; Japan and, 352, 353, *354*; Mongols and, 370; religion in, 369

Koryo dynasty (Korea), 369–370. *See also* Korea

Kosovo, Battle of (1389), 429

Kouros, 124

kowtow (ritual), *559*

Krishna (Indian god), *47*, 73

Kritovoulos, *524*

Kshatriya (class), 294

Kshatriya (Indian warrior class), 54, 56, 63, 66

Kukulcan (Toltec), 201

Kush, 32–33

Kushan Kingdom, 71; and Buddhism, 281; commerce in, 281; and Silk Road, *280*

Kushans, 280

Kyongju, Korea, 369

Kyoto, Japan, 351, 353, 355, 358, 366; Ashikaga shogunate, *569*; Golden Pavilion in, 366

Kyushu (Japan), 351, 353, 358, 569, 571

L

Labor: in Americas, 470; Aztec, 203; Inka, 211, 214; plague and, 434–435; in Roman Empire, 171, 176, 177. *See also* Forced labor; Industry; Peasants; Slavery; Slave trade; Workers

Lacquerware, 110

Laissez-faire (doctrine), 594

Lake Kisale, 269

Land bridge, between Asia and Americas, 192

Landlords: plague and, 434–435. *See also* Land(s)

Land(s): in Athens, 123; in China, 79–81; as fiefs, 383; in High Middle Ages, 386, 388; Holy Roman Empire and, 400–401; in South America, 209. *See also* Agriculture; Farms and farming

Landscape painting: in Japan, 366

Language(s): Afrikaans, 475; in China, 111–112; Germanic, 33; Greek, 33, 34, 124, 419; Indo-European, 33; in Japan, 364–365; Latin, 33, 156, 416; Olmec, 195; Persian, 33; Quechua, 214; Sanskrit, 33, 72; Slavic, 33; spoken, 51; in Vietnam, 373; Zapotec, 195. *See also* Writing; specific languages

Lao Zi, 93

La Plata, 466

Las Casas, Bartolomé de, 472–473

Last judgment, in Zoroastrianism, 45

Lateen sail, 457

Late Roman Empire, 177–178

Latifundia (estates), 161, 168

Latin America: from c. 1500 to 1750, *467*; colonies in, 462–469; marriages in, 498; state and the church in, 466; United States and, 83

Latin Empire of Constantinople, 411

Latin language, 33, 156; Justinian's Code in, 416, 419; Renaissance and, 438–439

Latium, 154, 156

La Venta: Olmec site at, 193

Law codes: of Hammurabi, 17–18; in Japan, 354; of Justinian, 415–417. *See also* specific codes

Law of Manu, 59

Law of nations, 169

Law(s): in Byzantine Empire, 423, 425; in China, 91; in England, 398, 399; Germanic, 379; Islamic, 225; Jewish, 38; Roman, 415–416; in Roman Empire, 169; in university studies, 407. *See also* Law codes

Lay investiture, 404

Leakey, Louis, 6, 192

Leakey, Mary, 6

Learning: in monasteries, 380, 381. *See also* Intellectual thought

Lebanon, 393

Lechfeld, Battle of, 383

Legalism, 91–92, 96, 99, 106, 184

Legions and legionaries, 161, 164, 166

Leo III (Pope), *376*

Leo IX (Pope), 427

Leonardo da Vinci, 441

Leo VI ("Leo the Wise," Byzantine Empire), 425

Lepanto, Battle of, 502

Lesbos, 118

Leyster, Judith, 516

Liberal arts curriculum, 407, 438

Li Bo (poet), 345
Libraries: in Alexandria, 148; in Andalusia, 236
Libya, 30
Libyan desert, 256
Life expectancy: of Germanic women, 379. *See also* Mortality rates
Limited (constitutional) monarchy, 513–514
Lineage group, 260
"Linked verse" technique, 364
Lion in Winter, The (film), 390–391
Lippman, Thomas, 238
Li Su (China), 96
Literature: Africa, 18–20; Arab preservation of, 245–247; in Byzantine Empire, 422–423; in China, 111–112; classics in, 489; in England, 516; Greek, 118; Hellenistic, 148; in India, 72–73; Islamic, 245–247; in Japan, 364–365; in Mesopotamia, 20; in Mughal culture, 550; Persian, 246; in Rome, 168–169; Safavid art and, 535–536; in Tokugawa Japan, 575–579; in Vietnam, 373. *See also* Poets and poetry; specific works and authors
Little ice age, 431, 504
Liu Bang, 99
Liu Ling (poet), 314
Livia, 164
Livy, 155
Li Yuan, 316
Li Zicheng (China), 556–557, *583*
Llamas, 214
Locke, John (1632–1704), 591
Lombards, 415
Longbows, 435
Long Count, of Maya, 199
Longshan culture (China), 79
Lord Chamberlain's Company, 516
Lords (Middle Ages), 388–389, 404. *See also* Nobility
Lord-vassal relationship, 382–385
Lost Cities of Africa (Davidson), 270
Lost-wax method, 275, 298
Louis VII (France), 389
Louis XI (Spider King, France), 443
Louis XIV (France), 508–511, *510*
Louis XVI (1774–1792) (France), 608–609, 622
Louis XVII (France), 622
Louis XVIII (France), 622
Love, marriage and, 498
Love poetry: Persian, 246
Lower Egypt, 22, 24, 25, 26
Loyola, Ignatius of (Saint), 500
Luba, 269
Luoyang, China, 85–86, 96, 327
Luther, Martin, and Lutheranism, 488, 491–493, 497; Ninety-Five Theses of, 491; Zwingli and, 493

Luxury goods, Harappan, 50
Lycurgus (Plutarch), 139
Lycurgus (Sparta), 122
Lydia, 42, 136
Lyons (France), 617

M

Ma'at (Egypt), 26
Macao, 554
Macartney (Lord), 560
Macedonia (ancient), 115, 140–144; Antigonid dynasty in, 144; Persia and, 44; Rome and, 160
Macedonian dynasty (Byzantine Empire), 424–425
Machiavelli, Niccolò, 443, 444
Machu Picchu, Peru, 212
Madagascar, Strait of, 257
Madras (Chennai, India), 542, 552
Magellan, Ferdinand, *458*, 462
Magellan, Strait of, 207
Magna Carta (England), 398
Magyars (Hungarians), 383, 402
Mahabharata (epic), 59, 72
Maharajas (great princes), 54
Maharashtra (India), 544
Mahavira (Jainism), 68
Mahayana, 284, 285
Mahayana Buddhism, 76
Mahmud of Ghazni, 287
Maimonides, 245
Maize (corn), 193
Majapahit (trading societies), 304
Majapahit kingdom (Hindu state), 454
Majlis (Arab council of elders), 220
Malabar, 295
Malacca: Portuguese and, 460, 461, 483; religion in, 483; Strait of, 302; sultanate in, 454
Malaya and Malay peninsula, 303–304, 483; commerce and, 454; sultan in, 483–484; tin from, 484
Malay Archipelago: buddhist religion and, 309
Malayo-Polynesian speakers, 301, 311
Malay peoples, *259*
Mali, 267–268, 275, 455
Mamallapuram, 298
Mamluks (Egypt), 235–236, 243, 525
Manchuria, 318; China and, 556; Korea and, 368
Manchus, 556–557
Mandate of Heaven (China), 86–87
Manichaeanism, 344
Manioc, 197, 216, 475, 480
Manors, 384–385, *385*
Mansa (chieftain), 267

Mansa Musa (Mali), 268, 455
Manuel I (Byzantine Empire), 428
Manufacturing: in China, 325; in India, 61–62
Manzikert, battle at, 233, 427
Maori, 311
Mao Zedong (China), 106
Maps: trade and, 241; voyages of exploration and, *458*
Marathon, Battle of, 44, 125
Marcus Aurelius, 174, 175
Maria Theresa (1740–1780) (Austrian Empire), 604, *623*
Marie Antoinette (France), 609
Marie Antoinette (2006) (film), *610–611*
Maritime empires: Portuguese, 458–462
Marius, 161
Markets: Aztec, 203; worldwide, 453–484
Marrakech, 240
Marriage: arranged, 498; in early modern world, 498; in Egypt, 31–32; of Germanic peoples, 380; in Hammurabi's Code, 18; in India, 59; Inka, 214; in Japan, 361; Luther on, 488; in Rome, 170; in Sparta, 122. *See also* Families; Polygamy; Polygyny
Mars (god), 179
Mary I (England), 496
Masaccio, 439
Massachusetts Bay Company, 601
Mastabas, 28
Material goods, 11
Mathematical Principles of Natural Philosophy (Newton), 587
Mathematics: Arabic numerals and, 76, 244; Mesopotamian, 20
Matrilinear lineage, 272
Mauryan Empire (India), 145, 537; India after, 70–72
Maximilian (Holy Roman Empire), 492
Mayan civilization, 192, 197–201, *200*; decline of, 200–201; writing of, 21, 198, 199
Mayors of the palace, 381
Meadows of Gold (al-Mas'udi), 247
Measles, 470
Mecca, 220
Medes, 39, 42
Medici, Cosimo de', 443
Medicine: Muslim, 245
Medieval China, ideological dispute in, 322
Medina, 223
Mediterranean region: agriculture in, 10; Muslims and, 228, 236, 455; Phoenicians in, 35; Rome and, 159–161; trade in, 220. *See also* specific countries
Megalithic structures, in Europe, 33
Megasthenes (Greek), *55*, 145

Mehmet II (r. 1451-1481) (Ottomans), 431, 522–523; fall of Constantinople, 522–523, *524*; Topkapi Palace, *527*, *531*
Mekong River, 302, *582*
Memphis, Egypt, 25
Men: Arawak, 217; in China, 107; Germanic society, 379; Neolithic, 12; Paleolithic, 8; patriarchy by, 12; in Rome, 172–173
Menander, 148
Mencius (Chinese philosopher), 91–93, 100
Menes (Egypt), 25
Mercantilism, 505
Merchants: in Africa, 480; on Silk Road, 167; to views of, 392–393
Merit system, in Japan, 353
Meroë, 33, 254
Merovingian dynasty, 377
Meru, Mount, 484
Mesa Verde, 216
Mesoamerica, 193–205, *194*. *See also* Central America
Mesolithic Age, 9
Mesopotamia, 1, 13; Assyria and, 39; city-states in, 15–18; civilization in, 14–20; culture in, 18–20; empires in, 16–18; Mongols in, 235; Persia and, 42; Roman rule of, 165; society in, 16–18; trade in, 13, 220; writing in, 19–20
Message, The (Muhammad: The Messenger of God) (film), 222–223, *223*
Messiah, 179
Mestizos, 466
Metal and metalwork: Aztec, 205; in China, 109–110; for Neolithic tools, 12
Mexico, 192, 466; Aztecs in, 201, *202*; Cortés in, 457, *463*
Michael Cerularius (Patriarch), 427
Michael III (Byzantine Empire), 424
Michael Paleologus, 429
Michael Romanov, 512
Michelangelo, 441, 442
Middle Ages: agriculture in, 386, 388; in Europe, *376*, 377–413; religious imagery in, *420*; society in, 488. *See also* Cities and towns; Trade
Middle East: agriculture in, 10; Alexander the Great and, 142, 144; Mongols in, 235–236; rug weaving in, 249; at time of Muhammad, *221*; trade in, 2; wealth in, 239–242
Middle Kingdom: Egypt, 25, 26; Europe, 381
Middle Passage, 477
Middle Path (Buddhism), 66–72
Middle way: in Buddhism, 66–68
Migration: into Americas, 192; Aryan, 52; Greek, 117–118, 120–121; of Slavic peoples, *402*
Mihrab (niche), 248
Milan, 396; duchy of, 443

Military: Abbasid, 233; Assyrian, 40; Aztec, 202; Byzantine, 423–429; as characteristic of civilization, 13; Chinese, 185; Egyptian, 29, 30; in Europe, 506–508; Greek, 120, 122, 123, 125; Hellenistic, 146; Inka, 214; janissary corps, 520–521; in Japan, 355–357; Persian, 42; Roman, 161, 176; service as vassal obligation, 384; Spartan, 122. *See also* Wars and warfare; Weapons
Millet, 528–529
Millet (crop), 10
Miltiades (Athens), 125
Minamoto Yoritomo (Japan), 357
Minerva, 179
Ming Dynasty (China), 98, 340–342, 554; art of, 568; attempt to deal with Russians, 559; brought to earth, 555–557; China and its enemies during late, 556; fall of, 562; later, 554; problems of, 556
Minoan civilization, 115–117
Minorities: in India, 63–64; in Ottoman Empire, 528–529
Minos (Crete), 115
Min River (China), 88
Missi dominici (messengers), 382
Mission,The (1986), 468–469
Missions and missionaries: Christian, 380; trade and, 241
Mobility: military, 522; social, 243
Moche culture, 209
Moctezuma (Aztecs), 463, 464
Moctezuma Xocoyotzin (Aztecs), 463
Modern Devotion movement, 491
Mogadishu, 264
Mohenjo-Daro, 13, 49, 49, 50, 52
Mole sauce, 196, 197
Mombasa, 264, 459, 473, 481
Monarchs and monarchies: in Athens, 123; Austrian, 512; in England, 398, 508–509; Hellenistic, 144–146; in Holy Roman Empire, 401; "new monarchies" and, 488; papal, 403–404. *See also* Kings and kingdoms; specific countries, rulers, and dynasties
Money: *wergeld* as, 379
Money economy, 391; in China, 88, 97; in India, 61
Mongols, 235–236; in Central Asia, 333–340; in China, 318, 333–340; historical impact of, 339–340; Islam and, 236; Japan and, 358; Korea under, 370; plague and, 431–432; in Russia, 403; trade and, 392
Monks and monasticism, 380; Christian, 379–380; in Japan, 361, 363. *See also* specific orders
Monogamy, in Egypt, 31

Monotheism, 35; of Hebrews, 35, 38; of Islam, 224; of Zoroaster, 45
Monte Albán, 194
Montesquieu (1689–1755), 593
Monte Verde (Chile), 208
Moorish population, 296
Moors, in Spain, 238
Morality: of Jewish law, 38; of slave trade, 476–480
Morocco, 232, 238, 481
Mortality rates: for plague, 432
Moscow: princes of, 403, 446. *See also* Russia
Moses (Bible), 35, 38, 222
Mosques: at Córdoba, 248; in Samarra, 248
"Mother" statues, 10
Mound-building cultures, in Cahokia, 215
Mount Kailasa, 298
Mount Meru, 484
Mount Olympus, 135
Mount Parnassus, 136
Mount Vesuvius, 52, 176
Movable type, 489
Mozambique, 474, 475, 480
Mu'awiya, 228
Mughals, grandeur of, 536–550, 538; Akbar and Indo-Muslim civilization, 537–539; Akbar's successors, 540–541; architecture, 549; culture, 548–550; economy, 547–548; founder (Babur), 536–537; gunpowder empire, 546; impact of European power in India, 542, 544–546; literature, 550; painting, 549–550; position of women, 548; society under, 546–548
Muhammad, 220–225; Arab empire after, 225–238; images of, 420, 421; teachings of, 224–225; trade and, 241; umma and, 239
Mulattoes, 466
Multiracial society, in Latin America, 466
Multiregional theory: of human development, 6–7
Mumbai (Bombay), 459
Mummification, in Egypt, 28
Mumtaz Mahal (Mughals), 540
Murad I (Ottomans), 429, 520, 551
Murasaki Shikibu (Lady Murasaki), 362
Muscovy, 512–513
Musical instruments, in Africa, 276
Muslims, 222, 481; in Andalusia, 236–238; Byzantines and, 424; Crusades and, 412; invasions of Europe by, 382; in Mediterranean region, 236; as Moors, 238; in Spain, 236–238
Mwene Metapa (Shona dynasty), 473–474, 481
Mycenaean Greece, 34, 117
Mystery religions, 151, 179
Mysticism, Sufism, 247

N

Nadir Shah Afshar, 535
Nagasaki, 571
Nanjing, 342, 554
Naples, 396
Napoleon Bonaparte (1769-1821) (France),
    618–622; domestic policies, 619–620;
    Empire, 620–622; fall of, 622; Grand
    Empire, 620–622, 622; rise of, 619
Napoleon's Civil Code, 620
Napoleon's Grand Army, 620
Nara period (Japan), 355
Nasrid dynasty, 525
National Assembly (France), 609–610, 623
Nationalism, modern (France), 617
Natural law, 169, 244, 591
Natural rights, 603
Nature: in Japan, 365
Navajo peoples, 216
Navigation, 450, 457
Navy: Athenian, 125–126
Neanderthals, 6
Near East, 15. See also Middle East; specific
    regions
Nebuchadnezzar II (Chaldean), 41
Necker, Jacques (France), 612
Neoclassical style, 176
Neo-Confucianism, 344, 564
Neolithic period in Japan, 352; megaliths in, 33
Neolithic Revolution, 9–12
Nero, 164, 171
Netherlands: United Provinces of, 502. See also
    Dutch
Neumann, Johann Balthasar, 596
Neustria, 379
New Comedy, 148
Newfoundland, Vikings in, 410
New Granada, 466
New Guinea, 326
New Kingdom (Egypt), 29–31
New Model Army (England), 513
New monarchies, 442, 488
New Spain, 466
New Testament, 181
Newton, Isaac (1642–1727), 587, 591
New World: European conquest of, 462–472;
    Spain in, 463–465, 464, 465
Nguyen dynasty (Vietnam), 583
Nicaea, kingdom of, 429
Nicene Creed, 424
Nicholas (Saint), 406
Niger River region, 481; Songhai Empire in, 455
Nika Revolt (Byzantine Empire), 417
Nile River region, 10, 13, 14, 20–33; trade in,
    476. See also Egypt

Nimrud, Assyria, 41
Nineteenth dynasty (Egypt), 30
Ninety-Five Theses (Luther), 491
Nineveh, Assyria, 39, 41
Ninhursaga (god), 19
Nirvana, 67
Nobility: Aztec, 204; in China, 105; in High
    Middle Ages, 388–389; in Japan, 256; in
    Korea, 370; medieval, 488. See also
    Aristocracy
Nobunaga. see Oda Nobunaga (1568–1582)
    (Japan)
No drama (Japan), 365, 576
Nogarola, Isotta, 439
Nok culture, 256
Nom (Egyptian province), 26
Nomadic peoples: Khitan and, 317; Kirghiz
    and, 318
Nomads, 3; Bedouins as, 220; in China, 81;
    Hebrews as, 35; Indo-European, 33–34, 34;
    Paleolithic, 8; settled peoples and, 9; Xiongnu
    as, 70–71, 97–98
Nomarch (Egyptian governor), 26
Noncentralized societies, 269
Norman Conquest (England), 398
Normandy: duke of, 399; in Hundred Years'
    War, 436; Vikings in, 383
Normans, 427
North Africa: Arabs in, 226, 228, 260–261;
    Carthage in, 35, 159; civilizations of, 256
North America: Eastern Woodlands cultures in,
    215; peoples and cultures of, 192, 207;
    Vikings in, 410
Northern Renaissance humanism, 490
Northmen (Norsemen), 383
Northumbria, monastery of Whitby in, 380
Norway: Vikings from, 383
Notre-Dame cathedral (Paris), 409
Novgorod, 403
Nubia, 27, 32–33, 253, 255
Nuclear family. See Families
Numerical systems, 76, 244
Nuns, 380; Christian, 380, 405
Nur Jahan (Mughals), 540
Nyame, 260

O

Oaxaca, Mexico, 194
Obsidian, 12, 195
Occupational groups, Ottomans, 529
Oc Eo port, Thailand, 302
Oda Nobunaga (1568–1582) (Japan), 569,
    582, 583
Odoacer, 178
Odyssey (Homer), 118, 119

Oeconomicus (Xenophon), 138
Oedipus the King (Sophocles), 129
Old Babylonians, 17
Old Kingdom (Egypt), *24*, 25–26
Old order (France), 608
Old regime (France): destruction of, 610–611, 615–616; social structure of, 607–608
Oleg (Kiev), 403
Oligarchies: in Greece, 121, 133
Olmec culture, 193–194, 197
Olympia, 115
Olympic Games, 136–137
Olympus, Mount, 135
Ometeotl (god), 204
One-Pillar Pagoda (Hanoi), 373
Onin War (Japan), 358
Optics, Muslim, 245
Oracle bones, in China, 81, 83, 89
Oracles, in Greece, 136
Orange, House of, William of Nassau and, 502
Oratory of Divine Love, 497
Ordeal, in Germanic law, 379
Ordos, 340
Oresteia (Aeschylus), 128
Orinoco River, 216
Orissa (India), 544
Orkhan I (r. 1326–1360) (Ottomans), 520
Orléans, battle at, 436
Osaka (Japan), 351, 353, 569, 571
Osiris (god), 27–28
Osmanli dynasty, 520
Osman (r. 1280–1326) (Ottomans), 520
Ostia, 167
Ostrogoths, 377, *416*
Otto I (Germany), 400
Ottoman Empire, 520–533, *521, 534*; administration of government, 528; advance into Western Asia and Africa, 523, 525; architecture, 531, 533; under challenge, 530; civilization in decline, 531; expansion of, 521–523, 525–526; face of warfare, changing, *522–523*; fall of Constantinople, 522–523, *524*; harem, 527; Mediterranean region and, 477; nature of Turkish rule, 526–528; Ottoman art, 531, 533; position of women, 529; religion and society in Ottoman world, 528–529; rise of Ottoman Turks, 520–521; role of Sultan, 526–527; social classes, 529; textiles, 533; treatment of minorities, 528–529; Turkish expansion in Europe, 525–526
Ottoman Turks, 236, 429–431; in Balkans and Anatolian peninsula, 523, 525; cross Bosporus, *551*; rise of, 520–521. *See also* Ottoman Empire; Turks
Out-of-Africa theory, 6–7

P

Pacal (Mayan), 198, 199
Pachakuti (Inka), 211
Pacific Ocean region: Japan in, 351; Magellan and, 462. *See also* Asia; specific countries
Padshahnama (Book of Kings),543
Paekche kingdom (Korea), 369
Pagan (Burmese state), 302
Pagoda in Yangon, 311
Paintings: Aztec, 205; Baroque, 515–516; in China, 568; Chinese, 347–348; Dutch, 516; Islamic, 249; in Japan, 365, 579–580; in Mughal culture, 549–550; in Renaissance, 443–444; wall paintings, 208. *See also* Art(s); Rock architecture
Pakistan, 48, *49*; Alexander the Great and, 142
Palaces, Islamic, 248
Palembang, 304, 454
Palenque, 198, 201
Paleolithic Age, 7–8
Paleologi dynasty (Byzantine Empire), 429
Palestine: Alexander the Great in, 141; crusader states in, 393
Pamir mountains, 327
Pandyas, 289
Panhellenic celebrations, 136
Panini (scholar), Sanskrit grammar by, 72
Pantheism, 260
Pantheon, 165, 179
Papacy: decline of Church and, 437–438; Luther on, 491; reform of, 403–404. *See also* Popes; specific popes
Papal States, 403, 490
Papal supremacy, Boniface VIII on, 437
Paper, 231
Papyrus, in India, 72
Paramesvara (Malacca), 454
Pariahs (outcastes), 57
Paris, cathedrals in, 409
Parliament: in England, 398, 496, 513; in France, 399
Parnassus, Mount, 136
Parsis, 296
Parthenon (Athens), 131
Pashas, in Ottoman Empire, 525
Pasta, 242
Pastoralists, in Africa, 474–475
Pataliputra (Patna, India), 54, 282
Paterfamilias, 169
Patriarchies, 12; in India, 58; in Mesopotamia, 18
Patriarchs, of Constantinople, 421, 422, 424
Patrician oligarchies, 600
Patricians, in Rome, 158
Patrilineal society, Mayan, 198

Paul III (Pope), 500
Paul of Tarsus, 181
Pax Mongolica, 340
Pax Romana, 165
Peace of Augsburg, 493
Peace of Westphalia, 507
Peasants: in Byzantine Empire, 427; in China, 97, 184; in Europe, 385, 385–388; in High Middle Ages, 386; in Islam, 242; in Japan, 355; lifestyle of, 388; medieval, 488–489; plague and, 435; in Rome, 161, 168. See also Revolts and rebellions; Serfs and serfdom
Peasant's Crusade, 410
Peasants' Revolt (England, 1381), 435
Peasants' War (1524), 492
Peking, 336
Peloponnesian League, 123
Peloponnesian War, 127
Peloponnesus region, 115, 118, 123
Pemba, 264
"People of the Book," 222
Pepin (Franks), 381
Pergamum, 145, 160
Pericles (Athens), 114, 126–127
Period of the Warring States, in China, 87, 95
Periplus, 257, 281
Persecution of Christians, 181
Persia: Abbasid dynasty and, 230–232; Arabs and, 226; Greece and, 42, 44, 125–126; Judah and, 38; literature of, 246; Mongols and, 236; Rome and, 176
Persian Empire, 2, 40, 41–45; Alexander the Great and, 140–141; Greece and, 42, 44; India and, 42, 44, 54; religion in, 45
Persian language, 33
Persians, The (Aeschylus), 125
Perspective, in Renaissance arts, 440
Peru: Caral civilization in, 14, 208–209; government of, 466; Moche in, 209
Peter (Saint), 380
Peter the Great (Russia), 512
Peter the Hermit, 410
Petit Trianon, 611
Petrarch, 438–439
Phalanx, in Greece, 120
Pharaohs (Egypt), 25, 26, 27; Ptolemaic dynasty of, 145
Philip II (Macedonia), 115, 125, 140
Philip II (Spain), 502
Philip II Augustus (France), 399, 411
Philip IV ("the Fair," France), 399, 437
Philippines, 454; Chinese traders in, 306–307; Spain in, 462; women of, 306–308
Philip VI (France), 435
Philistines, 36
Philosophes, 591–595

Philosophy: in Axial Age, 134–135; in China, 89–95; in Greece, 132–134; Hellenistic, 150–151; of history, 247; Islamic, 243–245
Phoenician alphabet, in Greece, 118, 124
Phoenicians, 34–35, 159
Phonetic script, 51, 111, 199
Photian schism, 424
Photius (Patriarch), 424
Physics, 76
Pictographs, 51, 111; in China, 111; Harappan, 50, 51
Pilate, Pontius, 180
Pillars (India), 73, 76
Pine Forest (Tohaku), 580
Pisa, 412, 428
Pisistratus (Athens), 124
Plantagenets (England), 399
Plantation agriculture, 242
Plataea, battle at, 126
Plato, 133
Platonic Academy (Athens), 244
Plebeians, 158–159
Pliny the Elder, 167
Plows, 386
Plutarch, Lycurgus, 139
Poets and poetry: Arabic, 245; Chinese, 316, 345; Homeric, 118–119; Inka, 214; in Japan, 364–365; Roman, 168–169. See also specific works and poets
Pogroms: against Jews, 434
Poitiers, battle at, 229
Poland, 446; Jews in, 434; Slavs in, 402
Polis (city-state), 119–121
Political order and global conflict in Europe, 603–607; Austrian Empire of Habsburgs, 604; changing patterns of war, 606–607; enlightened absolutism reconsidered, 606; Prussia, 604; Russia Under Catherine the Great, 604, 606
Political structures: in Africa, 480–481; Aztec, 201–203; as characteristic of civilization, 13; in China, 86–87, 96–97, 184; Harappan, 49–50; Hellenistic, 146; in Islam, 239; in Japan, 366; Mayan, 198
Politics: in Byzantine Empire, 425–426; in China, 558–559; France, 508–509; in German Reformation, 492–493; in Greece, 119–120; Hundred Years' War and, 435–436; in Southeast Asia, 483; wars of religion and, 501–504
Politics (Aristotle), 133, 139
Polo, Marco, 554
Polo family, 454; Niccolò and Maffeo, 392
Polyclitus (sculptor), 132
Polygamy: in India, 59
Polygyny, and Aztec, 204

Polynesia, 210
Polytheism, 19
Pompeii, 176
Pompey, 162–163
Pondicherry (India), 542
Popes, 380; Byzantine Empire and, 419–423, 424; Frederick II (Holy Roman Empire) and, 401; Reformation and, 490. *See also* Papacy; specific popes
Popular culture, 596–597
Population: of Baghdad, 395; Black Death and, 431–434; of China, 184; of Constantinople, 395; of Egypt, 432; in Europe, 396, 504; explosion in China and Europe, 563; of Japan, 368; movements of, 474; Neolithic growth of, 10; of Rome, 171
Po River region, 154
Portolani (charts), 457
Portraits, in Rome, 169
Ports, Italian, 167
Portugal: Africa and, 458; Americas and, 462–476; India and, 459; maritime empire of, 458–462; slave trade and, 477
Portuguese Empire, 466–471, 467
Poseidon (god), 136
Pottery, 50; Chinese, 109, 110
Praetorian guard, 164
Praetors, 157
Prakrit language, 72
Precolonial Southeast Asia, 483–485
Predestination, 494
Preface to the King's Accounts (1781) (Necker), 612
Primogeniture (Japan), 574
Prince, The (Machiavelli), 443, 444
Principia (Newton), 587
Printing: development of, 407; Reformation and, 489–490
Procopius (historian), 418, 423
Property, and women, 108, 170, 389
Prophets: Hebrew, 38; Muhammad as, 225
Prose writing, in Japan, 365
Protestant Reformation, 488–501; iconoclasm and, 420; spread of, 493–496; Switzerland, 493
Protestants and Protestantism: in Europe (by 1560), 499; Lutheranism, and, 491–493, 497; Lutheranism and, 488; Thirty Years' War and, 506. *See also* specific groups
Provinces: in China, 97; Indian, 55; Persian, 42; Roman, 160, 165–166, 379; Russian, 512
Prussia, 510–512, 604
Psalm, 37
Ptolemaic dynasty (Egypt), 145, 148; Ptolemy II, 148
Ptolemaic or geocentric theory, 586–587

Ptolemy (astronomer), 244, 245, 586
Public works, in Constantinople, 417
Pueblo Bonito, 216
Pueblo peoples, 215–216
Pugachev, Emelyan (Russia), 606, 623
Puja (personal worship), 287
Punic Wars, 159–160
Punishment: in China, 91–92, 97; in Code of Hammurabi, 18; Germanic, 379
Punjab (India), 49, 287, 537
Punt, 27
Purdah (India), 292–293, 548
Pure Land Buddhism, 354, 363, 369
Pure Land sect, 343
Puritans, in England, 513, 514
Pyongyang, 369
Pyramids: in Chiapas, 197; Egyptian, 27, 28–29, 196; in Teotihuacán, 195, 196

Q

Qianlong, reign of, 558, 583
Qibla, 248
Qin dynasty (China), 88, 95–99; empire of, 95–99; tomb of First Emperor, 110–111; Vietnam and, 370
Qing dynasty (China): art of, 568; China on eve of Western Onslaught, 559–561; daily life in China, 564–566; economy, 562–564; in eighteenth century, 560; greatness of, 557; military campaigns, 558; political institutions, 558–559; reign of Kangxi, 557–558; reign of Qianlong, 558
Qin Shi Huangdi (First Emperor of Qin, China), 96, 97, 98; Great Wall and, 98; tomb of, 109, 110
Qu (China), 95
Quechua language, 214
Queen Elizabeth I, 503, 513
Queens, Egyptian, 148
Quetzalcoatl (god), 201, 204, 463
Quipu (Inka record-keeping system), 214
Quraishi clan, 221, 228
Qur'an, 220, 222, 224, 225, 226, 227, 239

R

Rabe'a of Qozdar (Persian poet), 246
Radical Revolution (France), 616–618; equality and slavery (Haiti), 617–618; nation in arms, 616–617; Reign of Terror, 617
Raga, 300–301
Raja (prince), 54, 356
Rajputs (Hindu clans), 288
Rama (India), 73
Ramadan, 225

Ramayana, 72, 73
Ramcaritmanas, 550
Ramesses II (Egypt), 30
Rann of Kutch, 296
Raphael, 441
Rationalism, 589
Raw materials: from Americas, 468
Razzia (raid), 226
Re (god), 27
Realism: in Renaissance, 438
Reality, Plato on, 133
Reason: in Enlightenment, 591; in Roman law, 169; in scholasticism, 407–408. *See also* Rationalism
Reconquista (reconquest), 238, 399–400
Record keeping: Inka, 214; Mayan, 199
Red Fort, 540, 549
Red heads, 533
Red River, 370, 372; and the Mekong, 301; valley, 337, 582
Red Sea, 27, 220; Egyptian port city in, 241
Reformation: Catholic, 497–501; in England, 496
Reform(s): papacy of, 500; in Rome, 177
Reign of Terror (France), 617–618
Reims, 409
Reincarnation, in Hinduism, 63
Relics, 406; salvation through, 491
Religion: Aztec, 204–205; in Byzantine Empire, 419, 425; in Çatal Hüyük, 10; as characteristic of civilization, 13; in China, 89, 94; Egyptian, 27–28; exploration and, 457; in German Reformation, 492–493; in Greece, 135–137; of Hebrews, 35–36, 38–39; Hellenistic, 151; imagery of, 419, *420*; in India, 62–72; in Japan, 353, 361–363; in Korea, 369; Mayan, 198–199; Mesopotamian, 19; in Persian Empire, 45; Reformation and, 488; in Rome, 179–184; in Southeast Asia, 483–484; trade and, 241; in Vietnam, 373; wars of (16th century), 501–502
Religious art, in India, 76
Religious orders: Catholic, 377, 405–406; in Reformation, 497–501. *See also* specific orders
Rémy, Nicholas, 504
Renaissance (Europe), 438–446; artistic, 439–442; intellectual, 438–439; printing in, 489–490; society in, 488; state in, 488
Renaissance humanism, 438
Rentiers, 600
Renzong (emperor), 320
Republic, The (Plato), 133
Republic(s), in England, 514
Revolts and rebellions: Jewish, 179; Peasants' Revolt (1381) and, 435; by Roman slaves, 171. *See also* Revolution(s)

Revolution(s): Neolithic, 9–10
Rhapta, port of, 257
Rhetoric, 132
Rhine River region, 177
Ricci, Matteo, 564, *583*
Rice: in China, 88, 104
Richard II (England), 435
Richard I the Lionhearted (England), 411
Rigaud, Hyacinth, *510*
Rights: in Greece, 119; of women, 18, 361
Rig Veda, 53, 64, 72
Rites of Zhou, 86, 91, 112
Rituals, in Byzantine court, 422
River valley civilizations, 14
Roads and highways: in China, 97, 167; of Inka, 211; in Rome, 156, 157, 167
Robespierre, Maximilien (France), 616, 618, *623*
Rock architecture, 262
Rock chambers (India), 73, 76
Rock paintings, of Sahara, *259*
Rococo style (architecture), 595–596
Roman Catholic Church: church organization and, 379–380; Clovis and, 377; corruption in, 490; decline of, 437–438; doctrine of, 501; in Europe (by 1560), *499*; Orthodoxy and, 422; Reformation of, 497–501; salvation through relics and, 490–491; schism with Orthodox Church, 426; Thirty Years' War and, 506. *See also* Papacy; Popes; Reformation; specific orders
Romance of the Three Kingdoms (novel), 105, 347
Roman Confederation, 157
Roman Empire, 153–186; Augustus in, 163–165; Britain and, 165, 377; Charlemagne and, 382; China and, 184–186; Christianity in, 178–184; crisis in late period, 176–178; culture in, 168; early period in, 163–176; end of Western, 177–178; *vs.* Han empires, 184–186; Jews in, 179; law in, 169; nature of imperialism, 160–161; slavery in, 170–171; society in, 168–176; trade and, 167; women in, 170, 172–173. *See also* Roman Republic; Rome (ancient); Western Roman Empire
Romanesque architecture, 408–409
Roman language, 35
Roman law, 169; codification of, 415
Romanov family, 512
Roman Republic, 156–159; army in, 161; Carthage and, 159–160; decline and fall of, 161–163; government of, 158–159; Hellenistic world and, 160; Mediterranean region and, 159–161; Punic Wars and, 159–160; social divisions in, 158–159

Rome (ancient): Chinese silk exports, 167; civil wars in, 162; colonization by, 157; economy in, 162, 167; Etruscans in, 156–157; military in, 161, 176. *See also* Roman Empire; Roman Republic
Rome (city), bishops of, 379
Romulus and Remus, 156
Romulus Augustulus, 178
Ronin (unemployed warriors), 573
Rose Garden (Sadi), 246
Rotation of crops, 388
Rotation of earth, 149
Rousseau, Jean-Jacques (1712–1778), 594
Royal Road, 44
Rubaiyat (Omar Khayyam), 246
Rubber, 253
Rubens, Peter Paul, 515
Rudra (Vedic god), 65
Rugs, in Middle East, 249
Rules of Saint Benedict, 380, *381*
Rumi (poet), 247
Runnymede, 398
Rural areas: in Arab world, 242
Rus people, 403
Russia: to avoid Ottoman blockade, 535; under Catherine the Great, 604, 606; chariots in, 83; Christianity in, 425; fall of Napoleon, 622; Mongols in, 403; nobility, 606; second European coalition, 620; Slavs in, 402; state of, 512. *See also* specific wars
Rwanda, 475

S

Saba, 254–255
Sacks, of Constantinople, 428
Sacraments, 404, 406
Sacred edict of Kangxi, 565
Sacred Way, 156
Sacrifice: in Mesopotamia, 19. *See also* Human sacrifice
Sadi (Persian author), 246
Safavids, 533–536, *534*; art and literature, 535–536; battle in 1514, 525; collapse of dynasty, 534–535; politics and society, 535; rise of, 533–534
Safi's community, 533
Sahara Desert region, 253, 254, 256–257; commerce in, 480–481; migration from, 258; Muslims in, 455; rock paintings of, *259*; trade in, 241, 266
Sahel, Arabic, 264
Saikaku (1642–1693) (Japanese novelist), 575–576
Sailendra, 310
Saint Catherine, monastery of (Egypt), *421*

Saint-Denis, abbey of, 409
Saint-Domingue (French colony), 617–618
Saint Peter's Basilica (Vatican), 516
Saint Petersburg, 513
Saladin (Muslims), 235, 411, 428
Saleh, 267
Salvation: by faith (Luther), 490–491. *See also* specific religions
Salvo, 507
Salween, 301
Salween Rivers, 302
Samaria, 36
Samarkand (city), *291*, 431
Samarra, Mosque of, 248
Samudragupta, 282
Samurai (Japan), 355, 356, 357, 358, 363, 569, 572, 575
Sanchi, gate and stupa at, 76
San Lorenzo (Olmec site), 193
San Lorenzo, Church of (Florence), 440
San peoples, 270
Sanskrit language, 33, 53, 72
Santa Claus, 406
Santarem, 217
São Tomé, 477
Sardinia, 156, 236; Phoenicians in, 35
Sardis, 44
Sargon (Akkad), 17
Sarnath, 67
Sassanian (Sassanid) Empire, *221*, 226
Sassanid, 176
Sati (India), *59*, 293, 548
Satori (enlightenment), 363
Satraps and satrapies, 42
Saxons, 377, 400
Saxony: dukes of, 400; Holy Roman Empire and, 492
Scandinavia, trade in, 389
Schliemann, Heinrich, at Mycenae, 117
Scholargentry, 321; Vietnam, 373
Scholasticism, 407–408
School of Law (China), 91
School of Mind, 345
Science(s): Hellenistic, 149–150; in India, 76; Islamic, 243–245; Mesopotamian, 19–20
Scientific method, 591
Scientific Revolution, 586–590, *590*; in astronomy, 586–587; descartes and rationalism, 587–589; Europe, China, and, 589–590
Scorpion (Egypt), 51
Scribes: Aztec, 205; Mayan, 199
Scripts, Arabic, 249
Scrolls, in Japan, 361, 365
Sculpture: Aztec, 205; Baroque, 515–516; Egyptian, 29; Greek, 132; Harappan, 50;

Hellenistic, 149; kouros, 124; in Renaissance, 441; Roman, 169
Sea Peoples, 31, 34
Second Continental Congress, 602
Second Crusade, 411
Second Estate, 399, 488, 607–609
Second Punic War, 160
Secularism, 438
Secularization: Aztec, 204
Sedentary societies, 11
Seleucus and Seleucid kingdom (Syria), 145
Self-government: in medieval European cities, 394
Selim II (Ottomans), 530
Selim I (r. 1512–1520) (Ottomans), 525, 533
Seljuk Turks, 232–234, 410, 427, 428, 429, 520, 533
Semitic people and languages: Arabs and, 220; Assyrians and, 39; Phoenicians and, 35
Senate, Roman, 155, 158, 162–166
Seoul (Korea), 581–582
Separation of powers, 593
Serbs, and Ottomans, 429
Serfs and serfdom, in Europe, 385, 489
Servants, in Islam, 243
Seth (god), 27
Settlements: Greek, 120–121; Neolithic, 10, 12
"Seven sages of the bamboo forest" (Chinese writers), 314
Seventeen-article constitution (Japan), 353
Seven Years' War, 602, 606–607
Severan dynasty, 176
Seville, 236
Sex and sexuality: in Abbasid Empire, 232
Shah Jahan (r. 1628–1657) (Mughals), 540, 549; capture of Hoogly Port, 543; reign of, 540, 552
Shakespeare, William, 516
Shakuntala (play), 300
Shandong province, 89
Shang Di (god), 89
Shang dynasty (China), 81–85; bronze casting in, 84, 109–110; jade trade in, 88; religion in, 89
Shang Yang (China), 95
Shari'a, 528, 539
Shari'a (Islamic law), 225, 239
Sheba, 254–255
Sheikh, 220
Shen Nong (China), 79, 107
Shi'ite Muslims, 229, 231, 528, 533, 535; Fatimid, 232, 427
Shikoku (Japan), 351, 569, 571
Shinto, 361, 363, 368
Ships and shipping, 449; Harappan, 50; Phoenician, 35; trireme as, 125; Vikings, 383

Shiva (god), 65, 298, 299
Shoen (farmland), 355, 360
Shogun and shogunate (Japan), 357–358, 569. See also specific shogunates
Shohaku (Japanese poet), 364
Shona peoples, 473
Shotoku Taishi (Japan), 353, 355
Shwedagon, 311
Sichuan province, China, 85, 109
Sicily, 148, 156, 157, 159; kingdom in, 401; Phoenicians in, 35
Siddhartha Gautama (Buddha), 66–67, 74, 134, 241
Sidon, 35
Sierra Leone, 481
Sigiriya, paintings, 297
Sikhs and Sikhism, 48, 293, 547
Silk and silk industry, 103; in China, 88; in Constantinople, 425; Rome and, 167
Silk Road, 241, 280–282, 327; in China, 102–104; Chinese trade and, 88, 167; Kushan Kingdom and, 280; Kushan kingdom and, 280; plague and, 431; Rome and, 167
Silla kingdom (Korea), 369, 370
Silver, 84, 504, 505
Sima Qian (historian): on emperor's mausoleum, 110; Historical Records, 98; on Qin society, 95, 96, 98, 99
Sinai peninsula, 235
Sinan (Ottoman architect), 531
Sind (state), 287
Singapore, 454
Sinitic language, 112
Sino-Tibetan languages, 364
Sipahis, 528
Sistine Chapel, 442
Sita (Hindu mythology), 73
Sitar, 300
Skin color, in India, 55–56
Slave Coast, 481
Slavery: Africa and, 476–480; Aztec, 203; Islamic, 243; mortality rates and, 477–478; Portuguese trade and, 459; in Rome, 170–171; sources of slaves, 479; Sumerian, 16. See also Slave trade
Slave trade, 459, 476–480, 478; in Africa, 273; effects of, 479–480. See also Slavery
Slavic languages, 33
Slavic peoples, 401–403; migrations of, 402
Slovenia, in Austrian Empire, 512
Slums, 50
Smallpox, 432, 470
Smith Adam (1723–1790), 594
Socho (Japanese poet), 364
Social classes, in Ottoman Empire, 529
Social Contract, The (Rousseau), 594

Social mobility, in Islam, 243
Society: in Africa, 480–481; Arawak, 216–217;
   Assyrian, 41; Aztec, 201; Black Death and,
   434–435; in China, 83–85, 87–88, 97, 554,
   558, 561, 564–566, 567; civilization, 12–13;
   in Egypt, 26–28; European in eighteenth
   century, 599–600; of Germanic peoples, 379;
   Greek, 115; Harappan, 48–53; in India,
   55–58; Inka, 211; Islamic, 238–239,
   242–243; in Japan, 359–361, 571, 574–575,
   580; of Jesus (see Jesuits); Korea, 581; in
   medieval cities, 394; in Mesopotamia, 16–18;
   Mughals, 539, 546–548; Neolithic, 9–12; in
   Ottoman world, 528–529; Paleolithic, 7–8;
   Protestant Reformation and, 497–501;
   Renaissance, 488; Roman, 168–176;
   Safavids, 535; in Southeast Asia, 484–485;
   stateless, in Americas, 214–217; Sumerian,
   16; Vietnam, 582; in Vietnam, 373–374
Socrates and Socratic method, 132–133
Sofala, East Africa, 459, 473
Sogdians, Iranian-speaking, 327
Sogi (Japanese poet), 364
Soldiers: Assyrian, 40; in Greece, 120, 122;
   Inka, 214
Solomon (Israel), 36
Solomonids, 263
Solon (Athens), 123–124
Song Dynasty, 239, 318, 567, 573, 590;
   Vietnam and, 372
Songhai, 455, 455–456, 476, 481
Song of Lasting Pain (Bo Ju-yi), 347
Song of the South (China), 112
Song Ruozhao, 332
Song Taizu, 318
Son-Jara, 277
Sonjo (1567–1608) (Korean king), 582
Sonni Ali (Songhai), 455
Sophists, 132
Sophocles, 129
South Africa: Boers and, 475; Dutch in,
   475–476
South America: Arawak people in, 216–217;
   Europeans in, 462, 463–476; geography of,
   207–208; humans in, 192; peoples and
   cultures of, 192, 207; trade in, 208
Southeast Asia, 301–311; in 13th century, 303;
   buddhism in, 62, 309; China and, 301–302;
   daily life in, 305–308; economy in, 484–485;
   European exploration of, 462; family in,
   306–308; India and, 301–302, 304; Islam in,
   454; kingdoms in, 483–484; migration and,
   79; precolonial, 483–485; religion in,
   308–311, 483–484; rice in, 302; social
   structures, 305; society in, 305, 484–485;
   spice trade and, 302–304, 485–489; states of,
   302–304; women in, 306–308. See also
   specific countries
Southern Africa, 270–271
Southern Asia, and religions spread, 286
Spain: Americas and, 462–476; Arabs in, 228;
   Bourbon dynasty in, 509; Christianity in,
   399–400; exploration by, 461, 462; Moors
   in, 238; Muslims in, 236–238; in New
   World, 463–465, 464, 465; Phoenicians in,
   35; Reconquista in, 238; Rome and, 159,
   160, 162; Visigoths in, 377; voyages, 463.
   See also Americas; Colonies and colonization
Spanish Empire, 466–471, 467
Spanish Inquisition, 238
Spanish Netherlands, 502
Sparta, 115, 118, 122–123, 125, 127, 138–139.
   See also Greece
Spartacus, 171
Spice Islands (Moluccas), 459, 461, 505; Jesuits
   in, 500
Spices and spice trade: European commerce
   and, 505; Islam and, 454–455; Portugal and,
   459–461; Southeast Asia and, 485–489
The Spirit of the Laws (Montesquieu), 593
Spirits, in India, 60
Spoken language, 51, 112
Squadrons, 507
Sri Lanka (Ceylon), 48, 70
Srivijaya (trading societies), 304
Stamp Act of 1765, 602
Standard of living: in Southeast Asia, 484–485
Standing army, 507. See also Military
Starry Messenger, The (Galileo), 587
State (nation): church and, 496; in Japan,
   353–359; in Renaissance, 442–446; Spartan,
   122–123
State Confucianism, 99
Stelae, 276
Stirrup, 383
Stoicism, 150, 169
Stone of the Fifth Sun (Aztec), 205
Stone tools, 6
Storytellers, in Africa, 277
Strabo, 167
Strait of Sunda, 304
Strait(s): of Gibraltar, 228, 236; of Magellan,
   207
Strategoi (officials), 126
Streusand, Douglas, 546
Stuart dynasty, in England, 513
Stupas, 60, 68, 73
Subinfeudation, 384
Sublime Porte (PORT), 530
Sudras (India), 57, 63, 291
Sufism, 247, 455
Sugar and sugar industry, 469, 470

Suger (Abbot), 409
Sui dynasty, 315–316
Sui Wendi, China, 315
Sui Yangdi, 315
Sulawesi, 454
Suleyman I the Magnificent (r. 1520–1566)
    (Ottamans), 525, 530; at Battle of Mohács,
    526, 551; defeat of Turks at Vienna, 526, 551
Suleymaniye Mosque and Hagia Sophia, 532
Suleyman Kanuni. see Suleyman I the Magnifi-
    cent (r. 1520–1566) (Ottamans)
Sulla, Lucius Cornelius, 162
Sultan and sultanate, 233, 520, 524; role of,
    526–527
Sultanate of women, 527
Sumatra, 454, 482, 483, 485
Sumer and Sumerians, 15–16. See also
    Mesopotamia
Sunda, Strait of, 304
Sun Kings, in France and China, 510–511
Sunni Muslims, 230, 233, 528
Sun Temple at Konarak, 298
Sun Tzu, 523
Supe River valley (Peru), 14
Supreme Ultimate, 344–345
Suras (chapters): in Qur'an, 225
Surat (India), 462, 542, 552
Surpluses: as characteristic of civilization, 13; in
    Egypt, 24
Susa, 43, 44
Swahili, 257, 264
Swahili culture, 481
Switzerland, Reformation in, 493
Syr Darya River, 536
Syria, 27; Alexander the Great in, 141; Arab
    control of, 226; crusader states in, 393; Egypt
    and, 30; Phoenicians in, 35; Saladin in, 235;
    Seleucids in, 145

T

Tabula rasa (blank mind), Locke on, 591
Tacitus, 164
Tahuantinsuyu (Inka empire), 211
Taika reforms (Japan), 353–354
Taille (French tax), 443, 607–608
Taj Mahal, 531, 540, 549
Taklimakan Desert, 103, 280, 327
Tale of Genji, The (Murasaki Shikibu), 362
Tale of the Marshes (novel), 347
Tales from 1001 Nights (Arabian Nights), 246
Tamerlane, 289–290, 522, 533, 536, 551;
    empire of, 290
Tamil languages, 550
Tang Dynasty, 239, 316–318, 317, 522;
    Buddhism under, 342–344; Japan and, 353;
Korea and, 369; land reform and, 324–325;
    religion under, 342–345; Silk Road trade
    and, 327; women under, 331–332
Tang Taizong, 316, 332, 343
Tantrism, 343
Tanzania, 481
Tariffs, 505, 509
Tariq, 228
Tatami (woven-mat floor), 360, 366
Taxation: in China, 97, 185; in Egypt, 26; in
    Japan, 354, 355
Taxila, 281
Tea, 107
Teachers and teaching: in medieval universities,
    407
Technology: agricultural, 88; in Americas, 209;
    in High Middle Ages, 386; in metalwork,
    109–110; Neolithic, 12; spread of, India,
    326; transportation and, 241. See also
    Science(s)
Tehuacán valley, 193
Tell el-Amarna, Egypt, 30
Temple of Literature (Vietnam), 373
Temple of the Sun (Cuzco), 214
Temple(s): Egyptian, 29, 30; in Jerusalem, 36,
    38; Sumerian, 16
Temuchin, 333–334
Tenant farming: in China, 184; in Rome, 168,
    177
"Ten lost tribes," 36
Tenochtitlán, 201, 202, 204, 205, 463
The Ten Princes, (Dandin), 300
Teotihuacán, 195, 196
Terra-cotta figures: army, in China, 110;
    Harappan, 50
Territory of Macao, 554
Terror, in Assyrian warfare, 40
Thailand, 482, 483, 484; Ayuthaya in, 454
Thebes, Egypt, 30
Thebes, Greece, 115, 116, 129
Theme (Byzantine administrative unit), 419
Themistocles (Athens), 125
Theocracy, Sumerian, 16
Theocritus, 148
Theodosius, 184
Theology: Byzantine, 419, 425; study of, 407.
    See also Religion; specific religions
Theravada Buddhism, 284, 285, 483
Thessalonica, 429
Thessaly, 115
Third Coalition, Napoleon's war and, 620
Third Crusade, 411
Third Estate, 399, 489, 608–609
Third Punic War, 160
Thirty-Six Views of Mount Fuji (Hokusai), 580
Thirty Years' War, 506, 506–507

Thomas Aquinas (Saint), 408
Thrace, 44
Three-field system, in Europe, 386
Throne of Saint Peter (Bernini), 516
Thucydides, 128
Thutmosis III (Egypt), 30
Tian, 89
Tian Shan, heavenly mountains, 103, 327
Tiberius, 164
Tiber River, 155, 156, 167
Tibetan plateau, 80
Tidor, 462
Tigris River region, 14, 39, 147, 230, 232
Tikal, 196, 199, 200, 201
Timbuktu, 268, 455, 456, 481
Timur-i-lang. *See* Tamerlane
Titus, 175
Tlaloc (god), 204, 205
Tlaltelolco, *202*
Tlaxcallan, 464
Tobacco and tobacco industry, 469, 479
Togo (Togoland), 481
Tohaku (Japanese painter), 580
Tokugawa bakufu, 572, 574
Tokugawa Ieyasu (1598–1616) (Japan), 569,
    571, 582, *583*
Tokugawa Japan, 569–581, *570*; art,
    579–581; commercial expansion, 573;
    culture, 575–579, *578*, *579*; Daimyo and
    Samurai, 572; expulsion of Christians,
    571–572; in foreign trade, 572; great peace,
    572–574; great unifiers, 569–569; indus-
    trial activity, 573; land problems, 573–574;
    life in village, 574–575; literature of new
    middle class, 575–579; maxims for peasant
    behavior in, *577*; opening to west,
    570–571; persecution of Christians, 571;
    role of women, 574–575; seeds of capital-
    ism, 572–573
Tokyo, 351, 352, 357, 569
Toledo, 236
Toleration: in Andalusia, 236; in Rome, 181
Toltec people, 201
Tombs: in China, 82, 83; of First Emperor,
    110–111; Mayan, 199; pyramids as, 28–29;
    of Qin Shi Huangdi, 109, 110
Tools, 6; in High Middle Ages, 386; Neolithic,
    12; Paleolithic, 8; stone, 6. *See also* Technology
Topa Inka, 211
Topkapi Palace, 527, 531
Tordesillas, Treaty of, 461, 465
Tours, battle at, 229
Toussaint L'Ouverture, Pierre Dominique, 618,
    667
Toyotomi Hideyoshi (1582–1598) (Japan),
    582, *583*; edict prohibiting Christianity

in Japan, 571, *583*; invaded Korea, 569,
    583
Tozama daimyo (Japan), 572
Trade: African, 256–258; Arab, 226, 239–240,
    455; Assyrian, 41; in Axum, 255; Aztec, 203;
    in Byzantine Empire, 395, 423–424, 427; in
    China, 87, 102; Chinese, 167; civilization
    and, 241; in Egypt, 26–27; in gold, 473;
    Harappan, 13, 50; India and, 61–62; inter-
    regional, 241; Islam and, 220, 241, 454;
    Japanese, 359; of Kush, 32–33; in medieval
    Europe, 389–390, 395; in Middle East,
    239–242; Nubian, 32; Olmec, 194; outside
    Europe, 392–393; Phoenician, 35; plague
    and, 431, 433; Portuguese, 458–462;
    regional, 2; religion and, 241; Roman, 167;
    in Sahara, 241; in South America, 208;
    Sumerian, 16; to views of, 392–393; world-
    wide (1500–1800), *470*. *See also* Silk Road;
    Slave trade; Spices and spice trade; specific
    countries and regions
Trade routes, Hellenistic, 147
Trading companies, 391
Tragedies (Greek), 128–129, 148
Trajan, 165, 176, 182, 185
Translations: by Arabs, 244–245; of Middle
    Eastern literature, 246
Transportation: in Egypt, 24; Sumerian, 16;
    technology and, 241
Trans-Saharan trade, in slaves, 456, 459, 478,
    479
Transylvania, in Austrian Empire, 512
Travels of Sebastian Manrique, 1629–1649
    (Cabral), *543*
Treaty of Karlowitz, 530
Treaty of Nerchinsk, 559
Treaty of Paris, 602
Treaty of Utrecht, 601
Trent, Council of, 500
Trials, for witchcraft, 504
Tribes, Bedouin, 226
Tribunes of the plebs, 158
Tribute system, in China, 369, 372
Trinity, 408
Tripitaka (Buddhist writings), 70
Tripoli, 428
Trireme (ship), 125
Troy, 117, 118, 168
Trung sisters (Vietnam), 370, 374
Tsar (Russia), 512. *See also* specific tsars
Tudor dynasty (England), 444, 513. *See also*
    specific rulers
Tughluq dynasty, 289
Tullia, 170
Tulsidas (1532–1623), 550
Tumasik (Singapore), 454

Turkey: Hittites in, 34
Turkic-speaking people, 317
Turkmenistan, 14
Turks: at Battle of Mohács, *519*; defeat at
    Vienna, *551*; defeat Mamluks in Syria and
    seize Cairo, *551*; expansion in Europe,
    525–526; Hagia Sophia, 531; at Lepanto,
    502; Osman, 520; Ottoman, 236, 520–521,
    523, 525; out of Hungary, 526; rule, 525,
    526–528; seized island of Cyprus, 526;
    Seljuk, 232–234, 427, 520, 533. *See also*
    Ottoman Empire; Turkey
Tutankhamun (Egypt), 30
Tutsi people, 475
Twelve Tables, 169
"Twice-born" classes (India), 56–57
Two-field system, in Europe, 386
Typhus, 470
Tyranny and tyrants, in Greece, 121
Tyre, 35, 393
Tyrrhenian Sea region, 154

U

Uighurs, 317
Uji (Japanese clans), 353, 359
Ulama (Muslim scholars), 225, 484, 528
Umar, 228
Umayyad dynasty, 228–230 236
Umma (Islamic community), 223, 239
Umma, Mesopotamia, 15
Understanding Islam (Lippman), 238
United Provinces of the Netherlands, 502
United States Constitution, 603
Universal law of gravitation, 587
Universal mobilization, 616, 623
Universe: geocentric theory of, 586; Greek phi-
    losophers on, 132; heliocentric (sun-centered)
    theory, 586–587; heliocentric view of, 149;
    medieval conception of, 587–588, *588*; new
    conception of, 587–588
Universities and colleges: in Europe, 407
Untouchables (India), 57
Upanishads, 63, 134
Upper class, in Islam, 242
Upper Egypt, 22, *24*, 25, 26
Ur, Mesopotamia, 15, 16–17
Urban areas: in Arab world, 240; as character-
    istic of civilization, 13; poor workers in, 489;
    in Roman Empire, 168, 171. *See also* Cities
    and towns
Urban II (Pope), 410, 427
Urban VI (Pope), 437
Uruinimgina cone, cuneiform script and, 21
Uruk, Mesopotamia, 5, 15, 20
Utamaro (1754–1806) (Japanese artist), 580

Uthman, 228
Uxmal, *200, 201*
Uzbekistan, 14
Uzbeks, 533, 537

V

Vaisya (Indian commoner class), 56
Valencia, 236
Valley of Mexico, 195, 197, 201, *202. See also*
    Aztecs
Valois, house of (France), 501
Values, in Homeric Greece, 118–119
Vandals, *416*
Varanasi, 281
Varna (Indian classes), 56
Varna class, 305
Varuna (god), 62
Varus, 164
Vassals (Middle Ages), 356, 382–384, 388,
    403–404
Vatican, 516
Vault, 169
Vedas, 53, 62, 134
Vedic prose (India), 58
Veils, for Islamic women, 224
Veneration of ancestors, in China, 83
Venezuela: Arawak in, 216
Venice, 396, 443; Crusades and, 411; trade
    and, 389, 393, 428
Veracruz, 193, 199, 463
Versailles (France), 508, *610–611*
Vespucci, Amerigo, 458, 463
Vesuvius, Mount, 176
Vienna: second siege to, 526, *551*; Turks at,
    526, *551*
Vietnam, 370–374; China and, 97, 370,
    372–374; culture in, 373; government of, 373;
    perils of Empire, 582–583; society in,
    373–374. *See also* Southeast Asia
Vietnam War, *523*; First, 370
Vikings, 383
Villages: Harappan, 49; in Japan, 353;
    Neolithic, 10, 11–12
Villehardouin, Geoffrey de, 431, 433
Vindication of the Rights of Woman
    (Wollstonecraft), 595
Virgil, 168–169
Virgil (poet), 439
Virgin Mary, 406
Vishnu (god), 65
Visigoths, 178, 228, 236, 377
Vizier, 231; in Egypt, 26; Saladin as, *235*
Vladimir (Rus leader), 403
Volga River region, 403
Voltaire (1694–1778), 593

Von Bora, Katherina, 492
Voyages: of Columbus, 461; European, *458, 459–462*; of Zheng he, 454

W

Wallachia, 525
Walled cities, 12, 49; Sumerian, 15
Wall painting, in Amazon region, 208
Wang Anshi, 320
Wang Mang, 104
Wang Yangming, 345
Wari people, 209
Warka, mound of, 5
Warring States period, in China, 87, 95
Warriors: Almoravids as, 238; Germanic, 377; Japanese samurai as, 356, *357*; Mycenaean, 117. *See also* Samurai
Wars (Procopius), 418, 423
Wars and warfare: Assyrian, 40; in Byzantine Empire, 418, 423; changing face of, *522–523*; in China, 95, 96, 98; in Europe, changing patterns of, 606–607; in Greece, 120; Indian attitude toward, 72; knights in, 384; nobles, vassals, and, 383; in Rome, 156–157, 159–160; in Sparta, 118, 122; wars of (16th century), 502
Wars of Religion (France), 501–502
Washington, George (1732–1799), 602
Water: civilization and, 14; for crops, 88
Water mill, 386
Waterpower, 386
Watteau, Antoine (1684–1721), 596
Wayang kulit, entertainment, 304
Way of the Dao (Lao Tzu), 343
Wealth and wealthy: in Abbasid Empire, 232; in Americas, 466–470; in Arab Empire, 239–242; in China, 88; in Egypt, 30
Weapons: in Africa, 480; in Early Middle Ages, 384; Greek fire as, 419; in Hundred Years' war, 435–436; improvements in, 450; networks of, 450. *See also* Firearms; Gunpowder
Wei Rivers, 315
Well-field system, in China, 87
Wendi (emperor), 100
Wergeld, 379
West Africa, 256, 260, 265–268; agriculture in, 10; colonies in, 481; epic literature from, 277; gold from, 459; Islam in, 265, 455–456; metalwork in, 275; slave trade in, 480; trade and, *458*
Western Asia: empires in, 39–45; Hittites in, 34–35
Western Europe: Hundred Years' War, 443
Western Hemisphere, 192 *194,* 196; colonial empires in, 462–472; plants and animals in, 10

Western Roman Empire, 177–178, 377. *See also* Roman Empire; Rome (ancient)
Western world: Byzantine Empire and, 428; crises of 14th century in, 431–438; Southeast Asia and, 482. *See also* specific countries and regions
West Indies, 600; mortality rates in, 477–478
Westphalia, Peace of, 507
Wheat, 10, 11, 14
Wheel, 16, 33
Whitby, monastery of, 380
White Lotus Rebellion (1796–1804), 558, *583*
White Lotus sect, 343
William and Mary (England), 514
William of Nassau (prince of Orange), 502
William of Normandy (England), 397, 398
Wind exploration, 458
Winkelmann, Maria, *595*
Witchcraft hysteria, 504–505
Wittenberg, 491
Wollstonecraft, Mary (1759–1797), 595
Women: Arawak, 217; arranged marriages and, 498; in Athens, 138–139; Aztec, 204; in Byzantine Empire, 426; in China, 107–108, 172–173, 565–566, *567*; Christianity and, 183; defense of learning, 440–441; in Egypt, 32; Germanic society, 379; in Hellenistic world, 147–148; Homeric, 119; in India, 59–60; Inka, 213, 214; Islamic, 224, 243; in Japan, 360–361, 365, 574–575; Mayan, 198; in medieval Europe, 389, 396; in Mughal Empire, 548; Neolithic, 12; in Ottoman Empire, 529; Paleolithic, 8; in peasant society, 388; property and, 108, 170, 389; Protestant Reformation and, 496–497; in religious orders, 405; Renaissance and, 439; in Rome, 170, 172–173; as slaves, 479; in Sparta, 122, 138–139; in Vietnam, 374; witchcraft hysteria and, 504. *See also* Women's rights
Women's rights, 18, 361, 374
Woodblock print, 580
Woolen industry, 390, 434
Workers: in guilds, 396; poor, 489. *See also* Labor
World-machine (Newton), 587
World market, 453–484
World War I, 531. *See also* Peace; specific countries
Writing: ancient systems of, *53*; in Central America, 193; as characteristic of civilization, 13; Chavín society and, 208; in China, 81, 85, 91, *111,* 111–112; civilization and, 51; cuneiform, 20, 21; Egyptian, 29; in Greece, 118; Harappan, 50–51; Inka, 214; Mayan, 198, 199; in Mesopotamia, 19–20;

Phoenician, 35; purposes of, 51; in Vietnam, 373. *See also* Alphabets; Storytellers
Wrought iron, 84, 109
Wu people (China), 95
Wu Zhao, 329, 332

X

Xavier, Francis, 500, 570–572, *583*
Xenophon, 138
Xerxes (Persia), 125
Xia (Hsia) dynasty (China), 81
Xian, China, 83, 85, 97; tomb of First Emperor in, 110–111
Xianyang, China, 97, 107
Ximenes (Cardinal), 497
Xinjiang (China), 82, 316, 559
Xiongnu people, 70–71, 97, 186
Xuan Zang (Chinese missionary), 282, 295, 343
Xuanzong (Tang emperor), 317

Y

Yahweh, 38
Yalu River, 582
Yamato clan (Japan), 353
Yamato plain, 353, 355
Yan'an, China, 106
Yang and yin, 348
Yangban (Korea), 581–582
Yang Guifei, 317
Yang Jian, 314–315
Yangshao culture, China, 79
Yangzhou (China), 568
Yangzi River (China), 79, 81, 85, 88, 95, 97, 102, 105, 314, 318, 325, 342
Yarmuk River, battle at, 226, 419
Yayoi culture (Japan), 352, 359
Yellow Emperor (China), 79
Yellow River (China), 13, 14, 79, *80*, 81, 83, 85, 95, 97, 105, 315, 318, 342, 561
Yi dynasty (Korea), 370
Yi Jing, 89
Yin and *yang*, 89, 345
Yi Song-gye (Korea), 370, 581
Yi Sunshin (1545–1598) (Korea), 582
Yoga (union), 63

Yongle (Ming Dynasty), 554, 557, 564
Yongzheng, 558
Yuan dynasty, 336, *554*
Yuca, 216
Yucatán peninsula, 193, 197, 199
Yue (Chinese state), 95
Yueh (Vietnam), 370, 374
Yurts, 335

Z

Zagwe dynasty, 262
Zakat (alms), 225
Zama, Battle of, 160
Zambezi River, 269, 270, 473
Zamindars, 539, 545, 548
Zand dynasty, 535
Zanj, 263–265
Zanzibar, 264
Zapotec culture, 194–195
Zara (port), 428
Zazen, 363
Zemsky Sobor (Russian assembly), 512
Zen Buddhism (Japan), 364, 366, 578. *See also* Chan Buddhism
Zeno, 150
Zero, use of, 244
Zeus (god), 135–136
Zhang Qian, 102
Zheng He (Ming Dynasty), 341–342, 449, 454, 481, 554, *583*
Zhou Daguan (Chinese traveler), 306–307
Zhou (Chou) dynasty (China), 85–95, 569; agricultural technology in, 88; burial pit from, 82; family during, 105
Zhu Xi (neo-Confucian philosopher), *567*
Zhu Yuanzhang (Ming Dynasty), 338, 554, 557
Ziggurat, 16
Zimbabwe, 269–270, 473. *See also* Great Zimbabwe
Zoque culture, 197
Zoroastrianism, 45, 89
Zubaida (wife of Harun al-Rashid), 232
Zuni Indians, 216
Zürich, Zwingli in, 493
Zwingli, Ulrich, 493–495